THE FLOWERING PLANTS
OF
WESTERN INDIA

THE FLOWERING PLANTS
OF
WESTERN INDIA

BY THE REV.

ALEXANDER KYD NAIRNE
LATE BOMBAY CIVIL SERVICE

GYAN

Published by

GYAN

Gyan Publishing House
5, Ansari Road
Daryaganj, New Delhi-110002
Phone: 011-47034999, 9811692060
E-mail: books@gyanbooks.com

Distribution Network
gyanbooks.com
India, USA, Canada, UK, Australia, France

ISBN : 978-81-212-2198-6 (HB)
First Published, 1894

2nd Impression 2021

Printed at: Gyan Press, Delhi.

The Flowering Plants of Western India
Author: Alexander KYD Nairne

THE FLOWERING PLANTS

OF

WESTERN INDIA.

BY THE REV.

ALEXANDER KYD NAIRNE,

LATE BOMBAY CIVIL SERVICE.

"Science is a steep island surrounded by a few more rocks than are necessary, to which every savant makes it a pleasure and a duty to add some asperities. I pass people over in a light wherry. I transport them from the opposite shore, and land them on the beach of the island."—*Alphonse Karr.*

LONDON: W. H. ALLEN & CO., LIMITED

13, WATERLOO PLACE, S.W.

Publishers to the India Office.

BOMBAY: THE EDUCATION SOCIETY'S PRESS, BYCULLA.

DEDICATED

TO THE DEAR MEMORY

OF

M. F. N.

ERRATA.

In the first half of the book Sir E. Tennent's name is wrongly given as *Tennant.*

The name of the district of the Panch Mahâls is frequently spelt wrongly.

p. 17. '*Kabab*' should be '*Kadab.*'

p. 20. The generic description of *Pittosporum* should be given thus—"Petals erect with connate claws, ovary sometimes stalked."

p. 23. 'PORTULACÆ' should be 'PORTULACA.'

p. 33. '*Shamenla*' should be '*Shameula.*'

p. 46. Tribe 'Toddalicæ' should be 'Toddaliæ.'

" '*Acrorycnhia*' should be '*Acronychia.*'

p. 83. '*S. bigetmina*' should be '*bigemina.*'

p. 86. Pisum *satioum* should be '*sativum.*'

p. 98. 'Kásod' should be in italics.

p. 103. At the end of the description of *A. ferruginea* add—"Not in *D.* or *G.* Forests of Panch Mahâls and Konkan.—*Brandis.*"

p. 115. Under Psidium Guyava there should be a comma between *jámb* and *peru.*

p. 120. '*aquivala*' should be '*agnivala.*'

p. 123, near the bottom, 'Bixinea' should be 'Bixineæ.'

p. 149. *Dele* "many" before "small flowers."

p. 182. At the end of order Apocynaceæ add—"*Allamanda Aubletii* or *cathartica* is a milky climber with large yellow trumpet-shaped flowers: common in gardens; *jahari sontakká.*"

p. 185. '*skidodi*' should be '*shidodi.*'

p. 208. '*Kamain*' should be '*Kamuni.*'

p. 225. Under *S. suaveoleus dele* comma after 'flowers.'

p. 226. '*jingali*' should be '*jinjali.*'

p. 231. Under *H. spinosa dele* comma between 'calyx' and 'segments.'

p. 234. Under *B. asperrima* insert comma between '*atgan*' and '*akdá.*'

" 'Malaga' should be 'Malaya.'

p. 236. Under *B. cristata dele* comma between 'calyx' and 'segments.'

p. 239, line 5 from bottom, for 'of the genus Rostellularia' read '(formerly genus Rostellularia,).'

p. 242. Under *B. parviflora dele* comma after 'barren.'

p. 243. Under *Gymnostachyum glabrum* for 'fascicled or' read 'fascicled on.'

p. 256, last line, for '*Káj hár*' read '*Ká jhár.*'

p. 277, line 2, for 'olong' read 'oblong.'

p. 336. Under *Kæmpferia scaposa* after 'stem,' read 'leaves large, broad-lanceolate.'

PREFACE.

THIS book is intended mainly for the use of two classes. Firstly, Englishmen and Englishwomen, whose duty calls them to Western India, and who without being, or intending to become, scientific botanists, wish to know something about the trees and flowers which surround them. And among these I specially think of those district officers who have (as I had myself for many years) to spend several months in each year more or less in the jungle, and with very little of English or educated society. Secondly, the educated natives of the country, whose inclination directs them more and more to intellectual pursuits. The study of natural history has spread so greatly, both in England and India, during the last twenty-five years, that there are many in both of the classes mentioned, to whom it must seem a hardship that there are so few books to help them in the study of any branch of natural science in India. For it is obvious that large and expensive books are not generally within the reach of those I have mentioned, and that articles in magazines, gazetteers, and the journals of scientific societies are seldom available up-country, even if they were adapted for use in the field. Small unambitious books, of which there are now many relating to every branch of science in England, are wanted for India, and so far are not to be found.

The object of this book, then, is to enable any person of average education and very moderate powers of study to identify, by reference to this one volume alone, any flowering plant met with in the Bombay Presidency. For this purpose, not only a description of the individual plants is required, but also something like an outline of botany generally, and in particular an explanation of the scientific classification of plants, and of all the technical terms used. These will be found in the Introduction.

The explanation of my publishing this book so long as fifteen years after my retirement from India is that I found it impossible to make any part of it satisfactory without an authoritative work like Sir J. Hooker's to found it on. The last part of that great work necessary to my purpose appeared only four months ago.

That many mistakes and omissions will be found in the book is certain; and it is simple truth to say that I see more faults in it than any one is likely to tell me of. But I shall be greatly obliged to any who use the book if they will keep a list of the mistakes and omissions they find, and will from time to time communicate them to me.

Finally, I must express my thanks, not only to those whose names appear in the body of the work, but to many other gentlemen, mostly in the Bombay Presidency, who have written to me in elucidation of various points. I have used all the information I could get, with discrimination I hope, certainly with full appreciation of the ready help that I have received from many different quarters.

Coblenz:
January, 1894.

TABLE OF CONTENTS.

PRELUDE OF QUOTATIONS.

There is not so contemptible a plant or animal that does not confound the most enlarged understanding. . . . The workmanship of the all wise and powerful God, in the great fabric of the universe and every part thereof, farther exceeds the capacity and comprehension of the most inquisitive and intelligent man, than the best contrivance of the most ingenious man doth the conceptions of the most ignorant of rational creatures.—JOHN LOCKE.

When I look at the poor little herbs that arise out of the earth, the lowest of vegetables, and consider the secret spark of life that is in them, that attracts, increases, grows, and seminates itself and its kinds, the various virtues that are in them for the food, medicine, and delight of more perfect creatures, my mind is carried up to the admiration and adoration and praise of that God whose wisdom and power and influence and government is seen in these small footsteps of his goodness: so that, take all the wisest, ablest, and most powerful and knowing men under heaven, they cannot equal that power and wisdom of his that is seen in a blade of grass.—SIR M. HALE.

We may safely affirm of all those multiform tribes which have been animated by God, that they exhibit, without a single exception, the very nicest adaptation of means to an end, and that the greatest and least are equally proofs that it is a principle with the Creator to make nothing in vain. You cannot say that what is merely ornamental answers no purpose. Not in vain hath God clothed with beauty or gifted with melody, "the fowls which sing among the branches." Not in vain hath he painted the foliage and pencilled the flowers with which the earth is bedecked. Not in vain hath he given grandeur to the mountain and loveliness to the valley, and caused the diversified landscape to strike us by its sublimity or win us by its softness. It was every way worthy a benevolent Creator so to construct and furnish the dwelling which he designed for rational creatures, that in all its apartments there should be objects which should minister to their delight; and it further well became a wise Creator to surround beings whom he meant to engage in his worship with such manifestations of himself as are best calculated to gain their attention and remind them of a Deity.—CANON HENRY MELVILL.

Not alone the plant,
Of stately growth, and herbs of glorious hue,
Which strike even eyes incurious, but each moss,
Each shell, each crawling insect, holds a rank
Important in the plan of him who framed
The scale of beings: holds a rank, which, lost,
Would break the chain, and leave behind a gap,
Which nature's self would rue.—THOMPSON.

If we could open and unbind our eye,
We all, like Moses, should espy,
E'en in a bush, the radiant Deity.

. . . . .

Upon the flowers of heaven we wondering gaze,
The stars of earth no wonder in us raise,
Yet these perhaps do more than they
The human lives about us sway.—COWLEY.

Do not depreciate any pursuit which leads men to contemplate the works of their Creator. The Linnæan traveller who, when you look over the pages of his journal, seems to you a mere botanist, has in his pursuit an object that occupies his time and fills his mind and satisfies his heart. Nor is the pleasure which he experiences in investigating the structure of a plant less pure than that which is derived from perusing the noblest productions of human genius.—SOUTHEY.

It is good for a man perplexed and lost among many thoughts to come into closer intercourse with nature, and to learn her ways and catch her spirit. It is no fancy to believe that if the children of this generation are taught a great deal more than used to be taught of nature and the ways of God in nature, they will be provided with the material for far healthier and happier, and less perplexed and anxious lives, than most of us now living.—BISHOP PHILLIPS BROOKS.

Like a beautiful flower full of colour but without scent are the fine but fruitless words of him who does not act accordingly. But like a beautiful flower full of colour and full of scent are the fine and fruitful words of him who acts accordingly.—THE PATH OF VIRTUES. (Buddhist.)

The love of nature is a great gift, and if it is frozen or crushed out, the character can hardly fail to suffer from the loss. I will not indeed say that a person who does not love nature is necessarily bad, or that any one who does is necessarily good; but it is to most minds a great help. Many, as Miss Cobbe says, enter the Temple through the gate called Beautiful.—SIR JOHN LUBBOCK.

It cannot be too extensively known that nature is vast and knowledge limited, and that no individual, however humble in place or acquirements, need despair of adding to the general fund.—HUGH MILLER.

I hope we agree in considering all Europeans who visit remote countries, whatever their separate pursuits may be, as detachments from the main body of civilized men sent out to levy contributions of knowledge, as well as to gain victories over barbarism.—SIR JAMES MACKINTOSH (Address to the Bombay Literary Society).

Men that undertake only one district are much more likely to advance natural knowledge than those who grasp at more than they can possibly be acquainted with; every kingdom, every province should have its own monographer.—WHITE (of Selborne).

Do you wonder why poets talk so much about flowers? Did you ever hear of a poet who did not talk about them? . . . They will bloom over and over again in poems, as in the summer fields, to the end of time, always old and always new.—O. W. HOLMES.

. . . . .

Through primrose tufts in that sweet bower,
The periwinkle trailed its wreaths:
And 'tis my faith that every flower
Enjoys the air it breathes.

. . . . .

The budding twigs spread out their fan
To catch the breezy air:
And I must think, do all I can,
That there was pleasure there.

If this belief from heaven be sent,
If such be nature's holy plan,
Have I not reason to lament,
What man has made of man?

WORDSWORTH.

Within the tropics the wild luxuriance of nature is not lost even in the vicinity of large cities, for the natural vegetation of the hedges and hill-sides overpowers in picturesque effect the artificial labour of man. . . . Houses within the tropics are surrounded by the most beautiful forms of vegetation, because many of them are at the same time most useful to man. Who can doubt that these qualities are united in the banana, the cocoa-nut, the many kinds of palms, the orange, and the bread-fruit tree? . . . .

Epithet after epithet was found too weak to convey to those who have not visited the inter-tropical regions the sensation of delight which the mind experiences. . . . In my last walk I stopped again and again to gaze on those beauties, and endeavoured to fix in my mind for ever an impression, which at the time I knew sooner or later must fail. The form of the orange tree, the cocoa-nut, the palm, the mango, the tree-fern, the banana, will remain clear and separate, but the thousand beauties which unite these into one perfect scene must fade away; yet they will leave, like a tale heard in childhood, a picture full of indistinct but most beautiful figures.—DARWIN.

Fine and varied foliage rather than gay flowers is characteristic of those parts where tropical vegetation attains its highest development. In every locality a lengthened residence will show an abundance of magnificent and gaily-blossomed plants, but they have to be sought for, and are rarely at any one time or place so abundant as to form a perceptible feature in the landscape. I have studied and described individual scenes where vegetation was most luxuriant and beautiful, and fairly stated what effect was produced on them by flowers. And the result of these examinations has convinced me that the bright colours of flowers have a much greater influence on the general aspect of nature in temperate than in tropical climates. During twelve years spent among the grandest tropical vegetation I have seen nothing comparable to the effect produced on our landscapes by gorse, broom, heather, wild hyacinths, hawthorn, purple orchises, and buttercups.—WALLACE.

As regards the foliage of the trees, it might be expected that the variety of tints would be wanting which forms the charm of an English landscape, and that all nature would wear one mantle of unchanging green. But it is not so, and though there is no revolution of seasons, the change of leaf on the same plant exhibits colours as bright as those which tinge the autumnal woods of America. It is not the decaying leaves, but the fresh shoots that exhibit these brightened colours; the older are still vividly green while the young are bursting forth, and the extremities of the branches present tufts of pale yellow, pink, crimson, and purple, which give them at a distance the appearance of clusters of flowers.—SIR E. TENNENT, "Ceylon."

The branching of trees forms an admirable winter study, and one full of interest. It is sufficient to allude to the zig-zag branchlets of the oak with rounded terminal buds, the graceful straight twigs of the beech with lance-shaped buds, the bold stout branches of the horse-chestnut with ovoid buds, and the exquisite subdivided sprays of the elm, like lace-work against the sky. All these characteristic features are due to the form, direction, and setting on of twigs and buds, and are objects of equal interest to the botanist and the artist.—HOOKER.

The forms of leafless trees seen against a clear sky should be entertainment enough even to one who is now commencing the study of botany. If you persevere in that one line of observation, you will in time learn to distinguish the several kinds of trees as easily by their outlines in winter as by their leaves or fruits in summer.—SHIRLEY HIBBERD.

The colouring of flowers follows certain rules. The corollas of few or no plants present all the primary colours, and white alone occurs in most families of plants with coloured corollas. White and various shades of yellow and red are found in roses, tulips, and rhododendrons. Blue, yellow, and white are found in gentians, but very rarely red. Anemones are amongst the few plants in the different kinds of which red, yellow, blue, and white are found. Night-flowering plants have usually large white very strong-scented corollas, on purpose to attract moths. Certain lurid red and purple flowers both look and smell like putrid meat, and hence attract flies, which lay their eggs on them and fly away with the pollen.—HOOKER.

Pink and red flowers almost invariably revert in many individuals to white. Indeed, there is probably not a single blossom of these colours in England of which white specimens may not occasionally be gathered. . . . Almost all pink or red flowers become white with the greatest readiness under cultivation. . . . Blue flowers in nearly every case produce abundant red, pink, and white varieties in a state of nature. . . . In an immense number of cases blue appears as a late modification of red, the bud or young petals being still of that colour, and only deepening into blue as the flower opens.—GRANT ALLEN.

INTRODUCTION.

BOTANY is that division of natural science which comprehends the knowledge of all that relates to the vegetable kingdom. It is divided into several branches, of which it is sufficient here to mention the following :—

1. Structural botany, which has reference to the structure of plants and their various organs.
2. Descriptive and systematic botany, which has to do with the arrangement and classification of plants.
3. Geographical botany, or the distribution of plants over the globe.
4. Fossil botany, which has to do with the plants found in a fossil state in the various geological formations.
5. Economic botany, which has to do with the practical uses to which plants, or parts of them, and their products are put.

We have here only to do with the second and third of these branches, and to a smaller extent with the fifth; and with those only so far as relates to plants found in Western India, which I here take as synonymous with the Bombay Presidency, excluding Sind. To describe the chief phanerogamous, or flowering, plants in that part of India according to their scientific classification is the first object of this book; for I have not been able to include the flowerless orders, such as ferns and mosses, much less the seaweeds; and indeed I do not include all that are botanically called flowering plants, for I have stopped short before coming to the sedges and grasses, which, though the flowers consist only of bracts or scales, are yet included by botanists among the phanerogamous orders. But even with these limitations my task has been more than sufficient for my capacity.

" In botany the term Flora is a collective name for plants, and is used with regard to the vegetable kingdom in the same way as the term Fauna with regard to the animal kingdom. It is common to speak of the Flora of a country or district, and a work devoted to the botany of a country or district is often entitled a Flora of that region."—*Chambers' Encyclopædia.*

The following extract from Mr. Bentham's writings, reproduced by Sir Joseph Hooker at the beginning of the Indian Flora, gives the principles which have been kept in view in the purely botanical part of this book.

"The principal object of a Flora of a country is to afford the means of determining (i.e. ascertaining the name of) any plant growing in it. . . . With this view a Flora consists of descriptions of all the wild or native plants contained in the country in question, so drawn up and arranged that the student may identify any individual specimen which he may gather.

"These descriptions should be clear, concise, accurate, and characteristic, so that each one should be readily adapted to the plant it relates to, and to no other: they should be, as nearly as possible, arranged under natural divisions, so as to facilitate the comparison of each plant with those most nearly allied to it; and they should be accompanied by an artificial key or index, by means of which the student may be guided with the least delay to the individual description belonging to the plant under examination.

"Descriptions should be expressed as much as possible in ordinary well-established language. But for the purpose of accuracy, it is necessary not only to give a more precise technical meaning to many words used more or less commonly and vaguely, but also to introduce purely technical names for such parts or forms of plants as are of little importance except to the botanist.

"At the same time, mathematical accuracy must not be expected. Names cannot be invented for all the infinite forms and appearances assumed by plants and their parts. The same term is not only differently applied by different botanists, but the same writer sometimes gives somewhat different meanings to the same word. The botanist's endeavours should always be, on the one hand to make as near an approach to precision as possible, and on the other hand to avoid that prolixity of detail and overloading with technical terms which tends rather to confusion than clearness."

It should be understood at starting that no one can expect to get any considerable knowledge of the plants around him without taking the trouble to master two branches of the subject mentioned in the above extract: 1, the scientific classification of plants; 2, the technical terms used in botany. Further on in this introduction information will be found as to these two matters, sufficient, it is hoped, to enable any student to go pretty far in the identification of the plants around him. With regard to the second point, viz. the technical terms, a certain amount of apology seems necessary. It is certain that many people are repelled from the study of botany by the number of difficult and unusual words used to describe even the most familiar parts of common flowers. But "though most readers probably entertain at first a persuasion that a writer ought to content himself with the use of common words in their common sense, and feel a repugnance to technical terms and arbitrary rules of phraseology as pedantic and troublesome, yet it is soon found by the student of any branch of science that, without technical terms and fixed rules, there can be no certain or progressive knowledge. . . . Technical description is in reality the only description which is clearly intelligible, but that technical language cannot be understood without being learnt as any other language is learnt."—*Whewell.*[1]

In this book I have endeavoured to cut down the purely technical words to the smallest number possible, and I have dispensed with a good many commonly used by scientific botanists, without, I hope, increasing the difficulty of identification.

The mode in which the scientific part of this book is made up is as follows. The nomenclature and classification are entirely those of Hooker's "Indian Flora;" the descriptions of orders are mainly Hooker's, but with details from other writers; the descriptions of genera are Hooker's, very much compressed, firstly, by the omission of microscopical details, secondly, by the omission of all characteristics which do not apply to all the species of the genus—thus getting rid of the alternatives which so greatly abound in most purely scientific works. The descriptions of species are taken in the main from my own notes, as I was in the habit of writing a full description of each plant when I first saw it, and afterwards comparing

[1] Hist. Inductive Sciences, iii. 340.

other specimens of the same with this description. But I have, of course, compared all these descriptions of my own with those of the same plants already in print, especially Hooker's and Dalzell's, and in all cases of marked difference have done my best to find out the cause and clear up the discrepancy. It must be remembered that a certain amount of difference is inevitable, and does not mean generally that one observer or another has made a mistake since great variations are found, and are to be looked for, in different specimens of the same species, depending on different circumstances of soil, climate, etc.

Besides the short scientific description of each species, given in as easy technical language as may be, I have made special mention of any peculiarities likely to strike the unscientific observer when he first sees the plant, as the unusual size, shape, or colour of any particular part, unusual modes of growth, &c.

Following this are, in as many cases as possible, the native names of the plants, and as to these I have gone on a very simple principle, i.e. to set down all the names that I could find from any source whatever, provided they professed to belong to this side of India; and I have not thought it necessary, under this very inclusive arrangement, to give authorities for the names. But it is necessary to say that I do not myself attach very much importance to this matter of native names. In the case of very well-known trees or remarkable shrubs there are generally one or two names almost universally known; but as regards the rest, and I should say almost all herbs, the names are, I believe, not only very local, but also very indiscriminately applied. My experience is that very few natives know the names of more than a very few plants, and that they apply the few names they know with great latitude; in fact, I have sometimes suspected a facile villager of making up names on the spot for the benefit of the questioner. I quote the great authority of Sir Joseph Hooker in support of this view: "Throughout our travels in India we were struck with the undue reliance on the native names of plants and information of all kinds, and the pertinacity with which each linguist adhered to his own crotchet as to the application of terms to natural objects, and their pronunciation. It is a very prevalent but erroneous impression that savage and half-civilized people have an accurate knowledge of objects of natural history, and a uniform nomenclature for them."[1]

As this is in no respect a strictly scientific work, but intended mostly for unscientific flower-lovers, I have not hesitated to relieve its dryness by quotations both from prose writers and poets; and I believe that, so far as these are apt and in themselves good, they will be approved by those who will mainly use the book.

I may add one other point in which this work will be found to differ from a scientific Flora, i.e. that I have not thought it necessary to separate introduced but naturalized plants from those which are truly indigenous; but I have always, so far as I know, stated the fact. I have also included such garden flowers as I know under their respective orders; but the lists of these I fear will be found very imperfect, owing chiefly to the time that has elapsed since I left India.

There are, of course, a great number of the plants of Western India which I have never seen. These I have described altogether on the authority of Hooker, Dalzell, Graham, &c. It is difficult for any one man, unless he has nothing else to do, or is absolutely unfettered in his movements, to get hold of every plant, even of a single district, and not many officers in twenty years' service visit every part of even the smallest Indian presidency. I myself have never been in the Southern Maratta country at all, and my acquaintance with Guzerat is decidedly limited; and I have no doubt that more deficiencies will be found in this book with reference to plants peculiar to those provinces than in those of the Konkan, which I may claim to know pretty well (and that, with the Ghauts, which bound it on the east, is botanically the richest part of the Presidency), and of the Deccan, with which I have a fair acquaintance.

I should add that all plants which I have not myself seen I have marked with an asterisk. And I have added to the authoritative name of each species (Hooker's), the name under which it is to be found, when that is different, in Dalzell and Gibson's "Bombay Flora."

There are two or three points as to which it may seem that I ought to have given more information. As to the habitat of

[1] Himalayan Journals, 524. The same vagueness is found in old English herbals and flower books, a few common names being applied to many different plants.

the various plants described, i.e. the districts and places where they may be found, I did not keep as many notes as I might have done, and both Dalzell and Graham are rather short in this matter. I have, therefore, in most cases only put the provinces or districts in which the species are found, giving first the localities in which I myself have found them; then the habitats given by Dalzell, Graham, and other local authorities; and finally adding Hooker's habitat when the species is either widely spread through India or confined within very narrow limits in W. India.

The same deficiency, and for the same reason, will be noticed as to the time of year when the different species flower. And I have very rarely given the measurements of leaves, fruits, &c. They are given very fully in the "Indian Flora," but the specimens at Kew, from which these measurements are taken, come from such a very wide range of country that they would, I believe, when applied to plants found in a limited territory like the Bombay Presidency, be quite as often misleading as helpful. The variation in the growth of plants and in the development of their various parts, caused by differences of soil, climate, and other conditions, is so great, that it is almost impossible to give the *ordinary* size of any particular plant of wide distribution, or the average size of its leaves. The following extract from Hooker gives the chief causes of such variations as I have mentioned :—

"A bright light and open situation, particularly at considerable elevations, without too much wet or drought, tends to increase the size and heighten the colour of flowers in proportion to the stature and foliage of the plant. Shade, on the contrary, especially with rich soil and sufficient moisture, tends to increase the foliage and draw up the stem, but to diminish the number, size, and colour of the flowers. A hot climate and dry situation tend to increase the hairs, prickles, and other productions of the Epidermis, and to shorten and stiffen the branches. Moisture in a rich soil has the contrary effect. The neighbourhood of the sea, or a saline soil or atmosphere, imparts a thicker and more succulent consistence to the foliage and almost every part of the plant, and appears not unfrequently to enable plants usually annual to live through the winter.

"The luxuriance of plants growing in a rich soil, and the dwarf, stunted character of those crowded in poor soils, or in the cold, damp regions of high mountain tops, is well known.

Luxuriance, besides increasing the size of the whole plant and of individual parts, may increase the number of the branches, or of the leaves, or of the leaflets, when the leaf is compound."

There is, of course, an aggravating vagueness in the terms "large," "small," "middle-sized," &c., but there seems no alternative between using these and giving measurements that may often mislead. And it must be remembered that the terms "large" and "small" are often used relatively to other species of the same order, e.g. a flower may well be called small in Malvaceæ, an order of decidedly large flowers, which would be large for the next order, Tiliaceæ; or, to put it more popularly, a small rose would make a very large buttercup.

Having explained so far what is to be looked for in this book, I think it advisable to give a little practical advice to those who may have to begin the study of the plants around them without any previous knowledge of botany, and without anyone to help them through their difficulties. The technical terms and the principles of classification (already mentioned) can best be learnt by examination and comparison of individual plants; and for purposes of identification it is a good plan, I think, to begin with the commonest, giving the preference to those with large flowers; if neither English nor Latin name is known, ask for the native name, and look up the description of it in this book. Study the plant so as really to take in the description, not only of the species, but also of the genus and order, to which it belongs; if there is anything else of the same order very common, get that, and note the resemblances and differences between the two species. In this way both the eye and the mind will be quickly educated into the main distinctions that exist between flower and flower. Or, as a plan that may be tried concurrently with the above, collect as many species as possible of those orders which are very distinct, and of which the general appearance is known to almost everyone—the leguminous, the mallows, the labiates, and so on.[1] In the identification of these, and always in the case of plants which are quite unknown, the proper way is to proceed from the greater to the lesser divisions—that is, beginning with the order, go through the tribes until you find the one to which the

[1] I omit the compound flowers (Compositæ) from this list, as the genera and species are often very difficult for beginners to distinguish.

specimen seems to belong; then go through the genera in the same way, and when the genus is fixed on which seems to agree, go through its species. Only the beginner must not expect the description of either tribe or genus (and very often not of the order either) to be so plainly what is wanted as to enable him to reach his species without a good many mistakes and disappointments. But I believe that anyone who takes the trouble carefully to examine all the commonest species about him, and also all those he can get of orders which he knows, and to learn all he can about the families they belong to, will soon get a foundation which will enable him within a reasonable time to identify nearly everything he meets with. I say nearly everything, because, even after years of study and practice, plants occasionally come before one which, after a great deal of trouble, have still to be left unidentified.

But in this, as in most other studies, the advantage of two or three students working together, or, if they cannot work together, comparing notes as often as possible, can scarcely be exaggerated. And there is the further resource of preserving specimens and submitting them to well-known authorities. For this purpose proper botanical paper is generally necessary, and boards for pressing, at all events in the case of the larger plants. But I confess to an unscientific preference for paintings or drawings of plants to dried specimens. It matters not how rough the drawings may be, but they must be strictly accurate or they will be useless; any parts of the flowers that may be remarkable should be separately portrayed, and careful notes taken of place of growth, season of flowering, size of plant, etc.

With regard to carrying flowers home after they have been picked, a tin box of some sort is even more necessary in India than in England, as in the heat they wither so much more quickly. I have always thought a tin cylinder (a small map-case, in fact) more convenient than the oblong case generally used by botanists. The movable top excludes the air better than any sort of lid, and the cylindrical case is handier to carry when walking, or even when taking casual rides. No one, without trying it, would believe how much a case of this sort, of a size to go comfortably in the hand, will hold, or how fresh the flowers come out of it even after many hours.

I conclude with a list of the books available for botanical study in W. India, to all of which I have referred very freely.

Sir J. Hooker's "Flora of British India" is, of course, the authoritative work for all India, and invaluable for reference, though it is too large and expensive for those whom I desire to serve. Besides which, owing to the immense range of country it refers to (far greater than the limits of British India), it includes such a vast number of species as to make identification in very many cases difficult, except for very advanced botanists.

2. Professor Oliver's "First Book of Indian Botany" is useful for the study of the orders, &c., but it does not profess to describe more species than are sufficient to serve as examples of each order.

3. The "Bombay Flora" of Dalzell and Gibson, published in 1861, is the only work which professes to give a full list of the plants known in Western India up to that time. It is what I always worked with, for want of a better book; but its defects are very great, the chief being that it contains descriptions of species only, without any of orders or genera, so that it was next to useless without two or three other books to refer to. The language also is exceedingly technical, and there is an (apparently intentional) absence of everything in the way of popular description or information. The book is, I believe, out of print.

4. Graham's "Plants of Bombay" is, from its accuracy and easy style, a most valuable little book, but it is little more than a list of plants known nearly sixty years ago, as the author unfortunately died (in 1838) before the larger work which he proposed to bring out was well in hand. The book was difficult to get twenty years ago, and must be much more scarce now.

5. Roxburgh's "Flora Indica" contains the most full and admirable descriptions of the plants which he knew; but it contains only a fraction of the plants now known, and of that fraction only a small proportion are found in Western India.

6. Dr. Brandis's two books on Indian trees are most valuable as to all trees, including a good many which in one part of India or another are found only as shrubs. Smaller and more partial works I need not refer to.

DEFINITIONS.

THE following definitions are taken mainly from the "Indian Flora," but with many omissions, additions, and alterations.

1. "The *plant* includes, in its botanical sense, every being which has vegetable life, from the loftiest tree to the humblest moss, and extends even further, to the mould or fungus which attacks our provisions and the green scum which floats on our ponds." Putting aside these lower forms of vegetation, we have to do only with flowering (or *phanerogamous*) plants, which are divided into herbs, shrubs, and trees.

2. *Herbs* are those plants of which the whole or nearly the whole dies down after flowering. Of these *annuals* are those which spring up from seed, bloom, ripen their seed, and die within twelve months. *Biennials* spring up and produce leaves the first year, but do not produce flower or seed till the second, and then die. *Perennials*, springing up like the last in the first year, produce neither flower nor fruit till the third year at the earliest, and then live on for an uncertain period. Biennials and perennials have a woody stock and root, which live through one and several winters respectively.

3. *Shrubs* have a perennial woody portion, branching near the base, which forms the greater part of the plant, from which the flowering branches shoot out each year. *Undershrubs* are smaller, and the flowering branches form a larger proportion of the whole plant.

4. *Trees*, besides being larger than shrubs, have a distinct woody trunk, scarcely branching from the base.

But *note*, that the same botanical species may be an annual or perennial, a herbaceous perennial or an undershrub, an undershrub or a shrub, a shrub or a tree, according to climate, treatment, or variety.

5. Another classification of plants is into *terrestrial*, *aquatic*, or *parasitical*, according as they grow on earth, as by far the greater part do, in water, or on other plants. *Epiphytes* are distinguished from parasites by growing on the surface of other plants without deriving sustenance from them.

6. Trees or shrubs are called *deciduous* when they get and lose their leaves at a particular time of the year, *evergreen* when they remain clothed with leaves throughout the year.

7. The parts of plants which every one can recognize are the root, stem, leaves, flowers, and fruit. But the varieties of these, and the different parts of which they are made up, and their forms, require a good deal of explanation.

Note.—Here should be noticed a very common error. On asking for information about a tree or shrub, one is often told "it has no flower," or "it has no fruit;" the fact being that the flower is inconspicuous, or the fruit does not appear under the given circumstances. But every plant, except such low forms as ferns, mosses, lichens, seaweeds, &c., has a flower of some sort, and every plant, except those which are exclusively male (the female plants of the same species being then found separately), will under natural conditions produce fruit, or at least seed; though there are many which, when removed from their natural conditions, will not flower, and many more which, under similar circumstances, flower, but will not fruit.

8. I. The Root.—Roots which consist chiefly of slender fibres are called *fibrous*; those which consist mainly of one main tapering root going straight down are called *tap roots:* such fleshy roots as carrots and turnips are looked on as modifications of tap roots. Those which have the main root or its branches thickened into one or more fleshy or woody masses are called *tuberous*, as in the potato. *Bulbs*, which are commonly looked on as roots, are really subterranean buds growing on the lower part of the stem (*stock*) of perennial plants, and the real roots are the fibres at the bottom of the bulb.

Roots are sometimes given off from the stems of climbers or creepers, as in ivy, and more rarely from buds, which in some plants are produced on the edges of the leaves; see *Bryophyllum*. Aquatic plants sometimes bear *vesicles* or air-bladders on their roots, just as tubers are borne on the roots of terrestrial plants.

9. II. The Stem.—The stems of plants are mostly cylindrical (in ordinary language round), but sometimes angular or flat. In the great majority of plants they are *erect*, i.e. growing straight upwards without support. Of plants which are not erect, the stems sometimes climb by extending themselves over the surface of trees, walls, or other supports, and sometimes twine, by winding spirally round any object that they attach themselves to. *Creepers* are those whose stems lie flat on the ground, and put out roots at the joints. When the stems lie flat without thus rooting they are called *prostrate*, and when partially prostrate *procumbent*. Plants which are erect with a tendency to climb, are sometimes called *ascending*, and the same term is often applied to plants which first spread a little horizontally and then become erect.

Those points of the stem at which branches or leaves are given off are called *nodes*, and the same term is applied to similar points in the branches themselves.

10. When a plant has no proper stem, and the leaves are therefore all radical (i.e. from the root), the naked stalk which bears the flowers, as in the primrose, the hyacinth, &c., is called the *scape*.

11. III. The Leaf.—The stalk of a leaf, when it has one, is called the *petiole;* when it has none, the leaf is *sessile*. The point where the leaf, whether petioled or sessile, leaves the stem is called the *axil* of the leaf. This is, therefore, almost the same as the node of the stem.

Sessile leaves are called *stem-clasping*, when the base of the leaf is closely attached to the stem, *perfoliate* when the bases of two opposite leaves are so united that the stem seems to run through them, as in the common honeysuckle.

12. The petiole may have appendages on it quite distinct from the stem, as in the orange; these are called *wings;* but sometimes the lower part of the leaf, not shaped as a petiole, runs down into the stem, and forms a sort of wing on it; the leaf is then called *decurrent.* When the lower part of the leaf or the petiole expands into a sheath surrounding the stem, as in many plants of the orders *Scitamineæ* and *Commelinaceæ,* it is called *sheathing.* When the petiole is attached, not to the base of the leaf, but to its centre or some other part of the under-surface, the leaf is called *peltate,* as in many species of order *Menispermaceæ.*

13. The continuation of the petiole running generally through the middle of the leaf, and forming its back-bone, so to speak, is the *midrib.* The veins of leaves are either *reticulated,* i.e. forming a network running in all directions, or parallel to one another, and generally to the midrib. This is a distinction of the first importance in classification. The main veins are called *nerves,* and it is sometimes essential to describe leaves as 3-nerved, 5-nerved, etc. In fleshy leaves the nerves are often scarcely distinguishable.

14. *Arrangement of leaves with regard to the stem.*—When most of the leaves of a plant are arranged about the root they are called *radical,* those of the stem being then called *cauline;* when the leaves are in pairs all up the stem, one on each side of it, they are *opposite;* when they occur singly, taking each side of the stem in turn, they are *alternate;* when each pair of opposite leaves is at right angles to the next pair they are *decussate;* when the leaves are arranged one above the other in two opposite rows, one on each side of the stem or branch, they are called *distichous* or *bifarious.*[1] When three or more leaves surround the stem at one point they are called *whorled,* or *verticelled.*

Note.—Opposite, alternate, or whorled leaves are respectively characteristic of many orders, so that it is often essential to notice the arrangement.

15. *The division of leaves.*—Leaves are either simple or compound: *simple* when all in one piece, even though they be cut into *lobes* or segments, as those of the vine, and of most of the genus *Hibiscus; compound,* when they are composed of two or more pieces, looking each like a separate small leaf, as those of gram or the *nim* tree: these divisions are called *leaflets.* Simple leaves, which are oblong and deeply divided into segments on each side of the midrib are *pinnatifid:* if the terminal lobe of a pinnatifid leaf is much the largest it is called *lyrate:* those which are roundish and rather deeply divided into segments towards the petiole are *palmate,* those divided almost down to the petiole *digitate;* if the lobes are narrow and very irregular the leaf is *laciniate.* Of compound leaves, those which are

---

[1] A green branchlet, with leaves thus arranged, may sometimes be mistaken for a pinnate leaf.

composed of 3 separate leaflets, are called *trifoliate;*[1] those with 5 or 7 leaflets are expressed in this work as 5-*foliate or* 7-*foliate.*

16. *A pinnate* leaf is one composed of more than 3 leaflets arranged on each side of the midrib, or common petiole. If the number of leaflets be even, the leaf is said to be *evenly* or *abruptly pinnated;* if uneven, *unevenly* or *unequally pinnated.* In this case the odd leaflet is often called the *terminal* one.

The divisions of pinnate leaves are themselves sometimes pinnate, as in many of the Acacias. The leaf is then called *decompound,* or *bipinnate,* or *tripinnate,* as the case may be: the *pinnæ* are then the larger divisions of the leaf, the leaflets the divisions of the pinnæ.

Note, that leaflets may have all, or nearly all, the characteristics of simple leaves, i.e. they may be sessile or petioled, opposite or alternate on the common petiole or midrib, and may be very various in shape and the outline of their edges.

17. *The edges of leaves.*—When the edge is even, and without teeth or depressions of any sort, the leaf is *entire;* when it has small, sharp teeth, like a saw, it is *serrate;* if the teeth are rounded it is *crenate;* if deeply notched, *dentate;* if the edge is not toothed, but has broad and shallow depressions, the leaf is *sinuate;* if the depressions are shallower and less marked it is *wavy* or *undulate;* if the leaf is fringed with hairs it is *ciliated.* The above terms are also applied to petals, sepals, bracts, etc. The term *pectinated,* implying that the teeth are long and narrow, like a comb, is applied oftener to these smaller organs than to leaves.

18. *The shape of the leaf.*—The number of terms used in botany to express the different shapes of leaves is exceedingly great, but the following will, it is thought, be sufficient in a work of this sort.

The narrowest possible leaf, not tapering to either end, is called *linear,* though, of course, every leaf must have some breadth; equally narrow, but tapering to a point, *subulate* or awl-shaped; a narrow leaf, shaped like the head of a lance, is *lanceolate;* an egg-shaped leaf, i.e. broader than lanceolate and broadest in the middle, is *oval* (*ovate* is used variously by different authors, but may be taken as approaching oval, but broader); *elliptic* may be taken as something between oval and lanceolate; when the upper end is decidedly the broadest the leaf is *obovate;* when the leaf does not broaden in the middle it is *oblong;* when it tapers sharply from the middle to the base it is *cuneate,* or wedge-shaped; *spathulate* (ladle-shaped) when the top is broad, and the lower and narrow part long; *heart-shaped,* which explains itself, implies that the broad part is nearest the petiole or stem; *cordate* is applied to a leaf of any shape, if its base be like the broad part of a heart; kidney-shaped, or *reniform,* is roundish, broader than long, and cordate; *falcate* is curved, like the blade of a sickle. When the lower part of the leaf is prolonged into two acute lobes, it is called *sagittate,* or arrow-shaped; when these lobes are not acute, but rounded, and more or less ear-shaped, it is *auricled.* When the two sides of a leaf are unequal it is called *oblique;* this is often the case at the base of the leaf only.

---

[1] I retain this rather than the modern and more correct word *trifolioliate,* which seems needlessly pedantic for my purpose.

19. With regard to the end of the leaf, the terms used are *pointed; acute* when the point is sharp; *blunt,* or *obtuse; truncate* when the end is cut off more or less abruptly; *retuse* when, being blunt, it is also slightly indented. Leaves sometimes end in spines, or bristles, or *awns,* which are fine but stiff hairs.

Note.—When two terms are combined, as linear-lanceolate, oval-oblong, it is understood that the shape is something between the two, and in such cases the leaves generally vary, more or less, from one shape to the other.

20. The above terms apply not only to sepals, petals, bracts, etc., but also to *stipules,* which are leaf-like appendages (generally small) at the base of the petiole. *Stipels* are the stipules of leaflets.

Floral leaves are the small leaves which are often found close to the flower, especially in spikes and racemes. They are often scarcely distinguishable from bracts.

Note that "*sub*" is prefixed to adjectives of description (sub-lanceolate, sub-acid, etc.) to modify them, and is equivalent to "more or less," or "a little."

21. IV. THE FLOWER. A perfect flower should have the following parts present and capable of performing their functions, viz. calyx, corolla, stamens, pistil. The flower is considered imperfect if any of these are absent or imperfect. Each of these organs consists of several parts, which have their technical names.

22. *Calyx and Corolla.*—The *calyx* (or cup, so called from its usual shape) is the outer or protecting covering (or envelope), generally green, which encloses the other parts of the flower when in bud. The segments into which the calyx is generally divided are called *sepals,* which are either quite distinct or more or less united. The calyx very often falls off before the fruit matures; when it remains and is attached to the fruit it is called *persistent.* The position of the calyx with regard to the ovary will be mentioned under the latter organ.

23. The *corolla* is the inner or attractive covering or envelope, and being usually coloured and larger than the calyx, is that which generally gives the flower its beauty, and is, in fact, in common speech often called the flower. The divisions are called *petals,* and these may be all equal and symmetrical, in which case the corolla is *regular,* or unequal, in which case it is *irregular.* For examples of extreme irregularity see orders Balsamineæ and Orchideæ. On the corolla being all in one piece (*monopetalous*), or divided into several petals (*polypetalous*), a good deal depends in the classification of plants.

24. Of the monopetalous corolla, the lower part, which is entirely united, is called the *tube,* but this may be, and often is, so short as to have nothing tubular in appearance. The upper part of the corolla is then called the *limb,* and this is generally divided into *lobes* or *segments:* in practice, these lobes, if divided deeply, are often called, though not correctly, petals.

A corolla is called *tubular* when the whole or the greater part of it is in the form of a tube or cylinder, as in either of the *Plumbagos, bell-shaped* (*campanulate*) when more or less in the shape of a bell;

salver-shaped when the lower part is tubular and the lobes spread out horizontally, as in *Vinca rosea* and the English periwinkles; *funnel-shaped* when the tube broadens from the bottom and the lobes expand more or less horizontally.

25. The commonest form of irregular monopetalous corolla is *two-lipped*, or *bilabiate*, when the limb separates into two parts, something in the way of a mouth with lips, as in the various species of *Antirrhinum* and *Salvia*. In this case we speak of the *upper* and *lower lip* of the corolla, these lips being generally lobed or toothed; of the *palate*, which is the part, often raised and not unfrequently spotted or hairy, just within the lobes of the lower lip; and of the *throat*, which is the entrance to the tube.

Note.—The term two-lipped is also applied to some polypetalous corollas, if arranged so as to give that appearance, and also to the calyx of many plants.

A petal is said to be *clawed* when its lower part is suddenly narrowed into what to some extent corresponds to the petiole of a leaf, as in the genus *Lagerstrœmia*: *spurred* when it is produced downwards into a narrow cylinder or *spur*: *saccate* when expanded into a little bag or *sac*.

26. The arrangement of the petals in the unopened flower (often apparent also after it is opened) is called the *æstivation*, and sometimes requires to be noticed. If the edges of the different petals meet evenly the æstivation is said to be *valvate*, if the petals much overlap each other it is *imbricated* (this term is also much used with reference to bracts); if the petals are twisted together, it is *twisted*. When four opened petals are so shaped and arranged as to form a cross, they are called *cruciate*.

27. In many flowers either the calyx or corolla is wanting; the single floral envelope that exists is then generally called the *perianth*; its divisions are called *sepals*, as if it were the calyx. In some cases (e.g. orders *Liliaceæ*, *Iridaceæ*, etc.), though there is both calyx and corolla, yet from their being both coloured, and otherwise very much alike, the whole is often called the perianth.

28. When there are six or more separate petals (whether with or without calyx) they are sometimes so disposed as to be in two or three different rows, one outside the other; they are then said to be in two or more *series*, or rows. This term is applied also to sepals, bracts, etc. (see especially order *Compositæ*). Flowers, as roses, etc., which by cultivation or otherwise develop several rows of petals instead of stamens, are called *double*.

29. *Stamens and Pistil.*—The stamens and pistil, being the male and female organs of generation or reproduction, are really the most important parts of the flower, and occupy the centre of it, though they are by no means the most conspicuous parts. The modern view is to look on the calyx and corolla as meant mainly to protect these more important organs while forming, and to promote reproduction by means of insects when the stamens and pistil are mature.[1]

A flower that has no pistil (or female organ) is called *a male flower*;

[1] On this subject the unscientific reader may be referred to the works of Sir John Lubbock and Mr. Grant Allen.

one that has no stamens, *a female flower;* the great majority of flowers have both organs, and are therefore called *hermaphrodite.* Sometimes the male and female flowers are distinct, some being without pistil, others without stamens (see orders *Menispermaceæ* and *Cucurbitaceæ*). When the sexes are thus distinct but on the same plant, the flowers are called *monœcious*; when distinct but on different plants, *diœcious*; when male, female, and hermaphrodite flowers are all found either on the same or different plants, they are called *polygamous.*

30. Stamens, which vary from one to an indefinite number, are always for the whole or a great part of their length inside the corolla, but their attachment to corolla calyx or disk is a matter of importance in classification. Stamens are said to be *hypogynous* when they are inserted below the ovary; *epigynous* when inserted upon the ovary; *perigynous* when, by being attached to the calyx, they surround the ovary. The same terms are sometimes applied to petals under similar circumstances.

31. The stamen consists of stalk or *filament*,[1] surmounted by the *anther*, which is generally a round or oblong body. When the filaments are absent the anthers are *sessile.* The anthers are generally divided into two cells, comparatively seldom visible to the naked eye; these cells are sometimes distant from one another, and are then joined by a *connective* (see *Melastoma*). The anthers are filled and covered with a yellow dust, *pollen*, which fertilizes the pistil. The stamens are said to be *included* when more or less concealed in the corolla tube, *exserted* when they protrude beyond the level of the petals.

32. When several stamens are united either into a column (as in *Malvaceæ*) or into a tube (as in *Meliaceæ*), or more loosely, they are called *monadelphous*, when in two columns or parcels (as in many of the Leguminosæ) *diadelphous.* When there are four stamens in two pairs, one pair longer than the other, they are called *didynamous*, as in *Labiatæ* and other orders; when there are six stamens, two pairs longer and one pair shorter, as in *Cruciferæ*, they are *tetradynamous.*

33. The *pistil* occupies the exact centre of the flower, and though there is said to be never more than one, yet many flowers, e.g. all the Ranunculaceæ, have a number of *carpels* so slightly united as to appear to be so many distinct pistils, and these separate carpels sometimes produce separate fruits, e.g. Saccopetalum. Some authors call the pistil *simple* when it consists of a single carpel, compound when it consists of more than one. In the first case the terms pistil and carpel are synonymous.

34. The pistil when undivided consists of the *ovary*, the lowest part, the *style*, which corresponds to the filament in a stamen, and the *stigma*, which corresponds to the anther. Each carpel may be composed exactly as an undivided pistil, and a single ovary may have more than one style, and a style more than one stigma. In many cases the styles are wanting, so that the stigma is *sessile* on the ovary; and very often the stigmas are not to the naked eye

---

[1] From filum, a thread, from which comes also the the term *filiform*, or thread-like, applied to various very small and delicate parts of flowers.

distinguishable from the top of the style. So also it is often difficult for those who do not use a microscope to determine whether there is one style with several branches or several distinct styles, and whether one style has several stigmas or one stigma branched or lobed.

35. The *placenta* is the part of the inside of the ovary to which the *ovules*, which are the first germs of the future seeds, are attached. In all works of scientific botany the nature of the placenta and the position of the ovules are made much of, but these being mainly microscopical details, do not come within the scope of this work.

The main parts of the perfect flower having been described, some less important details have to be mentioned before the fruit is considered.

36. The stalk of the flower is called the *pedicel;* when a number of flowers are aggregated the common stalk is called the *peduncle*, each separate flower (unless sessile) having its own pedicel.[1] The extremity of the pedicel on which the corolla and ovary (and sometimes the stamens) are inserted is called the *receptacle, thalamus*, or *torus*. It is often not sufficiently enlarged to be readily noticed. The *disk* is a more or less circular enlargement of the receptacle, and may be entire, cut, or divided. It is always inside the calyx. When the parts of the disk are quite separate they are often called *glands.* In many of the orders of division *Disciflorœ*, the disk is very conspicuous, but in very many plants it is either absent or minute.

37. *Bracts* are leaf-like appendages to the flower, much as stipules are to leaves; they very often resemble the sepals in size and shape. Their most usual position is at the base of the flower, but sometimes they are on the pedicel or the main stem. There are sometimes larger bracts at the base of the pedicel and smaller ones at the base of the flower; these latter are then called *bracteoles.* When a number of bracts are united in a whorl they are called an *involucre*, a number of bracteoles similarly united an *involucel.* (See orders *Malvaceœ, Umbelliferœ*, and *Acanthaceœ.*) Bracts or other parts of the flower when from the first dry and withered looking are called *scarious.*

38. The way in which the separate flowers are arranged is called the *inflorescence* of the plant. If the flowers occur one by one they are said to be *solitary*, if two together *twin.* A number of sessile flowers arranged round a stem or branch is called a *whorl* (see order Labiatæ); collected into a round or oval cluster, a *head;* arranged on or round one main peduncle one above the other, a *spike.*

39. A number of stalked flowers arranged on or round a main peduncle one above the other is a *raceme*, arranged on a branched peduncle, a *panicle.* A panicle is *dichotomous* when each branch forks into two, and the same forking occurs again and again; *trichotomous* when each branch forks into three. When several branches or pedicels of the same length start from the same point of the peduncle (radiating like the ribs of an umbrella), the inflorescence is an *umbel.* (See order Umbelliferæ) The terms *cyme*

---

[1] When a flower is solitary its stalk is often called peduncle or pedicel indifferently.

and *corymb* are less definite than the above, and are used when the inflorescence is not exactly that of any of them, the flowers being all more or less level at the top. The corymb is considered to be a modification of the raceme, the cyme of the panicle. A *fascicle* may perhaps be best described as an imperfect whorl of stalked flowers. An *ament* or *catkin* is the spike of imperfect flowers characteristic of the old order *Amentacea*. A *spadix* is a fleshy spike, containing flowers only in the lower part, and enclosed in a large bract called a *spathe;* this arrangement is characteristic of *Aroideæ*, and two or three allied orders.

40. When the flowers, whatever the inflorescence may be, proceed from the axils of the leaves, they are said to be *axillary;* when occurring only at the top of the stem or branches, *terminal.*

41. Any part of a flower that quickly falls off is called *deciduous;* any part that is united to another part, as the calyx often is to the ovary, is called *adnate* to it: *connate* is used in much the same sense.

42. V. The Fruit.[1]—The enlarged ovary is, generally speaking, the fruit of the plant: in many cases, however, the ovary is so altered in shape, or by the adhesion to it of the calyx or other parts, that it can only be called the foundation or first form of the fruit. Generally speaking, a single perfect or female flower produces a single fruit; but where the ovary has several distinct carpels, distinct fruits are often found. On the other hand, where a number of flowers grow on a common receptacle, a single fruit sometimes results, as in the pine-apple, which is made up of the ovaries and floral envelopes of several flowers combined, and *Morinda citrifolia*, the fruit of which is composed of many drupes coalescent into a fleshy round head like an apple.

43. Any part of the flower which remains, and forms part of the fruit (as the calyx or part of it, or the style often do), is called *persistent.* Fruits are called *succulent* when they are fleshy or juicy; *dry* when they have neither flesh, pulp, nor juice; *dehiscent* when they open naturally to let out the seeds; *indehiscent* when they do not so open. In the last case the seeds are liberated by the rotting of the fruit, or by passing through the birds which eat the fruit.

44. The principal dehiscent fruits are the following: The *capsule*. a general name for a dry fruit: it most often splits into valves, but sometimes breaks up irregularly, sometimes opens like a lid from a box, when it is called *circumsciss;* the *legume*, or *pod*, having two valves, with the seeds attached to a placenta on one side (see order *Leguminosæ*[2]); the *silique*, which opens by two longitudinal slits, forming two valves, separating from a central frame, to which the seeds adhere (see order *Cruciferæ*); the *follicle*, also two-valved, but opening by one longitudinal slit only, and with the seeds variously

---

[1] The limitation of the word fruit to eatable products is not recognized botanically, every plant as a rule having its own fruit.

[2] Although the fruit of all leguminous plants are called legumes, there are some genera in which it is indehiscent, and others in which it separates into one-seeded joints (see gen. Pongamia and Desmodium).

distributed (see orders *Apocyneæ* and *Asclepiadeæ*). A solitary follicle seldom occurs, two or more generally forming one fruit. When a fruit is made up of two or three united one-seeded carpels, which finally separate, these are called *cocci*. (See order *Euphorbiaceæ*.) A capsule, or other fruit, having two equal rounded lobes is called *didymous*.

45. The principal indehiscent fruits are the *berry*, a fleshy fruit with many seeds, as the guava; the *drupe*, a fleshy fruit, with one seed, as the mango and peach:[1] the *nut*, a hard and dry shell, containing a single seed: the name *achene* is generally given to the same when the fruit is small and seed-like; the *samara*, a thin nut with an extensive wing.

46. The parts of the drupe called botanically *epicarp*, *mesocarp*, and *endocarp*, are in most cases commonly known as skin, flesh, and stone, the latter enclosing the kernel or seed. *Pericarp* is used of the whole of the fruit outside of the seed or seeds.

When the endocarp consists of several distinct stones or nuts these are called *pyrenes*. In some cases, as in orders Boragineæ and Labiatæ, these look like naked seeds.

47. The base of the seed, by which it is attached to the placenta, is called the *hilum*, the opposite extremity the *point* or *apex*, that part which becomes the root of the new plant is the *radicle*, which in order *Rhizophoreæ* (mangroves) is very remarkably developed. The seed is sometimes more or less covered by a skin or *aril*, which, being coloured, is often very conspicuous.

48. In a few orders, e.g. *Coniferæ*, the seeds are not enclosed in a fruit, but are naked: these orders are, therefore, called *gymnospermous*.

49. Before finishing with the fruit, it may be said that beginners often find it difficult to say under what designation a particular fruit should come. The walnut is a drupe, the eatable part being an unusally large lobed seed, the shell being a two-valved endocarp, and the green fibrous outer covering epicarp and mesocarp, which, being united, H. in this case calls exocarp. In the cocoa-nut, which is also called a drupe, the green fibrous covering is epicarp, the hard shell the endocarp, the eatable pulp the albumen, in which the embryo of the seed is embedded at the base of the fruit. The orange is a berry divided into a number of cells, the walls (or dissepiments) of which are membranous. The banana, or plantain, is a succulent indehiscent many-seeded fruit, properly speaking a berry. The name *pome* is given to the apple, pear, etc., in which the fleshy, eatable part is the swollen peduncle,[2] while the scaly cells, or core, enclosing the seeds are the endocarp. The acorn is a nut with a leathery shell, which the seed completely fills: the cup is not part of the fruit, but is formed by the union of many hardened bracts or floral leaves.

---

[1] Hooker does not entirely keep to this distinction between the berry and the drupe, but sometimes calls a fruit a berry-like drupe, considering any fruit to be a drupe if the seed or seeds are enclosed in a stone or other covering, a berry if the seeds are not so enclosed.

[2] This is the description in Hooker's "Primer;" other authors describe the formation of the pome differently.

50. The following minor parts of plants require to be mentioned:—*Tendrils* are either abortive petioles or peduncles, or else the ends of branches or of midribs of leaves, which by holding on to and coiling round any object within reach help to support the plant. Thorns, or *spines*, and prickles are produced on many parts of plants, sometimes on almost all parts of the same plant. "In all rocky and parched situations plants become more spiny, the free development of foliage being checked." *Hooker.* The term *armed* is frequently applied to plants which have either thorns or prickles.

51. The distinction between rough and smooth leaves or plants is apparent to every one, but many terms have been found necessary to describe the various sorts of hairs which clothe the leaves and other parts, and their density. Generally speaking, however, these terms will not be found in this book, the terms rough and smooth, hairy, very hairy, etc., being considered sufficient. The term *glabrous* is used to describe a plant, or part of it, that is free from hairs, *smooth* implying freedom from roughness of surface of every sort; *pubescent* implies a slight downiness. The terms *furrowed, wrinkled, ribbed, warty,* which describe variations from perfect smoothness, explain themselves.

52. The surface of a leaf or other organ is *glaucous* when it is of a pale bluish-green, often with a fine bloom; *glandular*, when more or less covered with *glands*, which are small, fleshy, watery, or oily bodies, sometimes mere dots. *Viscid, viscous,* or *glutinous* are the terms used when a surface is covered with a sticky or clammy exudation; *papillæ* are minute protuberances, often only visible as dots.

INDEX TO DEFINITIONS.

(*The numbers refer to the paragraphs.*)

CLASSIFICATION.

In classification it is necessary first to explain what is to be understood by a species. A species comprises all the individual plants which resemble each other sufficiently to make it apparent that they all are, or may have been, descended from a common ancestor, as for instance anyone would feel certain of this as to all the oak trees or all the mango trees that he may meet with from time to time. These individuals may often differ from each other in many particulars (as well as in the mere size of the plants), such as the colour of the flowers, the size of the leaves, etc.; but these differences would scarcely hide from any one the identity of the trees, and are such as experience shows are likely to occur in seedlings raised from the same tree or herb.

When a large number of individuals of a species differ from the others in any striking particular they constitute a *variety*; but it is almost needless to say that botanists constantly differ as to whether a particular variation is sufficient to make a separate species or merely to constitute a variety. Varieties are much more numerous and striking in well-known garden flowers (e.g. roses and tulips) than in wild flowers; because it is to the interests of florists in the case of garden flowers to make and perpetuate differences in the blossoms of some plants and the foliage of others.

The known species of plants (now near 100,000) are grouped into *genera*, a *genus* containing a number of species resembling each other in the most important points of structure. Each genus has a Latin (substantive) name; and each species belonging to the genus has that *generic* name, as it is called, with a Latin adjective joined to it, the two words forming the *specific* name. Thus the teak tree is *Tectona grandis*; the shoe flower and the vegetable *bhendi* are two species of the same genus, *Hibiscus*, the former being *H. rosasinensis*, and the latter *H.*

esculentus. This system of grouping and nomenclature was invented by the great Linnæus.

The genera, which number about 6000, had next to be divided into families or *orders.* Linnæus made his orders depend on the number and other peculiarities of the organs of generation, i.e. the stamens and pistils; but this arrangement, which is certainly the easiest for beginners, and therefore probably the most suitable when botanical classification was a new science, has now been generally abandoned. The system of division into orders now universally adopted takes into account all resemblances and differences, especially those of the flower and fruit, valuing them according to their evident or presumed importance, and is therefore called the natural system. These special characters of the orders are sometimes obvious to the common observer, as in the case of the carrot and the parsnip, or between the common pea and gram, the near relationship between which any one could see; sometimes they are similarities which cannot be recognized without botanical knowledge, as in the case of the potato plant and the tobacco plant, which, though so different in appearance, belong to the same order.

The natural orders have been further grouped into great divisions or *classes*, and all the classes brought into one of the two *sub-kingdoms* of flowering and flowerless plants.

Thus the general Flora of the world has been built up and classified by the learned, who have examined all the plants that are. It is the reverse process that we have to do with, and anyone wishing to identify any particular plant must work downwards from the greater to the lesser divisions. So it is necessary here to give short descriptions of the classes and orders in which the plants of Western India are found, the genera and species being described in the body of the book, with further particulars as to the orders.

The following are the classes into which plants are divided according to Bentham and Hooker's "Genera Plantarum," on which Hooker's "Flora of British India" is founded.

The first great division is into Dicotyledons and Monocotyledons, otherwise called Exogens and Endogens (the names which will be used in this book), under one or other of which denominations all flowering plants come. Dicotyledons are those whose seeds when the skin is removed separate into two lobes (cotyledons). At the hinge or point of junction of the two lobes may be seen the radicle, or incipient root, and the plumule, or incipient bud. A pea or bean or the seed of any large leguminous tree will give as good an example of this as can be, but the skin must be taken off carefully and the *embryo* (the inner part of the seed) handled tenderly. In small seeds it is difficult to distinguish the parts except with a microscope.

The other characteristics of Exogens are, firstly, that the stems in trees or other perennials are composed of pith, fibre in regular concentric layers, and bark; and secondly, that the leaves have a midrib, from which the veins branch out in all directions, forming a fine network.

In Monocotyledons or Endogens, on the other hand, the embyro on the skin being removed does not divide into two parts, and the young plant is developed from a sheath-like cavity on one side. A grain of wheat is a sufficient example. Besides this, the stems of endogens are not separable into pith, fibre, wood, and bark, but consist of fibre irregularly imbedded in cellular tissue with a firmly adherent rind outside. The leaves also, which are, as a rule, simple and entire, have generally no midrib, but simple and parallel veins running longitudinally.

The most obvious of the above distinctions to the ordinary observer is that of the veins of the leaves, but there are a few genera and species of Monocotyledons which have leaves with netted veins.

The first great division of Exogens is into polypetalous and monopetalous, i.e. those having a corolla of separate petals or of one piece respectively.

A. Exogens.

Polypetalous exogens, Polypetalæ, are described thus. Plants having the stamens and pistil surrounded within the calyx by separate petals, to which they are not attached.

But to the above definition there are various exceptions.

(1.) When the stamens are monadelphous the petals generally adhere more or less to the staminal tube or column.

(2.) In some orders, e.g. Olacineæ, Ilicineæ, etc., the petals adhere slightly at the base.

(3.) In a few small genera in various orders the corolla is

truly monopetalous, bearing the stamens, or is with the latter hypogynous.[1]

(4.) In many orders there are some genera or species without petals, especially in Ranunculaceæ, Sterculiaceæ, and Sapindaceæ.

Polypetalous Exogens include the first three sections given below.

I. THALAMIFLORÆ. (Orders Ranunculaceæ to Tiliaceæ.)

Sepals generally distinct, free from the ovary. Torus small, rarely expanded into a disk; petals inserted on the torus, and therefore below the ovary, or more rarely on the base of the calyx; stamens indefinite or definite, inserted as the petals, free from them, or slightly cohering at the base. Ovary superior.

Exceptions. (1.) The ovary is included or immersed in a fleshy torus in some genera of Nymphæaceæ.

(2.) The calyx tube is to some extent connate with the torus and ovary in Portulaceæ.

(3.) A cup-shaped disk bearing petals and stamens free from the ovary, but adnate to the base of the calyx, is found in a few genera of various orders.

(4.) The torus is expanded into a disk in some genera of Capparideæ, Bixineæ, and Tiliaceæ.

II. DISCIFLORÆ. (Orders Lineæ to Moringeæ.[2])

Sepals either distinct or partly united into a calyx, generally small and free from the ovary. Torus generally expanded into a disk. Petals generally equal in number to the sepals, or fewer by abortion. Stamens generally equal in number to the petals, sometimes double as many, or fewer by abortion, inserted round or within or upon the disk. Ovary generally superior or immersed in the disk.

Exceptions. (1.) In Lineæ, Malphigiaceæ, Zygophyllaceæ, Geraniaceæ, and Ilicineæ, the disk is either absent or inconspicuous.

(2.) The stamens are indefinite in Ochnaceæ.

(3.) The ovary is inferior or nearly so in some of the Rhamnaceæ and Olacineæ.

[1] I am not aware that there is any instance in this book of a plant coming under this exception.

[2] These orders are generally found under Thalamifloræ, and were first made into a separate division by Bentham and Hooker.

III. Calycifloræ. (Orders Connaraceæ to Cornaceæ.)

Sepals generally more or less united into a tube adnate to the ovary, very seldom altogether free; disk rarely apparent. Petals generally equal in number to the sepals, or fewer by abortion, inserted on the top of the calyx tube. Stamens definite or indefinite inserted on the calyx; ovary generally inferior, or included in the calyx tube, but occasionally exserted.

Exceptions. (1.) There is no calyx tube in a few genera of Leguminosæ, Rosaceæ, Samydaceæ, and Ficoideæ.

(2.) In Myrtaceæ, Umbelliferæ, and Araliaceæ there is a conspicuous disk.

IV. The next division of Exogens is Monopetalæ. (Orders Rubiaceæ to Plantagineæ.)

Petals within the calyx, more or less united into a lobed corolla; calyx generally persistent, of 4 or 5 sepals. Stamens usually few, affixed to the limb of the corolla or sometimes inserted with it. Leaves very rarely compound, generally, except in Rubiaceæ, without stipules.

Exceptions. (1.) There are a very few genera, especially in Oleaceæ, with distinct petals, but easily distinguished from polypetalous genera by other marks.

(2.) The calyx is apparently obsolete, being quite adnate to the ovary and without a limb in some Rubiaceæ and many Compositæ.

(3.) In some of the Sapotaceæ the lobes of the corolla are double, and in Plantagineæ the corolla is scarious.

(4.) In Styraceæ and Ebenaceæ the stamens are indefinite.

V. The absence of corolla marks the last division of Exogens.

Apetalæ or Monochlamyds. (Orders Nyctagineæ to Gnetaceæ.)

Plants without a corolla, the perianth generally without strong colouring, its lobes or segments in one or two series much alike.

Exceptions. (1.) Flowers with true petals inside the calyx are found in some genera of Euphorbiaceæ.

(2.) In some genera of Loranthaceæ the perianth is corolla-like, and there is an expansion of the pedicel which takes the place of calyx.

(3.) In some genera of Amarantaceæ there are staminodes looking like petals.

(4.) Plants with highly coloured flowers are to be found in Nyctagineæ, Thymeleaceæ, Loranthaceæ, and Santalaceæ.

(5.) The last order (Gnetaceæ) differs from all the rest in the male flowers consisting of a single stamen and the females of a naked ovary, with scarcely anything else distinguishable.

Note.—"The monochlamyds form a class neither natural nor well-defined; many of the orders with little affinity among themselves approach more nearly to some of the polypetalous orders. Many learned botanists have tried to distribute these orders among the Polypetalæ, but no better system than De Candolle's has yet been discovered."—*Genera Plantarum.*

VI. B. Endogens.

Stems herbaceous, rarely with woody stock, leaves parallel-veined. Perianth generally in two series. Stamens in one or two series. Parts of the flower generally 3 in each series.

Exceptions. (1.) Order Dioscoraceæ, and tribe Smilaceæ of order Liliaceæ, have reticulated leaves.

(2.) Order Scitamineæ have leaves pinnately nerved from the midrib.

(3.) Order Orchideæ has stamens and style united in a column, and perianth remarkably irregular.

(4.) Many of the orders, particularly those towards the end, have no perianth, and are otherwise very imperfect.

The one hundred and twenty-seven orders described in this book are thus grouped into five divisions of Exogens, and one of Endogens; and it will be found that the Monopetalous Exogens contain as many species as any two of the other divisions put together.

CONSPECTUS OF POLYPETALOUS ORDERS (EXOGENS).

I. THALAMIFLORÆ. Plants with hypogynous stamens, i.e. inserted on the thalamus and below the pistil, so that they remain behind when the calyx and corolla are pulled off.

Of the orders included in this book twenty-two come under this division, and in the greater part of these the flowers are regular, and the stamens very numerous, or indefinite.

Note.—The numbers are those under which the orders will be found. The descriptions here given do not always apply to the order generally, but sometimes only to the genera and species given in this book.

(*a*) Flowers regular: stamens indefinite.

1. RANUNCULACEÆ. Herbs or climbing shrubs; petals none (*except Naravelia*), carpels many, free.
2. DILLENIACEÆ. Trees with large simple leaves; petals and sepals 5.
3. MAGNOLIACEÆ. Trees: sepals and petals in whorls of 3.
4. ANONACEÆ. Trees or shrubs, sepals 3, petals 3 to 6, in two series.
6. NYMPHACEÆ. Water lilies.
7. PAPAVERACEÆ. Herbs; sepals 2, petals 4, soon falling off.
10. CAPPARIDEÆ (*except some genera with definite stamens*;) sepals and petals 4, stamens often on the stalk of the ovary.
12. BIXINEÆ (*except Hydnocarpus*). Trees or shrubs, sepals and petals 4, the latter sometimes wanting.
18. GUTTIFERÆ. Trees or shrubs with yellow juice, and generally beautiful flowers.
20. MALVACEÆ, tribe BOMBACEÆ. Trees, sepals and petals 5, stamens sometimes united below.
21. STERCULIACEÆ. Stamens generally more or less united; sepals and petals 5, or the latter wanting.
22. TILIACEÆ. Generally fibrous plants; flowers yellow or white, sepals and petals 5, or the latter wanting.

(*b*) Flowers regular, stamens definite.

5. MENISPERMACEÆ. Climbers: sepals, petals, and stamens usually 6.

9. CRUCIFERÆ. Stamens 6, tetradynamous, petals 4, arranged crosswise.
14. CARYOPHYLLEÆ. Herbs with opposite entire leaves and stems swollen at the joints; stamens 5, 8, or 10.
15. PORTULACEÆ. Herbs with entire leaves, and scarious hairy appendages at the joints; stamens 8 to 12, perigynous.
16. TAMARISCINEÆ. Shrubs with minute leaves, stamens 4 to 10.
17. ELATINEÆ. Small, inconspicuous herbs, stamens 4 to 10.
19. DIPTEROCARPEÆ. Leaves alternate, stamens 10, fruit winged.

Also some genera of CAPPARIDEÆ and BIXINEÆ.

(*c*) Flowers regular, stamens united into a column or tube.

20. MALVACEÆ (*except tribe Bombaceæ*), sepals 5, petals 5, twisted.

(*d*) Flowers irregular.

8. FUMARIACEÆ. Herbs with divided leaves, sepals 2 deciduous, stamens 6 in two bundles.
11. VIOLACEÆ. Sepals, petals, and stamens 5.
13. POLYGALEÆ. Leaves simple, entire, stamens 4 to 8 united into a sheath.

II. DISCIFLORÆ. Flowers generally with a conspicuous disk, on or about which the stamens, which are nearly always definite, are inserted. In the eighteen orders included in this division, the flowers are mostly regular.

(*a*) Flowers regular; disk conspicuous.

27. RUTACEÆ. Leaves dotted, sepals and petals 4 or 5, stamens very various.
28. SIMARUBEÆ. Like the last, but leaves not dotted.
29. OCHNACEÆ. Sepals 4 or 5, petals as many, or ten, stamens various, sometimes indefinite.
30. BURSERACEÆ. Trees or shrubs with compound leaves; sepals and petals 3 to 6, stamens as many or double.
31. MELIACEÆ. Trees or shrubs, generally with pinnate leaves; stamens united into a tube.
32. CHAILLETIACEÆ. Trees or shrubs with alternate leaves; sepals, petals, and stamens 5.

33. OLACINEÆ. Trees or shrubs with alternate leaves; petals 3 to 6, stamens 3 to 15.
35. CELASTRINEÆ. Trees or shrubs, sepals, petals and stamens 4 or 5 (*except tribe Hippocrateæ*).
36. RHAMNEÆ. Like the last, but the petals and stamens are inserted on the calyx tube.
37. AMPELIDEÆ. Like Celastrineæ, but generally climbing shrubs, with leaves usually lobed or compound.
39. ANACARDIACEÆ. Trees or shrubs with milky or acrid juice; sepals, petals, and stamens generally 4 or 5.

Also some genera of SAPINDACEÆ.

(*b*) Flowers regular; disk inconspicuous or none. (In this case the orders are practically Thalamifloral.)

23. LINEÆ. Sepals, petals, and stamens 5, styles 3 to 5.
25. ZYGOPHYLLEÆ. Sepals and petals 5, stamens 5, 10, or 15.
26. GERANIACEÆ (*except tribe Balsamineæ*). Leaves compound; sepals and petals 5, stamens 5, 10, or 15.
34. ILICINEÆ. Trees or shrubs, leaves alternate, stamens 4 or 5.

(*c*) Flowers irregular.

24. MALPHIGIACEÆ. Trees or shrubs, sepals and petals 5, stamens 10, fruit winged.
26. GERANIACEÆ, tribe BALSAMINEÆ. Sepals coloured, one spurred, stamens 5, very short.
38. SAPINDACEÆ (*with exceptions*). Sepals and petals mostly 4 or 5, stamens 5 to 10.
40. MORINGEÆ. Soft wooded trees with compound leaves; flowers somewhat papilionaceous; fruit pod-like.

III. CALYCIFLORÆ. Stamens (and petals) inserted on the calyx. The great majority of the twenty-two orders included in this division have regular flowers and definite stamens; but the latter are not so often five as in the last division.

(*a*) Flowers regular, stamens definite.

41. CONNARACEÆ. Trees or shrubs with compound leaves; stamens 5 or 10.
42. LEGUMINOSÆ, tribe MIMOSEÆ. Stamens usually 10.
44. SAXIFRAGEÆ. Sepals and petals 4 or 5, stamens double as many.

45. Crassulaceæ. Fleshy herbs or undershrubs, sepals and petals 4 to 8, stamens double as many.
46. Droseraceæ. Glandular herbs, petals, sepals, and stamens 4 or 5.
47. Halorageæ. Small herbs with minute flowers, often very imperfect.
48. Rhizophoreæ. Trees or shrubs, mostly of salt water swamps; stamens 8 to 30; (*in one genus indefinite*).
49. Combretaceæ. Trees or shrubs, stamens 4 to 10, fruit generally winged.
51. Melastomaceæ. Stamens 8 to 10, anthers with a connective.
52. Lythraceæ. Stamens very various, sometimes indefinite, ovary free at the bottom of the calyx tube.
53. Onagraceæ. Stamens various, often 8 or 10, ovary very notably inferior.

Note.—Hooker calls the flowers sub-irregular.

54. Samydaceæ. Trees or shrubs, flowers small and unattractive; stamens numerous.
55. Passifloreæ. Generally twining, stamens 5, calyx with a corona, ovary superior.
56. Cucurbitaceæ. Twiners with unisexual flowers, stamens generally 3, style one with 3 thick stigmas.
58. Datiscaceæ. Stamens 4, inserted round a disk, petals none.
59. Ficoideæ. Succulent herbs, petals small or wanting, stamens sometimes indefinite.
61. Araliaceæ. Stamens 5 to 7 inserted round a disk; styles more than one.
62. Cornaceæ. Like the last, but no disk and one style.

(*b*) Flowers regular, stamens indefinite.

42. Leguminosæ, tribe Acacieæ. Trees or shrubs.
43. Rosaceæ. Sepals and petals 5.
50. Myrtaceæ. Trees or shrubs with dotted leaves and conspicuous disk.

(*c*) Flowers irregular.

42. Leguminosæ, *except suborder Mimoseæ.*
57. Begoniaceæ. Succulent herbs with unequal-sided leaves, unisexual flowers, and no petals.
60. Umbelliferæ. Herbs with small flowers in umbels, generally with a conspicuous disk.

THE FLOWERING PLANTS OF WESTERN INDIA.

Note.—H stands for Hooker's "Flora of British India."
D „ Dalzell and Gibson's "Bombay Flora."
G „ Graham's "Plants of Bombay."
R „ Roxburgh's "Flora Indica."

Native names are in Italics at the end of the description.

An asterisk before the name of a plant means that it has not been seen by me.

ORDER 1. **RANUNCULACEÆ.**

Generally herbs, sometimes shrubs, leaves generally much divided and with dilated petioles; sepals 3 to 6, deciduous, petals 3 or more, sometimes wanting; stamens many, ovary generally of many distinct carpels; fruit of many one-seeded achenes, or many-seeded follicles.

This is an order of temperate regions, best known in England from the buttercups, but only slightly represented in W. India. There are five tribes, named respectively from the Clematis, Anemone, Ranunculus, Hellebore, and Pæony. There is nothing here belonging to the third and fifth tribes, and of the second and fourth only a single species each.

CLEMATIS. Climbing undershrubs with opposite leaves, sepals usually 4, petaloid, petals none; carpels many, fruit a head of achenes, with long feathery points.

Note.—The leaves and leaflets in this genus often vary a great deal in the same specimen, and the petioles are often twisted.

1. *C. Gouriana.* Nearly smooth, leaves pinnate or bipinnate, leaflets oval or oblong, flowers in large panicles, small, white, achenes hairy. *Morvel, ránjái.* Very variable (*H.*).

The Ghauts: very abundant about Násik. This strongly recalls *C. vitalba* of English hedges, known generally as "Traveller's joy" or "Oldman's beard," but also by various other names—

"The clematis, the favoured flower,
Which boasts the name of virgin's bower."—*Scott.*

2. *C. Wightiana.* A large hairy climber, leaves pinnate,

leaflets 3 to 5 lobed, toothed, flowers large and handsome, achenes very silky. *Morvel.**

The highest Ghauts (*D. & G.*). Mahableshwar (near the top only—*Dr. Cooke*). The colour of the flowers is a lovely pale gold, which, very strangely, is not mentioned in any book that I have seen.

Two other species much less common are given. *C. smilacifolia;* leaflets large, entire, oval, with a sudden point, very like the leaves of the common Smilax; flowers large, purple. Fonda Ghaut (*D.*). I have seen it (but not in flower), near Bassein. And **C. triloba*, with small, long-stalked leaves, simple or ternate, flowers large white, fruit not so much bearded as in some species. The Máwal districts (*D.*).

The following also are found :—

Naravelia. Differing from Clematis in having 6 to 12 petals, and in the terminal leaflet being often changed into a tendril. **N. zeylanica*, a climber, with solitary yellowish flowers, the hairy sepals twice as long as the smooth petals. Southern Ghauts (*D. & G.*).

Thalictrum. Erect herbs with sheathing petioles, and no petals, * *T. Dalzellii*, a small plant with white flowers in a small panicle; achenes with a long straight hooked beak. Harichander (*D.*).

Delphinium (Larkspur). Erect herbs with palmate leaves and irregular flowers, one of the five sepals being spurred. * *D. dasyacaulum*, a branched plant with bright blue showy flowers in a lax raceme, follicles short, hairy. Near Junar (*D.*).

Order 2. DILLENIACEÆ.

Leaves alternate, simple, sepals 5, persistent, petals 5, deciduous, stamens many in many series, carpels generally distinct, styles always so.

A small order, closely allied to *Ranunculaceæ*, but represented here only by two rather striking trees.

> "Rose as in dance the stately trees, and spread
> Their branches, hung with copious fruit."—*Milton.*

Dillenia. Trees with large leaves very strongly veined, and large flowers, carpels 5 to 20, cohering, fruit roundish, formed of the matured carpels enclosed in the thickened calyx.

1. *D. indica* (*D. speciosa*, D.). A fine tree with lanceolate leaves sharply serrated, collected at the end of the branches; flowers very large, white, solitary, the sepals roundish, thick and fleshy, the inner stamens arching over the outer; fruit size of a cocoanut, green, round, with shallow irregular lobes. *Mota Karmal, Karambali.*

The Konkans, not common. Cultivated in most parts of India.—*Brandis.*

"Dillenia, casting its enormous flowers, as big as two fists."—*Sir J. Hooker.*

* *Vel* is the common Maratta word for a climbing plant.

The calyx is eaten, and the fruit used as food for cattle. I rather think that this tree is sometimes by English people called the Magnolia.

2. *D. pentagyna.* A fine tree with leaves upwards of two feet long, oblong lanceolate, serrate; flowers on the branches, showy, yellow, but very much smaller than the last; fruit flesh-coloured, lobed like the last, looking like bunches of cherries. *Karmal, Karambal.*

Konkan, S. Ghauts, and S. Maratta country, not common. Forests throughout India (*H.*). Very noticeable for its

"Large foliage, overshadowing golden flowers."—*Cowper.*

They are the largest simple leaves that I know, except perhaps those of the teak tree, and are sold in bundles for chuppers.

ORDER 3. MAGNOLIACEÆ. The Magnolia Family.

Trees or shrubs often aromatic; leaves alternate, sepals and petals arranged in whorls of 3, very deciduous, stamens and carpels indefinite; fruit of numerous carpels, more or less distinct.

A small order, but distinguished for beauty and fragrance. In England the Magnolia, *M. grandiflora,* and the tulip tree, *Liriodendron tulipifera,* natives of N. America, are well known in gardens.

The only species of this order known in W. India is wild in the Himalayas and Nilghiris, but not with us.

MICHELIA. Trees; leaf buds enclosed in the twisted stipules, sepals and petals similar; fruit an elongated spike of carpels.

M. champaca. A fine tree with long, oval, pointed, waved leaves, shining above; sepals and petals 15 to 20, flowers yellow very fragrant; carpels roundish, oval sessile, many together at the end of a swollen stalk. *Pila champa, champaka.*

Commonly cultivated. The flowers are used by women to ornament their hair, and are offered in temples.

"The champak odours fail,
Like sweet thoughts in a dream."—*Shelley.*

"The pale yellow flowers have the sweet oppressive perfume which is celebrated in the poetry of the Hindus. From the wood of the champak the images of Buddha are carved for the temples."—*Tennant's "Ceylon."*

ORDER 4. ANONACEÆ. The Custard Apple Family.

Trees and shrubs, often climbing and aromatic, leaves alternate, simple, entire, without stipules, sepals 3, petals 3 to 6 in two series; stamens many, closely packed on a torus, filaments short or none, anthers with a long connective; fruit of numerous carpels, either quite distinct or united.

A tropical order, mainly distinguished by the peculiar anthers and carpels. It is much better known in W. India by the cultivated than by the wild species.

(*a*) Stamens many, close packed, the anther cells concealed by the connective; ovaries indefinite.

1. UNONA. Petals flat, spreading from the base, style recurved and grooved; carpels long, generally constricted between the seeds.

2. POLYALTHÆA. Like the last, but the carpels, when ripe, are one-seeded berries.

3. ANONA. Ripe carpels confluent into a fleshy, many-celled, many-seeded fruit.

(*b*) Stamens often indefinite, anther cells not concealed by the connective; ovaries indefinite.

4. SACCOPETALUM. Petals in two series, valvate, the outer smaller; carpels in fruit quite distinct and stalked.

(*a*)

1. UNONA.

* *U. discolor* (including D's *U. dunallii*). A shrub spreading or climbing, the young branches rough with white tubercles, leaves oblong or lanceolate, smooth or shining above, flowers yellow, strong-smelling, solitary; carpels stalked, with several joints, fleshy.

The Konkan and Wari country (*D.*). *H.* has four varieties. He gives the petals as about 2 inches by ½ inch.

Two less common species are given. **U. pannosa* (*U. farinosa*, D.) a tree with ovate lanceolate leaves, the petals covered with brown woolly hairs, the carpels not constricted—Párwar ghaut and Talawári, (*D.*) and * *U. Lawii*, said to be much like *U. discolor*, but the petals 2 to 3 inches long, and not ½ inch broad, leaves pale and downy beneath, carpels with 1 to 3 ovoid joints. Named after Mr. Law, C.S., a very distinguished botanist, who found it in the Konkan.

2. POLYALTHÆA.

* *P. cerasoides* (*Gualteria c.*, D.). A tree with light grey bark, leaves lanceolate or oblong, softly hairy beneath, petals dirty green, thick, leathery, half an inch long, carpels size of a small cherry, dark red, stalked. *Hum.*

Thall ghaut and Jawhár forests (*D. & G.*), W. Ghauts, and Sattara districts.—*B.* * *P. fragrans* found in the Wari country by Dalzell, has very fragrant yellow flowers with linear petals, carpels ovoid, stalked.

P. longifolia is a very handsome tree in gardens and elsewhere, with long lanceolate, shining, waved, leaves and yellowish-green flowers in dense umbels. *Áshoka, rátjámbul, devdár, Asupala.*

3. Anona.

1. *A. squamosa.* The custard apple. Sweet sop of the W. Indies. *Sitaphal.*

2. *A. reticulata.* Bullock's heart. Custard apple of the W. Indies. *Rúmphal.*

Both are natives of tropical America, but naturalized in India, the first especially in the W. Peninsula, the second in Bengal (*H.*).

"The quality of this fruit is well expressed by its English name, which it acquired in the W. Indies; for it is as like a custard, and a good one too, as can be imagined."—*Cook's "Voyages."*

Note.—The fruit of these two are utterly unlike those of all other species of the order found in India, as in these the carpels are amalgamated into a solid fruit, but in the rest the carpels remain separate.

Belonging to this section (*a*) is *Uvaria*, climbing shrubs with ovaries indefinite in number. **U. narum* is a large smooth climber with oblong lanceolate leaves, and large solitary flowers reddish or purple; carpels long-stalked scarlet. S. Ghauts (*D.*), Konkan (G.). H. makes D.'s *U. lurida* a variety of this.

(*b*)

4. Saccopetalum.

S. tomentosum. Tree with oval or oblong acute leaves, flowers in stalked cymes, greenish-yellow with brown streaks, carpels stalked, 3 or 4 together, size shape and colour of a plum, 3 or 4 seeded. *Hum, Kirni, Kari.*

The Konkan and Ghauts, not common. The carpels would naturally be taken for separate fruits.

To this section belongs *Bocaggea.* Trees with shining leaves, stamens 6 to 21 in 2 or more series, thick and fleshy. * *B. Dalzellii* (*Sageræa laurina*, D.), *G.* calls a very elegant tree with polished oblong leaves, something like the Portugal laurel; flowers small white crowded, carpels round smooth, stalked. *Sájeri, undi.* The Konkans (*D. & G.*).

Order 5. **MENISPERMACEÆ.**

Climbing or twining shrubs with small inconspicuous diœcious flowers, dull green or yellow; leaves alternate, often peltate, without stipules; sepals and petals generally 6, stamens as many; female flowers with 6 or more staminodes, ovaries generally 3, ripe carpels drupaceous.

This is a distinctly tropical order of little beauty, but the leaves are of a very marked character. The male flowers resemble some of the *Euphorbiaceæ*, but the female flowers and fruit are utterly unlike.

1. TINOSPORA. Sepals in 2 series larger than the petals filaments free, stigmas forked.

2. ANAMIRTA. Sepals 6 with 2 bracts, petals none, filaments united into a column; female flowers with 9 staminodes and stalked ovaries.

3. COCCULUS. Sepals in 2 series, the outer smaller, petals 6 smaller, stamens embraced by the petals; female flowers with 6 staminodes.

4. CISSAMPELOS. Male flowers with 4 sepals and petals, the latter united into a cup, anthers united round the top of the staminal column; female flowers crowded among the leafy bracts, with one sepal and one petal.

5. CYCLEA. Male flowers with 4 to 8 sepals and petals, the calyx inflated, stamens as in the last; female flowers with one sepal and one petal.

1. TINOSPORA.

T. cordifolia. A large twiner with light grey bark, leaves smooth, heart-shaped on long petioles, flowers in racemes very small, yellow, very deciduous; drupe very small, round or oval, bright red, glutinous inside. *Gulvel*, *ambarvel*, *garudvel.*

Konkan and Deccan. Throughout tropical India (*H.*). The stems, called *gulo*, throw out long thread-like roots, and are sold in the bazaar, and used in fevers (*D.*).

Largely cultivated in Ceylon. "Such is its tenacity of life that the Cinghalese to grow it simply twist several yards of the stem into a coil, and hang it on the branch of a tree, where it speedily puts forth its large heart-shaped leaves, and sends down its rootlets to the earth."—*Tennant.*

* *T. malabarica* ascribed by *D.* to the Konkan has white hairs scattered about it, ovate cordate pointed leaves and green flowers.

2. ANAMIRTA.

A. cocculus. A smooth twiner with thick corky bark; leaves heart-shaped or ovate with long petioles; flowers comparatively large, greenish, in very long panicles from the thicker branches; drupes roundish, smooth, black. *Kákmári ki bij.*

Common in the Konkan (*D.*). I have seen it only at Kew. The seeds are the *Cocculus indicus* of commerce, chiefly used in adulterating beer.

3. Cocculus.

C. macrocarpus. Climbing over high trees with round or kidney-shaped peltate leaves, smooth and long petioled; flowers very small, yellowish, in panicles from the older branches; fruit in clusters. *Rámrik, wátvel.*

This is the only very attractive native species in the order. The beautiful clusters of fruit, like grapes with a silvery bloom, are very noticeable, and the foliage is luxuriant, the bright green leaves often forming thick hanging masses. Abundant at Matherán; tolerably common on Konkan hills, and in the Ghauts. These great woody climbers were by old travellers called "lianas," a term first used in the French colonies (*Chambers*). In the same way the great creepers of tropical regions were called by the essentially English name of "supple-jacks." "In many parts the woods are so overrun with supple-jacks that it is scarcely possible to force one's way amongst them. I have seen several which were 50 or 60 fathoms long."—*Cook's "Voyages."*

2. *C. villosus.* A soft hairy climber, much smaller than the last, leaves oval rather triangular, short stalked; male flowers in nearly sessile clusters, female 3 together on a short stalk; fruit size of a pea, black, smooth, full of very black juice. *Hundir, wassanvel, tán.*

Common in hedges, Deccan and Konkan. Throughout tropical and subtropical India (*H.*).

4. Cissampelos.

C. pareira. A slightly hairy climber, leaves peltate, round-cordate or kidney-shaped; flowers yellowish minute, male in panicles, feathery looking, female in racemes with large round bracts; fruit red, downy, size of a pea. *Pahádvel, pahádmul.*

Common in hedges in the Konkan and elsewhere. Tropical and subtropical India (*H.*). It looks like a small edition of *Cocculus macrocarpus.*

5. Cyclea.

Note.—The species of this genus are easily distinguished by the cup-shaped calyx and corolla. *Cissampelos* has the corolla alone cup-shaped.

C. peltata. A climber, leaves peltate hairy, flowers very small green, male panicles very long; drupe kidney-shaped, hairy. *Párvel, pádel.*

The Konkan, Matherán, and Mahableshwar. **C. Burmanii* attributed to the Konkan and Ghauts by *D. & G.* is apparently very like this, but larger and less hairy.

Stephania. Sepals 6 to 10 in the male, 3 to 5 in the female, petals 3 to 5, ovary one, style 3 to 6 divided. *S. hernandifolia* has peltate triangular leaves, rounded at the angles, long petioled, pale below, flowers minute yellowish, crowded in short umbels on a long axillary stalk; drupe smooth, red.—At Dápolí. The Konkan (*D.*).

ORDER 6. NYMPHÆACEÆ. Water Lilies.

Aquatic plants with leaves usually floating, and often peltate, sepals 3 to 6, petals as many, or numerous; stamens many, disk fleshy, surrounding or enveloping the 3 or more carpels; stigmas as many as the carpels.

Here as in England the water lilies can scarcely be mistaken for anything else.

1. NYMPHÆA. Sepals petals and stamens indefinite, all inserted on the disc, which is confluent with the carpels, filaments petaloid, fruit a spongy berry ripening under water.

2. NELUMBIUM. Leaves well out of the water, peltate, sepals soon falling off, petals and stamens in many series, anthers with a clubbed appendage; ovaries many, sunk in a fleshy torus, which enlarges as the fruit ripens.

1. NYMPHÆA.

1. *N. lotus.* Leaves round, sharply sinuate or dentate, flowers large, red or white, sepals ribbed, white inside, oblong, petals the same shape, filaments broad at the base, stigmas with clubbed appendages.

This is the Egyptian lotus, as famous in the art and literature of Egypt as the Indian lotus in that of India. In later days and as regards one variety, "It was asserted that as a new star had appeared in the sky, so a new flower had blossomed on the earth at the moment of the death of Antinous. This was the lotus of a peculiar red colour, which the people of Lower Egypt used to wear in wreaths on his festival."—*J. A. Symonds.*

2. *N. stellata.* Leaves entire or slightly waved, sepals nerved but not ribbed, petals acute, anthers with long white appendages, stigmas horned, flowers red, white, or blue, smaller than the last.

Both sorts are common in tanks throughout the warmer parts of India, and are called *Kamal.*

2. NELUMBIUM.

N. speciosum. Much larger than either of the two last;

leaves one to two feet in diameter, petioles and pedicels 3 or 4 feet long, hollow; flowers red or white, sepals 5 with 2 bracts; fruit large, top-shaped, enclosing many carpels, the tops of which project like knobs.—*Kamal, poini, poira.*

Common in tanks throughout India.

"The large-leaved lotus on the waters flowering."—*Southey.*

This is the sacred lotus of India: Sanscrit *padmá;* and as Brahma, the self-existent, sprang from a lotus before the creation of the world, it may by some be considered the first of all vegetable forms.

"The black seeds in China, and some parts of India, are served at table in place of almonds, which they are said to resemble."—*Tennant's* "*Ceylon.*"

ORDER 7. **PAPAVERACEÆ.** Poppies.

Herbs with milky juice and radical and alternate leaves, flowers regular, sepals 2, concave, petals 4, stamens very many, style short or none, stigmas radiating.

A well-known order of temperate climes, with considerable resemblance to Ranunculaceæ. The petals and stamens fall off very quickly. There are no species wild in the plains of India, but that given below is one of the commonest of imported weeds.

ARGEMONE. Prickly with yellow juice and flowers; stigma 4 to 7 lobed, capsule many-seeded.

A. Mexicana. Mexican or prickly poppy. A stout, branched plant; leaves sessile, pinnatifid, sinuate, much variegated with white; flowers large, bright yellow; capsule oblong opening at the top usually bristly. *Dar-uri, Kánte-dhotra.*

"It has spread like a weed all over the tropics."—*Bentham.* Oil for lamps is extracted from the seeds, which are purgative and diuretic.

Papaver somniferum is the garden poppy of England, the opium poppy of India, fields of which, red, purple and white, may be seen occasionally in Guzerat, but in perfection in Central India.

"The poppy fields (near Chittagong) resembled a carpet of dark green velvet, sprinkled with white stars, or a green lake studded with water lilies."—*Hooker.*

ORDER 8. **FUMARIACEÆ.** Fumitories.

Herbs with divided leaves and very irregular flowers; sepals 2, small, deciduous, petals 4 in unequal pairs, stamens 6 in 2 bundles.

A small order with great peculiarities of petals. In the "Genera Plantarum" it is given as a sub-order of *Papaveraceæ.*

FUMARIA. Segments of leaves very narrow; petals, two

outer, one flat or concave, the other spurred at the base, the two inner clawed and keeled, fruit round, one-seeded.

F. parviflora. A small smooth branched plant with angular stem, leaves pinnatifid, segments flat, flowers in racemes whitish or rose-coloured, tips of petals cohering, fruit smooth. *Pitpátra.*

Deccan and Khandeish. "A weed of cultivation."—*H.*

This species is rare in England, but differs very little from the common English fumitory (*F. officinalis*) except by its smaller size. Lear when mad went

"Crowned with rank fumitor, and furrow weeds."

Corydalis has flowers of the same peculiar form.

ORDER 9. **CRUCIFERÆ.** Cressworts.

Herbs with radical and alternate leaves, without stipules; sepals 4, often enlarged at the base, petals 4, arranged crosswise; stamens 6, of which two pairs are longer and one pair shorter (this arrangement is called tetradynamous); disc with 4 glands opposite the sepals; fruit a silique, or in some genera indehiscent.

This is a large and very well-defined order, having its name from the appearance of a cross in the petals and stamens. The tetradynamous stamens and the peculiar fruit together distinguish it from any other order. It mainly belongs to the temperate parts of the world, and in England numbers of common weeds, and many common culinary vegetables, belong to the order. But only one inconspicuous species is found wild in W. India.

CARDAMINE. Sepals equal at the base, petals entire, clawed, silique linear.

C. hirsuta. A small plant, slightly hairy; leaves pinnate or pinnatifid, leaflets roundish ovate coarsely toothed, flowers small, white or yellow, silique smooth, erect, tapering.

This is the "hairy bitter cress" of England. *H.* has for it "all temperate regions of India," and it is found at Bombay, Poona, Mahableshwar and other places; but *D.* gave only "hills about Belgaum," and *G.* has not got it, so it may perhaps have spread of late years.

"In the common small form the stamens are usually reduced to 4."—*Bentham.*

Dr. Cooke has C. subumbellata at Mahableshwar, very like this.

The following are the best-known species of this order which are cultivated in W. India;—

Cheiranthus Cheiri. Wallflower.

Raphanus sativus. Radish—*mulé.*

Brassica oleracea. The original species from which all the varieties of cabbage, cauliflower, broccoli and nolecole have been produced. Of *B. campestris* one variety (*rapa*) is the turnip plant, and another (*napus*) that which produces rape-seed, from which colza oil is made. *B. nigra* and *alba* (formerly *sinapis*) mustard, *rái.*

Nasturtium officinale, water-cress.

Lepidium sativum, common cress.

Note.—Nolecole is the same plant as what is called Cole rubbi in England. The garden flower commonly called Nasturtium is a Tropæolum.

ORDER 10. CAPPARIDEÆ. Capers.

Herbs, shrubs or trees, leaves simple or palmately divided, sepals 4, petals 4, arranged crosswise: stamens often very numerous, and on or at the base of the stalk of the ovary (gynophore), style short or none; fruit a silique or berry.

This order is distinguished from Cruciferæ by the general difference in habit, by the stamens (in the Indian genera) being never tetradynamous, and generally very conspicuous. The gynophore is a very uncommon characteristic. The flowers are often very handsome. The so-called siliques of this order are more correctly siliquiform capsules.

TRIBE 1. CLEOMEÆ. Herbs.

1. CLEOME. Stamens sessile on the disk, ovary sessile or nearly so: fruit a silique.

2. GYNANDROPSIS. Leaves 5-foliate, petals long-clawed, stamens 6, rising from the gynophore.

TRIBE 2. CAPPAREÆ. Shrubs or trees.

3. MÆRUA. Climbing shrubs, petals smaller than the sepals, stamens many inserted high up on the gynophore: fruit necklace-shaped.

4. CRATÆVA. Trees, petals long-clawed, stamens indefinite, united to the base of the slender gynophore, stigma sessile, berry fleshy.

5. CADABA. Sepals unequal, petals clawed, disk tubular, from which the gynophore arises: stamens 4 to 6, inserted on one side of the gynophore: stigma sessile, silique slender.

6. CAPPARIS. Trees or shrubs generally thorny with simple leaves; stamens indefinite inserted on the disk at the base of the long gynophore: stigma sessile, fruit fleshy.

1. Cleome.

1. *C. simplicifolia* (*Polanisia S.* D.). Hairy plant with reddish stem and very rough ovate or obovate leaves, flowers pink, solitary or in leafy racemes, stamens 10 to 12, silique smooth pointed with the style.

Poona collectorate and elsewhere, common. H. calls it prostrate, which it does not seem to be in W. India.

2. *C. Chelidonii* (*Polanisia C.* D.). A tall strong plant, rather pretty, leaves radical, long-petioled, deeply 7-divided, upper trifoliate; flowers pink in racemes, stamens very numerous, silique 3 inches long, smooth.

Beds of Konkan rivers. Moist places in Deccan (*D.*).

3 *C. viscosa* (*Polanisia icosandra*, D.). A hairy and sticky weed, leaves 3 to 5 foliate, leaflets ovate or obovate, flowers small, yellow, in racemes: stamens many, silique long, rough, erect. *Kánphati, piwali tilwan.*

"Abundant throughout tropical and warm India, and the rest of the world," H. I found it growing by the lighthouse on the Vingorla Rocks, a good proof of uncommon hardiness.

* *C. monophylla*, called by D. a common weed, leaves oblong or lanceolate, flowers pink or purple, stamens 6, silique cylindric.
* *C. Burmannii*, much branched, prickly, leaves trifoliate, flowers solitary, purple, silique cylindric. A weed (*D.*).

Note.—H. and others give this as having 6 stamens, but identify it with R.'s *Polanisia dodecandra.*

C. speciosissima is a tall, very handsome garden plant, leaves 5 to 7 foliate, flowers large, rose-coloured, stamens very long, pink.

2. Gynandropsis.

G. pentaphylla. An erect plant, hairy, sticky, and strong-smelling, leaves 5-foliate, leaflets obovate or lanceolate, flowers in racemes, white or pink, stamens very long. *Tilwan tilparni, mábli.*

A common weed. Warm parts of India and all tropical countries (*H.*).

This is a good type of one large section of this order, from the long conspicuous gynophore and stamens.

3. Mærua.

M. arenaria (*Niehburia oblongifolia*, D.). Leaves oblong or oval, flowers white or greenish, stamens long, white, fruit constricted between the seeds.

Khair, Poona districts. Hedges Guzerat and Deccan (*D.*).

4. Crataeva.

C. religiosa (*C. Roxburghii and C. Narvala*, D.). A tree with long petioled leaves, leaflets ovate or obovate, lateral ones very oblique; flowers in racemes, white turning to buff, with long purple filaments; fruit large, round or ovoid, long-stalked. *Wárwan;* Sanscrit, *Wáras, háwarna.*

Very variable. (*H.*). Not uncommon, but generally planted; as it is throughout India (*Brandis*).

5. Cadaba.

C. Indica. A straggling much-branched shrub, leaves small, ovate or oblong, flowers dingy-white, stamens spreading out from the gynophore, silique linear, nearly black when ripe, seeds black with scarlet or orange-pulp.—*Kabab.*

Common in hedges in most parts, and not at all attractive.

6. Capparis.

1. *C. spinosa* (*C. Murrayana*, D.). A prostrate, rather downy shrub, flowers very handsome, solitary, white, with long purple filaments, sepals large and very convex, leaves alternate roundish-ovate, thorns small, orange-coloured, fruit ribbed, ovate or oblong.—*Kabar.*

This is the caper-plant, the flower buds of which are our capers. Found in every quarter of the globe. *H.* has 4 varieties, which between them extend over a great part of India. Beds of streams on the Ghauts (*D. & G.*). I have seen it only at Bátlod.

An old traveller says that the genus takes its name from the famous island of Capri, where "the caper-bush hangs from the walls and ledges of rocks, and adorns them with its white flowers, full of long lilac-coloured stamens."

2. *C. divaricata* (*C. stylosa*, D.). A thorny shrub or small tree with large white flowers tinged with yellow, solitary, on short stout stalks; leaves linear lanceolate, fruit size of a billiard-ball, scarlet, warted, with 6 ridges, seeds dark, embedded in pulp.

The above is as I have seen the flowers, but *D.* calls them green, *G.* red. Common all over the Deccan (*D.*). S. M. country (*G.*).

3. *C. aphylla.* A very thorny shrub or small tree, with innumerable green smooth branches; leaves only on the young shoots, linear subulate; flowers red, handsome, several together, buds whitish and mealy, fruit smooth, round, size of a cherry.—*Karil, Kerá.*

Very common in Guzerat, less so in the Deccan: a plant of very dry districts.

4. *C. Roxburghii.* A large climbing, thorny shrub, leaves lanceolate, more or less downy, flowers in racemes large, pure white, stamens long, fruit large round scarlet, rough and wrinkled, splitting from the top, seeds large, dark.—*Wágati, purvi.*

Waghotan. Ghauts and S. Konkan, not common (*D.*).

5. *C. pedunculosa.* A small thorny shrub, mostly smooth, leaves small, round-cordate pointed: flowers few together, white, small, delicate, umbellate on long stalks: fruit round on a short thickened stalk size of a cherry. *Kolisná.*

Mahableshwar, Matheran, &c.

6. *C. sepiaria.* A poor-looking thorny shrub, all parts more or less hairy, leaves roundish ovate or oblong, flowers small, white, with very long stamens, umbelled; berry two-lobed, size of a pea, black.

H. has 3 varieties, occurring in dry places nearly all over India. It is common all over the Western presidency, I believe.

7. *C. horrida.* A climber, rusty-brown all over the young parts, and covered with hooked thorns, leaves ovate or oblong with a short bristly point, flowers rather large, long-stalked, white, with long white stamens turning purple: fruit roundish, smooth, reddish-brown. *Tarti, taranti.*

Common in hedges. Brandis says it flowers so freely that the bush often looks like a mass of white and rose-colour, but I have generally seen it more in accordance with its specific name, and with the thorns far more noticeable than the flowers.

The following are less common. * *C. zeylanica* (*C. brevispina*, D.). A thorny shrub, flowers large, white, solitary, the two lower petals yellow; leaves oval lanceolate: fruit scarlet, size of a small orange. *Wágáti.* W. Deccan and Vingorla (*D.*). A southern species (*H.*).

* *C. heyneana* (*C. formosa*, D.). A shrub, flowers large, solitary, pale-blue with yellow base, leaves as the last, fruit ovoid, beaked. Chorla Ghaut (*D.*).

C. grandis. A small tree, leaves broad ovate, flowers white in corymbs, fruit purple, larger than a cherry. *Páchaonda.* Forts of Sholapore and Miraj (*D.*). * *C. tenera.* Shrubby, leaves ovate, flowers small, fruit pear-shaped. On the Ghauts, rare (*D.*).

ORDER 11. VIOLACEÆ.

Sepals, petals, and stamens 5, corolla irregular, the lower petal being dissimilar. Fruit a 3-valved capsule.

The above is the description of Tribe Violeæ, to which the violets and pansies, and the solitary species of the order found wild in W.

India belong. *Ionidium.* Sepals subequal. Lower petal larger than the others, clawed, saccate or spurred at the base: stigma oblique, capsule roundish. *I. suffruticosum* (*I. enneaspermum and I. hexaspermum*, D.). Six to twelve inches high, very variable, leaves narrow, flowers pink or red. S. Konkan and Belgaum (*D.*). *Ratanbaras.*

ORDER 12. BIXINEÆ.

Trees or shrubs with alternate leaves, flowers regular, sepals and petals 4 or 5, the latter sometimes wanting, capsule 3 to 5 valved.

This is a tropical order, not very easy to describe, and the genera here given differ very much from one another. Those with many stamens are said to bear some relation to Capparideæ and Tiliaceæ, those with few to Violaceæ. See also Samydaceæ.

1. COCHLEOSPERMUM. Stamens many on a disk, ovary round, stigma toothed, seeds cochleate, i.e. twisted like a snail-shell.

2. FLACOURTIA. Trees of small size and little beauty, flowers small without petals, stamens many, ovary seated on a glandular disk, fruit indehiscent.

3. HYDNOCARPUS. Flowers diœcious, sepals 5, free, petals 5 with a scale opposite each, stamens 5 to 8, stigmas 3 to 6, large and lobed, berry round.

1. COCHLEOSPERMUM.

C. Gossypium. A fine tree with smooth bark; leaves acutely lobed, flowers large and handsome, bright yellow at the end of the branches, capsule oblong, with 5 lobes and valves, full of silky cotton. *Gadbi, galgal, galeri, gunglai.*

Not in *D.* Khandesh and Satpura jungles, *G.* The flowers appear when the tree is bare. It has a strong general resemblance to the silk cotton tree, and was considered a Bombax by *R.*

"I found trees of Cochleospermum, whose curious thick branches spread out somewhat awkwardly, each tipped with a cluster of gold and yellow flowers, as large as the palm of the hand, and very beautiful: it is a tropical gum cistus in the appearance and texture of the petals and their frail nature. The bark abounds in a transparent gum, of which the white ants seem fond, for they had killed many trees."—*Hooker's Himalayan Journals.*

2. FLACOURTIA.

Note.—*H.* says that the species of this genus are excessively variable, and hard to distinguish, and no one who compares a number of specimens will doubt that this is so. The flowers of all are small, green, and few together, the stamens being the most conspicuous part.

1. *F. Montana.* A thorny tree, leaves smooth, hard, oval,

crenate, fruit size of a cherry, red, eatable, seeds 10 or 12, embedded in pulp.—*Atak.*

The Ghauts and hilly parts of the Konkan.

2. *F. sepiaria.* Very thorny, bark light-grey, leaves smooth, shining, obovate, on red petioles, stigmas 3 to 5, fruit size of a pea, purplish, seeds in 5 vertical pairs.—*Ataran.*

The Konkan.

What the *támbat* at Mahableshwar is it is beyond me to decide. It is almost exactly like this last, and I believe, and am well supported in thinking, that it is very often found unarmed. It may be a variety of *F. sepiaria*, or as *G.* makes it, *F. inermis*, which *H.* does not refer to this part of India. Mr. Birdwood calls it *F. ramontchi*, which *H.* makes wild or cultivated throughout India, and which *G.* calls the Mauritius plum.—*Káki, bhekal.* *D.* has also * *F. cataphracta* on the banks of rivers in the *Wári* country. Thorns large compound, berry size of a small plum, with very hard sharp-edged seed. —*Jagam.* Commonly cultivated, *H.* Dr. Dymock calls this also *ámbat.*

3. Hydnocarpus.

H. Wightianus (*H. inebrians*, D.). A fine tree, leaves long lanceolate, smooth and shining, flowers white in umbels or racemes, calyx and pedicels rusty, petals rounded, fringed with silvery hairs, scales brown, hairy and fleshy: fruit a rough, hard, rusty-brown ball, like the wood-apple. *Kauti, Kadu-Kawat.*

S. Konkan. Commoner apparently further S.

Scolopia. Flowers small, racemed, stamens many, berry 2 to 4 seeded. * *S. crenata* (*Phobera c.* D.). Leaves ovate or oblong, obtusely serrated or crenated, fruit round, green. S. Ghauts (*D.*). Excessively variable (*H.*) *Hintálu.*

To this order also belongs *Bixa orellana*, a handsome shrub or small tree commonly cultivated.—*Kisri, sendri.* The pulp which covers the seed is Arnotto, used as in England and Holland, for colouring butter and cheese. In the Spanish Main the Indians paint their bodies all over with it for full dress (Kingsley): and this use of it is said also to prevent mosquito bites.

Order 13. PITTOSPORACEÆ.

Trees or shrubs, leaves alternate entire, sepals and petals 5 imbricated, stamens 5, stigma 2 to 5 lobed.

* Pittosporum floribundum. A small tree, leaves lanceolate waved, flowers in racemes, dingy white, capsule 2-valved, size of a pea, seeds covered with reddish resin. *Yekadi, behkali, vikhári.*

Along the Ghauts (*D.*). Khandalla, pretty common (*G.*).

ORDER 14. POLYGALEÆ. Milkworts.

Leaves alternate simple entire, flowers very irregular, sepals 5, the two inner (wings) like petals: petals 3 unequal, the largest keel-shaped (keel); stamens 4 to 8 united into a sheath; capsule 2-celled, 2-seeded, frequently margined.

The shape of the flowers distinguishes this order from every other. They have a superficial resemblance to those of the pea family, but here the wings belong to the calyx. All the species found in W. India (as in England) are small herbs, and would be easily recognized by any one who knows the common English milkwort, *P. vulgaris.*

1. POLYGALA. Wings larger than the other sepals, petals united at the base with the staminal tube, which is split; keel generally crested; stamens 8.

3. SALOMONIA. Flowers minute in dense spikes; sepals nearly equal; stamens 4 or 5, united half way down into a sheath.

1. POLYGALA.

1. *P. elongata.* Erect, branched, 4 or 5 inches high, leaves linear or oblong, smooth, flowers in racemes yellow, wings obliquely oval, longer than the capsule, which is nearly round and notched.

H. includes in this *D.'s* P. campestris.
The Konkans. Coast of Kattywar (*D.*).

2. *P. Chinensis.* Generally procumbent; leaves from roundish to narrow linear, flowers yellow in short racemes, wings large pointed, longer than the roundish notched capsule.—*Negli.*

Guzerat, Deccan, &c. *H.* makes this most variable, includes in it three others of *D.'s* species, and ascribes it to the whole of India.

* *P. persicariæfolia* is called by Mr. Birdwood the Mahableshwar milkwort—erect, branched, leaves oval or oblong, flowers rose-colour, wings obovate, capsule obcordate, ciliate. Highest Ghauts (*D.*).

* *P. erioptera* (*P. vahliana,* D.) flowers yellow, wings longer than the notched capsule, seeds very hairy. Guzerat (*D.*). Very variable (*H.*).

2. SALOMONIA.

* *S. ciliata* (*S. cordata,* D.), 3 to 6 inches high, leaves sessile, cordate ovate; flowers red or purple, capsule with red filiform teeth, broader than long. *Bhui sána.*

Vingorla (*D.*). N. Konkan (*G.*). Kattywar and Sholapore, Mr. Jyekrishna Indraji.

Order 15. CARYOPHYLLEÆ. The Pink family.

Herbs with opposite branches, jointed, and thickened at the joints; leaves opposite entire, sepals and petals 4 or 5, stamens generally 8 or 10, sometimes 5, styles 2 to 5, fruit a capsule.

"There are no other exogens with polypetalous flowers, opposite undivided leaves without stipules, and stems swollen at the joints." *Lindley.*

This large order contains flowers, both wild and cultivated, well known to most English people, such as pinks and carnations, sweet-williams, catchflys, chickweeds, &c., but it is very poorly represented in India except in the Himalayas.

1. Saponaria. Leaves flat, calyx more or less tubular 5-toothed, petals 5, clawed, stamens 10, styles 2.

2. Polycarpæa. Leaves flat with scarious stipules, sepals 5 free, more or less scarious, petals and stamens 5, style trifid.

1. Saponaria. Soapwort.

S. vaccaria, a tall and pretty smooth plant, leaves long lanceolate connate at the base, with a scarious tip or margin; flowers long stalked pink, capsule broad oval included in the increasing calyx; seeds many, black.

This is not common, and is not given either in *D.* or *G.* "In wheat fields throughout India: a weed of cultivation" (*H.*). I have seen it only in watered fields. Any English flower-lover would at once recognize it as a near relation of the garden pinks.

2. Polycarpæa.

P. corymbosa. A plant with narrow linear leaves generally verticilled at the nodes, and flowers in much branched cymes, remarkable for the scarious silvery sepals which are longer than the petals and capsules.

Seashore S. Konkan and Guzerat: also in the Deccan (*D.*). *D.* calls this "rigidly erect with few branches." *H.* "erect or decumbent much dichotomously branched."

Arenaria (sandwort) sepals and petals 5, the latter entire, stamens 10 to 15, styles 3 or 4. * *A neilgherrensis* much branched, procumbent, flowers small, white. Belgaum and Dharwar collectorates, D.; but H., whose description differs a good deal, has it only at considerable elevations in the Himalayas and Nilghiris.

For genus Mollugo, often put in this order, see Ficoideæ.

Order 16. PORTULACEÆ.

Herbs with entire leaves and membranous or hairy appendages at the nodes; sepals 2, petals 4 or 5, styles divided, fruit a capsule.

In genus Portulaca the stamens are perigynous, and the order was therefore formerly included in Calycifloral. It comes near to Ficoideæ.

PORTULACÆ.—Succulent herbs, flowers terminal surrounded by a whorl of leaves, seeds numerous, kidney-shaped.

1. *P. oleracea.*—A small prostrate plant, smooth and fleshy, leaves alternate, sessile, flat, oblong, cuneate; flowers sessile yellow, petals 5, stamens 8 to 12, style about 5 parted. *Kurfá, mothi-ghol, Ghol báji.*

Commonly found in moist places in the rains. It is the English "common purslane," cultivated as a vegetable in many parts of Europe and Asia; found wild in all warm climates, *H.* In Cook's voyages, the finding of purslane in the Pacific Islands is always mentioned as a blessing to the ships' crews.

P. quadrifida, *ránghol raighol*, is so like this that it is distinguishable only on examination, but it has only 4 petals, a 4-cleft style, and leaves in whorls of 4. Common. * *P. tuberosa*, stems short and spreading, leaves linear, terete, flowers in terminal clusters, stamens 20 or more. Cutch, Palin, Sind, Stocks. *Junak.*

The garden Portulacas are well known for the brilliance of their blossoms.

ORDER 17. TAMARISCINEÆ. Tamarisks.

Bushes and small trees, leaves alternate, very minute, sepals and petals 5 or 10, stamens 4 to 10, ovary free, stigmas 2 to 5, capsule 3-valved.

The greenness of these bushes, though almost leafless, and their growth in the beds of rivers or on the sandy seashore, make the species easily distinguishable.

TAMARIX.—Leaves scale like, flowers in spikes or dense racemes, disk lobed, ovary narrower upwards.

1. *T. gallica.*—Leaves smooth subulate, not sheathing, flowers in slender racemes, pink and pretty, disk 5-lobed, stamens 5. *Jhao.* The galls are called *magiyá mai.*

This is the tamarisk commonly found, though scarcely wild, on the English coast. *D.* has not got it, but *H.* and *B.* both call it commom throughout India.

2. *T. ericoides* (*Trichaurus e.* D.).—A tall shrub, leaves sheathing; flowers in spikes, pink, heath-like, only half opening, stamens 10, style protruding, fruit over half an inch long, conical. *Karáti, sarub.*

Common in the beds of Deccan and Konkan rivers. * *T. dioica* is very like No. 1, but usually much smaller, and the foliage a greyer green. Not in *D*, common in the Deccan (*G.*); and found at Ahmedabad and Junagarh by Mr. Jyekrishna I.

Order 18. ELATINEÆ. Waterpeppers.

Small herbs or undershrubs, leaves opposite or whorled, flowers small, axillary, sepals, petals, and styles 2 to 5, stamens as many or twice as many; capsule 3 to 5 celled.

Bergia.—Flowers minute, all parts usually 5, sepals with herbaceous midrib and membranous margins.

1. *B. odorata* (*Elatine o.* D.) —A small, mean-looking plant nearly prostrate, more or less hairy; leaves less than inch long, oval oblong serrated, flowers inconspicuous, pinkish few together, stamens 10, styles 5.

Very variable: smells of camomile (*H.*).

Pretty common in Guzerat (*D.*). It grows in masses in cultivated fields in the Panah Mahals.

2. *B. ammanioides.*—Erect, branched 3 to 12 inches high, with rough stems and oblong lanceolate sharply serrated leaves, flowers minute reddish, several together, stamens 5.

Very like an Ammania, and growing in wet ground. Throughout India, *H.*

*** *B. verticillata* is apparently not so common. It has white flowers in dense sessile heads, and 10 stamens. Dr. Dymock calls it *hintál*, which probably will apply to the other species also.**

***Note.*—*G.* gives these two last species as Octandria trigynia.**

Order 18. GUTTIFERÆ.

Trees or shrubs abounding in yellow or greenish juice, leaves opposite, flowers regular, sepals and petals 2 to 6, stamens usually indefinite; fruit usually a berry or drupe.

This small order contains some of the most beautiful of Indian trees. It seems to have no particular affinities to other orders here given. In all the genera given below the flowers are male, female, and hermaphrodite. All here given are trees.

1. Garcinia.—Sepals and petals 4 or 5, anthers sessile, or on short thick filaments, stigma lobed, berry with leathery rind, seeds with pulpy aril.

2. Ochrocarpus.—Sepals 2, anthers erect, stigma 3 lobed, berry with 1 to 4 large seeds.

3. Calophyllum.—Leaves very finely veined, flowers in panicles, sepals and petals imbricated in 2 or 3 series, anthers erect, stigma peltate, fruit a drupe.

4. Mesua.—Flowers large, axillary, solitary, anthers erect, style long, stigma peltate, fruit 4-valved with 1 to 4 seeds.

1. Garcinia.

G. Indica. A very pretty tree with drooping branches and thick dark green foliage, the trunk black and grooved, leaves oval pointed entire, almost veinless, flowers fleshy, sepals in 2 unequal pairs, petals 4, mouth of corolla entirely filled with stamens, fruit size and colour of a plum. *Kokambi, rátambi.*

This has much of the general appearance of the Evergreen oak (*Quercus Ilex*). It is tolerably common in the Konkan, and often cultivated. The leaves when young are of a beautiful red. From the oil of the seeds is made the well-known salve *Kokam*. The fruit is good when cooked, though exceedingly acid.

* *G. Xanthochymus* (*X. pictorius*, D.). Leaves oblong or lanceolate, a foot long, flowers white, sepals and petals 5, roundish, stamens in bundles divided by fleshy glands, fruit size of an apple, pointed, bright, yellow. *Aont.* S. Ghauts (*D.*). Widely distributed (*H.*). *G. ovalifolius* (*Xanthochymus o.* D.), leaves oval, flowers greenish white, fascicled on the branches, sepals, petals and stamens as in the last : fruit oblong, smooth, green, the size of a walnut. The Ghauts : pretty common, *D. & G. Tavir, haldi, jaugali rámphal.*

G. mangostana is the mangosteen tree, native and cultivated in the Malay Peninsula and S. Tenasserim.

Gamboge comes from one of this genus, and most of the individuals of the order yield an inferior sort of gamboge (*R.*).

2. Ochrocarpus.

O. longifolus (*Calysaccion, l.* D.).—A handsome tree with small strong-smelling flowers clustered on the branches; leaves large, oblong, dark green, sepals and pedicels red, petals white, anthers yellow, stigma large, flat, white ; fruit small, oval, reddish, one-seeded. *Suringi undi, god-undi, punág, harkin.*

Ghauts and Konkans. The flower buds are exported for use in silk dyeing. They are round and red, and are called *támbadi náj-kesar.*

3. Calophyllum.

C. inophyllum. Trunk black and crooked, leaves large oval rounded entire; flowers in racemes small but beautiful, very fragrant ; sepals and petals 4 each, roundish pure white ; stamens in 4 bundles, anthers yellow, ovary large round red, fruit round green, size of a walnut. *Undi.*

Very common in the S. Konkan, often growing to a large size close to high-water mark. *H.* says it is cultivated throughout India, but I believe it never grows well away from the sea. *G.* calls it the "Alexandrian laurel." Oil is obtained from the fruit and commonly burnt in the S. Konkan, and the wood is valuable. In Java, as with us, it is planted about the houses both for shade and sweetness, and it is mentioned by Miss Gordon-Cumming as one of the splendid trees of the Fiji islands, growing there also down to the water's edge.

4. Mesua.

M. ferrea. Leaves oblong, lanceolate, shining above, whitish beneath, flowers solitary or twin, large, silvery white with bright yellow anthers; fruit oval pointed, with the calyx attached. *Nág champa;* Sans. *Nág kesara.*

Found wild in the Konkan, and cultivated elsewhere, but not so commonly as its beauty and fragrance deserve. There is no exaggeration in Sir W. Jones's description: "This tree is one of the most beautiful on earth, and the delicious odour of its blossoms justly gives them a place in the quiver of Cáma-deva." Tennant, who says it is planted in Ceylon near every Buddhist temple, describes the flowers as resembling white roses, and forming "a singular contrast with the buds and shoots of the tree, which are of the deepest crimson." It is described as growing 60 or 70 feet high in the Burrampooter valley, "a glossy green mass of foliage, beset with snowy, fragrant gold-centred flowers of the camellia character: its timber unmatched for weight and hardness by any other in all the immense wilderness of Ind." And no flower can better fit Wordsworth's lines—

> "A silver shield with boss of gold,
> That spreads itself some fairy bold
> In fight to cover"—

Here comes order Ternstræmiaceæ. It is very doubtful whether there is any species of it wild in W. India, but it is mentioned here as containing the genus Thea, from the leaves of various species of which all the tea is produced. *H.* makes Thea only a section of the genus Camellia, so well known for the beauty of the flowers, and calls *C. theifera*, which is wild in Assam, "possibly the wild stock of the tea plant."

Order 19. **DIPTEROCARPEÆ.**

Leaves alternate and simple, flowers regular, anthers 2-celled with connective.

I can make out no other constant characteristics of this small order, nor are the number of petals and sepals given of the only species belonging to W. India.

Ancistrocladus. Smooth climbing shrubs with short hooked tendril-like branches, leaves entire in tufts, calyx at first small, but increasing and becoming wings to the fruit, styles 3.

**A. heyneanus.* A handsome climber with sessile oblong dark green leaves and small white flowers in terminal racemes; calyx and corolla at first about equal, stamens 10, fruit small with 3 very long wings. *Kardal Kardondi.* The Ghauts, *D.* and *G.*

ORDER 20. MALVACEÆ. Mallows.

Leaves alternate, simple, generally lobed, stipulate, sepals 5 valvate, often with an involucre or outer calyx, petals 5 twisted, stamens many united into a tube or column, from the sides of which spring very numerous filaments, bearing one-celled anthers; ovary of several carpels united round a common axis, styles generally the same number as the carpels, more or less united.

The valvate calyx and stamens united into a column are the special characteristics of this great order (but see Abutilon polyandrum); in many cases the fruit, consisting of the enlarged carpels as above, is also very noticeable. Lobed leaves, jointed pedicels, and showy flowers are of very frequent occurrence.

Note 1. *H.* has included in this order as a tribe Bombaceæ, previously considered a distinct order, and to that the above remarks do not apply.

Note 2. In these and all other monadelphous genera, the petals are more or less united at the base, and so the flowers often appear to be monopetalous.

"The plants of the order are all wholesome, and yield much mucilage, while many produce useful fibres."—*Le Maout.*

(*a*) Fruit of ripe carpels, separating from the axis.

1. MALVA. Downy herbs, involucre of 3 distinct bracts.

2. SIDA. Flowers small, involucre none, carpels generally with 2 awns or beaks.

3. ABUTILON. Flowers yellow, generally large and handsome, involucre none.

4. MALACHRA. Herbs with flowers in dense heads, usually intermixed with bracteoles; sepals cup-like below, styles 10.

5. URENA. Flowers clustered, involucre of 5 bracts; styles 10, ripe carpels often bristly.

6. PAVONIA. Involucre of 5 or more bracts; ovary 5-celled, styles 10.

(*b*) Fruit capsular.

7. DECASCHISTA. Involucre of 10 bracts, ovary and capsule 10-celled, styles 10.

8. HIBISCUS. Flowers large, showy, leaves usually palmately

lobed, involucre of 5 or more bracts, capsule 5 valved, or apparently 10 valved.

9. THESPESIA. Involucre of 5 to 8 bracts, deciduous, sometimes obsolete, calyx cup-shaped, style one, club-shaped.

10. GOSSYPIUM. Involucre of 3 large bracts, calyx as in the last, stigmas 5, seeds densely woolly.

1. MALVA.

M. rotundifolia. Spreading much branched, leaves roundish heart-shaped, bluntly lobed, flowers small, pale, bracts very narrow, calyx increasing with the fruit.

This is the small-flowered Mallow of England; frequently found in the Deccan, and in various other parts of India.

2. SIDA.

All the species here given have small yellow flowers, and are found commonly through the hotter parts of India.

1. *S. humilis.* A low herb, softly hairy, leaves roundish cordate acute, flowers solitary, axillary rather pretty, carpels 5, enclosed in the angular calyx.

1. *S. rhombifolia* (*S. retusa*, D.) Shrubby, leaves obovate or rhomboid, serrated towards the top, carpels 7 to 10, as long as the calyx. *Sahadevi, Atibala.*

These two are common throughout the Presidency, and are very variable (*H.*).

S. spinosa (*S. alba*, D.). Shrubby and thorny. Bandora, Surat (*D.*).

S. *carpinifolia* (*S. acuta*, D.). Shrubby, nearly smooth, with lanceolate acute leaves. Málwan, Bombay, *D. Tukati, tupkariya. S. cordifolia*, shrubby and softly hairy. Málwan. No hab. (*D.*). *Chikná, lobirsir bháji.*

3 ABUTILON.

1. *A. polyandrum.* A tall hairy shrub, leaves long-petioled, deeply cordate, long-pointed, flowers handsome, yellow, streaked at the base with pink, carpels 5, forming a round fruit depressed at the top. *Mudám.*

The Ghauts; also in the Panch Maháls, I think. This is remarkable in this order from the stamens being not columnar, but joined only at the base. There is a clammy and strong-smelling variety, which I found on the S. Ghauts, and Dr. T. Cooke at Khandalla, but no mentioned in any of the books. It is very like *A. graveoleus*, but easily distinguishable by the separate stamens and the small number of carpels.

2. *A. Indicum.* Shrubby, all grey and velvety, leaves heart-shaped, slightly lobed, unequally toothed, carpels about 20,

hairy, forming a top-shaped fruit rising in the centre. *Petári, madmi, Karandi.*

3. *A. muticum* (*A. tomentosum*, D.). Hairy, leaves round, cordate not lobed, slightly serrated, flowers large, carpels kidney-shaped, very hairy, forming a nearly round fruit with a depression at the top. *Kasili, Karandi.*

These two species grow in similar places in the Deccan, and are common. They have a great general resemblance, but the fruit sufficiently distinguishes them. The latter is the larger plant, and not so grey as the former, which is much more widely distributed over India. The capsules are called *Mudrá*, from their resemblance to a seal.—*Dymock.*

D. had at Cambay * *A. racemosum* (*A. sidoides*, D.) with white bark, acutely lobed leaves, and very small yellow flowers, carpels glutinous, 2-beaked, 3-seeded.

4. Malachra.

M. rotundfolia. A hairy plant with rough round leaves slightly angled or lobed; flowers small yellow, short stalked, fruit roundish.

This is supposed to be a foreigner, but it is common about Bombay, and said to be so in many parts of India. It certainly was not introduced for its beauty.

5. Urena.

1. *U. lobata.* Herbaceous, more or less hairy, leaves rounded with 3 or more lobes, flowers pink 2 or 3 together, involucre segments linear or lanceolate as long as the calyx, fruit of 5 carpels, roundish, covered with soft hooked bristles. *Wanbhendi.*

2. *U. sinuata.* Like the last but shrubby, leaves downy, deeply lobed or pinnatifid; flowers larger and pretty. *Lichi, rám-kápshi.*

These two species are both common, and both said by *H.* to be widely distributed over India, and very variable. *D.'s U.scabrinscula* is by *H.* made a variety of *U. lobata.*

6. Pavonia.

* *P. zeylanica.* An erect shrub, much branched, glandular and hairy, leaves deeply lobed, flowers solitary, middle-sized, whitish, bracts 8 to 10 linear, carpels oblong, 3-sided, sharply winged.

Near Gogo (*D.*).

Two others are given from Cutch by General Palin. * *P. glechomifolia*, a rigid procumbent plant, leaves somewhat 3-lobed, crenate, flowers yellow, carpels 5, warty. * *P. odorata.* Erect, sticky, leaves much as the last, flowers pink, in clusters at the end of the branches; carpels obovoid. *Kálá válá.*

7. Decaschista.

* *D. trilobata.* A hairy shrub, lower leaves deeply 3-lobed, upper sometimes entire, flowers large, capsule rough.

S. Ghauts, *D.* Belgaum, near the Ghauts, (*G.*).

8. Hibiscus.

1. *H. furcatus.* A large climber covered with recurved prickles and prickly hairs, stem and branches much coloured, leaves long petioled palmately 3 to 5 lobed, serrated; involucre with leafy appendages on the back; flowers very large and handsome, yellow with purple throat, capsule brown conical, hidden in the calyx.

Common on the Ghauts; found also in the Konkan and Bombay. Hotter parts of India (*H.*).

H. describes it as shrubby erect, which is not true of this Presidency, and the flowers as 4 inches in diameter, which they are not with us.

2. *H. hirtus.* A shrubby hairy plant with 3-lobed or entire ovate leaves and pretty white flowers, solitary and long stalked; involucre of 5 to 7 subulate segments shorter than the calyx, capsule melon-shaped, seeds covered with white silky hairs.

Very common at the lower part of the Ghauts. Both plants and flowers of this are much smaller than those of most of the other species. It is often cultivated (*H.*).

3. *H. micranthus.* A strong shrubby rough plant, with petioled ovate leaves deeply serrated, flowers small solitary pink, capsule round, seeds as in the last.

Deccan, Kattywar, and Kaira in hedges. Hotter parts of India, *H.* He calls it variable, and quotes *R.* that it may be a variety of the last.

4. *H. cannabinus.* Tall, thick-stemmed prickly, leaves long petioled palmate, flowers very handsome, pale yellow with crimson or claret centre, involucre segments 5 or more, calyx much longer, hairy and warty; capsule nearly round, pointed, covered with silky stinging hairs. *Ambari.*

Cultivated for the fibre; the leaves eaten as a vegetable, and the capsules used for oil. The calyx and involucre become hard and bristly when dry.

5. *H. panduræformis.* A tall, much-branched very hairy

plant, leaves cordate unequally toothed, lower ones slightly lobed, flowers solitary yellow with purple bottom, bracteoles 7 to 10 linear shorter than the calyx, capsule ovoid.

Sholapore. Surat (*D.*). Hotter parts of India (*H.*).

6. *H. vitifolius.* Tall, softly hairy all over with lobed serrated long petioled leaves, flowers solitary sulphur-coloured with purple centre, bracteoles about 8 subulate, capsule covered by the calyx beaked, 5-winged.

Salsette, Malwan (*D.*). Ram Ghaut (*G.*). Hotter parts of India (*H.*). The leaves of the specimens that I have seen have no particular resemblance to vine leaves.

7. *H. tiliaceus* (*Paritium t.* D.) A tree with very broad strongly nerved leaves roundish cordate with a sudden point, crenulated, hoary beneath, flowers large bell-shaped, yellow with crimson centre, bracteoles 10, united half way up, capsule 5-valved, seeds small brown kidney-shaped. *Belapatá.*

N. Konkan. Rutuagherry and Teracoil river (*D.*). Bombay esplanade, G. Coasts of both peninsulas, and tropics of both hemispheres, usually near the coast (*H.*).

In the South Sea islands long strips of the bark of this tree are cut off and used as ropes, and Captain Cook saw one of these ropes nearly 30 feet long, and strong enough to bear the weight of a man scrambling from one ledge of rock to another. Matting is also made of the bark, some of which is as fine as a coarse cloth.

The following are less common :

**H. trionum*, a hairy herb, leaves roundish, flowers large yellow with purple base, calyx membranous, inflated, bracts many, linear, capsule oblong obtuse. Common, chiefly on black soil (*D.*). **H. surattensis,* hairy, covered with small prickles, leaves roundish lobed, stipules large, bracts linear with a spathulate appendage. Malabar Hill (*D.* & *G.*). **H. intermedius* (*H. scanden,* D.), leaves deeply lobed, flowers solitary, smallish, yellow, bracts strap-shaped. Coast of Kattywar (*D.*). Sind, Stocks. **H. radiatus* (*H. heptaphyllus,* D.) 4 or 5 feet high, prickly, leaves palmate, flowers large solitary, purple or yellow, bracts linear forked. E. side of the N. Ghauts (*D.*). *H. solandra* (*Lagunea lobata,* D.) small hairy plant, leaves rough, cordate or lobed, flowers white or yellow, generally without involucre. Poona. Near Belgaum (*D.*). *H. tetraphyllus* (*Abelmoschus t.* & *A. Warreensis,* D.) Tall, rough and slightly prickly, leaves cordate, lobed and toothed, flowers yellow with purple centre, bracts leafy; strongly resembles *H. esculentus.* Dapoli. Caranja and S. Konkan (*D.*). *Ranbhenda.* **H. punctatus,* hairy and glutinous, three or four feet high, leaves ovate or three-lobed, flowers rose-coloured, very small, bracts 8 to 10, capsule beaked. Broach collectorate, *D.* rare. Sind, Stocks.

The following are cultivated :

H. rosasinensis, the shoe flower, *jásud.*

H. mutabilis, the changeable rose : Inconstante amante (Portuguese) the flowers change from white to red in the course of the day.

H. subdariffa, roselle, red sorrel of the W. Indies. The jelly is made from the red, fleshy calyx, and involucre. *Lal ámbári, patwá.*

H. esculentus, the vegetable *bhendi.* The vulgar, but very appropriate name of 'slip go down' comes, I believe, from the Madras Presidency.

9. THESPESIA.

T. populuea. A tree. Leaves heart-shaped, pointed, entire, smooth; flowers yellow, sometimes reddish with purple or crimson centre, calyx 5-toothed, capsule oblong or roundish, depressed, the calyx adherent. *Bhendi, pimparui.*

An exceedingly common tree all about the coast, not growing well at any distance from the sea. It is sometimes called the Indian tulip tree, but the tulip tree proper (*Liriodendron*) belongs to the Magnolia family.

T. lampas, a shrub very like this, 3 or 4 feet high, has the leaves 3-lobed. *Rán bhendi.* Konkan and Ghauts.

10. GOSSYPIUM. Cotton.

G. Stocksii. Shrubby branching, leaves palmately 3 to 5 lobed, flowers small, yellow, involucre segments deeply and irregularly cut, capsule ovoid, cotton yellow, adherent to the seeds.

H. looks on this as the parent type of all the forms of Indian cotton. It is doubtful if it is found wild in Sindh; pretty certain that it is not in any other part of the Presidency. *G. herbaceum*, the cultivated form of this, produces the varieties of Indian cotton, *kapás ; G. barbadense*, the American varieties. It was cultivated in Egypt in very early times and found in India by Alexander the Great.

"Sir M. Noel told us of the dispute between him and the E. I. Company, whether calico be linen or not, which he says it is, having ever been esteemed so; they say it is made of cotton wool, and grows upon trees, not like flax or hemp. But it was carried against the Company, though they stand out against the verdict."—*Pepys' Diary, Feb.* 27, 1664. So the Germans to this day call cotton *Baumwolle*, tree wool.

Althæa rosea, the hollyhock, seems to be the only common garden flower of this order and tribe, not already mentioned :—

"With foxgloves and gorgeous poppies,
And great-eyed hollyhocks.—*G. Macdonald.*

TRIBE BOMBACEÆ.

Trees with leathery sepals, not generally united; stamens not united or only slightly so; otherwise like *Malveæ.*

1. KYDIA. Involucre of 4 to 6 bracts, increasing with the fruit; stamens united below, above divided into 5 bundles, each bearing 3 anthers, style 3 cleft, stigmas 3, capsule roundish 3-valved.

2. BOMBAX. Involucre none, stamens in 5 bundles below, above divided into many filaments, stigmas 5, capsule 5-valved, seeds woolly.

3. ERIODENDRON. Like the last, but each bundle of stamens bears only 2 or 3 anthers, stigma 1, obscurely 5-lobed.

1. KYDIA.

* *K. calycina.* Leaves rounded cordate, closely felted beneath, flowers in panicles, white, pink, or pale yellow, small, involucre segments oblong, downy, capsule size of a pea, hidden in the calyx. *Wárang, bhoti, potári.*

Common on the Ghauts (*D.*). Kennery forests (*G.*). I was unfortunate enough never to find it. "The fruit ripens in the cold season, and hangs on the tree for months, conspicuous by the brown, shining calyx and involucel" (*Brandis*). Tropical Hymalayas (*H.*).

2. BOMBAX.

B. malabaricum (*Salmalia M.* D.). Trunk and branches all covered with stout, hard prickles, leaflets 5 to 7, narrowing at both ends, petioled; flowers very numerous, large, deep red, calyx unequally lobed, fleshy; capsule woody when ripe, felted inside, full of silky cotton. *Shewa, Mocha.*

The well-known silk cotton tree, exceedingly common in the Konkan, less so elsewhere. Nothing can be more beautiful than the cotton shaken slowly out of a ripe capsule till it forms a downy heap. It makes very good pillows. "The Ceiba's crimson pomp" is Heber's description of the flowers. The gum is called *Mocha ras.*—(*Dymock.*) In the W. Indies it is looked on with superstitious respect as the haunt of evil spirits.—(*Kingsley.*)

3. ERIODENDRON.

E. anafractuosum. A tree with a general resemblance to the last, but less prickly; leaflets 5 to 8, peduncles 2 inches long, club-shaped; flowers like the last, but of a dirty white; capsule and seeds like the last. *Shamella, bhujaridhaman.*

Khandeish and Konkan, but not common, I believe. To this tribe also belongs *Adansonia digitata*, the fantastic-looking tree with immense swollen trunks, which never fail to attract the attention of newcomers to Bombay. The flowers are very large, white, and very handsome. It is found in various places up the coast and elsewhere, but is not supposed to be a native of India. In some parts of Africa the hollow trunks are said to be used as burial places for the bards (*Kirby*). Called the monkey bread tree, *baobab*, and *Gorakh chinch.*

ORDER 21. STERCULIACEÆ.

Leaves alternate with stipules; flowers generally regular, sepals 5, more or less united, often with bracteoles, petals 5 or none; stamens generally more or less columnar or tubular, anthers 2-celled; ovary generally of 3 or 5 carpels.

Some of the genera of this order are very near to Malvaceæ, others to Tiliaceæ. In all the genera here given the stamens are more or less united, though not so conspicuously so as in Malvaceæ.

1. STERCULIA. Trees or shrubs with palmate or digitate leaves, calyx tubular, 4 or 5 divided, petals none; staminal column bearing a head or ring of sessile anthers, ovary of 4 or 5 carpels, styles and stigmas as many, fruit of distinct carpels, sometimes stalked.

2. HELICTERES. Trees or shrubs with simple leaves; flowers often irregular, calyx tubular 5 divided, petals 5 clawed, stamens united half way up, ovary at the top of the staminal column 5-lobed, fruit of carpels more or less united.

3. PTEROSPERMUM. Trees or shrubs with oblique leaves, staminal column short, bearing the anthers and 5 staminodes, ovary within the top of the column 3 to 5-celled, stigma 5 furrowed, capsule 5-valved, seeds winged.

4. MELOCHIA. Leaves simple, stamens 5, tubular below, petals persistent after withering, styles 5, capsule 5-valved.

5. WALTHERIA. Herbs or undershrubs with simple leaves, stamens as in the last, stigma club-shaped, capsule 2-valved, one-seeded.

1. STERCULIA.

1. *S. urens.* A tree with white and pinkish papery bark; leaves large, 5-lobed, soft and velvety; flowers in panicles, green or yellow with purple throat, strong smelling and sticky; fruit of 5 carpels radiating like a star fish, when young like crimson velvet, the hairs bristly and stinging. *Sárdol, Sárdora, Karái, Káoli, pándruk.*

When the tree is without leaves in the cold weather, the white bark gives it the appearance of being dead. It is tolerably common in most jungles.

2. *S. guttata.* A tall, handsome tree, with large ovate or

oblong entire leaves, downy beneath; flowers in racemes covered with reddish down, the tips greenish and curled backwards; carpels about 3, large broad ovate or nearly round, splitting and showing the large black seeds. *Kukar, Koidáre, Goldár.*

The Ghauts and S. Konkan.

3. *S. colorata.* A large tree, with large, smooth, 5-lobed leaves, the lobes long-pointed; flowers in panicles, mealy, orange outside, dark red inside; fruit of 2 to 5 membranous follicles on a common stalk, opening very soon, and showing the unripe seeds attached to the edges. *Kháosi, Bháikoi.*

The Ghauts and Konkan. The remarkable-looking open follicles might be taken for dry leaves.

4. *S. fœtida, Rán badám.* A very fine tree, with digitate leaves; fruit size of a small mango; seeds size of a bean, eatable.

Planted (*D.* and *G.*), but wild in the Konkan (*H.*). "One of the noblest of Ceylon forest trees, producing from the end of its branches bunches of dark purple flowers of extreme richness and beauty, but emitting an intolerable smell."—*Tennant.*

All of these are remarkable trees, such as

"Spread
A roof of dark green glory o'er the hill."—*Sir E. Arnold.*

2. Helicteres.

H. isora. A poor-looking shrub with oval toothed roughish leaves; flowers 2 or 3 together, with yellow calyx and lanceolate bracts, petals dull red, 2 large and 2 or 3 small, all cohering; fruit of 5 long carpels twisted together into the shape of a screw. *Kewan, Dhámni, Murádsing.*

Konkan and Ghauts, not uncommon. *B.* calls it a shrub or small tree, but it is not even a large shrub with us.

3. Pterospermum.

P. glabrescens. A tree with large leaves of very various shapes, oblong, peltate, or cordate, irregularly-toothed, waved or lobed, underside and petioles light grey, with close down; flowers large white, capsule brown, oval, about 5 inches long, very rough and hard, splitting into 5; seeds very numerous, flat, brown. *Muchkunda.*

There are two or three fine trees of this on the Tanna maidán.

* *P. suberifolium,* a small tree with oblong leaves toothed or lobed;

flowers large, white, fragrant, capsule an inch or two long, slightly angular, Konkans (*D*). Very superior torches are made of its straight dried branches.—*Tennant.*

* *P. heyneanum* (*P. lawianum*, D.), larger than the last, leaves variable, sometimes sub-peltate. Dharwar and S. Ghauts (*D.*).

These two seem to differ but little from the first, and have the same native name.

4. Melochia.

M. corchorifolia (*Riedelia c.* D.). A stout, erect, rather hairy plant; leaves ovate serrate; flowers in terminal heads, pale pink with yellow throat, surrounded by subulate bracts, capsule round, hairy.

Konkan and Guzerat. Hotter parts of India (*H.*).

* *M. velutina* (*Riedelia tiliæfolia*, D.). A small tree with long petioled subcordate leaves, when young velvety; flowers small, pink, in pænicles; seeds winged. *Methuri.*

Bassein, Belgaum, Khandalla (*D.*). Hotter parts of India (*H.*).

5. Waltheria.

W. Indica. A tough plant, softly hairy; leaves lanceolate or ovate; flowers small, yellow, crowded, on a short peduncle, bracts 3 narrow; capsule very small, black.

Very variable. Common in all the hotter parts of India; a widely diffused tropical weed (*H.*).

Eriolæna. Staminal column short, bearing externally numerous oblong 2-celled anthers. * *E. Candolleii.* A tree, leaves ovate cordate, grey beneath, flowers crowded, downy, yellow, bracts deeply cut; capsule ovate, pointed. *Botku, Arang.* Ram Ghaut (*D.*).

* *E. Hookeriana* differs from this in the leaves being roundish cordate, and the capsule an inch long. *Buti.* Not in *D.* Along the Ghauts, not common (*G.*).

Buettneria. Flowers minute, limb of the petals with a long strap-shaped appendage, stamens 10, tubular below, 5 only being fertile. * *B. herbacea*, a small plant with ovate leaves, and red and yellow flowers, "the petals forming a circular dome over the pistil and nectary" (*G.*), fruit size of a pea, prickly. Common in Bombay (*D.* and *G.*).

Kleinhovia, staminal column dilated above into a bell-shaped 5 divided cup, each division with 3 anthers. * *K. hospita*, a tree with ovate entire leaves and very long petioles, capsule membranous, inflated, pear-shaped. "A doubtful native" (*D*), but pretty widely distributed in India (*H.*).

Theobroma cocoa, from the seeds of which chocolate is produced, belongs to this order. Gardens, Bombay (*D.*).

ORDER 22. TILIACEÆ. Lindens.

Leaves generally alternate; flowers regular, sepals 3 to 5, valvate, petals 3 to 5, stamens numerous, usually from a disk, ovary superior, fruit generally 2 to 10-celled.

Some of the genera in this order are very like mallows, but easily distinguished by the free stamens and 2-celled anthers. Many species have strong fibres. The flowers of all that are found in W. India are yellow or white, and though generally speaking not attractive, some of them remind one of "the lime tree's pale and fragrant flowers."—*Cowper*.

1. GREWIA. Trees or shrubs with entire strongly nerved leaves, sepals generally larger than the petals; fruit a drupe, not bristly, often lobed.

2. ERINOCARPUS. Petals clawed, fruit covered with bristles; otherwise like the last.

3. TRIUMFETTA. Herbs or undershrubs, generally hairy; flowers crowded, stigma 5-toothed, capsule spiny or bristly.

4. CORCHORUS. Strong fibrous herbs or undershrubs; leaves strongly serrated, the lowest serratures often produced into long points; flowers few together, small, yellow, style short, stigma cup-shaped.

5. ELÆOCARPUS. Trees. Stamens (in the species here given) rising from a raised torus, fruit a drupe.

1. GREWIA.

1. *G. tiliæfolia.* A tree with roundish leaves, cordate and oblique at the base, bluntly toothed, 5-nerved, stipules leafy, auricled on one side, peduncles 3 or 4 together, 3 or 4 flowered, sepals twice as long as the orange-coloured petals, drupes 2 to 4-lobed, blackish, smooth. *Dáman, Karkani.*

Konkan. Common in Bombay (*D.*).

2. *G. asiatica.* Small tree, much like the last, but stipules short, lanceolate, petals yellow, drupe round, hairy stalked. *Fulsi.*

Much cultivated in most parts of India, and very variable (*H.*). Wild in the Poona collectorate (*D.*).

3. *G. polygama.* A straggling shrub or small tree, leaves lanceolate, serrate, rather rough, 3-nerved; flowers polygamous, rather large and handsome, sepals covered with yellowish down, much larger than the white petals, drupe 4-lobed, or 2 together 2-lobed. *Gaoli.*

Konkan. Common on the Ghauts (*D.*).

4. *G. microcos.* A shrub or small tree with ovate or obovate bifarious leaves, papery and smooth, stipules large, wedge-shaped; flowers in terminal panicles, yellowish, drupe size of a pea, purplish, smooth. *Shiral, hausoli.*

The inflorescence of this is quite different from that of the other species found in this Presidency.

Konkan. Abundant in the hills about Parr (*G.*).

The following are all shrubby except the last. * *G. columnaris*, leaves oblong, rough; flowers small, the yellow sepals twice as long as the white petals, drupe purplish, top-shaped, bristly. Mahableshwar, Salsette, &c. * *G. orientalis*, scandent, leaves ovate lanceolate, flowers rather large, sepals and petals as in the last, drupe yellow, size of a small cherry. S. Ghauts (*D.*). * *G. populifolia*, much-branched, smooth; leaves cuneate, variable, flowers solitary or twin, petals white, drupes yellowish, eatable. *Gingo*; not in *D.* or *G.* Cutch, Palin; Sind, Stocks. * *G. pilosa*, leaves obovate, rough; flowers yellow, largish, petals bifid, drupes reddish-brown, hairy. *Khatkhati.* Deccan (*D.*), Guzerat (*B.*) * *G. villosa*, softly hairy almost all over; leaves roundish cordate; flowers nearly sessile in close tufts, white or yellowish, petals notched, drupe round, size of a cherry, pulp sweet, eatable. Deccan, Sind (*D.*). *G. hirsuta*, straggling and hairy; leaves ovate, oblique at the base; flowers pretty, greenish-white turning yellow, drupe smaller than the last. Not in *D.* Sattara and Mahableshwar. Salsette (*G.*). * *G. abutilifolia*, a small tree; leaves roundish cordate; flowers greenish-white, drupe yellow, hairy, 4-lobed. Deccan (*D.*).

2. Erinocarpus.

E. Nimmoanus. A small crooked tree with large roundish cordate leaves, lobed and rough when young, and with round glands at the lower serratures, flowers rather large yellow, the sepals longest, fruit triangular, bristly, the angles winged. *Chaora, Tivra, jangli bendi, cher.*

Common on the Ghauts and Konkan hills.

3. Triumfetta.

T. rhomboidea (*T. angulata*, D.). A small tough plant, hairy all over, rough-stemmed, leaves various in shape, generally angled, sometimes 3-lobed, flowers small, corolla nearly hidden in the reddish calyx, stamens 8 to 15, fruit nearly round, size of a pea, covered with smooth prickles. *Nichardi.*

H. includes in this *R.'s T. trilocularis*, which has a large fruit with hooked bristles (I had it at Dápoli), and considers *T. rotundifolia*, D., which has roundish unequally-toothed leaves, to be possibly only a form of this. Poona, Deccan, and Surat (*D.*). *H.* calls the plant very variable, and common through hotter India. * *T. pilosa*, a rough plant, flowers much larger than in the other species, leaves as in the first, fruit round with hooked prickles. *Kutre wândre.* Wári country (*D.*). Throughout tropical India (*H.*).

4. Corchorus.

Note.—The capsules vary very greatly in the different species, and are the best distinction.

1. *C. capsularis.* Leaves oblong, lanceolate, the appendages to the lower serratures very fine, capsule round, flattened at the top, wrinkled, ribbed, 5-celled. *Chouchen.*

2. *C. olitorius.* Tall and strong, tinged with red, leaves much as in the last, capsule cylindric; erect, 2 or 3 inches long, 10-ribbed, sometimes with 5 obscure blunt points. *Tánkla, chunch.*

These are both common in the Konkan, and many other parts of India, and are cultivated for their fibre—jute. They are widely spread over the hot parts of the world: and the second, which is used as a potherb all over tropical Africa, is commonly known as Jew's Mallow.

3. *C. acutangulus.* Leaves oval pointed, crenated, capsules erect, 5 or 6-angled, some of the angles winged, and with a two or three-pointed beak.

Rutnagherry. A common weed (*D.*).

C. Trilocularis. Leaves crenated, capsule with 3 or 4 angles and valves, covered with prickly points. Deccan, Guzerat (*D.*). *Kadu chunch*: the seeds *Rájjiren.* * *C. fascicularis.* Peduncles opposite the leaves, 2 to 5 flowered, capsule very small, cylindric. Surat (*D.*). *Bahuphalli, hirankhori.* *C. antichorus* (*C. humilis*, D.), very small, shrubby, prostrate, leaves ovate, capsule linear oblong, 3 or 4-celled. Panch Mahals. Kattywar and Deccan (*D.*). *Bahuphalli.*

* Of these *H.* makes *C. acutangulus* and *fascicularis* common throughout the hotter parts of India; the others have a narrower range.

5. Elæocarpus.

* 1. *E. ganitrus.* Leaves lanceolate or elliptic, flowers white in drooping racemes, petals much cut, drupe round, purple, size of a cherry, stone tubercled, grooved, 5-celled. *Udrach, rudraksh.*

The higher Ghauts (*D.*). S. Konkan (*G.*). The stones are used by Fakirs for necklaces.

* *E. oblongus*, leaves lanceolate or elliptic, flowers in racemes, white, petals fringed, drupe oblong, stone tubercled. *Khás, Khásas.* S. Ghauts, rare (*D.*). "When in full bloom this is a very beautiful tree, the foliage is frequently tinged with red" (*G.*).

* *E. tuberculatus* (*Monocera t.* D.). Leaves obovate, flowers in rather large erect racemes, petals much cut, anthers with a long awn, drupe oval, stone tubercled and furrowed. Ram Ghaut (*D.*).

II. DISCIFLORÆ.

ORDER 23. LINEÆ. The flax family.

Herbs or shrubs, with alternate simple leaves and regular flowers, sepals, petals and stamens usually 5, styles 3 to 5.

This order outwardly most resembles *Caryophylleæ*, and like *Tiliacea* is chiefly valuable for its fibres.

1. LINUM. Herbs; petals twisted deciduous, with 5 glands united to the staminal ring, ovary and capsule 5-celled, styles 5.

2. REINWARDTIA. Undershrubs, stamens with 2 or 3 glands and alternating staminodes, ovary 3 to 5-celled, styles 3 or 4.

1. LINUM. Flax.

1. *L. usitatissimum*, the common flax plant, cultivated chiefly for the oil throughout India, and in England for the seed, linseed. *Alsi, jawas.* Supposed to have been first cultivated in Egypt.

It is one of the prettiest of crops. "The flax was in full bloom; it had pretty little blue flowers, as delicate as the wings of a moth, or even more so."—*Hans Andersen.*

2. *L. Mysorense.* A small, smooth, branched plant, leaves oblong, blunt, flowers yellow, petals much separated, capsule roundish, ribbed, enclosed in the calyx. *Wundri, bâmburti.*

Leaves variable (*H.*) It has much superficial resemblance to a mustard. Konkan, Deccan, and Ghauts.

2. REINWARDTIA.

R. trigyna. Smooth, leaves lanceolate, flowers bright yellow, handsome, with bracts, sepals much imbricated, capsule size of a pea. *Abai.*

Mira hills (*D.*). Koina Valley (*Dr. Cooke*). Common in gardens.

Hugonia. Stamens 10, styles 5, drupe round.

* *H. nystax.* A large climbing shrub with tendrils, and with much brown hair, flowers large, pale yellow, leaves ovate entire, stamens alternately long and short. Málwan taluka (*D.*).

ORDER 24. MALPHIGIACEÆ.

Trees or shrubs, often climbing, leaves opposite entire, calyx 5 divided, often furnished with large glands, petals 5, stamens 10, fruit winged.

This, which is a large American order, is by form and position of the parts of the flower, and by the samaroid fruit very like *Sapindaceæ*, but differs from that in having no disc to speak of.

HIPTAGE. Flowers in racemes; calyx with one gland, united to the pedicel, petals clawed, four white, one coloured, one stamen much larger than the rest, ovary 3-lobed.

H. madablota. A beautiful climber, leaves large, oval, pointed, shining, flowers large and very fragrant, petals finely fringed, pure white, but the fifth with base and centre sulphur yellow; carpels 3, each with 3 unequal wings. *Halad vel, dhasra chi vel, bokhi, piloka, utimukhta.*

Ghauts and Konkan, not uncommon.

The beauty of the whole plant is very striking, and the want of symmetry in the flowers and fruit not less so. It is mentioned in the Sakuntala and other Sanscrit works under the name of *Mádhavi.* "When it meets nothing to grasp it assumes the form of a sturdy tree" (*Sir W. Jones*), and may be seen so in gardens.

Aspidopterys. Calyx without glands, ovary 3-lobed, styles 3.

* *A. Roxburghiana*, a slender climber, leaves ovate, smooth, flowers small, white or yellow, with rusty hairs, carpel with a broad wing like hops (*G.*). Khandalla and Konkans (*D.*).

* *A. cordata*, like the last, leaves rounded cordate, with an abrupt point, flowers in panicles, carpel roundish winged. Near Penu (*D.*).

ORDER 25. ZYGOPHYLLEÆ.

The description of this order is so full of alternatives that the only features approaching to constancy seem to be sepals and petals 5 each, stamens 5, 10, or 15. It is also said to be closely allied to the last order, and to be with difficulty distinguished from *Rutaceæ*.

1. TRIBULUS. Herbs, leaves opposite pinnate, stamens 10, inserted on the base of a 10-lobed annular disk, 5 longer, the other 5 with a gland outside, ovary hairy, lobed, style short, stigmas several.

2. FAGONIA. Leaves simple or trifoliate with spiny stipules, stamens 10, inserted on a short inconspicuous disk, ovary 5-cornered tapering into the style, fruit 5-cornered dividing into 5.

1. Tribulus.

T. terrestris. A pretty plant, all grey and hairy, often quite flat on the ground; leaflets about 6 pair, oblong oblique, flowers stalked yellow, fruit comparatively large, irregularly lobed and angled, with several sharp spurs standing out horizontally. *Gokhru, Saráte.*

Deccan, Guzerat, Kattywar. Throughout India and the warm regions of the globe (*H.*). The English name of the genus is Caltrops, from the shape of the fruit.

2. Fagonia.

F. arabica (*F. Mysorensis,* D.). A small much-branched undershrub, all covered with glandular hairs and very thorny; 2 small oblong leaves and 4 thorns in a whorl, and one pink flower in each axil, fruit deeply 5-lobed with a sharp point at the top. *Dhamásá.*

The Deccan.

Guiacum officinale, the wood of which is lignum vitæ, belongs to this order.

Order 26. GERANIACEÆ.

With this *H.* includes the two old orders *Oxalideæ* and *Balsamineæ* as tribes. The three families have such very decided characteristics of their own that it seems well to separate them as much as possible.

Tribe Geranieæ. Geraniums.

Sepals and petals 5, stamens two or three times as many, disk of 5 small glands, ovary 5-lobed, styles 5, fruit 5-lobed, generally with a long beak.

This family, so well known in England both by wild flowers, stork bills, crane bills, &c., and by the cultivated pelargoniums and tropæolums (Indian cress, but often called Nasturtium), is represented in W. India by various species and varieties of the two last mentioned genera, but by only a single wild species.

Monsonia, stamens 15, united below. * *M. Senegalensis,* a small diffuse plant, leaves ovate or cordate, hairy, long-stalked; flowers solitary, pink, capsule hairy, with a beak often as long as the whole plant. Dry pastures in the Deccan, not common (*D.*).

Note that *Tropæolum* has the capsule not beaked, and one petal is spurred.

Tribe Oxalideæ. Wood sorrels.

Leaves compound, flowers regular, sepals and petals 5, stamens 10, 5 longer, styles 5, capsule 5-celled.

1. Oxalis. Herbs with trifoliate leaves, ovary 5-lobed, stigma capitate bifid, seeds bursting elastically.

2. Biophytum. Herbs with pinnate leaves more or less radiating from the top of the stem, leaflets oblique, otherwise like Oxalis.

1. Oxalis.

O. corniculata. A small more or less hairy weed, leaflets broad obcordate, flowers yellow, more or less umbellate, calyx persistent, capsule like a silique, erect angular, very hairy, seeds many. *Nálkarda, ambuti.*

A common weed. Cosmopolitan and very variable (*H.*). I have found it in Sussex and S. Italy, as well as in India. The leaves are characteristic of the genus, and would remind any one of the English wood-sorrel, *O. acetosella.*

2. Biophytum.

B. sensitivum. A small plant with a whorl of pinnate leaves at the top of the stem, leaflets many pairs oblong, flowers yellow, several together on peduncles of various lengths, sepals tipped with red, capsule roundish, many-seeded. *Lájri.*

H. gives three varieties. The leaves are very sensitive; very common.

To this tribe also belongs *Averrhoa;* trees with pinnate leaves, of which two species are cultivated, *A. carambola karmal, karambal;* the fruit like a plantain, but acutely angled, has a (to me) delicious flavour, though very acid: and **A. bilimbi, bailimbi, dhákta anvála,* the obtusely angled fruit of which grows on the trunk and branches.

Tribe Balsamineæ. Balsams.

Leaves simple, flowers very irregular, sepals and petals 3 to 5, sepals coloured, one spurred, stamens 5, very short, anthers more or less connected, capsule 5-valved, bursting with great force.

Impatiens. Succulent herbs, generally with showy flowers, two lateral sepals small green, the third (lip) large, petal-like, generally ending in a hollow spur; two lateral petals (wings) 2-lobed, the third (standard) large, style none, stigma 5 divided.

The flowers of this genus are unlike anything else, and therefore easy of recognition, but it is often difficult to identify the species, of which *H.* gives no less than 123, many of them with varieties. Of these 14 are attributed to this Presidency, confined to the Konkan and the Ghauts, as the balsams are essentially plants of moist climates.

1. *I. acaulis.* A smooth low plant, leaves roundish crenated, flowers pale pink, large, long-stalked, wings with 2 lobes, one longer, spur very long, capsule acute at both ends.

A most lovely plant, which I have seen only on the Waranda Ghaut, growing in the spray of waterfalls. Matheran and Mahableshwar (*Birdwood*). **I. scapiflora* (*G.*) having wings with three broad segments, and **I. rivalis* with the same feature, but very variable, *H.* considers scarcely to differ from this.

2. *I. Kleinii.* Small, smooth, leaves opposite, ovate lanceolate, with two large glands near the petiole, flowers pink, solitary or twin, sepals linear, spur long and slender, capsule narrow with round black seeds.

Variable (*H.*). A plant of little beauty, and the only species besides *I. balsamina*, which is very common in S. Konkan.

3. *I. inconspicua.* Small, smooth, leaves opposite, ovate lanceolate, flowers minute, white tinged with purple, sepals very long and narrow, wings with a large rounded clawed lobe, and a smaller one, lip small without spur.

D. Without hab. Mahableshwar, *Dr. Cooke.* Very variable (*H.*). **I. oppositifolia* so closely allied as to be not always distinguishable from this, but it has a short stout incurved spur. Very common in the Konkan (*D.*).

4. *I. balsamina.* Mostly smooth, leaves alternate, lanceolate, rather rough, flowers generally stalked, lip funnel-shaped with slender spur. *Tirda, shirda.*

The common balsam, the original of the garden flower of England. "Brought by the Portuguese from India in the sixteenth century, and still blooming everywhere in Italy."—*Hehn.* Very common throughout the Konkans. On rocks close to the sea, where it often grows so abundantly as to colour them; it is there frequently not more than two or three inches high, with a few flowers crowded together at the top. **I. scabriuscula*, allied to this, but much smaller and leaves broader (*H.*). S. Konkan (*D.*).

5. *I. pulcherrima.* Stout, smooth, nearly two feet high, leaves ovate, pointed with bristly serratures, petioles long, glandular in the upper half, flowers large rose-colour, wings deeply divided, spur long.

This is a most beautiful plant: Shady jungles in the Wári country (*D.*) and no other authority (*H.*). I have found it at Wándri, and one or two other places in the Rutnagherry district.

6. **I. Dalzellii.* A large species with yellow flowers, lip saccate with a short spur.

S. Konkan (*D.*). Mahableshwar, dying down early in October.—*Dr. T. Cooke.*

**I. Stocksii* very small, leaves round or broad ovate, lip boat-shaped, scarcely spurred, wings 3-lobed. S. Ghauts (*D.*). **I. Chinensis*, a variable and beautiful plant, all smooth, stem angled, leaves opposite oblong, flowers rose purple or white, spur very long, incurved, wings auricled. Konkans (*D.*).

**I. Lawii*, small, much branched, smooth, leaves opposite oblong, flowers large, lip small without spur, wings 3-lobed. A very beautiful species. S. Konkan (*D.*), *I. tomentosa*, small, leaves opposite oblong, rough above, flowers purple, one or two in each axil, on longish hairy stalks, lip inflated into a very short spur. Mahableshwar. Fonda Ghaut (*D.*). **I. latifolia*, stout, two or three feet high, smooth, leaves ovate lanceolate, flowers large solitary, pale purple with green lips and spur. Konkan, common (*D.*).

Any one who could collect all the species obtainable in the Presidency, and get them properly identified, would do a great service. It would have to be done mostly in the rains.

ORDER 27. RUTACEÆ.

In this order *H.* has included Aurantiaceæ, which, from its very decided characteristics, I think it well to keep separate as much as possible.

TRIBE RUTEÆ. Rues.

Herbs, rarely shrubby, flowers regular, disk thick, ovary deeply 3 to 5-lobed.

PEGANUM. Leaves alternate, petals 4 or 5, stamens 12 to 15, inserted at the base of the disk, some without anthers.

Note.—This genus, unlike the order generally, has neither glands nor smell.

**P. harmala.* A large smooth-branched plant, with thick foliage, leaves multifid, segments linear, acute, flowers solitary in the axils, white with green veins, capsule round, 3 or 4-celled. Syrian rue. *Harmára, ispand.*

Bijapore and Indapore, and very abundant in Sind. Widely distributed through the least fertile parts of the world (all over Affghanistan, *Bellew*); and in a barren part of Morocco Hooker found it forming at intervals green patches among the general barrenness. "The Turks use the seeds both as a spice and for dyeing red."—*Chambers.*

Ruta graveoleus. Common rue, *Santáp, santuri* is commonly cultivated.

"Rank-smelling rue."—*Spenser.*

"Sour herb of grace
Rue even for ruth."—*Richard II.*

This is thus explained by *C. Knight* : "The rues like the oranges abound in oil glands, but with a different result, the smell in that case being as disagreeable, as in most of the orange family it is sweet. From this fact rue is said to express ruth or sorrow, and then, by the connection between sorrow and Christian grace, was called 'The herb of grace.'"

Rue is used by Arabs in Palestine and Syria as a preventive of the ill effects of water drunk at unaccustomed springs: they either chew the leaves, or soak the plant in water.—*Fullerton.*

TRIBE ZANTHOXYLEÆ. Shrubs or trees; flowers regular, usually polygamous, ovary deeply 2 to 5-lobed; carpels capsular.

ZANTHOXYLUM. Leaves alternate, disk small, stamens 3 to 5, fruit of 1 to 5 round one-seeded carpels, separating or not.

Z. Rhetsa. A tree entirely covered with prickles, bark grey, leaves pinnate, leaflets 8 pair or more, oval pointed, unequal sided, smooth; flowers very small yellow in large terminal panicles, all parts 4, carpels rough black, size of a pea, splitting open. *Tirpál, Sisal, tisal, Kochli.*

Konkan and Ghauts, not very common. The seeds are very aromatic, and are used as pepper.

Evodia, leaves opposite, stamens 4 or 5, stigma 4-lobed, fruit of 4 three-valved cocci. **E. Roxburghiana* (Zanthoxylum triphyllum (*D.*). A small unarmed tree, leaves large, of three oblong obovate leaflets: flowers small, white, in cymes or panicles. All along the Ghauts (*D.*). The books vary very much in the description of this tree.

(Tribe Toddalicæ) *Toddalia,* leaves alternate, flowers unisexual. **T. aculeata,* shrub or small tree, leaves trifoliate, flowers small, white, in cymes, calyx glandular, petals, stamens, and stigma-lobes 5, fruit grooved orange colour, size of a small cherry. *Ranmiri,* S. Konkan and Ghauts sparingly: Canara, plentiful (*D.*). The whole is hot and pungent. *H.* includes in this *D's Limoniaoligandia,* which has fruit size of a pea. *Acrorycnhia,* calyx, lobes and petals 4, stamens 8, inserted under a thick 8-angled disk, stigma 4-grooved. **A. laurifolia* (*Clausena simplicifolia,* D.) tree or shrubby, leaves oval oblong, flowers yellowish-white, fragrant, sepals much rounded, petals oblong from a broad base. Tulkut Ghaut (*D*).

TRIBE AURANTIEÆ. The orange family.

Shrubs or trees abounding in a volatile oil, the leaves dotted with transparent glands.[1] Flowers regular, generally white, calyx lobes and petals 4 or 5, disk within the stamens, fruit a berry, usually pulpy.

The very visible oil glands in the leaves, and the flowers generally resembling orange blossoms, enable one to identify most species of this family, which belongs almost entirely to tropical Asia. The flowers of all species here given are white, except Feronia.

[1] Other orders which have dotted leaves, more or less generally, are Myrtaceæ, Myrsineæ, and Burseraceæ.

1. Glycosmis. Unarmed, leaves pinnate, leaflets alternate, stamens 8 to 10 inserted round a disk, style short, berry small, 1 to 3-seeded.

2. Murraya. Like the last, but stamens 10 alternately shorter, disk elongated, ovary narrowed into a long deciduous style, berry 1 or 2-celled and seeded.

3. Atalantia. Leaves alternate simple, stamens 6 to 8 inserted round a disk, style deciduous, stigma capitate, berry roundish with thick rind.

4. Feronia. Leaves alternate, unequally pinnate, stamens 10 to 12 inserted round a short disk, style none, fruit large, one-celled, many-seeded.

5. Ægle. Trees, leaves alternate, 3-foliate, stamens very numerous arranged round an inconspicuous disk.

2. Glycosmis.

G. pentaphylla. An erect poor-looking smooth shrub, leaflets 3 to 5 oblong, lanceolate slightly serrated, petioles thick ; flowers in short panicles small, scarcely opening, filaments flat, berry size of a pea, flesh coloured. *Kirmira.*

H. describes this as exceedingly variable, and as "one of the commonest plants in India, if the shrubby and arboreous forms are the same species." It is found with us, as a shrub only I believe, in the Konkan and Ghauts, and not very common there I should say.

2. Murraya.

M. Kœnigii (*Bergera k.* D.) A small tree, leaves very strong smelling, leaflets many, ovate serrate shining, flowers small in panicles, stigma capitate grooved, fruit in close clusters, oval pointed, dark red, about an inch long. *Kadu nim, Kadu-páb, jhirang.*

The Ghauts. Very common at Matheran.

H. makes the leaflets variable and the fruit black.

**M. exotica* (*M. Paniculata*, D.). Leaflets 3 to 8 smooth, very oblique at the base, flowers rather large, sepals glandular, berry round or ovoid, red. *Pándari, Kunti.* Higher Ghauts and Rohe (*D.*). Matheran *Birdwood.* A variety is found in gardens.

Clausena is very like *Murraya*, but the leaflets uneven in number, ovary stalked, and berry small. **C. Indica* (*Piptostylis*, I. D.) leaflets 7 to 11, ovate oblique, flowers small in panicles, berry round, yellow. **C. Wildenovii*, very like this, but leaflets fewer, fruit size of a pea, whitish green pellucid. Both are rare, and found in this Presidency only on the S. Ghauts.

3. Atalantia.

A. monophylla. A large smooth thorny climber, leaves shining oval, flowers small in fascicles, calyx splitting irregularly, filaments forming an irregularly cleft tube with broad anthers at the top, fruit like a lime, long stalked. *Rán limbu, mákar limbu.*

Ghauts and Konkan. It seems not always to climb, and *H.* has it also as a small tree.

4. Feronia.

F. Elephantum. A thorny tree, leaflets 2 to 7 obovate, smooth, common petiole winged : flowers small in racemes, pale with large dark anthers; fruit like a large ball, grey, very hard. *Káota.*—(See Hydnocarpus.)

Commonly called the wood-apple tree. Pretty common and often cultivated throughout India. In favourable situations, e.g. Surat, it is a very handsome tree.

5. Ægle.

Æ. marmelos. A tall thorny tree, with grey rough bark, leaflets oval, smooth, crenulate, flowers in panicles rather large, fruit large, round, or pear-shaped, smooth pulpy, the rind full of oil glands, seeds many. *Bil, bela.*

Cultivated throughout India, and said to be wild in the Deccan. The pulp of the fruit is much used in dysentery.

Limonia, leaves and leaflets with winged petioles, stamens 8 to 10, berry round. * *L. acidissima,* a thorny, smooth shrub, leaflets obtuse or retuse, crenated, flowers small, sepals and petals 4 : fruit size of a pea or larger, very acid, with flesh-coloured pulp. Padshahpore and Falls of Gokak (*D.*). *Nhaibel.*

Luvunga. Calyx and disk cup-shaped, stamens as in the last, berry 2 or 3-seeded. * *L. eleutheranda,* leaflets, 3 abruptly acuminated, flowers large, berry size of an olive. The Ghauts, common (*D.*).

Paramignya. Stamens 8 to 10 surrounding a columnar disk. *P. monophylla,* a large thorny climber, leaves ovate oblong, flowers large, filaments broad, stigma large and capitate, berry hairy, yellow, size of an apple. *Karwa wágati, rányid.* S. Konkan. As far N. as the Savitri (*D.*).

The genus *Citrus,* which has from 20 to 60 stamens, and petioles often winged, contains the trees which make the order famous. *C. medica* (wild here and there on the W. Ghauts, (*Brandis*) ; I had it on the Párpoli Ghaut), is said to be the original of the cultivated citron : and of this *var. limonum* is the lemon ; *var. acida* the lime, *limbu ; var. limetta,* the sweet lime.

C. aurantium is the orange, *nárangi*, in all its varieties: *C. decumaná* the pumelo, "pumplemoeses, which in the W. Indies are called shaddocks."—*Cook's voyages.*

When the scientific cultivation of fruit is seriously taken up in India, may we not hope that gardens of oranges will enliven at least such districts as the cooler parts of the Konkan and the eastern slopes of the Ghauts? It is true that Hooker says of the Indian climate generally that, "being marked by one season of excessive humidity, and the other of excessive drought, it can never be favourable to the production either of good European or tropical fruits. Hence there is not one of the latter peculiar to the country, and perhaps but one which arrives at full perfection, viz. the mango."—*Himalayan Journals.* Yet tolerable oranges are even now to be had.

"He hangs in shades the orange bright,
Like golden lamps in a dark night."—*A. Marvell.*

"What garden tree can rival the orange in beauty and nobility? . . . Every traveller who is happy enough to have seen the lemon grove in the neighbourhood of Poros in the Peloponnesus, the agrumi of Messina at the foot of Etna, and those of Reggio on the opposite coast of Calabria, the gardens of Sorrento, near Naples, and the enchanting orange woods of Milis in the island of Sardinia, thinks of them ever after with delight."—*Hehn.*

Triphasia trifoliata is a thorny shrub common in gardens, *China limbu*, leaves trifoliate, berry oblong, size of a sloe.

ORDER 28. **SIMARUBEÆ.**

Trees or shrubs, leaves alternate mostly very large and pinnate; flowers usually unisexual, regular and small, calyx 3 to 5-lobed, petals 3 to 5, stamens as many, or twice as many inserted at the base of the disk: styles 2 to 5.

A small order said to differ from Rutaceæ mainly in having bitter bark and leaves without oil glands.

1. AILANTHUS. Large trees, leaves unequally pinnate, calyx segments and petals 5, disk 10-lobed, stamens 10, but in hermaphrodite flowers only 2 or 3, ovary deeply 2 to 5-lobed, fruit of 1 to 5 one-seeded, winged nuts.

2. BALANITES. Leaves of two leaflets, calyx and segments and petals 5, disk thick conical, stamens 10, ovary entire, fruit a large fleshy oily drupe.

1. AILANTHUS.

A. excelsa. A fine tree with very large pinnate leaves collected at the end of the branches, leaflets very large, unequal at the base, deeply and irregularly toothed, flowers yellowish in large cross panicles, carpels podlike winged, swollen in the middle, crowned with the long curled styles. *Máruk, Adusa.*

Deccan and Guzerat. The leaves are very strong smelling.

2. BALANITES.

B. Roxburghii. A small thorny tree with whitish bark, leaflets oval entire, flowers greenish in small cymes, disk notched round the edge, fruit size of an egg, 5-lobed, smooth. *Hingen, hingor, penda.*

Deccan and Guzerat, drier parts of India (*H.*). Omitted by *D.*; but it is a common tree in some parts.

Samadera, disk large, conical, ovary deeply lobed, drupe winged. **S. Indica*, a small tree with large lanceolate fleshy leaves, flowers small white in long dense umbels, filaments very long, drupe oval. Not in *D.* S. Konkan (*G.*).

Quassia amara, "which occupies the first rank among bitter medicines," belongs to this order.

ORDER 29. OCHNACEÆ.

Smooth trees or shrubs with alternate simple leaves with stipules, and conspicuous flowers, sepals 4 or 5, petals 4, 5, or 10, disk enlarged after flowering, stamens inserted on it, fruit fleshy.

OCHNA. Flowers yellow, sepals coloured persistent, petals deciduous, stamens numerous, disk and ovary lobed, fruit of 3 to 10 drupes seated on the enlarged disk.

O. pumila (*O. nana*, D.). A small straggling shrub with narrow lanceolate leaves slightly serrated: flowers rather large in small clusters from the branches; fruit enclosed in the calyx, carpels only slightly attached to the enlarged disk.

This is, in this Presidency, found only in the S. Konkan, and not common there, I think. It is a remarkable-looking plant, the anthers being 2 or 3 times as long as the filaments, and the generic arrangement of the carpels being unique, as far as I know. The same peculiarities exist in O. squárrosa, a garden tree with us, but wild in some parts of India, with oblong shining leaves, and yellow flowers. G. had *Gomphia angustifolia*, a shrub with flowers and leaves agreeing in description with *O. squarrosa*, and about 5 pea-like carpels seated on a broad disk: S. Konkan, but *D.* could never hear of it.

ORDER 30. BURSERACEÆ.—The Myrrh family.

Trees or shrubs, producing balsam or resin, leaves alternate, pinnate or trifoliate, flowers regular small in racemes or panicles, sepals and petals 3 to 6, stamens as many or twice as many, inserted on the edge of the usually conspicuous disk; ovary free, fruit or drupe containing 2 to 5 kernels (pyrenes).

This order is closely allied to Anacardiaceæ, and chiefly known for its balsamic qualities.

1. BOSWELLIA. Leaflets opposite, calyx teeth and petals 5, disk annular, crenate, stamens 5 long and 5 short, stigma 3-lobed.

2. BALSAMODENDRON. Calyx segments and petals 3 or 4, stamens usually 4 long and 4 short, disk erect cup-shaped, style short.

3. GARUGA. Leaflets alternate, stamens 10 equal, stigma 4 or 5-lobed, disk ample lining the calyx.

1. BOSWELLIA.

B. serrata. A very pretty tree with grey papery bark, and drooping branches; leaves and flowers collected about the end of the branches, leaflets 6 to 15 pairs oval crenate or serrate; flowers small white, disk red, anthers yellow, drupe 3-cornered, splitting into 3. *Gugal, Sálai, dup-sálai, Sálphalli.*

Jungles in various parts. I have seen it only in the Panchmaháls. *D.* has omitted it. *H.* has a variety with entire leaflets. The gum is the olibanum of commerce, and probably the frankincense of scripture. "Conspicuous by its pale bark and spreading curved branches, leafy at their tips; its general appearance is a good deal like that of the mountain ash. The gum, celebrated throughout the east, was flowing abundantly from the trunk, very fragrant and transparent." —*Hooker: Himalayan Journals.*

2. BALSAMODENDRON.

**B. mukul* (*B. Roxburghii*, D.) A small thorny tree, the bark pealing off; leaves simple or trifoliate, ovate smooth and shining; flowers small, red, fascicled, disk toothed, drupe red ovate. *Mukul, guggal.*

Berar and Khandesh (*D.*). Sind, Kattywar and Rajputana (*Brandis*). The balm or balsam of scripture is the gum of B. Gileadense (*Hooker*), and from another species, B. Myrrha, is produced myrrh. So from their products the trees of this and the previous genus are sometimes called Incense trees.

"And there were gardens bright with sinuous rills,
Where blossomed many an incense-bearing tree:
And here were forests, ancient as the hills;
Enfolding many spots of greenery."—*Coleridge.*

3. Garuga.

G. pinnata. A rather fine tree, most parts hairy, leaflets 4 to 9 pairs, oblong pointed, slightly serrated, panicles large of small yellow flowers, calyx bell-shaped 5-furrowed, whitish, fruit edible round waxy yellowish green, size of a gooseberry. *Kurak, Kunak, Kánkad.*

Ghauts and Konkan hills. Found in many parts of the country, but nowhere in great quantity (*D.*). Throughout India (*H.*).

Order 31. MELIACEÆ.

Trees or shrubs with alternate leaves, usually pinnate and without stipules, sepals and petals 3 to 6, stamens united into a tube, and inserted below the disk, anthers erect, usually sessile on the tube, ovary superior.

The very perfect staminal tube is as strong a distinguishing mark of this order (except gen. Cedrela and Chloroxylon), as the staminal column is of Malvaceæ. Otherwise, the order is nearly allied to Rutaceæ. The genera are mainly distinguished by differences in the tube, the disk and the fruit. The flowers are generally small, pale in colour, and in panicles.

1. Turræa. Leaves simple, staminal tube toothed, the anthers inserted just within the mouth, disk small, style long, capsule 4-celled or more.

2. Melia. Trees, tube dilated at both ends, 10 or 12-toothed, anthers inserted near the top, disk annular, style slender within the tube, fruit a drupe.

3. Dysoxylon. Staminal tube toothed or crenulated, anthers included or slightly exserted, disk tubular, capsule roundish.

4. Heynea. Staminal tube deeply divided, lobes linear toothed, the anthers between the teeth, disk fleshy, capsule 2-valved.

5. Soymida. Staminal tube short, cup-shaped, 10-cleft, lobes toothed, anthers sessile between the teeth, disk flat and wide, capsule 5-celled.

6. Cedrela. Stamens distinct, 4 to 6, at the top of the lobed disk, capsule 5-celled.

7. Chloroxylon. Stamens 10, free, inserted in the depres-

sions of the 10-lobed disk, in which the ovary is immersed, capsule 3-celled.

1. Turræa.

T. virens. A shrub with smooth oval pointed leaves, flowers few together pure white, the staminal tube tipped yellow, petals long, rather unequal, capsule very small, hairy. *Kápur-bhendi.*

Pretty common on the Ghauts (*D.*). An evergreen (*H.*), but I have seen it as *G.* mentions in flower, while still leafless, and this is confirmed by others. Its flowers are much larger than those of any other member of the order that I have seen.

2. Melia.

M. azadirachta (*Azadirachta Indica,* D.). Leaflets 9 to 15, unequal sided, serrated smooth, flowers in panicles very fragrant; drupe oblong one-seeded.

The common *neem* or *limb* tree, well known throughout the greater part of India, and sometimes called the Indian lilac. It has nothing to do with the real lilac, which is a Syringa.

M. azedarach is the *bokhayan*, often called the Persian lilac, much cultivated throughout India, and in the N. taking the place of the *nim*.

M. dubia. (*M. Composita,* D.) Leaves very large, twice or thrice pinnate, leaflets smooth oval crenated, flowers white or tinged with purple, panicles mealy; fruit yellow, size of a small plum. Konkan and Ghauts, often cultivated. *Nimbára, limbára.*

3. Dysoxylon.

D. binectariferum (*Epicharis exarillata,* D.). A fine straight tree, leaves very large of 7 to 11 alternate leaflets, lanceolate, unequal-sided, smooth; flowers pale-green or yellow: capsule smooth, size of an apple, brick-red with hard rind, splitting into 4, and showing bright gamboge flesh, and 4 large olive-shaped seeds. *Yerindi; burumbi.*

This is not common, being known in W. India only on the Ghauts: but it is a striking looking tree; the disk is inside the staminal tube, one third of its length, and like it yellow and 8-lobed. This arrangement was called by the old botanists a double nectary—a designation which had the merit of expressing something uncommom.

4. Heynea.

*H. *Trijuga.* A small smooth tree with 3 to 6 pairs of ovate or lanceolate pointed leaflets, flowers white, panicles long-stalked, lobes of the staminal tube alternately shorter, capsule round, red, like a cherry, opening from the apex, one-seeded. *Limbára, tisul.*

Common all along the Ghauts (*D.*) and (*G.*).

5. Soymida.

**S. febrifuga.* A large smooth tree, leaflets 3 to 6 pair, oval or oblong obtuse : flowers greenish-white, petals clawed obovate spreading, capsule size of a small apple, black when ripe, opening from the apex. *Ruhin, potára.*

Jungles, in many parts. The bark is bitter and medecinal, and the wood dark-red.

6. Cedrela.

**C. toona.* A large and handsome tree, leaves very large about the end of the branches, leaflets oblique long pointed, stamens often alternating with staminodes, flowers small white, fragrant, capsule oblong, splitting from the apex, seeds winged. *Tuna, thorala nim, Kunan.*

Rohe, Khandala, &c. (*D.*). Most hilly districts of India (*H.*).

7. Chloroxylon.

** C. Swietenia.* A beautiful tree, leaflets 20 to 40, obtuse, very oblique, pellucid dotted, flowers greenish-white, capsule smooth oblong dark brown, seeds brown, angular winged. *Billu, halda, bheriya.*

Indian satin wood. Various hilly parts throughout the S. of the Presidency.

"The satin-wood in point of size and durability is by far the first of the timber trees of Ceylon. For days together I have ridden under its magnificent shade. . . It grows to the height of 100 feet, with a rugged grey bark, small white flowers, and polished leaves with a somewhat unpleasant odour."—*Tennant.*

Swietenia Mahogani is the mahogany tree, and the wood of other species of the same tribe is often called cedar.

The remaining species of the order are all trees or shrubs, confined in this Presidency, except when otherwise stated, to the S. Ghauts, and belonging also to S. India and Ceylon.

Naregamia, staminal tube inflated above, obsoletely crenated, disk annular. **N. alata*, small undershrub, leaves trifoliate, petioles winged, capsule roundish. Panwell and Vingorla. *Kápurbhendi, pitvel, timpáni.*

Cipadessa, staminal tube with 10 deep bifid lobes, disk cup-shaped. **C. fruticosa* (*Mallea Rothii*,! D.), a much-branched shrub, leaflets several pair, unequal-sided, flowers small, white, in panicles : fruit red, much like the rowan berry. *Naorungi.*

Amoora, staminal tube roundish or bell-shaped, slightly crenated, no disk. **A. cucullata.* Bark ash-coloured, leaflets few pair, unequal-sided, male flowers in long drooping panicles, female in racemes, calyx lobes and petals 3, fruit roundish with orange-coloured aril. *G.* had at Khandála a solitary tree of **A Rohituka* with leaves about 3 feet long, fruit like a ball of Windsor soap, opening from the apex, seeds solitary scarlet. *Rohitak, haramkháni.* It is widely spread over the E. and S. of India (*H.*). **A. Lawii* (*Nemedra Nimmonii* (*D.*), flowers small, white, scaly, scarcely opening, fruit size of a plum, abounding in white juice. *Burumb.* S. Konkan (*D.*).

Walsura, disk fleshy, stigma toothed. **W. piscidia*, leaves trifoliate, staminal tube deeply cleft, the divisions bifid, flowers very small and numerous, yellowish-white, berry dark-brown, velvety, one or two-seeded.

Chickrassia, staminal tube crenate, disk none, ovary short stalked, **C. tabularis* (*C. nimmonii*, D.). A very fine tree, leaflets 10 to 16 ovate, flowers yellowish or red, capsule woody, size of an apple, 3 to 5-valved, seeds winged. *Pabh, Chikrás.* Tungár hills (*G.*). Rohe jungles (*D.*).

The three orders which follow are small ones, chiefly tropical; and the species found in W. India are nearly all trees, and neither common nor in any way remarkable. They have all simple alternate leaves and small flowers, and unless otherwise stated are found only on the Ghauts.

ORDER 32. CHAILLETIACEÆ.

Sepals, petals, and stamens 5 with a disk.

Chailletia, petals 2-lobed narrow, disk of 5 scales.

**C. gelonoides.* Leaves broad lanceolate, pointed, flowers in numerous small fascicles, ovary broad woolly, fruit size of a nutmeg, 2-lobed, downy, with red aril.

ORDER 33. OLACINEÆ.

Petals 3 to 6, stamens 3-15, anthers erect, disk cup-shaped.

1. *Olax*, calyx cup-shaped increasing with the fruit, stigma 3-lobed. *O. Wightiana*, leaves ovate, oblong, flowers white in racemes, fertile stamens 3, with 5 staminodes much larger: fruit smooth oblong, half covered by the calyx. *Kálagonda.* *H.* mentions a variety found by Mr. Law with large leafy bracts. * *O. scandens*, a large prickly climber, leaves ovate oblong, flowers white in racemes, petals irregularly cleft, fertile stamens 3, staminodes bifid, drupe yellow like an acorn, nearly hid in the calyx.—*Harduli, archiri.* Khandala and Ghauts (*G.*). Sátpuras (*B.*). Not in *D.*
2. *Strombosia*, petals and stamens 5, disk 5-lobed, fruit surmounted by the calyx lobes and style. * *S. Zeylanica* (*Sphærocarpa leprosa*, D.). Bark greyish, leaves large oblong, flowers in nearly sessile clusters, fruit roundish, purple, wrinkled and scaly.

3. *Gomphandra,* corolla campanulate 4 or 5-lobed, stamens 5, drupe surmounted by the remains of the disk. * *G. axillaris.* (*Platea a.* D.) leaves lanceolate, flowers whitish in very short cymes, calyx minute, fruit half an inch long, smooth.

4. *Mappia,* calyx lobes, petals and stamens 5, disk cup-shaped. * *M. oblonga.*—Leaves oblong pointed, flowers yellowish in panicles, hairy and fetid, drupe small succulent, olive-shaped. *Gur, kalgur, gánera.*

5. *Sarcostigma,* climbing shrubs with diæcious flowers, stamens 5, drupe with corolla and calyx attached at the base. **S. kleinii,* leaves oblong, fruit oval, size of a large nutmeg, bright orange-red, wrinkled, in long pendant racemes.

ORDER 34. **ILICINEÆ.** The holly family.

Flowers clustered, without disk, ovary free.

Ilex, calyx lobes and stamens 4 or 5, corolla rotate, anthers oblong. * *I. malabarica* (*I. Wightiana,* D.). Leaves oval or oblong, entire, leathery, flowers white in very short umbels, drupe size of a pea, red, with 5 or 6 stones. *Ilex aquifolium* is the holly of English woods and shrubberies. The Ilex tree or evergreen oak, *Quercus ilex,* has nothing to do with this order. From the leaves of various species of this genus the liquor maté is produced, much used in S. America as tea, called there the herb of Paraguay, and the Caa tree. The Abbé Raynal describes the process, and Southey speaks of the tree as more fatal than the Upas, owing to the great mortality which took place among the natives sent, "through many a land of mines and slavery," to pick the leaves.

The next three orders form a very natural group, having all woody stems, small greenish flowers and conspicuous disk, and (except tribe Hippocrateæ) 4 or 5 petals and stamens. Many of the species are of a climbing habit.

Order 35. **CELASTRINEÆ.**

Trees or shrubs, leaves simple, petals sometimes wanting, inserted below the disk : seeds usually with an aril.

Tribe 1. Celastreæ. Stamens 4 or 5.

1. CELASTRUS. Climbing shrubs with alternate leaves and polygamous flowers: disk broad concave, ovary free from the disk, stigma 3-lobed, capsule roundish.

2. GYMNOSPORIA. Leaves alternate, stamens inserted below the broad disk with which the ovary is united, style 2 or 3-lobed, capsule roundish.

Tribe 2. Hippocrateæ. Leaves opposite, stamens 3, inserted on the face of the disk.

3 HIPPOCRATEA. Disk conical or cup-shaped surrounding the ovary, stigmas 1 to 3, fruit of 3 flattened carpels joined at the base, seeds winged.

4. SALACIA. Ovary immersed in the disk, fruit a berry, seeds large and angular.

Note.—The 3 stamens found in the genera of this tribe are an uncommon peculiarity in exogenous plants.

1. CELASTRUS.

C. paniculata. A large straggling shrub all smooth, branches warty, leaves broad ovate with a short sudden point slightly serrated. Flowers in long compound racemes greenish-yellow, petals turned back, ovary large, capsule 3-celled. *Pengi, Kángoni, Karang-Kángoni.*

Common in the Konkan and Ghauts; and throughout the hilly parts of India (*H.*).

2. GYMNOSPORIA.

G. montana. (*Celastrus m.* D.). A shrub or small tree with white smooth bark and long stout thorns: leaves small, smooth, ovate or obovate, minutely crenate, flowers in short panicles, small, white, pretty and fragrant, capsule 3-lobed, size of a pea. *Mál-Kángoni, Zekadi.*

Konkan and W. Deccan. Also Guzerat and Sind (*D.*).

A variable plant ranging from the Mediterranean, through tropical Africa, to India (*H.*).

* *G. Rothiana* (*Celastrus R.* D.) a shrub, sometimes armed, leaves obovate crenulate, flowers greenish-yellow, capsule obovate, red, 3-lobed, seeds brownish-orange. Konkan hills and Ghauts (*D.*). * *G. emarginata,* leaves emarginate, flowers below them, fruit pear-shaped, red, 3-celled. Not in *D.*, common on the Ghauts (*G.*). Both of these are called *Yenkal, ingli, Ikari.*

The four following genera, consisting of trees and shrubs with usually opposite leaves, also belong to this tribe.

Euonymus, disk large fleshy, 4 or 5-lobed, ovary sunk in it, capsule angled or winged. * *E. Indicus,* leaves oval lanceolate, petals fringed, rust coloured, fruit obovoid, small. Gangellee Ghaut (*D.*). To this genus belong the English spindle tree, and other species, commonly planted as hedge shrubs in gardens near the sea in England.

Lophopetalum, disk entire or lobed, capsule angled, not winged. * *L. Wightianum,* a tree with leathery oblong wings, and flowers in panicles, disk 5-lobed, petals crested, fruit 4 inches long, sharply triangular, seeds winged. No hab. (*D.*). *Bolpále.*

Pleurostylia, disk thick and crenulate, ovary half immersed in it. * *P. Wightii*, leaves entire, oblong, whitish, petals much larger than the sepals, fruit small, indehiscent, seeds with an aril. The Ghauts (*D.*).

Elæodendron, disk thick, ovary attached to it. * *E. glaucum* (E. *Roxburghii*, D.), leaves ovate, crenate, shining, flowers small, yellow in lax cymes, drupe yellowish-green, size of a cherry, tipped with the style. *Támrug*, *Bhutápal.* Ghauts (*D.*). Common over a considerable part of India (*B.*).

3. Hippocratea.

* *H. Grahamii.* Climing over high trees, leaves oval acute, shining, flowers minute in long panicles, calyx lobes rounded crenated, carpels 2 or 3 inches long, flat, like a paper cutter, *Zewati, danshir.*

Common along the Ghauts (*D.* & *G.*).

* H. Indica appears to differ in having smaller panicles, and the calyx lobes triangular, entire, fruit oblong an inch long. *Kájuráti, tiroli.* Ghauts (*D.* & *G.*).

4. Salacia.

S. prinoides. Inclining to climb, leaves small, smooth, oblong, finely crenated, disk large roundish, anthers red, fruit roundish, red, fleshy, one-seeded with the disk adhering. *Ingli, nisal bundi.*

The Konkan, not uncommon, I think. Khandalla (*G.*).

D. has 3 other species found on the Ram or Chorla Ghauts. * *S. brunonia*, branches black and rigid, flowers fewer together than in the last. * *S. Roxburghii*, branches pale brown, leaves almost if not quite entire, fruit 2 or 3-seeded. * *S. oblonga*, flowers nearly sessile, rather larger than in the others, fruit size of a small orange, 8-seeded.

Order 36. **RHAMNEÆ.** Buckthorns.

Shrubs or trees frequently thorny, leaves simple, usually leathery and very strongly nerved, flowers small greenish, petals and stamens 4 or 5 inserted on the calyx tube and alternate with its teeth, the petals hooded or with edges turned in, disk large and fleshy or lining the calyx tube: fruit a capsule or drupe.

The general thorniness, the strongly nerved leaves, and the petals and stamens inserted on the calyx tube (unlike all other orders of the Thalamifloræ and Discifloræ) make the identification of this order tolerably easy. The flowers, however, are much like some of the species of Ampelideæ.

Note.—All the species here described have 5 sepals, petals and stamens, and all except Scutia have alternate leaves.

1. VENTILAGO. Climbing shrubs, disk 5-lobed, ovary sunk in it, style very short, fruit winged, with persistent calyx.

2. ZIZYPHUS. Thorny shrubs or trees, leaves generally bifarious, petals sometimes wanting, disk lobed filling the calyx tube, ovary sunk in it, styles 2 to 4, fruit a drupe with hard stone.

3. SCUTIA. Smooth shrubs with opposite leaves or nearly so, disk fleshy filling the calyx tube, ovary sunk in it narrowing into a short 2 or 3-cleft style, drupe with adherent calyx.

4. COLUBRINA. Like the last, but leaves alternate and the calyx surrounds the fruit below the middle instead of at the base.

1. VENTILAGO.

V. madraspatana. A large climber with grooved branches, leaves smooth ovate or roundish, unequal at the base, bifarious, flowers in slender panicles at the end of the branches; fruit size of a pea, light green with a flat wing about 2 inches long. *Bika, lokandi, Kánvel.*

The Ghauts and N. Konkan. The junction of the wing with the fruit is like the closing of a lid.

V. Bombaiensis differs in the young parts being tawny with hairs, and the flowers fascicled in the axils. Chorla Ghaut (*D.*). I believed that I had it at Mahableshwar; but it seems more likely that that was *V. Calyculata,* which Mr. Birdwood has in his list under the name of *Karkandi chá yel, Kányel,* and which *H.* attributes to all the hotter parts of India.

2. ZIZYPHUS.

1. *Z. jujuba.* A thorny tree with small leaves ovate or roundish, dark and shining above, woolly below, flowers in short cymes, strong smelling, fruit round, size of a cherry, smooth yellow. *Bher, bhor.*

Varies greatly in shape and size of fruit, shape and downiness of leaves and general habit. *Brandis.*

Throughout India wild and extensively cultivated; but Z. vulgaris, not known in W. India, is also called the cultivated *bher.*

This is thought by some to be the *Sidra* of the Koran, the tree which Mohammed in his miraculous night journey found growing at the further limit of the seventh heaven, but others think that to be Z. lotus. (*Sprenger*).

2. *Z. mummularia.* A small low shrub, leaves small roundish finely serrated, underside and branches woolly, thorns in pairs, one long and straight, the other short and curved,

flowers sessile, many together, quite flat greenish-white, berry like the last. *Gangar, jangra.*

Common in Guzerat, Sind, and other parts.

3. *Z. œnoplia.* Slightly climbing, all covered with hairs, leaves oval lanceolate acute, very unequal-sided, flowers short-stalked axillary, petals very small, soon falling off; fruit round, size of a currant, turning from yellow to black. *Chunibher, kánare.*

Common in the Konkan, also in the Deccan. When out of flower this is very like Briedelia scandens, but the thorns and unequal-sided leaves distinguish it.

4. *Z. xylopyrus.* A shrub or small tree with or without thorns, leaves broad oval or round, downy beneath, finely serrated, flowers in a close cyme, fruit size of a cherry, round, hard, 3-celled. *Guti, bhurguti.*

Konkan, common in the Ghauts (*D.*), and all over S. India. *Brandis.*

5. *Z. rugosa.* A straggling shrub with large panicles of small white flowers without corolla, leaves broad oval, serrate, shining; fruit small, white round or obovate, eatable. *Turan.*

Konkan, common on the Ghauts.

Z. lotos, common in N. Africa, is the tree from which the Lotophagi of the Odyssey took their name, the fruit of which is the lotos:—

> "Which whoso tastes
> Insatiate riots in the sweet repasts,
> Nor other home nor other care intends,
> But quits his house, his country and his friends."
>
> *Dryden.*

> "The Lotos blooms below the barren peak;
> The Lotos blows by every winding creek."
>
> *Tennyson.*

3. Scutia.

S. Indica. A straggling thorny shrub with small smooth obovate leaves and very small flowers in umbels, which are axillary or arranged round the stem, fruit obovate or roundish, 2 to 4-celled and seeded. *Chimát.*

The Ghauts, common.

4. Colubrina.

C. Asiatica. An unarmed smooth shrub with shining ovate crenate leaves unequal at the base; flowers in short cymes, fruit size of a pea, very smooth. *Guti.*

Konkan and the Ghauts.

This and *Zizyphus xylopyrus* (also called *Guti*) may easily be mistaken when not in fruit, but the smooth shining leaves distinguish this.

Rhamnus, disk thin lining the calyx tube, ovary free. * *R. Wightii*, unarmed leaves long, narrow, pointed, flowers in fascicles, fruit size of a pea with calyx adherent. *Raktzorar*. N. Ghauts (*D.*).

Gouania, stamens enclosed in the hooded petals, disk fleshy filling the calyx. * *G. leptostachya*, smooth, climbing, unarmed, leaves ovate, flowers in panicles or racemes, fruit triangular winged, crowned by the calyx. Wari country (*D.*).

Paliurus aculeatus is Christ's thorn, from which the crown of thorns is traditionally said to have been made; common in the S. of Europe and about Jerusalem.

ORDER 37. AMPELIDEÆ. Vines.

Shrubs, usually climbing and with tendrils, leaves generally much lobed, flowers regular, calyx cup-shaped, entire or 4-5 lobed; petals 4 or 5, stamens as many, inserted on or beneath the disk; filaments and style short, fruit a small berry.

This order differs from the last mainly in its climbing habit, tendrils, and lobed or sometimes compound leaves. The small flowers are generally in large clusters, and when not otherwise stated are greenish.

1. VITIS. Climbing shrubs, tendrils opposite the leaves, berry oval or round, one or two-celled.

2. LEEA. Shrubs not climbing, without tendrils, with very large leaves and sheathing petioles: calyx lobes, petals, and stamens 5, ovary inserted in the disk, stigma swollen.

1. VITIS.

Note.—*H.* has 70 species of Vitis, having included in it the old genus Cissus, which has 4 petals and stamens, whereas Vitis has 5.

Note.—In many cases the climbing tendency is but slight.

(*a.*) Petals and stamens 4.

1. *V. quadrangularis* (*Cissus q.* and *C. edulis*, D.). An extensive climber, very fleshy and cactus-like, stems thick, 4-sided, jointed and often winged, leaves large ovate, variously toothed, berry roundish, red. *Harsánkal, mhaisvel, Khárbuti.*

Common in hedges throughout hotter India (*H.*). The leaves are frequently 3-lobed, and the stems without wings. Good specimens, as at Surat, are very handsome, but more often it is with us a poor-looking and scraggy plant.

"Its stem, like that of another Vitis (*V. Indica*), when freshly cut, yields a copious draught of pure, tasteless fluid." *Tennant.* The stems are eaten in curries.

2. *V. repanda* (*Cissus r.* D.). Hairy, stems woody, leaves large, cordate roundish, coarsely-toothed, stipules oblong, tendrils forked or none, flowers in compound umbels, fruit pear-shaped black, tipped with the persistent style. *Gendal.*

3. *V. aduata* (*C. latifolia,* D.). Is very like the last, but not so stout, with stipules oval, adnate. *Nádena.*

H. considers that these two are difficult to distinguish. They are both found in the Konkan, and probably in the Ghauts, in the rains. The latter only is in Mr. Birdwood's list.

4. *V.* . A stout, woody shrub, not generally climbing, leaves large, smooth, heart-shaped with incurved serratures and umbels opposite to them; petals recurved, berries black, one or two-seeded.

Common in the Deccan, as a roadside bush; not at all attractive. This is *D.'s C. vitiginea*, but I have not been able to identify it with any of *H.'s*.

5. *V. carnosa.* Fleshy, leaves trifoliate, petioles rather long, leaflets ovate, coarsely serrated, tendrils forked, flowers in panicles green, glands, disk and stamens white, style conspicuous, fruit black and juicy, 2 to 4-seeded. *Támánya.*

Very common on the seashore, in the Konkan, growing among the rocks. There it is quite smooth, but inland is often coarse and hairy. Common in most parts of India.—*Brandis.*

6. *V. auriculata.* A stout and handsome climber, young stems, petioles, &c., thickly downy, light-green, leaves with 5 or more oblong or ovate serrated leaflets; stipules ear-shaped, tendrils forked, flowers in large long-stalked panicles, yellowish, berry red or plum-coloured, shining, size of a sloe. *Ambári, jangli Kájorni.*

Plentiful about Ghorabunder. Vingorla (*D.*). Matheran, *Birdwood.* * *V. repens,* smooth and glaucous, leaves cordate, ovate, bristle-toothed, flowers in compound umbels, fruit round. The Konkans (*D.*). * *V. glauca,* very doubtful how this differs from the last. *D.* has not got it. The Konkans (*G.*). * *V. Rheedii* (*C. trilobata,* D). Smooth, leaves trifoliate, leaflets oblong, bristle-toothed, fruit round. *Vansa.* Konkan (*D.* & *G.*). * *V. setosa.* Fleshy, covered with long bristly hairs, leaflets 3, long oval, fruit one-seeded, red. Junar (*D.*). *V. elongata.* A very large climber, smooth and succulent, leaflets 5, oval lanceolate, flowers in panicles white, berry size of a cherry, blackish. Mahableshwar. Not in *D.* * *V. lanceolaria* (*C. Muricata,* D.). A woody climber, branches warty, leaves 5-foliate, stipules large, flowers in compound umbels, yellowish, fruit size of a cherry, white when ripe. S. Ghauts and Canara (*D.*). *Khájgoli cha vel.*

V. discolor, with leaves much blotched with white above, purple and shining beneath, is attributed by *D.* to shady jungles in the Konkan, has been found by Mr. Woodrow in the Dangs, and is in Mr. Birdwood's list. *Nága vel, teli cha vel.* It is also an old-fashioned plant of English greenhouses, where other species of Vitis and Cissus are cultivated for the foliage.

(*b.*) Petals and stamens 5.

7. *V. latifolia.* A very handsome climber, mostly smooth, the dark stems shooting out to a great length, leaves large round cordate with about five acute lobes serrated, petioles and tendrils long, flowers in close clusters, claret-coloured with yellow anthers, fruit black, 2-seeded. *Golinda.*

This is not in *D.*; I have found it at Rutnagherry and in the N. Konkan, and *Brandis* ascribes it to the Sátpuras also. It and V. auriculata shoot out before the rain begins to fall.

8. * *V. pedata.* A large weak climber, leaflets 7 or more, long petioled, lanceolate acute serrated; flowers covered with grey hairs, fruit white, 4-lobed, 4-seeded.

Konkan and Ghauts (*D.*).

* *V. Indica.* Stems slender and hairy, leaves heart-shaped: flowers in cylindric spikes or racemes, greenish-purple, style none, fruit round (*D.*). *Pálkanda,* the Konkans (*G.*). **V. araneosa,* slender, covered with deciduous down, leaflets 3, unequal-sided, flowers brownish-red in umbels with long woolly peduncles, fruit, black. Highest Ghauts W. of Junar (*D.*)., and very little known elsewhere. *Bendarvel, Ghorvel:* the root *Chamarmusli.*

From *V. vinifera* and its varieties all (or almost all) wine-making grapes are produced. Its native country is unknown, but the oldest books extant testify to its value, having been found out very early. In Judges ix. the olive, the fig, and the vine are the three trees given as most worthy of sovereignty over the rest. In the New Testament still greater honour is put upon the vine and its fruit (Luke xxii. 18).

The twining of the vine round a forest tree is a common symbol of marriage in old English writers, the vine being one of the most ancient symbols of fertility:—

"Thou art an elm, my husband, I a vine,
Whose weakness, married to thy stronger state,
Makes me with thy strength to communicate."
Comedy of Errors.

"They led the vine
To wed her elm: she, spoused, about him twines
Her marriageable arms."—*Milton.*

"So doth the humble vine creep at the foot of an oak, and leans upon its lowest base, and begs shade and protection, and leave to grow under its branches, and to give and take mutual refreshment, and pay a kindly influence for a mighty patronage; and they grow and dwell together, and are the most remarkable of friends and married pairs of all the leafy nation."—*Bishop Jeremy Taylor.*

The same figure occurs in Hindoo poetry. In Sákuntalá, a jasmine growing over a mango tree is used for the same comparison.

'To sit every man under his vine' (Micah iv. 4, etc.) refers to the custom, common in Palestine as in Italy, of training vines over a trellis (pergola) in front of the house.

2. Leea.

1. *L. sambucina* (*L. staphylea*, D.). A large shrub mostly smooth, with pinnately compound leaves; leaflets narrow, lanceolate serrate, flowers in large flat cymes, stamens coloured, fruit round, black. *Dinda.*

Very common in S. Konkan. Widely spread through hotter India (*Brandis*). The young leaves are of a lovely bronze pink, opening out of a pouch. The heads of flowers and leaves rather resemble the English elder (*Sambucus*).

2. *L. macrophylla.* Very like the last, but the very large leaves are simple, broad ovate subcordate, smooth, the flowers more decidedly white.

The Konkan, much less common than the last; also called *dinda.*

The next two orders are sufficiently alike to be grouped together.

Order 38. SAPINDACEÆ.

Leaves mostly pinnate, flowers small, usually white, calyx 4 or 5-lobed, often unequal, petals 4 or five, stamens 5 to 10 (oftenest 8), fruit sometimes lobed or winged.

This large order comes nearest to Celastrineæ, but the flowers are often irregular, and the stamens generally more than 5. The maples are by *H.* put in a tribe of this order, and one of its beauties is the horse chestnut, Æsculus hippo-castaneum, "said to be indigenous in N. India, but not now known in its wild state" (*H.*). "It migrated from the N. parts of Asia to England by Constantinople, Vienna, Italy, and France."—*Loudon.*

Note (1.)—All the genera here given, except *Dodonæa* and *Turpinia*, belong to the sub-order Sapindeæ, and have alternate leaves without stipules, and stamens inserted inside the disk.

Note (2.)—All here given, except the two species of *Cardiospermum*, are trees or shrubs.

1. Cardiospermum. Climbing herbs, flowers irregular, sepals and petals 4, one pair of each larger, disk of 2 glands, stamens 8, 4 shorter; style trifid, capsule 3-celled, inflated.

2. Hemigyrosa. Leaves pinnate, flowers irregular, disk one-sided, stamens 8, stigma 3-cornered, fruit indehiscent, not lobed.

3. Allophylus. Leaves simple or trifoliate, flowers irregular, sepals and petals 4, disk one-sided with 4 glands opposite the petals; stamens 8.

4. Schleichera. No petals, disk annular, stigma 3 or 4-cleft.

5. Sapindus. Flowers regular, sepals in 2 rows, disk annular, fleshy, stigma 2 to 4-lobed, fruit deeply lobed.

6. Dodonæa. Flowers as the last, but no corolla, capsule with several angles and valves.

1. Cardiospermum.

C. halicacabum. A small and beautifully delicate climber, all smooth, leaves twice ternate, leaflets like miniature vine leaves with pointed lobes; flowers in threes, white; capsules conspicuous, leafy, much inflated, seeds 3, black with a white spot. *Bodha, Sibjal.*

Common in hedges in the Konkan and elsewhere. Most tropical and sub-tropical countries (*H.*). Called by *G.* heart-pea, and balloon-vine. Every part of this little plant is beautiful, though the very small flowers, " with curling tendrils gracefully disposed," might easily be passed without notice.

2. Hemigyrosa.

H. cænescens (*Cupania c.* D.). Small tree or spreading shrub, leaflets 2 to 4 pairs, like polished mango-leaves, flowers small, white, in close racemes, capsule ovoid, triangular, brown, and velvety. *Karpa.*

S. Konkan, Ghauts (*D. & G*).

3. Allophylus.

A. Cobbe (*Cardiospermum schmiedelia* and *C. villosa*, D.). A small tree or large shrub, sometimes climbing, all hairy, leaves ternate on long stalks, leaflets large, ovate, pointed, serrated, flowers very small, white, clustered on the racemes, fruit round, red, shining, one-seeded. *Tipin, Mendri.*

Very variable with many synonyms (*H.*).

Konkan and Ghauts, tolerably common; abundant at Mahableshwar.

4. Schleichera.

S. trijuga. A tree with three pairs of oblong or lanceolate entire leaflets, and very small green flowers in short racemes, 2 or 3 together : ovary with irregular points on it, style long exserted, stigmas 3 : fruit about an inch long, beetle-shaped, with blunt prickles. *Kusimb, Kun, Kocham.*

Konkan and Ghauts, common. The young leaves appear in the hot weather, of a beautiful lake turning to copper colour.

5. Sapindus.

S. trifoliatus (*S. laurifolius* and *emarginatus*, D.). A tree with about three pairs of ovate lanceolate entire leaflets, sometimes nearly a foot long, very papery: flowers very small, dingy white, scarcely opening, in large compound panicles: petals and stamens very woolly : fruit 3-lobed, rough, reddish-brown. *Ritta.*

There are two varieties distinguished by the greater or less hairiness of the leaves and petioles, and by the leaflets being pointed or emarginate. The fruit is used as soap, and called soap-nut.

Common in various parts : cultivated in Bengal (*H.*).

6. Dodonæa.

D. viscosa (*D. Burmanniana*, D.). A shrub, climbing or straggling, leaves oblong, oval, more or less clammy, flowers small, yellow, fragrant, in short cymes, disk hairy, capsules oblong, winged. *Dhásera, dawa ka jhár, latchmi, jakhmi.*

S. Konkan. Khandalla and Belgaum (*D.*). Throughout India and in all warm countries (*H.*). On the mountains in S. India it is a small tree (*Brandis*)—and in Afghanistan common in the low hills, and used for thatching.—*Bellew.*

It is much like one of the Combretums in appearance.

Erioglossum, leaves odd-pinnate, petals 4, unequal, stamens 8. *E. edule* (*Sapindus rubiginosa*, D.), a tree with leaves resembling the ash, very soft, flowers white, very fragrant, young parts reddish, hairy. Mahim Woods, planted (*D. & G.*).

Nephelium. Flowers regular, stamens 5 to 10. *N. longanum.* Tree with 2 to 5 pairs of leaflets, flowers yellowish-white in panicles, fruit reddish, size of a cherry, warty when young. *Wumb, lungám.* Parr and Rám Ghauts (*D.*). *N. litchi* produces the *litchi* fruit, and is found in gardens. The contrast between the dark red rind and the pearly pulp within is very striking; but the flavour in Bombay scarcely comes up to the description of the same in China.

Turpinia. Flowers regular, sepals, petals and stamens 5. * *T. pomifera* (*T. nepalensis*, D.). Leaves opposite, leaflets 3 to 5 lanceolate, flowers white in panicles, berry size of a large pea, 3-celled. Párwar Ghaut (*D.*).

ORDER 39. ANACARDIACEÆ.

Trees or shrubs with milky or acrid juice, leaves alternate without stipules, often pinnate, flowers small, regular, often unisexual or polygamous; sepals and petals 3 to 5, stamens as many or more up to 10, inserted on or under the disk; fruit usually a drupe, 1 to 5-celled.

This order is mainly distinguished from the last by the flowers being regular. The foliage and fruit are generally more noticeable than the flowers. The species also have often strong resinous juice, and, from this being used for varnishing and lacquering, some trees of the order have got the name of Varnish trees.

1. MANGIFERA. One stamen usually large and perfect, the rest smaller or imperfect, ovary oblique, style lateral, drupe large and fleshy, stone compressed.

2. ANACARDIUM. Sepals and petals 5, stamens 8 to 10, disk filling the base of the calyx, fruit formed of the enlarged disk and flower stalk, with nut growing outside.

3. BUCHANIANA. Disk round, 5-lobed, stamens 10, ovary of 5 or 6 carpels, but only 1 perfect, styles short, drupe small.

4. ODINA. Leaves odd pinnate, flowers unisexual, disk annular, 4 or 5-lobed, stamens 8 to 10, styles 3 or 4, drupe small reniform crowned by the styles.

5. SEMECARPUS. Stamens 5 or 6 inserted at the base of the broad annular disk, styles 3, drupe fleshy, seated on the much enlarged peduncle.

6. HOLIGARNA. Petioles with spur-like appendages, flowers polygamous, stamens 5 inserted on the edge of the disk, styles 3 to 5.

7. SPONDIAS. Leaves odd pinnate, calyx deciduous, disk cup-shaped crenate, stamens 8 to 10 inserted beneath it, styles 4 or 5, drupe fleshy.

1. MANGIFERA.

M. Indica. The mango tree. All smooth, leaves oblong lanceolate, flowers in panicles greenish-yellow or white, petals twice as long as the sepals, partly orange-coloured, disk fleshy, 5-lobed, anther of the one perfect stamen purple or red. *Amb.*

Grows all over India, and thought to be indigenous in the W. Ghauts, and a few other places. It is to the Portuguese that the excellence of the fruit on the W. coast is due, the only Indian fruit, perhaps, which can be called "delectable both to behold and taste" (*Milton*). At Manilla the best grafted varieties are said to be equal, if not superior, to those of Bombay (*Burbidge*). In the Konkan, during the early part of the rains, the inchoate trees growing out of the stones that have been thrown away, well sucked, by the sides of the roads are as beautiful and interesting objects as one could wish to see.

The smell of the flowers is often quite overpowering at night, as any one will find who drives along a well planted road like that between Indore and Mhow. "There is a variety of the common mango tree, or perhaps a distinct species, which bears fruit nearly as large as a man's head; the tree grows about Savanoor, and in Canara" (*Graham*). I have heard of this at Dápoli, but never saw it. It should be either H.'s *M. fragrans* or *M. macrocarpa.*

2. Anacardium.

A. occidentale. The cashew-nut tree. Leaves smooth ovate or obovate; flowers small, yellow streaked with red, in panicles with numerous leafy bracts; fruit red, very juicy, very much larger than the kidney-shaped nut. *Káju, hijali badám.*

A native of Brazil introduced by the Portuguese, and sometimes called the Goa almond; common on many parts of the coast, particularly in Salsette and the S. Konkan. "Its fruit, an apple with a nut below," is one of the curiosities of the vegetable kingdom. The apple, though tempting to the eye, is excruciating to the palate, though Oliver calls it eatable. Miss Bird speaks of the immense spread of its branches in the Malay Peninsula, but with us it is always a small tree. The shell of the nut contains a very acrid oil (from which anacardic acid is made), the fumes of which (Kingsley says) will blister the face if the cook bends over the fire. I never heard of this difficulty in India.

3. Buchaniana.

B. latifolia. A good-sized tree with large leaves, broad ovate or obovate, hairy, with short petioles, flowers in large hairy panicles, drupe compressed ovoid. *Pyál, chároli, chár.*

Found in all parts of the Presidency, but not particularly common. The kernels are called *chéronji*, and are eatable.

4. Odina.

O. wodier. Leaflets 3 or 4 pairs oblong ovate pointed, panicles hairy or mealy terminal, flowers very small, tinged with purple or red, fragrant, stamens filling the mouth of the corolla; drupe kidney-shaped, red when ripe. *Shimti, mowa, moini.*

Very common (*D.*); but I think it is widely distributed rather than common. The leaves fall in the cold weather when the flowers appear. "A handsome tree when in full foliage, an eyesore when leafless."—*Brandis.*

4. Semecarpus.

S. anacardium. The marking nut tree. A good-sized tree with large leaves oblong rounded or obovate, whitish and strongly veined below; flowers in large cross panicles, very small, greenish-white, drupe black, heart-shaped, deeply seated in the yellow apple-shaped receptacle which is about the same size. *Bibu, behelu, kardin.*

Said to be common in Deccan, Konkan, and Guzerat; but I should scarcely call it so. The receptacle of the fruit is eatable, and the acid whitish juice, which is used for marking linen, comes from the pericarp.

5. Holigarna.

H. Grahamii (*Semecarpus G.* D.). A tall tree with leaves over a foot long collected at the end of the branches, smooth above, hairy below; panicle and calyx rusty and hairy; drupe and receptacle like the last. *Ran bibu.*

Ghauts and Konkan hills. The shape of the leaves is very peculiar; the broadest part is above the middle, thence tapering very gradually to the base, less so to the point.

**H. Arnottiana* (*H. longifolia*, D.) Leaves very long and tapering, flowers very small in large panicles, drupe obliquely oblong, an inch long, with thick acrid juice. *Bibu, hulgari.* Canara (*D.*), Konkan (*G.*).

6. Spondias.

S. mangifera. All smooth, leaflets 4 to 5 pairs large, oblong, pointed, entire, panicles very large, flowers greenish-white or yellow, fruit like a small mango. *Ranámb, ámbára, dolamba.*

Often found planted, but a doubtful native. It flowers when bare of leaves. The fruit is eatable, and sometimes called the hog plum, the W. Indian name of another species.

**S. acuminata* differs from the above chiefly in smaller leaflets with longer points, a very short panicle, and probably a smooth stone. Not in *D.* Kennery Caves (*G.*).

Nothopegia, sepals, petals, stamens and disk lobes 4 or 5. **N. Colebrookiana* (*Glycocarpus racemosus*, D.). Small tree, leaves simple, oblong entire, racemes short, flowers minute, drupe size of a cherry, with thick edible pulp. *Amberi.* Ghauts (*D.*).

D. mentions that there were at Hewra "many large trees" of *Schinus mulli* belonging to this order, and that it thrives well in India and ripens its fruit. If this is so, it is a pity it is not commonly cultivated, for it is a most beautiful and elegant tree, with large clusters of small red waxy-looking fruit. It is very common in Naples and other places in S. Italy, where it is called *pepe*, or pepper tree. *Pistacia vera* is the tree of which the fruit is the pistachio nut, much imported into India, a native of the warmer parts of Central Asia, and supposed to be the nuts of Gen. xliii. 11. Mastic is produced from another tree of the same genus. And another species, *P. terebinthus*, is said by Hooker to be what is variously called in the Bible the turpentine tree, the teil tree, the elm and the oak: elsewhere called the Terebinth.

Order 40. **MORINGEÆ.**

Deciduous trees with soft wood; leaves alternate pinnate, with glands at the base; flowers irregular in panicles, calyx cup-shaped with 5 unequal petaloid segments, petals 5 unequal; stamens 5 perfect and 5 imperfect inserted on the edge of the disk, ovary stalked, style slender tubular, capsule angled, corky within.

Perhaps the smallest of all orders, as it contains but one genus and three species. Outwardly they are very like some of the Leguminosæ, but the fruit is not really a pod, and there are other differences which make Bentham and Hooker call the genus absolutely anomalous.

Moringa—genus as the order.

1. *M. pterygosperma.* The horse-radish tree; sometimes also called the drumstick tree. Leaves very large, twice or thrice pinnate, leaflets very small, oblong or oval, smooth; calyx as well as petals white, capsule pod-like, a foot long, slender, 3-angled, 9-ribbed, the seeds 3-cornered, winged at the angles. *Shevga, shekta, sonja.*

Cultivated all over India, the pods used as vegetables, the root as horse-radish. From the seeds oil of ben, used by watchmakers, is produced (*Balfour*).

2. *M. Concanensis.* Like the last, but leaves and panicles larger, leaflets also larger oval, roundish, flowers sweet-scented, petals yellowish, red streaked at the base. *Sainjna, mua.*

Wild at various places in the Konkan; also in Sind and Rajputana (*B.*).

III. CALYCIFLORÆ.

Order 41. **CONNARACEÆ.**

Trees or shrubs with alternate compound leaves without stipules, flowers regular or nearly so, calyx lobes and petals 5, stamens 5 or 10, fruit generally 1-seeded. A small order with doubtful affinities.

1. Rourea. Sepals round imbricate, increasing with the fruit, stamens 10, ovaries 5, 4 usually imperfect.

2. Connarus. Sepals imbricate, not increasing, stamens 10, 5 shorter, sometimes imperfect; ovaries as in the last, capsule oblique stalked.

1. Rourea.

R. santaloides. A smooth climber, leaflets 5 to 9, ovate shining, flowers in racemes small, white and fragrant, capsule size and shape of an acorn, splitting from the top and showing the orange-coloured aril. *Wagáti, wákeri, wardhára.*

Matheran, S. Konkan and Ghauts (*D.*). I noted that the young plants are prickly.

2. Connarus.

C. monocarpus. A handsome erect shrub or small tree, leaflets 5, oval, pointed, shining; flowers in long panicles, hairy, yellowish-white, very fragrant; fruit in clusters, slightly kidney-shaped, bright red, size of a bean, splitting from the top. *Gudri, nágudri, Sundar.*

Southern Ghauts. Matheran (*Birdwood*).

**C. Wightii*, apparently like the last, but the capsule pale chestnut colour, shining, much narrower than the last. Not in *D.* S. Konkan, Stocks, *H.*

**C. Ritchiei.* Flowers smaller, capsule about half the size of No. 1, dark coloured, the base rounded. Same as last, and Rám Ghaut Ritchie, *H.*

Order 42. **LEGUMINOSÆ.**

This is the second largest of all the natural orders, and might very well be divided into three, the second and third of the sub-orders being very different as to the appearance of the flowers from the first. The plants of the sub-order Papilionaceæ are very easily recognized by the flowers, which are all more or less like those of the common pea, while the fruit in this, as well as in the other sub-orders, is a pod.

Hooker, in mentioning the absence of leguminous plants in a certain part of the Himalayas, says that "cool, equable, humid climates are generally unfavourable to the order." *Journals* 76.

Dr. Cooke notices as remarkable that there is not a single tree of the order at Mahableshwar, though several at Matheran.

General description of the order. Leaves very often compound, with stipules, the leaflets frequently with stipels, sepals 5, often unequal, petals 5: stamens generally 10, free or variously combined (but in tribe Acacieæ they are indefinite) ovary superior, style simple, fruit usually the pistil grown into a pod, with the calyx attached, but very various in shape.

I. SUB-ORDER PAPILIONACEÆ. Flowers papilionaceous (butterfly shape), consisting of a large upper petal (the standard), which embraces the rest in the bud, 2 lateral petals (wings), and two usually more or less coherent by their lower margins (the keel), which enclose the stamens and pistil; stamens almost always 10, and monadelphous or diadelphous.

The sub-order is further divided into a large number of tribes distinguished mostly by the divisions of the leaves, and the nature of the pod.

(*a*) GENISTEÆ. Stamens monadelphous; leaves simple or digitately trifoliate.

1. HEYLANDIA. Stamens united into a tube, split above, style long, pod short, ovate compressed, one or two-seeded.

2. CROTALARIA. Flowers generally yellow, style long, bearded above, pod straight, generally inflated.

(*b*) TRIFOLIEÆ. Stamens diadelphous, leaves trifoliate, leaflets toothed.

3. TRIGONELLA. Flowers yellow, standard and wings narrow, keel shorter, pod many-seeded.

4. MELILOTUS. Flowers in long racemes, style much incurved, pod short, round or oblong, indehiscent.

5. MEDICAGO. Pod spirally twisted, indehiscent.

(*c*) GALEGEÆ. Stamens usually diadelphous; leaves various.

6. CYAMOPSIS.—Stamens monadelphous, pod linear straight, divided internally by partitions.

7. INDIGOFERA. Keel spurred on each side near the base, pod usually linear or cylindrical.

8. PSORALEA. Leaves simple, dotted with glands, petals all clawed, pod ovoid or oblong, one-seeded, indehiscent.

9. TEPHROSIA. Petals clawed, pod linear, flat, many-seeded.

10. SESBANIA. Herbs or softwooded shrubs, leaflets very numerous, deciduous, petals long-clawed, pod very long and narrow.

(*d*) HEDYSAREÆ. Pod either one-seeded or made up of many separate joints, and so not easily recognized as a pod.

11. TAVERNIERA. Undershrubs, leaves simple or trifoliate, ovary stalked, pod of 3 or 4 joints, or simple.

12. GEISSAPSIS. Leaflets 2 pairs, flowers with conspicuous membranous bracts, pod of 2 turgid joints, or simple.

13. ALHAGI. A low thorny shrub with simple leaves, pod of several joints.

14. ZORNIA. Leaflets one or two pairs, flowers with large bracts, pod of several round flat warty joints.

15. SMITHIA. Leaflets many, small, pod of several flattened joints folded together within the calyx.

16. ÆSCHYNOMENE. Leaflets as in the last, pod straight, exserted from the calyx, stalked, and with several flat joints.

17. PSEUDARTHRIA differs from the last in the pod not being jointed but linear, one to six-seeded.

18. URARIA. Flowers very numerous, small, pod of about 4 joints, twisted or pressed together within the calyx.

19. ALYSICARPUS. Diffuse plants, leaves generally simple, calyx quite as large as corolla, pod of several joints, not flattened or twisted.

20. OUGEINIA. A tree, leaves trifoliate, pod linear flat, of two to five large joints.

21. DESMODIUM. Leaves trifoliate or simple, pod of several joints often straight on one edge, divided on the other.

(*e*) VICIEÆ. Vetches. Leaves even-pinnate ending in a tendril, pod dehiscent, not jointed.

22. ABRUS. Climbing shrubs with only 9 stamens, united into a tube split above, style short incurved.

23. CICER. Leaflets toothed, flowers solitary, pod sessile, turgid, tipped with the style.

(*f*) PHASEOLEÆ. Usually climbers with trifoliate leaves, pod as in the last tribe, stamens usually diadelphous.

24. SHUTERIA. Stipules and bracts conspicuous, wings spurred, pod flat recurved.

25. MUCUNA. Flowers large, usually dark purple, keel larger than the standard and wings ; pod covered with stinging hairs.

26. ERYTHRINA. Trees with prickly branches and red flowers, ovary stalked, pod turgid.

27. GALACTIA. Leaflets 3 to 7, pod linear, 4-sided.

28. SPATHALOBUS. Woody climbers, pod linear, thin, with one seed at the point.

29. BUTEA. Trees or climbing shrubs, flowers large and showy, keel much curved, pod as the last.

30. CANAVALLIA. Flowers showy, standard large, roundish, pod thick, 3-keeled on the upper edge.

31. PUERARIA. Standard usually spurred, pod linear, flattish.

32. PHASEOLUS. Bracts usually conspicuous, keel elongated, much twisted, style twisted with it, pod more or less cylindrical.

33. VIGNA, like the last, but with the style and keel shorter and much less twisted.

34. CLITORIA. Flowers very showy, leaflets up to 7, standard spoon-shaped, very large, ovary stalked.

35. DOLICHOS. Petals usually equal in length, pod flat recurved.

36. ATYLOSIA. Leaves gland-dotted, pod generally swelling, seeds with a large grooved aril.

37. CAJANUS. An erect shrub, petals equal in length, pod straight, tipped with the style.

38. CYLISTA. Corolla enclosed in a large scarious calyx, petals equal in length, pod small oblique, enclosed in calyx.

39. RHYNCOSIA. Leaves dotted with glands beneath, pod compressed.

40. FLEMINGIA. Generally shrubs, leaves sometimes simple, petals equal in length, pod swollen, one or two-seeded.

(*g*) DALBERGIEÆ. Trees or climbing shrubs, leaves odd, pinnate, pod not jointed, indehiscent.

41. DALBERGIA. Leaflets alternate, flowers white or pale, small, only half opening, pod thin and flat.

42. PTEROCARPUS. Leaflets alternate, petals long-clawed, pod roundish, winged.

43. Pongamia. Leaflets opposite, pod woody, oblong, flattened.

44. Derris. Climbers: as the last, but the pod thin, flat, and more or less winged.

(*a*) Genisteæ.

1. Heylandia.

H. latebrosa.—A small prostrate hairy plant with very oblique cordate ovate leaves, flowers small, yellow, solitary or nearly so in the axils.

Common in most parts. (See the next species.)

2. Crotalaria.

Note.—Where not otherwise specified the flowers are yellow and in racemes. *H.* has 77 species.

1. *C. filipes.*—A small prostrate slender-stemmed plant covered with long hairs, leaves oblique, cordate oblong, peduncles very slender, bearing one or two flowers, pod oblong, much inflated, 8 to 10-seeded.

Konkan and Deccan. This much resembles the last and grows at the same time of year (the rains) and in similar situations. *H.* has 3 other species closely resembling this, known only from Stocks's herbarium, and attributed to the Konkan, viz. *C. trichophora*, clothed with long silky brown hairs, pod smooth; *C. Stocksii*, nearly smooth, leaves linear oblong; *C. vestita*, densely silky, leaves equal-sided, pod 15 to 20-seeded.

2. *C. linifolia.* Branched from the base, hairy and silky, leaves oblong obtuse, broader upwards, sometimes linear, racemes long, many-flowered, pod ovoid smooth, scarcely as long as the calyx.

Dapoli. Surat and Khandalla (*D.* & *G.*).

3. *C. retusa.* A short undershrub, branched, nearly smooth, leaves oblong, broader upwards, stipules subulate, flowers many, large and handsome, veined red, pod linear, oblong, stalked, 1 or 2-seeded. *Ghágai.*

Konkan, Ghauts and Guzerat, common.

This and the next two are much alike, and have all a general resemblance to the English broom (*Sarothamnus scoparius*). *C. triquetra*, with 3-sided branches, is also much like *C. retusa*, but much smaller. Dapoli. Malwan districts (*D.*), Mahableshwar (*Dr. Cooke.*) *Ghati.* *C. albida* (*C. epunctata*, D.) is also like *C. retusa*, but smaller and mean-looking, silky, leaves linear, oblong or obovate, pod sessile. S. Konkan.

4. *C. Sericea.* Stem angled, stipules and bracts large, leafy, leaves silky beneath, larger than C. retusa, flowers not so large.

Along the B. B. & C. I. Railway line at the end of the rains. Pasture grounds in Bombay (*D.*).

5. *C. Leschenaultii*, a very handsome tall shrub, mostly smooth, leaves narrow, obovate, silky beneath, stipules minute, racemes and flowers large, bracts small half way up the pedicel, pod like the two last. *Dingala, Dayali.*

Matheran and the Ghauts, common.

6. *C. verrucosa.* A stout herbaceous much-branched plant, smooth, with square and winged stems and branches, leaves broad ovate, narrow at the base, stipules half-moon shape, flowers pale blue, bracts subulate, pod nearly cylindric, light-brown. *Tirat.*

Very common on the sandy seashore, and easily known by the colour of the flowers. *H.* gives it a wide range in India, and makes the flowers yellow and white, as well as blue.

7. *C. juncea.* Sun hemp. A tall erect branched shrub, shining and silky, leaves linear or oblong, racemes very long, calyx densely covered with rusty hairs, pod sessile, oblong, broader upwards, many-seeded. *San, tág.*

Commonly cultivated for the fibre. "(Near Chittagong) Fields of poppy and san formed the most beautiful crops, the latter 4 to 6 feet high, bearing masses of laburnum-like flowers."—*Hooker's Himalayan Journals.*

8. *C. orixensis*, a procumbent hairy herb, leaflets 3 lanceolate, ovate, or obovate, flowers small long-stalked, bracts cordate, pod short, cylindric smooth.

Konkan, Deccan, and Guzerat, but not common, I think.

9. *C. notonia.* (*C. rostrata*, D.) Shrubby, rigid, much-branched with much fine short hair on it, leaflets obovate or obcordate, small, racemes short terminal, pod roundish ovate, 2-seeded with reflexed beak. *Kulai.*

Konkan, Guzerat, Kattywar, Cutch.

H.'s only habitat for this is Nilgherry and Pulney Mountains, but I believe there is no doubt that it is *D.'s* plant.

The following are less common. When not otherwise stated the leaves are oblong, very frequently broader upwards.

* *C. Burhia*, a low undershrub with close entangled woody branches, leaves rigid, corolla with red veins. Cambay (*D*), Cutch

and Sind (*H.*). * *C. bifaria*, prostrate, hairy, leaves sometimes roundish, flowers one or two together, pod ovoid, much swollen. Belgaum and Ram Ghaut (*D.* and *G.*). * *C. nana*. A foot high, hairy and silky, flowers pale yellow, pod ovoid, sessile black. Malwan (*D.*), Mahableshwar (*Cooke*). *C. umbellata*, D. is included in this, having a dense terminal umbel of flowers and round legumes. Vingorla and Ram Ghaut (*D.*). * *C. calycina* (*C. anthylloides*, D.) covered with silky brown hairs, leaves linear or lanceolate, calyx large with long teeth, corolla shorter, pod included in the calyx, 20 to 30-seeded. S. Konkan; the flowers open in the evening (*D.*). * *C. lutescens*. (*C. peduncularis*, D.) Erect, tall, smooth, flowers an inch long, distant, standard much veined, pod cylindric oblong. S. Konkan (*D.*). *C. fulva*. Stiff, erect, much branched, thickly hairy, calyx large, yellowish, teeth broad, leafy, pod included. Ram Ghaut (*D.*). * *C. laburnifolia*. Erect, smooth, leaves trifoliate, leaflets broad, flowers in long racemes long-stalked, pod cylindrical, many-seeded. S. Konkan (*D.*). * *C. quinquefolia*, a tall herb with hollow stems, leaflets 5 linear lanceolate, racemes long, flowers lax. Rice fields, Salsette (*D.* and *G.*).

(*b*) TRIFOLIEÆ.

3. TRIGONELLA.

T. Fœnugræcum. Erect, robust, stipules entire, leaflets lanceolate oval or obovate, flowers pretty, pod long, thin, and pointed. *Methi*.

Commonly cultivated for *baji*, as it is also in S. Europe. It was adopted as fodder by the Romans from the Greeks; hence the specific name.

4. MELILOTUS.

M. parviflora. A small erect delicate plant, leaflets roundish, lanceolate or obovate, stipules linear pointed, flowers pale yellow, very small, pod nearly round, finely wrinkled. *Van metika, jhir*.

Pastures in the cold weather. This and *M. alba*, which is much larger with white flowers, found in irrigated lands, are European plants. *M. officinalis* is the English Melilot.

5. MEDICAGO.

M. sativa. Stem usually erect, leaflets oblong, flowers somewhat racemed, usually purple, pods downy and loosely spiral.

Purple medick, or lucerne, not wild in India any more than in England, but widely cultivated.

Hehn says that the name *medicago* (originally *medike poa*) shows that the plant came originally from Media, and quotes the following strong eulogy from Columella, a Spanish writer on agriculture in the reign of the Emperor Claudius: "Lucerne once sown lasts ten years; it is mown four times a year regularly, sometimes six; it does not exhaust the soil, but rather enriches it; it makes lean cattle fat, and heals the sick; one acre of it will keep three horses the whole year."

(*c*) GALEGEÆ.

6. CYAMOPSIS.

C. psoraloides. Erect, robust, leaflets 3 ovate, acute, dentate, flowers very small and numerous in racemes, purple, blue, or white, pod warty, about 6-seeded. *Gauri, matki.*

Cultivated for the pods, which are eaten, cooked like French beans. A doubtful native.

7. INDIGOFERA. Indigo.

Note.—This is an unattractive genus. Most of the species are more or less covered with close-pressed hairs. The flowers of all here given, when not otherwise specified, are red or reddish-purple, and in racemes. *H.* has 40 species.

1. *I. linifolia.* A grey prostrate plant, much-branched, hairs silvery, leaves lanceolate or linear, varying to obovate, racemes very short, pod round one-seeded. *Burburra, bhángra, torki.*

Deccan, Cutch, and elsewhere, common. The fruit outwardly is not the least like a pod. The seeds are eaten.

2. *I. cordifolia.* Of the same habit as the last, hairs long and white, leaves broad ovate, cordate; flowers very small in sessile heads, pod oval, 2-seeded. *Godádi, bechaka, bodaga.*

Deccan and Konkan, and probably elsewhere, often growing in masses. The seeds are eaten.

Two other simple-leaved species, both very small and procumbent, are * *I. echinata,* branches angular, leaves obovate, pod crescent-shaped, bristled, beaked, seed one, kidney-shaped. Very common (*D.*), but no hab. * *I. triquetra,* stem 3-edged, leaves oblong, pod swollen, linear 4-winged. Malwan district (*D.*).

3. *I. glandulosa.* A small diffuse species, leaflets 3, ovate or obovate, deeply pitted with glands beneath, pod brown or reddish, very short, angled and with toothed wings, seeds 1 to 4. *Bekhariyo, baragadan.*

The Deccan and elsewhere. On black soil it becomes woody and much branched.

4. *I. enneaphylla.* Small, branched and trailing, leaflets about 9, obovate or oblong, pod oval, 2-seeded. *Bhuiguli.*

Deccan, Guzerat, and Cutch. This and No. 2 grow together on the maidán at Poona; this is the stouter of the two.

5. *I. trita.* A small undershrub, stiff-branched, leaflets 3, ovate or obovate, flowers crowded; pod long, straight, rigid,

horizontal, slightly 4-sided, sharp-pointed; seeds about .6-angled.

Common. This much resembles No. 3, but the habit is different and the leaves not pitted.

6. *I. hirsuta.* A coarse erect herb, leaflets 5 to 11, large, obovate oblong, racemes long, dense, flowers pink, corolla not much larger than calyx, pods crowded, straight, bent down, 4 to 8-seeded.

Bombay, S. Konkan, Guzerat, Cutch.

All the three last species are ascribed by *H.* to the plains of India from the Himalayas to Ceylon.

7. *I. tinctoria.* Cultivated indigo. A shrub, hairs silvery, leaflets 9 to 13, oblong, obovate, flowers greenish or yellowish-red, pod nearly straight and cylindrical, about 10-seeded. *Nil, bhui tarvar, guli.*

Apparently wild in the Konkan (*D.*). *H.* doubts it being wild in India at all.

8. *I. pulchella.* A tall shrub, racemes long, erect, flowers pink or light purple, branches angled, leaflets 13 to 21, broad, pod straight, cylindrical or turgid, sharp-pointed, 8 to 10-seeded. *Chimnáti, Nirda.*

Mahableshwar and the higher Ghauts; the one handsome member, as far as W. India is concerned, of a very plain family.

The following are also found. The leaves of all are odd-pinnate, except the last two. The leaflets are always lanceolate, ovate, or obovate, very generally varying from one of these shapes to the other.

* *I. tenuifolia*, a diffuse herb, leaflets 7 to 9, racemes few flowered, pod straight, cylindrical, compressed between the seeds. Ankaleshwar (*D.*). * *I. trifoliata,* small, shrubby, leaflets 3, racemes short, crowded, pod short, straight, bordered. Domus (*D.*), Cutch. *Bekárhriya.* * *I. paucifolia.* A tall shrub, leaflets 3 to 5, sometimes reduced to one, racemes many flowered, long, pod linear recurved. Guzerat, Cutch, and Sind. * *I. endecaphylla (I. kleinii,* D.), a trailing herb, flowers violet-purple, pods crowded, straight, linear, 4-angled, with rigid point. Bombay, S. Konkan, Guzerat, Cutch. * *I. argentea* (*I. cœrulea,* D.), shrubby, with silvery hairs, leaflets 7 to 11, large, flowers reddish-yellow, pods very short, curved upwards. Broach Collectorate (*D.*) Sind. * *I. Wightii,* a low shrub, hoary, leaflets 11 to 21, silvery, racemes short, dense, pod turgid, straight, sharp-pointed. Belgaum (*D.*). * *I. uniflora,* a prostrate herb, leaflets 3 to 7 digitate, sometimes reduced to one, flowers long-stalked, very small, pod straight, linear. S. M. Country (*D.* and *G.*). * *I. aspalathoides.* Shrubby, young parts whitish, leaflets 3 to 5, pods straight cylindrical. Deccan and Belgaum (*D.*).

8. Psoralea.

P. corylifolia. A tall straggling plant with ovate or roundish irregularly-toothed leaves, flowers small violet, tipped darker, in close long-stalked spikes. Calyx segments unequal, covered with granules; pod small included in it. *Báwarchi.*

A common weed in the Deccan, and throughout the plains of India (*H.*), especially in cultivated fields. *H.* calls the flowers yellow.

9. Tephrosia.

T. purpurea. A much-branched erect half-shrubby plant, with a most offensive smell, more or less hairy, leaflets 6 to 10 pair, oblong or obovate, flowers red or purple in long racemes, legume slightly curved, short-pointed, 6 to 10-seeded. *Sirpakhá, unhála, utáti.*

A very disagreeable weed, often called bastard indigo, which springs up very freely in the rains in company with *Cassia occidentalis.* Everywhere in the tropics (*H.*).

* *T. incana* in Cutch (Palin) *H.* makes a var. of *T. villosa*, which has the habit of *T. purpurea*, but more hairy and pods more densely silky. * *T. tenuis*, a small delicate plant, leaves linear or elliptic, flowers solitary or twin, long-stalked, purple, pod straight. Konkan (*D.*) and Sind. * *T. senticosa*, shrubby, leaflets one to three pairs, narrow, flowers few, orange-red, pod with recurved tip. Konkan Hills (*D.*), Sind.

10. Sesbania.

S. aculeata. A tall weak herb, rather pretty, sometimes half shrubby, stem and petioles with soft prickles, leaflets 20 to 40 pair, obtuse, flowers in racemes on slender pedicels, yellow, dotted with purple, calyx nearly entire, pod nearly cylindrical, sharp-pointed. *Rán shevari, chinchani.*

Common; known by its wonderfully rapid growth, springing up to 8 feet or more in a very few weeks.

* *S. procumbens*, a straggling plant with prickles like the last, leaflets minute, 15 to 20 pair, flowers 2 or 3 together, pod much smaller than the last. Bombay, Cutch, and Kattywar.

S. Egyptiaca, shevri, jayanti, Sándeslar, a tree very like *S. aculeata* is with us considered to be a foreigner, but *H.* has it as wild throughout the plains of India.

S. grandiflora, ágási, hadjá, basna, a tree with very large white flowers, and pointed pods; cultivated for both. Native of the Indian Archipelago, and of N. Australia.

To this tribe belong: *Milletia*, petals long-clawed, pod woody. * *M. racemosa* (*Wisteria r.* and *W. pallida*, D.). A woody climber, leaflets 5 to 7 pair, ovate or obovate, with petioles and stipels, flowers in long slender racemes, pod linear narrow, bulging at the seeds. At Belgaum with large rose-coloured, and in the Dangs with pale yellow flowers. *Mundulea;* standard long-clawed, wings adhering to the keel. * *M. suberosa* (*Telphrosia s.*, D.). Small tree or shrub, leaflets 6 to 10 pair, oblong or lanceolate, flowers rose-coloured in close silky racemes, pod long, straight, thin with thickened border. *Supi, supti.* Belgaum districts (*D.* and *G.*). N. Konkan, Lisboa.

(*d*) HEDYSAREÆ.

11. TAVERNIERA.

T. nummularia (*T. cuneifolia*, D.). A smooth, stiff under-shrub with soft green stems and branches, and small broad oval veinless leaves or leaflets; flowers 2 or 3 together, nearly sessile or in racemes, pink, striped; pod covered with soft bristles. *Jetimad.*

Deccan, Kattywar, Sind. The root said to be used as a substitute for liquorice. I have seen the shrub so eaten down by cattle that a perfect leaf could not be found.

12. GEISSAPSIS.

G. cristata. A trailing plant, leaflets small obovate, stipules adnate, flowers small orange and brown, each with a large roundish bract edged with stiff brown hairs; joints of pods roundish. *Barki.* (See also *Zornia.*)

Common, growing in grass; a noticeable plant, though small.

13. ALHAGI.

A. maurorum. Camel thorn. A low shrub with green branches and strong hard thorns, one to each leaf; leaves sessile oblong or obovate, rather fleshy, flowers small, red or purple, in short racemes ending in a bristly point, joints of pod irregular. *Jawás, kás, yavásá.*

Very common in Guzerat and Sind, less so elsewhere; used for making tatties. It grows in the deserts of most eastern countries, and an exudation from the leaves and branches is made into the Persian manna of commerce. The English name is due to camels eating it regardless of the thorns.

14. ZORNIA.

Z. Diphylla (*Z. angustifolia* and *Z. zeylonensis*, D.). A small diffuse plant; leaflets one pair, oblong lanceolate at the end of a long stalk, stipules large; flowers small, yellow, with red spot at the base of the standard, nearly hidden in the ovate acute bracts, which are attached by the middle; joints of pod round, prickly, very loose. *Barki, nálabarki.*

Common, growing in grass. There is some resemblance but plenty of difference between this and *Geissapsis*. *H.* has two varieties.

15. Smithia.

Note.—Out of 12 Indian species of this interesting and ornamental genus, 9 are found in this Presidency, and all those apparently within a very limited range, viz. S. Konkan and S. Ghauts, and one or two species about Belgaum; and all that I have seen appear in the rains. The flowers of 7 out of the 9 species are bright yellow, and almost all have, according to my observation, one or two red spots at the base of the petals. This characteristic is, however, partly denied, and partly looked on as trivial at Kew, so I should be glad to be confirmed on this point, and also to hear of the last species mentioned under this genus.

1. *S. sensitiva.* A slender branched herb, leaflets about 4 pairs, sensitive, bristly on the edges and midrib, flowers in short racemes without the red spot; joints of the pod several, warty. *Kaola.*

H. has a separate species, * *S. geminiflora*, which differs from the above in having the flowers in pairs in the axils. *D.* considered this the commonest variety.

2. *S. blanda* (*S. racemosa*, D.). Erect, covered with spreading yellow hairs, leaflets 3 to 7 pairs, obtuse bristle-tipped, flowers in dense terminal panicles, corolla with 2 red spots; pod 4 to 6-jointed. *Moti barki.*

These are the two commonest species in the S. Konkan, and are frequently found together. The latter at Mahableshwar.—*Dr. Cooke.*

3. *S. pycnantha.* Erect, bristly, leaflets 3 or 4 pairs, linear or oblong, flowers with red spot in short rather dense racemes, pedicels and calyx glandular and hairy, pods about 4-jointed.

This also is very common about Dápoli in the rains, growing all along the roadsides with the two last species.

"Yellow and bright, as bullion unalloyed,
Their blossoms."—*Cowper.*

I have no doubt that this is *D.'s S. hirsuta*, though *H.* has not so identified it.

4. *S. setulosa.* A stout hairy plant, 3 or 4 feet high, leaflets about 5 pair, oblong obtuse, smooth except the edges, flowers in terminal panicles large, with red spots, calyx segments very unequal, pod about 10-jointed.

This is one of the handsomest plants of the rains, but I believe rare. *D.* has only Párwar Ghaut; I have found it near Mandangarh, in the Dápoli taluka, *Dr. Cooke* at Mahableshwar.

The other species are * *S. purpurea*, smooth, erect, slender, flowers in racemes, purple with white spot, pod 10 to 12-jointed. Mahableshwar, *Dr. Cooke.* Lanoli, *Mr. Jyekrishna I.* Plains of Konkan (*H.*); but where are they? *S. bigetmina*, small, branched, hairy, leaflets 2 pairs, flowers few in long-stalked racemes, pod of about 7 joints. Dápoli and Mahableshwar: near Poona, Jaquemont (*H.*) * *S. capitata*, erect, leaflets 9 to 15 pair, flowers in a dense round head, purplish, bracts large. Párwar Ghaut (*D.*). *S. dichotoma*, mostly smooth, leaflets 2 or 3 pair, flowers rather few and large in a lax panicle; pod of 10 or 12 joints; not in *D.* I had a species at Dápoli, where it is common, very like this, with the pod of about 20 joints completely hidden in the calyx. Nothing was known of this at Kew.

16. Æschynomene.

Æ. Indica. A smooth procumbent plant with slender branches; leaflets 15 to 30 pairs, linear obtuse sensitive, stipules rather large adnate, flowers pale yellow streaked with red, pod straight on one side, indented on the other, warty.

Guzerat and the Konkans. Everywhere in the tropics of the old world (*H.*). He says that the peduncles and pedicels are usually viscid.

* *Æ. aspera*, growing in many parts of India, is the *Sola* or pith plant, from which hats and many other things are made.

17. Pseudarthria.

* *P. viscida.* A diffuse hairy herb, leaves trifoliate, leaflets oval rounded, flowers purple, distantly fascicled in threes, calyx minute, pods downy, slightly notched on both sides. Common (*D.*), (without hab.).

18. Uraria.

U. picta. A tall, erect hairy, half-shrubby plant, leaves simple or with several pairs of leaflets, which are as much as 9 inches long, linear lanceolate obtuse, nearly smooth, stipules large; flowers small, violet or reddish-purple, in rigid spikes as much as 18 inches long; joints of pod about 5, loose.

Himalayas to Ceylon (*H.*); but seems to be uncommon in this Presidency; *D.* had it near Penn, *G.* in jungles S.E. of Surat; I had it in Salsette on the B. B. & C. I. railway line.

The specific name refers to the leaves being variegated.

19. Alysicarpus.

1. *A. vaginalis.* Rather hairy, leaves cordate from oval to lanceolate, stipules large, flowers in racemes red, whitish

beneath, calyx large, 5-divided, much shorter than the pod, which is thickened at the joints and not much divided. *Chái, Hiroli, pudza, dhákta dhámpta.*

In fruit the large chaffy calyx is the most conspicuous feature. *H.* makes *D.'s A. nummularifolius*, which has roundish leaves and almost cylindrical pods, a variety of this, and has two other varieties.

The Konkan, Matheran, Deccan, and Guzerat. See *Desmodium diffusum.*

2. *A. longifolius.* Leaves linear lanceolate with large stipules; flowers small, pale, in very long racemes, calyx 4-divided, nearly equalling the pod, which has about 5 veined joints. *Jangli gaulya, dhámpta.*

They seem to vary very much in habit and size. Mr. Jaikrishna Indraji says that it reaches 9 or 10 feet in height at Kundwa.

Bombay, S. Konkan, Matheran, and Deccan.

3. *A. rugosus* (*A. Styracifolius*, D.). Much branched, prostrate or ascending, very hairy, leaves small oval, flowers in racemes like those of No. 1. Calyx of 4 large smooth sepals nearly the same length as the pod, which has 3 to 5 deeply separated joints.

D. had this only at Surat: I had it at Poona. *H.* makes one or other of the 3 varieties, one of which grows a yard high, common almost throughout India.

**A. bupleurifolius*, smooth leaves linear lanceolate, flowers in pairs on the raceme, small, red or pale, pod as in No. 1. Common (*D.*) (without hab.). **A. pubescens*, erect, hairy, leaves linear lanceolate, spikes close and long, pod 3 or 4-jointed, covered by the calyx. **A. Belgaumensis*, hairy, leaves often trifoliate, racemes long, pod as the last. These two depend almost entirely on *Dalzell*, who had them at Rám Ghaut and Belgaum.

20. Ougeinia.

**O. dalbergioides* (*Dalbergia oojinensis*, D.). A large tree with slender grey branches, leaflets large, roundish or oval with grey margins, flowers small, whitish or rose-coloured, in short close racemes, pod two or three inches long. *Tanaz, tánia, telas, tiwas.*

N. Konkan, Dangs and Canara.

21. Desmodium.

1. *D. triquetrum.* A shrubby rather hairy plant, with triangular branches, leaves ovate with winged petioles, stipules

large lanceolate, flowers in long erect racemes, purple or violet, pod of about 6 irregular joints beaked, divided on the lower suture. *Kákyánja, ghorachijibh.*

Common and easily recognizable.

2. *D. gangeticum.* A shrubby plant with irregularly angled stems covered with rigid white hairs, leaves broad ovate, rather cordate, stipules and bracts triangular long-pointed, flowers in long racemes violet, pod about 6-jointed deeply divided. *Sálwan, sálparni, dai.*

Bombay and S. Konkan, over a great part of India (*H.*). He has a large and a small variety.

* D. latifolium, very like this, but leaves broader, roughish, raceme dense, shorter, pod crenate on one side, deeply divided on the other. Konkan Hills, (*D.* and *G.*).

3. *D. diffusum.* A tall, straggling herb, all hairy, the stem and branches variously angled, leaflets oval or obovate, stipules leafy auricled and stem clasping, bracts similar but smaller, flowers very small, red, long stalked on very long racemes, pod of about 6 joints, rough and hairy.

This is not in *D.* or *G.*, but is found in both Konkans, and is common at Nasik. *H.* calls the flowers the smallest of all the 49 Indian species In general appearance it much resembles Alysicarpus vaginalis.

4. *D. triflorum,* small, creeping, stem and calyx very hairy, leaflets roundish or obcordate, flowers 3 together in the axils, purple, pod about 6-jointed, slightly curved, hairy. *Ránmethi.*

Very common. Everywhere in the plains of India (*H.*).

* *D. umbellatum.* A tall shrub, leaflets broad oblong, flowers white, 6 to 12 together in umbels, pod about 4-jointed with thick margins, indented on both edges. S.E. of Surat and near Belgaum (*D.* and *G.*). *D. cephalotes* (*D. congestum*, D.). Shrubby, branches angular, leaflets oval lanceolate, stipules large, flowers whitish in crowded heads or umbels, pod about 5-jointed, slightly indented. The Konkan. *D. laxiflorum,* a small shrub, leaflets oval, flowers very pretty in 2's or 3's on long racemes, wings and keel blue, standard white, pod very thin, thickened at the joints, not indented. *Jangli ganga.* Not in *D.* S. Konkan. *D. polycarpum.* Stout plant, half shrubby, leaflets ovate or obovate, petiole slightly winged, flowers bluish-purple in crowded conical racemes, pod about 6-jointed, straight on one side, deeply notched on the other. Dápoli. Near Penn and Rám Ghaut (*D.*). Everywhere in the plains of India (*H.*). He has a var. with large bracts. *D. parviflorum* (Alysicarpus p. *D.*). Erect or diffuse, leaves oblong or trifoliate, flowers pink in long racemes, each flower nearly hidden in a large deciduous bract, pod falcate about 5-jointed. Vingorla. Fonda Ghaut (*D.*). **D. reniforme,* slender, creeping, smooth,

leaves roundish or reniform, flowers solitary or in racemes, pod about 4-jointed, straight on one side, indented on the other.

Pycnospora, leaves trifoliate, pod turgid, not jointed. **P. hedysaroides* (*P. nervosa*, D.) diffuse, leaflets obovate, flowers small purplish in racemes, bracts scariose, pod oblong. Near Vingorla (*D.*). *Lourea*, leaflets 3 or less, pods about 4-jointed, within the enlarged calyx. **L. verspitilionis*, erect herb, leaflets shaped more or less like the wings of a bat, flowers small, purple or white in long racemes, calyx inflated. In gardens, and doubtfully wild. Waste places throughout India (*H.*).

(*e*) Vicieæ.

22. Abrus.

A. precatorius. A small twiner with woody stem, leaflets numerous, oblong, blunt, flowers pale in crowded racemes, pod flat beaked, seeds round, scarlet with black spot. *Gunj, chánoti.*

Very common in hedges. The very pretty seeds are used as weights by goldsmiths, each seed being said to weigh exactly one grain. A var. has white seeds with black spot.

This may be considered as the representative of the vetches (in Scripture 'fitches') or tares, so common in various species in England.

> "Among the rustling ears, too closely blending,
> Are rank and wasteful tares."—*H. Goodwin.*

> "What landscapes I read in the primrose's looks,
> And what pictures of pebbled and minnowy brooks
> In the vetches that tangled their shore."—*Campbell.*

In America the leaflets of this plant are said to predict changes of weather by their movement, from which it is called the weather plant.

23. Cicer.

C. arietinum, gram, chick pea, *harbara, channa,* has generally a terminal leaflet instead of a tendril.

Lathyrus sativus, chickling vetch, *láng*, is cultivated in Guzerat as in some countries of Europe, and there as here, the grain is said to have deleterious effects on human beings. L. odoratus, the sweet pea, will scarcely grow in W. India.

Ervum lens, massur is the lentile (or one of them) of the Bible: in our time it has become known as Revalenta Arabica; and from being a common food for fast days in Roman Catholic countries it is thought by some to have given its name to the season of Lent.

Pisum sativum is the garden and field pea of Europe, now much grown all over India.

(*f*) PHASEOLEÆ.

Note.—The leaflets are three, except when otherwise stated.

24. SHUTERIA.

S. vestita. Small and slender, very hairy, leaflets roundish, flowers very small, purplish, in dense racemes, pod long with a rigid turned-up point, 5 or 6-seeded.

The flowers have the mouth closed, like Snapdragon. S. Konkan, Deccan, Bombay. Ghauts (*D.*).

25. MUCUNA.

M. pruriens. Hairy, twining, leaflets ovate, unequal-sided, flowers large, lurid purple in drooping racemes, pod curved into the shape (more or less) of S, 5 or 6-seeded. *Kawaj, Kuhili, Kuyeri.*

Common in hedges. From the Himalayas to Ceylon (*H.*). The pods are disagreeable to touch owing to the stinging hairs. *H.* says that a variety with velvety pod is cultivated. The seed is called donkey's eye.

**M. monosperma,* a woody climber, racemes of 6 to 12 flowers similar to this, pods 3 inches long, half oval, much wrinkled and bristly. *Moti Kuhili.* *G.* mentions this as cultivated under the name of Negro bean.

26. ERYTHRINA.

E. Indica. Indian coral tree. Bark light and greenish, prickles black, petioles very long, leaflets smooth, more or less cordate, flowers large, bright scarlet in racemes, pod several inches long, black when ripe, very protuberant at the seeds, and with a hooked point. Seeds large, smooth, dark-red. *Pángara, Mándár.*

Very common, especially in the Konkans. A white flowered variety is said to grow in Salsette.

The flowers appear when the tree is bare, which it is for several months in the year. In Java, coffee is cultivated under its shade (*Forbes*). In Trinidad, where "it blazes against the blue sky with vermilion flowers," it is called "Bois immortelle" (*Kingsley*). In Ceylon it is planted for fences.

**E. stricta,* like the last, but prickles white, flowers smaller, pod lance-shaped, slightly protuberant. S. Konkan (*D.*). Ghauts (*G.*). *E. suberosa,* often without thorns, flowers smaller and lighter than *E. Indica,* and pod more like the last. N. Konkan, not common. Ghauts, Khandesh and Guzerat (*D.*).

27. GALACTIA.

**G. tenuiflora.* (*Leucodictyon Malvense*, D.). A slender twiner, leaflets oblong, white veined, flowers solitary or twin, purple, pod linear flattened (*D.*).

Málwan (*D.*).

28. SPATHALOBUS.

S. Roxburghii (*Butea parviflora*, D.). Petioles long, leaflets very large, ovate or obovate, lateral ones oblique, flowers small, white or red, 3 together, in large panicles, corolla not much larger than the calyx, pod velvety, of a rich reddish-brown. *Phalsan, pallas.*

Hills in Salsette and other parts of the Konkan. From the Himalayas to Ceylon (*H.*).

29. BUTEA.

B. frondosa. Petioles long, leaflets large, roundish ovate, flowers large, many together on long racemes, orange-red and silky, calyx and pedicels deep bottle-green, pod thin, downy. *Pallas, Kákria.*

Common in most parts but not in the S. Konkan. The flowers appear before the leaves, completely covering the upper part of the tree. In the Pauch Mahâls, where it is commoner, and attains a better size than in any other district I know, it very frequently grows out of the hollow trunk of a *wad* tree, and gives a character to the whole landscape in the cold weather, having

"Flowers that with a scarlet gleam
Cover a hundred leagues, and seem
To set the hills on fire."—*Wordsworth.*

A pale yellow-flowered var. is mentioned as rare in Bombay.—*N. H. Soc.'s Journal*, vol. 6.

**B. superba*, "a gigantic climber, very like this, but leaflets and flowers larger, the latter of a gorgeous orange colour" (*B.*). N. Konkan forests (*D.*). *Palasvel, tivat.*

30. CANAVALLIA.

C. ensiformis. (*C. virosa* and *C. Stocksii*, D.). A large smooth twiner, leaflets ovate pointed, petioles swollen at the base, flowers rather large, of a beautiful pink, sometimes purplish, in long-stalked racemes, pod large, plantain-shaped, seeds 6 to 8. *Gáora, Kismári, abai.*

Pretty common in hedges. Everywhere in the tropics (*H.*). One var. is commonly cultivated for food, though parts of it are thought poisonous.

31. PUERARIA.

P. tuberosa. A large hairy climber, root large, tuberous, leaflets large, oval roundish, with stipels, lateral ones unequal-sided, flowers in long stiff racemes of a delicate lilac, the wings deep blue, pod 3 to 6-seeded, much contracted between the seeds. Vingorla.

Caranjah, etc., pretty common (*D.*).

32. Phaseolus.

1. *P. trilobus*, straggling, leaflets ovate, usually 3-lobed, flowers small, yellow, in long-stalked racemes or heads, pod 6 to 12-seeded. *Arkmath, jangli math.*

Common all over India (*H.*). It varies greatly as to hairiness.

2. *P. trinervius.* Twining, hairy, leaflets ovate acute, sometimes slightly lobed, flowers yellow in cylindrical long-stalked heads, pod horizontal, about 12-seeded. *Matki, mukni, mungir.*

Common. Closely allied to P. mungo (H.).

**P. grandis*, bristly in most parts, leaves and stipules very large. **P. pauciflorus*, slender, climbing, leaflets ovate, flowers small, 2 or 3 together at the top of a slender stalk. These two, known only to Dalzell and Stocks, were found in the highest Ghauts and the S. Konkan respectively.

The following are cultivated—*P. vulgaris*, French bean; *P. mungo*, *urid*, *mung*—wild in many parts. *H.* includes in this *D.'s P. setulosus*, and has 3 vars. *P. rostratus*, *halaonda*, *halaola*. *P. acontifolius*, *math.*

P. coccineus is the scarlet runner.

33. Vigna.

V. vexillata (*Phaseolus sepiarius*, D.). Twining with broad ovate acute leaflets, lateral ones unequal-sided, flowers largish, pink, few together at the end of a very long stalk, pod 3 or 4 inches long, many-seeded, hairy. *Birambol, halula.*

The handsome flowers of this plant, which is pretty common in the Konkan and found at Mahableshwar (cosmopolitan in the tropics, *H.*), remind one strongly of the sweet pea, but without its delicacy or fragrance.

V. cattiang (*Dolichos sinensis*, D.) with flowers very like the last, is the cultivated *chaoli*, also called *safed* or *hariya lobeh.*

34. Clitoria.

C. ternatea. A beautiful climber, leaflets 5 to 7, ovate, flowers solitary, deep blue and white, with long bracts, pod straight and thin. *Bhovera, Kájali, Gokarni.*

Common in hedges in many parts, and at once noticeable by the size and shape of the standard. Grows abundantly in the Moluccas near the shore, with *Vinca rosea* (*Forbes*), and in Trinidad, scrambling over shrubs and walls (*Kingsley*).

C. biflora, very like this, but a stout, erect plant, flowers 2 together and smaller, is not common in the Konkan, and is attributed by *H.* to no other locality in India.

35. Dolichos.

D. lablab (*Lablab vulgaris*, D.) cultivated in the Konkan as a cold weather crop, *pauti, valpápri, ávri.*

D. biflorus (*Johnia congesta*, D.) cultivated in the Deccan, *Kulti.* Allied to this is Psophocarpus tetragonolubus, chevaux-de-frise bean, *chandhari, chárpatti,* flowers very pretty, lilac, with large standard, pod large with membranous jagged wings.

36. Atylosia.

1. *A. lineata* (*A. Lawii*, D.). A hairy shrub, leaves palmately trifoliate, long petioled, leaflets small, obovate, flowers solitary, axillary yellow-streaked, pod short, brown, 2 or 3-seeded. *Rán tur.*

Mahableshwar and the Ghauts. It may easily be mistaken for a Crotalaria.

2. *A. scarabœoides* (*Cantharospermum pauciflorum*, D.). A slender climber, hairy all over, leaflets ovate or obovate, wrinkled and strongly nerved, flowers small, yellow, 2 or 3 to a peduncle; seeds 4 to 6, shining, cream-coloured, with large black divided base.

Common in the Konkan. Plains throughout India (*H.*). In this and the next the petals fall off before the pods form.

3. *A. rostrata* (*Cajanus glandulosus*, D.). A very handsome climber, all covered with short hairs, petioles long, leaflets more or less ovate, as broad as long, with brown glands below, flowers large, bright yellow in erect racemes, pod linear, nearly straight, constricted between the seeds. *Kula, Kuili.*

This seems to be an essentially Konkan species. *D.* has Málwan and Wághotan; there is a good deal of it in the B.B. and C.I. Railway hedges in Salsette in September, but the flowers go off so quickly that it is probably not as often noticed as its beauty deserves. So the broom, "which blazes for a week or two, and is then completely extinguished, like a fire that has burnt itself out."—*Hamerton.*

This plant is wrongly identified in *H.* with A. mollis, but this is to be corrected in future editions.

**A. geminifolia*, hairy, leaflets roundish with scattered golden glands, stipules large auricled, flowers stalked in pairs, pod almost membranous, rough; known only to Dalzell, and no definite hab. given. **A.*

sericea shrub, hairy, leaflets lanceolate, flowers small, red, in pairs, Konkan, Stocks, etc. (*H.*). Not in *D.* **A. Kulnensis.* (*Cajanus K.* D.) Hairy, leaves rhomboid, ovate with waxy glands below, racemes of about six yellow flowers, bracts round. Wári country (*D.*). *A. barbata* (*Cajanus Goensis*, D.) A large twiner, softly hairy, leaflets roundish or ovate, with waxy glands, racemes very long, flowers yellowish, standard large, purple, streaked, pod rather inflated. Bandora and Nasik. Chorla Ghaut (*D.*). On this the callosity at the base of the wings, which *D.* made a special mark of, Gen. Cajanus, is very apparent, but *H.* does not mention it.

37. Cajanus.

C. Indicus. Pigeon-pea. An erect shrub, silky, leaflets oblong lanceolate, flowers yellow, often veined with red, pod 2 or 3 inches long. *Tur, dál.*

Doubtfully wild, but cultivated all over India for the grain, and the stalks used in making gunpowder.

38. Cylista.

C. scariosa. A climber with ovate wrinkled downy leaves, flowers in racemes, the calyx large and withered-looking, hiding the rest of the flower, a bract of the same shape soon falls off, corolla yellow, red-streaked, pod almost semicircular, one-seeded. *Rán gevra.*

The Konkan. Very common in Salsette, and easily recognizable : also in the Ghauts.

39. Rhyncosia.

R. minima (*R. medicaginea*, D.). A slender twiner, leaflets ovate cuneate, flowers in racemes, yellow, streaked with brown, pod scimitar-shaped, 2-seeded, much longer than the calyx.

Common in hedges. Everywhere in the plains of India (*H.*).

R. Cyanosperma (*Cyanospermum tomentosum*, D.). A woody hairy climber, leaflets with large stipels, flowers yellow, red or white, calyx lobes broad leafy, bracts large, pod of 2 round lobes, each with one large dark-blue seed. S. Ghaut (*D.*). I have seen it only at Kew.

40. Flemingia.

F. strobilifera. A tall, straggling shrub with simple ovate leaves, and racemes of small white flowers streaked with violet, enclosed in large green-veined bracts, which are roundish, deeply cordate and folded close together : pod short. *Bundar, Kán phuti.*

Common on the Ghauts and Konkan hills; and throughout India (*H.*).

* *F. congesta* (including *D.'s F. procumbens.*) Racemes dense, short, often fascicled, flowers streaked with purple, calyx brown silky, pod 2-seeded. *Daudaula*, Wári jungles and Fonda Ghaut (*D.*). *H.* has 4 vars., one with winged petioles, another with flowers in roundish heads—widely distributed. *F. tuberosa*, creeping and spreading, long-branched, very hairy, leaflets lanceolate, panicles large, flowers few, small, lilac, pod short, enclosed in the calyx. Dapoli. Malwan districts (*D.*). Rare, apparently.

Glycine. Leaflets 3 to 7, stamens monadelphous, pod linear. * *G. pentaphylla*, slender, twining, leaflets lanceolate, rather hairy, flowers very small, reddish, in spikes or racemes, pod smooth, flat. S. Konkan (*D.*). *Teramnes*, like the last, but alternate stamens barren, pod linear, hooked with the style. * *T. labialis* (*Glycine l.* and *wareensis*, D.) Nearly smooth, leaflets ovate, flowers small, reddish, pod 8 to 12-seeded. *D.* without hab. Plains of India (*H.*). *Grona*, leaves simple, pod linear, turgid. * *G. dalzellii* (*Galactia simplicifolia*, D.). A twiner, leaves ovate, flowers small, purple, in dense sessile heads, with bracts, pod straight, hairy. Talawári and Harichandra: known only to Dalzell and Stocks.

(*g*) Dalbergieæ.

41. Dalbergia.

1. *D. latifolia.* The blackwood tree. Leaflets 3 to 7, roundish, either with a small point or notched: flowers yellowish-white, in small close panicles, pod lanceolate. *Sissu, Kálaruk, táli.*

Common in the S. Konkan and S. M. country: also on the Ghauts.

The *Sissu* or *Shisham* of N. India is a different tree, D. Sissu. It may be met with cultivated in many parts, and is thought by *B.* to be indigenous in Guzerat.

2. *D. Sympathetica.* A very large climber, running over trees, with strong blunt thorns, often curiously twisted, leaflets 11 to 15, hairy, obovate or emarginate: flowers in very dense axillary panicles white and fragrant, pod oblong obtuse, short-stalked. *Pendkul, Titábli, yekyel.*

3. *D. volubilis.* Similar to the last in habit and leaves, branches round and green, panicles spreading, rather flat and hairy, with numerous floral leaves, flowers pale lilac, pod oblong, narrowed to a point, long-stalked. *Alei, Munganvel.*

These two are found in the Konkan and Ghauts.

There are two other climbers, * *D. Stocksii*, known only from Stocks's herbarium, leaflets 11 to 15, oblong, flowers in panicles large, "pod quite characteristic, thin, oblong, smooth, the usually solitary seed filling up the greater part." * *D. monosperma*, leaflets 5 to 7, unarmed, with black branches, flowers white, pod brown, crescent-shaped. *Garudgal.* Hills in Málwan district (*D.*). Matheran (*Birdwood*).

4. *D. paniculata.* A tree with light-grey smooth bark, leaflets 5 or 6 pair, ovate or obovate, flowers in large panicles tinged with blue, and with bright yellow pollen, calyx segments unequal, greenish-white, pod lanceolate pointed. *Pási, pádri.*

Mawal districts, Matheran, N. Konkan and Panchmahals; in the latter district it is a common and pretty tree, rather resembling the *Káranj.* It is deciduous, and the new leaves appear just after the flowers.

**D. lanceolaria.* A tree, leaflets 11 to 15, oval, panicles large, flowers larger than in other species, pale blue, pod lanceolate, bright-brown. *Dándus, gengri, haráni.*

42. Pterocarpus.

P. marsupium. A tree, leaflets 5 to 7, ovate, waved, panicles large, terminal, calyx large, white, 2-lipped, petals yellowish, pod with woody centre, and waved membranous wing. *Bibla, honi.*

Ghorabandar. Konkan, Dangs, and S. M. country (*D.*).

43. Pongamia.

P. glabra. Leaflets 5 to 7, ovate, smooth, rather large, flowers in axillary racemes, pale, deciduous, the standard large, calyx entire brown, pod more or less oval, with short beak, 1 or 2-seeded. *Káranj, Sukhchain.*

One of the commonest and handsomest trees in the Konkan: not seen with us at any distance from the coast. Extends to China, the Fiji Islands, and tropical Australia. Oil is extracted from the seeds.

44. Derris.

1. *D. scandens* (*Brachypterum s.* D.) A large and handsome climber, all smooth, leaflets about 11, oblong or lanceolate petioled, flowers like *Káranj* in long racemes, standard deeply divided, calyx brown, with 2 bracts, pod lanceolate pointed, with a narrow margin along the upper edge and 2 rather large seeds.

Konkan and Ghauts. Extending to Burmah, China, and N. Australia.

2. *D. uliginosa.* Smooth, leaflets 3 to 5, oval, rather blunt and fleshy, flowers small, pretty, pale rose-colour in small erect panicles, calyx reddish-brown, with shallow teeth, pod nearly round, veined, winged at the upper edge and with a hooked point.

Common in the Konkans near the sea: but found in other parts also apparently.

D. heyneana, smooth, woody, leaflets 3 to 7, oval entire, flowers very pretty, white or rose-colour, smaller than the last, calyx red, pods smooth, oblong, veined, winged on both edges. Párpoli Ghaut,

Konkan and Mysore (*H.*). * *D. canariensis* (*Brachypterum c.* D.). Woody, rather hairy, leaflets 15 to 21, flowers of a beautiful pink in 3's on racemes or panicles, pod oval, winged on both edges. Gersappa falls (*D.*), and no other authority. * *D. oblonga*, leaflets 9 to 15, racemes short and close, pod broad, 1-seeded. * *D. brevipes*, leaflets 5 to 7 obovate, flowers red in crowded panicles, pod broad oblong, silky. Both these found in the Konkan by Stocks.

Sophora (tribe *Sophoreæ*) stamens diadelphous, but almost free, corolla much exserted. * *S. Wightii* (*S. heptaphylla*, D.), Shrub, leaflets 11 to 17, margins recurved, flowers large yellow in lax racemes, calyx brown silky, pod leathery, much contracted between the seeds. Hills E. of Belgaum (*D.*). * *S. tomentosa*, common in gardens, an ornamental shrub, leaflets 15 to 19, flowers yellow in racemes, pod necklace-shaped.

II. SUB-ORDER CÆSALPINEÆ. Mostly trees or shrubs: flowers not papilionaceous, but the petals generally slightly unequal: stamens generally free, sometimes more than 10.

This sub-order contains many species of remarkable beauty, but the genera vary a good deal, so that it is difficult to mention any particular plant as typical.

(*a*) EUCÆSALPINEÆ. Leaves evenly bipinnate.

45. CÆSALPINIA. Prickly shrubs with showy yellow flowers, calyx deeply cleft, the lowest lobe largest and hooded, petals spreading.

46. MEZONEURUM. Woody and prickly climbers, calyx very oblique, lobes as in the last, petals spreading, pod large, thin and winged.

47. POINCIANA. Erect unarmed trees, differing from Cæsalpinia in having a valvate calyx of 5 equal segments.

48. WAGATEA. Flowers in long spikes, calyx with deep segments, the lowest the longest, pod thickened at the edges.

(*b*) CASSIEÆ. Leaves pinnate, calyx tube short.

49. CASSIA. Sometimes herbs, flowers rather large, yellow, some of the stamens often imperfect or obsolete, the petiole or midrib often with one or two conspicuous glands.

(*c*) AMHERSTIEÆ. Leaves evenly pinnate, disk at the top of a prolonged calyx tube.

50. SARACA. Corolla none, calyx coloured with 4 unequal segments, stamens 3 to 8, long exserted, pod flat, leathery.

51. TAMARINDUS. Petals 3, the upper hooded, stamens 3, monadelphous, the rest mere bristles, pod pulpy within.

(*d*) BAUHINEÆ. Leaves simple, deeply 2-lobed.

52. BAUHINIA. Flowers showy, petals generally clawed, stamens sometimes imperfect or absent, pod linear flat.

(*a*) EUCÆSALPINEÆ.

45. CÆSALPINIA.

1. *C. bonducella* (*Guilandina Bonduc*, D.). A large climber, pinnæ 4 to 8 pair, leaflets about 4 pair, smooth, oblong obtuse, flowers in racemes, each with a lanceolate bract, calyx rusty, pod ovate, swelling, very prickly, seeds 2, large. *Ságargota, Káchki, Karbat.*

Common in hedges: most so in Guzerat, I think.

"The fever nut widely spread throughout the tropics."—*Brandis.* "Rounded prickly pods, which, being opened, proved to contain the grey horse-nicker beads of our childhood."—*Kingsley.* "The seeds are so strongly coated with silex that they are said to strike fire like a flint."—*Tennant.*

2. *C. nuga* (*C. paniculata*, D.). Spreading smooth, thorns short and curved, pinnæ and leaflets 3 or 4 pair each, leaflets large, ovate shining above, flowers in terminal panicles fragrant, calyx lobes larger than the petals arising from a broad fleshy tube, pod brown, woody, irregularly oval, nearly flat, 1-seeded.

Tolerably common in the S. Konkan: always, I believe, growing near the sea or tidal creeks.

3. *C. sepiaria.* A similar shrub, pinnæ 6 to 10 pairs, leaflets 8 to 12 pairs, linear oblong obtuse, racemes large erect, calyx coloured, pod linear oblong smooth, with a long abrupt point, 4 to 8-seeded. *Chillar.*

Common in the Deccan. It forms an impenetrable fence, and was planted by Tippoo Ali round fortified places, and therefore (presumably) called Mysore thorn.

C. mimosoides, straggling or climbing, every part thorny and rusty, pinnæ 12 to 30 pair, leaflets 8 to 10 pair, flowers smaller than the last in long racemes, pod short, inflated with short recurved point. Rajapore. Wári jungles (*D.*).

Cæsalpinia pulcherrima (*Poinciana p.* D.). The common gold mohur tree, *Gulmohar.* The well-known flower fence of the W. Indies, also called "Barbadoes pride." *C. coriaria* is the *libi* or *dividivi* tree, cultivated for the pods, which are used in tanning. **C. sappan* produces the valuable wood sappan, and the dye *gulál*: said to be found in gardens. Other species produce what is called Brazil wood.

46. MEZONEURUM.

M. cucullatum. An immense thorny climber, with large leaves of about 4 pinnæ, and 3 pairs of leaflets, both stalked; leaflets oval pointed, smooth and shining, flowers small, yellowish-green in racemes or panicles, calyx as large as the corolla, upper petals fleshy, dark, hooded, pod leafy, 1-seeded, with wing exactly similar to the pod itself. *Rági.*

Common on the highest Ghauts (*D.*). Matheran (*Birdwood*). I have seen it only at Lanoli. Its great size and peculiar calyx make it remarkable. *H.* has a variety in which the leaflets are 3 or 4 inches long.

47. Poinciana.

P. elata. A tree with 10 to 16 pinnæ and 30 to 40 leaflets, flowers in racemes white, changing to yellow, with long dark filaments, pod several inches long. *Sandesrá.*

Gardens (*G.* and *D.*), but *H.* calls it wild in the W. Peninsula.

P. regia is the large flowered *gulmohar*, one of the trees which make Bombay compounds so beautiful in the cold weather, called by the French in the W. Indies "Fleur de Paradis." It is planted along the roads at Batavia (*Forbes*), and I have also heard of it as one of the beauties of Nassau in the Bahamas.

Parkinsonia is closely allied to this genus, but has a necklace-shaped pod. *P. aculeata* is a very common thorny shrub, with yellow flowers, without admixture of red: the leaflets fall very soon, and leave a large rachis like the phyllodes in some acacias. Native of tropical America. *Vilagatibábul, Kesribábul.*

48. Wagatea.

W. spicata. A small thorny shrub, sometimes slightly climbing, pinnæ and leaflets 5 to 7 pair, leaflets oblong obtuse, flowers very handsome in close erect spikes, the calyx scarlet, petals orange, pod red, much swollen at the seeds. *Wagáti, wákiri, wámera.*

Ghauts and S. Konkan. Tolerably common and very noticeable from the length and elegant shape of the spikes.

(*b*) Cassieæ.

49. Cassia. Senna.

1. *C. Fistula.* Tree, leaflets 4 to 8 pair, large ovate, pointed smooth, flowers in long drooping racemes, stamens perfect, but the anthers of 2 or 3 larger than the rest, pod perfectly cylindrical, brown, smooth, from 1 to 2 feet long. *Báwa, garmála, chimkani.*

The Ghauts and Konkan. Common throughout the forest tracts of India (*B.*).

One of the most noticeable of jungle trees, the flowers like "laburnum, rich in streaming gold," to which the Germans give the beautiful name of "Golden rain." But the pods, which are little less remarkable, are said to have procured for the tree the less romantic name of "pudding pipe tree." The medicinal cassia comes from the pulp surrounding the seeds. *Suvarna* of Sanscrit poetry.

(*a*) Stamens 7 perfect, the rest without anthers.

2. *C. occidentalis.* A large smooth annual, leaflets 3 to 5 pair, ovate lanceolate acute, leaf with one large gland close to the petiole, flowers long-stalked, the upper ones racemed, pod long, thin, nearly cylindric. *Thorala tákla, Kásoda, Kasumdro, Kochinda.*

Abundant nearly everywhere, springing up very quickly in the rains, generally with *Tephrosia purpurea.* It has a strong and offensive smell, and is in every way the greatest contrast to the last. *H.* gives the petals as pale lilac, and says it was probably introduced. In W. Africa, as with us, "it thrives in wild and stinking luxuriance," and is there called "Negro coffee," the seeds both of this and of *C. tora,* roasted and ground, making very good coffee, and being quite harmless.—*Moloney.*

3. *C. sophora.* A smooth shrub, leaflets 6 to 12 pair, lanceolate, gland as in the last, pod more swollen, particularly towards the top, many-seeded.

Common: closely allied to the last, and known by the same names. Cosmopolitan in the tropics (*H.*).

4. *C. tora.* A shrubby plant of the same general appearance as the two last, leaflets about 3 pair, obovate, with glands between the leaflets, pod very long and slender, 4-sided, sharp-pointed. *Tákla, tarwatá.*

Common: universally spread through our limits (*H.*).

5. *C. auriculata.* A shrub, leaflets 8 to 12 pair, oval obtuse, glands as in the last, stipules large, leafy, obliquely cordate, flowers large and showy in racemes, pod thin, strap-shaped, brown, few-seeded. *Tarwad, áwal.*

Common in the Deccan and Guzerat.

"The Singhalese pull the twigs and hold them in their hands, or apply them to their heads for the coolness which they diffuse: and they use the leaves in the S. of the island as a substitute for tea."—*Tennant.*

(*b*) Stamens 5 to 10, all perfect.

6. *C. absus.* A hairy plant about a foot high, the stems often reddish, petioles long, leaflets 2 pair oval, unequal-sided; flowers solitary or in a short raceme, pale yellow, with one bract at the base and two half way up the pedicel, pod nearly straight, strap-shaped, bristly, few-seeded. *Chimar, Chaken.*

Everywhere in the tropics of the old world (*H.*). It is very common both at Bandora and Dápoli, and I believe elsewhere, and is a very distinct species: but strange to say, neither *D.* nor *G.* have it. The leaves are said to be purgative, as are those of several other species, and the seeds are used in Egypt to cure chronic ophthalmia.

7. *C. pumila.* A low or procumbent plant, leaflets 10 to 30 pair, very small, unequal-sided, with a smooth gland between the lowest pair, flowers one to three together above the axils, pod flat linear. *Sarmal.*

Common generally.

C. Kleinii, like the last, but more robust, downy or hairy, leaflets four pairs or more, pod linear, broader at the top. Bandora. Not in *D.* * *C. obovata* (*C. senna*, D.). Tall, nearly smooth plant, leaflets 4 to 6 pair, without glands, very glaucous, flowers pale yellow in erect racemes, pod much curved. *Mendi ál.* Guzerat, E. Deccan and Sind (*D.*). * *C. Montana.* Shrub or small tree, leaflets 10 to 15 pair, bristle-pointed, without glands, flowers in long panicles, pod linear straight. Ghauts (*D.*).

The following are cultivated: *C. glauca*, a tree with a heavy smell, *Kárud*: wild all over India (*D.*). *C. augustifolia*, a shrub, produces the drug senna, *sona mukhi*; nowhere wild in India (*H.*). *C. sumatrana*, a handsome tree, Kásod, *Siras.*

Note.—For the bark Cassia see under Cinnamonum. *Cynometra*, flowers minute, pod turgid, oblique. * *C. ramiflora*, shrub or tree, leaflets 1 to 3 pair, oblong, oblique, racemes few flowered, sessile on the branches, pod fleshy, nearly semicircular, warty. Konkan, very rare (*D.*). Gardens, Bombay (*G.*).

Hardwickia, flowers minute, calyx with scarcely any tube, corolla none. * *H. binata*, a tree, leaflets oblique, two, flowers greenish-yellow in racemes, pod strap-shaped with one seed at the top. *Anjan.* Khandesh, Nimar and Central India.

(*c*) AMHERSTIEÆ.

50. SARACA.

S. Indica (*Jonesia Asoka*, D.) A small tree, leaflets 3 to 6 pair, flowers orange-coloured changing to red, in large round heads, calyx tube long, stamens long, rising from the edge of the calyx tube, bracts peduncles and pedicels coloured, pod broad, flat, straight or scimitar shaped, 8 to 10-seeded. *Ashoka, jásondi, asupálá.*

Konkan and Ghauts: not very common.

No one looking at the flowers would suspect that this was a leguminous tree. Sir W. Jones found the stamens to vary from 6 to 9, even in flowers from the same tree, and thought that no part of the plant is constant. He says, " The vegetable world scarce exhibits a richer sight than the Ashoka tree in full bloom," which is rather higher praise than any specimen I have seen deserves. He hoped that botanists would retain the Sanscrit name Ashoka, " as it perpetually occurs in the old Indian poems and treatises on religious rites;" and the Indian botanists of the last century improved on this suggestion by naming the genus after " the most enlightened of the sons of men " himself;[1] thus making the tree Jonesia Asoka. But

[1] Sir W. Jones was so called by Dr. Johnson.

the Indian Flora has made short work of this pleasing sentiment, and the present name is as commonplace as those of most other beautiful trees.

51. TAMARINDUS. Tamarind.

T. Indica. Leaflets very numerous, obtuse, flowers few together in lax racemes, pale yellow, beautifully streaked with red, pod thick, more or less curved. *Chinch, amli.*

Very common: but a doubtful native of India (*H.*). Though the flowers are not conspicuous they are exceedingly beautiful when examined; and in favourable districts, as the Konkan and Guzerat, this is by shape and foliage one of the noblest of trees. The W. Indian Tamarind is a different, but closely allied species.

(*d*) BAUHINIEÆ.

52. BAUHINIA. Mountain ebony.

Note.—This genus has leaves of a shape almost unique, nearly circular, but divided into two equal lobes from the top, sometimes close down to the petiole.

1. *B. racemosa.* A small crooked tree, leaves deeply divided, flowers in racemes yellow or white small, calyx spathulate split on one side, stamens 10, all fertile, pod linear, woody, thick, seeds oval, brown. *Apta, ásandra, wanrája.*

Common in most parts of India.

2. *B. Vahlii.* A very large climber with large leaves downy beneath, divided not far down, but deeply cordate, flowers large white, in long-stalked racemes, fertile stamens 3 to 5, pods very long and thin, rusty and downy, 8 to 12-seeded. *Chámbuli, máwali.*

Common in some parts of the Konkan and Ghauts, but I have seen it only in the palm house at Kew. The leaves are large enough to be used as plates, and the right to collect them is (or was) sold in the Colaba collectorate.

* *B. lawii*, a climber, leaves deeply cordate, not deeply lobed, racemes dense, downy, stigma large peltate. * *B. diphylla*, a smooth twiner with curled tendrils, flowers large, pod many-seeded. These two are attributed by *H.* to the Konkan, but very insufficiently described. *B. malabarica*, shrub or small tree, leaves slightly cordate, not deeply lobed, flowers large, creamy white, stamens all fertile, alternately shorter, pod long-stalked, slightly falcate. *Kánchan, Koral, amli.* Matheran (*Birdwood*); W. Ghauts (*Brandis*).

In gardens *B. purpurea, devkanchan, atmáti*, flowers large, deep rose-colour, and *B. variegata, Kanchan*, flowers white or variegated with red or yellow. *B.* calls them wild in most parts of India.

SUB-ORDER III. MIMOSEÆ.

Leaves (in all here given) bipinnate, flowers very small but many together, petals regular, usually united above the base.

Note.—There is a great general resemblance between the many species of this sub-order, so that anyone who knows any of the Acacias would be able to recognize without much difficulty most of the species here mentioned as belonging to the family.

(*a*) MIMOSEÆ. Stamens generally 10.

53. NEPTUNIA. Herbs with flowers in dense round heads or spikes, stamens exserted.

54. XYLIA. A tree with flowers in round heads and large woody pod.

55. ENTADA. Woody climbers with tendrils, calyx minute, pod very large, jointed outwardly.

56. ADENANTHERA. Trees, pod strap-shaped, swelling at the seeds.

57. PROSOPIS. Prickly trees or shrubs, pod turgid, spongy inside.

58. DICHROSTACHYS. Prickly shrubs, the lower flowers of the spike with long staminodes, pod strap-shaped, indehiscent.

59. MIMOSA. Shrubs or herbs with sensitive leaflets, flowers in dense round heads, pod flat and jointed.

(*b*) ACACIEÆ. Stamens indefinite, much exserted.

60. ACACIA. Prickly shrubs or trees with yellow or white flowers in round heads or cylindrical spikes; stamens free, pod various.

61. ALBIZZIA. Large unarmed trees, flowers in round heads, stamens united at the base several times as long as the corolla, pod long, thin, strap-shaped.

(*a*) MIMOSEÆ.

53. NEPTUNIA.

N. triquetra. Prostrate, creeping, with flattened sometimes angular stems, and occasional small thorns, pinnæ 2 to 3 pair, leaflets 8 to 15 pair, oblong obtuse, heads of flowers on very long stalks which have one or two bracts half way up. Corolla green or yellow, staminodes of lower flowers bright yellow, pod linear, very thin.

This is abundant in ditches and pastures at Surat, which is the only habitat given by either *D.* or *G. H.* has W. peninsula and Bandalkand. It is not an aquatic plant, though growing in moist places.

N. oleracea, floating, pinnæ 2 to 3 pair, leaflets 8 to 15 pair, obtuse, stipules obliquely cordate, flowers in spikes, pod oblique, very thin. Tanks in the Konkan (*D.*).

54. XYLIA.

X. dolabriformis. Tree with whitish bark, pinnæ 2, with a gland between, looking like separate leaves, leaflets 4 to 10, lanceolate large, with a gland between each pair, flower-heads size of a gooseberry, greenish, fragant, pod very hard, five or six inches long. *Jámba, yeral, suria.*

S. Konkan and Canara. The white filaments with yellow anthers, and the pod, curved and widening at the end, are very noticeable.

55. ENTADA.

E. scandens (*E. pursætha*, D.). An immense woody climber, the main stem often with a spiral wing, pinnæ one or two pair, leaflets 2 to 5 pair, ovate or obovate, spikes erect, axillary about six inches long; flowers white, becoming yellow; pod a yard long, hard and woody, reddish-brown, seeds nearly round, about two inches in diameter. *Gárbi, Kárdal, Khairi.*

The Ghauts and Konkan hills.

The flowers of this may often be seen so high up as to be quite inaccessible; a difficulty which very commonly troubles botanists in great tropical forests. The immense jointed pods must be known to many who have never seen the tree. The seeds are both eatable and medicinal.

Called in Ceylon 'the great hollow creeper'; the pods sometimes five feet long and six inches broad, the seeds used as tinder boxes when hollowed out.—*Tennant.*

56. ADEMANTHERA.

A. pavonina. Pinnæ 4 to 6 pair, leaflets 6 to 9 pair, flowers in pretty yellow spikes, pod long, curved, seeds scarlet, large. *Thorala ganj.* Sanscrit, *Kuchandana.*

Khandesh and Guzerat (*B.*).

The seeds are used as goldsmiths' weights and made into necklaces.

57. PROSOPIS.

P. spicigera. A tree with short stout thorns, branches very drooping, foliage small and pale, pinnæ 1 to 3 pair, leaflets 8 to 12 pair, linear obtuse, smooth, flowers yellow in long slender spikes, several together, very pretty; pods slender, cylindrical or contracted between the seeds. *Sumri, shema, kandi, saundar.*

Guzerat, Cutch and Sind, common: less so in the Deccan and N. Konkan. The pulp is eatable.

58. Dichrostachys.

* *D. cinerea.* A pretty thorny shrub, pinnæ 5 to 10 pair, leaflets 12 to 20 pair, strap-shaped, flowers yellow in drooping cylindric spikes, the staminodes conspicuous, red, pod partly jointed. *Sigamkáti.*

Common in the Deccan (*D.* and *G.*). Cutch.

59. Mimosa.

M. hamata. A thorny shrub, pinnæ 3 to 5 pair, leaflets 6 to 10 pair, oval or oblong; heads of flowers pink, long-stalked, pod curved with a border on each edge, and large hooked prickles. *Arkar.*

Deccan, Guzerat, and Cutch: pretty common.

M. rubricaulis, closely allied to this, but flowers reddish, becoming white, pod longer and thinner; Malabar Hill (*D.* and *G*). E. Deccan. *Arái.*

M. pudica, lájálu lájári, generally called the sensitive plant, is said by *H.* to be spread through the hotter parts of India, possibly introduced from tropical America. Often cultivated on account of the sensitive leaves,

> "For the sensitive plant has no bright flower,
> Radiance and odour are not its dower."—*Shelley.*

"Some sensitive plants were formerly called 'humble plants,' because not only the leaflets close, but the whole leaf bends down."—*Martyn.*

"One of the Mimosas drops its branches whenever any person approaches, seeming as if it saluted those who retire under its shade. This mute hospitality has so endeared the tree to the Arabians that the injuring or cutting of it down is strictly prohibited."—*Niebuhr.*

To this tribe belongs *Parkia biglandulosa, chenduphul*, a striking and beautiful garden tree, but not very common, the flowers forming large balls, like brown velvet when in bud, hanging down from a long stalk.

(*b*) Acacieæ.

60. Acacia.

Note.—Most or all of the species have glands on the petiole, or between the pinnæ, or both, but they do not seem constant enough in number or position to make it necessary to describe them.

(*a*) Flowers in round heads, thorns straight.

1. *A. Arabica.* A tree with white thorns, pinnæ 2 to 6 pair, leaflets 10 to 20 pair, linear nearly smooth, heads of flowers yellow, fragrant, stalked, with broad membranous bracts half way down the peduncle; pod flat, linear, downy, depressed between the seeds. *Bábul.*

This well-known tree is common in most parts except near the coast, as it, like the majority of the genus, is essentially a tree of dry regions. Covered with dust in the hot weather it is not a lovely object to the traveller, "thirsting in a land of sand and thorns," but under favourable conditions its beauty is undeniable. *A. Farnesiana* (*Vachellia F.* D.), *Eri bábul, guya bábul, Kankar*, closely resembles this except that the pod is short, thick, cylindrical and pulpy inside. It is a doubtful native, but common in the Deccan, Cutch and Sind.

A. Arabica and some other species yield gum arabic, and other sorts used in medicine :

"One whose subued eyes
Drop tears as fast as the Arabian trees
Their medicinable gum."—*Othello.*

"The shittim tree of Scripture is without doubt one of the acacias, and A. Arabica may be included in the name."—*Dict. of Bible.*

* *A. eburnea*, also very like the *bábul*, but with fewer leaflets, and a very narrow flat pod ; flowers golden-yellow : *Marmat*, Deccan (*D.*). *Rámkânta*, which *D.* calls a var. of the *bábul*, is a tall broom-like tree, with close ascending branches. I have not identified it in *H.*

2. *A. leucophlæa.* A tree with strong twin thorns on the young parts, pinnæ 6 to 12 pair, leaflets 15 to 30 pair, blunt, very small ; the small heads of pale yellow flowers are in large panicles, which distinguishes it from the rest : pod linear, sometimes curved, hairy, about 15-seeded. *Hewar, nimbar, pándhari bábul.*

Khandesh, E. Deccan, S. M. country and Cutch.

(*b*) Flowers in stalked axillary spikes.

3. *A. Suma* (*A. catechu*, D.). A small tree with white bark and hooked thorns in pairs, pinnæ 10 to 20 pair, leaflets 30 to 50 pair, flowers white, calyx very downy, pod strap-shaped, straight, 6 to 8-seeded. *Khair, Khaderi.*

This is the common species in the Konkan as the *bábul* is in the drier parts. It is a delicate-looking and pretty tree. From this chiefly, *Káth* is made from which the Konkan tribe of Kathkaries get their name. *A. Sundra, lálkhair, H.* calls scarcely more than a variety of this, but it is generally with us a much larger tree, has dark bark, a hairy calyx, and narrower and thinner pods. It is common in the Deccan.

4. **A. ferruginea* also closely resembles *A. suma*, but is a large tree with dark bark, thorns sometimes absent, flowers yellow, pod dark-brown, smooth, the upper edge narrowly winged. *Kaigar.*

5. *A. latronum.* A shrub or small tree, bark dark, spotted with white, thorns very large, white and straight, united at the base ; pinnæ 2 to 5 pair, leaflets 6 to 15 pair, minute, linear, flowers white, turning yellow, fragrant, pod oblong, thin, flat and curved, 2 to 4-seeded. *Bhes, devbábul.*

Common in the barren parts of the Deccan. Often gregarious, forming formidable thorny thickets (*B.*). I have not seen it, but am consoled by finding it called, by a botanist who had, "frutex horridissimus." It is the buffalo thorn of Ceylon.

(*c*) Large climbing shrubs with round heads of flowers in panicles.

6. *A. concinna.* Prickles numerous, hooked, pinnæ 4 to 8 pair, leaflets 12 to 25 pair, oblong, oblique, smooth, stipules and bracts ovate cordate, panicles very downy, flowers yellow or white, fragrant, pod strap-shaped, thick and succulent, contracted between the seeds. *Chikakai.*

Common in the Konkan and Ghauts. The legumes are sold and used as soap, &c.

A. Intsia, stout and straggling, with small curved prickles, pinnæ and leaflets much like the above, flowers white, pod smooth, dark red or purple, very thin. *Nitári.* Dápoli. Cambay and Ankaleshwar (*D.*). Konkan and Ghauts (*H.*). *H.* has 2 vars., one of which is *D.*'s * *A. cæsia*, pinnæ and leaflets more numerous, but not so many as the next.

7. *A. pennata.*—Thorns straight or slightly curved, pinnæ 8 to 20 pair, leaflets 30 to 50 pair, narrow, linear, smooth, flowers yellow, pod straight, strap-shaped, thin, smooth or with reddish down. *Shembi.*

Common in the Konkan. The bark is used for dyeing nets.

Note.—The so-called Acacia tree in England is *Robinia pseudo-acacia.*

Note.—There are a number of Australian species of Acacia, which have no leaflets, but only a flattened and enlarged petiole, called a phyllode. This may easily be taken for a simple narrow leaf. Some of these phyllodineous Acacias are said to have been introduced in S. India.

61. Albizzia.

1. *A. lebbek.* Pinnæ 2 to 4 pair, leaflets 4 to 9 pair, oblong, very obtuse, unequal-sided, flowers white, very fragrant, in large long-stalked heads and irregularly racemed; pod nearly a foot long, smooth, straw-coloured, seeds flat oval, with a horse-shoe depression. *Siras, farári, hareri.*

Common in the Konkan and elsewhere. Widely spread over the globe, except in Europe.

This is the *Sirisha* of Sanscrit poetry:—

> "Fair maids, the chosen of their hearts to please,
> Entwine their ears with sweet Sirisha flowers."
>
> *Sakuntala* (Sir M. Williams' transl.).

2. *A. procera.* (*Acacia p.* D.) Bark light, pinnæ 3 to 6 pair, leaflets 6 to 12 pair, oblique, oblong, smooth, flowers yellow in round heads panicled, pod pointed, 8 inches long, red and leafy, seeds small oval. *Kinai, kilai, gurár.*

Konkan, Ghauts and E. Guzerat.

3. *A. stipulata.* Pinnæ 6 to 20 pair, leaflets 20 to 40 pair, very narrow unequal-sided, stipules large acute reddish flowers in panicles, the heads many-flowered, the long brush-like stamens are pink in the upper half, pod flat, reddish-brown, smooth. *Shembar, lallei, udal.*

Ghauts and S. Konkan. This is a most beautiful flat-topped tree, and grows in perfection at Matheran. I have seen it also in full bloom in gardens in N. Italy. It must surely almost bear comparison with trees

"Crowning the glorious hills of Paradise."—*Wordsworth.*

* *A. amara*, generally downy, pinnæ 4 to 11 pair, leaflets 20 to 40 pair, very narrow, flowers yellow in heads, pod opaque, grey-brown. *Lallei.* Mahableshwar (*D.*). Deccan, Lisboa.

* *A. odoratissima.* Like *A. procera*, but leaflets and heads of flowers more numerous, flowers small pale yellow, pods shorter and broader with thickened margins. *Rán siras, sirsa.* Konkan (*D.* and *G.*). Panch Mahals (*Brandis*).

To this tribe belongs *Pithecolobium dulcis* (Inga d. *D.*), a widely-spread tropical tree, but introduced into India, and freely planted about Bombay and elsewhere. It has drooping branches and very small white flowers in small round long-stalked heads, pods twisted into 2 or 3 coils, full of a white edible pulp. It is generally called *Viláyati chinch.*

P. bigeminum, an unarmed tree, pinnæ one or two pair, leaflets two or three pair, ovate pointed, heads few-flowered in irregular panicles, flowers white, silky, pod in one or two coils. *Káchlora.* S. Konkan (*D.*), but doubtfully wild.

ORDER 43. **ROSACEÆ.** The Rose family.

Leaves alternate with stipules, flowers regular, calyx 4 or 5-lobed or more, petals 5, inserted under the margin of the disk; stamens indefinite, perigynous; ovary of one or more carpels, generally separate.

This great, important, and well-known order of temperate regions is but very slightly represented in W. India, but it is as well to describe it at some length, on account of the many fruits, which are cultivated more or less in this country, but come to perfection only in cooler climates.

In *H.* the order is divided into nine tribes, but considering the few species we have it seems sufficient to give the simpler division of Lindley, which is followed by Bentham in his English Botany, and by Oliver.

1. *Roseæ.* Carpels several, distinct from each other and from the calyx. This tribe, besides the many roses (Rosa), includes the strawberry (Fragaria), the raspberry and blackberry (Rubus), and the well-known garden flowers Spiræa, Potentilla, &c.

2. *Pomeæ.* Calyx superior, ovaries one to five, more or less adherent to the calyx and to each other; fruit containing about five seeds in separate cells in the centre (endocarp), surrounded by a thick fleshy mass (epicarp and mesocarp). This fruit, which is crowned by the calyx segments, is called a pome, from poma, an apple, which is the best type of the fruit. The pear, quince, mountain ash, and hawthorn, also belong to this tribe.

3. *Amygdaleæ.* Calyx inferior, carpel solitary, fruit a drupe. To this belong the almond, cherry, plum, peach, apricot, sloe, etc.

The first of the two genera given below belongs to the third tribe, the second to the first.

1. Pygeum. Evergreen trees or shrubs: flowers small in racemes, calyx 5 to 10, toothed, petals minute or none, filaments slender, incurved.

2. Rubus. Prickly and straggling shrubs, carpels many on a convex receptacle, fruit of many fleshy one-seeded carpels crowded on a conical receptacle.

1. Pygeum.

P. Gardneri (*P. zeylanicum* D.) A fine tree with large oval long-pointed smooth leaves, calyx yellowish-white, stamens 12, short, fruit broader than long of 2 round lobes, smooth, size of a small plum, long-stalked.

Mahableshwar.

2. Rubus. Bramble.

R. lasiocarpus. A large shrub, stems smooth glaucous, prickles curved, leaves digitate, leaflets 5 to 7 pleated oval, serrated, white beneath, flowers in terminal racemes red, fruit in appearance between a mulberry and a raspberry, hairy, black when ripe. *Gauriphal.*

This appears to be the sort called country raspberry, found, as are the two following, at Mahableshwar and on the highest Ghauts. *H.* calls it very variable. * *R. moluccanus* (*R. rugosus*, D.), prickles small, leaves cordate, 3 to 5-lobed, downy beneath, stipules jagged, petals white, shorter than the calyx, fruit small round, red or black. Very variable (*H.*). * *R. ellipticus* (*R. Wallichianus*, D.) nearly erect with short hooked prickles and dense brown hairs all over, leaves trifoliate, leaflets roundish, petals white, fruit round, yellow.

The strawberry is *Fragaria elatior;* the almond tree, *badám, Prunus amygœalus;* the peach tree, *P. persica.* These are all cultivated in the Deccan, as well as various roses. *Eriobotrya japanica* is the loquat tree, sometimes found in gardens, a fruit very common in the S. of Europe, and well worthy of careful cultivation.

ORDER 44. SAXIFRAGEÆ. Saxifrages.

Flowers quite regular, sepals and petals 4 or 5, stamens as many or double the number, ovary of two or more carpels, fruit a capsule with minute seeds.

This order comes near to Rosaceæ, but differs by the carpels and definite stamens. Most of the species are herbs of mountainous and temperate regions. Besides the single wild species given below, we have in gardens in India, as in the south of England, Hydrangea hortensis. Currants and gooseberries (genus Ribes) also belong to this order, according to the most modern arrangement.

VAHLIA. Herbs with opposite entire leaves, calyx tube quite adherent to the ovary and afterwards to the capsule, calyx lobes, petals, and stamens 5 each, styles 2, seeds numerous.

V. viscosa. A small common-looking leafy plant, hairy and slightly glutinous, leaves sessile, oval, lanceolate, flowers yellow or white in pairs, almost sessile, or terminal aggregated, calyx larger than the petals, capsule and calyx nearly round.

The Konkans and Guzerat.

The large ovary covered by the tubular calyx is the noticeable feature of this plant. *H.* says that both Oldenlandia and Mitreola may easily be mistaken for this when in fruit, and that the leaves of this often have a connecting line as if falsely stipulate.

ORDER 45. CRASSULACEÆ. Stone crops.

Herbs or undershrubs, usually having fleshy stems and leaves, calyx with 4 to 8 divisions, petals and carpels as many, stamens as many or double, fruit of two or more follicles.

The remarkable fleshy habit and the exact regularity of the flowers are the chief characteristics of this order, many species of which remain green in the most arid countries. The house leek (Sempervivum) which grows on the roofs of English cottages, and the many garden Sedums, generally preferring rocks and walls to softer beds, belong to this order.

In the two genera here given the corolla is monopetalous.

1. BRIOPHYLLUM. Tall erect herbs with opposite crenate leaves, flowers large, drooping, calyx and corolla tubular about

the same length, 4-divided, stamens 8, carpels narrowed into a long style; follicles 4.

2. KALANCHOE. Stout erect herbs with erect flowers, corolla much longer than the calyx, follicles membranous, many-seeded, otherwise like the last.

1. BRIOPHYLLUM.

B. calycinum (*Kalanchoe pinnata*, D.) Stem red and thick, leaves simple, ovate or 3-partite, crenated and dark-edged; flowers in terminal panicles, yellowish-red and purple, calyx inflated enclosing the fruit. *Gháyál, gháipál, parnabij, pánphui.*

This very strange-looking plant is very common in gardens, but grows wild in the S. Konkan and at Mahableshwar, and is said to be common near Belgaum and the Ramghaut, and to grow throughout the tropics of the world (*H.*). Buds are formed in the edges of the leaves, from which young plants are produced.

2. KALANCHOE.

1. *K. brasiliensis* (*K. olivacea*, D.). Of a pale olive colour all over, stem spotted with red, leaves ovate or broad lanceolate, unequally crenated, pedicels, calyx and flowers glandular, viscid and hairy, calyx divided to the base, corolla tube swelled at the base, segments ovate pointed, pink, carpels narrow upwards.

The above is my description of a remarkable-looking plant which I found at Singarh growing on the rocks, and *D.* at two or three other hill forts. The above identification was made at Kew, but *H.'s* description does not agree very well with my plant or *D.'s*.

2. * *K. glandulosa* (*K. Ritchieana*, D.). Stem thick, the upper part glandular, leaves oblong obovate, stem clasping, racemes panicled, corolla much longer than the calyx.

Between Belgaum and Sholapore (*D.*).

*** *K. laciniata*, leaves pinnatifid or deeply gashed, coarsely toothed, flowers yellow, pretty in panicles. Hills about Dharwar, and Pandugarh (*D.*).**

Tillæa, petals free or connate. * *T. pentandra*, a small smooth herb, stem creeping, branched, leaves lanceolate flat, flowers white axillary. Not in *D.* Konkan, *Stocks*.

ORDER 46. DROSERACEÆ. Sun dews.

Small herbs, more or less covered with glandular sticky hairs, the young leaves and flower stems curled inwards like ferns; flowers regular, sepals, petals and stamens 4 or 5 each, styles 3 to 5, capsule valves as many, seeds many.

H. calls this small order one quite by itself, but some authorities make it a tribe of Saxifrageæ. The stamens he calls almost hypogynous. The curious glandular hairs on the leaves is the great outward distinction; "the clammy sundew's glistening glands" being a fatal trap to small flies. Three species are known in Europe.

DROSERA. As the order.

1. *D. Burmanii.* Stemless, a good deal tinged with red, leaves radical crowded nearly flat on the ground, wedge-shaped or obovate, flowers on a slender scape in a one-sided raceme white, sepals red, pointed, styles 5, undivided.

2. *D. Indica.* Stem three or four inches high, simple or branched, leaves alternate linear, fringed with long hairs; flowers in racemes red or pink, styles 3 bifid to the base.

I have had these at Dápoli and one or two other places in the Rutnagherry collectorate, and they seem not to occur out of the Konkan in this Presidency, though *H.* gives them a wide range in India.

ORDER 47. HALORAGEÆ.

Small plants, often aquatic, with small and inconspicuous flowers, calyx lobes and petals 4 or none, stamens 8, 4 or 1, ovary inferior, styles 4, 2 or 1.

This is the order to which the Mare's tails of English ponds and ditches belong, and is neither interesting, beautiful, nor useful. In many cases the flowers are, as to some of their parts, quite rudimentary.

MYRIOPHYLLUM. Herbs with floating stem and whorled leaves, flowers small, sessile or nearly so.

* *M. Indicum* (*M. tetrandum*, D.) A small water plant, leaves narrow lanceolate, the lower ones divided into many hair-like segments, flowers white, solitary in the axils, upper male, lower female; all parts of the flower 4, but styles sometimes 2.

Common in tanks (*D.* and *G.*). This is the only species of W. India, although by some authorities Trapa has been put in the order.

ORDER 48. RHIZOPHOREÆ. Mangroves.

Trees or shrubs, usually but not always, growing in the salt mud of tidal rivers, leaves opposite smooth, with stipules (except one tribe not here mentioned), flowers regular, calyx variously lobed, petals as many, stamens usually double as many: fruit crowned by the calyx, one-seeded.

The true mangroves are known by the remarkable way in which the seed germinates and is thrust down into the salt-water mud. But the order also contains forest trees with no special peculiarity, one of which is given below.

1. RHIZOPHORA. Calyx lobes 4, petals 4 entire, disk fleshy, stamens 8, stigma bifid. The radicle of the seed pierces through the apex of the fruit before the fruit drops.

2. BRUGUIERA. Petals 8 to 14 bifid, embracing the stamens, anthers about as long as the filaments; ovary included in the calyx tube: germination as in the last.

3. CARALLIA. Jungle trees, calyx lobes 5 to 8, petals as many on the edge of a finely crenated disk, clawed, roundish, stamens inserted with the petals, fruit round, one-seeded, germinating in the usual way.

1. RHIZOPHORA.

R. mucronata. A small tree or large shrub, leaves ovate with a long sudden point, fleshy, veinless, chiefly about the ends of the branches, flowers white, fragrant, calyx yellowish, segments triangular, anthers large, erect, radicle nearly cylindrical, pointed. *Kándal, hariya.*

Very common along the coast S. of Bombay, where many of the creeks have a broad belt of mangrove swamp. The radicles, nearly a foot long, are washed up in quantities all along the beach. (*Brandis* says they are often 2½ feet long). This is often called 'the black mangrove.' These radicles would naturally be taken for the fruit, but they should be examined while still upon the tree.

"The sea-loving mangrove with its sickening ooze, and fantastic centipedal roots."—*H. M. Stanley.*

"The aerial roots, as they are called, which are also seen in Pandanus, often raise the main trunk much above its original level, and give the tree the appearance of being supported upon stalks."—*Balfour.*

"As far as the eye could pierce into the tangled thicket, the roots interlaced with each other, and arched down into the water in innumerable curves by no means devoid of grace, but hideous just because they were impenetrable."—*Kingsley.*

2. BRUGUIERA.

B. parviflora (*Kanilia p.* D.). Like the last, but smaller every way, leaves blunt or obovate, flowers in nearly sessile clusters, small, greenish, calyx segments and petals 6 or 8, radicle like the last, but smaller.

Found in similar situations, but not nearly so common.

* *B. gymnorhiza.* A similar tree, with large red solitary flowers. *Kánkra.* Also said to be common on the coast.

Note.—Oliver speaks of this genus as having a 12-lobed calyx.

The name mangrove (Mar. *tivar*) is popularly applied to many shrubs and trees growing along the shore, as well as to those of this order. (See Lumnitzera, Avicennia, Sonneratia, Exæcaria.)

3. Carallia.

C. integerrima. A small tree with ovate or obovate polished leaves, flowers very small white in trifid stiff peduncles; fruit in clusters, red, soft, like cranberries. *Fansi, ranfannus.*

The Ghauts, Matheran, &c.

In the younger trees the leaves are often serrated, in the older quite entire, and otherwise very variable.

Order 49. COMBRETACEÆ.

Trees or shrubs: leaves simple entire without stipules, calyx tubular, segments 4 or 5, petals as many or none, stamens double as many, on the calyx, ovary altogether inferior, fruit a drupe often prominently winged, one-seeded.

This order contains in genus *Terminalia* some of the commonest and most useful trees of W. India. In most of the species found here the flowers are small, white or pale coloured, and the fruit in masses much more conspicuous.

(*a*) Petals none.

1. Terminalia. Trees, leaves with glands at the back of the leaf, on or just above the petiole, flowers in spikes or racemes, stamens 10, fruit sometimes winged.

2. Calycopteris. A diffuse shrub, calyx segments 5, stamens 10 in 2 series, fruit ovoid, crowned with the enlarged calyx.

3. Anogeissus. Flowers in dense round heads, calyx segments 5, stamens as in the last, fruit 2-winged, aggregated into heads.

(*b*) Calyx segments and petals 4 or 5.

4. Lumnitzera. Salt marsh trees like mangroves, leaves entire, stamens 10 or less, fruit woody, crowned with the calyx.

5. Combretum. Large shrubs more or less climbing, fruit with 4 or 5 wings, angles, or ridges.

1. Terminalia.

Note.—The leaves and flowers of the species here given are very much alike, but they can be easily distinguished by the fruit. The leaves are often collected at the end of the branches, whence the generic name.

(*a*) Fruit not winged.

1. *T. belerica.* A large, spreading tree, leaves large, broad ovate or obovate, long petioled, flowers yellowish-green in spikes with a very sickly smell, fruit nearly round, size of a damson, dark, covered with grey silky down. *Bahira, bhirda, vela, bábra.*

Common throughout India. It has 3 varieties, one without glands on the petiole.

2. *T. chebula.* A large tree with ovate or oblong leaves more or less cordate at the base, spikes of flowers often panicled, fruit oval, smooth, about the size of an olive. *Hirda, chambári hirda, rangári hirda.*

Common in the Ghauts and Konkan. It has 6 varieties, one or other found all over India. The fruit of this and other Indian species are the myrobolans of commerce, but those of this species are the most valuable. The nuts with sulphate of iron make capital ink. —*Hooker, in Le Maout.*

(*b*) Fruit with 5 wings.

3. * *T. arjuna.* A large tree with smooth bark and oval leaves often cordate, spikes of flowers usually panicled, fruit ovoid, nearly smooth, truncated or suddenly narrowed at the top. *Arjun, arjun Sádara, shárdul, pinjal.*

Common in jungles S.E. of Surat and about Belgaum (*D.*). Also found in the Konkan and at Matheran. *H.* includes in this *D.'s T. Berryii*, which has narrower leaves.

4. *T. tomentosa* (*T. glabra*, D.). A small tree, leaves linear oblong obtuse, somewhat cordate, with a pair of top-shaped glands on the midrib, flowers in large cross panicles, wings of fruit broad. *Ain, Sádri, Asan.*

This is, perhaps, the commonest tree in the Konkan, and one of the most useful; common also over a great part of India in one of its 3 varieties (*H.*).

(*c*) Fruit with 3 wings.

5. *T. paniculata.* A small tree very like the last, but with whitish flowers becoming purplish, calyx segments reddish-brown, the fruit dark-red, the wings unequal. *Kinjal, honal.*

Very common in the S. Konkan and elsewhere with the *ain*, but it has a much narrower range. The clusters of dark-red fruit make the tree conspicuous.

T. catappa, bengali badám, a fine tree in gardens; kernels eatable.

2. CALYCOPTERIS.

C. floribunda (*Getonia f.* D.). A shrub with elliptic or oval opposite leaves, flowers in panicles greenish-white, downy outside; calyx divided nearly to the base, stamens small in the mouth of the calyx. *Uksi, báguli.*

This would generally be called a climber, though *H.* says it is not. From the great abundance of its light flowers it is conspicuous in hedges. *H.* has 2 varieties.

Very common in the Konkan and Ghauts.

3. ANOGEISSUS.

A. latifolia (*Conocarpus l.* D.). A small tree with light bark and oval smooth leaves, flowers small greenish, the heads long-stalked, fruit very small, roundish, beaked. *Dháura, dábria, dindaga.*

Deccan and Konkan hills; common in some places. The wood is reckoned one of the best in India (*H.*).

A. pendula differs from this by very small leaves of a beautiful reddish-brown when the tree is in fruit. N. Guzerat and Sátpuras (*Brandis*). *Kardáhi.*

4. LUMNITZERA.

L. racemosa. A pretty shrub or small tree with sessile obovate slightly crenated leaves, flowers in spikes, white, strong-smelling, calyx thick with 2 bracts, the petals inserted in the tube; drupe oval.

Creeks in S. Konkan, growing with mangroves.

5. COMBRETUM.

1. *C. ovalifolium.* A large climber with oval entire leaves and short spikes of very small yellowish flowers; calyx filled with the hairy disk, the tube not longer than the ovary, fruit smooth, red, with 4 oval or semicircular wings. *Yelosi, mádhvel, vededhaus, piloka.*

Common in the Konkan and Ghauts.

C. extensum (*C. Wightianum,* D.) is of the same habit, the calyx tube much longer than the ovary, the fruit much larger, red and handsome; *piloka.* Vingorla. Hilly parts of the Konkan (*D.*).

Quisqualis Indica, so named on account of its doubtful affinities, *lál chámeli, Rangoon cha vel, bármási,* is one of the commonest garden bushes, and often found growing luxuriantly "where once a garden smiled;" the long, drooping spikes of long-tubed flowers vary from white to orange and red. I have not heard of its fruiting in W. India. "It is the most profuse of bloomers, and in the Sulu Archipelago forms bushes about four feet high, the slender branches being actually borne down to the ground by the weight of the flowers."

Poivrea coccinea, is a very beautiful climber, tolerably common in gardens, with one-sided spikes of crimson flowers.

ORDER 50. MYRTACEÆ. Myrtles.

Trees or shrubs, leaves simple, entire, flowers regular, calyx tubular, 4 or 5 divided, petals as many, inserted on a disk within the calyx; stamens numerous, ovary adherent to the calyx tube, fruit usually crowned with the limb of the calyx.

Two very distinct tribes are by *H.* united in this order. The first is that of the myrtles, properly so called.

TRIBE MYRTEÆ. Leaves usually opposite, full of transparent glands, and with veins running into a nerve parallel to the margin; fruit a berry or drupe fleshy.

There is always something agreeable about the myrtles, as there is in the name to English ears. *Myrta communis*, the myrtle of gardens and cottages at home, is also found in Indian gardens, and its leaves used in native medicine (*H.*). There is no plant with wider associations, for it is also the myrtle of Scripture, and in Isa. xli. and lv. is mentioned as one of the accompaniments of prosperity and civilization. Among the Greeks, too, "it was beloved on account of its sweet scent, evergreen leaves, white blossoms, and aromatic berries, and was everywhere to be seen planted about temples, and at last adorning the rocky shores of Greece."—*Hehn.*

Note.—The dotted leaves and some similarity in the flowers may lead beginners to take some of this tribe for species of *Aurantiaceæ*, but the numerous perigynous stamens (by which this order approaches *Rosaceæ*) make an easy distinction.

1. EUGENIA. Calyx tube more or less round, its lobes and petals generally 4; fruit a berry.

H. has no less than 131 species; but the majority belong to Malaya or Ceylon. All given below are very suggestive of the common myrtle.

1. *E. caryophillæa* (*Syzigium c.* D.). A small smooth tree or large shrub, leaves obovate or ovate obtuse, flowers small white in trichotomous cymes, fruit round, size of a pea, one-seeded. *Karkas, rán lavang.*

On the banks of streams in S. Konkan and Ghauts. Leaves variable (*H.*).

2. *E. jambolana* (*Syzigium j.* D.). A large, handsome tree, all smooth, leaves large oval or oblong, pointed, flowers white

in cross panicles, petals deciduous, berry size and shape of an olive, purple. *Jámbul.*

A very well-known tree in the Ghauts and Konkan. *B.* calls it common throughout India, except in Sind and S. Punjab, and very variable in shape of leaves, size of fruit, and other respects.

The other species are trees, generally small, confined to the higher Ghauts.

* *E. lanceolaria* (*Jambosa l.* D.), leaves narrow lanceolate, flowers fascicled, large, rosy, fruit size of a small apple, irregularly lobed. *Dhakti sheran.* * *E. læta* (*Jambosa pauciflora*, D.) leaves ovate lanceolate with long slender point, flowers large, solitary, crimson or white, the stamens crimson or purple, berry ovoid. *E. zeylanica* (*Syzigium z.* D.), leaves oval oblong, flowers white, large, in terminal corymbs, calyx white, elongated, berry round, white. * *E. rubicunda* (*Syzigium r.* D.) leaves narrow oblong, flowers minute in corymbs, calyx 4-lobed, short. *E. heyneana*, leaves shining, lanceolate, blunt-pointed, flowers white, in panicles, calyx white, long-tubed. * *E. bracteata* (*E. wildenovii*, D.), leaves ovate, shining, flowers stalked, solitary, or few together, calyx short-tubed, bracted, berry round. Very fragrant; the pear-shaped fruit has exactly the flavour of roses. *Jámbli, guláb jámb, sákara jámb.*

E. malaccensis, also in gardens, with very handsome red flowers and fruit like a pretty streaked apple, but absolutely dry and tasteless.

> "Like to the apples on the Dead Sea's shore,
> All ashes to the taste."—*Byron.*

Cloves are the dried flowers of *E. caryophyllata*, and allspice the dried berries of *Pimenta acris*, also belonging to this tribe, and much cultivated in India (*H.*). *Psidium Guyava*, the guava (a corruption of the American name), probably introduced by the Portuguese, *jámb peru*, is grown everywhere.

TRIBE 2. BARRINGTONEÆ. Fruit indehiscent, leaves alternate, not dotted.

2. BARRINGTONIA. Trees; calyx tube scarcely longer than the ovary, lobes 2 to 5, petals 4, much imbricated, stamens very many, all perfect, united at the base, fruit one-seeded, fibrous.

3. CAREYA. Calyx tube as in the last, lobes and petals 4, stamens as in the last, but some of them without anthers; fruit large, fleshy, many-seeded.

2. BARRINGTONIA.

1. *B. racemosa.* A tree with very large ovate lanceolate leaves, quite smooth, finely serrated; flowers large, in long drooping racemes, calyx reddish-brown, petals pale pink, long

and pointed, with the edges turned back, stamens long, pink, fruit ovoid. *Karpa.*

I have only seen this tree once, in a salt marsh near Vingorla; *D.* has it in Severndrug taluka rare, in Canara common. I thought the blossoms as beautiful as anything I had ever seen :

> " Flowers worthy of Paradise, which nature boon
> Poured forth profuse."—*Milton.*

2. *B. acutangula.* A tree with cuneate, obovate, finely serrated leaves, and slender, drooping racemes of small pink flowers with scarlet stamens, the 4 petals wax-like with edges turned back, fruit oblong with 4 sharp angles. *Tivar, ingar, ijal ;* the fruit *Sámudraphal, Sáthphal.* (*Dymock.*)

S. Konkan, not uncommon.

The flowers of this also are very beautiful, though small. They fall off very easily, making the ground all red below. So the guelder rose at home

> " In a great stillness drops, and ever drops,
> Her wealth about her feet."—*Jean Ingelow.*

3. Careya.

C. arborea. A tree all smooth with large, obovate finely serrated leaves, flowers few, very large white, sepals and petals 4, the latter curled, stamens sometimes red, fruit large, round or somewhat pear-shaped. *Kumba.*

Common in S. Konkan. Grows to an immense size in the mountains of Coromandel (*R.*). Said by *H.* to be called the Indian oak. The size of the leaves, flowers and fruit make the tree very noticeable, but there is not much beauty about it. The alternative name *Wai-Kumba* belongs, *Dr. Dymock* says, to the unripe fruit.

To other tribes of this large order belong the genus *Eucalyptus*, Australian gum-trees, and *Bertholletia excelsa*, the seeds of which are Brazil nuts.

Order 51. **MELASTOMACEÆ.**

Flowers regular, calyx lobes and petals 4 or 5, stamens (in all here given) twice as many, calyx more or less adherent to the ovary, and afterwards enclosing the fruit, seeds minute, very many (except Memecylon).

This large S. American order is closely allied to the last, and also to the next, differing from *Myrtaceæ* in the stamens being definite, and from *Lythraceæ* in the manner of their insertion. Three of the species given below are strikingly beautiful, and easy to identify. The name of the order arose from the trivial fact of the fruit of the early-known species staining the mouth black.

1. Osbeckia. Stamens with a connective, ovary inferior, capsule opening at the top, seeds much curved.

2. Melastoma. Shrubs, stamens very unequal, the alternate ones with a long connective, fruit bursting irregularly, seeds much curved.

3. Memecylon. Shrubs or trees with opposite leaves, calyx campanulate, entire or shortly 4-lobed, petals 4, berry one-seeded, crowned with the margin of the calyx, seed large.

1. Osbeckia.

O. truncata (*O. leschenaultii*, D.). A small erect plant, all hairy except the petals, stems square, leaves oval, prominently 3-nerved, flowers in small terminal heads, nearly sessile, pink or purple, the petals cruciate, calyx and apex of the ovary bristly, capsule very small ovoid.

Dápoli. The Konkan (*D.*). Throughout the Deccan peninsula (*H.*).

2. Melastoma.

M. malabathricum. A very handsome low shrub, leaves broad lanceolate, very bright green, strongly ribbed, more or less rough, petioles very hairy, flowers very large, rose-coloured, 3 to 5 together, almost sessile, fruit small, round. *Sarkoli, lákheri, pálore.*

S. Konkan, generally near water; S.M. country. On the Ghauts it grows to 6 feet, but is not then so handsome as when dwarf. "Indian rhododendron" of the English (*H.*).

The strongly-ribbed leaves and handsome flowers with large curved connective to some of the stamens well distinguish this plant, which ought to be cultivated.

3. Memecylon.

M. amplexicaule. An erect shrub with long, smooth, leathery leaves, cordate and stem clasping; flowers in fascicles or very short-stalked umbels from the branches, pedicels and calyx reddish, petals bright blue, larger than in the next, fruit a berry, crowned with the nearly entire calyx.

Not in *D.* or *G.* Penang; and a var. in the Nilgherries (*H.*). I had it on the tank at Dhámapor, S. Konkan, a lovely spot, and a fine hunting ground for botanists;

> "Where the fair trees look over, side by side,
> And see themselves below."—*Longfellow.*

The shrub is well worth looking for.

2. *M. edule.* A small handsome tree with ovate entire polished leaves, flowers very small in dense heads or umbels from the naked branches, calyx red inside, white outside, petals purple or blue, fruit round, red or purple. *Anjan, yálkí, lokhandi.*

Very common at Mahableshwar, and on the Ghauts, less so in S. Konkan. Called the iron-wood tree (*G.*), and the wood *Kurpa*. *H.* has 12 varieties, but only attributes it to Eastern peninsula and Ceylon.

From the mode of growth the flowers look almost as if they were parasitical on the tree. The colours blend in a lovely manner, and a poetical forest officer aptly described them to me as forming "globes of pink and blue and white, like living opals."

Note.—The name 'Iron-wood tree' is applied in different places to a variety of trees.

* *M. terminale,* a low shrub, leaves sessile lanceolate, flowers unbelled blue, fruit like a large pea. E. Ghauts and Canara (*D.*).

Sonerila. Small herbs, calyx, teeth, petals, and stamens 3, the latter with a connective. * *S. scapigera,* stemless, leaves radical, ovate, long-petioled, flowers unbelled, mauve, capsule bell-shaped. Ghauts and Konkan hills (*D.*).

ORDER 52. LYTHRACEÆ.

Leaves simple, entire, generally opposite, without stipules, calyx tubular, lobes 3 to 6, often with additional smaller ones, petals as many: ovary free at the bottom of the calyx tube; capsule crowned by the calyx; seeds many.

It is characteristic of this order that the petals are inserted on the top of the calyx tube, and the stamens a little lower down. The order has on this side of India some very poor-looking herbs (tribe Ammanieæ), and some very beautiful trees and shrubs (tribe Lythreæ). So in England the beautiful purple loose strife (*Lythrum salicaria*) is balanced by the insignificant water purslane (*Peplis portula*).

TRIBE 1. AMMANIEÆ. Low or aquatic herbs with small flowers and membranous calyx.

1. AMMANIA. Stems often 4-sided, flowers axillary often sessile, stamens 2 to 8.

TRIBE 2. LYTHREÆ. Trees or shrubs, calyx herbaceous.

2. WOODFORDIA. A shrub, calyx long, tubular, 6-toothed, petals 6, very small, or none; stamens 12.

3. LAWSONIA. A smooth shrub, calyx tube very short, lobes and petals 4, stamens 8 in pairs between the petals, style very long, capsule round, breaking up irregularly.

4. LAGERSTRÆMIA. Trees or shrubs of great beauty, calyx lobes 6, petals 6, conspicuously clawed, stamens very many exserted, capsule 3 to 6-valved, seeds winged.

5. SONNERATIA. Trees growing near the sea, smooth, leaves entire, calyx thick, lobes and petals 4 to 6, stamens very many, berry roundish with calyx attached.

Note.—Where not otherwise stated the leaves are opposite.

1. AMMANIA.

(*a*) Small and low, or creeping, herbs; (1) calyx teeth and petals 4.

1. *A. rotundifolia* (*Ameletia r.* D.). Spreading, tinged with red, branches erect, leaves rounded sessile, spikes crowded square decussate, flowers red, each with a cordate bract, sepals and petals alike but the petals narrower, capsule 4-valved elliptic, seeds brownish-yellow.

Common in rice fields, etc. Throughout the plains of India (*H.*). He says that there are two types of flowers, one with stamens included and long style, the other with stamens exserted and short style.

2. *A. floribunda* (*Ameletia f.* D.). Erect, leaves alternate linear or oblong, stem-clasping, branches very slender, flowers bright red in short racemes, capsules and seeds as in the last.

The highest Ghauts and Sivapore are the only habitats known for this. At Mahableshwar it grows on the rocks in masses, looking like a heath. The small green bracts might be taken for calyx.

* *A. peploides*, leaves obovate, flowers in numerous sessile spikes, calyx tube long, pink petals wanting or small, capsule 2-valved. Hab. as in No. 1. "This is abundant on wet soil in some part of the Himalayas, and gives a heath-like colour to the turf with its pale purple flowers."—*Hooker*. * *A. Ritchiei*, aquatic, leaves elliptic, flowers solitary, calyx long, petals rose-colour, capsule 4-valved. Not in *D.* or *G.* Rice-fields at Belgaum (*H.*). Not otherwise known. * *A. tenuis* (*Ameletia t.* D.). Erect, very slender, leaves ovate or roundish, spikes dense, capsule 2-valved. Banks of the Penu river. (*D.*).

(2) Calyx lobes and petals 3 to 5.

* *A. rotala* (*Rotala verticillaris*, D.). Growing and creeping in water, leaves in whorls of 3 to 6, linear, flowers minute solitary, capsule 2-valved. Ditches, tanks, etc. (*D.* and *G.*). *A. pentandra.* Leafy, much branched, with thick square stems, leaves very small, linear or lanceolate, close pressed together with the solitary flowers, calyx lobes, petals, and stamens 5, all bright red, capsule 3-celled. Málwan. Not in *D.* or *G.* Throughout tropical India (*H.*).

(*b*) Erect, height up to one or two feet.

3. *A. baccifera.* Stem sharply angled, leaves often alternate, lanceolate, narrow at the base, flowers minute sessile, whitish in dense clusters, petals none, capsule round, seed black. *Agiya, Aginbuti, bharjámbhul.*

Common; the leaves are very acrid. Throughout tropical India in moist places (*H.*).

4. *A. salicifolia.* Leaves lanceolate sessile, flowers red, sessile or nearly so, calyx lobes 4 or 5 broadly triangular with horns between, petals sometimes wanting, capsule as in the last.

D. has only Málwan for this. *H.* has it widely distributed. I had it at Dápoli and Bandora, at the latter place growing in masses.

A. multiflora, stems sharply quadrangular, leaves linear lanceolate, auricled, flowers minute red in sessile clusters, calyx teeth 4, petals none or small Deccan. Throughout the plains of India (*H.*). * *A. octandra*, much like the last apparently, but stamens 8, and capsule not so round. Common in wet ground (*D.*).

2. Woodfordia.

W. floribunda (*Grislea tomentosa*, D.). A small handsome shrub, leaves narrow lanceolate pointed, dotted with black glands beneath and strongly nerved, flowers very numerous, bright red, tubular, curved, stamens of the same colour long exserted, capsule oblong covered by the withered calyx. *Dháuri, dháusi, dháiti.* Sanscrit, *Dhátri pushpika, aquivala.*

Exceedingly common in S. Konkan and the Ghauts, and throughout India (*H.*).

3. Lawsonia.

L. alba. A twiggy smooth shrub, with small oval lanceolate leaves and small dingy strong-smelling flowers in dense panicles, capsule size of a pea, 4-lobed, seeds many-angled. *Mendi.*

Commonly cultivated: "perhaps wild in W. India" (*H.*). It is much like the English privet, and the leaves produce *henna*, in common use all over the East and in Egypt. It is said to be the plant referred to in the beautifully sounding verse, "My beloved is unto me as a cluster of *camphire* in the vineyards of Engedi."—*Cant.* i. 14.

A red flowered variety is mentioned.

4. Lagerstræmia.

1. *L. parviflora.* A large tree with grey bark, leaves hard, shining, strong nerved, oval acute, pale beneath, flowers very

numerous, small white in panicles, calyx lobes and petals triangular; capsule small oblong. *Náneh, bondháre, kákria.*

A very pretty tree both as to flowers and foliage, which appear together. The wood is called *benteak.*

Common in the Konkan and Ghauts.

2. *L. lanceolata.* Leaves smooth lanceolate, flowers pure white in axillary racemes, calyx and pedicels covered with dense grey down, capsule small oval. *Bondar, bodága, sukutya.*

Very like the last, but more elegant and beautiful, the flowers larger, the capsule smaller. The tree may be seen from a distance when quite covered with flowers,

> " As white as Mount Soracte,
> When winter nights are long."—*Macaulay.*

It is common on the Ghauts and in some parts of the Konkan.

3. *L. flosreginæ.* Leaves lanceolate ovate smooth, flowers large and very handsome, purple or mauve, in large and numerous panicles, calyx downy furrowed, fruit oval, 6-lobed. *Táman.*

This is a very noticeable tree from the mass of colour it often gives, but not so elegant as the last. It is tolerably common in the Konkan. *H.* has a variety with leaves 15 inches long.

L. Indica, China mendi, is a pretty shrub with bright pink flowers, common in gardens; originally from China (*H.*).

5. Sonneratia.

1. *S. apetala.* A pretty slender tree with thick veinless oval oblong leaves and white flowers, calyx 4-lobed thick and fleshy, stigma remarkably large, umbrella-shaped, fruit round with short hard point. *Amthi.*

Not in *D.* or *G.*, but common in the salt marshes of the S. Konkan, growing with the mangroves.

2. *S. acida.* A small tree, leaves opposite entire, thick and veinless oval, flowers large, solitary, red, fruit nearly round, slightly flattenened, seated in the hardened calyx, much larger than that of the last. *Tivar.*

Common in salt marshes. Very different from the last. *H.* has *S. Griffithii,* "probably an apetalous form of this," which I believe I had, but have lost my note of it.

To this tribe also belongs (but put by Oliver and others in Myrtaceæ) *Punica granatum, Ánár, dálimb,* the pomegranate, wild in Afghanistan and Beluchistan.

"What should we do but sing his praise,

. . . . .

Who does in the pomegranate close
Jewels more rich than Ormus shows."—*A. Marvell.*

"As in Asia so in Greece, the tree and its fruit served as the symbol of fructification and procreation, and again of death and resurrection."—*Hehn.*

Browning called one of his collections of poems "Bells and pomegranates" (in allusion to Ex. xxxix. 24 to 26), "to indicate an endeavour towards something like an alternation or mixture of music with discoursing, sound with sense, poetry with thought. . . . Giotto placed a pomegranate in the hands of Dante, and Raffaelle crowned Theology with blossoms of the same."

ORDER 53. ONAGRACEÆ.

Herbs, calyx tubular of 2 to 6 valvate lobes, united to the inferor ovary; petals 2 to 6 inserted on the calyx, stamens as many or double, similarly inserted; fruit a capsule or berry.

This not a large order, but contains some well-known and beautiful flowers, both wild and cultivated, as the fuchsias, the evening primroses (Ænothera), and the willow herbs (Epilobium). The most noticeable feature in plants of this order is the very inferior ovary, which is well below the calyx, and in many cases looks like a flower stalk much swollen in the upper half. Most of the species grow in water, or in moist situations.

1. JUSSIÆA. Marsh plants with alternate undivided leaves and solitary flowers, stamens double the petals, style short, stigma 4 or 5-lobed, capsule 4 or 5-celled, many-seeded.

2. LUDWIGIA. Leaves alternate undivided, stamens as many as the petals, capsule linear or oblong, many-seeded.

3. TRAPA. Floating herbs, calyx lobes 4 persistent, becoming spiny on the fruit, petals and stamens 4, fruit bony, 4-angled, beaked, one-seeded.

1. JUSSIÆA.

1. *J. repens.* Floating and spreading in tanks, the stems rooting at the joints, and bearing clusters of conspicuous white fleshy vesicles, leaves smooth, obovate oblong, flowers very pretty, erect, long-stalked, white with yellow base, calyx lobes and petals 5, capsule cylindric, woody.

Common on the edges of tanks,

"Where rosy-winged flamingoes fish all day
Stalking amid the lotus blossoms fair."—*J. Ingelow.*

Very common throughout India and Ceylon, and distributed over the warmer parts of the whole world (*H.*).

2. *J. suffruticosa* (*J. villosa*, D.). Tall and erect, softly hairy almost all over, leaves lanceolate tapering into the petiole, flowers almost sessile yellow, calyx tube very long with 2 bracts, lobes and petals 4, capsule bluntly 4-angled with innumerable seeds. *Pánlavang.*

The Konkan and Ghauts: not particularly common, I believe; but *H.* makes it as common and as widely distributed as the last.

The flowers recall the evening primrose.

2. Ludwigia.

L. parviflora. A small plant, erect, smooth and branched, leaves lanceolate, flowers 2 or 3 together, small, yellow, nearly sessile, calyx lobes and petals cruciate, capsule slightly 4 or 5-angled, seeds red.

In moist places in the Konkan and Guzerat. Throughout India (*H.*).

3. Trapa.

T. bispinosa. Stem thick; submersed leaves in thread-like segments, floating leaves whorled, broad reniform or angular, covered with brown hairs beneath, the petioles with large oval vesicles, flowers white, disk angular, yellow and hairy, fruit long-stalked with two straight barbed spurs. *Shingari.* Sanscrit, *Sringáta.*

The water-chestnut, a very pleasant eatable nut. "The Hindoos were so fond of its nut that they placed it among their lunar constellations."—*Sir W. Jones.*

Common in tanks, especially in Guzerat.

Several species of evening primrose (Ænothera) and of Fuchsia are found in gardens.

Order 54. **SAMYDACEÆ.**

Trees or shrubs, with simple alternate often bifarious leaves, flowers small, inconspicuous, regular, petals often wanting, fruit 2 to 5-valved.

This is small and uninteresting tropical order, differing from the last in the ovary being almost or altogether superior. It resembles a tribe of Bixinea (*H.*).; but Balfour put it in the Monochlamyds.

Casearia.—Flowers clustered in the axils, pedicels short, jointed, calyx 4 or 5-lobed, petals none, stamens about double the calyx lobes, more or less united, with staminodes alternating seeds many, with a flesh-coloured aril.

1. *C. graveolens.* Large shrub or small tree, leaves elliptic acute, mostly smooth, stipules lanceolate pointed, flowers numerous green with a disagreeable smell, fruit almost round, smooth, shining. *Chillá.*

Konkan hills, Bombay, Bandora, Canara.

2. *C. esculenta* (*C. lævigata*, D.). Mostly smooth, leaves large oblong, acuminated entire or obscurely serrated, thick and shining, flowers numerous, greenish, fruit size of an acorn with woody stalk, splitting into three and showing a brilliant red aril. *Mori, bokra.*

Common at Matheran and Mahableshwar; Konkan hills (*G.*).

* *C. rubescens*, "distinguished from the last only by the minute pubescence of the pedicels" (*H.*).; but *D.* makes the leaves suddenly and obtusely acuminated, with the midrib bright red. S. Ghauts (*D.*). *C. tomentosa* (*C. anavinga*, D.). Small tree, leaves oblong, slightly oblique and cordate, stems and petioles reddish, flowers on the leafless branches, fruit oval, shining, size of a nutmeg. *Chillá, marsai, Karai.* Rajapore. Also Caranja (*D.*). Common throughout India (*H.*).

Note.—The native names given above are probably interchangeable.

The very small order Turneraceæ must be mentioned here on account of a common garden plant *Turnera ulmifolia, bhinjra*, with alternate simple leaves, and rather large yellow flowers growing on the leaf-stalk; calyx segments, petals and stamens 5, styles 3, stigmas divided brush-like.

ORDER 55. PASSIFLOREÆ. Passion flowers.

Twining herbs or shrubs: leaves alternate with stipules, flowers regular, calyx tubular with 5 segments, petals as many or none, corona generally conspicuous, stamens 5, ovary superior, styles one or three.

This order is allied to Cucurbitaceæ, but differs from that in the superior ovary, and the central corona arising from the calyx.

MODECCA. Climbers with unisexual flowers, disk with 5 glands opposite the sepals, staminodes 5, forming a membranous cup surrounding the base of the ovary, dividing above into filaments, and so forming a corona.

* *M. palmata.* Root large and woody appearing above the ground, leaves cordate acuminate, usually 3 to 5-lobed with glands beneath, flowers rather large, yellow, bell-shaped with rather deep lobes, fruit round, size of a crab apple, bright orange: tendrils on the peduncle. *Undal.*

Malwan and S. Ghauts; rare (*D.*).

A good many species of Passion flower (*Passiflora*) are cultivated in India as in England. Of these, *P. fœtida* is very common, and runs wild in many places. It is a hairy plant, with small white flowers. The name "Passion flower" was due to resemblances, which the mystical Fathers of the Church discovered more readily than we can. The five anthers represented the five wounds of our Saviour, the triple style the nails, the stalk of the ovary the main pillar of the cross, and the thread-like corona, the glory round His head.

Carica papaya, the papaw tree, *papawa*, belongs to this order (*H.*). The fruit makes a very fair imitation of apple pie. The curious fact seems well-established, that meat hung up under its shade quickly becomes tender.

ORDER 56. CUCURBITACEÆ. Gourds.

Climbing or prostrate herbs or shrubs, with solitary lateral tendrils, leaves alternate petioled, generally cordate and lobed, frequently rough; flowers unisexual, either on the same or different plants, yellow or white, regular; calyx tube wholly united to the ovary, 5-lobed, petals 5, more or less united; stamens usually 3, filaments short and thick, style one with 3 thick stigmas; fruit generally fleshy crowned by the scar of the calyx, seeds many.

This well-known order is extremely well represented all over India. It is easily recognized as well by its foliage and tendrils as by the structure of the flowers (*Bentham*); but from the great general resemblance that runs through the family, it is often difficult to distinguish the genera except by the fruit, which, in the large majority of the species here given, is eatable.

Note.—The stamens in the genera here given are 3, except in *Luffa*, where they are sometimes, and in *Zanonia* always, 5, but the filaments are often so combined as to make a definite statement on this point misleading. Of the anthers one is generally one-celled, and the others two-celled.

1. TRICHOSANTHES. Flowers white, males in racemes, females solitary, petals much fringed at the margin, calyx tube long, anthers long linear, ovary at the base of the calyx, seeds packed in pulp.

2. LUFFA. Calyx tube short, stamens sometimes 5, stigma 3-lobed, fruit fibrous when dry, opening by a lid at the top.

3. MOMORDICA. Calyx tube and filaments short, style long, fruit indehiscent or 3-valved.

4. CUCUMIS. Flowers yellow, males clustered, females solitary, calyx top-shaped or bell-shaped, style short.

5. CITRULLUS. Flowers all solitary, calyx cup-shaped with long teeth, style short, stigmas reniform.

6. CEPHALANDRA. Flowers white, all solitary, calyx tube

short, bell-shaped, style long with 3 bifid stigmas, fruit oblong, more or less cylindric.

7. BRYONIA. Flowers small, male and female clustered in the same axils, calyx widely bell-shaped, teeth 5, small, style slender, 3-divided at the top, fruit round.

8. MUKIA. As the last, but style thick.

9. ZEHNERIA. Flowers all corymbose, or the females solitary, calyx bell-shaped, style cylindric, 3-lobed, surrounded at the base by an annular disk.

10. CORALLOCARPUS. Flowers very small, males long peduncled, females sessile or nearly so, stamens nearly sessile at the mouth of the calyx tube, berry ovoid, splitting near the base.

11. CTENOLEPIS. Flowers minute, males in racemes, females solitary in the same axils, filaments very short, seeds margined.

Note.—All gourd-like fruits tend to vary very much in shape: bottle gourds (and probably other sorts) may be made to take various shapes by strings or other compresses being fastened round them when young.

Note.—I recommend, as specially interesting, the chapter on Cucurbitaceæ in Hehn's "Wanderings of plants and animals."

1. TRICHOSANTHES.

1. *T. palmata.* A very large climber, running over trees, with trifid tendrils and deeply-lobed toothed leaves, flowers large and handsome, calyx lobes deeply toothed, fruit like a small orange. *Mukál, Kaundal.*

The Konkans and Ghauts, not very common.

The thickly fringed petals mark this genus, but there may possibly be a confusion in the identification of this, and of *Modecca palmata.*

2. *T. Cucumerina.* Climbing in hedges, tendrils trifid, leaves broad cordate, lobed or angled, toothed, flowers delicate and pretty, ovary hairy, fruit oblong pointed, orange-coloured when ripe. *Padval, karu padval, jangli parol.*

One of the commonest climbers in Guzerat: in S. Konkan comparatively rare. Throughout India and Ceylon (*H.*).

T. Anguina, the snake gourd, *Chikonda, parol*, is cultivated for its very long curiously twisted fruit.

2. LUFFA. Towel gourds.[1]

1. *L. Ægyptiaca.* A large climber, tendrils bifid, leaves

[1] From the fibrous fruits being used as flesh rubbers.

smooth at first, afterwards very rough, broad, 5 to 7-lobed with small teeth, flowers long, yellow, often veined, stamens 5, fruit several inches long, cylindric, striped when young, seeds oval, blackish, with membranous margin. *Gousáli, párosi.*

D. and *G.* have this only as cultivated, with the next. *H.* has it as wild throughout India and Ceylon, and I believed it to be so in N. Konkan.

2. *L. acutangula.* Leaves 5 to 7-lobed, rough, flowers like the last, stamens 3, fruit long, 10-angled; flowers bright yellow of middle size. *Turái, dodki.*

This is the vegetable so commonly cultivated, and *H.* makes *L. amara rán turai, Karu dodki,* only a variety of it, the leaves being softly hairy when young, and the fruit with 10 sharp ridges. It is a pretty climber, exceedingly common in hedges in Guzerat. The flowers open in the afternoon.

* *L. echinata,* sparingly rough and hairy, leaves roundish, cordate, or kidney-shaped, sometimes deeply cut, flowers small white, fruit roundish, densely prickly. *Devdangri, Kukurvel.* Guzerat (*D.*). Sind (*H.*).

3. MOMORDICA.

1. *M. charantia.* Rather a pretty twiner, stems hairy, sometimes angular, leaves palmately 5-lobed, sinuate, toothed, flowers small, solitary, long-stalked, pale yellow; a reniform bract half way up the pedicel in the male flower, and near the base in the female, fruit oblong ovate, covered with ridges and tubercles. *Kareli, parwad, omble.*

Commonly cultivated. A well-known vegetable.

2. *M. dioica.* A large climber, nearly smooth, leaves cordate entire or lobed, flowers large yellow, long-stalked, males with a large hooded bract covering the calyx, females with a small one near the base of the pedicel; fruit ovate pointed, covered with soft bristles, seeds truncated black with bright red aril. *Kartoli.*

S. Konkan. Very common (*D.*); throughout India (*H.*).

3. *M. cymbalaria.* Root a large turnip-shaped tuber, stems slender, smooth, leaves cordate, 5 to 7-angled, flowers white or yellow, pedicels longest in the female, fruit like *turai,* but smaller and 8-angled without a lid. *Kadawanchi.*

Sholapore districts. Also reported from Igatpuri, Sattara and the Konkan; but not in *D.* or *G.* Deccan peninsula (*H.*).

4. CUCUMIS.

C. trigonus. Rough all over, leaves variously lobed, female flowers few, larger than the male, ovary hairy, fruit at first slightly 3-lobed, and striped in light and dark green, but when ripe, smooth, level, and yellow. *Jangli Kakri, Kárit, Kátvel.*

Common throughout India. The pulp is bitter. *H.* includes under this *D.'s C. pubescens chibar, takmak,* common in the Deccan, Cutch and Sind: the fruit is covered with small bristles.

C. sativus is the cultivated cucumber, *Kakri, Khira.*

"The prickly and green-coated gourd
So grateful to the palate."—*Cowper.*

C. melo is the melon *Kharbuz, chibur,* of which there are many varieties, and which *H.* says is perhaps the cultivated form of *C. trigonus.* Dr. Lansdell and Vambery speak of the melons of Central Asia, and especially of Khiva, as probably the best in the world, which indeed is pretty much what Marco Polo said. The melon was brought from Jamaica and cultivated in England, certainly since 1570: the cucumber was introduced in 1573.—*Don.*

5. Citrullus.

C. colocynthus. A large rough creeper, with leaves so deeply gashed as to be almost pinnatifid, male and female flowers alike, middle-sized, yellow, long-stalked, fruit round, smooth, size of an orange, yellow variegated with green. *Indrayan, indrafal, Kadu kakri.*

Throughout India, cultivated and also very often apparently wild (*H.*). It is one of the characteristic plants of the desert region, extending from Arabia and Palestine across the whole of N. Africa (*Hooker* in 'Marocco'). The old commentators considered that the 'wild vine' of 2 Kings iv. 39 was the Colocynth (from Kolokunthe, the Greek name). The pulp is called by English chemists, 'bitter apple': and the fruit is mentioned by old writers as a typical bitter—"That which is unrighteous is as hateful to the child of God as colócynth to the taste."—*Bishop J. Taylor.*

C. vulgaris is the water melon, *tarbuz, Kalingar.* The mounds of them piled up inside the town gates and elsewhere in Italy in the late summer, give one some idea of the easiness of their growth. It is by some considered to be indigenous in India. "A traveller in the East," says Kitto, "who recollects the intense gratitude which the gift of a slice of melon inspired while journeying over the hot and dry plains, will readily comprehend the regret with which the Hebrews in the Arabian desert looked back on the melons of Egypt," —(*Num.* xi. 5.)

A variety of *C. vulgaris* is the *dilpasand.*

6. Cephelandra.

C. Indica (*Coccinea I.* D.). A smooth climber, leaves 5-angled, or more or less deeply lobed, sometimes fleshy, flowers large, petioles and peduncles short and thick, fruit 2 or 3 inches long, red, at first marked with white streaks. *Kutrund, dilori, tondli, bimbi.*

Very common, especially in Guzerat, the N. Konkan, and Cutch. The fruit is eatable.

7. Bryonia.

B. laciniosa. A pretty climber, leaves 3 or 5-lobed, petioles long, sometimes warty, flowers yellowish-green, males stalked, females nearly sessile, fruit smooth, size of a gooseberry, at first green with white streaks, afterwards dull red. *Sivlinga, popti, Kandori.*

Deccan, Konkan, Guzerat, and Cutch.

B. dioica is the well-known green-flowered bryony of English hedges. Darwin's descriptions of its tendrils would no doubt apply to many other plants. "I have gone out to watch the bryony on an exposed hedge, as the branches were tossed to and fro by the wind. Unless the tendrils had been exceedingly elastic they would have been torn off, and the plant thrown prostrate. As it was it safely rode out the gale, like a ship with two anchors down, and with a long range of cable ahead to serve as a spring as she surges to the storm."

8. Mukia.

M. scabrella. Twining, very rough all over, leaves cordate, lobed or angled, flowers very small, sessile, yellow, berry like a scarlet pea. *Chiráti.*

Very common and pretty; with Corallocarpus this is probably the smallest species of the order in W. India.

9. Zehneria.

Z. umbellata. (*Bryonia u.* D.). Smooth or nearly so, leaves cordate and sagittate at first, afterwards various, flowers very small, the corolla scarcely exceeding the calyx; fruit oval, red, size of a pigeon's egg. *Gometta.*

Common in hedges. Very common throughout India (*H.*). * *Z. baueriana* (*Bryonia Mysorensis*, D.), seems to be much like the last, but the male and female flowers frequently in the same axils, and the fruit much smaller. *Waráli.* Wári country (*D.*), Mahableshwar, *Dr. Cooke.*

10. Corallocarpus.

C. epigeia (*Æchmandra e.* D.). Twining, rather fleshy, greyish or glaucous, leaves deeply lobed, toothed, petioles very thick, flowers few together, yellowish-green, calyx nearly as large as the corolla, fruit stalked, beaked, orange or scarlet with green base. *Kadoindi, Karvinai.*

This is another very small species, found in hedges in the Konkan, Guzerat, and Sind.

* *C. conocarpa* (*Æchmandra c.* D.) differs from the last in the sessile conical fruit; the seeds not margined, as the others are slightly. *Máhádevi, Shivaling.* Guzerat (*D.*).

* *Rhyncocarpa fœtida* (*Æchmandra rostrata,* D.) appears to be very like the last two, but hairy and strong-smelling, the leaves round or ovate cordate, toothed, seeds margined, stamens with a crested connective. Guzerat (*D.*).

11. Ctenolepis.

C. Garcinii (*Zehneria g.* D.). Leaves bristly, rather rough, lobes deep rounded, bracts large, kidney-shaped, pectinated, flowers salver-shaped white, calyx scarcely visible, fruit red, horizontally egg-shaped. *Jháli.*

Surat. Guzerat, Cutch and Deccan. It is a small species, a good deal like Corallocarpus.

* *C. cerasiformis* (*Zehneria c.* D.) like the last, but the round scarlet fruit is in clusters, seeds 2, rather large. Guzerat and Sind: known apparently only to Dalzell and Stocks.

Zanonia. Flowers in large panicles, males stalked, females subsessile, stamens 5 on a fleshy disk. * *Z. Indica,* smooth, leaves large, oval, flowers pale yellow, females much the largest, fruit the shape of a candle extinguisher, about 4 inches long. Near Vingorla (*D.*).

The following also are cultivated :—

Cucurbita maxima, the common gourd, *dudhi bhopali; C. moschata,* the musk melon, *Kali dudki: C. pepo,* the pumpkin, *Kaula, dámgar: C. ovifera,* the vegetable marrow: *Lagenaria vulgaris,* the white pumpkin or bottle gourd, *haria kaddu.* A variety of this is the *bhopla,* used for crossing rivers, but I rather think that this name is used for all sorts of gourds, to many of which G. Sand's fanciful description might apply: " The pumpkins, haughty leviathans of this verdant sea, ponderously sprawled their great orange-coloured stomachs over their broad and sombre leafage."

Order 57. BEGONIACEÆ.

Succulent herbs, leaves simple, alternate, unequal-sided with stipules, flowers unisexual without corolla; male calyx of 2 unequal pairs of sepals, females of 5 to 2 segments; stamens indefinite, ovary inferior, styles 2 to 4.

A tropical order variously placed by botanists. The unequal-sided leaves and coloured flowers without corolla, some showy and some delicately beautiful, are easily recognizable. " Leathery melastomæ, and succulent-stemmed, lop-sided leaved, flesh-coloured begonias are typical of tropical American forests."—*Belt.*

Out of 65 Indian species of Begonia given by *H.*, only one is at all common in this Presidency.

The Begonias have in a very high degree the power of reproduction by their leaves; as it is stated that a leaf placed on damp soil and cut across the nerves, will produce roots and buds at every incision. —*Le Maout.*

BEGONIA: as the order.

B. crenata. A very pretty and delicate little plant, leaves ovate, unequally crenated, with a few stiff hairs, flowers pink, stamens 8 to 16, monadelphous, capsule 2-celled with irregular wings. *Mutia.*

Abundant in S. Konkan, growing in crevices of rocks, walls, and wells, also in the Ghauts. Grows also on trees (*D.*).

* *B. integrifolia*, leaves ovate, oblong, dark red below, flowers small, white, stamens about 50, monadelphous, capsule with one broad and two very narrow wings. * *B. trichocarpa*, leaves ovate, cordate, flowers large, white, few together, stamens about 40 free, capsule with 3 nearly equal wings. These two on rocks on the Ghauts (*D.*). * *B. concanensis*, leaves ovate, acute, sometimes lobed, flowers rose colour, stamens as in the last, capsule with the larger wing triangular. Konkan and Ghauts (*D.*).

The order Cacteæ must here be mentioned, though there are no plants native to W. India belonging to it. But *Opuntia Dillenii*, commonly called the broad-leaved prickly pear, *nág-phanna*, *chappal*, is quite naturalized, and is generally looked on in the Deccan as a nuisance. It is nearly if not quite the same species as that on which the cochineal insect is reared in Teneriffe (*H.*) In Mexico, where apparently cochineal was first produced, the plant is called *nopal*, and the plantations *nopalries*. The species so common in S. Italy, *O. vulgaris*, is to all appearance the same, and there, as in America, the fruit is called the Indian fig. Hehn eulogizes the plant in a manner which reads strangely to those who know it only in India.

Note.—"In India there are no indigenous cactuses: what people take for thickets of cactus are really cactus-like spurges. In the dry soil of India many spurges grow thick and succulent, learn to suppress their leaves, and assume the bizarre appearance of the true cactuses. In flower and fruit, however, they are euphorbic to the end; it is only in the thick and fleshy stem that they resemble their noble and more beautiful Western rivals."—*Grant Allen.*

Many species of cactus have large and splendid flowers:

"And cactuses a Queen might don,
If weary of a golden crown,
And still appear as royal."—*E. B. Browning.*

To this order also belongs the genus *Cereus*. *C. grandiflorus*, grown in Indian verandas, is, as regards its flowers, one of the most beautiful objects of the vegetable world; and that its splendid blossom lasts but the few hours of a single night, perhaps enhances its value.

"Do you wish to see the prettiest thing you ever saw in your lives? . . If so, come this moment to my conservatory. My night-blowing Cereus has her coming-out party to-night." (A long and rather high-flown description follows.)—*The Bread-winners.*

ORDER 58. DATISCACEÆ.

Flowers small, unisexual, calyx tubular with 3 to 9 teeth, petals none, ovary adherent to the calyx, capsule opening at the top between the styles.

One of the smallest orders, resembling Begoniaceæ, but without the succulent habit.

TETRAMELES. Stamens 4, inserted round a depressed disk, styles 4, short.

* *T. nudiflora.* A large tree, leaves long petioled, roundish or ovate, sometimes lobed, downy beneath, flowers small yellow in panicles, stigmas thick, obliquely truncate, capsule very small, ovoid, glandular. *Jangli bhendi.*

The Ghauts (*D.*) The flowers appear before the leaves.

ORDER 59. FICOIDEÆ.

Succulent herbs with simple generally opposite leaves and regular flowers, calyx of 4 or 5 segments, free, petals none or small.

A rather uninteresting order, though the Mesembryanthemums (with very numerous petals) are ornamental garden plants. M. crystallinum is the ice plant.

Note.—All the genera here given are without petals.

1. SESUVIUM. Leaves fleshy, calyx tubular, stamens many or 5, inserted round the top of the calyx tube, capsule 3 to 5-celled, circumciss.

2. TRIANTHEMA. Diffuse, prostrate, leaves in pairs, one large and one small, the petioles dilated and joined at the base, flowers from the dilated petioles, stamens inserted near the top of the calyx tube, capsule 1 or 2-celled, circumciss, more or less beaked.

3. MOLLUGO. Leaves entire, with scarious stipules soon falling off, flowers axillary; calyx deeply 5-divided, stamens hypogynous, ovary free, capsule membranous, 3 to 5-celled.

1. Sesuvium.

S. portulacastrum. A smooth, very fleshy prostrate plant, much tinged with red, stems rooting at the joints, very thick, leaves oval spathulate, flowers axillary, solitary stalked, calyx within and stamens pink, ovary 3-lobed, styles 3 thread-like. *Dhápa.*

On the sea-shore, Salsette, Bassein, &c.

2. Trianthema.

T. monogyna (*T. obcordata*, D.). Creeping, with thick stems much tinged with red and hairy on one side, leaves obovate, petioles hairy, with 2 bract-like processes, flowers solitary sessile, sepals 5, pinkish, stamens 15, style one, capsule somewhat 4-pointed, seeds 4 to 6, black. *Kápra, narmá.*

Common on rice fields, Bombay, Salsette, Cutch.

T. crystallina, stamens 5, style 1, capsule about 2-seeded. Poona. Cambay (*D.*). Cutch, very common. **T. decandra*, stamens 10, styles 2, capsule 4-seeded. Bombay and elsewhere. **T. hydaspica*, stamens 5 to 7, styles 2, capsule 10 to 15-seeded. Not in *D.* or *G.* Bombay and Sind (*H.*) *T. pentandra* like *T. crystallina*, but with 2 styles and about 4 seeds. Poona. In Sind, *Dr. Dymock*, and called *fasarláni*, but not ascribed to this Presidency by any of the books.

3. Mollugo.

1. *M. hirta* (*Glinus lotoides*, D.). A mean-looking prostrate plant, covered with white down, leaves small ovate or obovate, fascicled in unequal sizes, flowers few together of a dirty pink, stamens 10 or 12, styles 5, capsule oblong, seeds with a long bristly appendage. *Kothak.*

A common weed. Throughout India, *H.* He has 3 varieties.

2. *M. stricta.* Erect with angular branched stems, leaves linear lanceolate to obovate, verticelled, veinless, flowers in panicles small, white, stamens 3 or 5, styles 3, capsule round, seeds without appendages.—*Jharas.*

A common weed throughout India. *H.* includes in this *M. pentaphylla* of *D.*, *R.* and others.

Note.—The genus Mollugo was formerly included in Caryophylleæ and this plant suggests that order.

Order 60. UMBELLIFERÆ.

Herbs often with hollow and furrowed stems, leaves usually divided into many segments, petiole generally sheathing at the base, flowers very small in umbels, generally compound, and with numerous bracts, calyx adnate to the ovary, petals 5, often unequal, inserted round a fleshy disk, stamens 5 epigynous; styles 2, fruit of 2 carpels, united until ripe, generally ridged and furrowed.

This large but very plain family is very well known in England, but has few representatives in W. India, and those few not common. It is one of the most natural orders, the umbellate arrangement of small white or yellow flowers, and the apparently 2-lobed dry fruit being very characteristic. But it is often very difficult to distinguish the genera and species, so that Rousseau compared the plants of this order to a number of relations, with so great a family likeness that outsiders could be sure of the close relationship without being able to distinguish individuals.

Note.—The outer flowers of the umbels are generally more irregular than the others, the outer petals being the largest.

The cultivated species are far better known than any of the native Indian ones; and any one can get a good idea of the peculiarities of the order by carefully comparing the flowers and fruit of two or three of the species here given, viz.:

Apium petroselinum—parsley.
A. graveolens—celery, *Karfas, bori ajmod.*
Fœniculum vulgare, fennel, *barishoph, waryáli.*
Pastinaca sativa—parsnep.
Daucus carota—carrot—*gánjar.*
Coriandrum sativum, coriander—*dhangá, Kothmir.*
Peucedanum graveolens—dill—*sowá.*
Cuminum cyminum—cummin—*jirá.*

Note.—Out of 13 native species attributed by *H.* to this Presidency, 8 are given on the authority of Dalzell, Stocks and Law alone, and apparently not known otherwise.

Note.—The first of the genera here given is by no means a typical Umbellifer, the umbels being not very pronounced; the flowers, in the species here given, dark, and the leaves simple.

1. Hydrocotyle. Prostrate herbs, rooting at the nodes, leaves entire, umbels simple, small, fruit laterally compressed, the achenes flat, nearly round.

2. Carum. Petals retuse or emarginate, fruit laterally compressed, ovate or oblong.

3. Pimpinella. Impossible to give any constant and appreciable distinctions from the last.

4. Peucedanum. Fruit much dorsally compressed, achenes winged on the margin.

5. HERACLEUM. Bracts few or none, petals obovate emarginate or bifid, fruit roundish, much dorsally compressed.

1. HYDROCOTYLE. White rot.

H. asiatica. A small plant, leaves round or kidney-shaped, crenated, long-stalked, umbels short, flowers few, dark-coloured, near the root, fruit roundish. *Bráhmi, Káringa, Kárivaná.*

S. Konkan, Mahableshwar, and elsewhere in moist places, not common. Throughout India, *H.*, and in the warmer parts of the globe. The leaves are like those of violets.

2. CARUM. Caraway.

C. Roxburghianum (*Pimpinella involucrata*, D.). Erect; leaves much divided, segments linear, flowers white, umbels long-stalked of 6 or 8 rays, bracts both general and partial various; fruit warted. *Ajmod, Karonga.*

This *D.* calls very common in the Konkans. Throughout India, extensively cultivated (*H*). I had it only at Sattara, and do not feel certain of the identification. Two or three other species are cultivated, the leaves being used for parsley, and the seeds for caraway.

3. PIMPINELLA. Burnet saxifrage.

1. *P. lateriflora.* A smooth delicate plant; leaves twice or thrice ternate, segments linear-lanceolate, umbels about 8, general bracts about 8, partial about 4, flowers tinged with violet or pink, fruit warted.

Poona. Ravines in the Deccan, common (*D.*).

2. *P. adscendens.* A slender smooth plant, radical leaves many; leaflets about 6 pair oval, serrate cuneate at the base, stem leaves few; flowers white, bracts small linear, fruit not warted.

Panchganni. Banks of Konkan, rivers and elsewhere (*D.*). The plant smells like parsley.

P. monoica. Six or eight feet high, smooth, umbels in many branches at the top, leaves trifoliate, the upper leaflets variously divided; fruit at first woolly. *Bhálga.* Mahableshwar. Highest Ghauts (*D.*). **P. heyneana,* two feet high, smooth, leaves, and sometimes leaflets, ternate, umbels long-stalked, without bracts, fruit roundish. Konkan (*D.*).

4. PEUCEDANUM. Hog's fennel.

* *P. grande* (*Pastinaca g.* D.). Three feet high, thick-stemmed, smooth, leaves mostly radical bipinnate, leaflets of

3 large rounded lobes, flowers yellow, fruit large, broadly ovate *Búphali.*

Matheran and Konkan hills; the fruit is sold in Tanna bazaar. Ghauts near Bombay (*D.*).

**P. dhana* (*Pastinaca glauca*, D.). Leaves radical, pinnate, leaflets 3 to 5, generally deeply lobed, bracts few and various, flowers small, yellow, fruit broad oval. *Koland.* The root, like a carrot, is eaten. Near Belgaum (*D.*).

5. Heracleum. Cow parsnep.

H. pinda. One to two feet high, hairy, leaves mostly radical bipinnate, segments coarsely toothed, umbels with 6 to 8 unequal rays, flowers white, external petals large, deeply lobed. *Pinda.*

Lanoli. Mahableshwar, *Dr. Cooke.* Ghauts (*D.*).

**H. concanense*, larger, all hispid with spreading hairs, leaves twice ternate. Konkan hills (*D.*).

**H. rigens* (*H. sprengelianum*, D.). 2 or 3 feet high, leaves with 3 to 7 roundish leaflets, fruit roundish, reddish brown. Between Belgaum and Ram Ghaut (*D.*).

Polyzygus tuberosus, a smooth herb, leaves twice ternate, segments ovate, variable, flowers white, petals turned in, fruit smooth shining. Dápoli. Malwan (*D.*).

**Bupleurum mucronatum* (*B. falcatum*, D.). Diffuse, much-branched, leaves oblong, linear, long-pointed, rays 5 to 8 with 8 to 12 flowers, fruit strongly ribbed. Dharwar Collectorate (*D.*).

Assafœtida, *hing*, called devil's dung by the old travellers, is a gum from one or two species of *Ferula*, which grow in Beluchistan, Persia, &c.

Order 61. **ARALIACEÆ.** The ivy tribe.

Trees or shrubs, often climbing, leaves alternate, flowers regular, small, calyx tube united with the ovary, petals 5 to 7, stamens as many, inserted round a disk.

This is a small order coming near to the last, but the flowers are imperfectly umbelled, and the fruit succulent. *Hedera helix* is the English ivy, found also in the Himalayas.

Heptapleurum. Large shrubs or trees, umbels panicled, fruit a berry-like drupe, roundish, 5 or 6-angled.

**H. Wallichianum* (*Hedera w.* D.). A strong woody climber, leaves digitate long-stalked, leaflets 5 to 10, oblong, entire leathery, flowers pedicelled, panicles very large, berry 6-celled, crowned by the much enlarged pentagonal disk.

Foot of Ram Ghaut and similar places, pretty common (*D.*). *H.* calls it a large glabrous tree. It is a southern species.

To this order belong two very common garden shrubs, *Panax cochleatum*, shell-leaved panax, with simple large and very hollow leaves, and *P. fruticosum* with large supra-decompound leaves.

Order 62. CORNACEÆ.

Trees or shrubs, with small regular flowers, calyx tube united to the ovary, stamens inserted with the petals into a fleshy disk, ovary inferior, style single.

This is a small order of the northern hemisphere, allied to the two last, but differing from Umbelliferæ in the flowers not being in umbels, and from Araliaceæ in having a single style. The cornel or dog-wood (Cornus sanguinea) is a well-known shrub or small tree of English hedges. The wood throughout the order is very hard.

Alangium. Leaves alternate entire, petals 5 to 10, stamens twice as many, style very long, stigma large capitate, fruit a berry crowned by the calyx limb.

A. Lamarckii. A small tree with grey bark and occasional thorns, leaves oblong or lanceolate, slightly hairy, flowers in small fascicles on the naked branches very fragrant, calyx teeth minute, petals varying in number, yellowish white, curled back; stamens about 20, long, white, bearded at the base, disk white and fleshy, berry like a gooseberry, dark red with one large seed embedded in pulp. *Ankul, Kála akol.*

Konkans. Also Deccan and Guzerat (*D.*). Throughout India, very common (*H.*).

IV. MONOPETALOUS EXOGENS.

PLANTS having a corolla with united petals, the stamens inserted on it, and very generally definite in number.

The thirty orders which are included in this great division of plants can be separated for the most part into two very distinct groups—

1. Flowers, generally regular, with 4 or 5 stamens, and the same number of calyx and corolla lobes; the stamens as a rule alternate with the corolla lobes.

2. Flowers with an irregular 2-lipped corolla, and either 2 or 4 (didynamous) stamens, generally the latter.

Note 1.—It must be remembered that in many cases, particularly in the earlier orders of this division, the petals are united very low down, and so may at first sight easily be looked on as separate.

Note 2.—Throughout this division the stamens are on the corolla, except when otherwise stated.

CONSPECTUS OF ORDERS.

I. STAMENS 4 OR 5: LOBES OF CALYX AND COROLLA AS MANY.

(*a*) Stamens 5, corolla regular.

67. PLUMBAGINEÆ. Herbs or undershrubs; ovary superior.
68. PRIMULACEÆ. Herbs.
69. MYRSINEÆ. Shrubs or trees, leaves alternate undivided, without stipules.
75. APOCYNEÆ. Generally shrubs, leaves opposite entire, without stipules; fruit often of 2 follicles.
76. ASCLEPIADACEÆ. Generally twiners with milky juice; stamens combined into a mass, fruit of 2 follicles.
81. CONVOLVULACEÆ. Twiners, leaves alternate, ovary superior.
82. SOLANACEÆ. Herbs or shrubs, leaves alternate, without stipules.

(*b*) Stamens 5, corolla irregular.

65. GOODENOVIÆ. A shrub, corolla oblique.
66. CAMPANULACEÆ. Tribe Lobelicæ. Herbs, ovary inferior.

(*c*) Stamens 4; flowers regular.

74. SALVADORACEÆ. Trees or shrubs, leaves opposite entire.
92. PLANTAGINEÆ. Herbs with radical leaves; stamens long and weak, anthers large.

(*d*) Stamens 4 or 5; flowers regular.

63. RUBIACEÆ (except Randia and Gardenia). Leaves simple entire, stipulate, ovary inferior.
77. LOGANIACEÆ. Leaves opposite, ovary superior.
78. GENTIANACEÆ (except Canscora). Herbs, leaves opposite, all parts symmetrical.
79. HYDROPHYLLACEÆ. Differs from the last in having alternate leaves, and imbricated corolla lobes.
80. BORAGINEÆ. Rough plants, leaves alternate, fruit often of 4 nutlets.
66. CAMPANULACEÆ. Tribe Campanuleæ. Herbs.

II. FLOWERS BILABIATE: STAMENS 4, DIDYNAMOUS, OR TWO.

83. LENTIBULARIEÆ. Herbs of moist places, corolla spurred, stamens 2.
84. SCROPHULARINEÆ.
85. OROBANCHACEÆ.
86. GESNERACEÆ.
87. BIGNONIACEÆ.
88. PEDALINEÆ.
89. ACANTHACEÆ.
90. VERBENACEÆ.
91. LABIATÆ.

(84–91) For distinctions see explanations preceding these orders.

III. ORDERS NOT INCLUDED IN THE ABOVE.

64. COMPOSITÆ. An order quite by itself; flowers composed of many distinct perfect florets.
70. SAPOTACEÆ.
71. EBENACEÆ.
72. STYRACEÆ.

(70–72) Trees; almost all with many stamens.

73. OLEACEÆ. Trees or shrubs, flowers regular, stamens 2.

Note.—In some cases the short descriptions given above refer not to the order generally, but only to those genera and species here described.

ORDER 63—RUBIACEÆ.

Trees, shrubs, or herbs, with simple entire leaves, opposite or whorled, with stipules (except *Rubia*), often sheathing, calyx tube adherent to the ovary, corolla regular tubular, 4 or 5-

lobed (but see *Randia and Gardenia*), stamens as many inserted on the corolla.

This is a large and important order, mainly tropical, generally characterized by great symmetry in all parts of the plants. The best known species are the Coffee shrub, the various species of Chinchona, and the ornamental Gardenias.

The distinctions between the genera here given are often obscure, and a considerable number of the species may be called inconspicuous weeds.

Note.—*H.* has made a great number of tribes, which, owing to the slight differences, I have been unable to follow. I have grouped the genera as well as I can, but those of group (*e*) have no noticeable characteristics apart from those of the order.

(*a*) Trees or shrubs, flowers small in dense round heads.

Note.—This is a very distinct group. All here given, with two other species, were formerly in one genus, Nanclea, of which *H.* has made four.

1. ANTHOCEPHALUS. Calyx and corolla tubular and 5-lobed, style exserted; fruit fleshy, round, composed of the aggregated pyrenes of many separate flowers.
2. ADINA. Like the last, but the fruit of each flower separate and capsular.
3. STEPHEGYNE. Like the last, but the calyx limb entire.

(*b*) Shrubs or small trees, flowers in spikes or racemes.

4. HYMENODICTYON. Parts of the flower 5, capsule many-seeded.
5. WENDLANDIA. Stamens between the corolla lobes, capsule small, round.

(*c*) Small inconspicuous plants; parts of the flower 4, when not otherwise stated.

6. DENTELLA. Parts of the flower mostly 5, corolla lobes with 2 or 3 teeth.
7. HEDYOTIS. Stigma one, bifid or two-lobed.
8. OLDENLANDIA. Stipules acute or bristly, stigmas 2.
9. ANOTIS. Stigmas 2 to 4, capsule 2-lobed

(*d*) Trees or shrubs, anthers sessile or nearly so, fruit fleshy.

10. MUSSÆNDA. Calyx lobes and petals 5, one lobe of the calyx very large and leaf-like.
11. RANDIA. Corolla lobes and stamens usually 5, berry 2-celled, many-seeded.
12. GARDENIA. Flowers white, often large, corolla lobes and stamens 5 to 12, the latter in the tube, style short and stout.

13. CANTHIUM. Flowers small axillary, ovary 2-celled, style stout, stigma large.
14. VANGUERIA. Like the last, but ovary 3 to 6-celled, and fruit larger.
15. IXORA. Corolla tube long and very slender, lobes 4, twisted in bud, style filiform exserted, fruit quite small.
16. PAVETTA. Like the last, but stipules more or less sheathing, and style much longer.
17. MORINDA. Flowers white on a common receptacle; calyx altogether united to the ovary and without a limb, and therefore not easily distinguishable, corolla lobes 4 to 7, fruit of the whole head of flowers united into one large berry.

Note.—From the peculiarities of calyx and fruit this is a very difficult genus to identify.

(*e*)

18. HAMILTONIA. Flowers small, numerous, corolla tube long, filaments short, ovary 5-furrowed, style 5 divided, capsule 5-valved.
19. SPERMACOCE. Flowers small, corolla lobes 4, fruit of 2 united achenes.

(*f*) Herbs with angular stems and entire leaves in whorl without stipules.

20. RUBIA. Straggling or climbing, fruit didymous, fleshy.

Note.—This last genus alone belongs to the tribe by which the order is known in England; and which is sufficiently distinct to have been made a separate order (Stellatæ) by Bentham.

1. ANTHOCEPHALUS.

A. cadamba (*Nauclea c.* D.) A very fine tree with large long-stalked cordate ovate leaves, flowers in large stalked showy heads, fragrant, orange coloured with white exserted stigmas, calyx tubes growing together, corolla tube long, fruit size of a small orange, yellow. *Nhiv, nipa, Kadamba.*

Not uncommon about villages in the Konkan, and frequently planted about temples. Wild or cultivated throughout India (*H.*).

This tree is held in great reverence both by Hindoos and Buddhists. The ancient Indians compared the smell of the flowers to that of new wine, from which they called the tree *Halipriya* (*Sir W. Jones*): the flowers also having an irresistible power of recalling the absent lover. From its seed the tree of Buddha is said to have sprung, and to have grown in a moment to an enormous size. (*Dymock.*) It is also much connected with the unedifying history of Krishna, and therefore held in reverence by his devotees.

2. Adina.

A. cordifolia (*Nauclea c.* D.) A stout tree with large round cordate slightly hairy leaves tinged with red, flowers in smaller heads than the last, buff coloured, strong smelling, calyx very small, capsule small, wedge-shaped, many-seeded. *Hedu, haldwa, aldu.*

The Konkans, tolerably common. Dry forests throughout the hilly parts of India (*H.*).

3. Stephegyne.

S. parvifolia (*Nauclea parviflora,* D.) A nearly smooth tree with oval leaves, heads of flowers much smaller than the last, the peduncle with 2 small leaves at the base, flowers light yellow, calyx lobes very short, capsule very small. *Kadam, halwan.*

The Konkans. Throughout the drier parts of India (*H.*).

Nauclea. Gen. as the last. **N. missionis.* Small tree, leaves elliptic with winged petioles and sheathing stipules, flowers yellowish-white. Chorla Ghaut (*D.*]. Konkan, *Stocks* (*H.*).

(*b*) 4. Hymenodictyon.

* *H. excelsum,* leaves oblong or roundish, flowers greenish-white in large panicles, floral leaves large oblong, coloured, capsule oblong on thick curved pedicel, *kadwa, dondru, dándelu.*

Along the Ghauts (*D.*) Panchmahals (*B.*). * *H. obovatum,* leaves smooth obovate, flowers in racemes, white or greenish, strong smelling, floral leaves lanceolate, coloured, capsule small erect. *Kadwai, Sirid.* Ghaut jungles, common (*D.*).

5. Wendenlandia.

W. notoniana. A very handsome small tree or shrub, with long oval nearly smooth leaves, stipules leafy, flowers in thick heads or panicles of interrupted spikes, pure white, long tubed, very fragrant ; capsule enclosed in the calyx.

Near Mahableshwar and in other parts of the Ghauts, not common. Hills of the Deccan peninsula, common (*H.*) Wight calls the flowers reddish white, and *H.* says the leaves are usually in threes.

(*c*) 6. Dentella.

D. repens. A small creeping plant with oval ciliated leaves and small white flowers, nearly sessile, solitary or in pairs, capsule compressed oval 2-celled.

Common in moist places.

7. Hedyotis.

H. auricularia. Prostrate, slightly hairy, leaves lanceolate or ovate, strongly nerved below, stipules membranous, edged with long hairs, flowers small, white, sessile, with short broad tube, capsule very small, crowned by the calyx segments. *Gaimaril.*

Dápoli. This is not in *D.*, but *G.* has it common in the rains. Nearly all over India with several very distinct-looking vars. (*H.*).

8. Oldenlandia.

1. *O. corymbosa* (*Hedyotis burmaniana*, D.). A small weak plant, leaves linear or lanceolate, stipules bristly, peduncles often divided, bearing from one to four white flowers, corolla tube short, capsule didymous, smooth. *Phápati.*

Common. Very common at Mahableshwar in October (*Dr. Cooke*). An abundant weed throughout India, varying from a diminutive straggling herb to an erect one a foot or more high (*H.*).

2. *O. Heyneii* (*Hedyotis h.* D.). Like the last, but larger and stronger, branches acutely angled, flowers solitary or in pairs, corolla tube long, capsule opening across the top. *Kájhuri, párpati.*

Konkan, common. These two probably run into one another.

O. trinervia, (*Hedyotis t.* D.) procumbent, straggling, leaves ovate or roundish, flowers solitary or clustered, corolla rotate, white or purplish, capsule small, hairy. S. Konkan. *O. aspera* (*H. aspera*, D.), small and rough, leaves narrow linear, stipules sheathing, bristly, flowers long-tubed, pale blue, capsule roundish. Poona. Deccan and Surat. (*D.*) **O. umbellata*, stem woody, much-branched, leaves often fascicled, linear, flat, peduncle stout, capsule as in No. 1. Not in *D.*, but *G.* calls it Indian madder, common in Konkans. **O. Senegalensis* (*Hedyotis s.* D.) a foot high, leaves linear, flowers short-pedicelled, distant, few, dingy white, capsule hemispheric. Barren places in the Deccan (*D.*).

9. Anotis.

A. fœtida. (*Hedyotis f.* D.). Erect, smooth, leaves linear or narrow lanceolate, flowers purple in threes or fives at the end of long peduncles, very fetid, capsule broader than long.

Konkan and Canara (*D.* and *B.*). At Poona there is a species or variety very common, and agreeing with this except that it is all hairy and the leaves oval. At Kew I found specimens with hairy, but not oval leaves.

**A. Leschenaultii*, stems straggling, hairy, leaves broad ovate, stipules bristly, flowers blue, long-tubed, calyx increasing and becoming leaflike after flowering. Belgaum (*D.*). **A. lancifolia*, erect, leaves lanceolate, flowers in heads of 5, long-tubed, capsule rough, much broader than long. **A. Rheedi* (*H. latifolia*, D.), a large species, stems square, leaves ovate hairy, flowers minute, pale rose colour, capsule very small. Málwan (*D.*) **A. carnosa* (*Hedyotis c.* D.) smooth thick and fleshy : Malwan (*D.*); supposed by him to be only a seashore variety of *A. fœtida*. **A. Ritchiei*, very slender, acutely angled, leaves lanceolate, rough, flowers purple, tube very slender. Konkan and Belgaum (*H.*). Not in *D.*

Note.—The last three genera run into one another a good deal, and *H.* has 97 species between them; so the student may expect to be puzzled.

To this group belong *Argostemma*, flowers white, panicled or umbelled. **A courtallense* (*A. Cuneatum*, D.). About three inches high, leaves in pairs or fours ovate, umbels short, bracts leafy: on rocks at Chorla Ghaut (*D.*). **A. verticellatum* (*A. glaberrimum*, D.), leaves sessile in fours, lanceolate ovate, unequal-sided, all parts of the flower 5, filaments swollen at the points, adhering. Trees in Wári (*D.*). Canara (*H.*). *Ophiorrhiza*, all parts of flower 5, disk very large, capsule girt in the middle by the calyx tube. **O. harrisiana*, herbaceous or half shrubby, leaves ovate lanceolate, stipules with one or more long points, flowers white in corymbs. Ram Ghaut (*D.*).

Knoxia (here inserted out of *H.'s* order), fruit very small of 2 cocci. **K. corymbosa*, erect, slender, leaves lanceolate, stipules bristly, sheathing, flowers very small, white or purplish, fruit 4-angled. Near Vingorla (*D.*).

(*d*) 10. Mussænda.

M. frondosa. A shrub, inclining to climb, leaves oval, flowers small in terminal cymes, rich yellow, one of the calyx segments like a white leaf, the other segments long linear, fruit smooth obovoid. *Sarwad, láuchut, bhutkesh, shivardoli.*

Common in the Konkan and on the Ghauts; handsome and easily recognizable by what seems a leaf growing out of the flower, "white with the whiteness of what is dead." By this the plant departs very remarkably from the symmetrical character of the order. *H.* gives 6 varieties.

11. Randia.

R. uliginosa. A small smooth tree, branches rigid, 4-angled, thorns short and few, leaves large, shining, ovate or obovate, narrow at the base, flowers large, white, solitary, sessile, very fragrant, petals 5 to 8, rounded, stigma large, yellow, fruit size and shape of a guava, yellow, smooth, with deep depression left by the calyx. *Pendharey, Kaurio.*

S. Konkan, S. M. country, Panchmahals. All parts of the flower are more or less fleshy, and the fruit is eatable. *H.* says that the flowers are of two forms, either large and sessile with stigma 2-cleft, or small and peduncled with stigma entire.

2. *R. dumetorum.* A rigid shrub or small tree, smaller in all points than the last, thorns stout, leaves smooth, shining, oval, narrow at the base, flowers solitary, terminal, white, fragrant, turning to yellow as they fade; fruit size of a small apple, green. *Ghela, pairálu, mindhal.*

Very common on the Ghauts and other hills: also in most parts of India (*Brandis*). Very variable in habit and size. *H.* includes in this *D.'s R. longispina*, with long straight thorns and fruit size of a small wood apple. Khandesh jungles.

The fruit is used for poisoning fish, but when ripe is roasted and eaten.

12. Gardenia.

1. *G. lucida.* A large shrub or small tree, leaves oval, smooth, hard and shining, flowers large, long tubed, white, solitary, stamens erect, stigma thick and protruding, fruit size of an acorn, smooth green, striped longitudinally, crowned with the lanceolate calyx lobes. *Dekámáli, Karanji.*

Konkan, and further South.

The *dekamáli* ointment is the yellow strong-smelling gum which exudes from the young shoots of this and of **G. gummifera*, a similar tree called *Kamari*, found in the S. M. country and Canara. Its leaves are sometimes obovate, flowers 2 or 3 together almost sessile, fruit much larger, oblong, smooth, with a stout beak (*D.*). **G. latifolia*, leaves opposite or in threes, large broad oval, stipules large, connate, flowers large, solitary, long-tubed, fruit large, round, greenish speckled. *Pándru, pápur, Ghogari.* Khandesh, Konkan, Belgaum (*D.*). **G. turgida* (*G. montana*, D.), thorns straight, leaves oblong obovate, flowers 3 to 6 together, white, short-tubed, fruit roundish or ovoid, rough, grey. *Kurphendra.* The Atavisi, Mr. Law (*H.*).

13. Canthium.

C. umbellatum. A handsome tree with smooth oval entire leaves, flowers white in short-stalked umbels, corolla lobes and stamens 5, fruit larger than a pea with square calyx mark on the top. *Arsul, tup.*

G.'s C. didymum, Málya, warsangi, common along the Ghauts, which seems to be less of a tree, and the flowers in compressed cymes instead of umbels, is probably not a different species (*H.*). This is found at Mahableshwar and on the Ghauts. **C. Rheedii*, a thorny shrub, leaves ovate lanceolate, flowers small, greenish, fascicled or in racemes, tube very short and broad with acute lobes, fruit roundish. Konkan (*G.*). Near Sivri Fort (*D.*). **C. angustifolium* (*C. Leschenaultii*, D.) *H.* thinks to be only a glabrous variety of *C. Rheedii.* Foot of Rám Ghaut (*D.*). *Chápyel.* **C. parviflorum*, shrubby, often very thorny, leaves ovate to roundish, corolla and calyx lobes and stamens 4, flowers very small, yellowish. *Kirni.* S. Ghauts and S. M. country (*D.*). Near Ellora (*G.*)

14. Vangueria.

V. spinosa. A small handsome tree, more or less thorny with broad ovate highly polished leaves, flowers small, greenish, in short cymes, corolla very hairy within, stamens scarcely longer than the hairs, calyx very small at the base of the corolla tube, fruit when ripe brown and rotten like a medlar, eatable. *Alu, Chircholi.*

Common in the Konkan and Ghauts.

H. makes *V. edulis*, which is cultivated and has the same native name, a different tree. It is unarmed.

15. IXORA.

1. *I. parviflora.* A shrub or small tree with rather large oblong blunt shining leaves, cordate at the base, and small pink or white flowers in cross-armed panicles with bracts at the intersections, style very hairy, berry round, smooth, size of a pea. *Kurát, ráikura, guávi-lakri, mákri che-jhár.*

Ghauts and Konkan. The green branches are used for torches, whence it is called "the torch tree."

2. *I. coccinea.* A shrub with smooth obovate leaves, upper ones stem-clasping, flowers bright scarlet in close terminal umbels or corymbs, calyx very small, corolla lobes broad-pointed, berries scarlet, turning to purple. *Bakora, ábuli, pendkul.*

Exceedingly common on the seashore of the S. Konkan, and strikingly beautiful. From the general resemblance of the flowers to the scarlet geranium it is often called "jungle geranium."

> "Where, gemming oft the sacred gloom,
> Glows the geranium's scarlet bloom."—*Heber.*

Also called "Flame of the woods"; probably *bandhuka* of Sanscrit poetry. Cultivated throughout India (*H.*).

3. *I. nigricans.* A handsome shrub with long lanceolate leaves, which turn black in drying, flowers delicate, white, in very large heads, calyx and pedicels reddish, fruit size of a pea. *Kátkuri, lokhand, átkura.*

The Ghauts.

**I. elongata* (*I. pedunculata*, D.). A shrub with slender smooth branches, leaves elliptic, smooth, leathery, flowers small, pink, in a loose panicle, fruit slightly 2-lobed. Ghauts (*D.*). Konkan and Canara (*H.*)

16. PAVETTA.

P. Indica. A smooth shrub of no beauty, leaves lanceolate, obovate, flowers dingy white in crowded heads, corolla tube very long, berry size of a pea. *Pápat, tartari.* "Matheran coffee." (*Mr. Birdwood.*)

Konkan and Ghauts, very common. "Throughout India; one of the commonest and most variable of Indian small trees or bushes" (*H.*). He includes in this *D.'s P. Brunonis*, which is softly hairy more or less all over.

**P. hispidula* (*P. siphonantha*, D.). Very like the last, but with flowers usually much larger and yellowish. Párpuli Ghaut (*D.*).

Webera, filaments short or none, stigma long. **W. corymbosa* (*Stylocoryne Webera*, D.), leaves oblong lanceolate, shining, flowers small, white, in corymbs, corolla bearded in the mouth, stigma 10-ribbed, berry size of a pea. *Káre.*

Diplospora, flowers diœcious, calyx and corolla tube short. **D. apiocarpa* (*Discospermum a.* D.). Middle-sized tree, leaves ovate elliptic, flowers small, sessile in the axils, stamens much exserted, fruit pear-shaped with a circular ring below the top. **D. sphærocarpa* (*Discospermum s.* D.), like the last, but the fruit round, fetid, 2-celled. These two depend chiefly on Dalzell, who has "Ghauts, lat. 16°."

17. Morinda.

1. *M. tinctoria* (*M. citrifolia*, D). A shrub or small tree, branches 4-angled, leaves oval, shining, flowers white in short-stalked heads, corolla lobes and stamens 5, fruit round or ovoid, fleshy. *Al, bártondi.*

"Cultivated and wild (?) throughout the hotter parts of India and Ceylon" (*H.*). Fields of it are cultivated in Khandesh and other places, for the roots, from which a red dye is made.

H. includes in this *D.'s M. bracteata*, which has heads of flowers bracted, and calyx often with one long leafy lobe. (See *Mussænda.*)

2. *M. citrifolia* (*M. tomentosa*, D). A shrub or small tree, most parts downy with handsome shining ovate leaves, flowers few together, white, long-tubed, fragrant, fruit round and smooth, size of an apple, showing the marks of the separate berries of which it is composed. *Nágkura, aseti.*

The Konkan and elsewhere, often planted.

H. strangely puts the fruit of this as one inch in diameter, though it is described and figured as above by various authors. There appears to be much confusion between this species and the last, and many varieties are found throughout India. The tree is very widely spread. Captain Cook says that the fruit is eaten in the South Sea islands in time of scarcity. At Sierra Leone it is called the brimstone-tree, and attains a great size.

(*e*) 18. Hamiltonia.

**H. suaveolens* (*H. mysorensis*, D.). A small erect rigid shrub, leaves oval lanceolate, flowers small, white or blue, calyx teeth very variable, often with intermediate gland-tipped processes, capsule very small, elliptical, seeds 3-sided. *Gidisa, gitsai.*

Caranjah and the Ghauts, pretty common (*D.* and *G.*).

H. calls this shrub 'fetid when bruised,' which seems scarcely consistent with the specific name, still less with R.'s description of it as "a charming fragrant-flowered shrub."

19. Spermacoce.

1. *S. stricta.* A small erect rough plant with square hairy stems, leaves sessile linear lanceolate, flowers very small, short-tubed, white, crowded in the axils, capsule roundish, crowned by the calyx, smooth below, rough above.

Common in the rains at Rutnagherry, Bombay, and other places, and throughout India (*H.*). Not in *D.* or *G.*

2. *S. hispida.* A rather trailing plant, all rough, stems square, reddish, leaves ovate sessile, flowers very small, few, in axillary whorls, corolla long-tubed, blue or white, capsule as in the last. *Madnaghauti, Ghautiche báji, dhoti.*

I noted the corolla tube as white, lobes lilac.

A common weed. Throughout India (*H.*).

Psychotria, shrubs, fruit of 2 pyrenes. **P. truncata* (*Grumilea vaginnans*, D.). Smooth, with large obovate leaves and very large sheathing stipules, flowers small, white, fruit like black pepper. Chorla Ghaut and Mahableshwar (*D.*). Matheran (*Birdwood*). *H.* has also in Canara and southwards, *P. Dalzellii*, with very large broad oblong or roundish stipules, and large persistent bracts.

Chasalia, shrub, corolla tube long, curved. **C. curviflora* (*Psychotria ambigua*, D.). Smooth, leaves oblong lanceolate, flowers white in cymes, fruit size of pea. Parwar Ghaut (*D.*).

Geophila, small herbs, corolla tube long. **G. reniformis*, creeping, leaves roundish, deeply cordate, flowers very small, corolla lobes recurved, fruit small, round, purple. Vingorla (*D.*).

Saprosma, shrub, calyx limb dilated. **S. Indicum.* Smooth, with sessile oblong leaves, stipules sheathing, flowers few, terminal, berry ovoid, blue, crowned with the calyx teeth, very fetid. Chorla Ghaut (*D.*).

(*f*)

20. Rubia.

R. cordifolia. A rough straggling climber, leaves in 4's, long-petioled, ovate cordate pointed, strongly nerved, flowers minute white, usually 5-cleft in large compound panicles, fruit size of a small pea, black, sometimes twin. *Manjit, itári.* Indian madder.

Mahableshwar and the higher Ghauts. Throughout the hilly districts of India, very variable (*H.*).

This is very much in the style of the common English goose grass (*Galium aperine*), found also in the Himalayas.

Coffea arabica, the coffee shrub, *Kawa, bun,* belongs to the same tribe as Ixora, &c. Sir E. Tennent describes the great beauty of the shrub at every season.

The cinchonas, now much cultivated in India, belong to a tribe of which no other species is found in W. India. The discovery of the virtues of Peruvian bark, as it was formerly called, was, according to Dr. Darwin, accidental: trees cut down for other purposes having impregnated the water into which they fell with quinine, and this having cured of fever some workmen who drank the water.

ORDER 64. **COMPOSITÆ.** Composites.

Herbs or shrubs, leaves generally alternate (except in tribe 5), without stipules, flowers composed of many small florets inserted on a broad receptacle, which is often furnished with chaffy scales (paleæ), and surrounded by an involucre of many bracts often in several series.

Description of florets. Calyx superior, but curiously modified, as it adheres closely to the ovary and is indistinguishable from it (except Echinops); the limb if present composed of bristles or hairs (pappus), corolla either tubular with 4 or 5 lobes or strap-shaped (ligulate); stamens as many as the corolla lobes, within the tube, anthers generally cohering, style slender and bifid, fruit an achene, crowned by the pappus, if there is one.

This is the largest of all the orders, containing, it is said, one tenth of all the flowering plants known, and is also the most natural, so that one can seldom mistake a species of this order for anything else.

The description given above needs some explanation. If what is commonly called a flower in this order be picked to pieces, it proves to be made up of a number of many small flowers (florets), each complete in itself. Hooker has therefore given up the old mode of description, given above, for one more technically correct, and so describes a daisy or sun-flower[1] as a head of flowers, and each floret as a flower, and so throughout the order. But I have retained the old method of description as easier for those who are not scientific.

The shape of the flowers is either rayed, i.e. having a centre of erect tubular florets, and a margin of strap-shaped florets, all turning outwards (e.g. the sun-flower), or disciform, having a more or less round and flat top of erect florets without any margin (e.g. the groundsels in England, and Blumeas in India). Unfortunately for the classification flowers of both shapes occur in most of the tribes, and even in many genera.

[1] A flower of *Guizotia*, *Kálatil*, or of *Zinnia*, is an equally good example.

The flowers are composed either 1° of tubular florets only, 2° of strap-shaped florets only, 3° of tubular and strap-shaped mixed. Jussieu classified the genera on this principle, which is I think certainly the simplest for beginners. But this arrangement has gone out of date, and Hooker has adopted De Candolle's, modified by Cassini, in which the shape of the styles is made the determining feature. This arrangement is, I believe, not easy even for scientific botanists, and for the unscientific it is scarcely possible. I have therefore not attempted to describe this feature, nor to give *H.'s* description of the florets as homogamous or heterogamous; and I fear that thus cut short the tribal distinctions here given will not be found of any great use.

It is not possible to allot *H.'s* genera to Jussieu's tribes, mentioned above, but I believe that it is correct to say that in what follows

Tribes 1 and 2 have florets all tubular: no rays.

Tribe 9 the same, but with flowers of the thistle type.

Tribe 10, florets all strap-shaped; no disk: flowers of the dandelion type.

The remaining six tribes have flowers with or without rays. There is, however, a difficulty to beginners, that a flower may be called rayed when it has only 3 or 4 (perhaps minute) florets differing from the rest, and so to an ordinary observer would appear not rayed.

The peculiarities of the involucre usually afford generic distinctions. This generally clasps the flower like a calyx, and is often (as in the thistles) very conspicuous. I have called the segments of the involucre bracts, and bracts of the ordinary sort when present, which is not often, floral leaves.

The number of plants of this order with which we have to do is small in proportion to the whole number; a gratifying circumstance when we remember the small average of beauty, and the frequent difficulty of recognition. There are few attractive plants among those wild in W. India. The dahlias, zinnias and sunflowers are foreigners.

"Nearly all the compositæ (and cruciferæ), wild or cultivated, are used as salad in the East."—*Hooker*. "They have all more or less bitterness, which is sometimes associated with astringent, acrid, and narcotic qualities."—*Balfour*.

TRIBES 1 and 2. VERNONIEÆ and EUPATORIEÆ. Florets all tubular and hermaphrodite, corolla never yellow (occasionally orange).

1. VERNONIA. Bracts in many series, inner longest, achenes generally ribbed or angled, pappus of many hairs.

2. ELEPHANTOPOUS. Rigid herbs, flowers of 2 to 5 florets clustered into heads, bracts about 8, dry and stiff, corolla equally 4-lobed, cleft on one side, achenes truncate, 10-ribbed, bristles of pappus rigid.

3. ADENOSTEMMA. Smooth or glandular herbs, leaves mostly opposite, bracts many in one or two series, tube of florets short, achenes 5-ribbed glandular, pappus hairs few and short.

4. AGERATUM. As the last, but bracts in 2 or 3 series, achenes 5-angled, pappus various.

TRIBES 3 and 4. ASTEROIDEÆ and INULOIDEÆ. Flowers usually yellow, florets all tubular, or the outer (female) ligulate, inner hermaphrodite (except Cæsulia), receptacle almost always naked.

5. DICROCEPHALA. Annuals, flowers very small, not rayed, outer florets in many series, bracts in one series, achenes compressed without pappus.

6. CYATHOCLINE. Strong smelling annuals, flowers small, not rayed, receptacle elongated concave at the top, bracts in one or two series, florets as in the last, achenes minute, oblong, smooth, without pappus.

7. GRANGEA. Softly hairy herbs, flowers roundish, not rayed, outer florets filiform, tube very slender, bracts in few series, outer herbaceous, pappus cup-shaped.

8. CONYZA. Ray florets filiform, rarely strap-shaped, 2 or 3-toothed, inner tubular 5-toothed, involucre bell-shaped.

9. BLUMEA. Glandular pubescent or woolly herbs, flowers in racemes or panicles, outer florets many filiform, inner few tubular, bracts in many series, narrow.

10. LAGGERA. As the last, but centre of many florets.

11. SPHÆRANTHUS. Low branched annuals with winged stems, flowers in close round clusters, bracts mostly chaffy, achenes large, angled.

12. GNAPHALIUM. Hoary or woolly herbs, florets all fertile, outer filiform and numerous, bracts scarious in many series.

13. VICOA. Flowers woolly, ray florets narrow, involucre bell-shaped, bracts in many series narrow, inner scarious.

14. PULICARIA. As the last, but bracts in few series, narrow, pointed or awned, pappus double.

15. CÆSULIA. A smooth marsh herb, flowers in axillary sessile round heads, surrounded by floral leaves, florets tubular, bracts only two, pappus none.

TRIBE 5. HELIANTHOIDEÆ. Flowers rayed or not, receptacle paleaceous, pappus slight or none.

Note.—Though the sunflower is the type of this tribe, the flowers of many of the genera and species here given are not rayed: in all except the first genus they are yellow.

16. LAGASCA. Leaves mostly opposite, flowers in leafy balls not rayed, florets all hermaphrodite, and tubular, involucre tubular of 5 united bracts.

17. SIEGESBECKIA. Glandular herbs with opposite leaves, flowers partly rayed, ray florets female, in one series short tubed, disk florets hermaphrodite, bracts few herbaceous, outer spathulate spreading.

18. ECLIPTA. Leaves opposite, flowers small peduncled, rayed, of female and hermaphrodite florets, bracts in one or two series herbaceous, outer large and broad.

19. WEDELIA. Rough or hairy herbs or undershrubs, leaves opposite, flowers rayed, ray florets large, strap-shaped, disk florets tubular with elongated limb, bracts few, outer usually herbaceous, inner dry.

20. SPILANTHES. Leaves opposite, flowers long-stalked, rayed or not, bracts in one or two series, receptacle convex elongate.

21. GUIZOTIA. Leaves mostly opposite, flowers stalked, decidedly rayed, tube of all florets short and woolly, bracts in one or two series, outer leafy, inner chaffy, receptacle convex or conic.

22. GLOSSOCARDIA. A smooth herb with much divided leaves, flowers small, scarcely rayed, florets very few, bracts few, inner oblong with membranous margins.

23. BIDENS. Leaves opposite, outer bracts short and leafy, inner membranous.

TRIBE 6. HELENIOIDEÆ. Flowers as in the last, receptacle naked, flowers yellow.

24. FLAVIERIA. Leaves opposite, florets of disk solitary or few, of ray solitary or none, bracts in one series equal, free, pappus none.

TRIBE 7. ANTHEMIDEÆ. Flowers rayed or not, bracts dry or with scarious tips, pappus none or slight.

25. ARTEMISIA. Strong-smelling herbs or shrubs, flowers not rayed, in racemes or panicles, outer florets female, very slender, bracts in few series, outer shorter.

TRIBE 8. SENECIONIDEÆ. Like the last, but flowers all yellow, and pappus more decided.

26. EMILIA. Florets generally all hermaphrodite and tubular, pappus white.

27. NOTONIA. Fleshy undershrubs, flowers large, florets all hermaphrodite, bracts in one series equal.

28. SENECIO. Bracts in one or two series, equal, with a few shorter outer ones, pappus soft, white.

TRIBE 9. CYNAROIDEÆ. The thistle and artichoke tribe. Flowers all tubular, bracts imbricated, frequently bristly, receptacle bristly, leaves often spinous.

29. ECHINOPS. Flowers in dense involucred heads, each floret with its own calyx distinct from the ovary, pappus bristly.

30. TRICHOLEPIS. Unarmed herbs, florets all hermaphrodite and fertile, bracts narrow, pappus bristly, unequal, receptacle densely bristly.

TRIBE 10. CICHORACEÆ: the chicory and dandelion tribe. Herbs, usually with milky juice, florets all strap-shaped, truncate, tip 5-toothed.

31. LACTUCA. Involucre narrow, bracts in few series, receptacle flat, naked, pappus abundant.

32. SONCHUS. Involucre broad at the base, bracts in many series, outer smaller, receptacle and pappus as in the last.

33. LAUNEA. Involucre bell-shaped or cylindrical, otherwise as in the last.

(1) VERNONIEÆ.

1. VERNONIA.

1. *V. cinerea.* A common-looking rather weak plant, with oval or oblong rather hairy leaves, toothed, flowers small, dull purple in corymbs, bracts lanceolate, achenes not angled or ribbed. *Moti sádori, sahádevi.*

A common weed all over India: very variable in habit and foliage, but uniform in flowers (*H.*). He seems to include *D.'s V. conyzoides* in this.

2. *V. divergens* (*Eupatorium d.* D.). A tall shrub with large broad toothed leaves, narrowed into the petiole, flowers very numerous in small heads, panicled, light purple, corolla tube curved, achenes smooth, 10-angled or ribbed. *Bundár.*

The Ghauts. From Central India southwards (*H.*).

This much resembles the English hemp agrimony, Eupatorium cannabinum.

**V. anthelmintica.* Large, stout, leaves lanceolate, coarsely serrated, flowers purple in corymbs, bracts linear with broad purplish tips. *Kala jira.*

2. Elephantopous.

E. scaber. Coarse, rough and hairy, leaves large obovate radical, flat on the ground, flowers purple, floral leaves cordate, acute, spinous. *Mháka, páthri.*

Common in the Konkan and Ghauts. Throughout India (*H.*). The leaves, in growth and shape like those of the primrose, appear at the beginning of the rains, and raise hopes of something good. Nothing more appears till about September, when a tall and promising stem shoots up, and, after further waiting, develops as plain and uninteresting a flower as could be seen.

Centrantherum, bracts in many series, inner dry, outer herbaceous. *C. phyllolænum* (Decaneurum molle, *D.*). Erect, branched, leaves ovate, roughish above, woolly below, bristle-serrated, flowers solitary purple, rather handsome. Dapoli, S. Konkan (*D.*). The other species are not in (*D.*). **C. tenue,* very like this, but more slender with smaller flowers, and only one or two of the leafy bracts. Konkan (*H.*). Matheran (*Birdwood*). **C. courtallense,* similar, but leaves often quite entire, and coarse hairs all about ; Canara (*H.*). **C. Ritchiei,* branches smooth, sometimes shining, the outer leafy bracts 2 to 6, large cordate ; Konkan and Canara (*H.*). **C. Hookeri.* Stiff, branches angled and grooved, leaves linear lanceolate, flowers red, involucre with no leafy bracts. Konkan (*H.*).

Lamprachænium, bracts in many series all dry, pappus hairs few and short. **L. Microcephalum,* erect branched annual, leaves white beneath, elliptic, flowers small in heads or panicles, bracts acute, pappus reddish. Parwar Ghaut (*D.*). Smells of chamomile. Very like *Centrantherum tenue* (*H.*).

Adenoon, bracts in many series awned, outer shorter, pappus none. **A. Indicum,* erect, branched, stems angular and grooved, leaves broad ovate, glandular, flowers panicled, blue. *Kusumb, Moti Sonki.* Parwar Ghaut and Belgaum, (*D.* and *G.*) : Mahableshwar (*Cooke*).

(2) Eupatorieæ.

3. Adenostemma.

A. viscosum (*A. latifolium* and *A. rivale,* D.). A tall, strong-smelling weed, hairy or viscid, with rough nettle-shaped leaves coarsely serrated, and heads of small white flowers in panicles, bracts narrow, about equal ; achenes often warted. *Rangiran.*

Konkan, Deccan and Cutch. Throughout India, and varying very much, especially as to hairiness, breadth of leaves and wartiness of achenes (*H.*).

4. AGERATUM.

**A. conyzoides.* Rough, hairy and strong-smelling, leaves ovate, cuneate, flowers small, pale purple in dense terminal corymbs, bracts linear, about equal, achenes black. *Ganera, osádi.*

Not in *D.*, but *G.* calls it one of the commonest weeds in gardens at Belgaum, Bombay, and elsewhere. Throughout India and in all hot countries (*H.*).

(3) ASTEROIDEÆ.

5. DICROCEPHALA.

D. latifolia. Erect, about a foot high, all hairy, leaves obovate, toothed, lobed at the base, flowers in very small heads of many minute florets, the centre ones yellow, the outer silvery or lilac.

Mahableshwar and elsewhere in the Ghauts. Widely spread in India: leaves very variable (*H.*).

6. CYATHOCLINE.

1. *C. lyrata* (*C. stricta*, D.). A delicate, leafy, greyish plant, erect, covered with clammy white hairs, leaves much divided, lobes serrated, flowers in small rather flat corymbs, purple. *Gangotri.*

Banks of streams in Konkan and W. Deccan.

2. *C. lutea* (*C. Lawii*, D.). A very pretty delicate-looking plant, with pinnatifid or much divided leaves pressed flat on the ground, stem about four inches high, almost leafless, branched, flowers bright yellow, button-shaped.

"A curious and very beautiful little plant" (*H.*). The leaves are like miniature copies of those of the well-known English "milfoil" or "yarrow."

Lanoli. The Ghauts and Konkan: and nowhere else (*H.*).

7. GRANGEA.

G. maderaspatana. Prostrate, much branched, covered with white clammy hairs, leaves sinuate or pinnatifid, flowers bright yellow in nearly round flat-topped heads; florets very numerous minute. *Mashipatri.*

In rice fields and similar places in the cold weather. Throughout India (*H.*).

8. CONYZA.

C. stricta (*C. absinthefolia*, D.). A handsome erect plant, stem leaves crowded, narrow, the lower coarsely toothed, flowers small yellow, in flat-topped panicles, bracts linear, pointed.

Leaves sometimes pinnatifid (*H.*). The Ghauts, Matheran. "The commonest composite at Mahableshwar."—*Cooke.*

C. adenocarpa, rough and hairy, much branched, leaves spathulate, stem-clasping, flowers small yellow in corymbs, achenes with yellow glands. Highest Ghauts (*D.*).

Erigeron. Flowers rayed, outer bracts green, narrow, pappus often double. *E. asteroides*, hairy plant, leaves stem-clasping, ovate or oblong, flowers solitary, rather large, disk yellow, rays lilac. *Márndi, Sousáli.* Poona. Konkan (*G.*). Not in *D.*

Note.—The daisy (*bellis*) and *Aster* are the best known flowers of this tribe; but, except *Erigeron*, the genera given above have flowers not rayed.

(4) INULOIDEÆ.

9. BLUMEA.

"The species of this genus may be called the groundsels of India. . . . There is no more unsatisfactory genus . . . the divisions here proposed are most unsatisfactory, and I fear that the scientific diagnosis is not much better. . . . The foliage is sportive to an extraordinary degree, as is the pubescence; gland-hairs are common to most species, but the amount varies with the dryness of the locality' (*H.*).

This will explain the difficulty of identifying the species; and I may add that there is so little beauty or usefulness in the genus, as far as I know it, that if it disappeared from the face of the earth altogether, instead of increasing and multiplying as it does, there would be very little to regret.

Mr. Jaikrishna Indraji, who gave me a good deal of information about this genus, says that the strong-smelling species are called generally *bhámurda, chauchar mori*, and *Kákharunda.*

Note.—The flowers are yellow, unless otherwise stated.

*1. *B. amplectens.* Branches spreading, leaves oblong, coarsely toothed, flowers stalked, solitary, or in pairs, bracts very slender.

Common on roadsides (*D.*). *H.* has a variety near the sea, bushy, smooth and glandular.

**B. bifoliata* is like this, but the leaves serrate, and tips of the bracts not hair-pointed (*H.*). Common about Surat (*D.*).

2. *B. glomerata.* All grey and hairy, leaves obovate or lyrate, serrate, flowers in clusters all along the branches, sometimes in interrupted spikes.

Konkans and Ghauts. I take this to be the common Matheran species. *H.* includes in it *D.*'s *B holosericea* and *leptoclada.*

3. *B. lacera* (*B. leptoclada*, D.). Hairy, glandular and strong-smelling, leaves obvate oblong, serrated towards the top, flowers clustered, bracts narrow-pointed, achenes smooth.

This I take to be the common strong-smelling species growing all over dry rice fields. Throughout the plains of India (*H.*).

Very like this are **B. laciniata*, usually taller and smoother, scentless and with laciniate leaves; rare in the Konkan (*H.*); and **B. Wightiana*, often prostrate with ascending branches, flowers small, pink or purple, achenes hairy. Bombay, and plains of Indiá (*H.*).

4. *B. membranacea* (*B. muralis*, D.). Tall and slender, hairy and glandular, leaves lyrate toothed, flowers very small, oblong, bracts slender and shining.

On roadsides and old walls. Throughout India in 6 varieties (*H.*). **B. virens* closely resembles this, but is perfectly smooth, sometimes 4 feet high. Konkan and Canara (*H.*). **B. oxyodonta*, a small species, prostrate or diffuse, branched, leaves obovate, spine-toothed, flowers few, peduncles slender. Not in *D.* Bombay (*Mr. J. Indraji*). *H.* has **B. eriantha*, Konkan, Law, perhaps a variety of this, very slender, peduncles and involucres with long silky hairs, *nimurdi*. **B. Malcolmii*, like these two, " the stout habit, dense silvery woolly clothing, and sparse often peduncled heads are its most prominent characters" (*H.*). Konkan and Belgaum (*H.*). Matheran (*Birdwood*). **B. Belangeriana*, woolly, branches a foot long, often red-brown; Konkan (*H.*). **B. Malabarica*, leaves membranous with a distinct petiole, flowers half an inch in diameter; Canara, &c., Law (*H.*). **B. spectabilis* (*B. Longifolia*, D.). Six to eight feet high, leaves oblong, petiole often winged, flowers in a pyramidal panicle with floral leaves, pappus red. Tallawári (*D.*). Canara (*H.*).

10. Laggera.

1. *L. alata* (*Blumea a.* D.) A stout leafy plant with reddish hairs, stems winged, leaves oblong-toothed decurrent, flowers purplish in racemes, drooping, outer bracts often recurved, inner long, straight.

Ghauts (*D.*).

2. *L. aurita.* Rather slender, stem not winged, leaves lanceolate or half pinnatifid, shortly decurrent, flowers pink, bracts soft and slender. *Jangli muli.*

Not in *D.* or *G.* Common in Bombay.

11. Sphæranthus.

S. Indicus (*S. mollis*, D.) A small prostrate plant, all hairy and strong-smelling, stem petioles and peduncles irregularly winged, leaves oblong, broader at the top, toothed, flowers purple in round heads, florets many minute, bracts shorter and slender. *Mundi, Kharak-shepu, nai.*

Common in rice fields in the cold weather.

12. Gnaphalium. Cudweed.

G. Indicum. A small diffuse weed, branched from the root, all covered with white cotton, leaves oblong or linear, heads of flowers small in spikes with scarcely any colour, but becoming brown and rough when withering.

Common throughout India (*H.*). It is very like the English *G. uliginosum.*

G. hypoleucum, very similar, but leaves stem clasping and auricled, flowers yellow. Wára in the Poona districts. Abu (*Dalzell*). Not in *D.* Mr. Birdwood has at Matheran *G. leucoalbum*, smaller than this and the leaves not auricled.

13. Vicoa.

V. auriculata (*V. Indica*, D.). Erect branched, leaves sessile, lanceolate, auricled, much wrinkled, flowers small, solitary or twin, long-stalked, like camomile.

Deccan, Konkan, Cutch. Drier parts of India (*H.*).

**V. cernua*, like this, but lower leaves petioled, flowers drooping, bracts with recurved margins. Konkan Hills and Belgaum (*D.* and *H.*).

14. Pulicaria. Fleabane.

P. Wightiana (*Callistephus w.* D.) Strong erect branched, leaves sessile linear oblong, flowers solitary long-stalked, yellow, outer bracts leafy.

Common in the Deccan. Peduncles swollen upwards (*H.*). **P. angustifolia* (*Callistephus concolor*, D.). Much smaller in every respect, "the ligules very deciduous, if indeed they are always present" (*H.*). Málwan (*D.*), Cutch (*Palin.*).

Note.—Most of the English fleabanes are woolly, but the above are not so.

To this tribe also belong—*Pluchea*, florets as in Blumea, but the few central florets are sterile, bracts ovate, broad, dry. **P. Wallichiana.* A tall shrub, glandular, hairy and rough, leaves sessile, obovate, flowers pink in corymbs. Dhej, Guzerat (*D.*). Sindh (*H.*). **P. Indica*, 6 or 8 feet high, hedges in Cutch (*Palin.*).

Nanothamnus, florets as in the last, but very few of either sort, bracts in many series lanceolate, dry, pappus none. **N. sericeus*, a small rigid woolly herb, stems very many, leaves lanceolate, pungent, flowers in dense clusters, subsessile. Not in *D.* or *G.* Konkan Hills, Dalzell (*H.*).

Epaltes, outer florets in many series, female, filiform, centre hermaphrodite, bracts in many series, pappus none. *E. divaricata*, small prostrate, much-branched herb, leaves oblong, broader above, slightly decurrent, flowers one or two together, flat topped, containing an immense number of pink florets. Malwan in rice fields. *H.* calls it erect, 4 to 8 inches high.

Blepharispermum, flowers in close round clusters, bracts mostly chaffy. **B. subsessile* (*Leucoblepharis s.* D.). A smooth under shrub, leaves ovate or elliptic shining, clusters of flowers with large leafy floral leaves. Ghauts (*D.*), Dharwar (*G.*), Konkan and Canara (*H.*).

Helichrysum, very like *Gnaphalium* in generic features. **H. Buddleioides*. A shrub 4 to 6 feet high, densely cottony, leaves large sessile lanceolate, flowers yellow in many round clusters, inner bracts with a scarious blade. Along the Ghauts (*H.*). Not in *D.* or *G.*

Inula. Flowers rayed, outer bracts herbaceous. **I. Grantioides*, a low stout, woody shrub with balsamic smell, leaves fleshy trifid, flowers large, solitary, yellow, rays few and short, bracts hairy and sticky. Not in *D.* Cutch and Sind.

15. Cæsulia.

Note.—I have put this at the end of the tribe, as being very unlike all the other genera; it is in fact not easy to recognize it as belonging to the order, and the same may be said of Flavieria.

C. axillaris. A rather pretty plant, often prostrate, stem purple and mottled, leaves lanceolate, dilated into a broad stem-clasping base, which contains the sessile heads of pale-coloured flowers: the leaf bases and the few floral leaves are violet and veined, style black.

Bombay, Konkan and Deccan; common in wet ground. Throughout N. India (*H.*).

(5) Helianthoideæ.

16. Lagasca.

L. mollis. A common-looking much-branched herb, leaves ovate acuminate silky, flowers in round long-stalked heads of many white florets, heads surrounded by floral leaves.

A South American plant, now very common about Poona and elsewhere.

17. Siegesbeckia.

S. orientalis. A branched plant with woody stem, leaves ovate, coarsely toothed, softly hairy, flowers small, yellow, solitary, short-stalked, with few florets, inner bracts united enclosing the florets, outer 5, linear slightly dilated at the top; achenes angular black.

Poona districts. Near Belgaum (*D.*). Throughout India and all over the world in warm climates (*H.*).

H. has in the genus 'flowers subradiate in leafy panicles,' but my description agrees with *R.*'s.

18. Eclipta.

E. alba (*E. erecta* and *E. prostrata*, D.). A small rough weed, erect or diffuse, leaves lanceolate or oval, narrow at both ends, flowers white, solitary or twin enclosed in a large soft involucre, outer florets very narrow. *Máka, bángra.*

Common in most parts. Throughout India, and in all warm climates; leaves very variable (*H.*).

From the predominance of narrow strap-shaped florets the flowers look like those of a chickweed.

19. Wedelia.

W. urticæfolia (*Woolastonia biflora*, D.). Shrubby spreading, branches angular grooved, leaves ovate pointed, serrated, peduncles generally two together, of which one is longer, flowers rather large yellow, ray florets few, bracts lanceolate dry, achenes with black spot in the middle. *Sunki.*

Very common on the Ghauts; covering the roofs of houses at Khandalla (*G.*). *D.* has no habitat. I had it at Malwan close to the sea, and *H.* has *W. biflora* as a coast species very like this but a climber; so some differences may be allowed for.

W. calendulacea, straggling, hairy, leaves lanceolate ovate, flowers large, solitary, long-stalked, bright yellow, ligules few, disk florets crowded on convex receptacle, outer bracts about 5 large. *Pivala máká.* G. I. P. railway hedge about Lasalgaum. No hab. (*D.*).

20. Spilanthes.

S. acmella. A leafy plant with ovate lanceolate leaves and small ovoid yellow flowers on very long stalks, ray florets small and few; achenes more or less rough. *Acharbondi.*

Deccan, Konkan and Ghauts. Throughout India (*H.*).

H. has 4 varieties, one of which has flowers in panicles, and one or two are cultivated as pot herbs.

21. Guizotia.

G. Abyssinica (*G. oleifera*, D.). An erect leafy plant, leaves sessile or stem clasping, ovate lanceolate, serrate roughish, flowers bright yellow, large and handsome, long-stalked, solitary or in pairs, ray florets few and broad, bracts broad ovate. *Rám til, Kála til.*

A native of tropical Africa, commonly cultivated for the oil; a field of it in full flower is a bright and splendid object. On the Konkan hills it is often seen growing high up on steep and apparently inaccessible slopes.

Note.—That the *black* seeds of Sesamun Indicum, which are comparatively rare, are also called *Kála til* (*Lisboa.*)

22. Glossocardia.

G. linearifolia (*G. Bosvallea*, D.) A very small diffuse plant, stem angled, leaves of many filiform segments, petioles long and channelled, flowers solitary, short-stalked, yellow, ray florets only one or two. *Fattarsuva.*

Poona, Cutch. Common (*D.*). Has the smell of fennel (*H.*).

23. Bidens. Bur marigold.

B. pilosa (*B. Wallichii*, D.). A tall, rather lax, slightly hairy plant, leaves pinnate, or pinnatifid, leaflets or segments ovate deeply cut, petioles long and channelled, flowers yellow, long-stalked, solitary or corymbose, ray florets very few or none achenes with hooked awns.

Deccan, Bombay, &c. Throughout India, exceedingly variable (*H.*). It has the general appearance of the common agrimony, rather than of the English species of this genus.

To this tribe belong *Sclerocarpus*; flowers rayed, ray florets neuter in one series, disk florets hermaphrodite, bracts few outer spreading, receptacle raised. *S. Africanus*, straggling branched, rough, leaves broad ovate, flowers solitary yellow, disk florets about 12. Nasik, Junar Hills (*D.*), Konkan (*H.*) The achenes which are covered by the skin-like pales develop early, and separate the ray florets.

Blainvillea, herbs, ray florets female, few or none, disk florets tubular, hermaphrodite, bracts few, outer herbaceous, inner passing into the dry scales of the receptacle. *B. latifolia*, erect rough, leaves ovate, flowers mostly sessile small white, ligules few, 2-cleft, outer bracts about 5, soft oblong. Poona, &c. No hab. (*D.*). Cutch, Palin. *Glossogyne*, flowers small, scarcely rayed, florets very few, bracts few, inner oblong with membranous margins. **G. pinnatifida*, smooth erect, leaves mostly radical, pinnatifid or pinnate with narrow segments, flowers small yellow, bracts linear obtuse, achenes deeply grooved. S. M. country (*D.*)

H. also puts in this tribe *Xanthium*, which has generally had a tribe to itself, as being anomalous. Upper flowers round of many tubular male florets, females below of 2 apetalous florets; bracts of female flowers closing and covering the achenes. **X. strumarium* (*X. Indicum*, D.). A coarse rough herb, leaves heart-shaped or 3-lobed, florets dull purple, fruit ovate 2-beaked, covered with hooked bristles. Common, especially about rivers in S. M. country (*G.*). Hotter parts of India (*H.*). *Shankeswar.* Found in England, but not commonly.

The sunflower is *Helianthus annuus.*

. . . "the sunflower, shining fair,
Rays round with flame her disk of seed."—*Tennyson.*

The seeds are much eaten in Central Asia and in Russia. "The Russian peasant is never completely happy unless he is cracking and chewing the seeds of the sunflower."—*Harper's Mag.* It is an American plant, as is *H. tuberosus*, the Jerusalem artichoke. The dahlias also belong to this tribe.

(6) HELENIOIDEÆ.

24. FLAVIERIA.

F. repanda. Prostrate or spreading with jointed stems, leaves stem clasping, lanceolate, dilated at the base with very small sessile yellow florets clustered there, bracts 4, leaf-like.

An imported plant, not given by *H.* nor by *D.* or *G.*, but common in gravel walks, &c., at Poona and elsewhere. It is not easy to identify as belonging to this order, as the florets appear to be quite independent. It resembles Cæsulia in this and other respects.

(7) ANTHEMIDEÆ.

25. ARTEMISIA. Wormwood.

A. vulgaris (*A. Indica*, D.). Tall strong plant, the stem and underside of flowers covered with white down, leaves pinnatifid or much lobed, toothed and cut, flowers in panicles or racemes very small, the yellowish florets almost hidden in the involucre, outer bracts leafy, inner dry. *Daona, mastáru, surband.*

Deccan hills. Common at high elevations (*H.*). This, as *H.* has identified it, is the common Mugwort of waste places in England. Wormwood closely allied to this is several times mentioned in the Old Testament as symbolical of calamity or distress. Absinthe is made from other species.

* *A. parviflora*, leaves cuneate, often lobed or pinnatifid, with a pair of stipule-like lobes at the base, flowers green, drooping, bracts broad, the edges scarious. *Dauni.* Mahableshwar and Ghauts (*D.* and *H.*).

The chrysanthemums and camomiles (*Anthemis*) belong to this tribe.

(8) SENECIONIDEÆ.

26. EMILIA.

E. sonchifolia. A common and variable weed, smooth or slightly glaucous, leaves lyrate or pinnatifid, stem-clasping, sometimes auricled, leaves in small umbels purple, florets very numerous, involucre about as long as the flowers. *Sádhi-mandi.*

Common in many places. Throughout India (*H.*), but not in *D. H.* has three varieties.

E. flaminea (*E. sagittata*, D.). A garden species very like this, but with showy red flowers, is said by *H.* to be very commonly cultivated, and probably not a native of India.

27. NOTONIA.

* *N. grandiflora.* A small fleshy shrub with thick stem and branches, leaves oblong or obovate entire, flowers large, long-pedicelled, pale yellow, corymbose, achenes smooth. *Wúndar rotti, gaidar.*

Kandalla, Mahableshwar and other high places: and common in gardens.

* *N. Balsamica,* very like this, but distinguishable by the pappus, which is of stiff flattened hairs, while those of *N. grandiflora* are slender and round. *Gaozabán, pirang.* The Ghauts, rare (*D.*). Both are called the cabbage tree.

28. SENECIO. Ragwort.

This genus contains about 900 species, of which *H.* has 60 as found in India. All the species here given belong to a section with rayed flowers, ligules broad and long, bracts in one series, and pappus rigid, scabrous, often reddish.

1. S.—— (*Doronicum reticulatum*, D.). Erect, slightly rough, leaves somewhat quadrangular toothed, flowers small yellow, about 2 together on long stalks, outer florets 10 to 12, bracts linear, receptacle convex. *Sonki.*

The Konkan.
This description is of a species that, according to *D.*, has no pappus, and I have found it so at Dápoli: but the point mentioned makes it difficult to identify with any of *H.'s*, as it does not agree otherwise with *S. Belgaumensis.*

The following, except *S. Newrensis* and *Belgaumensis*, are not in *D.* or *G.* Most of them are known only to Dalzell and Law, and the hab., when not otherwise given, is Konkan and Bababudin hills.

* *S. ludens,* 'a most sportive plant,' herbaceous, leaves more often lyrate pinnatifid, the bases or petioles broad auricled. "Konkan specimens very stout, stem a foot high, as thick below as the little finger" (*H.*). * *S. tenuifolius.* Slender, smooth, leaves sessile pinnatifid, flowers few, long-peduncled. W. Ghauts. **S. Newrensis* (*Doronicum h.* D.). A small leafy plant, leaves oblong, auricled, toothed or subpinnatifid, flowers on long slender peduncles, ligules three, very small, disk florets about 12. Rocky places near Junar (*D.*). **S. Edgworthii,* a very cottony herb, leaves cordate, rhomboid or

ovate with auricled petiole, ligules 10 to 14, pappus white. Central India, &c. (*H.*). **S. Dalzellii*, herbaceous, more or less cottony, leaves linear or lanceolate, ligules 10 to 15 narrow. **S. Lawii*, very like the last, but much more slender with hair-like peduncles and smaller heads. Konkan and Severndrug (*D.*). **S. Belgaumensis*, erect, branched, leaves rhomboid, auricled, cottony below, peduncles long, pappus none. Belgaum. **S. Grahamii*, very like the last, but with double pappus of long and short hairs; also much like *A. Lawii.* **S. Gibsoni*, very similar, but leaves narrow, more membranaceous, and not white below.

Anyone who could get specimens of all the species of this genus and of Blumea that can be found in W. India, and get them identified, would do a good work. Blumea is a tropical and sub-tropical genus, Senecio of temperate climes, and therefore usually found in India only at high elevations.

Gynura, succulent herbs with bracts below the involucre, florets generally all hermaphrodite and tubular, bracts in one series equal, narrow. **G. angulosa* (*G. simplex*, D.) tall, erect, stem angled, leaves large oblong ovate, sometimes auricled, flowers many and large, deep orange, involucre bracts linear acute. *Dahu.* Junar hills (*D.*). Mahableshwar (*Cooke*): Konkan and Belgaum (*H.*).

The next tribe is Calendulaceæ, with only one genus Calendula. *C. officinalis*, the common Marygold, is found in the Punjaub and Sind, doubtfully wild, more or less cultivated elsewhere. *Makmal.*

"The Marygold that goes to bed with the sun,
And with him rises weeping."—*A Winter's Tale.*

(9) Cynaroideæ.

29. Echinops. Globe thistle.

E. echinatus. Erect, much branched, leaves sessile pinnatifid, woolly below, lobes sinuate and prickly, florets pale lilac, forming a prickly ball, segments of corolla linear, curled back. *Kántechubak.*

Common in the Deccan and elsewhere.

This has a very thistly appearance, but is still more like the English sea holly (*Eryngo*), which, however, belongs to the Umbelliferæ.

30. Tricholepis.

1. *T. radicans.* Smooth, much branched plant about a foot high, stem angular, leaves from linear to ovate, sometimes pinnatifid, dotted, with distant bristly teeth, flowers small, long-stalked, florets few, purple or lilac, outer bracts recurved.

Deccan and Konkan.

2. *T. glaberrima.* Erect, quite smooth, greyish, with

linear lanceolate bristle-toothed leaves, flowers small and slender, more or less panicled, florets few, purple, bracts erect. *Motabor*.

Deccan and Konkan, Mahableshwar and Ghauts. It often grows on cultivated fields.

T. amplexicaulis, a large stout plant, quite smooth, leaves elliptic obovate, flowers larger than *T. radicans* and with more florets, outer bracts recurved, inner longer, bristle-pointed. *Dáhán*.

Dapoli and above Lanoli, where it grows four or five feet high. Not in *D.*, Konkan (*H.*). I believe that the three species run into one another.

Carthamus tinctorius, belonging to this tribe, is safflower, cultivated in all black soil districts. *Kusumba*. There is a prickly var. called *Kurde*. From the flower a dye is made, which is often called bastard saffron. The true saffron comes from the common yellow crocus, and the colour is frequently used by the poets to describe the early morning sky, and otherwise.

"There let Hymen oft appear
In saffron robe."—*Milton*.

Goniocaulon, flowers narrow of few florets, all hermaphrodite and fertile, bracts very narrow, not spinous. **G. glabrum* (*Amberboa Indica*, D.), smooth, erect, stem furrowed and angular, leaves sessile lanceolate or obovate, flowers rose-purple, florets about 5. Guzerat (*D.*). Central India and Deccan (*H.*). *Volutarella*, outer florets in one series neuter, disk florets hermaphrodite, involucre ovoid or round. *V. divaricata* (*Tricholepis procumbens*, D.) branched, straggling or procumbent, more or less hairy, leaves lyrate or pinnatifid, bristle-pointed, florets about 12, bracts flat, bristle-pointed. Poona districts. Guzerat (*D.*). Cutch, Palin.

In tribe Mutisiaceæ the florets have generally a bilabiate corolla, but the genus here given belongs to a sub-tribe with sub-equal corolla, and separated from Cicoraceæ by minute differences.

Dicoma, flowers sub-sessile on the branches, disciform, receptacle flat, naked. *D. tomentosa*, erect, woolly, leaves sessile narrow, entire, flowers on short axillary branches, florets many, straw-coloured, with tufts of stiff white hairs among them, bracts long, narrow and very bristly.

Sholapore. Deccan and Gogo (*D.*).

(10) Cichoraceæ.

31. Lactuca. Lettuce.

L. Heyneana (*Brachyrampus*, *H.*, D.). A tall, smooth weak plant, radical leaves pinnatifid with rather broad lobes and saw-like serratures, stem leaves few, small and stem-clasping, flowers yellow, very narrow, racemed, florets few and small, involucre oblong, outer bracts much shorter. *Sádhimandi.*

Growing out of walls in many places: on the sea-sands in the N. Konkan: common in fields (*H.*). *L. remotiflora* (*Brachyrampus sonchifolius*, D.). Smaller, smooth, leaves stem-clasping, auricled, bristle-serrate. *Undirkani.* Sattara, common (*D.*).

L. sativa is the cultivated lettuce. The milky juice is narcotic.

32. Sonchus. Sow thistle.

S. oleraceus. Smooth or with scattered glandular hairs, leaves lanceolate entire or pinnatifid, acutely auricled, flowers crowded, more or less umbelled, achenes ribbed and wrinkled. *Mhátára.*

Not in *D.*, but common. Throughout India in fields and cultivated places (*H.*).

This is the "common annual sow thistle" of England. It is used for salad in many places. "The asinine feast of sow thistles and brambles."—*Milton.*

33. Launea.

L. pinnatifida (*Microrhyncus sarmentosus*, D.). A small glaucous creeping plant with many roots, radical leaves sinuate and pinnatifid; flowers solitary, bright yellow, with scales or bracts on the short peduncles, involucre bracts from long to very short. *Almiro, páthri.*

Very common on the sandy sea-shore, Bombay and Konkans; and on many other tropical shores (*H.*).

* *L. nudicaulis*, not in *D.* or *G.*, is ascribed by *H.* to the Deccan and Sind, with flowers sometimes 6 to 10 in a cluster, otherwise very much like the above.

Note.—The next five orders agree in having leaves without stipules, and calyx and corolla lobes and stamens 5.

Order 65. **GOODENOVIÆ.**

Shrubs or herbs, calyx tube adherent to the ovary, stamens inserted at the base of the corolla, stigma large and fleshy.

Scævola. Corolla oblique, split to the base behind, fruit a drupe.

S. Kœnigii (*S. Taccada*, D.). A large shrub with thin loose bark and handsome fleshy leaves, collected about the ends of the branches, obovate, smooth and shining, flowers white, tinged with purple in short cymes, calyx segments oblong, enlarging in fruit, stigma hairy, drupe roundish, fleshy, white. *Bhadrak.*

Close to the sea in the Rutnagherry Collectorate, and widely distributed in similar situations (*H.*).

It is easily recognized by the cleft one-sided corolla.

ORDER 66. CAMPANULACEÆ. Bell flowers.

Herbs or undershrubs, calyx superior, seeds very many. In this two orders are included which outwardly are very different, as in the Lobelias the corolla is irregular. The stamens are inserted on a ring at the base of the corolla. Canterbury bells and the harebell of the poets are the best-known plants of the order.

TRIBE LOBELIÆ. Corolla 2-lipped, anthers united.

1. LOBELIA. Leaves alternate, corolla oblique, tube cleft to the base behind, upper lip 2-lobed, lower 3-lobed, capsule 2-valved.

TRIBE CAMPANULEÆ. Corolla generally bell-shaped, anthers free, filaments dilated at the base.

2. WAHLENBERGIA. Ovary top-shaped, stigma 3-lobed.

1. LOBELIA.

1. *L. trigona.* Smooth, small, rather straggling, leaves roundish or ovate crenated, flowers blue or white, pedicels angled, stamens protruding through the cleft back of the corolla, capsule oval.

Konkan, in rice-fields, &c. At Mahableshwar and in the Panch Mahals. Small specimens might be taken for a Vandellia, but for the protruding stamens.

2. *L. nicotianæfolia.* Five or six feet high, stem hollow, leaves mostly radical, very long, lanceolate, flowers white in racemes, capsule roundish, covered by the calyx. *Dawal, devnal, boknal.*

Common on the Ghauts : a handsome plant.

The whole plant is exceedingly acrid, and its touch to be avoided. A West Indian species, *L. longifolia,* is described as much worse.

"Where fell Lobelia's suffocating breath
Loads the dark pinion of the gale with death."—*E. Darwin.*

* *L. radicans* (*Pratia r.* D.). Annual, smooth, creeping, leaves

sessile, linear oblong, flowers green with pink marks, stigma long, green, 2-lobed. A native of China, but now common in gardens (*D.*).

The small blue lobelia used for edgings in English gardens is *L. cælestis.*

2. Wahlenbergia.

W. gracilis (*W. agrestis,* D.). Nearly all smooth, leaves narrow linear with waved margins nearly entire, flowers white or blue, sometimes tubular, calyx lobes erect, very narrow, bracts about half as long as the pedicels, capsule ovoid.

Matheran, Mahableshwar, Konkan. Throughout India, a common weed (*H.*). This is in all respects an ordinary-looking plant, and has no apparent claim to its specific name.

Cephalostigma. Corolla deeply lobed, capsule within the persistent calyx teeth. **C. schimperi* (*C. hirsutum,* D.), a small rigid erect plant, branched at the top, hairy, leaves lanceolate, crisped, flowers bluish, in racemes, capsule roundish, and **C. flexuosum* very similar, but with ascending instead of horizontal branches and pedicels longer. The Konkans (*D.*). *Sphenoclea,* flowers in dense bracted spikes, stigma 2-lobed. **S. zeylanica,* a herb, leaves narrowed at both ends, flowers small, white, with bracts, capsule top-shaped, angled, circumsciss. Not in *D.* Rice-fields (*G.*). Swamps throughout India (*H.*).

Order 67. PLUMBAGINEÆ.

Herbs or undershrubs, flowers regular, bracted, calyx inferior tubular, 5 to 10 ribbed, stamens 5, anthers oblong, styles 5, capsule membranous, included in calyx.

This order includes Statice, Sea-lavender, and Armeria, thrift, well-known in English gardens.

Plumbago. Flowers in spikes, calyx covered with stalked glands, corolla tube long and slender, capsule circumsciss near the base.

P. zeylanica. A straggling climber, leaves ovate, suddenly narrowing, flowers white, spikes glandular, hairy and sticky, bracts 3. *Chitrak.*

Guzerat, common in hedges, less so in the Konkan. The flowers are sometimes umbellate.

P. rosea (*P. coccinea,* D.) *lálchitrak,* flowers red, leaves more tapering is perhaps only a cultivated variety (*H.*), but I have seen it apparently wild. *P. capensis, udichitrak, kála chitrak,* with flowers of a peculiar and beautiful blue, is one of the commonest garden climbers in W. India, and well-known in English conservatories.

Vogelia, small shrubs, calyx 5-winged, capsule circumsciss at the very base. * *V. Indica* (*V. arabica,* D.) whitish, leaves ovate to roundish, sessile or perfoliate, spikes long and slender, flowers small and dense. Hanamant Ghaut, Abu and Canara (*D.*).

ORDER 68. PRIMULACEÆ. The Primrose family.

Herbs, flowers regular, calyx inferior, style one, stigma capitate, capsule valved.

Note.—This and the next order are distinguished by the stamens being opposite to the corolla lobes, instead of alternate with them, as in other regular monopetalous flowers.—*Bentham.*

The primrose, almost the earliest, and perhaps the most popular of all English wild flowers, is of course unknown in the Tropics: while the only representative of the order found in W. India seems to be rather a doubtful native, and is, at all events, much better known at home.

ANAGALLIS. Leaves opposite entire, capsule round.

A. arvensis. Small, erect, branches square and winged, leaves ovate, stem clasping, flowers solitary axillary, long-stalked, scarlet or deep blue.

This is the common pimpernel, or shepherd's weather-glass. It is found occasionally in the Deccan in moist places, and is common in the Páshan valley (*Mr. Woodrow*) and in the S. Ghauts (*Dr. De Crespigny*). But it is the blue flowered variety, comparatively rare in England, which is oftenest found.

ORDER 69. MYRSINACEÆ.

Shrubs or small trees, leaves alternate undivided, flowers regular, calyx inferior, anthers oblong, acute.

A small order allied to the last, but different in habit. The leaves are generally dotted with glands, as in Rutaceæ and Myrtaceæ.

1. MÆSA. Calyx 2-bracted, nearly enclosing the round many-seeded berry.

2. ARDISIA. Calyx often enlarged in fruit, bracts small deciduous, corolla segments twisted in bud, filaments very short, anthers ovate lanceolate, style long, fruit roundish, one-seeded.

3. EMBELIA. Flowers small, mostly diœcious, fruit small, round, one or two-seeded.

4. ÆGICERAS. Flowers in umbels without bracts, calyx lobes imbricate, corolla lobes twisted in bud, filaments long, anthers cordate lanceolate, fruit cylindric, curved, one-seeded.

1. MÆSA.

M. Indica. A tall shrub, with large polished leaves, oblong, coarsely serrated, flowers small, pure white, bell-shaped, fragrant, in very numerous short spikes or racemes, corolla lobes rounded and reflexed, berry size of a pea. *Átki*, *átak.*

Common in the Ghauts.

H. gives several varieties, depending chiefly on the size and shape of the leaves, and calls it an erect tree 30 feet high, or a shrub on lands gone out of cultivation, neither of which alternatives seem to be correct for W. India.

2. Ardisia.

A. humilis. A handsome shrub, quite smooth, leaves long, ovate or lanceolate, shining, flowers pale pink, waxy in umbels or racemes, anthers very large, meeting in a point at the top, fruit black. *Dikna.*

Southern Ghauts. Throughout India (*H.*). This is the only one out of forty-five species attributed to this Presidency.

The unopened pink buds are very beautiful. The anthers are like those of Solanum. The specific name humilis is particularly inappropriate.

3. Embelia.

* *E. ribes.* A large scandent shrub, stem rough and knotty, leaves ovate, narrowed at both ends, flowers white or greenish-yellow, very many in panicles, fruit like peppercorns. *Karkani.*

Common in Salsette and on the Ghauts (*D.*). The fruit, *waiwarang*, is collected and sold for medicinal purposes.

* *E. robusta* (*E. basaal*, D.), like the last, but the flowers in short racemes, and the fruit red, when ripe. *Amti*, *bárbati*, *gondali*. Konkan, Khandalla, &c. Throughout India, very common (*H.*).

4. Ægiceras.

Æ. majus. A handsome shrub with laurel-like leaves, obovate, blunt, smooth, and pure white fragrant flowers, petals recurved, anthers large, erect, fruit like a miniature curved carrot. *Chip*, *fungali*, *cháwir.*

Growing in salt marshes with the different sorts of mangrove. Tropical shores nearly of the whole world (*H.*).

Note.—Of the next three orders all the species here given are trees, almost confined (as to this Presidency) to the W. Ghauts, and nearly all have many stamens.

Order 70. SAPOTACEÆ.

Leaves alternate, entire, leathery, without stipules, flowers axillary, clustered without bracts, calyx lobes 4 to 8 much imbricated, or in 2 series; corolla with as many lobes or 2 or 4 times as many, stamens on the corolla tube, filaments short, fruit indehiscent 1 to 8-seeded, with calyx attached.

Chiefly a tropical order: most of the species are milky and have edible fruits.

1. SIDEROXYLON. Lobes of calyx and corolla 5, imbricated, stamens 5, attached to the base of the corolla, berry fleshy.

2. BASSIA. Calyx segments 4 in 2 series, corolla bell-shaped, lobes 6 to 12, stamens 12 to 40, anthers with connective.

3. MIMUSOPS. Calyx segments 6 to 8 in 2 series, corolla lobes 18 to 24 in 2 or 3 series, stamens 6 to 8 with as many staminodes.

1. SIDEROXYLON. Iron-wood. (See also Mesua.)

S. tomentosum (*Sapota t.* D.). A stiff branched thorny tree of no beauty, most parts hairy, leaves small oval, dull grey, flowers dingy-white, fruit oval, size of a plum, full of milk, seeds large dark, about 3. *Kumbel, Káula Kumli.*

Very common at Matheran, and on the Ghauts generally. The thorns are not unfrequently absent.

2. BASSIA.

1. *B. latifolia.* A large handsome tree all full of milk and in most parts densely hairy, leaves large, oval to roundish obovate, flowers white fleshy, corolla cup-shaped, filaments none, style long, berry oblong, smooth, size of a small apple with calyx attached. *Mowa, mowra.*

Most abundant in the jungles of Guzerat, less so in the Konkan. Throughout Central India (*H.*).

This is a most useful tree, the wood being hard and durable, the flowers edible, though they have a most disagreeable mousy smell; when dried they produce the mowra spirit: the fruit is also eatable and is used in making bangles. The oil produced from the seeds is called *dhulia*, and from it bassic or stearic acid is obtained.

* 2. *B. longifolia.* Leaves lanceolate, narrowed at both ends, smooth, flowers whitish in dense clusters near the ends of the branches, corolla lobes and stamens generally fewer than

in the last, berry yellow, like a large plum, densely hairy when young. *Mowa, ippi, ilupi.*

Dharwar, Canara, and the South of India generally, where the flowers and seeds are used for the same purposes as those of the last further north. *H.* calls this and another species "Indian butter trees."

3. Mimusops.

1. *M. elengi.* A handsome tree but growing to no great size, leaves elliptic oblong, dark green, shining, flowers white, fragrant, calyx rusty, berry size of an acorn, one or two-seeded. *Bakhor, bársoli, taindu, wáoli.*

Ghauts and S. Konkan, not very common, but often cultivated for the flowers. Deccan common (*H.*). Sometimes called the Indian medlar tree. Sanscrit, *kesára.*

2. *M. hexandra.* A small stiff tree of no beauty, leaves leathery, smooth and shining, obovate or emarginate, flowers small, white, berry like an acorn, yellow, seeds one or two oblong black. *Ráyan, ránjan, karni.*

Very common in N. Konkan and Guzerat. Deccan peninsula (*H.*).

Chrysophyllum, calyx and corolla lobes and stamens 5 or 6. * *C. Roxburghii,* a very large tree, leaves lanceolate acute, flowers minute, pale yellow, corolla rusty with hairs, fruit like a small apple, yellow, pulpy. *Tarsi, tarsiphal.* Chorla Ghant and Sunda jungles (*D.*). *Isonandra,* calyx and corolla lobes 4, stamens 8. * *I. candolleana,* a small tree, leaves oblong blunt-pointed, flowers small, dull white, rusty, berry oblong, small. *Dichopsis,* calyx lobes 6 in 2 series, corolla lobes 6, stamens 12 to 18 with connective. * *D. elliptica,* (*Bassia e.* D.) leaves elliptic or obovate, flowers 4 to 8 together, filaments hairy, berry oblong, fleshy. *Panchoti, pallá.* Bombay and Canara. This is called the Indian gutta-percha tree, the milky juice of D. gutta being the true gutta-percha.

Order 71. EBENACEÆ. The Ebony family.

Leaves alternate entire without stipules, flowers regular, axillary, usually unisexual, pedicels jointed under the flower, calyx and corolla 3 to 7 lobed, stamens various, fruit fleshy with calyx attached.

Ebony, from which this order (which is nearly allied to the last) takes it name, is the heart wood of different species of Diospyros, and is remarkable for its great weight and hardness, as well as for its blackness, which has long been proverbial—

"By heaven, thy love is black as ebony."—*Love's Labour Lost.*

1. MABA. Corolla lobes 3 or 4, stamens 3 to 22, anthers oblong, female flowers often with staminodes.

2. DIOSPYROS. Calyx and corolla lobes 4, occasionally 5, stamens often 16, anthers linear, female flowers often with 16 staminodes, styles 1 to 4, fruit with enlarged often woody calyx.

1. MABA.

1. * *M. nigrescens.* A small tree with rigidly erect branches and a good deal of tawny hair about it, leaves small ovate or lanceolate, shining above, flowers small, males 1 to 5 together, females one or two, stamens about 9, fruit half an inch long, ellipsoid with cup-like calyx. *Raktrora.*

A tree in sheltered situations, a shrub in the plains. *Lisboa.* Western Ghauts (*H.*).

2. * *M. micrantha* (*Holochilus m.* D.). Leaves oblong, narrow at both ends, female flowers minute, white, sessile, solitary, with 6 staminodes and 3 styles, fruit oblong, hard and dry, with funnel-shaped calyx.

S. Ghauts: "male flowers not seen" (*D.* and *H.*).

2. DIOSPYROS.

H. has 59 species, besides some imperfectly known. The male flowers in all the species here given are in short cymes or clusters, the female solitary or nearly so, and the fruit eatable. The stamens seem to vary very much, even in the same species.

1. *D. montana.* Leaves ovate or oblong, obtuse, shining, female flowers with several staminodes, fruit size of a cherry, round, smooth. *Goindu, hádru, lohári.*

Common in the Ghauts. *H.* includes in this *D.'s D. Goindu.*

2. *D. assimilis* (*D. nigricans*, D.). Leaves smooth, oval or oblong, stamens 24 or more, fruit round, seated in a large fleshy green calyx, the lobes standing out horizontally. *Malya.*

Matheran, common. Chorla Ghaut (*D.*). This comes very near to *D. ebenum,* the true ebony, which is wild in S. India (*H.*).

3. *D. tupru* (*D. exsculpta*, D.). Rough almost all over, leaves oval, blunt, flowers very small, white, fruit round, size of a large plum, brown or yellowish, with glutinous pulp. *Timburni, tartara.*

The Konkan.

I find that Colonel Beldome and Dr. Dymock agree with me in

thinking that *D.'s* tree described above is wrongly identified in *H.*, and should be *D. embryopteris*, which *H.* ascribes to the whole of India, and identifies with *G.'s D. glutinosa. Timbori, mákar kendi.*

* *D. pruriens*, leaves narrow, oblong, fruit ovoid, size of a large cherry, covered with fulvous stinging hairs, the calyx scarcely enlarged. Ghauts and Canara (*D.*). * *D. chloroxylon*, sometimes thorny, leaves small oblong or obovate, flowers small, white, female with about 8 staminodes and 4 styles, fruit smooth, size of a large pea. *Ninei.* Surat and Nasik districts. Fruit size of a cherry. *Lisboa.* * *D. Candolleana*, large shrub or small tree, smooth, leaves oblong, female flowers with about 5 staminodes, fruit ovoid, hard, size of a nutmeg. The Ghauts, common. * *D. paniculata*, leaves oblong, obtuse at both ends, calyx and corolla lobes 5, stamens 20, male panicles black, velvety, fruit ovoid, covered with red hairs, calyx much enlarged. Chorla Ghaut and Raigarh (*D.*).

ORDER 72. **STYRACEÆ.**

Leaves alternate without stipules; flowers regular in racemes or spikes, calyx persistent, bell-shaped, 4 or 5-lobed, corolla 5-lobed, stamens united to the petals, fruit a drupe.

A small order, having generally stimulant and aromatic qualities. Storax and benzoin are exudations from two of the trees.

SYMPLOCOS. Stamens numerous in several series, ovary inferior.

H. has 64 species; both of those found in this Presidency have stamens free, or nearly so.

1. * *S. spicata* (*Hopea s.* D.). Leaves oblong, lanceolate, smooth, flowers yellowish-white, small, crowded, bracted, stamens about 40, drupe like a small fluted pitcher.

The Ghauts, pretty common (*D.*).

2. * *S. Beddomei* (*Hopea racemosa,* D.). Leaves as in the last, petals sometimes 8, stamens indefinite, fruit ovoid crowned by the calyx, dark blue or purple. *Lodra, hura, khádra.*

Mahableshwar and Ghauts. "A very beautiful tree, the scent like almond blossoms." (*G.*).

ORDER 73. **OLEACEÆ.** The Olive Family.

Trees or shrubs, leaves opposite without stipules, flowers regular, calyx small, corolla segments 4 to 9, stamens 2.

The two stamens distinguish this order from all others having regular flowers. *H.* has made 4 tribes, named respectively after the jasmine, the lilac, the ash, and the olive. The third of these is not represented in W. India.

TRIBE 1. JASMINEÆ. Shrubs more or less twining, flowers fragrant, corolla lobes much imbricated, and twisted in bud.

1. JASMINUM. Calyx 4 to 9-divided with funnel-shaped tube, corolla salver-shaped, stamens included, stigmas 2.

TRIBE 2. SYRINGEÆ. Seeds winged.

2. SCHREBERA. Leaves unequally pinnate, corolla salver-shaped.

TRIBE 3. OLEINEÆ. Trees, corolla lobes 4.

3. OLEA. Calyx 4-divided, corolla tubular, drupe one-seeded.

4. LIGUSTRUM. Calyx truncate or shortly 4-toothed, corolla funnel-shaped, drupe one to three-seeded.

1. JASMINUM.

The flowers in all given below are white, and the calyx generally pubescent. They are all much like the English favourite, *J. officinale*, which has pinnate leaves.

1. *J. sambac*. Leaves oval, slightly cordate, racemes with opposite flowers, calyx segments 7 to 10 subulate, long; corolla lobes as many, oblong, often double, fruit round, black. *Mogri, bhat mogri.*

Frequently cultivated, but wild in many parts. "Called (in Europe) Tuscan jasmine, from having been introduced at Pisa from Goa" (*Don*); also Arabian jasmine.

2. *J. pubescens*. All more or less hairy, leaves ovate lanceolate, flowers terminal in cymes or umbels, rather large, tinged with pink, calyx teeth long subulate, 6 to 9, corolla lobes oval pointed, fruit oval, smooth. *Vikmogra.*

S. Konkan. From Himalaya to Ceylon, common (*H.*). He includes in this *D.'s J. bracteatum.*

3. *J. arborescens* (*J. latifolium*, D.). A shrub, all smooth with heart-shaped long pointed leaves and large flowers in terminal cymes, calyx lobes 5 to 7 subulate, shorter than the corolla tube, corolla lobes 8 or more, lanceolate or abruptly pointed, fruit ovoid or oblong, often unsymmetrical. *Kusar, ránjai, Kund.*

The Ghauts and hilly parts of the Konkan; the commonest species. It grows luxuriantly, and suits very well Tennyson's description—

"Growths of jasmine twined
Their humid arms, festooning tree to tree."

* *J. Rottlerianum*, hairy, leaves elliptic acute, flowers solitary, or subpanicled, bracts white lanceolate, prominent. Jungles in Wári (*D.*).
* *J. Ritchiei*, smooth or nearly so, leaves long ovate, flowers in lax cymes, long pedicelled, corolla lobes long and narrow. Not in *D.* or *G.* W. Ghauts and Belgaum (*H.*). The fruit carpels are large and round.

Several other species are found in gardens. *Nyctanthes arbortristis*, the night-blowing jasmine, is common, but not wild, a shrub or small tree with rough leaves, flowers white with orange tube, very strong-smelling, falling off very freely in the early morning. *Har, singahar, párijatak.* "This gay tree (for nothing sorrowful appears in its nature) spreads its rich odour to a considerable distance every evening."—*Sir W. Jones.*

2. Schrebera.

* *S. swietenioides.* A large tree, leaflets 5 to 7 ovate acute, flowers in cymes, small white with brown marks, capsule pear-shaped, rough with white specks. *Moka, mokádi.*

The Ghauts, Jowhar and Sind (*D.*). Widely diffused, but not abundant (*H.*).

The lilacs belong to this tribe, but not the beautiful garden shrub commonly called *Syringa*, which is *Philadelphia coronarius.*

3. Olea.

O. dioica. Leaves oval, flowers in panicles very small, white, calyx minute, corolla bell-shaped, fruit oval, like a sloe. *Párjámb, Karamba.*

The Ghauts; very common at Matheran. It is very like the *jámbul* tree, but the fruit is exceedingly bitter. Sometimes called the wild olive; but see *Eleagnus.*

The cultivated olive is *O. Europæa*, which I used to dream long ago of introducing into the S. Konkan. But from what I have since read, I fear it would be a hopeless experiment. Apart from the extraordinary usefulness of the tree, it would be delightful to see on these shores

"The wan grey olive woods, which seem
The fittest foliage for a dream."—*E. B. Browning.*

"No plant yields so much for man's use, and the bulk of its produce is enormous."—*Hooker.* An olive branch has from ancient times been the symbol of peace.

4. Ligustrum.

L. nilgherrense. A small tree, leaves oval acute, smooth and shining, flowers white and fragrant in panicles at the end of the branches, drupe small, oblong, dark plum colour with white bloom. *Lokhandi, marsingha.*

All along the Ghauts. The Nilgherry privet of Mahableshwar (*Dr. T. Cooke*).

L. vulgare is the English privet. (See *Lawsonia.*)

Order 74. SALVADORACEÆ.

Trees and shrubs differing only from tribe Oleineæ of the last order in having 4 stamens.

Salvadora. Calyx and corolla bell-shaped, 4-lobed, style none, stigma truncate, drupe round.

S. persica. Branches very straggling, leaves oval, variable, fleshy, scarcely veined, flowers in large cross panicles, very small, greenish, corolla and calyx scarcely separable, fruit like a minute red currant. *Miraj, mirjoli, Kabar, pilu.*

The Konkans and Guzerat; said to be a salt marsh tree in N. Konkan. All over India, often planted, and wild in Syria, Arabia, Egypt, &c. (*H.*). It is said by most authorities to be the mustard tree of Scripture (and is so marked in the museum at Kew), the berries being aromatic and eatable.

> . . . "the mustard tree,
> That hath its seed so little, and its boughs
> Widespreading."—*Sir E. Arnold.*

Azima, thorny shrubs, flowers unisexual, petals 4, free, stamens hypogynous, stigma large, bifid. * *A. tetracantha*, branches 4-sided, leaves elliptic, sometimes spiny, flowers axillary, yellow, berries round, white. Dharwar and the Habshi's country (*D.*). It somewhat resembles the common furze (*G.*).

Order 75. APOCYNACEÆ. Dogbanes.

Shrubs often twining, occasionally trees or herbs, usually abounding in milky juice, leaves generally opposite, entire and without stipules, flowers regular, calyx inferior, 5-lobed, persistent, corolla tube generally short, lobes 5, twisted in bud, stamens 5, anthers long, stigma bifid, fruit generally of 2 narrow follicles, seeds often tufted with long hairs.

This is a large and distinct order, chiefly tropical. Many of the plants are poisonous, and many of considerable beauty. The flowers of some, and the fruit of most, resemble those of Asclepiadeæ, but the remarkable arrangement of the stamens so conspicuous in that order does not occur in this.

The great majority of the plants here given have white or pale yellow flowers.

TRIBE 1. CARISSEÆ. Anthers free from the stigma, ovary of 2 wholly combined carpels, fruit a fleshy berry, seeds without hairs.

1. CARISSA. Erect armed shrubs, stamens included in the tube, anthers lanceolate, berry 2-seeded.

TRIBE 2. PLUMERIEÆ. Anthers free from the stigma, ovary of 2 distinct carpels united by the style, fruit generally of 2 follicles.

2. RANWOLFIA. Smooth shrubs, leaves in whorls, corolla lobes broad, stamens included, disk large, fruit a twin drupe.

3. VINCA. Disk of 2 large glands.

4. ALSTONIA. Trees with leaves in whorls.

5. HOLLARHENA. Trees or shrubs, follicles incurved.

6. TABERNÆMONTANA. Trees or shrubs, follicles pulpy.

TRIBE 3. ECHITIDEÆ. Anthers forming a cone round the top of the style, cells spurred, ovary as in the last tribe; follicles with hairy seeds.

7. WRIGHTIA. Throat of corolla fringed.

8. NERIUM. Leaves whorled, throat of corolla fringed, stigma broad and tubercled.

9. ANODENDRON. Mouth of corolla contracted, style very short, stigma thick conic, seeds large beaked.

Note.—Milky plants like those of this and the next order are commonly called *dhudi*.

1. CARISSA.

C. carandas. A smooth shrub, thorns long and straight, leaves oval, shining, flowers white or slightly tinted, fragrant, fruit round or oval, deep purple, the pulp exceedingly sticky. *Karanda, hartundi.*

Very common in many parts. Throughout the dry, sandy, and rocky soils of India (*H.*).

The stickiness of the fruit is a serious drawback, but the flavour is very good, and it is perhaps the best in this country of

"Such cooling fruit,
As the kind hospitable woods supply."—*Milton.*

D.'s C. spinarum appears not to be in *H.* It is a shrub in gardens almost exactly like the *Karanda*, except that the fruit is the size of an olive, and cherry-coloured.

* *C. spinarum* (*C. hirsuta* D.), "probably a state of the first" (*H.*), but smaller in most points and slightly hairy. Hills E. of Belgaum (*D.* and *G.*). * *C. macrophylla* (*C. lanceolata*, D.). A large shrub, thorns very strong and curved, leaves lanceolate, acute, fruit size of

a plum, purple. Ram Ghaut (*D.*). From *H.* it seems that it may sometimes be unarmed.

2. Ranwolfia.

R. serpentina (*Ophioxylon s.* D.). A shrubby plant, leaves long lanceolate in threes, corolla long tubed, pure white, calyx and pedicels bright red, the double berry ovoid black. *Chándra, chotá chánd.*

The Konkan. Not common. "Few shrubs in the world are more elegant" (*Sir W. Jones*). The names are due to a belief in the efficacy of the plant against snake bites.

* *R. densiflora* (*Ophioxylon Nilgherrense*, D.). Larger than the last, leaves often in 4's, flowers rosy or white, berry oblique, wrinkled. W. Ghauts (*H.*). *Dr. Cooke* says this is the only representative of the order at Mahableshwar. * *R. decurva* has small leaves crowded at the tips of woody branches, decurved peduncles and small flowers. Konkan, &c. (*H.*).

3. Vinca.

V. pusilla. A herb, quite smooth with square stem, slightly winged, leaves lanceolate, corolla white with long narrow tube, sepals very narrow, follicles erect.

The Deccan. Except for the corolla this has all the appearance of a gentian.

V. major and *minor*, the periwinkles, very common in gardens at home, and often half wild, are the English representatives of the order; and *V. rosea, sadáful*, is one of the commonest garden plants in W. India, the flowers very like the periwinkle, but red.

4. Alstonia.

A. scholaris. A large handsome tree, leaves in whorls of 5 to 7, obovate oblong, narrow at the base, shining, flowers small, greenish-white, hairy in the throat, broad tubed, follicles pendulous, very slender, a foot long. *Sátwin, Shaitán, Saptáparni.*

Not uncommon in the Konkan. Extends to the Indian Archipelago, Queensland, and tropical Africa (*H.*).

Boards cut from this tree are used as slates in schools, hence the specific name. Natives have a superstitious fear of it (*G.*), which accounts for the second of the native names given above. The appearance of the tree is however altogether pleasing.

5. Hollarhena.

H. antidysenterica. A tall shrub, leaves oblong or ovate, pale green, flowers rather large in cymes, follicles a foot long, very slender, hairs of seeds brown and silky. *Kura, pándhra-kura.*

One of the commonest shrubs in S. Konkan: also in the Ghauts, tropical Himalaya, and throughout the drier forests of India (*H.*). The seeds are called *Indarjáo*; the bark gives the specific name.

6. Tabernæmontana.

1. *T. coronaria.* A shrub, leaves smooth, shining, lanceolate, unequally paired, flowers large, pure white, fragrant, in dichotomous cymes, follicles horizontal like a pair of horns, with scarlet aril. *Tágári, tágái, nándet.*

Very common in gardens, and the flowers generally double; wild on the Mira hills near Penn (*D.*); nowhere wild in India (*H.*).

* 2. *T. crispa.* Very like the last, but the leaves very long, the margin of corolla crisped, and the follicles without the red aril. *Taital.*

Matheran. Ghauts, pretty common (*D.*).

Mr. Birdwood has in his Matheran list *T. dichotoma*, with the same native name as the last, and Colonel Beddome ascribes it to the W. Ghauts; a small tree, flowers white with yellow tube, follicles orange-yellow.

To this tribe also belong,—

Cerbera, leaves alternate, corolla funnel-shaped, fruit round or ovate. * *C. odollam*, a small tree or large shrub, leaves lanceolate, shining, flowers in large cymes white with red or yellow throat, fruit ovoid, 3 or 4 inches long: *Sukanu*, salt swamps in Konkan (*G.*), but introduced (*D.*). *C. thevetia* a garden shrub, flowers yellow, trumpet-shaped, leaves lanceolate, fruit size of a crab-apple. *Pila Kanher.*

Ellertonia, stigma linear, bifid, fruit of 2 follicles, seeds winged. * *E. Rheedii*, a climber, leaves elliptic, sometimes whorled, flowers in short cymes, tube inflated in the middle, follicles horizontal. Wári country (*D.*).

Plumieria acutifolia, *Khair champa*, a common tree in gardens, ugly when out of leaf from the swollen truncated branches, but beautiful when adorned with large lanceolate leaves and white flowers with yellow throat, very fragrant. It does not seed.

7. Wrightia.

1. *W. tinctoria.* A pretty, small tree, leaves oval, lanceolate, smooth, flowers white in panicles, the fringe almost like double petals, follicles long, the tips at length cohering. *Kála Kura.*

Hills in S. Konkan. The seeds are called *goda inderjao.*

2. *W. tomentosa.* A small tree, leaves lanceolate, downy on both sides, flowers larger than the last, follicles a foot long, rough, with brown specks. *Támbada kura, Kála inderjao.*

Panch Mahals. N. Ghauts (*D.*). *H.* says the flowers are given differently as yellow, rosy and purple. I have seen them white only.

8. Nerium. Oleander.

N. odorum. A large shrub, leaves long linear, lanceolate, flowers red, fragrant in racemes, follicles 8 or 9 inches long. *Kanher.*

Not in *D.* River beds and banks in Khandesh and the Deccan, W. Himalayas, Central India and Sind (*H.*). White flowers are found sometimes, yellow rarely. Scarcely any shrub is more beautiful or delightful.

"Where oleanders flush the bed
Of silent torrents, gravel spread."—*Tennyson.*

Perhaps only a variety of the common *N. oleander* of the Mediterranean, which extends eastwards to Persia (*H.*). "In Greece and Italy the oleander, or rose laurel, not only adorns gardens, but fringes the roads and the dry beds of rivers with its fragrant rose-like blossoms, and the faint brilliancy of its long evergreen leaves" (*Hehn*). "It seems in Palestine to revel in the rough and shingly bank, along which the winter torrent rushes." (*Fullerton*). So Hooker considers that "the willow of the brook" in Scripture is the oleander. "The wood, flowers, and leaves are very poisonous, death has followed from using the wood as meat skewers"—*Hooker* in *Le Maout.*

9. Anodendron.

A. paniculatum. A very large smooth climber, with very thick green stems, leaves much polished, oval with short point, flowers numerous, small, pale yellow, calyx very small, corolla lobes much twisted, follicles horizontal, 5 or 6 inches long, tapering from a thick base to a blunt point. *Lamtáni, Káuli.*

Ghauts and S. Konkan.

To this tribe belong, *Parsonsia,* filaments twisted, disk of 5 lobes, follicles united when immature. *P. spiralis* (*Heligma Rheedii,* D.), a large, smooth climber, leaves ovate, flowers small, yellow or white, in cymes, calyx segments edged purple, corolla segments hairy within, anthers long, arrow-shaped, follicles grooved lengthways. Vingorla. Wári country (*D.*).

Vallaris, as the last, but filaments very short, not twisted, disk various. * *V. Heynii,* climbing, bark pale, leaves elliptic, flowers rather large, pure white, fragrant, stamens woolly, follicles tapering to a stiff point. Konkans and Deccan (*D.*).

Beaumontia, flowers very large with leafy bracts, disk deeply 5-lobed, fruit long, thick and woody, at length dividing into 2 follicles. * *B. Jerdoniana.* A large, woody climber, leaves obovate, flowers 4 inches long, follicles cylindric. Wari, S. M. country, and Canara (*D.*). This *H.* thinks is probably only a var. of *B. grandiflora,* an immense climber found in gardens with white flowers like *datura,* but much larger. It is a native of the Himalayas. "The magnificent

Beaumontia was in full bloom, ascending the loftiest trees, and clothing their trunks with its splendid foliage, and festoons of enormous funnel-shaped white flowers."—*Hooker.*

Chonemorpha, flowers large, filaments broad, short and hairy, disk thick, follicles 3-sided. * *C. macrophylla*, a large climber, leaves broad, oval, or roundish, very large, flowers white and fragrant in erect cymes, follicles a foot long. Wári country (*D.*).

Aganosma, disk 5-lobed, stigma columnar. * *A. cymosa* (*A. Doniana*, D.). A rambling creeper, leaves oblong, flowers small in crowded cymes. Fonda Ghaut (*D.*). * *A. caryophyllata*, nerves of the leaves red, flowers white in terminal panicles: a very ornamental garden shrub (*D.*). Deccan (*H.*).

Ichnocarpus, disk 5-lobed, stigma columnar. * *I. frutescens*, a large climber with small elliptic leaves, and cymes of small white or purplish flowers covered with red hairs, follicles very slender curved. Wári and S. M. country (*D.*).

ORDER 76. **ASCLEPIADEÆ.**

Shrubs, sometimes herbs, generally twining and abounding in acrid milky juice, leaves opposite, entire, flowers regular (except Ceropegia) more or less umbelled, calyx inferior, 5-lobed, persistent, corolla tubular 5-lobed, the throat often fringed, stamens 5, cohering round the pistil in a solid mass, and with the appendages forming a 5-lobed crown (*corona*), pollen in masses within, fruit of 2 follicles, seeds with a brush of hairs at the hilum.

A very large and distinct tropical order, often with handsome flowers. It comes near to the last, but the staminal crown, which outwardly is not the least like the stamens and pistil in any other plants, is quite peculiar to this order. The first three genera here given, however, are without this distinguishing mark.

Note.—When not otherwise stated, the species here described are twining shrubs, smooth or nearly so.

(*a*) Staminal crown none, or very small.

1. HEMIDESMUS. Filaments distinct, anthers united at the tip, stigma 5-angled.

2. CRYPTOLEPIS. Filaments united at the base, anthers united at the tip, and adhering by the base to the stigma.

3. GYMNEMA. Filaments columnar, 5 fleshy processes sometimes found on the corolla in place of a corona, stigma large, exserted.

(*b*) Corona conspicuous.

4. OXYSTELMA. Calyx small, an annular corona at the base of the corolla in addition to the staminal one.

5. CALOTROPIS. Erect shrubs, corolla broad, bell-shaped, follicles short and thick.

6. PENTATROPIS. Corolla deeply divided, follicles thick, acute.

7. DÆMIA. Corolla lobes large, spreading, follicles covered with soft prickles.

8. HOLOSTEMMA. Corona low, annular, 10-lobed, follicles short and thick.

9. TYLOPHORA. Flowers small, corolla short-tubed, lobes spreading, follicles smooth, pointed.

10. COSMOSTIGMA. Flowers small, greenish, coronal scales united to the base of anthers, leafy, 2-cleft; follicles large, obtuse.

11. DREGEA. Flowers green, coronal scales diverging from the column like the spokes of a wheel; follicles thick, hard.

12. HOYA. Leaves thick and fleshy, coronal scales 5, large, margins usually recurved, column short.

13. LEPTADENIA. Corona double, of 5 scales between the corolla lobes, and a raised waved wing at the base of the anthers.

14. CEROPEGIA. Corolla tube very long, swollen and curved at the base, lobes often joined at the tips, corona 5 or 10-lobed, with 5 strap-shaped processes.

Note.—In the above arrangement of genera, I have ignored *H.'s* tribes, which depend mainly on peculiarities in the anthers. He says that the analysis of plants in this order is most difficult; and it is certainly not easy to identify genera and species, though there can seldom be doubt about the family.

Note.—Dr. T. Cooke says that the name *Kauli* is given generally to all plants of this order.

1. HEMIDESMUS.

H. Indicus. Small, leaves variable, narrow, often variegated with white, flowers nearly sessile crowded, purple inside, anthers and stigmas combined into a large round knob, follicles very slender, spreading. *Anantamul, uparsál.*

Common; springs up in the Konkan very abundantly at the beginning of the rains, but takes a long time to flower, and often dies away without doing so. Called "Country Sarsaparilla" on the Coromandel coast.

Note.—The true Sarsaparilla is produced from various species of Smilax.

2. CRYPTOLEPIS.

C. Buchanani. Bark cracked and brown, flowers in nearly sessile cymes, pale yellow, petals long and narrow, leaves elliptic, with a short point, very strongly veined, whitish beneath, follicles horizontal, united at the base, very gradually tapering. *Wákhandi.*

Common; throughout India (*H.*).

3. Gymnema.

G. sylvestre. Stout, leafy, leaves small, ovate or lanceolate, flowers yellow, in crowded umbels, follicles cylindrical, tapering. *Wákhandi, káli kardori, pitáni.*

S. Konkan, Ghauts and S. M. country; common; when out of flower it looks rather like honeysuckle. Its leaves when chewed are said to destroy for a considerable time the power of tasting sweet things. * *G. montanum* (*Bidaria elegans*, D.), smooth leaves, cordate, ovate or lanceolate, follicles very thin. Higher Ghauts (*D.*).

4. Oxystelma.

O. esculentum. A delicate and beautiful twiner, leaves long, linear lanceolate, grass-like, flowers long-stalked, 2 or 3 together, nearly white, streaked and shaded with purple inside, follicles cylindrical, smooth, tapering. *Dhudika, dhudáni.*

"The lovely twining Asclepias."—*Sir W. Jones.*

Deccan and Konkan; often on milkbush; throughout the plains and lower hills of India (*H.*).

5. Calotropis.

1. *C. gigantea.* A large stout shrub with large ovate, cordate or stem-clasping leaves, downy beneath, corolla pale, purple or mottled, occasionally white, lobes reflexed, follicles ovoid, green, 3 or 4 inches long, hair round the seeds very silky. *Arak, madár, rui.*

2. *C. procera.* Very likely the last, but smaller, leaves said to be more oblong and acute, and the corolla lobes erect. *Lál madár, Támbada ákar.*

These are among the commonest shrubs in India, and almost always in flower. I never could make out the difference between the two species, as the distinctions given seemed to me to be not only trifling, but also not constant; and *R.* knew of only one species. There are also various differences of opinion among the authorities as to the distribution of the two species. One or both of these shrubs has the property of maintaining a very low temperature, Hooker having found the fresh milky juice to be 70°, when the soil surrounding the roots was from 90° to 104°, and the exposed leaves 80°, when the surrounding earth was about 105.—*Himalayan Journals.*

One of the broomrapes, Cistanche tubulosa, is said to be parasitic on these bushes.

6. Pentatropis.

P. microphylla. Small, leaves oval, nearly veinless, flowers greenish, 3 or 4 together in short-stalked umbels, points of the corolla curled up, follicles tapering at both ends. *Singrota.*

Common; growing close to the sea; very plentiful at Surat.

The flowers are a good deal like those of Cryptolepis, and the leaves are variable in breadth, and often much variegated.

7. Dæmia.

D. extensa. A middled-sized hairy twiner with roundish cordate pointed leaves, and dull white drooping flowers on long slender pedicels and peduncles; calyx very small, anthers large pure white, follicles cylindrical beaked. *Utarni, hirandori.*

A very common and unattractive plant with a disagreeable smell; specially common in Guzerat. Throughout India (*H.*).

8. Holostemma.

H. Rheedii. Large leaves deeply cordate, ovate pointed, flowers fleshy in umbels, anthers and column large and remarkable, follicles large, ovate. *Skidodi, tultuli, dudurli.*

"The flowers are a mixture of red, green, and white, agreeably fragrant" (*G.*). The bark is full of a very fine fibre.

S. Konkan. Common in hedges about Bombay, where children eat the flowers (*Dymock*). Hills about Poona (*Dr. Cooke*).

9. Tylophora.

D. has 4 species, but gives no hab. I have unfortunately never identified any one of them, though I believed I had the first as an erect shrub. * *T. fasciculata,* climbing among grass, leaves ovate lanceolate, flowers white, more or less umbelled, corolla lobes broad ovate, fleshy, follicles ovoid lanceolate. S. Konkan, &c. * *T. tenuis,* very slender, quite smooth, leaves small, fleshy, ovate, flowers very small, dark purple, in small umbels from a common peduncle, follicles poniard-shaped. Deccan peninsula (*H.*). * *T. Dalzellii* (*T. carnosa,* D.), smooth or slightly downy, leaves ovate, fleshy, shinning, very variable, flowers very small, purple, sometimes in a crowded round head, follicles as in the last. Konkan (*H.*). Mahableshwar (*Dr. Cooke*). * *T. asthmatica,* leaves ovate, flowers in small umbels, dull yellow and purple, follicles very variable. *Antamul, pitvel.* Deccan peninsula (*H.*).

10. Cosmostigma.

C. racemosa. A good-sized climber, leaves large, broad ovate or rounded, flowers in umbels or racemes, small, yellow with rusty dots, follicles oblong, obtuse. *Jati, shendori, ghárphul.*

Dapoli. Common in hedges (*D.*).

11. Dregea.

D. volubilis (*Hoya viridiflora*, D.). Large, bark light grey, leaves oval or cordate, flowers in drooping umbels, green, fleshy, follicles 3 to 5 inches long, seeds with delicate silky tufts. *Hirandori*, *ámbri*.

Common in hedges. Perhaps the commonest twiner of the order except Dæmia. It is a rather remarkable-looking plant, and has no smell, and not milky, but watery juice.

12. Hoya.

H. Wightii (*H. pallida*, D.). A climbing parasite, leaves oval acute, dead-looking, flowers in umbels white or cream coloured, pretty, follicles 4 inches long, slender, straight. *Amri*, *dudhvel.*

Mahableshwar and elsewhere, pretty common. Very like the well-known wax plant (*H. carnosa*), but paler in colour.

* *H. retusa*, parasitic, very slender, leaves very narrow at the base, gradually dilating to a broad tip, flowers few together, white, shining, corona pink. Dandelly jungles (*D.*) Matheran, *Birdwood ;* he calls it "Golden fringe" and *dhákti ám bri.*

* *H. pendula*, a stout climber, leaves ovate, flowers white, drooping, corolla lobes silky. S. Konkan (*G.*) Very imperfectly known.

13. Leptadenia.

L. reticulata. More or less hairy, lower parts woody with corky bark, upper pale green, leaves flat oval, flowers yellowish in stalked umbels, petals much bearded and folded back at the edges, anthers free on the dark corona, follicles plantain-shaped. *Raidori*, *shinguti*, *khárkodi.*

Common: often growing on milkbush.

* *L. spartium* (*L. Jacquemontii*, D.). An erect much-branched shrub, leaves narrow linear, flowers yellow in short-stalked umbels, follicles slender, beaked. *Kip.* Seashore S. of Gogo, and Sind (*D.*).

14. Ceropegia.

Of this genus, which differs very much in the shape of the flowers from anything else in the order, *H.* gives 36 species, and ascribes 9 of them to W. India, having reduced *D.'s* 11 to 6, and added 3. I have seen only one of these wild, but it seems that all the species, except *C. odorata*, have the corolla of the same peculiar form and colouring, viz., a long tube much swollen at the base, the lobes combined and "representing the head of a snake with green snout and eyelike spots."—(*Botanical Magazine.*)

1. *C. oculata.* Leaves ovate acuminate, rather hairy, flowers 4 to 6 on a peduncle, hairy, 2 or 3 inches long, corolla lobes lanceolate, follicles stiff, tapering, 4 or 5 inches long.

Near Rutnagherry. Bombay (*D.*). In the specimens which I had, the base of the corolla was very pale, the middle part dark green mottled, and the lobes nearly black.

* 2. *C. bulbosa* (including *C. Lushii*, D.), very slender, leaves from roundish to narrow linear, flowers several together, corolla tube less than an inch long, straight, follicles 4 inches long, slender.

Bombay and Malwan (*D.*). The roots, like small turnips, are eaten and called *khapparkaru, gayela* (*Dymock*).

* *C. attenuata* (including *C. angustifolia*, D.). Erect, less than a foot high, leaves narrow, flowers usually solitary, corolla tube straight, 2 inches long, lobes very narrow. Malwan and Vingorla (*D.*). * *C. Lawii*, erect, leaves ovate, peduncles many-flowered, corolla tube slightly curved, base scarcely swollen, lobes incurved, coronal lobes 10. S. Konkan (*H.*). * *C. juncea*. Stem stout, leaves few and small, lanceolate, flowers pretty large, lobes erect. Kasersai jungles (*D.*). *Kanvel.* * *C. tuberosa* (including *C. acuminata*, D.). Stem slender, leaves from roundish to lanceolate, corolla tubes straight, lobes ligulate, more or less adherent throughout, coronal lobes very short. Dharwar and Konkans (*D.* and *G.*). * *C. hirsuta* (*C. Jacquemontii, &c.*, D.). A coarse climber, leaves lanceolate or ovate, corolla nearly 2 inches long, lobes sub-erect, forming a crown over the throat. Konkan (*D.*). Ganesh Khind (*Dr. Cooke*): and found at Karli by *Jacquemont*. * *C. Stocksii*, closely resembling *C. oculata*, but the corolla lobes are long linear. Konkan (*H.*). * *C. odorata*, slender, leaves lanceolate, peduncles many-flowered, corolla yellow, fragrant, an inch long, straight, base not swollen, lobes very narrow, erect. Konkan (*G.* and *H.*).

Genianthus. Calyx minute, corolla rotate. * *G. laurifolius*, (*Toxocarpus crassifolius*, D.), twining, leaves oval acute, cymes sessile, corolla lobes sometimes densely bearded with white hairs, follicles very slender. Ghauts, Konkan and Canara (*D.*). *Cynanchum*, follicles long, often slightly winged. * *C. pauciflorum*, leaves ovate pointed, the base cordate and auricled, flowers in umbels rusty-coloured. Deccan and Dharwar (*D.*). * *C. alatum* in *G.* very like this, but more or less hairy with leaves narrow at the base. S. Konkan.

Heterostemma, corona of 5 large lobes spreading horizontally from the column. *H. Dalzellii* (*H. Wallichii*, D.). A large climber, leaves large, fleshy, ovate, flowers small flesh-coloured in stalked umbels, follicles bulged above the base. Dapoli. Malwan and Vingorla (*D.*).

Oianthus, corolla lobes very short, broad, corona cup-shaped, spreading, fleshy. * *O. urceolatus* (*Heterostemma u.* D.), stem purple, leaves ovate, lanceolate, corolla pitcher-shaped, purple, corona lobes 3-toothed. Belgaum, Rewadanda (*D.*).

Frerea, fleshy erect, flowers large, corona a ring round the column with 5 broad lobes, and 5 narrow processes. * *F. Indica*, leaves oblong sessile, flowers solitary or in pairs, corolla rotate purple. Ghauts near Hewra (*D.*). *Caralluma*, fleshy, erect, nearly leafless, corolla bell-shaped, corona annular 5-lobed. * *C. fimbriata*, stems and branches 4-angled and toothed, flowers drooping, yellow-green and purple mixed, divisions of corolla fringed, *Mákarsing*, Deccan (*D.*): has something the habit of a diminutive cactus (*G.*). Lisboa calls the flowers white and pink.

The following also belong to this order—

Asclepias Curassavica, "Negro ipecacuanha" of the W. Indies, "gayest and commonest of weeds" (*Kingsley*); an erect herb with reddish orange flowers and leafy corona. Common in gardens.

The beautiful bridal Stephanotis, also found in Bombay gardens.

Pergularia minor (*P. odoratissima*, D.) in gardens; a climber with roundish or ovate leaves and very fragrant yellow or green flowers, with double coronal scales.

The three next orders have simple leaves, and flowers of the ordinary 4 or 5-divided type.

ORDER 77. LOGANIACEÆ.

Leaves opposite undivided, flowers regular, calyx inferior, small, 4 or 5-lobed, as is the corona, stamens 4 or 5 on the tube, fruit a capsule or berry.

This tropical order is most like Rubiaceæ, but has a superior ovary, and the leaves instead of stipules have generally connecting lines. It is also closely connected with Gentianeæ, but its properties are very different, many of its species producing deadly poisons.

1. BUDDLEIA. Shrubs with small flowers densely crowded together, lobes of calyx and corolla and stamens 4; stipulary line very distinct, capsule 2-valved.

2. STRYCHNOS. Climbing shrubs with short tendrils, or trees, flowers white or yellowish, stamens 5, berry round or oblong.

1. BUDDLEIA.

* *Note.*—This genus was by some authorities put in Scrophularineæ.

B. Asiatica. A shrub or small tree, leaves lanceolate, acuminate, hairy beneath; flowers in long dense spikes, white, corolla tube much longer than the bell-shaped calyx, capsule and seeds oval.

Throughout India, very common (*H.*); but *D.* has only "hills near Penn," and *G.* has not got it. Dr. T. Cooke, however, has had it at Mahableshwar.

B. globosa is a shrub of old-fashioned English gardens, with dense balls of very small orange-coloured flowers, very fragrant, sometimes called "Honey-ball."

2. STRYCHNOS.

1. *S. nux vomica.* A tree without tendrils, leaves ovate, smooth, shining, flowers greenish white in cymes, corolla tube much longer than the calyx, fruit like a small orange, seeds many, light grey, silky. *Kájra, Kuchla.*

Common in S. Konkan. Throughout tropical India (*H.*).

The seeds, which are commonly sold in the bazaar, and look like flat, round buttons, produce strychnine, and the bitter woody root is also used medicinally.

"Among the Malabar immigrants to Ceylon there is a belief that the seed, if habitually taken, will act as a prophylactic against the venom of the cobra: and I have been assured that the Indian coolies accustom themselves to eat a single seed a day with that object."—(*Tennent.*)

2. * *S. potatorum.* A tree with elliptic acute smooth leaves, flowers small, white or greenish yellow, corolla tube as in the last, berry black, seeds one or two, hemispherical. *Gájra, nirmala, nivali, katák.*

Konkan, Matheran, Ghauts, and elsewhere. Called the clearing nut tree, from the seeds being used to clear water. "These seeds are constantly carried about by the more provident of our officers and soldiers in time of war, to enable them to purify their water. They are easier to be obtained than alum, and probably less hurtful to the constitution."—*Roxburgh.* Tennent mentions the same use in Ceylon.

* *S. colubrina*, a large climber, leaves ovate, smooth, flowers small in short cymes, fruit size of an olive, one-seeded. *Kanal, Kájarvel, taral.* S. Konkan (*D.*), Matheran (*Birdwood*). * *S. Dalzellii* (*S. axillaris*, D.), flowers in short dense cymes, berry much larger than the last, and many-seeded. Konkan and Deccan (*H.*). Not in *D.* or *G.*, and apparently not much known.

Mitreola. Herbs, with small white flowers, styles 2, short, under one hairy stigma. * *M. oldenlandioides*, small, erect, leaves narrow at both ends, flowers subsessile, capsule shape of a mitre, seeds 3-cornered. Caranjah (*D.*), Central Provinces, &c. (*H.*).

Mitrasacme. As the last, but all parts 4 instead of 5, capsule round. * *M. alsinoides* (*M. pusilla*, D.), 6 inches high or less, smooth, leaves linear subulate, flowers solitary or twin white, capsule shorter than calyx. Malwan (*D.*). Widely scattered (*H.*).

ORDER 78. GENTIANACEÆ. Gentians.

Herbs, generally erect, and very symmetrical in all parts (except *Canscora*), stems generally 4-sided, leaves opposite, simple, 3 or 5-nerved or ribbed, without stipules, calyx free, persistent, generally 3 to 5-lobed, corolla lobes as many, twisted to the right, stamens as many, anthers erect, style single, stigmas 2, small.

The plants of this order, abounding especially in tropical and temperate mountains, are known in most parts of the world for the beauty of their flowers. They have generally bitter and tonic qualities. Most of the species are absolutely symmetrical (using the word in the ordinary, not the botanical sense) in all parts; and in this and some other respects they resemble outwardly many of the Rubiaceæ.

1. Exacum. Calyx deeply 4-lobed, generally winged, corolla tube and filaments short, anthers large, capsule round.

2. Enicostema. Flowers small, sessile, clustered in the axils, calyx deeply 5-divided, stamens on the upper part of the corolla tube.

3. Erythræa. Calyx tubular with 5 keeled teeth, stamens near the top of the tube, filaments short, capsule oblong.

4. Canscora. Flowers irregular, calyx 4-toothed, keeled or winged, corolla lobes more or less unequal, stamens 1 large and perfect, 3 smaller, stigmas 2, capsule 2-valved.

5. Swertia. Calyx 4-lobed, corolla with deep depressions or pits at the base of each lobe, stamens on the lower part of the corolla, stigmas 2.

6. Limnanthemum. Aquatic herbs with deeply cordate leaves, sometimes alternate, peduncles clustered at the nodes, corolla tube glandular or hairy.

1. Exacum.

1. *E. bicolor.* A tall smooth plant, leaves sessile, ovate, lanceolate acute, flowers very beautiful, white tipped with blue, with large yellow anthers; lobes of calyx and corolla pointed. *Udichiráyat.*

Konkan and Ghauts. Not common.

This is

"A woodland treasure,
You could not look at without pleasure,
All in artistic harmony."—*Shelley.*

2. *E. pumilum.* A small branched plant, leaves sessile, ovate, obtuse, scarcely veined, flowers dark blue and handsome. *Jatáli.*

Konkan and Belgaum (*D.* and *H.*), but an allied form, *E. pedunculatum*, is found throughout India; and I presume this is much the same as * *E. Lawii*, which is described under the same native name as growing among grass at Matheran and Mahableshwar. I have found the former growing in masses in rocky ground or in grass.

3. *E. petiolare.* Larger than the last, very pretty, leaves ovate petioled, flowers lilac, white, or light blue, with golden anthers, calyx wings broad.

This seems to be *G.'s* No. 935, which he calls abundant on pasture lands between Panwell and Khandalla; also above the Ghauts and about Belgaum. *D.* had it only at Caranja, Birdwood at Matheran, I at Mandangarh.

2. Enicostema.

E. littorale (*Hippion orientale,* D.). A leafy plant, 6 or 8 inches high, much branched, stem 4-sided, slightly winged, leaves sessile, long, lanceolate, blunt, flowers white, sessile, about 3 in each axil, calyx with 2 bracts, capsule round. *Mamijwá, naichápála.*

Guzerat and N. Konkan. Common throughout India (*H.*). He makes the height up to 20 inches.

3. Erythræa.

E. Roxburghii. About 4 inches high, lower leaves obovate, upper linear acute, flowers very pretty pink or white in dichotomous cymes, anthers often spirally twisted. *Kadu nai, lantak.*

The Konkans. Pretty common. Throughout India (*H.*). It is much like the English *E. centaureum,* common centaury, but smaller.

4. Canscora.

1. *C. diffusa.* Much branched, leaves lanceolate or ovate, the lower running into the petiole, the upper stem clasping, bracts leafy, flowers pink, corolla 2-lipped, the upper deeply cleft with 3 stamens, the lower notched with one. *Mhátára cha gavat.*

Very common in the Konkans on rocks, walls, &c., also at Matheran and Mahableshwar. Throughout India (*H.*).

It is difficult to recognize this and the next as Gentians, owing to the very irregular corolla and stamens.

2. *C. perfoliata* (*C. alata,* D.). Smooth, a foot or more in height, stem 4-winged, leaves lanceolate acute, bracts perfoliate, roundish, flowers rather large for the size of the plant, of a delicate pink, calyx large and winged, upper lobes of corolla the largest.

S. Konkan. Deccan peninsula, Bombay to Travancore (*H.*).

C. decurrens, very doubtfully distinct from *C. diffusa* (*H.*), leaves more or less decurrent, bracts in the upper part small or linear, corolla rose-coloured or white. Vingorla. Rice-fields in S. Konkan (*D.*). *C. pauciflora*, stem winged; leaves ovate or oblong, sessile; flowers few, white, long-stalked, in a loose panicle, capsule as long as the calyx. S. Konkan. * *C. Concanensis*, slender, not above 5 inches high; leaves ovate; flowers red, calyx winged, scarious in fruit. Not in *D.* or *G.* The Konkan (*H.*).

5. Swertia.

S. decussata (*Ophelia multiflora*, D.). Stem 4-winged, leafy, leaves ovate, stem clasping, smooth, decussate, flowers white, pencilled, in thick heads, petals divided to the base, depressions at the base covered with a fringed scale, stamens twisted, surrounding the ovary, anthers black. *Chiretta, karvi, kauri.*

Ghauts and Dharwar; at Mahableshwar, but not common,—*Dr. Cooke.* From this an inferior chiretta is made, but *S. chirate*, from which the genuine drug comes, is a Himalayan plant.

* *S. Corymbosa* (*Ophelia pauciflora D.*). Stem square or 4-winged; leaves sessile ovate, calyx segments very narrow; corolla white or pale blue, a fringed scale at the base of the corolla lobes. *Kadvi nai.* Ghauts (*D.*).

6 Limnanthemum.

This genus also is not much like the typical gentians. *H.* has of the tribe to which it belongs, "leaves radical or alternate." The English buckbean, Menyanthes trifoliata, belongs to the same tribe, and is found in the W. Himalayas.

1. *L. cristatum.* Leaves round, glandular beneath, long-stalked, flowers crowded, pretty, white, with orange-coloured bearded throat, and a crest running the length of each petal. *Khátára, kamadu, kumbhráj.*

Tanks in the Konkan. Throughout India (*H.*).

D. has capsule one or two-seeded, as I have found it, but *H.* has seeds 10 to 20, and *R.* many.

From the round floating leaves this and the other species are often called water-lilies. "*Kumudá*, or delight of the water, seems a general name for beautiful aquatic flowers."—*Sir W. Jones.*

2. *L. Indicum.* Leaves round or kidney-shaped, long-stalked, flowers white, fringed but without crest, umbels immediately below the leaves, capsule ovate, seeds smooth.

Tanks in the Konkan and Deccan. Throughout India, very common (*H.*).

Both these species throw out roots from the nodes of the stem. *H.* has "corolla yellow towards the base within," which does not agree with *D.*, nor with my observation.

L. aurantiacum, leaves smooth, round, deeply cordate, long stalked; flowers in umbels, fringed, orange-coloured inside, capsule roundish. Málwan only (*D.*), near which I had it. Deccan peninsula (*H.*). * *L. parvifolium*, leaves round, cordate, pedicels numerous, just below the leaf; flowers white, bearded, capsule oblong. Very common in tanks, but so small as to be difficult to find (*D.*).

Pleurogyne, corolla rotate. * *P. minor* (*Ophelia*, *M.* D.), small, leaves ovate, flowers in cymes of a beautiful blue, with white spot at the base of the lobes; all parts 4. Highest Ghauts opposite Bombay (*D.*). From the descriptions it is not clear whether the calyx segments are equal or not.

Order Polemoniaceæ, which comes in here, contains no species wild in W. India, but the genus *Phlox* belongs to it, very well represented in gardens both in England and India.

Order 79. HYDROPHYLLACEÆ.

Differs from Gentianaceæ by having alternate leaves and imbricated corolla lobes.

Hydrolea. Herbs with regular 5-divided flowers, calyx divided nearly to the base, corolla widely campanulate, stamens five, attached to the very short tube of the corolla, anthers arrow-shaped, styles 2, stigmas capitate, capsule roundish.

H. zeylanica. Erect or procumbent, much branched, mostly smooth, stems round, leaves lanceolate ovate, flowers in short racemes, handsome, dark blue, with white anthers and blue styles, petals rounded, capsule enclosed in the calyx.

This is the only Indian species of the order. The Konkans in wet places. Throughout India (*H.*), and very widely distributed except in Europe. The flowers, both in form and colour, are like those of the common speedwell, but much larger. The petals are divided so low down that they may easily be looked on at first sight as quite distinct. The garden *Nemophila* belongs to this order.

Order 80. BORAGINEÆ. The Borage Family.

Herbs, shrubs, or trees, generally rough with coarse hairs, leaves without stipules, calyx inferior persistent, lobes 5 or more up to 8, corolla with 4 to 8 divisions, often with hairy scales in the throat, stamens as many as the corolla lobes inserted in the tube.

The old order Boraginaceæ had very decided characteristics, viz. rough stems and leaves, a 4-lobed ovary, the style between the lobes, and fruit of 4 seed-like nuts. In these respects it was very like Labiatæ, differing from that by the flowers being more or less regular, and the leaves alternate. But there is now included with this the old order Cordiaceæ, which has an entire ovary and varying fruit. The first three tribes here given do not therefore belong to the Borage family in the old acceptation of the term.

TRIBE 1. CORDIEÆ. Trees or shrubs, fruit a drupe.

1. CORDIA. Flowers in corymbs or clusters, calyx with very short irregular teeth, corolla lobes and stamens 4 to 8, style dividing into 2 or more branches, calyx increasing with the fruit.

TRIBE 2. EHRETIEÆ. Fruit of 2 or 4 nutlets.

2. EHRETIA. Trees or shrubs, corolla tube short, lobes 5, style bifid.

3. COLDENIA. Prostrate herbs, corolla funnel-shaped, styles 2, sometimes slightly adherent, drupe of 4 pyrenes.

4. RHABDIA. Calyx and corolla 5 parted, style 1, drupe of 4 pyrenes.

TRIBE 3. HELIOTROPIEÆ.

5. HELIOTROPIUM. Herbs with small flowers, stamens hidden in the corolla tube, fruit of 4 nutlets.

1. CORDIA.

1. *C. myxa.* A good sized tree, leaves broad oval, rough beneath, leathery, flowers white, fragrant, calyx cup-shaped, with many teeth, petals 5, curled back, stamens and pistil exserted, fruit size of a cherry, in stalked clusters, flesh-coloured, the stone imbedded in transparent pulp. *Bhokar, lessuri.*

Deccan and Konkan. Throughout India and often cultivated (*H.*). He has 2 varieties, and calls the leaves very variable in form and size.

The fruit under the name of *Sebesten* or *Sepistan* is used in medecine. The tree has been cultivated in Egypt from time immemorial.—*Le Maout.*

2. *C. obligera* (*C. latifolia*, D.). A tree much like the last, leaves large, broad, ovate, slightly waved, nearly smooth, fruit like a plum, smooth and yellow, full of glutinous pulp. *Bargund, gedori, dahivan.*

Guzerat and Sind; common; Deccan.

H. includes in this *D.'s C. Wallichii*, of which the calyx is described as velvety, and the underside of the leaves as densely tomentose and white.

3. *C. Rothii.* A poor-looking tree; leaves sub-opposite,

lanceolate or oblong, obtuse; flowers small, white, in panicles, petals curled back, stamens and styles 4 each, exserted; fruit larger than a pea, orange yellow, full of glutinous pulp, seated in the cup-like calyx. *Godan, gondani, dyár.*

D. calls this common everywhere, which I do not think it is. I believe that I have seen it only in the Deccan. Guzerat also (*G.*). W. India, frequent (*H.*).

* *C. Macleodii*, all softly and densely hairy, leaves ovate, cordate, obtuse, calyx tubular, clavate, berry ovoid, acute, very small. *Dahivan.* * *C. fulvosa*, the same, except for its much less tomentose corymbs and leaves (*H.*). These two are not in *D.* or *G.* Konkan and Belgaum (*H.*). * *C. Sebestena*, a small S. American tree, with showy red flowers, is frequent in gardens in Bombay (*Dr. W. Gray*).

2. Ehretia.

E. lævis. A tree with broad oval entire leaves, often unequal-sided, flowers very small, white, panicled. Calyx lobes 5, very short, drupe very small, red turning black. *Dátrang.*

Malwan, S.E. of Surat, and Bhimashankar (*D.* and *G.*). Common throughout hotter India (*H.*).

3. Coldenia.

C. procumbens. A small plant, grey and very hairy, lying close to the ground, stem thick, leaves obovate, deeply pleated, unequal at the base, flowers white, solitary sessile in the axils, fruit rough pyramidal pointed. *Tripakshi.*

Common on rice-fields in the cold weather. Throughout India, a weed (*H.*). It is a plant of quite the same character as Heliotropium.

4. Rhabdia.

R. lycioides (*R. viminea*, D.). A twiggy much-branched shrub, the branches frequently creeping and rooting, leaves obovate cuneate small, flowers small pink in axillary corymbs, berry smaller than a pea, orange-red.

Konkan, in the beds of rivers. India generally, in the same situations (*H.*). I have found this as *D.* describes with smooth leaves, thus differing from the order, but Brandis calls them more or less hairy with adpressed white hairs.

5. Heliotropium.

The common explanation of the name is found in the lines—

"The heliotrope that turneth
Towards her lord, the Sun."—*A. A. Proctor.*

From which also the common English name Turnsole. But Tournefort denies this interpretation, and says that it is so called from flowering about the time of the summer solstice, when the sun turns towards the equinoctial. Heliotrope was formerly supposed to possess the power of counteracting poison, and rendering the bearer invisible.

> "Among this swarm, most loathsome to survey,
> Ran spirits naked and with terror pale,
> No hiding place, no heliotrope had they."
> *Wright's* "Dante." Inferno xxiv. 92.

1. *H. supinum.* A small branched hairy plant, prostrate or ascending, leaves oval, velvety, deeply pleated, calyx large, corolla very small, almost hidden in it, white, capsule smooth, almost round, nutlets 2 or 4. *Wadásuri.*

Common in rice-fields, Konkan and Deccan; also in Cutch and Sind. The whole plant is sometimes thickly covered with white hairs.

2. *H. marifolium.* Prostrate, much branched, leaves lanceolate, calyx large, enclosing the fruit, which is sometimes distinctly 4-lobed, sometimes almost entire.

On the sea sands, S. Konkan.

* *H. bracteatum* is very like this (*H. laxiflorum*, D.), but erect, and much branched from the root. Poona. Bombay and Deccan (*D.*).

3. *H. Indicum* (*Tiaridium, I.* D.). A coarse, erect much-branched plant, very hairy all over except the fruit, leaves oval, wrinkled, running into the petiole, opposite or alternate, flowers white or lilac arranged in 2 rows up one side of the spike, fruit with the attached calyx mitre-shaped, separating into 2 halves, each 2-seeded. *Suryakamal, bhurundi.*

A weed often found on rubbish. Throughout India in the moister parts (*H.*).

This is a much larger plant than the other species.

**H. zeylanicum* (*Tournefortia subulata*, D.). Erect, branched, hairy, leaves lanceolate, sessile, spikes long and slender, flowers yellowish, nutlets 2. Near Gogo (*D.*). Throughout India (*H.*). *H. ovalifolium* (*H. coromandelianum*, D.) much like *H. supinum*, but erect, spikes in pairs, flowers in a waved row along them. Wara. Bhimashankar (*D.*). * *H. Rottleri.* Woody and rough with stiff horizontal branches, leaves very small, oblong, racemes long and stiff with distant flowers and ovate bracts, fruit round. Donus (*D.*). The commonest heliotrope of English and Indian gardens is *H. peruvianum.*

Tribe 4. Borageæ.

Herbs, ovary distinctly 4-lobed, style simple or bifid arising from between the lobes, fruit of 4 nutlets. The flowers are often arranged on only one side of the spike or raceme.

6. TRICHODESMA. Coarse herbs, calyx 5-parted, auricled at the base, increasing in fruit, anthers very large and hairy, joining in a cone : leaves sometimes opposite.

7. PARACHARYUM. Calyx deeply 5-cleft, corolla with mouth closed by 5 scales.

8. SERICOSTOMA. Small branched shrubs, sepals 5, narrow, mouth of corolla wide, closed with hairs, nuts ovoid, stony.

6. TRICHODESMA.

1. *T. Indicum.* (*T. zeylanicum*, D.). A very rough plant with bristly stem, the hairs springing from tubercles, leaves nearly sessile oblong, narrowed at the base, flowers lilac, calyx lobes ovate lanceolate. *Zinghi, gaoza.*

2. *T. amplexicaule.* Probably a mere form of the last (*H.*) but the lower leaves are oblong, the upper broad ovate cordate, stem-clasping and auricled. *Chota Kalpa.*

Both are common weeds throughout India ; the second I believe is the larger of the two, notwithstanding the native names.

7. PARACHARYUM.

P. cœlestinum. (*Cynoglossum c.* D.). A handsome straggling plant, as much as 5 feet high, not very rough, lower leaves broad ovate, long-stalked, upper narrower and sessile, flowers in long spikes or racemes, white with blue eye, calyx lobes ovate, nutlets flattish surrounded by a hairy ring. *Nisurdi.*

S. Konkan, Mahableshwar and Matheran : called the "Mahableshwar forget-me-not."—*Dr. Cooke.*

* *P. malabaricum* and **P. lambertianum* are said by Dr. Cooke to be tolerably common at Mahableshwar : both resemble *P. cœlestinum*, but the first is stouter, more hairy, and with larger flowers and fruits. Canara (*H.*). The second, which *H.* identifies doubtfully, has a quite different fruit, the nutlets ⅓ of an inch in diameter, ovate depressed. Neither are in *D.* or *G.*

8. SERICOSTOMA.

S. pauciflorum. Low and much branched, covered with rough hairs, leaves linear lanceolate, small, flowers solitary or racemed white, calyx large and thick.

Kelvi-Mahim. Coast of Kattywar, very common (*D.*). Sind (*H.*).

Cynoglossum, leaves mainly radical, corolla rotate, the mouth almost closed with a fringe of scales. *C. lanceolatum* (*C. micranthum*,

D.). A tall rough plant, leaves lanceolate acute, flowers in compound racemes small, blue with white eye, calyx lobes nearly as long as the corolla. *Lichardi.* Waranda Ghaut. Konkan, Khandalla, &c. (*D.* and *G.*). **C. denticulatum* (*C. glochidiatum*, D.). Stem softly hairy, tubercled, branches rather angular, leaves ovate, lanceolate, fruit with a hairy ring surmounted by long teeth with recurved hooks. Parr Ghaut (*D.*). *H.* has doubtfully *C. Ritchiei*, found at Belgaum by Dr. Ritchie, closely resembling this. This genus has, in English as in Latin, the name of Hound's tongue, from the long leaves resembing (more or less) the tongue of a dog.

The various Forget-me-nots (*Myosotis*) of English river banks and gardens belong to this tribe; also the Comfreys, of which *Symphytum asperrimum*, prickly comfrey, has been of late years cultivated in W. Indian for fodder.

ORDER 81. CONVOLVULACEÆ. The Convolvulus family.

Herbs or shrubs, generally twining, leaves alternate without stipules, flowers regular, generally showy with bracts; calyx persistent of 5 lobes, which are generally imbricated, and often distinctly unequal; corolla generally bell-shaped or funnel-shaped, often pleated; stamens, 5 on the corolla tube, 2 often shorter than the other 3; anthers oblong, ovary superior, styles one or two, stigma 2-lobed or branched, fruit not more than 4-seeded.

This is a tropical order of plants of singular beauty; and I think it a matter of congratulation that our Presidency has so great a number of its species: for it is not one of the large orders, though so well known. Most of those species, which cannot properly be called beautiful, have still "A sweet attractive kind of grace;" and members of this family can scarcely be mistaken for any other.

Note.—*H.* does not mention among the characteristics of the order either the imbricated calyx or the unequal stamens, but both are certainly found in the majority of the species here given.

Note.—The great majority of the large and handsome species are found in genera Nos. 1, 2, and 4. *Cuscuta* differs very much from the other genera given.

(*a*) Large climbers (except *Argyreia cuneata*), often shrubby; fruit indehiscent.

1. RIVEA. Flowers large white, long-tubed, about 3 together, stamens included, stigmas 2, linear oblong, fruit roundish.

2. ARGYREIA. Generally covered with silky hairs, flowers generally rose-coloured or purple, corolla with very short lobes, stamens included, style long, stigmas 2, round.

3. LETTSOMIA. Like the last, but stamens sometimes exserted.

(*b*) Mostly herbs, but including some large climbers: capsule 2 to 4-valved, or fragile, and soon breaking up.

4. IPOMŒA. Corolla very shortly lobed; stigma entire or 2-lobed; capsule round or ovoid, generally 4-valved.

5. CONVOLVULUS. Corolla vase-shaped, limb nearly entire, pleated, stamens included, stigmas 2, oblong.

6. EVOLVULUS. Not twining, corolla salver-shaped, scarcely lobed; styles 2, each with 2 linear stigmas.

7. PORANA. Large climbers, sepals in fruit much enlarged and scarious.

8. CRESSA. Not climbing, very small, flowers sessile, stamens exserted, styles 2.

(*c*) Leafless twining parasites.

9. CUSCUTA. Flowers fascicled, calyx and corolla much alike.

1. RIVEA.

R. hypocrateriformis. Stem and branches more or less clothed with white hairs, leaves large, round, cordate or kidney-shaped, sepals ovate, obtuse, corolla limb silky outside, fruit yellowish-brown, nearly dry. *Kalmiluta, fanjá.*

Bombay and the Konkans. *H.* includes in this *R. bonanox* (D.), which has large night-blowing flowers with a strong smell of cloves, strongly resembling the Moon creeper, but smaller, and said to be called "the Midnapore creeper." I thought the two were quite distinct.

* *R. ornata* very much resembles this, but the sepals are larger and more pointed, the stems more hairy and whiter. Higher Ghauts W. of Junar (*D.*).

2. ARGYREIA.

1. *A. tiliæfolia.* A very extensive climber, leaves round, cordate or kidney-shaped, long-stalked entire; flowers about 3 together, handsome, rose-coloured, streaked darker, sepals broad, ovate, much imbricated, increasing with the fruit and covering it, capsule round, brown, seeds 4, downy.

Not in *D.* or *G.*, but abundant and luxuriant at Kelvi Mahim and Belapore, and probably in other places, as *H.* has "India, except in the Western dry portion, very common in Bengal, and near the sea." It is very noticeable for its large flowers and fruit, the latter quite covered up by the calyx. *R.* calls it *Convolvulus gangeticus.*

2. *A. speciosa.* Elephant creeper. A very extensive climber, leaves very large, heart-shaped or ovate, cordate ; flowers large, rose-coloured in heads, with large white leafy bracts, berry dry, 4-celled, 4-seeded. *Samudra shok, gugali.*

Bombay and elsewhere near the sea, common; less so inland. From Assam to Belgum and Mysore.

3. *A. sericea.* Very like the last, but not so large ; leaves broad, heart-shaped, very white and silky below, bracts large and leafy, enveloping the heads of flowers, which are hairy outside ; berry orange-coloured, pulpy. *Gável.*

South Konkan and Ghauts. Matheran.

A. argentea I took to be a variety of this. It is not in *D.* or *G.*, but I found it at Poona, and Dr. Dymock has the name *Mhaisvel* for it. Peduncles leafy, bearing numbers of flowers at the end.

4. *A. malabarica.* Very large and woody, leaves heart-shaped, slightly hairy, flowers in heads many together, very large, white, with purple bottom.

One of the handsomest of the order, confined in this Presidency to the Ghauts, but abundant there from almost the beginning of the ascent. Malabar and Coromandel (*H.*).

5. *A. cuneata.* An erect shrub, nearly smooth, leaves obovate cuneate, nearly sessile, flowers deep purple, few together, sepals ovate obtuse, bracts very small, berry oval, with brown smooth outer shell, seated in the calyx.

This differs in habit from all the large species of the order found in this Presidency, and it can scarcely be called handsome. It is common in some parts of the Deccan and near the Ghauts. Deccan peninsula, common (*H.*).

* *A. involucrata*, nearly smooth, leaves large, ovate, pointed ; flowers in heads, large, rose-purple, sepals with scarious margins, bracts large, oblong, persistent. Not in *D.* or *G.* Bombay, Konkan, etc. (*H.*).

3. Lettsomia.

L. elliptica (*Argyreia e.* D.). Woody, leaves ovate, elliptic, flowers in long-peduncled panicles, rose-coloured or pale purple, with dark base, berry roundish, orange-coloured. *Bándvel, Kedári.*

Common on the Ghauts.

* *L. aggregata* (*Argyreia a.* D.). 'Hoary or woolly, leaves ovate cordate obtuse ; flowers in heads, small pink, bracts many roundish. anthers exserted ; capsule round, red. S. M. country, Mr. Law (*D.*),

* *L. setosa* (*Argyreia s.* D.). Covered with close pressed stiff hairs, leaves as the last, flowers rose-coloured or whitish, in dense long-stalked corymbs, stamens included; berry ovoid, red. *Sámbhar vel.* Near Viziadrug and Surat (*D.*). Matheran (*Birdwood*).

Note.—The flowers of this genus are generally smaller than in the Argyreias, from which it is difficult to distinguish those species which have the anthers included.

Erycibe, sepals about equal, roundish; corolla lobes 10, equal, style none; stigma large, round; berry fleshy.

* *E. paniculata*, a large climbing shrub, covered with tawny hairs; leaves oblong; flowers yellow in long terminal panicles, very small for the order; berry oblong, black. Konkan jungles (*D.*). Throughout India (*H.*). By the descriptions it must be a very variable plant.

(*b.*) 4. IPOMŒA.

Out of 57 species given in *H.*, 29 are found in this Presidency.

1. *I. bonanox* (*Calonyction speciosum*, D.). Moon creeper. A large climber, leaves large, smooth, heart-shaped, pointed; petioles very thick; peduncles long, with one to five large long-tubed white flowers, very fragrant, capsule smooth, 3 or 4-seeded. *Gul chándani, soma vel, banya bauri, Chandra kánt.*

Throughout India, but very often cultivated. A delightful plant, but rather aggravating from the very short life of the flowers, as they open at sunset, and close once for all soon after sunrise.

> . . . . "The midnight flower,
> That scorns the eye of vulgar light,
> Begins to bloom for sons of night,
> And maids who love the moon."—*T. Moore.*

Called by negroes in America "The lady of the night."

I. muricata was included by *D.* in this, but is called by *H.* clearly distinct, as it certainly is to an ordinary eye, the stems being covered with soft prickles, the flowers smaller, and pale purple. It is attributed to Bombay and S. Konkan.

2. *I. coccinea* (*Quamoclit Phœnicia*, D.). A beautiful twiner, all smooth, leaves ovate cordate acute, sepals long-pointed, flowers small, bright scarlet or crimson, long-tubed, limb spreading, capsule ovoid with four densely furred seeds. *Ishak-pech.*

3. *I. quamoclit*, like the last, but the leaves pinnate with very numerous linear segments, seeds nearly smooth. *Ganesh-vel, Sitache kesh.*

These two are natives of America, but are called by *H.* quasi-wild throughout India. They run wild in gardens, and the first is common in hedges in Guzerat. Of the second there is a white-flowered variety.

Sir W. Jones called the second the most beautiful of the order, and applied to its blossoms Milton's beautiful words, "Celestial rosy red, love's proper hue;" but surely "the affable archangel" never blushed so deep a red as these flowers generally are in W. India.

4. *I. hederacea.* A hairy twiner, leaves ovate cordate, 3-lobed, flowers large, of a lovely light blue, sometimes streaked darker, stamens included, capsule nearly round, smooth, 3-celled. *Nila pushpi.*

Also a doubtful native, but common in most parts. It is "the Morning glory" of the W. Indies, as it shuts early in the day. "In one piece of wild wood (in Bermuda) the morning glory vines had wrapped the trees to their very top, and decorated them all over with couples and clusters of great blue bells."—*Mark Twain.*

H. has two vars., one with entire leaves.

5. *I. digitata* (*Batatas paniculata*, D.). A large handsome climber, nearly all smooth, leaves large long-petioled, with 5 to 7 deep ovate lanceolate lobes, peduncles long, with many large and broad bell-shaped purple flowers, capsule 4-celled, seeds with long hairs. *Bhuikohola*, *vidárikand.*

Bombay and the Konkans: very common in railway hedges in Salsette. Tropical India (*H.*).

The young tubers are called *Asgand* (*Dymock*).

6. *I. pentaphylla* (*Batatas p.* D.). Much smaller than the last, every part except corolla and capsule very hairy, leaves digitate, leaflets broad lanceolate entire, petioles and peduncles long, flowers large, white, sepals unequal, covering the round smooth 4-celled capsule.

D. calls this a common weed, which I think is too strong. *G.* calls it common on Malabar Hill, &c., and it grows in Salsette. Besides India (chiefly W. India) it grows in Africa, Polynesia, and tropical America, and is often cultivated (*H.*) for the roots, I presume, like the next.

7. *I. batatas.* Hairy, with cordate-lobed leaves, flowers large, white tinged with red, long peduncled, sepals as in the last. *Rátálu*, *rátanvel*, *Sákarkand*, *Kángi.*

This is the sweet potato, commonly cultivated in India and all tropical countries, and it is what old English writers mean when they refer to the potato, our common potato being then called the Virginian potato (*Whewell*, Hist. Inductive Sciences). This (the sweet potato) was imported into England by way of Spain, and sold as a delicacy (*Chambers*). Both the Latin and the English name are corruptions of the West Indian and American names.

8. *I. pestigridis.* Twining, hairy all over, leaves palmately 5 to 7-lobed, lobes lanceolate or ovate, flowers small, delicate, white or slightly tinted, in heads surrounded by several ovate bracts.

Common in hedges. Throughout India (*H.*). *H.* has two varieties with leaves varying to ovate cordate entire.

Note.—There are two other species distinguished by very prominent bracts, both small and hairy, *I. pileata*, with several pink flowers within a large boat-shaped perfoliate involucre, and *I. pilosa*, with small purple-pink and white flowers in heads surrounded by bracts. Both belong to the S. Konkan.

9. *I. eriocarpa* (*I. sessiliflora*, D.). Small, covered with hairs, leaves ovate cordate pointed, flowers quite or nearly sessile axillary, pinkish, sepals large, points curled back; capsule quite round, large.

For this *H.* and *R.* have ovate or linear bracts larger than the calyx, which *D.* does not mention, and I did not note. *D.* has for habitat only Severndrug. I had it near Malwan, and about Bombay and Bandora. *H.* calls it common throughout India.

10. *I. obscura.* A climber, more or less downy, leaves heart-shaped acuminate, petioles and peduncles long, peduncles jointed and bracted at the joints, and bearing two or three cream-coloured flowers with purple throat, sepals ovate pointed.

This is perhaps the commonest of the order in W. India, occurring everywhere in hedges; and *H.* calls it common throughout India. In this case the specific name is very appropriate, for it is an eminently common-place and unnoticeable plant.

* *I. Clarkei* very like this, but flowers larger and sepals narrow lanceolate. Konkan (*H.*).

11. *I. sepiaria.* Like the last but larger, stems a little hairy, leaves heart-shaped, peduncles many-flowered, thick, flowers pinkish with darker throat, sepals ovate oblong. *Amti.*

This also is very common in hedges, and frequent throughout India (*H.*). The leaves are frequently dark about the midrib.

12. *I. aquatica* (*I. reptans*, D.). Creeping and floating, mostly smooth, stems hollow, leaves lanceolate sagittate,

petioles long, flowers large, rose-coloured, several to a peduncle, sepals ovate. *Pánvel, nári, nálichi báji.*

Common in tanks, Konkan and Guzerat. Throughout India common, often cultivated as a vegetable (*H.*).

13. *I. turpethum.* An extensive twiner, all covered with hairs, stem angled and winged, leaves various, cordate or sagittate or lobed, peduncles two or three together, each with three or four rather large white or pinkish flowers, sepals broad ovate, concave enlarged in fruit, seeds black, size of a pea. *Dudh kalmi, tevari, ted, nishottar.*

Remarkable in this order for being full of milky juice. Guzerat, Deccan, and Konkan. Throughout India, common (*H.*).

14. *I. biloba* (*I. pescapræ*, D.). Goat's foot convolvulus. Large, creeping on the ground, leaves of two round lobes joined on the inner edge (like Bauhinia), flowers peduncled, large, reddish purple, sepals ovate lanceolate, capsule round, smooth, seeds very hairy. *Chágal kun, dobati luta, maryádvel.*

Very common on the sea-shore, covering large patches of sand. It is said to grow all round the world in the tropics, and was the first plant that Kingsley saw in the W. Indies, growing just as with us.

15. *I. vitifolia.* A large climber, rather hairy, leaves like those of the common vine, long petioled, peduncles long, flowers large of a very delicate yellow, capsule much smaller than the calyx, seeds grey. *Nauli.*

One of the most beautiful of the order, but not common, I think. S. Konkan. Throughout India (*H.*). "In Deccan gardens pretty common" (*G.*); but I have not seen it so.

* *I. laciniata* (*Pharbitis l.* D.), slender, leaves digitate with seven narrow serrated or pinnatifid lobes, sepals thick and fleshy, flowers large, white, tube long, purple within, capsule 3-celled. Málwan, Belgaum, Bombay, etc. (*D.*). * *I. dissecta* (*I. coptica*, D.) prostrate, hardly twining, leaves much as the last, flowers very small, white, sepals wrinkled, muricated, capsule 6-valved. Khandala, creeping among grass (*D.*). *I. uniflora* (*Aniseia u.*, D.), small, leaves oblong, linear, flowers solitary, small, white, long-stalked, capsule ovoid. S. Konkan. Throughout India (*H.*); varies greatly in hairiness apparently. *I. calycina* (*Aniseia c.* D.), hairy, leaves ovate, cordate, acute, flowers one to three together on short peduncles, small, white, the outer sepals sagittate. Guzerat. Deccan (*H.*). *I. angustifolia* (*I. filicaulis*, D.), small, creeping, smooth, stem angular, leaves narrow, hastate and toothed at the base, flowers small, yellow, with dark throat. Konkan and Deccan. *I. tridentata*, small, prostrate, with many stems from the root, leaves very small and narrow, auricled

and toothed at the base, flowers solitary long-stalked, yellow. Never twining (*H.*). Bhoria. Bassein and Ghorabandar (*D.*). *I. chryseides*, a very delicate and pretty climber, leaves heart-shaped, pointed, sometimes lobed, flowers small, yellow, few to a peduncle, capsule wrinkled, rough. Dhámapore. Wari country (*D.*). Throughout India (*H.*). * *I. reniformis*, small, stems creeping close to the ground, leaves kidney-shaped or ovate cordate, flowers very small, yellow, outer sepals smaller, seeds dark chestnut. *Undirkáni.* In places where water has lodged, Konkan and Deccan (*D.* and *G.*). *I. campanulata*, a large climber, smooth or nearly so, leaves large, cordate acute, long petioled, flowers large and handsome in corymbs, rose-coloured or purple, always prominently lobed. *Mádvel.* I am not certain of my identification of this, but *D.* and *G.* have it in the hilly parts of the Konkan and the Ghauts. * *I. rhyncorhiza*, a smooth climber, leaves deeply 7-lobed, lobes often pinnatifid, peduncles long, with one or two large yellow flowers. Konkan, Syhadris, and Ghauts. Dalzell and Stocks; not known otherwise.

Jalap (from Xalapa, a city of Mexico) is made from the root of *I. purga.*

5. Convolvulus.

1. *C. microphyllus.* A small prostrate plant, covered with white or tawny hairs, leaves lanceolate or oblong, flowers small, solitary, or few together, pale pink, capsule smooth.

Guzerat, N. Konkan, and Sind.

2. *C. arvensis.* A twiner, leaves narrow, sagittate, auricled, flowers pink and white, beautifully blended, one or two to a penduncle, bracts 2, distant from the flowers, capsule smooth. *Haranpag.*

The common English field bindweed. Common in Guzerat and the Deccan. A weed of cultivation (*H.*).

"A low breath
Of tender air made tremble in the hedge
The fragile bindweed bells, and briony rings."—*Tennyson.*

"In all fair hues from white to mingled rose,
Along the hedge the clasping bindweed flowers,

. . . . . .

Along the hedge, besides the trodden lane
Where day by day we pass, and pass again."—*A. Webster.*

C. Rottlerianus, erect, branched, hairy, leaves sessile linear, flowers small, star-like, pink, capsule size of a small pea, seeds warty. Deccan. Kattywar also (*D.*).

* *C. parviflorus*, a weak twiner, leaves ovate, cordate, acute, flowers numerous, white or pink in cymes or umbels, lobes acute, capsule and seeds smooth. Caranjab, Surat, etc. (*D.*).

6. Evolvulus.

E. alsinoides (*E. hirsutus*, D.). A small hairy prostrate plant with several stems from the root, leaves very small, ovate-pointed, flowers very small, long peduncled axillary, of a beautiful bright blue, with white throat and anthers, sometimes violet or white, bracts about half-way up the peduncle. *Shankveli.*

Growing in grass, common. Throughout India, very common, and throughout the world in and near the tropics (*H.*).

"The beautiful Evolvulus, with its profusion of blue flowers, that reminds one of the English forget-me-not."—*Tennent.*

7. Porana.

* *P. malabarica* (*P. racemosa*, D.). Leaves cordate acute, long-petioled, flowers small, funnel-shaped, pure white, in panicles, with large cordate bracts at the forks.

The Ghauts, common (*D.*). Matheran and Mahableshwar.

Mr. Birdwood calls this the snow-creeper, but the plant which bears this name in the Himalayas (*P. racemosa*) must by the description be much more beautiful.

8. Cressa.

C. cretica. A small shrubby unattractive plant, prostrate and spreading, all covered with white hairs, leaves oval-pointed, flowers solitary or in terminal heads very small, white or pinkish, the corolla lobes with long tips, seeds smooth. *Khardi, cháwel.*

Rice-fields in the cold weather. Konkan. In the bed of the Mula river, near Kirkee.—*Woodrow.*

Throughout India, not common (*H.*).

Hewittia, a hairy twiner, sepals enlarged in fruit, corolla bell-shaped, stigma deeply 2-lobed. * *H. bicolor* (*Palmia b.* D.), leaves ovate cordate, angular or lobed, flowers an inch long, generally solitary, yellow with purple base, bracts on the peduncle leafy, capsule round, hairy. The Konkans ; near Penn (*D.*).

Breweria, corolla wide-tubed, styles 2, united below. *B. cordata* (*B. Roxburghii*, D.). A strong twiner, covered with rusty hairs, leaves ovate cordate, flowers middle-sized, white, capsule larger than the calyx, thick, seeds brown, angular. Vingorla.

(c.) 9. Cuscuta. Dodder.

C. reflexa. Stems yellow, succulent, flowers very small, white in lax racemes, bracts small and fleshy, styles with 2 long stigmas. *Akaspáwan, ámarvel.*

Not in *D.* Konkan, Mahableshwar, and Guzerat; growing over trees or shrubs. Throughout India, common (*H.*). It is very like *Cassytha filiformis*, forming tangled masses like string. * *C. chinensis*, like the last, but smaller, styles 2 with capitate stigmas. Not in *D.* Common in gardens, adhering to greens, etc. (*G.*).

Jacquemontia violacea, common in gardens, with small light blue flowers, and heart-shaped leaves, preserves the name of the gifted French botanist, who died at Colaba in December, 1832, from exposure during his excursions in Salsette too soon after the close of the rains. His remains were removed to France within the last ten years.

There are probably many other species of this order to be found in gardens.

Order 82. SOLANACEÆ. Nightshades.

Herbs, shrubs or soft-wooded trees, leaves alternate, without stipules, flowers regular without bracts, calyx inferior, persistent, generally 5-cleft, corolla more or less funnel-shaped, lobes generally 5, stamens 5 on the corolla, anthers ovate or oblong, fruit a capsule or berry, many-seeded.

The leaves are described by *H.* as never opposite, but often in pairs on the same side of the stem, an arrangement sometimes called geminate. Similarly the flowers are often not in the axils, but above them, and so-called extra-axillary.

This is a large order, chiefly tropical, well known for its strong narcotic properties, and therefore much used in medicine. There are also a great number of food-producing plants, the most famous of which is the potato, but most of these, as well as the medicinal species, are poisonous in some of their parts. Tobacco may be looked on as the champion of the narcotic species, as the potato is of the food producers.

As to external characteristics it does not seem possible to mention any by which the species of the order may be easily distinguished; but two marks are very usual, 1° the pleating of the corolla, as in many of the Convolvulaceæ, and 2° the union of the long anthers at their apex, so as to form a cone surrounding the pistil. This last feature, which is very noticeable, occurs only in the genus Solanum, the flowers of all the species of which much resemble those of the potato, and as the Solanums are not only the main part of the order as regards W. India, but are said also to be nearly twice as many as all the remaining species of the order all over the world, these characteristics may be looked on as tolerably general.

1. Solanum. Corolla divided almost to the base, lobes spreading, filaments short, anthers oblong, meeting at the points, style columnar, berry round, or nearly so.

2. Physalis. Herbs, corolla bell-shaped, berry round within the enlarged and inflated calyx.

3. Withania. Unarmed shrubs, otherwise much as the last.

4. Datura. Large, coarse herbs, calyx and corolla long-tubed, stigma 2-lobed.

1. Solanum.

Note.—All the species here given are prickly, except the first.

1. *S. nigrum.* Black nightshade. An erect leafy plant, unarmed, leaves ovate waved or bluntly lobed, flowers small, more or less unbelled, drooping, white, calyx teeth small, berry round, black, sometimes red or yellow. *Gháti, Kámain, Máko, Kákmachi.*

Not in *D.* Poona, Mahableshwar, etc. Thoughout India (*H.*). It is common in England. "This very common plant has followed the footsteps of man over all the world.—*Lindley.*

2. *S. giganteum.* A shrub, leaves smooth, variously and irregularly lobed and waved, mealy beneath, as are the young shoots, flowers purple or violet in cymes, berries red, size of a pea, in handsome bunches. *Channajhad, Kutri.*

Mahableshwar, very common, and the higher Ghauts.

3. *S. Indicum.* Tall and shrubby, prickly all over, leaves greyish sinuate or lobed, sometimes pinnatifid downy, flowers purple in racemes, berry round, size of a gooseberry; at first variegated with light and dark green, finally yellow. *Dorlin, chinchurdi, ringani, bhui-vángi.*

Common in most parts. Throughout tropical India, very common (*H.*).

4. *S. xanthocarpum* (*S. Jacquinii*, D.). A spreading herb, procumbent, prickly all over, leaves ovate oblong, pinnatifid with acute segments, more or less hairy, flowers solitary or in racemes like those of the last, fruit yellow, size of a plum. *Bhuiringani, Kánteringani.*

As common as the last throughout India (*H.*). The prickles of this are said to be straight, and of Nos. 3 and 5 curved, but I do not think that this can be depended on.

5. *S. trilobatum.* A climbing under-shrub, all prickly, leaves smooth, variously and irregularly lobed and waved, flowers purple, berry red, size of a currant. *Mothi ringani.*

Hedges, Guzerat and the Deccan.

S. verbascifolium, a shrub or small tree, mealy in many parts, leaves large, ovate entire, woolly (like Mullein), flowers small, white in dichotomous cymes, berry size of a small cherry, yellow. *Kotri.* Sattara. Near Dharwar (*D.* and *G.*). Throughout India, in and near the tropics. *S. bigeminatum* (*S. Meesianum*, D.). Shrub unarmed, leaves lanceolate, rough above, flowers in clusters, calyx entire or nearly so, berry size of a pea, red. Fonda Ghaut (*D*). * *S. torvum*, a shrub, 3 or 4 feet high, leaves ovate, waved or lobed, flowers white in dense racemes, berry yellow, round, much exceeding the calyx. S. M. country. Throughout tropical India (*H*). It appears to come near to the *brinjal.*

Also *S. tuberosum*, the potato, *álu*, *batáta;* grown in fields, as in England, in the Khair and Junar talookas, in sandy river beds in Guzerat, and elsewhere in gardens. *S. melongena*, the egg plant or brinjal, *bengan*, *vánge;* also called mad apple, Jew's apple, and apple of Sodom. *S. lycopersicum*, the tomato or love apple, *wálwánge*, soon running wild if left to itself. *S. macrophyllum*, the potato-tree, very ornamental, covered with flowers just like those of the potato. A native of S. America. I have heard of it growing in the open air in Ireland.

2. Physalis.

P. minima. An erect hairy plant, leaves ovate waved or toothed, flowers small, yellow, sometimes spotted with purple, calyx segments triangular, berry smooth. *Thán mori.*

Konkan and Deccan. A common annual (*G.*). Throughout tropical India (*H.*), but not in *D.* *H.* makes the 5-angled calyx in fruit the mark of a variety.

P. peruviana is the Cape gooseberry, common in gardens, *phopti, tankári.* Other species cultivated in English gardens are called winter cherry.

3. Withania.

W. somnifera (*Physalis s.* D.). A small erect grey shrub, leaves 2 together but not opposite, ovate; flowers small green in sessile clusters, berry red, smooth, size of a pea, stamens forming a ring round the pistil. *Asgund, tilá, kanchuki.*

Deccan, Konkan, and Guzerat. Throughout drier sub-tropical India (*H.*). It appears to have been described by different authorities as a tree and a herb, as well as a shrub.

4. Datura.

D. fastuosa. A tall, coarse plant, leaves smooth, ovate, entire or deeply toothed, flowers very large, wide mouthed, limb of corolla shortly toothed, capsule large, roundish, covered with prickles. *Dhátara.*

A very common and conspicuous weed, useful to poisoners and sufferers from asthma.

> "The broad dhatura bares her breast,
> Of fragrant scent and virgin white,
> A pearl around the locks of night."—*Heber.*

H. includes in this *D.'s D. alba* and *D. hummatu*. He makes this to differ from *D. Stramonium*, the English thorn apple (the Virginian fireweed, from the plant there springing up in places cleared by fire), in the flowers being usually larger, and the capsule nearly indehiscent instead of 4-lobed. There are also smooth varieties of *D. fastuosa*.

* *Lycium Europæum*, the box thorn, a thorny shrub, leaves linear oblong, flowers from purple to nearly white, corolla much longer than calyx, berry small, red or yellow. *Gángro, chirchitta.* A native of S. Europe, ascribed by Stocks to salt soil in W. India (*H.*).

The following are cultivated. Several species of *Nicotiana*, tobacco, "plant divine of rarest virtue" (*Lamb*): in England also as garden and conservatory plants. The *Petunias*, equally common in English and Indian gardens. *Capsicum frutescens, chili, lál mirch;* C. Nepalense, yellow pepper; and other species. *Brugmansia candida, mota dhátara*, a large climber with white flowers six inches long, like a gigantic datura: common in Indian gardens and English conservatories, and growing luxuriantly about Mahableshwar. *Hyoscyamus niger*, common henbane, *Khorasáni ajwan*, a weed in England, though not very common.

> "Then in the outskirts, where pollutions grow,
> Pick the rank henbane."—*Coleridge.*

Probably the 'cursed hebenon' of the Ghost in Hamlet. "It bears poison in its looks" (*G.*).

Finally *Mandragora officinalis*, the mandrake of Scripture, "fabled Mandragore," which grows wild throughout Palestine (an allied species is found in the Himalayas), belongs to this order.

> "Not poppy, nor mandragora,
> Nor all the drowsy syrups of the world,
> Shall ever medicine thee."—*Othello.*

Order 83. LENTIBULARIEÆ.

Note.—In *H.* this order comes between Scrophularineæ and Gesneraceæ, but I have put it here, so as to keep all the didynamous orders together.

Herbs growing in water or wet places, leaves radical inconspicuous, sometimes root-like with vesicles or air bladders; flowers very irregular, calyx inferior, 2 to 5 lobed, corolla 2-lipped spurred, upper lip usually smaller, lower lip 3 to 5 lobed, stamens 2 on the base of the corolla, filaments broad, ovary round, stigma unequally 2-lobed, capsule round.

"The spurred flowers of this order have a general resemblance to those of Linaria (Scrophulariaceæ), though the ovary and capsule are those of Primulaceæ" (*Bentham*). The species found on this side of India are, like the English Utricularias, very small plants, rarely exceeding 6 inches in height: but they are all delicately beautiful; and it is specially true of plants that

"In small proportions we just beauties see,
And in short measures life may perfect be."—*B. Jonson.*

UTRICULARIA. Pedicels bracted, calyx of 2 lobes, entire or minutely toothed, often enlarged in fruit.

Note.—I have found great difficulty in identifying my plants with the species either in *D.* or *H.*

1. *U. stellaris.* Leaves submerged, verticelled, much divided into hair-like segments with oval vesicles among and above them, flowers yellow on long erect pedicels, calyx lobes ovate, blunt, hairy, lips of corolla nearly equal, spur short and thick, capsule hairy.

Tanks in the Konkan. Throughout India (*H.*). He has a variety with white flowers, striped violet.

R. calls this plant leafless, looking on the hair-like masses as roots; and some of the other species have been so described.

2. *U. albocærulea.* Growing in masses, with the stems often much intertwined, leaves small at the base of the scape soon falling off, flowers deep blue, with white spot on the lower lip, which is much the largest, and twice as long as the acute spur. *Kajat cha ghás, Sita chi ásre* (Sita's tears).

This is essentially the Konkan species, *H.* having no other habitat. It grows in quantities at Rutnagherry (where it is called the Rutnagherry violet), Vingorla, &c., in little pools on the barest sheet rock; also in rice-fields at the end of the rains. Dr. T. Cooke has it also at Mahableshwar, under the first native name given, but I think it possible that that may be a different species from the Konkan one.

The second Maratta name was given me many years ago by a blue-coated Rutnagherry policeman, when guiding me to some out-of-the-way place, with this legend: "When Sita was brought back from Ceylon by her husband Ráma, after the expedition in which Hanumán took so great a part, her tears falling upon the bare rocks caused this lovely little flower to spring up."

* *U. cærulea* and *U. reticulata* must both be very like this; the latter, Dr. De Crespigny says, grows with *U. albocærulea* on the laterite rock. *U. reticulata* is variable in habit and size of flowers. The larger forms are twining, the smaller rigid and erect (*Oliver*). The flowers are distant, purple or blue, the throat veined darker, spur conical about equal to the lower lip, calyx lobes broad, pointed. Mahableshwar.

3. *U. arcuata.* Leaves as in the last, flowers blue-purple lower lip of corolla much the largest, spur long, slender, curved.

Konkan and Belgaum. Said also to have been found in Bombay

(*D.*). A specimen sent to me by Dr. T. Cooke, as being common at Mahableshwar, was identified as this at Kew. The species which I found at Mahableshwar I took to be U. reticulata, but the descriptions vary only in the spur of the latter being conical and shorter; and if the plants are different species they are certainly very much alike.

4. *U. orbiculata.* One or two inches high, very slender, leaves round petioled, flowers few, blue with yellow throat, sepals rounded about equal, lower lip with 5 obtuse equal lobes, spur rather thick, curved forwards.

S. Konkan. Very common in the Bhore Ghaut.—*Dr. T. Cooke.* Almost throughout India in the hills (*H.*).

U. exoleta, two inches high, slender, leaves of many capillary segments, flowers yellow with orange streaks, one or two at the top of the scape, sepals unequal, spur blunt. Not in *D.* or *G.*, but it is, I believe, *R.'s U. biflora.* I had it at Dapoli. * *U. affinis* (*U. decipiens,* D.), like *U. arcuata,* but smaller in all parts, and the spur straight or only slightly curved. Vingorla (*D.*). *U. racemosa* (*U. nivea,* D.), flowers few, scattered, white, spur conical, twice as long as the lower lip, scales attached to the scape by the middle. Vingorla (*D.*). *H.* has corolla blue or whitish, lower lip of corolla obscurely 4-lobed.

The eight orders which follow form a very natural group, containing all the plants with what Rousseau in his "Lettres elementaires sur la botanique," called "fleurs en gueule," which may be described as those having a two-lipped corolla and didynamous stamens. It is not that all the plants contained in these eight orders have these two peculiarities, for there are in them a number of genera or species with flowers either regular or obscurely two-lipped, and others with stamens not didynamous. But by far the greater number of species contained in the eight orders, which between them make up at least 700 genera, have these distinctions.

The stamens in these orders, as in corollifiorals generally, are placed on the corolla. The other characteristics of each order are given in the usual way, but the following short statement of obvious differences will be found useful. It refers not to all the species or genera contained in each order, but to the plants found in W. India, and described in this book.

1. SCROPHULARINEÆ. Herbs, the greater part inconspicuous. Stem generally round, fruit generally a many-seeded capsule.

2. OROBANCHEÆ. A small order of leafless parasites, which can scarcely be taken for anything else. There are only six species in W. India.

3. GESNERACEÆ. Also a very small order, with only five species known in W. India, and those rare. Their characteristics are much the same as those of Scrophularineæ.

4. BIGNONIACEÆ. Trees, generally remarkable by the large size of their leaves, flowers, and fruit. There are also some well-known climbers belonging to the order in gardens.

5. PEDALINEÆ. A very small order of herbs, of which only two species are found in W. India.

6. ACANTHACEÆ. Mostly shrubs, many of them very strong-smelling and viscid. Leaves opposite: flowers generally crowded together in spikes or racemes, surrounded by many bracts.

7. VERBENACEÆ. Mostly trees or shrubs, leaves opposite, fruit a drupe or berry.

8. LABIATÆ. Aromatic herbs, rarely shrubs; stems square, leaves opposite, ovary composed of 4 deeply separated lobes, developing into a fruit of 4 one-seeded nuts, always visible at the bottom of the calyx tube.

Note.—In small species it may sometimes be difficult to decide whether the stamens are didynamous or equal, and in a good many cases the corollas are obscurely 2-lipped. In the latter case the fact is mentioned either under the genus or the species.

Note.—Wherever the stamens are not didynamous in these orders it is so stated in the description of the genus: no mention of the stamens meaning that they are didynamous.

As far as exogenous dichlamyds are concerned, plants with two stamens are found, outside these orders, only in Oleaceæ and Lentibulariaceæ.

ORDER 84. SCROPHULARINEÆ.

Herbs, leaves without stipules, flowers usually irregular: calyx inferior usually persistent and with 5 often unequal lobes: corolla generally tubular and 2-lipped, stamens generally didynamous, sometimes 2, anthers often with 2 distinct cells, fruit capsular, seeds numerous.

Note.—There are shrubs and a few trees in the order: but none of these are found in W. India. There are also genera with five stamens, but none of these occur within these limits. This large order is somewhat disappointing to the English botanist in India, for though it is well represented as regards numbers, a very large proportion of the species found here are very small and insignificant. In England it is very different, the order there including many popular favourites among wild flowers, such as Foxglove "herb of pride," the lovely bright-blue Speedwell, Eyebright and Snapdragon : and, among garden and greenhouse flowers are the Calceolarias, Pentstemons, Mimulus, and many others, so that Figuier says, " this order presents us with a galaxy of flowers such as scarcely any other can produce."

1. CELSIA. Erect woolly: leaves alternate, corolla lobes broad, spreading horizontally, stamens 4 equal, filaments bearded.

2. LINARIA. Leaves usually opposite, sepals imbricate, corolla spurred in front, 2-lipped, the mouth closed by a projecting palate, stamens included, capsule 2-celled.

3. LINDENBERGIA. Flowers yellow, calyx bell-shaped with 5 short divisions, upper lip of corolla broad, lower 3-lobed, stamens included, anther cells separate stalked, capsule 2-grooved.

4. STEMODIA. Leaves opposite or whorled, sepals 5, sometimes increasing, corolla 2-lipped, stamens and capsule as in the last.

5. LIMNOPHILA. Plants more or less aquatic, leaves opposite or whorled, corolla tube broad and straight, lobes nearly equal, stamens generally as in the last.

6. HERPESTIS. Very small smooth marsh plants, calyx segments unequal, corolla with wide throat 2-lipped, capsule 2 or 4 valved.

7. DOPATRIUM. Of the same character as the last, and generally like it, but stamens 2 with 2 minute staminodes.

8. TORENIA. Leaves opposite, calyx tubular winged or deeply ribbed, corolla tube broad above, stamens sometimes equal, anthers joining in pairs, capsule linear or oblong.

9. VANDELLIA. Very small plants with opposite toothed leaves, stamens sometimes equal, upper pair of filaments arched and the anthers joining.

10. BONNAYA. Very small smooth plants, leaves opposite, sepals narrow, perfect stamens 2, the anthers meeting, and 2 staminodes, capsule linear.

11. VERONICA. Calyx 4 or 5 parted, corolla tube very short, lobes spreading, stamens 2 exserted.

12. STRIGA. Small rough plants, usually with square stems, calyx tubular strongly ribbed, corolla with slender bent tube, stamens included, anthers one-celled.

13. RAMPHICARPA. Erect smooth plants, calyx bell-shaped,

corolla tube long and slender, lobes equal, stamens included, capsule beaked.

14. Centranthera. Rigid and rough, calyx large, more or less 2-lipped with 2 bracts, corolla long-tubed, wide-mouthed, with five spreading lobes about equal, anthers meeting in pairs and spurred.

15. Sopubia. Corolla short-tubed, broad-mouthed, with 5 spreading lobes about equal, anthers with only one cell perfect.

1. Celsia.

C. Coromandelliana. A stout strong-smelling plant covered with sticky hairs, and with many leaves from the root, lower ones pinnate or pinnatifid with unequal lobes, upper ovate, flowers in a long erect spike, yellow, with a leaf-like bract to each flower, sepals toothed or with intermediate segments, capsule ovate smooth. *Kutki, Kolhal.*

Waste places. Deccan and Konkan. Throughout India (*H.*).
This plant is very like one of the English Mulleins, and the genus only differs from that (Verbascum) by having 4 stamens instead of 5.

2. Linaria. Toadflax.

L. ramosissima. A smooth delicate prostrate plant, much branched, leaves triangular or lobed, flowers small, yellow, solitary and long-stalked, spur short, curved, sepals linear lanceolate.

The Deccan and elsewhere. Throughout India on rocks and stony places (*H.*).

This is easily recognized by its likeness to the English *L. cymbalaria*, called "Mother of Thousands," "Creeping Jenny," and other names—

"The little flower that clings
To the turrets and the walls."—*Tennyson.*

3. Lindenbergia.

L. urticæfolia. A very downy plant, leaves small, ovate, serrate, flowers axillary, solitary or in pairs, the throat spotted, calyx much shorter than corolla, and as long as the capsule. *Dhol, gazdar.*

Common on walls, and hence called by *R.* (Stemodia) muralis. Throughout India; varies much in hairiness and disposition of the flowers (*H.*).

4. Stemodia.

S. viscosa. An erect plant, hairy, sticky, and strong-smelling, stem square, leaves stem-clasping, oblong or fiddle-shaped, flowers axillary solitary or terminal, dark blue, the throat nearly closed, calyx with 2 linear bracts as long as the ovate capsule.

Deccan, Konkan, and Guzerat, often found on dry rice-fields. It is sometimes less hairy, and with pale flowers.

* *S. serrata*, viscid, usually densely branched from the base, leaves sessile, obovate, serrated above, flowers smaller than the last, capsule linear oblong. Not in *D.* or *G.* Konkan (*H.*).

5. Limnophila.

1. *L. conferta.* A rather succulent procumbent plant, leaves sessile, ovate, serrate or crenate, flowers pretty, purple or pink, axillary generally solitary with 2 bracts, calyx segments lanceolate, capsule broad elliptic.

Marshes at Málwan (*D.*), where I also found it. Throughout the Deccan. Very variable, the larger variety having slightly petioled leaves and spiked flowers (*H.*).

2. *L. gratioloides.* Erect or diffuse, with a smell of turpentine, leaves verticelled, lower submerged and divided into many hair-like segments, those just above water pinnatifid, upper lanceolate, flowers solitary, axillary stalked, pale purple; capsule round. *Turti.*

Deccan and Konkan. Throughout India in swamps, rice-fields, &c. It is very variable, and *H.* says the normal form is with pinnatifid leaves only. The flowers are rather like those of a Linaria.

* *L. racemosa*, smooth, erect, stout-stemmed, flowers bluish or purplish in dense racemes, calyx segments with slender points. Konkans and Belgaum (*G.*). Matheran, *Birdwood.* The small states of this are with difficulty distinguished from the last (*H.*). * *L. gratissima*, leaves in 3's, linear lanceolate, calyx and peduncles glandular and hairy, capsule oblong acute. *D.* and *G.* without hab. or colour of flowers. * *L. Roxburghii* (*L. menthastrum*, D.), erect with many stems, leaves oblong serrated, flowers axillary, solitary or in heads, purple, calyx lobes lanceolate, capsule elliptical. No hab. (*D.* and *G.*). Konkan (*H.*).

Note.—*H.* has apparently not identified *D.'s L. Roxburghii*, and he says that the genus is a very variable one, the foliage and habit of the species depending on the depth, &c., of the water in which they grow.

6. Herpestis.

Note.—The Indian species all belong to the section, with sub-equal corolla lobes and stamens, and capitate 2-lobed stigmas (*H.*).

H. monniera. A succulent plant, leaves obovate entire, flowers solitary stalked, pale blue, calyx with 2 small bracts, corolla lobes nearly equal, capsule ovoid. *Bámb, nirbráhmi.*

Deccan and Konkan; Mahableshwar.—*Dr. Cooke.* Marshes throughout India and in all warm countries (*H.*). Generally to be met with on the margins of tanks (*G.*).

H. Hamiltoniana, small stout erect, leaves lanceolate entire, flowers sessile axillary, upper lobe of calyx very broad cordate, capsule round. At Málwan, plentiful (*D.*).

7. Dopatrium.

D. junceum. Stem naked, leaves mostly radical, thick, oblong lanceolate blunt, stem leaves like scales, flowers solitary sessile or on slender stalks, pink, capsule round.

S. Konkan. Swampy places, common (*D.*). Throughout India (*H.*).

8. Torenia.

T. Asiatica. Diffuse or prostrate,.leaves petioled, triangular crenate serrate, calyx 2-lipped, winged, flowers shaded, lateral lobes and lower lip dark purple.

I take this to be the common and handsome garden plant, often called "the Belgaum violet," and found wild in S. Konkan; and I suppose it to be *D.'s T. bicolor*, though *H.* does not so identify it. *T. cordifolia* is erect or trailing, with square stem, leaves ovate crenate, not cordate, flowers of 2 shades of purple, calyx winged. S. Konkan. **T. bicolor* has flowers dark blue, or violet and white, and the calyx not winged. *H.* says that the species are imperfectly characterized, and I can throw no light on them from the specimens I have seen.

9. Vandellia.

1. *V. crustacea.* Diffuse, smooth, with square stem, leaves ovate, coarsely crenated, flowers light purple, calyx segments lanceolate ribbed, capsule oval as long as the calyx.

Growing everywhere. Throughout India, a weed, and throughout the tropics of the old world (*H.*). It is very like a diminutive of Torenia cordifolia.

2. *V. hirsuta.* Erect, branched, stems square, pedicels and calyx hairy and glandular, leaves sessile ovate crenated, flowers dull white in long racemes, capsule ovate or roundish.

In watercourses, S. Konkar. Vingorla (*D.*).

V. scabra (*V. laxa*, D.) prostrate, branched, leaves broad ovate, toothed above, flowers larger than in the other species, white, sometimes with a yellow spot in the throat, capsule as long as the calyx. Dapoli. Vingorla (*D.*). Tropical India (*H.*). * *V. pedunculata*, smooth, procumbent, leaves ovate crenate, flowers long-stalked, white or pale blue, capsule much longer than calyx. *Gadagvel.* Vingorla (*D.*). Rice swamps throughout India (*H.*).

10. Bonnaya.

1. *B. brachiata.* Erect, branched, stem 4-sided, leaves sessile, obovate or oblong, deeply serrated, flowers in terminal racemes, pink, lower lip spotted with white, bracts lanceolate, capsule linear, long.

Common in pastures. Throughout India (*H.*).

2. *B. veronicafolia.* From creeping to nearly erect, stems square, leaves oblong lanceolate, entire or distantly and shallowly serrated, flowers in racemes, long-stalked, violet or light-blue, the throat much contracted, capsule long, erect. *Shewál.*

Common. Throughout India (*H.*).

H. includes in this, as varieties, two others, which *D.* made species, *B. grandiflora*, with short, stout branches, and flowers chiefly axillary, and *B. verbenæfolia*, with long, slender branches and flowers often in long naked racemes.

* *B. reptans*, stems creeping and rooting, slender, leaves obovate, sharply serrated, flowers in racemes, light purple, capsule long and slender. S. Konkan (*D.*). * *B. oppositifolia*, much smaller than any of the preceding, erect, much-branched, leaves sessile, oblong, slightly serrated, flowers small, blue, capsule very small. Konkans (*D.*).

Note.—"Several species of *Bonnaya* so closely resemble others of *Vandellia* as to render the validity of this genus very doubtful" (*H.*).

11. Veronica.

V. anagallis. A smooth, succulent plant with hollow stems, leaves sessile, linear oblong, cordate at base, flowers small in long racemes, white or pink, pedicels and bracts short, capsule ovate.

Not in *D.* or *G.* I found it in watercourses at Khair (Deccan). *H.* has for W India, "The Deccan peninsula, in the Konkan only;" but without any Bombay authority. It is remarkably like *V. beccabunga*, the common English brook-lime, and seems to be pretty common (with three or four varieties) in the N. of India and countries adjacent. *V. chamædrys* is the common speedwell—one of the best-known and most popular of English wild flowers.

12. Striga.

Note.—In this genus *H.* lays great stress on the number of striæ, or ribs, on the calyx. I doubt if this is a very reliable distinction for unlearned observers.

1. *S. orobanchioides.* Stem thick, leaves minute or scale-like, flowers spiked, pink or lilac, corolla tube long, calyx with 5 ribs. *Tambadi kari cha gavat.*

Deccan and Konkan, common; either growing on rocks or as a parasite on species of Lepidagathis and Euphorbium. It is reddish all over. Mr. Birdwood says the divisions of the corolla have a white spot at the base.

2. *S. lutea* (*S. hirsuta*, D.). Leaves linear, or lower ones lanceolate, flowers white or yellow, calyx with 10 or 15 ribs.

Konkan and Deccan. Very common (*D.*). Throughout W. India and the Deccan (*H.*). He makes it from 6 to 18 inches high, but I have seen it not more than 2 or 3. He has it also with flowers red or purple.

3. *S. euphrasioides.* Leaves linear, entire or slightly toothed, flowers mostly axillary and solitary, white, bracts lanceolate, longer than the 15-ribbed calyx.

Deccan. Very common (*D.*). Throughout India (*H.*). "Very variable in habit, from a simple filiform stem 4 to 6 inches, to a stout branched herb of 2 feet" (*H.*). I have seen only the small form.

* *S. densiflora*, leaves linear lanceolate, spikes dense, flowers white, bracts lanceolate, longer than the calyx, which has 5 striæ. About Surat (*D*). * *S. sulphurea*, distinguished from *S. euphrasioides* by the calyx being about double the length, with divisions long and exactly linear. Known only to Dalzell, who had it at Shivnar.

13. Ramphicarpa.

R. longiflora. A pretty, small, erect plant, leaves divided into many linear or thread-like segments, flowers white, generally solitary, very large for the size of the plant, capsule swelling, with slender curved beak.

Very common in S. Konkan, growing in grass. Ghaut pastures (*D.*). Matheran (*Mr. Birdwood*). Belgaum (*G.*). *H.*, who attributes it only to the Deccan peninsula, calls it very variable in habit and stature. At Dápoli, on the maidán, it succeeds Habenaria rotundifolia in the rains.

14. Centranthera.

C. hispida. About a foot high, leaves opposite, sessile, nearly linear, pointed, flowers solitary, nearly sessile, purplish-red or nearly white, filaments bearded, capsule round.

The Konkans. Matheran. Throughout India (*H.*).

15. Sopubia.

S. delphinifolia. A handsome, erect plant, branched, and mostly smooth, leaves pinnatifid with filiform segments, flowers axillary, solitary or in pairs, large, rose-coloured, the throat darker, bracts 2, linear, calyx teeth long and narrow, sometimes with intermediate teeth, capsule oblong. *Dudháli.*

Konkan and Guzerat. Mahableshwar. *H.* makes it as much as 3 or 4 feet high. I have not seen it more than half that.

Artanema, leaves opposite, corolla bell-shaped, upper stamens with long arching filaments. *A. sesamoides*, a tall plant with 4-sided stems, leaves lanceolate acute, flowers blue or purple in racemes; like those of Sesamum, but smaller. Konkan.

Ilysanthes, slender marsh plants, leaves opposite, 2 upper stamens only perfect, the anthers meeting. * *I. hyssopioides*, stem diffuse or erect, leaves oblong lanceolate, flowers pale blue, long-stalked, corolla much longer than calyx, flowers pink in racemes, the lower lip spotted with white, capsule linear long. Common in the rains (*D.*).

Glossostigma, flowers solitary, axillary, minute, calyx bell-shaped, 3 or 4-lobed, stamens 2 or 4. * *G. spathulatum*, very small, creeping, rooting at the joints, leaves fascicled, linear, spathulate, flowers blue on long pedicels, capsule as long as calyx. Margins of tanks, &c. (*D.*). *R.* says it grows at the bottom of clear running water.

Buchnera, rigid, black when dry, calyx tubular, nerved, ribbed, and toothed, with 2 bracts, corolla tube very slender, with 5 nearly equal lobes, capsule oblong. *B. hispida*, all rough, height up to 2 feet, leaves lanceolate, lower ones toothed, flowers small, lilac, in slender spikes, corolla tube slender, curved, capsule as long as calyx. Hirni. Caranja (*D.*).

Pedicularis zeylanica is in Mr. Birdwood's Matheran list, with tall erect leafy stems, leaves lobed or subpinnatifid, flowers in racemes pink, bracts pinnatifid. Konkan mountains, Stocks (*H.*). *P. sylvatica* is the common English lousewort.

In gardens. *Antirrhinum*, in varieties—Snapdragon. The genus differs from Linaria in having no spur. *Maurandya Barclayana*, a delicate climber, leaves heart-shaped or triangular, flowers violet-purple. *Russellia juncea*, *Kesh*, half shrubby, very common, the green branches divided into many filiform segments, leaves few, low down, ovate, flowers scarlet.

Order 85. OROBANCHACEÆ. Broomrapes.

Succulent leafless herbs growing as parasites on the roots of other plants. Stem scaly, corolla with curved tube and lobed limb, more or less two-lipped, stamens 4, didynamous on the corolla tube, ovary of 2 connate carpels, style long, fruit a capsule.

The few species of this order will always attract attention by their strange appearance, and cannot well be taken for anything else. The plants are generally of a uniform colour all over, either brown (and then looking like withered plants) or else dull blue or purple. Several species are found in England of the same general appearance as those here given.

1. Æginetia. Flowers large, without bracts, calyx spathaceous deeply split in front, corolla tube broad, lobes nearly equal, 2 upper united.

2. Orobanche. Flowers in spikes or racemes, calyx divided to the base, 2, 4 or 5-lobed, corolla 2-lipped, upper erect, lower 3-lobed, capsule 2-valved.

1. Æginetia.

Æ. Indica. A curious-looking plant, all purple, like a tobacco pipe standing on end, the large curved flower forming the bowl, calyx about as long as the corolla tube, corolla lobes very small, capsule smooth, round, jointed at the top.

Dapoli, Khandala, Salsette, &c. (*D.*). Throughout India (*H.*). The scapes grow 2 or 3 together.

2. Orobanche.

* *O. Indica* (*Phelipæa I.* D.). Sometimes branched, scales very few, calyx 4 or 5-toothed, corolla tube slender, funnel-shaped, purple or blue, ciliate, bracts ovate, anthers woolly.

There is some confusion about this plant, which is what *D.* and *G.* say is common on tobacco plants in the Deccan; but *H.* says "throughout the plains of India, especially in mustard crops," and Mr. Clarke confirms this. On the other hand *H.* has *O. nicotiana*, which *D.* and *G.* have not got, as common in and distinctive of tobacco plants. He describes it as thick-stemmed, pale brown, many-flowered, scales few acute, calyx of 2 distinct segments, corolla tube contracted in the middle, lobes small, pale blue, crenate; bracts as long as the corolla tube.

Christisonia, calyx tubular, 5-cleft corolla, long-tubed, lobes 5, nearly equal, stigma large. * *C. Lawii*, stems stout, thicker upwards, clothed with scales, calyx dark brown, corolla much larger, pale purple and yellow, anthers acutely spurred. From the figure and description the corolla is much the largest part of the plant. * *C. calcareata* (*C. Stocksii*, D.), "probably a more fully developed state of the last," the pedicels longer, the corolla bluish white. Both were found by Mr. Law in Salsette, the first also between the Rám Ghaut and Belgaum.

Cistanche, flowers in dense spikes, corolla tube long and curved. * *C. tubulosa*, one to five feet high and often as thick as the wrist! Corolla one or two inches long, much incurved, lobes short. Not attributed to this Presidency in the books, except to Sindh by *H.*, and to Kattywar on the roots of grasses and of *Calotropis procera* by Dr. Gray.

ORDER 86. GESNERACEÆ.

Herbs or undershrubs, leaves without stipules, flowers bracted, generally irregular, calyx segments 5, corolla tubular generally 5-lobed, two-lipped in all the genera occurring in this Presidency, stamens didynamous on the corolla tube; seeds very many minute.

This is a small order (included by Bentham in Bignoniaceæ), better known by the beautiful Gloxinias and Achimenes than by anything that is found wild in W. India. The flowers outwardly are much like those of the 2-lipped genera of Scrophularineæ, and all those found in this Presidency are of somewhat succulent habit.

1. ÆSCHYNANTHUS. Epiphytic undershrubs, leaves opposite, ovary superior, stalked, stigma peltate.

2. KLUGIA. Leaves alternate, unequal-sided, calyx 5-angled or winged, ovary ovoid, stigma obliquely dilated, capsule included, 2-valved.

1. ÆSCHYNANTHUS.

* *Æ. Perotettii.* Branches sometimes much compressed, smooth, leaves lanceolate acuminate, umbels 2 to 6 flowered, corolla 2 inches long, narrow scarlet, the lobes marked with purple; calyx lobes small.

Párwar Ghaut (*D.*). On trees in the Koina Valley.—*Dr. Cooke.* Other similar situations (*H.*).

* *Æ.* grandiflora seems to be very much the same, but the leaves and capsule larger. It rests as to W. India only on the authority of Nimmo in *G.*, and is described by him as having flowers like the fox-glove, and swollen joints, from which fibrous roots issue. On trees in the S. Konkan.

2. KLUGIA.

K. Notoniana. A pretty plant; a line of hairs runs down

the stem, leaves large oval acute, slightly rough, flowers in a one-sided drooping raceme, dull blue, lower lip of corolla broad, bract filiform longer than the pedicel.

This and *K. scabra*, which *H.* makes only a variety, seemed to me very different. *K. scabra* is much rougher, the leaves not so unequal at the base, flowers of a brighter blue, lower lip of corolla with an acute triangular apex. This I had at Khârepátan, and I believe at other places: *D.* in the Wári country. Both grow out of rocks and walls.

Chirita, leaves often unequal, stamens 2 perfect and 2 or 3 barren, filaments flattened, bent, the anthers usually applied to the oblique stigma. * *C. hamosa* (*Didymocarpus cristatus*, D.), herbaceous, erect, fleshy, leaves large, broad ovate cordate, peduncles connate with the petiole, flowers white, the mouth of corolla oblique and slightly coloured, capsule long, slender, curved. Rocks near Párwar Ghaut (*D.*). *Epithema*, succulent herbs, flowers in racemes, which have each one large one-sided hooded bract, stamens 2 perfect, anthers cohering. * *E. cernuosum* (*E. zeylanica* D.), hairy, lower leaves alternate petioled, upper opposite, sessile, ovate cordate, spikes of small blue or white flowers, bracts dentate. S. Ghauts (*D.*).

ORDER 87. BIGNONIACEÆ. Trumpet flowers.

Trees with opposite leaves, generally much divided and very large, flowers showy irregular, calyx bell-shaped, 2 to 5-lobed, corolla broad-tubular, two-lipped, 5-lobed, stamens didynamous (except Oroxylum) on the corolla, style long smooth, stigma of 2 elliptic lobes, capsule often podlike, generally very large, seeds winged.

This is a tropical order, differing from the other didynamous orders in the species being all trees and remarkable for the size of their leaves, flowers, and fruit. Their trumpet-shaped flowers "are the glory of the places they inhabit."—*Figuier.*

1. OROXYLUM. *Stamens* 5, leaves twice pinnate, corolla lobes about equal, round, crisped and toothed, capsule linear, compressed, 2-valved, seeds thin, discoid winged all round except at the base.

2. DOLICHANDRONE. Leaves pinnate, calyx spathaceous, cleft to the base on one side, corolla lobes about equal, seeds broadly winged at the sides.

3. HETEROPHRAGMA. Leaves pinnate, calyx ovoid, irregularly lobed, corolla lobes about equal, seeds winged at the sides.

4. STEREOSPERMUM. Leaves once or twice pinnate, calyx

ovoid, truncate, or shortly and unequally lobed, corolla lobes as in No. 1, seeds as in No. 4.

1. Oroxylum.

O. Indicum (*Calosanthes I.* D.). Leaves very large, pinnæ 3 pair, leaflets smooth, ovate, acute, petioled, flowers in large panicles, thick, fleshy, dark-coloured, pod about 2 feet by 6 inches, straight and flat, calyx adherent. *Taitu, phalphára, jagdalá.*

The Konkan and Ghauts. Throughout India (*H.*). *R.* calls the leaves 4 to 6 feet long, which I think is larger than we have them.

The tree loses its leaves in the cold weather, and then, with the long dark pods hanging from the ends of the branches, has a very weird appearance. They are like a harlequin's wand, and if struck send out an abundant shower of large thin seeds.

2. Dolichandrone.

D. falcata (*Spathdœa f.* D.). A small tree, leaflets 5 to 7, oval rounded, slightly hairy, flowers in racemes, calyx oblique, corolla white, about an inch long, fragrant, capsule linear, curved and pointed, more than a foot long by $\frac{3}{4}$ of an inch broad. *Netasing, marsingi.*

Guzerat, Konkan, and S.M. country : not common.

* *D. Lawii*, considered by Dr. Brandis to be a smooth variety of the last, the leaflets often larger, and generally very shortly acuminated. Not in *D.* or *G.*, Bombay and Konkan, Law (*H.*). **D. arcuata* (*Spathodea crispa*, D.), leaflets 9 to 11, roundish elliptic, velvety on both sides, corolla pure white, long-tubed, pod linear twisted, pendulous. Known only to Mr. Law in W. India. Buddi on the Gatparba.

3. Heterophragma.

H. Roxburghii. A large tree, leaves 2 or 3 feet long, smooth, leaflets 4 or 5 pair, ovate, flowers in downy or velvety panicles, white or pinkish, the margin wrinkled and curled, pod thick, linear, about 12 inches by 2, 4-celled. *Wáras, pálang.*

Common on the Ghauts and elsewhere.

Forests from Khandeish to Canara.—*Brandis.* This, found at Mahableshwar, is the only one of the order in Mr. Birdwood's list.

4. Stereospermum.

1. *S. chelonoides* (*Heterophragma c.* D.). A large tree, nearly smooth, leaflets 7 to 11, elliptic acuminate, flowers

yellowish, or flesh-coloured, fragrant, in large panicles, capsule obscurely 4-sided, one to two feet long. *Púdel, pádri.*

Ghauts and S. Konkan. Throughout moister India (*H.*). "The flowers are compared by the poets to the quiver of Káma, the God of Love" (*Sir W. Jones*). It is the fragant *pátala* of Hindoo poetry.

2. *S. suaveolens* (*Heterophragma, s.* D.). Leaves one or two feet long, leaflets 5 to 9, large oval, flowers, in viscous, hairy panicles, dull purple or crimson, hairy in the throat, very fragrant, capsule cylindric, 18 inches long. *Paral, Kalgori.*

I believe this tree to be common at Tungár and Ságargarh, but did not see the flowers. Deccan (*G.*). Common in the Dandelly jungles (*D.*). Throughout moister India (*H.*).

3. **S. xylocarpum* (*Bignonia, x.* D.). Leaves twice pinnate, petiole sharply angular, leaflets oblong, acute, large, flowers whitish, fragrant in large panicles, corolla oblique, short-tubed, pods 2 or 3 feet long, woody, linear or cylindrical. *Kharsing, bersingi.*

Ghauts, Konkans, Dangs, &c. (*D.*). Deccan peninsula, common (*H.*).

Tecoma, leaves simple, corolla lobes about equal, capsule very narrow, two-valved, seeds thin, discoid, with broad wings. **T. undulata*, leaves narrow, oblong, flowers few together, corolla bright orange, capsule 8 inches long, very narrow, curved. *Loheri Rakt-roera.* Khandish and Guzerat, rare (*D.*). Sind hills (*B.*). "A tree with drooping branches like the weeping willow: when in flower few trees can present a more noble or beautiful sight" (*G.*). *T. stans*, a tall, woody shrub, flowers yellow, streaked with red, common in gardens.

Of introduced species, *Millingtonia hortensis*, a native of Burma, has been much planted about the roads in Poona (and probably elsewhere). It is a grand tree, tall and straight, with large, much-divided leaves, and white, fragrant flowers, with very long tubes. *H.* describes it in its native jungles as 80 feet high, lanceolate in outline, with drooping branches. "Such a tree, a vast pillar of glossy green, placed on the summit of a lofty hill, would be a beacon to all the country round" (*O. W. Holmes*).

Bignonia radicans is the climbing trumpet flower of Bombay gardens, with large bunches of long-tubed, scarlet-orange flowers. Other species are also cultivated.

ORDER 88. PEDALINEÆ.

Herbs, with irregular flowers; corolla tubular, much bulged, 5-lobed, obscurely 2-lipped; stamens 4, didynamous; capsule 2 to 4-celled.

This very small order is sometimes included in Bignoniaceæ, but the habit and fruit are different. The species here given would naturally be taken to belong to *Scrophularineæ*.

1. PEDALIUM. Calyx small, 5 divided, capsule hard, spinous, indehiscent, 2 or 3-celled, with one or two seeds in each cell.

2. SESAMUM. Calyx as in the last, capsule without spines, 2 to 4-valved, seeds many in each cell, obliquely oblong.

1. PEDALIUM.

P. murex. A low, thick-stemmed, succulent herb, nearly smooth, leaves oval, obtuse, waved, or slightly lobed, flowers small, solitary, yellow, with 2 black glands at the base of the pedicel, fruit ovoid, with four conical spurs from the base. *Karontia, goksurak.*

Sandy shores of Guzerat, Katywar, and N. Konkan. Fruit called *gokru* (*D.*). The root is deep orange-coloured, and the whole plant has an odour of musk (*Don.*).

"The plant has the peculiar property of thickening milk or water. If bits of the stem, leaves, and roots be mixed for a few seconds in milk or water, the liquid turns thick and mucilaginous, so that it can be raised several feet out of the basin by the hand, and this, without acquiring colour, taste, or smell. The Singhalese in this way thicken the milk sent round for sale to Europeans."—*Tennent.*

2. SESAMUM.

S. Indicum. Erect, slightly hairy, leaves ovate, oblong, lower ones often lobed, flowers axillary, solitary, large and handsome, with an offensive smell, capsule oblong, erect, somewhat 4-sided. *Til, tilli,* the oil *jingali.*

Commonly cultivated for the oil produced from the seeds: native country doubtful (*H.*). The flower is very like that of foxglove, but smaller, and varies in colour from purple to rose and white. "The lamp-black, which is the chief ingredient of Indian ink, is said to be made in China, by collecting the smoke of the oil of sesame" (*Chambers*).

The seeds are celebrated in literature. "Open sesame," *Arabian Nights.* "That old enchanted Arabian grain, the sesame, which opens doors, not of robbers, but of king's treasures," *Ruskin*, who gave to his lectures on "the treasures hidden in books," the fantastic name of "Sesame and the lilies."

To this order also belongs *Martynia diandra*, an American weed, common in gardens and waste places, called tiger's claw, devil's claw, and locally, *Vinchu ákara.* The name-child of the devil, a tiger and a scorpion, ought to bear evil in its looks, but this is, in fact, a harmless-looking plant, with large, cordate, glutinous leaves, and handsome flowers, much like those of Sesamum. The capsule, to which the names refer, is very hard, beetle-shaped, with two sharp hooks. Another species seems to be called the unicorn plant.

Order 89. ACANTHACEÆ.

Herbs or shrubs, with opposite undivided leaves without stipules; flowers with tubular corolla, generally 2-lipped, sometimes of 5 nearly equal lobes, the calyx usually small and surrounded by bracts, which are often very conspicuous, and also by bracteoles; stamens on the corolla, 4, didynamous, or 2, anthers generally 2-celled, often conspicuously so; ovary superior; fruit a capsule, the seeds generally attached to hooks (retinacula) which form part of the placenta.

This is a very large order, almost confined to the tropics, and there are far more species in W. India belonging to it than to any of the other didynamous orders, and an unusually large proportion are decidedly common. On the other hand, scarcely any species are cultivated either for their flowers or for useful products. The bracts are in very many cases sufficiently conspicuous to mark the order from others having similar flowers, and many species are glandular and strong-smelling. So Milton speaks correctly of—

"Acanthus, and each odorous bushy shrub."

The undivided ovary distinguishes the order from Labiatæ, the fruit and seeds generally from Scrophularineæ, the same parts and the habit from Bignoniaceæ.

Note 1. I have not found any help from *H.'s* division into 5 tribes, and in order to keep the diandrous and didynamous genera separate have slightly varied *H.'s* order.

Note 2. I have not generally thought it necessary to describe bracteoles as well as bracts. The bracteoles usually resemble the calyx segments.

Note 3. In many species the anther cells are so separated as to give the appearance of double, or, as the old writers called them, twin anthers.

Note 4. As regards the genera described below:—

In gen. 1 and 16 there are no retinacula.

In gen. 2, and in some species of 11, the leaves are much divided.

In all the genera from 8 onwards, except 18 and 19, the capsule is 2 or 4-seeded, generally the latter.

In gen. 10, 11, and 13, the corolla has only one lip.

A large proportion of the plants have flowers either white or some shade of blue and purple. At the foot of the Himalayas, and at a small elevation, Hooker found "the white or lilac blooms of the Convolvulus-like Thunbergia and other Acanthaceæ to be the predominant features of the shrubby vegetation, and very handsome."—*Himalayan Journals.*

(*a*) Stamens didynamous:

1. THUNBERGIA. Climbers; calyx very small annular or with many teeth; bracts 2, covering the calyx, corolla lobes 5, nearly equal; capsule round, beaked.

2. CARDANTHERA. Herbs, often with divided leaves; corolla tube short, limb long 2-lipped; anther cells parallel; capsule narrow, many-seeded.

3. HYGROPHILA. Herbs, calyx 4 or 5 parted, segments narrow, one pair of stamens sometimes smaller or obsolete, anthers oblong, capsule as in the last.

4. RUELLIA. Herbs or undershrubs, bracts large, exceeding the calyx, corolla lobes about equal, anther cells oblong, capsule solid below, with large thin seeds in the upper part.

5. PETALIDIUM. Flowers solitary, or crowded on short lateral branches, bracts large and leafy, anther cells parallel, spurred at the base.

6. PHAYLOPSIS. Prostrate herbs with flowers in densely bracted one-sided spikes; sepals 5, one ovate, the rest linear; corolla tube slender, anther cells parallel, capsule 4-seeded.

7. HEMIGRAPHIS. Herbs or shrubs, bracts large, crowded, corolla tube long, swelling above, anthers oblong, stigma of one linear and one very short lobe.

8. STROBILANTHES. Shrubs or herbs, calyx deeply 5-cleft, corolla tube bulging, lobes nearly equal, anthers oblong.

9. CALACANTHUS. Calyx segments unequal, corolla deeply 2-lipped, otherwise as the last.

10. BLEPHARIS. Rough creeping or prostrate plants with verticilled leaves and crowded bracts; sepals 4, in 2 unequal pairs, corolla of short fleshy tube and lower lip only, which is 3-cleft, anthers 1-seeded.

11. ACANTHUS. Shrubs or herbs, leaves spinous, sometimes pinnatifid, otherwise as the last.

12. BARLERIA. Shrubs or large herbs with showy flowers; sepals in opposite pairs, the outer pair much the largest; corolla lobes 5, often divided into 4 and 1; stamens 2 perfect with 2-celled anthers, and 2 rudimentary, capsule with seeds in the lower half.

13. CROSSANDRA. Undershrubs, bracts crowded, sepals 5, 2 much smaller, corolla long-tubed, one-lipped, the lip 5-lobed, anthers 1-celled.

14. Asystasia. Undershrubs, sepals narrow, corolla lobes 5, about equal; anthers oblong, 2-celled, ovary very hairy, capsule with solid contracted base.

15. Lepidagathis. Herbs or undershrubs, often prostrate, generally bristly; calyx of 2 large and 2 or 3 small segments; corolla tube swelling in the middle, limb 2-lipped, anthers 2-celled, oblong.

(*b*) Stamens two:

16. Nelsonia. A diffuse herb, calyx 4 parted, anther cells distinctly separate, capsule oblong, with the seeds in the lower part.

17. Dædalacanthus. Corolla tube long and narrow, limb of 5 nearly equal segments, anthers narrowly oblong, 2-celled, capsule with solid base.

18. Andrographis. Herbs or very small shrubs, bracts very small, sepals narrow, anthers with 2 parallel cells exserted, capsule 6 to 12-seeded.

19. Haplanthus. Herbs, flowers more or less whorled, with small bracts and verticilled thorns, capsule 6 to 16-seeded from the base.

20. Justicia. Herbs or shrubs, often with leafy bracts, calyx with 4 or 5 narrow segments, corolla short-tubed, anther cells separate, the lower one with a white appendage.

21. Adhatoda. Shrubs with leafy bracts, very like the last, but the anther cells are acute and scarcely spurred.

22. Rhinacanthus. Shrubs, with small narrow bracts, calyx small with narrow segments, corolla tube very long and narrow, anther cells one above the other.

23. Ecbolium. A small shrub, with large crowded bracts and narrow calyx segments, corolla tube long and slender, upper lip narrow, bifid, capsule long-stalked.

24. Rungia. Diffuse herbs, flowers small, bluish or white, in dense spikes, bracts with scarious margins crowded, capsule short-stalked.

25. Dicliptera. Diffuse herbs, calyx equally 5-parted, covered with 2 large unequal bracts, corolla with slender tube and gaping mouth, anther cells one above the other, capsule club-shaped.

26. Peristrophe. Differs from the last in the bracteoles forming an outer calyx, with one or more oblong bracts twice as long.

1. THUNBERGIA.

T. fragrans. Leaves oblong, acute, angular, and slightly lobed at the base, bracts large, ovate, flowers solitary, large and handsome, pure white, long-stalked, calyx with 12 teeth, capsule 2-lobed, beak flattened, pointed. *Erivel.*

Pretty common in the Konkans; and on the Ghauts as high up as Pánchgani (*Dr. Cooke*). Throughout India (*H.*). The flowers are not fragrant with us. *H.* has three varieties.

* *T. mysorensis* (*Hexacentris m.* D.). Leaves elliptic, oblong, toothed or crenate, flowers large and handsome, orange or red, in a long, pendulous raceme, calyx a mere ring, bracts purplish-green. S. of Dharwar (*D.*).

T. grandiflora, a large and beautiful climber, a native of Bengal, very common in Bombay gardens; calyx a mere ring, flowers very large, pale blue.

T. alata, about the size of *T. fragrans*, and calyx as in that; flowers much smaller, yellow, or bright buff, with dark eye; sometimes called "Black-eyed Susan." Also common in gardens.

Note.—The habit and calyx in this genus are so different from anything else in the order, that the species might not be identified by beginners as belonging to it.

2. CARDANTHERA.

C. pinnatifida (*Nomaphila p.* D.). A much-branched, leafy plant, all glandular and hairy, leaves pinnatifid, or deeply toothed, lobes linear-lanceolate, flowers few, small, purple, spotted with white, calyx segments subulate.

Growing in masses in beds of Konkan rivers: also in Canara and W. Deccan peninsula (*H.*). I found at Sattara a variety with white flowers, and lobes of leaves broader.

3. HYGROPHILA.

1. *H. serpyllum* (*Physichilus s.* D.). A small, creeping plant, covered with stiff, grey hairs; leaves nearly round, rough, bracts and floral leaves oblong-lanceolate; flowers solitary, or nearly so, rather large for the size of the plant, bright blue, the lower lip blistered, and spotted with white, capsule as long as the calyx. *Rántevân.*

The Konkans and Ghauts. At Lanoli, in the cold weather, it covers the rice-fields, and colours them. W. Deccan peninsula (*H.*). He has a variety, found by Law and Stocks in the Konkan, a larger plant, with minute, bristly hairs, instead of long ones.

2. *H. salicifolia*. A strong, erect plant, leaves long, lanceo-

late, or ovate, smooth, waved, or slightly crenate, bracts ovate-lanceolate, flowers axillary, nearly sessile, about 7 together, pale blue, capsule within the calyx.

In the S. Konkan growing in swamps, with the next, and rather like it, but smaller every way, and without thorns. Very common throughout India and Ceylon (*H.*). He has 2 varieties.

3. *H. spinosa* (*Asteracantha longifolia*, D.). A stout, rough plant, with sessile, blue flowers among verticils of lanceolate leaves and thorns, calyx, segments, and bracts lanceolate, lower lip of corolla with a yellow spot. *Koráta, Kalsanda.*

Very common in swamps; much more so than the last. Throughout India (*H.*). The seeds are called *Talimkhána.*

* *H. Stocksii* differs from *H. serpyllum*, chiefly by being larger, and the stem leaves spathulate. Konkan (*Stocks*) and nowhere else (*H.*). Not in *D.*

4. Ruellia.

R. prostrata (*Dipteracanthus dejectus*, D.). Straggling, prostrate, or climbing in hedges, leaves long-petioled, ovate, often acute, flowers solitary, or nearly so, purple or blue, bell-shaped, bracts like the young leaves, seeds about 12, flat, roundish, light brown.

Very common in Guzerat, the Konkan, and Deccan. Throughout India, very common (*H.*).

H. makes this a variety of the species which is prostrate, but not straggling, and with blunt leaves; and has a separate species, *R. patula* (*Petalidium, p.* D.) resembling this, but densely and closely pubescent.

5. Petalidium.

P. barlerioides. A straggling, rather handsome shrub, leaves ovate, pointed, crenated, flowers large, white or pale blue, with veined throat; calyx hidden in 2 leafy, veined bracts, corolla tube narrow with wide mouth, lower lip bearded.

N. Konkan and Panch Mahals. Ghauts and Panwell (*D.* and *G.*).

This sufficiently resembles a *Barleria* to justify the specific name. I had noted the calyx as viscid, which is not mentioned in any of the books; but this viscidity of some of the parts is a frequent characteristic in shrubs of this order, and apparently not a constant one, but depending a good deal on situation.

6. Phaylopsis.

P. parviflora (*Ætheilema reniforme*, D.). Much-branched, hairy, leaves ovate, unequal at the base, bracts membranous, sometimes kidney-shaped, flowers whitish, scarcely longer than the calyx, capsule small. *Waiti, rán-maushi.*

S. Konkan and Ghauts. Throughout India (*H.*). This also I have found as a sticky and strong-smelling plant, as *G.* and *R.* describe it, but not *D.* and *H.*

7. Hemigraphis.

1. *H. dura* (*Ruellia, d.* D.). Prostrate and creeping, hairy and bristly, stem 4-sided, leaves oblong, obtuse, flowers large, bluish purple, in roundish heads, surrounded by 4 floral leaves ; calyx segments with scarious margins, capsule shorter than the calyx, 6 to 8-seeded.

N. Konkan and Sholapore districts. Surat (*D.*). Bombay, Belgaum, &c. (*H.*).

2. *H. latebrosa* (*Ruellia elegans*, D.). Hairy, erect, slightly viscid, flowers very pretty, light blue, streaked with red, and whitish tube, nearly sessile, and nearly solitary, leaves and bracts oval, serrated, covered with white hairs, capsule as long as calyx, 6 to 8-seeded.

Ghauts and Konkan. Found in most parts of the Presidency, but not very common. * *H. ebracteolata* scarcely differs from this, but is hispid, with scattered white hairs (*H.*). Ghauts (*D.*).

8. Strobilanthes.

H. has no less than 146 species of this genus, and they differ widely, he says, in habit, inflorescence, and size of flowers. *D.* had 8, as belonging to this Presidency, and of these ascribed 4 to the Ghauts, and 2 to the Wári country.

1. *S. Ixiocephalus* (*S. neesianus*, D.). A small shrub, very strong-smelling, leaves lanceolate, acuminate, unequal at the base, crenate, or serrate, hairy, or rough, bracts elliptic, leafy, flowers in ovate heads white, or pale lilac, bristly within, all covered with viscid hairs, calyx and bracts enlarged in fruit. *Kárvi, chit-Kárvi.*

Konkan hills and Ghauts. There is probably often some confusion between this and the next, though they are quite distinct; the peculiarity of flowering after seven years, and then dying, which is ascribed by different authorities to one or another species, Colonel

Beddome thinks to be common to several. Tennent says the same of the Ceylon species.

2. *S. callosus.* A tall shrub, branches warty, or tubercled, leaves large, elliptic, acute, crenate, long-petioled, spikes conical, sometimes compound, flowers large, hairy within, deep blue, bracts roundish, calyx increasing in fruit. *Kárvi.*

The Ghauts and Central India.

H. includes in this *D.'s C. Grahamianus.* This is, no doubt, the well-known Mahábleshwar shrub, and is viscid and strong-smelling.

3. *S. perfoliatus* (*Endopogon integrifolius*, D.). A shrub with a very powerful smell, leaves narrow lanceolate, running with a wing into the petiole, quite smooth and entire : flowers in a 4-sided raceme, bracts and calyx segments linear or lanceolate, hairy and viscid, corolla large, blue or purple. *Ránbokri.*

S. Konkan. Very common at Matheran (*Birdwood*). The leaves are never perfoliate (*H.*). I noticed what I have seen put down as a generic distinction in Endopogon (but not in *H.*) that there is in the corolla a depressed hairy channel which holds the style. (See *Hypæstes lanata.*)

* *S. barbatus* (*S. tetrapterus*, D.). Stem and petioles often winged, leaves large oval, flowers in short dense spikes, white, bracts cuspidate, green. Wári country (*D.*). * *S. wareensis*, leaves oblong acuminate, spikes short, drooping on hairy jointed peduncles, but erect in fruit with the calyx enlarged, corolla small white, purple-spotted. Wári country, Belgaum, &c. (*D.*). * *S. lupulinus*, woody and hairy, leaves elliptic acuminate, spikes short, sometimes umbelled, bracts concave, hairy, calyx scarious, bristly. Konkan and near Belgaum (*H.*) * *S. heyneanus* (*S. asperrimus*, D.), herbaceous, about a foot high, hairy, leaves elliptic acuminate, spikes short, roundish, flowers pale blue, bracts convex. *Akrá.* The Ghauts. * *S. scrobiculatus*, woody, with long much-divided branches, covered with flowers and leafy only at the tips, leaves as the last, corolla an inch long, pale below, of a beautiful blue upwards, lobes crenulate. Ghauts. "It appears to be the most beautiful of all the species, and is allied to *S. ixiocephalus*" (*H.*). * *S. asper*, a shrub, softly hairy, leaves ovate crenate, spikes oblong, panicled or fascicled, bracts ovate or oblong, reddish. Konkan, *Stocks* (*H.*). * *S. sessilis* (*S. sessiloides*, D.), a low undershrub, hairy, leaves sessile ovate acute, bracts large, the same shape, or broad cordate, flowers large and handsome, blue or pale purple. The Ghauts (*D.*).

9. Calacanthus.

* *C. Dalzelliana* (*Lepidagathis grandiflora*, D.). A shrub, stem quadrangular, leaves large, oval, acute, smooth, spikes long and slender, densely woolly, bracts, bracteoles, and upper

calyx segments oblong, flowers large, purple, with 2 lines of yellow hairs: capsule 2-seeded. *Motayé.*

The Ghauts (*D.*). Canara (*H.*). "The magnificent Calacanthus grows in profusion on the wet rocks on the road up to Matheran."—*Dr. Cooke.*

10. Blepharis.

1. *B. asperrima.* Diffuse with weak straw-coloured stem, every part covered with bristly hairs, leaves ovate, bracts trifid cuneate or lanceolate, whitish with green veins, flowers blue or white sessile, solitary or in pairs, capsule 4-seeded. *Páhadi-átganakdá.*

Very common on the Ghauts: also in the Konkan. The flowers are often seen on the Ghauts covering the ground like snowdrops.

2. *B. boerhaavifolia.* Leaves in fours, one pair smaller, lanceolate, bracts edged with long bristles broader upwards, calyx segments the same shape, but not bristly, flowers white, pale-blue or pink with white spot on lower lip, capsule 2-seeded.

Common in Guzerat. From Mount Abu to Ceylon (*H.*).

3. *B. molluginifolia.* Leaves in fours, one pair smaller, oblong, rather obovate, rough on the margin, bracts many, pressed flat against the calyx, boat-shaped, with one stiff and many short bristles, flowers blue, like those of No. 1, but smaller; capsule 2-seeded. *Kánte-máka.*

The Konkans, growing freely near the sea. Deccan peninsula (*H.*).

11. Acanthus.

A. ilicifolius (*Dilivaria i.* D.). A small handsome thorny shrub, with leaves like holly, sinuate, spinous-toothed, and large bright blue flowers; bracts small ovate, calyx segments ovate rounded, corolla lip nearly entire, anthers large, thickly bearded. *Nivgur, márandi.*

Very common on the sea coast. Also in Ceylon, Malaga, the Philippines, and Australia (*H.*). *G.* calls it sea holly, a very appropriate name, but it must not be confounded with the plant which bears that name in England (Eryngo).

The rather dismal salt marshes are often beautified by this handsome shrub, just as bare woods in England are by the true holly—

"When the bare and wintry woods we see,
What then so cheerful as the holly tree?"—*Southey.*

A. mollis is a noble plant, sometimes found in English gardens, called by Tournefort "this gentle thistle." Its leaves are very large and handsome, and are believed to have been the model on which the capital of the Corinthian columns was formed. At Nazareth

"the painted grouse
Lays her eggs there in carved Acanthus leaves."—*Sir E. Arnold.*

"To watch the emerald-coloured water falling
Through many a wov'n Acanthus wreath divine."—*Tennyson.*

The plant being thus well known gave its name to the order.

12. Barleria.

H. has 26 species of this beautiful and well-marked genus, and ascribes 14 of them to W. India, but 7 of these are not given by *D.*

1. *B. prionitis.* Shrubby and thorny, leaves elliptic, narrow at both ends, bracts subulate, larger calyx segments ovate entire, spinous-pointed, flowers axillary, spiked or whorled, buff-coloured, soon falling off. *Kholeta, kalsunda, pivala koránta.*

Konkan and the lower Ghauts, very common. Also in Guzerat and the Deccan. Tropical India (*H.*).

H. has * *B. cuspidata* in the Konkan, "exceeding near to *B. prionitis*, but a lower, harsher and more prickly undershrub."

2. *B. montana.* A large smooth plant, leaves narrow ovate, flowers large and beautiful, rose-coloured, mauve or blue, solitary and sessile in the axils, larger calyx segments elliptic entire, smaller and bracts very small linear, seeds densely silky. *Kolista, ikhari.*

Bombay (where I have seen no good specimens), Konkan and the Ghauts: not uncommon. *H.* has * *B. Gibsoni* over a great part of the Presidency "so exceedingly like the last that it has always been mixed therewith," but with smooth seeds, "thus differing from all others of the genus." Mr. Birdwood has this under the name of *Gura* at Matheran, with corolla tube white, limb pale lilac.

3. *B. grandiflora.* A shrub or tall herb nearly all smooth, leaves elliptic acuminate, flowers pure white, 4 inches long, solitary in the opposite axils, larger calyx segments ovate acute, smaller ones and bracts, which are half way up the pedicels, subulate.

This is said to be wild in the Konkan and Ghauts, and is in Mr. Birdwood's Matheran list. I have only seen it planted. Two other species, * *B. longiflora* and *B. Lawii*, appear to be very much like it, but both are hairy: the first had ovate leaves rounded at the base (Matheran, Khandalla, *G.*), the second elliptic leaves narrowed at both ends. The Ghauts, &c., *Law* (*H.*).

4. *B. cristata.* A shrub, erect or diffuse hairy, leaves ovate, flowers in the axils nearly sessile, 2 or 3 together or in heads blue or white; anthers violet; larger calyx, segments ovate, pectinated, veined, smaller segments and bracts lanceolate.

The white variety, which is *D.'s B. dichotoma*, is commonly planted about temples and in gardens, and is called *Pándhari Koránti.* The blue is said to be wild in Bombay and the Konkans.

5. *B. strigosa* (*B. terminalis*, D.). Shrubby, erect, rough nearly all over, leaves ovate, running down with a wing into the long petiole; flowers large, blue, crowded together in terminal spikes; outer sepals ovate, acute, bracts lanceolate. *Wáhiti, Kála Koránta.*

S. Konkan and Ghauts: common at Matheran. *H.* has 2 varieties, and says it is much cultivated. Mr. Birdwood says, "flowers blue, tube of corolla much paler than the limb, stigma purple."

* *B. buxifolia*, a small very prickly undershrub, leaves small, ovate, mucronate, no bracts, and spines instead of bracteoles, flowers rather large, purple, rose or white, larger calyx segments enlarging in fruit. Konkan, *Law*, &c. (*H.*). * *B. involucrata* (*B. elata*, D.). Six feet high, leaves elliptic unequal, long-petioled, flowers very large, long-tubed, blue, in short racemes or spikes, bracts linear lanceolate, leafy. Fonda Ghaut (*D.*). * *B. sepalosa*, leaves elliptic acute, covered with yellow hairs; outer sepals very large, broadly elliptic acute, one bifid. An imperfectly known species. Konkan, *Gibson* (*H.*). * *B. Courtallica*, a large shrub, leaves oblong or obovate, smooth and shining, spikes short, hairy and glandular, larger sepals very hairy, veined, flowers blue and yellow, or white. Chorla Ghaut (*D.*). Dr. Dymock gives this the same native names as *B. montana.* * *B. Stocksii*, a small undershrub, flowers solitary, axillary, leaves elliptic acute, bracts small, narrow oblong. Bombay and Bababudin hills, *Stocks* (*H.*).

13. Crossandra.

C. undulæfolia (*C. axillaris* and *C. coccinea*, D.). A shrubby plant, leaves smooth, ovate, waved, long-petioled, often in fours; flowers in 4-sided spikes, red or orange, bracts much imbricated, with the larger calyx segments ovate, pointed, bracteoles and smaller segments linear. *Abholi.*

Said to be wild about Dhárwar, but known generally as a garden-flower.

14. Asystasia.

A. violacea. A shrubby plant, softly hairy, stem jointed, leaves ovate or oblong acute, lower ones narrowed into the petiole, upper rounded at the base; flowers in one-sided racemes, large, violet, the lower lip dark purple and spotted, protruding.

The Konkans and Ghauts. Very common at Matheran, less so at Mahableshwar—*Dr. Cooke*—who doubts whether it is distinct from * *A. coromandelliana*, which *H.* calls a procumbent weed, grey pubescent, but *D.* erect, almost smooth—very common. *A. Lawiana*, a tall rough plant with 4-sided stems, thicker just above the joints, leaves oblong acute, flowers small white in short spikes, bracts lanceolate, leafy. Nasik. Near Dharwar (*D.*).

15. LEPIDAGATHIS.

The majority of the 10 species found in this Presidency are confined to the Ghauts, and known only to Dr. Stocks or Mr. Dalzell.

1. *L. cristata.* Prostrate, leaves lanceolate, they and the calyx and bracts sharp-pointed, flowers pale, streaked darker, in dense round heads near the root; calyx segments and bracts oblong or ovate. *Bhuiterda, Kolhe che chutar.*

Guzerat and the Deccan. Bombay (*G.*).

2. *L. prostrata.* Creeping and rooting from the joints, all silky or hairy; leaves small, sessile, ovate, bristle-pointed, bracts the same shape, densely imbricated, bracteoles and calyx segments narrow; flowers in short spikes, pink, streaked, capsule 2-seeded. *Bakrá.*

S. Konkan. About Rutnagherry it grows abundantly on the bare sheet rock. Canara (*H.*). This is probably what *G.* (No. 1175) calls common at Mahableshwar.

3. *L. rigida.* An erect undershrub, glutinous, leaves ovate, pointed, narrowed into the petiole, rough, bracts and larger calyx segments ovate, bracteoles and smaller segments narrow, all hairy and spinous-pointed; flowers yellowish white in dense spikes, capsule 4-seeded.

Ghauts (*D.*). Sind (*H.*). I had it at Párpoli Ghaut, where it is abundant and very strong-smelling. * *L. mitis* is closely allied to No. 1, but nearly smooth, and the flower heads not prickly, flowers white, spotted with pink and yellow. Fonda Ghaut (*D.*). * *L. trinervis*, leaves linear lanceolate, 3-nerved, flowers white, either in short spikes or in a conglomerated ball like the last; bracts (but not calyx) with long spinous points. Ghauts, Guzerat and Konkan (*H.*). * *L. lutea*, stems erect, leaves and inflorescence as in the last, both bracts and calyx spinous pointed, flowers yellow, stems and flower heads velvety. Malwan and Ghauts (*D.* and *H.*). * *L. clavata*, stem erect, leaves sessile ovate, bristle-pointed, bracts densely imbricated in 4 rows, flowers pink-streaked, in short spikes. Ghauts (*D.*). It is very like *L. prostrata.*

The last four are two-seeded, the next two four-seeded. * *L. hyalina*, an erect herb, leaves ovate viscid, bracts lanceolate, acuminate, flowers white, with brown spots. Konkan, Canara, &c. (*H.*). * *L. fasciculata* (*L. Goensis* D.), herbaceous, diffuse, hairy, leaves ovate, crenate serrate, spikes short, panicled, flowers as in the last. Wári country. The last two apparently have no spines.

Three more genera belong to the didynamous section. *Ebermaiera*, herbs, leaves sometimes alternate, corolla lobes 5, short, styles 2-lobed, the lower lobe often divided. * *E. glauca*, erect, leaves oblong, mostly alternate, flowers small, purplish, striped, in long lax spikes; one sepal much larger, bracts stalked and leaf-like. S. Konkan (*D.*). * *E. zeylanica* (*Erythracanthus elongatus*, D.) branches trailing, leaves oblong, oval, spikes dense short, calyx and corolla nearly as in the last. Wári jungles (*D.*).

Calophanes, herbs, calyx tubular, with 5 narrow teeth. * *C. vagans*, calyx teeth long, hairy, flowers in hairy cymes, bluish, the palate pleated across, anther cells parallel with prominent white spurs. Konkan and Belgaum (*H.*). * *C. Dalzellii*, closely resembling the last, but cymes denser, calyx teeth broader, flowers larger, and no spurs to the anthers. Konkan and Poona (*H.*).

Neuracanthus, calyx 2-lipped, corolla limb nearly entire. *N. trinervius*, a shrubby plant, leaves ovate lanceolate, bracts round ovate, white with hairs, flowers small blue in hairy 4-sided spikes, calyx segments very narrow. Bhándup. Near Alibag (*D.*). *N. sphærostachyus*, stout, unbranched, rough, leaves ovate, bracts roundish, silky, flowers pretty, blue, in close round sessile heads, corolla throat and tube streaked with white. Dhánu. Konkan and Bombay (*D.*). For these two *H.* has no other habitat than the Konkan and Ghauts.

(*b*) Stamens 2.

16. Nelsonia.

N. campestris (*N. tomentosa*, D.). Very downy, with numerous stems and branches pressed close to the ground; leaves oval entire, rather glutinous, flowers small, lilac or purple in spikes, bracts ovate, crowded.

Pauchmahàls. Wari jungles (*D.*). Throughout India (*H.*)

17. Dædalacanthus.

D. purpurascens (*Eranthemum nervosum*, D.). A shrub more or less hairy; stem 4-sided, leaves ovate, flowers in stiff spikes, handsome purplish blue, the throat streaked darker, bracts large imbricated all up the spike, oval pointed, veined ciliated, bracteoles and calyx segments very small, whitish. *Gulshám.*

The Konkans and Ghauts. Bombay (*G.*).

* *D. montanus*, a leafy herb, attributed by *D.* to the Ghauts near Dharwar, *H.* calls a variable species, best distinguished by the long

green viscidly hairy calyx teeth, otherwise very like the above; and he has a variety of this called *Konkanensis*, found by Mr. Law, with compound panicles, the spikes linear interrupted, bracts ovate, abbreviated.

* *D. roseus* (*Eranthemum, r.* D.). Leaves elliptic smooth, spikes linear, bracts imbricated glandular, with green nerves, corolla over an inch long, rose-coloured. Round Bombay (*D.*).

18. Andrographis.

* *A. paniculata.* Annual, erect, 4-sided, smooth, leaves lanceolate entire, racemes long, flowers distant, white spotted with purple, or rose-coloured, bracts linear, capsules subcylindric. *Kreát, kalpa, kála meti, mahátiti.*

Throughout India (*H.*). Common in gardens (*G.*). *D.* has it as wild, but with no habitat. It is much used in native medicine as a bitter.

* *A. visculosa,* undershrub, scarcely a foot high, leaves lanceolate smooth, flowers in panicles, which are covered with viscid brown hairs. Not in *D.* Konkan (*H.*). * *A. echioides,* annual, hairy, leaves sessile oblong, racemes numerous, axillary, anthers much exserted. *Rán chimani.* Deccan ravines (*D.*). S. Konkan (*G.*).

19. Haplanthus.

H. verticillaris. A shrubby plant, the upper parts covered with long white glutinous hairs, flowers small, purple or lilac, subsessile among bifid verticilled thorns, leaves very long-petioled ovate, narrow at both ends, seeds rough. *Jakára, Kála ákara, Kála kiráit.*

The Ghauts. Khandalla (*G.*). *D.* has no habitat. W. Deccan peninsula frequent, extending N. to Mount Abu (*H.*).

H. tentaculatus. A smaller species than the last, very like it, but with short-petioled oval leaves, rounded at both ends, a little hairy; grows commonly near the sea, also in Guzerat and Belgaum.

D. calls this a much stouter plant than the first, which I think is not the case; and *H.* has an ambiguous remark on the subject; so I have described the plants as I found them.

20. Justicia.

A great number of species were formerly included in this genus, which have now been removed to others. The last four species here given belong to a separate section of the genus Rostellularia, which *H.* defines as small, closely allied weeds, abundant in the tropics.

1. *J. betonica* (*Adhatoda ramosissimum,* D.). A tall smooth shrub, leaves ovate to lanceolate, blunt pointed, flowers in

spikes, dull white, streaked with pink, bracts rather large, oval pointed, green-veined, capsule protuberant at the seeds, which are nearly round and light brown.

Common on the higher Ghauts (*D.*). Matheran. I have seen this as described at Khair in the Poona districts, but in the S. Konkan as a weak shrubby prostrate plant. The latter *H.* makes a variety, and calls it *ramosissima.* He calls both forms common throughout India.

2. *J. trinervia* (*Adhatoda t.* D.). A smooth plant, erect or procumbent, much smaller than the last; leaves as in the last or fleshy, and slightly crenate, flowers in terminal spikes, bracts much veined, lanceolate long-pointed, 3-nerved. *Sut.*

Mahableshwar and S. Konkans. Matheran. Near the sea I have found this all fleshy. One authority makes it a small variety of the last.

3. *J. Wynaadensis* (*Adhatoda w.* D.). A shrub with long and slender branches, which with the leaves are much tinged with purple, leaves lanceolate, quite smooth, spikes somewhat interrupted, hairy, flowers small, white spotted with purple, bracts smaller than the calyx segments.

Vingorla. Jungly parts of the Konkan, common (*D.*). Belgaum (*H.*). *H.* calls it very variable as to hairiness. *D.* has "bracts ovate deciduous, bracteoles linear, subulate shorter than the calyx." These last are all that I saw, and all that *H.* mentions.

J. Gendarussa, tiv, bákas, a species said by *H.* to be cultivated all over India, and by *D.* to be very common in gardens, strong scented and of a purple hue, seems to me to differ only from *J. Wynaadensis* in being a herb.

J. montana (*Hemichoriste m.* D.). A tall handsome shrub, leaves large oval, narrow at both ends, entire polished, flowers large white, spotted with purple, in large racemes, bracts hairy, capsule with seeds near the top. Máchál. Ghauts (*D.*). * *J. heterocarpa.* A small herb, grey, leaves ovate, flowers minute in clusters, capsules of two kinds in almost every axil, one oblong 4-seeded, the other winged and crested, one-seeded; not in *D.* Deesa and Kurrachee, *Stocks* (*H.*). Not nearly allied to any other species (*H.*).

4. *J. procumbens* (*Rostellularia p.* D.). A small weed, hairy, branched; leaves ovate to lanceolate, ciliated, flowers in spikes, more or less 4-sided, pale purple, sepals 4 scarious, with green midrib, bracts and bracteoles lanceolate or linear, about as long as the calyx and corolla. *Tharambal, ghátipitpápara.*

The three other species of this section are apparently very difficult to distinguish from one another. * *J. micrantha* (*Rostellularia* *crinita*, D.), leaves ovate hairy, spikes short, flowers rose or purple, sepals broader than the rough, hairy, bracts. Vingorla (*D.*). * *J quinquangularis* (*R. peploides*, D.), branched, diffuse, often 4 or 5-angled, smooth and glaucous, leaves oval to linear lanceolate, spikes rather long, bracts and sepals spathulate. Watercourses in the Deccan (*D.*). * *J. diffusa* (*R. d.*, D.), stem 4-sided, leaves lanceolate ovate, spikes slender compressed, flowers pale purple, bracts and sepals lanceolate. In pastures (*D.*). *H.* has several vars. of this.

21. Adhatoda.

A. vasica. A large shrub of little beauty, with oblong elliptic leaves, narrowed at both ends, smooth; flowers large, white with brown spots; spikes several together, bracts smooth ovate, with white veins. *Adusa, bákas, vasuka.*

This is a very common shrub, used for hedges in Guzerat, the Konkan, and the Ghaut districts. Common all over India (*H.*) It is sometimes called the Malabar nut, and is so closely allied to *Justicia* Nos. 1 and 2 that it seems a pity they have been separated, particularly as this opinion is also expressed in *H.* It may be seen in Italian gardens.

22. Rhinacanthus.

R. communis. A shrubby plant 3 or 4 feet high, leaves large ovate oblong, obtusely pointed, flowers small white in axillary and terminal panicles, trichotomously divided, anthers exserted. *Nágamálli, jawái-panás, gajkarni.*

S. Konkan. Mahableshwar (*D.*). Throughout India, commonly cultivated (*H.*). A medicinal plant.

23. Ecbolium.

E. Linnæanum (*Justicia Ecbolium*, D.). A small shrub, nearly smooth, with elliptic acute leaves, flowers in dense 4-sided spikes of a pale sea-green, bracts ovate, green, often dark-veined, capsule much compressed. *Odu-játi, ránabholi, dhákta ádulsa.*

The Konkans, but scarcely common. Very common at Matheran (*Dr. Cooke*). *H.* has three varieties, one of which has roundish leaves, and another toothed bracts. The colour of the flowers is very delicate, but of so uncommon a hue that I find it described by different authorities as follows: Greenish or azure, pale blue, greenish livid, greenish blue or purplish, lurid or steely green-blue. All these are suggestive of the colour of the sea in one aspect or another; or perhaps one of Dr. Darwin's indefinite similes may suit it—"precisely the colour of a seraph's plume."

24. Rungia.

1. *R. repens.* An extensive much-branched creeping weed, leaves nearly sessile, oblong lanceolate, spikes crowded with almost smooth roundish pointed bracts, broad-margined, corolla white, blue or pink, spotted darker. *Ghátipitpápara* (see *Justicia procumbens*).

Very common almost everywhere. Throughout India, common (*H.*). *R. elegans*, *H.* considers as possibly a large form of this, but what I had in Salsette (agreeing with *D.'s* description) was very different, flowers of a beautiful blue, large for the genus, bracts with broad scarious margin, not white; the whole plant a foot high. Hills round Junar (*D.*).

2. *R. parviflora.* A small straggling plant, leaves oval or oblong, rather blunt, flowers small in small spikes, bright blue, streaked darker, fertile bracts roundish, oval, barren, narrower and less margined.

Common. Mahableshwar.—*Dr. Cooke.*

H. includes in this as var. pectinata, *D.'s R. polygonoides*, and calls it a universal weed throughout India. * *R. crenata* he makes allied to this, but with much larger flowerless bracts; they are hairy with narrow margins, oblong acute, those with the flowers roundish. Not in *D.* Konkan, Canara, and Belgaum (*H.*).

There is a considerable general resemblance between the species of this genus and the Rostellularia section of Justicia, and a more special resemblance in the white margins of the bracts.

25. Dicliptera.

1. *D. zeylanica* (*D. bivalvis*, D.). A tall weak plant, with 6-angled stem and branches, leaves ovate, pointed rough, flowers rather small, pink in trifid heads, bracts broad ovate, calyx and bracteoles much imbricated.

Guzerat, Konkan and Ghauts. Inflorescence variable (*H.*). *G.* calls it "Green-loden."

2. *D. leonotis* (*D. Burmanni*, D.). A low straggling plant, with angular and woolly branches, leaves oval pointed, somewhat unequal-sided, almost smooth, flowers pink with white tube and spotted throat; bracts ovate, bristle pointed.

S. Konkan. *H.* is doubtful about the identification of this plant and *D.'s*: my description above agrees thoroughly with *D.'s*, who gave no hab. *H.* has Guzerat and Ajmeer. I noted "both lips of corolla entire or nearly so."

* *D. micrantha*, leaves ovate pointed, nearly smooth, flowers in heads of three, umbelled, small and slender, bracts oblong and obovate,

cuspidate. Guzerat and Sagargarh (*D.*). * *D. Roxburghiana*, leaves ovate, acute at both ends, umbels 4 or 5 together, of 3 to 5 flowers, bracts obovate with a small point, veined, capsule hairy. This is *D.*'s description (without hab.), as *H.* only doubtfully identifies *D.*'s plant with his. One or other of the vars. is common throughout India.

26. Peristrophe.

P. bicalyculata. A tall poor-looking rough weed, with 6-sided stems; leaves ovate, hairy, flowers pink in panicles like candelabra, anthers red, bracts much longer than the flower heads, capsule pointed at both ends with seeds in the upper half.

Common in waste places. Tropical and sub-tropical India, very common (*H.*).

I have seen this with one bract only (besides the outer calyx), which gives the flower a curious appearance, and *D.* implies that this is usual, of which however *H.* says nothing. *H.* has a var. with the flowers in very short heads.

The following also have 2 stamens: *Elytraria*, herbs, leaves alternate or radical, scape covered with imbricated bracts, calyx 4-divided. * *E. crenata*, leaves obovate, oblong crenated, scape long and slender, bearing a spike of white flowers, bracts ovate with scarious margins. Broach collectorate (*D.*).

Eranthemum, very like Asystasia but for the 2 stamens, and the ovary often smooth. *E. malabaricum* (*E. crenulatum*, D.). Shrubby, leaves broad lanceolate, narrow at both ends, crenate, flowers in long slender spikes white, spotted and tinged with red, bracts and sepals very small, glandular and rough. S. Konkan. Wári jungles (*D.*).

Gymnostachyum, herbs or undershrubs, bracts very small, corolla tube slender, capsule many-seeded. * *G. glabrum* (*Cryptophragmium, g.* D.), leaves large ovate, narrow at both ends, running into a winged petiole, flowers fascicled or the panicles white, purple-spotted, bracts linear lanceolate. * *G. latifolium* (*Crypt. l.* D.), leaves very large ovate, very long petioled, panicles comparatively short, flowers solitary or clustered on them, yellow or green, bracts linear. These two in the Konkan and Ghauts, the latter also in Canara (*D.*).

Hypæstes, bracts 2 to 4, enclosing one perfect and some obsolete flowers, calyx scarious, corolla tube slender. * *H. lanáta*, undershrub, leaves lanceolate, slightly rough, petiole sometimes winged, spikes long, running into terminal panicles, covered with white wool, flowers light purple, rather large, bracts very hairy, linear. Konkan and Ghauts (*D.*). Unknown elsewhere. Superficially resembling *Strobilanthes perfoliatus*, but the corolla and stamens distinguish it (*H.*).

Gratophyllum hortense (*Justicia picta*, D.) is a shrub in gardens throughout India; leaves ovate lanceolate, much variegated, flowers large crimson or purple. *Kála* or *Karad adulsá.*

ORDER 90. **VERBENACEÆ.** Vervains.

Trees or shrubs, rarely herbs, with opposite leaves, without stipules, flowers mostly small, but in large cymes or panicles, calyx tubular persistent, corolla tubular, 2-lipped or with 5 nearly equal lobes; stamens generally didynamous, sometimes 2, 5, or 8. Ovary superior, style one, fruit a drupe or berry.

This is a considerable order, mainly tropical, with some very important and some beautiful species; but the greater part of those given below are not very remarkable.

The species of this order are distinguished from those of Scrophularineæ by their habit, and generally by their fruit. "They have the flowers of Labiatæ, except that the ovary is entire with the style proceeding from the top."—*Bentham.*

Note.—I have altered *H.'s* arrangement of genera so as to bring them together according to their stamens.

(*a*) Stamens didynamous.

1. LANTANA. Straggling shrubs with small flowers in heads, calyx small, entire or slightly lobed, bracts larger, corolla tube slender, lobes 4 or 5 spreading, drupe of 2 pyrenes.

2. LIPPIA, as No. 1, but fruit a capsule separating into 2 pyrenes.

3. PREMNA. Flowers small, often polygamous, calyx small, cup-shaped, persistent, corolla 2-lipped.

4. GMELINA. Flowers large, calyx bell-shaped, shortly 5-toothed or nearly entire, corolla tube short, lobes 5, anther cells separated, drupe succulent.

5. VITEX. Leaves digitate, flowers small, calyx as in the last, corolla 2-lipped, the lower lip unequally lobed, anther cells more or less twisted, calyx more or less enlarged in fruit.

Note.—*Avicennia* below is by some authors said to have didynamous stamens.

(*b*) Stamens 4, equal.

6. CALLICARPA. Calyx very small, minutely 4-lobed, corolla regular 4-lobed, anthers exserted, drupe round, of 4 or less one-seeded pyrenes.

7. CLERODENDRON. Calyx as in No. 4, corolla tube long and slender, lobes 5, spreading, anthers long, exserted, drupe roundish, 4-grooved, separating into pyrenes.

8. AVICENNIA. Calyx segments 5, concave, imbricated, corolla 4 or 5-lobed, capsule broad, one-seeded.

(*c*) Stamens more than 4, equal to the corolla lobes.

9. TECTONA. Trees, calyx and corolla 5 or 6-lobed, corolla tube short, anthers exserted oblong, drupe enclosed in the enlarged calyx, 4-celled.

10. SYMPHOREMA. Climbing shrubs, flowers surrounded by an involucre of 6 oblong bracts enlarging in fruit, calyx short, 4 to 8-toothed, corolla 6 to 16-lobed, anthers exserted, fruit included in the calyx, one-seeded.

1. LANTANA.

L. camara (*L. aculeata*, D.). A straggling scandent shrub, with square prickly stems, leaves ovate acute, flowers in small heads pretty, pink-orange or lilac, and of many shades in the same plant. *Ghúneri.*

This plant, which has a strong smell of black currants, is a native of America, but has run wild nearly everywhere in W. India, and still more so in the S., being in the Madras Presidency a recognized nuisance, as the prickly pear (opuntia) is with us.

L. Indica (*L. alba*, D.), called by *H.* common throughout India and Ceylon in the warmer parts, appears to be much like this, and is said by *D.* to be thinly scattered about Dharwar and other parts of the Deccan. Many species of *Lantana* are used as tea in Brazil.—*Le Maout.*

2. LIPPIA.

L. nodiflora. A small creeping plant, tough and hairy, leaves cuneate serrated in the upper half; flowers in ovoid heads very small, bracts overlapping.

The flowers are arranged so closely together as to seem to be on a common receptacle.

Deccan and S. Konkan. Common in grassy and sandy places (*D.*). Abundant throughout India (*H.*). Tennent (in Ceylon) speaks of the thickly matted verdure of this, so well adapted for imparting consistency to the soil.

3. PREMNA.

1. *P. coriacea* (*P. scandens*, D.). A large strong-smelling climber, nearly smooth, with very large ovate oblong or obcordate leaves pointed, entire, shining, petioles long, channelled, flowers very small greenish white in large panicles, one of the lobes of the corolla much larger than the rest, drupe size of a pea, black. *Chambári, dhánsar, arani.*

The Konkan and Ghauts.

2. *P. latifolia.* An erect straggling shrub, leaves broad oval, blunt, shining, entire or toothed in the upper part, flowers as in the last, but upper lip of corolla larger and whiter, calyx 2-lipped, petioles and young plants rusty. *Chambári, ghanori.*

Common in the Konkan, growing chiefly near the sea.

H. has 4 varieties, and as he has not referred to *D.* it is not certain whether the plant ought to be named as above, or *P. integrifolia*, as *G.* has it. The differences between the two, however, appear to be very slight.

* *P. corymbosa* (*P. cordifolia*, D.), a thick bushy shrub, leaves ovate cordate entire, flowers greenish white, in short dense panicles, drupe like a pea, 3 or 4-seeded. Khandalla (*D.* and *G.*).

4. Gmelina.

G. arborea. A tree, hairy in most parts, leaves long-petioled, heart-shaped, cordate, entire, flowers rather large, brown and yellow, in racemes, lobes of corolla broad roundish, curled back, the lower one much larger and protruding; anthers attached to the filaments by a point only, fruit larger than an olive, oval, yellow. *Shewan, Kumar, gumbár.*

Konkan, and less common in the Deccan. Matheran, but not Mahableshwar (*Dr. Cooke*).

H. says that it sometimes attains sixty feet.

Two species are found in gardens, *G. villosa*, a small thorny tree or shrub, with bright yellow flowers, and *G. asiatica*, a shrub like the last but less thorny, with scolloped and shining leaves instead of nearly entire and somewhat hairy ones.

5. Vitex.

1. *V. negundo* (*V. bicolor*, D.). A tall shrub with grey foliage, leaflets 3 to 5 lanceolate, the underside with the branches white and downy, flowers very small, lilac or light-blue in panicles, berry black, size of a pea. *Nirgund, Indráni, lingur.*

This is perhaps the commonest shrub in the Konkan. Very common also in the Ghauts. Throughout India (*H.*).

The crushed leaves have a very strong and unpleasant smell, said to be equally so to insects.

2. *V. leucoxylon.* A small tree, leaflets 3 to 5 entire smooth, flowers whitish in dichotomous panicles, lower lip of corolla

large and bearded with violet hairs, fruit oval or obovate, smooth, black. *Shiras.*

S. Konkan, Ghauts, and S. M. country.

* *V. altissima*, a large tree, branches compressed and channelled, leaves trifoliate, the long petiole sometimes winged, leaflets lanceolate, soft; flowers small, white tinged with blue, in hairy panicles, fruit size of a pea, black: *Banalgay:* S. Konkan and Canara, plentiful (*D.*). "A beautiful tree when in flower" (*G.*). * *V. alata* scarcely differs from the last, but the wing of the petiole is more pronounced, and leaflets sometimes 5, flowers pale-yellow, or tinged blue. S.M. country and Wári (*D.*). Konkan (*Lisboa*).

Priva (belonging to this section), erect herbs, calyx shortly 5-toothed, limb of corolla oblique, fruit of 2 two-seeded pyrenes.

* *P. leptostachya*, leaves ovate crenate, flowers small, white, in long interrupted spikes, calyx enlarged in fruit with small hooked spines on the back. Old walls at Dapori (*D.*).

(*b*) Stamens 4, equal.

6. Callicarpa.

C. lanata (*C. cana*, D.). A tall shrub, more or less covered with white wool; leaves very large, lanceolate or ovate pointed, wrinkled, flowers quite regular, small, pale-red in dichotomous cymes, anthers white. *Yesar, wákhora, ishwar.*

One of the commonest shrubs on the Ghauts; also on the Konkan hills. *H.* has it as a tree 30 or 40 feet high, but I have neither seen nor heard of it like that.

Note.—There is nothing in this species to justify the generic name.

7. Clerodendron.

1. *C. inerme.* A weak straggling shrub with a strong smell, leaves small, smooth, ovate or obvate entire, flowers long-tubed, white, in panicles, stamens very long, purple, ovary obsoletely 4-lobed. *Tatkari.*

Grows in most places near the sea, and extends to Australia, China, &c. Said to be sometimes called *tivar*, like many other coast plants.

To me it is a very unattractive shrub, but *G.*, whose opinion I always quote with respect, calls it very ornamental.

2. *C. phlomoides.* A large shrub of light-grey hue and downy nearly all over; leaves ovate, broad at the base, rather triangular, irregularly serrated about the middle, flowers white, fragrant, in racemes or panicles, drupe obovoid. *Iran, arni.*

Common in Deccan hedges; also in Guzerat and Sind.

3. *C. serratum.* A tall and handsome shrub, stem square and furrowed, leaves often in threes, obovate oblong, remotely serrated, papery, flowers in panicles, rather large, light-blue, stamens long and arched. *Bhárangi, borsangi.*

The petals in this are almost papilionaceous. The Konkan and Ghauts. Widely spread in India; very common in Bengal (*H.*).

* *C. infortunatum*, undershrub, leaves from round ovate to broad oblong, flowers white or tinged red in large erect panicles, calyx enlarging and turning red, with black drupe inside. S. Konkan and Belgaum (*D.*). * *C. siphonanthus*, shrubby, leaves linear lanceolate, flowers with white long fleshy tubes. In gardens, and said to be wild on hills E. of Ahmednuggur. *C.*   , a very common pot plant, in gardens, with creamy flowers and bright-red calyx. Also in English conservatories.

8. Avicennia.

A. officinalis. White mangrove. A small tree with thick, nearly veinless leaves, oval pointed entire, shining above, whitish below, peduncles long and thick, one from each axil, flowers small, dull-yellow, rather crowded, capsule oval-pointed, seed nearly heart-shaped. *Tiwar, cheria.*

Not in *D.* The wood is called *bakol.*

Very common in salt marshes; on black rocks covered by every tide it grows as a stunted shrub, and is said to grow in the same way on the coasts of the Red Sea, Africa, Australia, and S. America.

(*c*) Stamens as many as the corolla lobes.

9. Tectona.

T. grandis. The teak tree. Leaves ovate pointed, short-petioled, downy beneath, flowers small, whitish, in large terminal cross-armed panicles, which are brownish and hoary, bracts 2, small and narrow, drupe more or less 4-lobed, very hard, covered with furry down. *Ság, ságwán.*

Common in most jungly parts, but seldom attaining any particular size in this Presidency except in Canara. The size of the leaves is remarkable, especially in young plants; they are really "broad as amazonian targe."

10. Symphorema.

S. involucratum. A woody climber with oval blunt-pointed irregularly serrated downy leaves, involucre large, greenish-yellow, spreading horizontally, flowers several together, small, white, petals narrow, curled back, filaments curved, rising from the top of the tube, petals and stamens generally 7 or 8.

Konkans (*G.*) It appears to be rare. *D.* had it between Nagotna and Alibag; I at two places in the Rutnagherry collectorate. It has some resemblance to Getonia floribunda.

* *S. polyandrum*, like the last, but larger in all its parts and more hairy, leaves up to 9 inches long; corolla 14 to 18-lobed. Not in *D.* Konkans and Dharwar (*G.*). Extends northwards to Belgaum (*H.*).

Of cultivated plants, *Duranta Ellisii* is a large shrub, very common in gardens, with panicles of small bright-blue flowers, lighter in the throat. It is called "pigeon berry" in the W. Indies.

Petræa volubilis, a very handsome climber, with blue corolla and lilac-coloured calyx.

Stachytarpheta Indica, herbaceous, with spikes of blue flowers, in and about gardens. Of the common verbena, *V. officinalis*, there are varieties in several colours in gardens. It is wild in some parts of India, and was held in superstitious veneration both in classical and mediæval days. *Aloysia citriodora*, the lemon plant, or lemon-scented verbena, is also well known.

ORDER 91. LABIATÆ. The mint family.

Herbs, rarely shrubs, usually abounding in oil glands, and therefore strong-smelling. Stems generally square, leaves simple, opposite or whorled, without stipules; flowers irregular, usually small, very frequently in whorls, calyx persistent, 4 or 5-cleft, often 2-lipped, corolla tubular, limb 4 or 5-lobed, generally distinctly 2-lipped; stamens 4 didynamous, or 2, generally exserted, ovary free, deeply 4-lobed, style rising from between the lobes, stigma usually bifid, fruit of 4 small seed-like nuts at the bottom of the calyx tube.

> "Here's flowers for you:
> Hot lavender, mints, savory, marjoram;
> . . . . . these are flowers
> Of middle summer, and, I think, they are given
> To men of middle age."—*A Winter's Tale.*

This is a great order, both from size and importance, and is spread over the whole globe, though most abundant in the temperate regions of the Old World. "Labiatæ form one of the most natural groups of plants; the characters of its members are so uniform that it may be called monotypic, as if all the species could be comprehended in a single genus, and the discrimination of its genera is hence often very difficult" (*Le Maout*). The order is distinguished from others of this group by the deeply 4-lobed ovary, which can always be seen at the bottom of the calyx tube, and by the fruit of 4 small nuts similarly situated, looking like, and described by Linnæus as, naked seeds. Lavender and Salvia for their flowers, and Coleus for foliage, are old-fashioned favourites in gardens; but perhaps the sweet herbs of the kitchen garden are still better known—sage, balm, thyme, besides those mentioned by Shakspeare above.

I have not been able to make use of *H.*'s distinctions of tribes and sub-tribes, but have mentioned, as they occur, any characteristics common to two or three genera. The generic distinctions chiefly depend on the calyx and corolla.

No. 11 is the only genus here given which has only two stamens.

1. OCIMUM. Racemes bearing whorls of 6 to 10 flowers; calyx with upper tooth very large and decurrent, corolla tube short, upper lip equally 4-lobed, lower lip entire; calyx deflexed in fruit, stigma bifid.

2. ORTHOSIPHON. Racemes bearing whorls of 6 flowers or less, calyx with upper tooth broad, membranous, decurrent, corolla tube often long, upper lip 3 or 4 divided, lower entire concave, calyx deflexed in fruit; stigma entire.

3. PLECTRANTHUS. Calyx 5-toothed, 2-lipped, the upper lobe broad, enlarged in fruit, upper lip of corolla 3 or 4 divided, lower much longer, boat-shaped, filaments free.

4. COLEUS. As the last, but the filaments combined below into a sheath round the style (which distinguishes this genus from all others in the order.—*Don*).

5. ANISOCHILUS. Flowers in dense spikes, calyx inflated below the middle, corolla tube slender curved, upper lip short, lower long concave, disk lobed.

6. LAVANDULA. Leaves divided, flowers in spikes, calyx 5-toothed, upper lip of corolla bifid, lower trifid, lobes spreading, stamens included.

7. POGOSTEMON. Spikes or contracted racemes bearing whorls of many very small flowers crowded together; calyx equally 4 or 5 cleft, corolla lobes 4, lower usually the longest, filaments bearded.

8. DYSOPHYLLA. Small plants generally with whorled leaves, flowers in dense spikes, calyx ovoid equally 5-toothed, corolla equally 4-lobed, filaments bearded.

9. COLEBROOKIA. A densely woolly shrub, whorls dense in spikes or panicles, calyx teeth long subulate feathery, corolla minute, lobes 4, about equal, stamens included.

10. MICROMERIA. Whorls axillary or in terminal spikes, upper lip of corolla erect flattish, entire or nearly so, lower spreading 5-lobed, anthers with a connective.

11. SALVIA. Whorls of flowers in racemes or spikes, calyx 2-lipped, upper lip of corolla erect arched, lower 3-lobed, stamens 2, anthers with a connective.

12. SCUTELLARIA. Calyx 2-lipped, completely closing over

the fruit, upper lip with a large shield or plate on the back, upper lip of corolla entire or notched, lower broad 3-lobed, ovary oblique.

13. ANISOMELES. Tall coarse herbs, calyx equally 5-toothed, upper lip of corolla entire erect, lower 3-lobed, spreading.

14. LEUCAS. Generally woolly or hairy plants with white flowers in axillary whorls, calyx 6 to 10-toothed, the mouth often oblique, upper lip of corolla erect, hooded, lower spreading with very large middle lobe.

15. LEONOTIS. Flowers in dense axillary whorls with many slender bracts, calyx 8 to 10-toothed, upper lip of corolla long, hooded, lower very small, spreading, concave.

1. OCIMUM. Basil.

1. *O. basilicum.* Erect, smooth or nearly so, leaves ovate, bracts similar, spikes long, whorls rather close, flowers white, pink, or purplish, stamens long exserted, nuts black. *Sabza, Ajwala.*

This is the sweet basil, very widely cultivated, and with many varieties, making it difficult to fix its characteristics. It is the plant to which Keats's beautiful but rather revolting poem, "Isabella, or the Pot of Basil," refers—

> ". . . The basil tuft, that waves
> Its fragrant blossoms over graves."—*Lalla Rookh.*

H. says that it differs chiefly from *O. canum*, hoary basil, in the much larger size of all its parts, and in being smooth or nearly so. The latter, with white corolla, is considered to be wild in the plains and lower hills of India, and, like the next, is called *Rám tulsi.*

2. *O. gratissimum.* A shrub several feet high, nearly smooth, leaves ovate, acute crenate, or coarsely toothed, bracts sessile lanceolate from a round base, corolla scarcely larger than the calyx, pale yellow. *Rám tulsi, tulsi bij, rám duti.*

Common in gardens; doubtful if wild (*H.*). He has a variety with leaves softly hairy.

3. *O. sanctum.* Holy basil. Herbaceous, erect, softly hairy, leaves ovate obtuse toothed, petioled, floral leaves sessile, corolla very small, pale purple, hardly longer than the calyx, nuts reddish brown. *Kála tulsi.*

Very commonly cultivated, particularly about temples and in Brahmins' gardens: doubtfully indigenous (*H.*).

The plant is often purplish all over.

* *O. adscendens*, stem prostrate, branches ascending, leaves ovate, obtuse, floral leaves lanceolate, deciduous, corolla pale rose, filaments twice as long as corolla; nuts red brown. The Deccan in sandy places; very variable in habit (*H.*).

2. ORTHOSIPHON.

O. pallidus. Small, low, much-branched, smooth, leaves pale green, ovate obtuse or triangular, coarsely toothed, the base cuneate and entire, corolla white, calyx whitish, about the same length, stamens included, nuts pale, nearly smooth.

Near Poona. Very common in the Deccan (*D.*). Very like an Ocimum, and, *H.* says, "with difficulty distinguished from *O. adscendens*, the calyx being nearly identical." The latter, which is very variable, and, *H.* says, from 4 to 16 inches high, is found in the Deccan.

* *O. tomentosus* (*O. glabratus*, D.), leaves broad ovate, cordate, toothed, long-petioled, flowers light purple, corolla tube very long. Deccan (*D.*). A most variable plant, particularly as to hairiness (*H.*).

The four genera which follow are, like the two just given, in subtribe Euocimeæ, and have the lower lip of the corolla flat or nearly so. *Geniosporum*, whorls many-flowered in long lax racemes, corolla as in *Ocimum*. * *G. prostratum*, stems slender, many, from a woody stock, leaves oblong, very variable, corolla minute, hairy, bracts ovate acute, reflexed. Not in *D.* S. Konkan (*G.*).

Platystoma, small annuals, whorls many-flowered, corolla lips about equal. * *P. flaccidum*, erect, leaves ovate serrate, racemes slender, stiff, as long as the whole plant, calyx lobes ovate, nuts black. The Konkan, and on the Kála naddi (*H.*).

Acrocephalus, flowers whorled in dense heads, corolla lobes 4, about equal, stamens included. * *A. capitatus*, procumbent, leaves ovate lanceolate, flowers pale purple, heads with imbricated bracts. Alibág districts and S. M. country (*D.*).

Moschosma, flowers 6 to 10 together in panicles, corolla tube very short, stamens included. * *M. polystachyum*, slender, much-branched, erect, leaves ovate acute, crenate serrate, flowers purplish or flesh-coloured, nuts black, smooth. The Konkans (*D.*). This was made an Ocimum by *R.*, following Linnæus.

3. PLECTRANTHUS.

P. incanus (*P. cordifolius*, D.). A tall handsome plant, softly hairy all over, leaves broad ovate or roundish, deeply cordate, crenate, flowers small lilac, or light blue in racemes or panicles, corolla tube curved, nuts large, roundish. *Lál ághára.*

Dapoli. Sawant Wári (*D.*). "Grows in great abundance throughout Khandalla village, also on the ruins of Rosa near Ellora; and generally everywhere near the habitations of man" (?) (*G.*).

* *P. Stocksii* (*P. Wightii*, D.). Erect, branched, slender, leaves ovate cordate, panicles pyramidal, calyx incurved, striated, corolla tube short and broad. Konkan, Belgaum, &c., (*D.*). *P. rotundifolius* (*D.* and *G.*) *H.* cannot identify, procumbent at the base, leaves smooth, thick, ovate cordate, flowers blue in rather lax verticils, tubers edible. Konkans.

4. Coleus.

1. *C. spicatus* (*C. zatarhendi*, D.). Rough and hairy, stem very stout, leaves fleshy, broad ovate or roundish, flowers large and handsome bluish purple, about 6 to a verticil, upper lip of corolla very small, calyx very hairy, bracts concave pointed, soon falling off.

This plant I had at Lena, near Nasik, and *H.* has "S. Deccan, on low rocky hills, common," but I much doubt *H.'s* identification of it with *D.'s C. zatarhendi*, which he ascribes to the sandy coast N. of Bassein. The large boat-shaped lower lip of the corolla is very noticeable.

2. *C. barbatus.* Hairy, leaves ovate broad at base, crenate, flowers in drooping racemes of 6 flowered verticils, rather one-sided, corolla very light purple, lower lip not so prominent as in the last; bracts much the same. *Garwal.*

Dapoli. Caranjah and Deccan hills, (*D.*). On rice-fields in Guzerat (*G.*). Deccan peninsula, common (*H.*). Both *D.* and *G.* state on Mr. Law's authority that it is cultivated for the sake of the roots which are pickled, but from *H.* it seems likely that this may refer to another species.

I noted the calyx as bright red, contrasting well with the corolla. This probably is not constant, but in a figure in Maund's "Botanist" the stem is tinged with red, and the calyx described as more or less violet-coloured.

C. aromaticus, country borage, *páthar chur*, *pánachá onvá*, with fleshy and very aromatic leaves, is common in gardens.

Many species of *Coleus* are cultivated in England for the sake of the beautifully variegated foliage.

5. Anisochilus.

1. * *A. carnosus.* Stem stout, leaves thick and fleshy, ovate rounded, crenated, petioled, flowers pale purple in long-stalked spikes, upper lip of calyx large broad entire. *Vova, káporli, choronva.*

2. *A. eriocephalus* (*A. decussatus*, D.). Stem round, red, leaves broad-ovate, deeply cordate, long-petioled, glandular below, flowers small, bluish-purple, velvety, in long-stalked cylindrical or pyramidal spikes, anthers blue, lower lip of corolla large and boat-shaped.

The first of these, which is said to be called thick-leaved lavender, I have not seen. *D.* and *G.* have it, but without habitat. *H.* has it "throughout Central and Southern India," and makes it a very variable plant. The second I had at Lena, and *D.*, who attributes it to the highest Ghauts opposite Bombay, describes the dark red spike and "the leaves sprinkled on both sides with ruby-coloured glands." This would certainly be a considerable exaggeration if applied to my plant; but *H.* thinks this is perhaps only a state of *A. carnosus.*

Two species, which are not in *D.*, are given by *H.* on the authority of Dalzell, Law, &c. * *A. plantagineus,* dwarf and shrubby, leaves sessile, oblong obovate entire, spikes solitary long, on very stout peduncles, calyx woolly, bracts 3-lobed. Bábabudin Hills. * *A. verticillatus,* softly hairy, stem stout, leaves mostly whorled, sessile, narrow lanceolate, flowers very pale blue in a large terminal spike, calyx lips truncate, bracts large lanceolate. Konkan and S. Ghauts. *D.* has *A. adenanthus,* near Dhárwar and Bábabudin Hills, but the description is very imperfect, and *H.* could not identify it.

6. Lavandula.

1. *L. Gibsoni* (*L. Perottettii*, D.). A tall plant, all softly hairy, leaves pinnatifid, segments oblong or linear, flowers pale lilac in dense spikes, calyx long, segments lanceolate.

2. *L. Burmanni.* Less leafy and hairy than the last, leaves bipinnatifid, segments linear, spikes dense, flowers dark blue or white, bracts subulate with a broad base. *Gorea asmáni.*

Both these species (which are the only ones in India) are sufficiently like the favourite garden lavender of England (*L. vera*) to be at once recognized, and they have almost the same lovely smell.

> "Crowned lilies, standing near
> Purple spiked lavender."—*Tennyson.*

The first seems to be rare. *D.* has only hills at Sattara, where I also found it. *H.* adds to this "the Konkan." *G.* has Fort of Pándugarh; Mr. Birdwood, the Ghauts: on the Mahableshwar road. The second is tolerably common in the Deccan. Other species are found in gardens.

7. Pogostemon.

Note.—This genus and the two following approximate to the mints.

1. *P. purpurascens.* Herbaceous erect, much-branched, softly hairy all over, stem furrowed, leaves ovate petioled, doubly serrated, flowers in crowded clusters on large stout spikes, pink or white, calyx teeth short triangular, bracts longer ovate, glandular, stamens long, lilac.

Lanoli. Common in shady woods in the Konkan (*D.*). Canara (*H.*). Matheran, but rare (*Dr. Cooke*).

H. has corolla white with purple upper lip.

2. *P. parviflorus* (*P. purpuricaulis*, D.). A strong coarse half-shrubby plant, mostly smooth, stem and branches purple, leaves ovate, doubly serrated, flowers small, pale, in close pyramidal heads, bracts broad ovate. *Pángli.*

There seems no doubt that this, which has a strong smell of black currants, is the S. Konkan *pángli*, exceedingly common there, and also on the Ghauts and very unattractive in appearance. But even in flowers it must perhaps be conceded that "Pretty is all very pretty, but it's prettier far to be useful" (*Clough*), and if the reputation which this plant has for curing *fursa* bites is deserved, its merits must be fully acknowledged. The difficulty of identification lies in this, that *H.* calls No. 1 probably a large form of this, the next probably only a variety of this, and says that this most resembles a fourth and shrubby species, *P. plectranthoides*, which is hoary with ovate cuneate leaves doubly serrated, and clustered spicate flowers, bracts and calyx glandular. Chikli (*D.*). Konkan and Canara (*H.*). So there is undoubtedly a very strong resemblance between all these.

3. *P. pachouli* (*P. heyneanus*, D.). An erect branched herb, leaves ovate, long-petioled, crenate or toothed, flowers very small, whorls forming interrupted spikes, bracts about as long as the calyx. *Pách.*

From Bombay southward wild and cultivated. A common Indian garden plant, often much altered by cultivation (*H.*). Held sacred by the natives (*G.*).

"The odour of patchouli was known in Europe before the material itself was introduced, in consequence of its use in Cashmere to scent the shawls, with a view to keeping out moths; hence the genuine Cashmere shawls were known by their scent, until the French found out the secret, and imported the herb for use in the same way" (*Chambers*).

The patchouli of commerce is the dried branches of this plant, the perfume being said to be a very favourite one all over Asia.

* *P. paniculatus*, 3 to 5 feet high, branched, downy, leaves ovate, irregularly cut, spikes long, bracts very variable, imbricated membranous. S. Konkan (*D.*).

* *P. mollis*, a low growing plant, branched from the woody base, softly hairy, leaves roundish or oblong, crenate, flowers very small white in dense spikes. Not in (*D.*). Konkan (*H.*).

8. Dysophylla.

Don makes this genus differ from the last, principally in the more regular corolla. The generic name, meaning "ill-smelling leaves," is not, strictly speaking, applicable to all the species, and many people would think it quite as well bestowed on the patchouli plant.

1. *D. myosuroides.* A pretty erect plant, like a small mint, all silky, branched, leaves oblong or lanceolate, not whorled, flowers minute reddish, calyx teeth short and straight. *Shewal.*

Common in the beds of watercourses at Mahableshwar. This and the Bábabudan hills seem to be the only places recorded for it in W. India.

2. *D. stellata.* Erect or slightly creeping, slightly hairy, leaves linear, 5 to 7 in a whorl, quite entire, smooth, flowers red or purple in short spikes, floral leaves larger than the calyx, rather thick, calyx segments rather acute. *Marvá.*

3. *D. tomentosa.* Softly hairy with erect branches from prostrate stems, leaves lanceolate or linear, 6 to 9 in a whorl, bracts similar, flowers purple in close spikes, calyx segments obtuse.

These two are very much alike, and are both found in rice-fields in the cold weather. They differ chiefly in hairiness and in the calyx segments, and *H.* considers the second to be the larger species. It is abundant about Malwan, and *H.* has no other habitat. The first is a Southern species: from Belgaum southwards (*H.*). Also in S. Konkan and at Matheran.

Another species, * *D. gracilis*, which grows in patches at Mahableshwar, and flowers in October (*Mr. Birdwood*) is probably only a tall form of *D. stellata* (*H.*), and * *D. erecta*, hardly distinguishable leaves up to twelve in a whorl, near Malwan (*D.*). * *D. salicifolia*, stem one or two feet high, hairy or silky, leaves linear lanceolate, not whorled, otherwise like No. 1. Not in *D.* Mahableshwar, Konkan, &c. (*H.*). * *D. quadrifolia* (*D. rupestris*, D.), a stout undershrub, 2 to 4 feet high, hairy and silky, leaves 4 in a whorl, linear lanceolate, spikes long of innumerable small rose-coloured flowers. Near Vingorla (*D.*). Many other parts of India (*H.*). * *D. Stocksii*, very stout, erect, nearly smooth, leaves narrow, linear obtuse, spikes slender. the mouth of the calyx closed by the minute teeth. Not in *D.* Konkan, *Stocks* (*H.*).

Perilla belongs to the sub-tribe Menthoideæ (Mints). Calyx much enlarged in fruit, 2-lipped, upper broad 3-toothed, corolla bell-shaped, disk a large gland. * *P. ocimoides*, coarse, strong-smelling, 2 or 3 feet high, leaves ovate or rounded, serrate or crenate, flowers small, white or blue in racemes. Not in *D.* Ghauts and Mahableshwar (*G.*). *Pángli.*

9. Colebrookia.

C. oppositifolia (*C. tenuifolia*, D.). A small shrub, all soft and hairy, leaves verticilled in threes, elliptic, narrow at both ends, serrulate, flowers minute, dirty white, in very small lax spikes. *Báhmani, dasai, dasari káj hár.*

Very common on the Ghauts and Konkan hills. The spikes are suggestive of (Indian) squirrels' tails.

10. MICROMERIA.

M. capitellata (*M. Malcolmiana*, D.). A slender erect hairy plant, leaves small ovate obtuse, crenated, reddish, flowers small violet in twin stalked spikes, upper lip of corolla paler.

Streams at Mahableshwar. W. Ghauts (*H.*) It has both the smell and appearance of a mint.

11. SALVIA. Sage.

S. plebeia. A stout branched hairy plant, leaves oblong or ovate wrinkled, blunt, stalked, floral leaves very small ovate, flowers very small violet in verticils of about 6, upper lip of calyx entire, lower 2-lobed, almost closing after flowering. *Kamarkas.*

Sattara and Dhánu. Khandalla and Caranjah (*D.*). Throughout India (*H.*).

This has a strong mint-like smell and the general appearance of an Ocimum. I noted it as sticky, which is a common, if not a general, characteristic of the Salvias. Also that the calyx eventually almost shuts up like that of a Scutellaria.

S. officinalis, sage, *Salbia, Sefakas*, is cultivated as a kitchen herb. *S. Indica, Seoti*, also said to be cultivated; but is not a native of India (*H.*). Several species are also cultivated as garden flowers.

12. SCUTELLARIA. Skull-cap.

* *S. discolor.* Stem ascending from a creeping root-stalk often naked above, leaves ovate obtuse or roundish cordate, strongly nerved and purple below, flowers white in long slender racemes.

Matheran and Mahableshwar (*Birdwood*). Ghauts, Konkan and Canara (*D.* and *H.*). Two species are tolerably common in England.

13. ANISOMELES.

1\. *A. Heyneana.* A tall untidy straggling plant, more or less hairy all over, stems, branches and peduncles acutely 4-angled, leaves ovate crenate, narrow at the base, upper lanceolate with a hairy stipulary ring, cymes long-stalked, few-flowered, one-sided, flowers white or greenish, lower lip tinged pink, calyx dark-coloured. *Chandhára.*

The Konkan: very common in Salsette. *H.* has Western Ghauts, and suggests, "Perhaps only a variety of the next:" but the plants when living appear very different.

2. *A. ovata.* A large handsome plant, leaves soft and downy, ovate crenate, flowers in dense whorls on spikes, light-coloured with deep purple lower lip, calyx teeth lanceolate acute. *Gopáli.*

Most variable in hairiness (*H.*). It has a strong smell of camphor.

Very common, Guzerat, Deccan, and Konkan.

3. *A. malabarica.* Large and shrubby, all covered with hair or wool, leaves oblong lanceolate, acute crenate, bracts and floral leaves subulate, flowers pale purple or lilac in whorls or cymes, calyx teeth narrow, lanceolate. *Gojibhá, Guligaozabán.*

The Ghauts.

I believe that this plant must vary very much in hairiness and wooliness, for *H.* calls the branches sometimes most densely clothed with snow-white adpressed wool and Mr. Birdwood says it may be recognized by this. But *R.* and *D.* put it much less strongly, and my observation agrees with theirs.

14. Leucas.

This genus and the next approximate by the upper lip of the corolla to the dead nettles (*Lamium*). This is an unattractive but very prolific genus. *H.* has 38 Indian species, of which about 11 are attributed to W. India, and of these several are very common and widespread.

1. *L. lanata* (*L. collina,* D.). More or less woody below, branches 4-angled, leaves ovate or lanceolate, coarsely toothed, whorls many-flowered, calyx mouth about equal, with 10 teeth alternately shorter, bracts linear.

Guzerat and S. Konkan. Deccan peninsula (*H.*).

2. *L. biflora.* Small, erect or procumbent, leaves ovate or lanceolate serrated, flowers 2 in each axil erect, calyx mouth equal, 10-toothed.

Sattara and the Konkans.

Easily distinguished from other species by the few and comparatively large flowers. *H.* has, however, * *L. procumbens*, attributed to Canara, with as few flowers, but more nearly smooth and with shorter calyx teeth.

3. *L. stelligera.* A tall plant with large dense whorls of flowers, leaves oblong, distantly serrated, calyx with 10 soft and spreading teeth, bracts many subulate. *Burumbi, gumá.*

The Ghauts, Konkan and Belgaum. The commonest species of the order both at Matheran and Mahableshwar.—*Dr. Cooke.*

4. *L. cephalotes.* Tall, stems grooved, leaves ovate or lanceolate serrate, whorls large, terminal round, the uppermost leaves coming through the whorl, calyx mouth oblique, teeth short, bracts oval lanceolate, long-pointed imbricated membranous, surrounding the whorl. *Tumbá.*

Sattara, and common in Guzerat. Coast of Kattywar (*D.*). Through the Deccan (*H.*). The bracts distinguish it from other species.

5. *L. aspera.* Rough and hairy, about 6 inches high, leaves oblong or lanceolate, whorls small, dense, bracts subulate, calyx curved, smooth below, ribbed above, mouth oblique, teeth short. *Tumbá.*

S. Konkan on the sea-shore. Plains of India: very variable (*H.*). It much resembles the next.

6. *L. linifolia.* Smooth or nearly so, leaves linear or oblong, whorls dense, calyx mouth oblique, elongated above, lower teeth very short, bracts few and short.

This is the common species of cultivated fields, and in many places is very abundant and conspicuous when the crops are off. Konkan, Guzerat, and Deccan. Plains of India (*H.*).

So in the Himalayas. "In poor soil a white-flowered Leucas monopolized the space, like our charlock and poppy: it was apparently a pest to the agriculturist, covering the surface in some places like a sprinkling of snow."—*Hooker.*

* *L. urticæfolia*, finely hairy, leaves ovate, coarsely toothed, whorls many-flowered, round, distant, calyx mouth oblique, split above: Cambay (*D.*). *L. longifolia*, stem 4-angled, leaves very narrow linear, whorls of about 6 flowers, rather large for the genus, calyx with 10 short equal teeth, bracts minute. About Poona. Konkan (*H.*). * *L. ciliata*, tall, leaves ovate lanceolate, coarsely serrated, whorls round, large and dense, calyx teeth 10, spreading, the upper lip of the corolla covered with dense yellow-brown hairs. *Burumbi.* Konkan and Ghauts (*D.*). Mahableshwar.—*Cooke.*

15. Leonotis.

L. nepetifolia. A strong handsome annual, 6 or 8 feet high, with square and furrowed stems, leaves ovate crenate with channelled petioles, whorls large and distant, corolla orange coloured, hairy, especially the upper lip, calyx teeth bristle-pointed. *Mátisul, ekri, dipmál.*

A doubtful native, but pretty common. Especially abundant about Agási and Tárapore in N. Konkan, and in some Deccan hill forts.

G. and *D.* mention two other species as found in gardens, which should be very handsome—the flowers of the one, * *L. leonurus*, large scarlet, of the other, * *L. tartarica*, rich pink, variegated with white.

Nepeta, catmint, calyx 15-ribbed, 5-toothed, corolla throat inflated, upper lip straight, lower 3-lobed. *N. bombaiensis*, small, erect, hairy, leaves ovate, obtuse, crenated, flowers small, pale, 5 or more to a peduncle, corolla scarcely larger than calyx. Old rocks and walls, at Shivner Fort (*D.*). I had this, as I believed, at Chámpanir. *H.* has no other hab. than *D.'s*, but mentions a plant sent by Mr. Woodrow from Poona, apparently coming between this and a much commoner species, *N. ruderalis*. *N. cataria* is a well-known English plant.

The following are cultivated :—

Mentha viridis, and *M. arvensis*, mint, *padina*, *watalao*. *M. pipirita*, peppermint. *Meriandra Bengalensis*, Indian sage, *shevti*.

Rosmarinus officinalis, rosemary : a very common shrub in the S. of Europe.

"There's rosemary : that's for remembrance."—*Hamlet*.

And with the same idea, perhaps, it is associated with death—

"All must be left when death appears,
In spite of wishes, groans and tears,
Nor one of all thy plants that grow,
But Rosemary will with thee go."

G. Sewell (17th century).

Origanum vulgare—marjoram, *Márva*, *Márda kush*.

Thymus vulgaris, common thyme : (*not* the wild thyme of poets) : *ipán*, *hásha*.

Note.—In Sir J. Lubbock's "Beauties of Nature," and "Flowers and Insects," will be found a very interesting account of the use of each part of various labiate flowers, with reference to their fertilization by insects.

Order 92. PLANTAGINEÆ.

Herbs, with radical strongly-nerved leaves and inconspicuous flowers in a scape; sepals 4 persistent, corolla hypogynous, chaffy, 4-lobed; stamens 4, long and weak on the corolla, anthers very large, slightly attached, ovary free, capsule membranous.

A very small but well-marked order, not at all resembling any that have gone before. The long weak stamens and disproportionately large anthers are the most conspicuous part of the flowers.

Plantago. Characters of the order.

This, the only genus found in India (and there are only two others in the order), is in England called plantain, a name which, to avoid confusion, it is better to drop in the tropics.

P. maior. Leaves petioled oblong, somewhat toothed, spike long and slender, bracts equalling the calyx, capsule 2-celled, with 4 to 8 seeds in each cell. *Bártang.*

Not in *D.* or *G.* This is the greater or broad-leaved plantain of England, common by the side of every dusty road, and a pest in lawns. It seems to be found here and there in most parts of India, and is ascribed to Bombay and Mahableshwar. The old English name is Way-bred, and it is said so surely to follow the footsteps of migratory man as to have got in some colonies the name of the "Englishman's foot."

B. "Take thou some new infection to the eye,
And the rank poison of the old will die."

R. "Your plantain leaf is excellent for that."
Romeo and Juliet.

"The hedgehog underneath the plantain bores."
Tennyson.

(In Sikkim) "I attended an old woman who dressed her ulcers with plantago (plantain) leaves, a very common Scotch remedy, the ribs being drawn out from the leaf, which is applied fresh: it is rather a strong application."—*Hooker, Himalayan Journals.*

Two other species, * *P. amplexicaulis* and * *P. ovata*, are found in Sind (*H.*).

We have now come to the end of those orders in which the flowers have generally all their parts perfect. The orders which follow have flowers wanting in corolla or calyx, or both; and the first great division of these is called Monochlamyds (i.e. having a single floral envelope) or Apetalous; because, where there is only one floral envelope, botanists consider that it is the corolla which is wanting, whether the part which exists is coloured or not, and this part is called indifferently perianth or calyx. But as in the Dichlamydeous orders there are many exceptions in the way of genera and species which want either calyx or corolla, so in these Monochlamydeous orders there are plants which have both.

In the orders now to be described the male and female organs are oftener found on separate plants or in separate flowers than in the earlier ones, and this in itself is an imperfection. And from the absence of petals the flowers are, in the majority of cases, small and green, "though flowers which have lost their corolla (according to the theory of degeneration) often tend to re-develop brilliant colours in their calyx; while flowers that have lost both corolla and calyx often tend to re-develop such colours in bracts, involucres, or leaves, as in Jatropha and Poinsettia."—*Grant Allen.*

V. APETALOUS EXOGENS.

It seems scarcely possible to make any groups of the seventeen orders contained in this division, but the following points are to be noticed:—

(1) The first seven orders are, as far as W. India is concerned, composed almost entirely of herbs, and have no trees. Euphorbiaceæ and Urticaceæ have herbs, shrubs, and trees; the remaining seven orders have shrubs and trees only, and no herbs.

(2) The orders containing species with highly-coloured flowers are Nyctagineæ, Thymeleaceæ, Loranthaceæ, and Santalaceæ.

(3) Flowers with calyx as well as corolla are to be found in Loranthaceæ and Euphorbiaceæ.

(4) The species with lobed or divided leaves are very few indeed.

CONSPECTUS OF ORDERS.

93. NYCTAGINEÆ. Leaves usually opposite entire, perianth petaloid monopetalous, anthers twin.
94. AMARANTACEÆ. Leaves simple without stipules, flowers with conspicuous chaffy bracts, sepals and fruit dry.
95. CHENOPODACEÆ. Mostly succulent herbs, often tinged with red, leaves alternate without stipules.
96. POLYGONACEÆ. Leaves generally alternate with conspicuous sheathing stipules, sepals imbricated, nut hard.
97. PODOSTEMONACEÆ. Minute aquatic plants with very imperfect flowers.
98. ARISTOLOCHIACEÆ. Leaves alternate without stipules, perianth superior, generally large and tubular.
99. PIPERACEÆ. Aromatic herbs or shrubs, flowers minute in a catkin-like spike, with a bract, but no perianth.
100. MYRISTICEÆ. Trees, generally aromatic, leaves alternate without stipules, perianth 3-lobed, fruit fleshy.
101. LAURINEÆ. Aromatic trees or shrubs, leaves gland-dotted without stipules, perianth usually 6-cleft.
102. THYMELEACEÆ. A shrub, leaves without stipules, perianth coloured, regular, 4 or 5-lobed.
103. ELEAGNACEÆ. Flowers regular, perianth tubular, fruit enclosed in the tube.
104. LORANTHACEÆ. Parasitic shrubs, generally with complete calyx and corolla, leaves generally thick and fleshy, fruit a one-seeded berry or drupe.
105. SANTALACEÆ. Leaves without stipules, perianth more or less tubular.
106. EUPHORBIACEÆ. Plants generally full of milky and acrid juice, flowers very various, often with conspicuous involucre and glands.
107. URTICACEÆ. Leaves generally rough, flowers minute, often crowded on a fleshy involucre.
108. SALICINEÆ. A tree, flowers in catkins.
109. GNETACEÆ. A large climber with male flowers consisting of a single stamen, and females of a naked ovule, in catkins.

ORDER 93. **NYCTAGINEÆ.**

Leaves usually opposite quite entire, without stipules, one of each pair being generally smaller than the other, perianth monopetalous, tube persistent, covering the fruit, limb 3 to 5-lobed, stamens hypogynous, anthers twin or distinctly 2-celled, ovary free, fruit membranous.

This small tropical order has two garden species sufficiently well known and beautiful to make it famous, but it would take a tolerably good botanist to discover the relationship between them, or between either of them and the other plants of the order here given. One of these is the Marvel of Peru, Mirabilis dichotoma, generally called in India, as in America, "four-o'clock," from the time of the flowers opening, and thence *chár baje.* The other is perhaps the most conspicuous feature of Bombay gardens, the grand climber, Bougainvillea spectabilis, introduced from the Cape little more than forty years ago. The flowers are very small and yellow, the large leafy involucres which surround them giving the plant its brilliant colour. It is often seen in English conservatories, but the colour there is always (as far as I have seen) more or less washed out, so as to afford no idea of the beauty of the tropical plant. The native species of the order have no such attractions as these two foreigners.

BOERHAAVIA. Herbs, with very small flowers on jointed pedicels, stamens 1 to 5, ovary oblique stalked, stigma peltate.

1. *B. repens.* A prostrate and spreading plant with thick stem and petioles, leaves ovate oblong or roundish, often cordate at the base and with waved red edges, often white with hairs below, flowers pink, in small heads or umbels, fruit oval ribbed, viscid, stamens 2 or 3. *Punarnavá, Khápará.*

Very common. Throughout India (*H.*). He has two varieties, one of which is *D.'s B. diffusa* (*B. procumbens*, R.), which *G.* says is generally monandrous. When in fruit and withering this plant looks much like a bedstraw (*Galium*).

2. *B. repanda.* Climbing in hedges, all smooth, leaves petioled cordate sinuate, sometimes red-edged, flowers few together in long-stalked umbels, like a miniature pink convolvulus with long-exserted stamens, fruit oblong, broader at the top, rough all over with glandular knobs. *Sátura, punarnavá.*

Pretty and delicate, very common in Guzerat, less so in the Deccan. Konkan (*Stocks*).

* *B. verticillata* (*B. stellata*, D.), which seems to have been found in most parts of the Presidency, but not common, is described as very like this, but the flowers smaller, white or pink, the fruit club-shaped with large glands round the top (*H.*). *Sátura.*

* *B. fruticosa,* shrubby erect, all viscid and hairy, leaves small ovate, flowers umbellate, pink, pedicels long and slender, fruit linear oblong, warty. Sivner and Ghauts E. of Bombay (*Dalzell*). No other Indian authority.

Pisonia, trees or shrubs, flowers diœcious, perianth of male flower funnel-shaped, of female flower tubular, stamens 6 to 10, ovary oblique sessile. * *P. aculeata*, woody, often climbing, prickly, leaves elliptic obtuse, flowers small, greenish white in panicles, fruit oblong or club-shaped, ribbed and glandular. Not in *D.* S. Konkan and elsewhere (*G.* and *H.*).

P. alba, a native of the Andamans, where it grows to be a tree 30 or 40 feet high, is the lettuce plant or tree lettuce, common in tubs in Bombay, and owing its name to its light green leaves, which *D.* says grow darker away from the light, contrary to the usual rule. *Chinai Sálib.*

The next two orders contain very many of the plants which are used as potherbs, or *bháji.*

Order 94. AMARANTACEÆ.

Herbs, rarely shrubs, leaves without stipules simple, flowers usually in terminal spikes with chaffy bracts and bracteoles, sepals rigid or dry, generally 5, sometimes 2 or 3, separate or slightly connected, persistent, stamens 1 to 5, styles 1 to 3, fruit dry, generally one-seeded.

This is an uninteresting order though useful for food. It is closely allied to the next, but distinguished from it by the dry bracts, which are often more conspicuous than the sepals.

Note.—The anthers are 2-celled in all the Indian genera except Alternanthera and Gomphrena.

(*a.*) Leaves alternate.

1. Celosia. Flowers white or pink shining, sepals chaffy, stamens 5 united below into a cup, fruit circumsciss.

2. Digera. Flowers in threes, the two outer reduced to crested scales, stamens 5, ovary oblong, truncate. Style filiform, stigmas 2 curved back, fruit a roundish nut.

3. Amaranthus. Flowers small unisexual, ovary compressed, style short or none, stigmas 2 or 3, fruit compressed.

(*b.*) Leaves opposite (except Nos. 5 and 6 partially).

4. Pupalia. Perfect flowers few, surrounded by imperfect ones, which are reduced to bristly hooked awns, stamens 5, fruit compressed.

5. Nothosærua. Branched from the base, flowers most minute, woolly, sepals colourless 3 to 5, stamens 1 or 2.

6. Ærua. Woolly herbs or undershrubs, leaves sometimes alternate, flowers very small, sometimes polygamous, sepals and stamens 4 or 5, the latter united below with staminodes into a cup.

7. Achyranthes. Flowers in spikes, bracts spinous, sepals 4 or 5 shining, becoming hard and ribbed, stamens 2 to 5, united at the base to as many square staminodes.

8. ALTERNANTHERA. Usually prostrate, flowers small, white in heads, sepals 5 unequal, stamens 2 to 5, united into a short cup with or without staminodes, anthers one-celled.

1. CELOSIA.

C. argentea. Smooth, branched, leaves linear lanceolate, flowers silvery tinged with pink, in long-stalked spikes, sepals larger than the bracts, fruit ovate or pear-shaped, seeds black and shining. *Limri, Kudhu, Kunjir.*

This is the silver-spiked cockscomb, called in Mr. Birdwood's list, Quailgrass. Very common in cultivated fields. Throughout India and Ceylon (*H.*). In Borneo and the Malay archipelago "it forms compact little bushes 2 feet high, every branchlet terminated by a rose-tipped spike of silvery bracts."—*Burbidge.*

C. cristata, the garden cockscomb, *lál murgha, rájagiri, H.* looks on as a form of this, and doubts it being anywhere wild in India. It assumes many forms under cultivation, from which many spurious species have resulted (*H.*).

2. DIGERA.

D. arvensis. A pretty, rather procumbent plant, leaves ovate tinged with red, petioles long and hairy, flowers red, in erect spikes several inches long. *Getaná.*

Leaves very variable, flowers greenish (*H.*).

Poona, Bandora, Surat. I had what I believed to be this, growing on the sea-shore in S. Konkan, very large with fleshy leaves, and the long spikes drooping.

3. AMARANTUS. Amaranth.

It seems quite unsuitable that so uninteresting a set of plants as those which come under this genus should bear the name of that

> "Immortal amaranth . . . which once
> In Paradise, fast by the tree of life,
> Began to bloom, but soon for man's offence
> To heaven removed, where first it grew, there grows,
> And flowers aloft, shading the fount of life."—*Milton.*

> "The only amaranthine flower on earth
> Is virtue."—*Cowper.*

1. *A. spinosus.* Smooth, dark-coloured, thorny, leaves oblong obtuse petioled, variegated behind, flowers in dense axillary clusters and terminal spikes, green, sepals and stamens 5, utricles as long as the calyx. *Kántebháji, Kántemáth.*

A common weed. Throughout India and Ceylon in waste places; the plant varies in colour from green and red to purple (*H.*).

2. *A. blitum* (*Euxolus oleraceus*, D.). Tall, smooth, stem succulent reddish, leaves ovate, very obtuse or retuse, spike

terminal, erect, rather thick, flowers closely clustered, pale green, sepals 3, stamens 3 to 5. *Ránmáti, támdulja, mát támbari.*

A variable weed, cultivated and wild in most parts of India (*H.*). There are apparently several varieties. This is the only species of the order found wild or half-wild in England.

3. *A. polygamus* (*Amblogyna polygonoides*, D.). Only a form of the last (*H.*) with small usually obovate leaves with a soft point, flowers fewer in a cluster, sepals larger, more subulate, utricles smaller, more acute. *Cháuli.*

This appears to be the species most commonly used as *bháji.* Very common in all cultivated lands (*D.*). But Dr. Dymock thinks that the next is the commonest species and the most used.

4. *A. gangeticus* (*A. tristis*, D.). Erect, smooth, branched, tinged with red, leaves long-petioled, waved, ovate or lanceolate obtuse, spikes rather obtuse, sub-erect, the terminal one longer and slightly drooping, flowers crowded, small, green, sepals and stamens 3. *Máti, chulai.*

The following species all seem to be cultivated more or less, and found in cultivated ground, but I have not identified them, and *D.* throughout this order very rarely gives any habitat. The native names are, I think, of very little use in distinguishing the species, and Dr. Dymock gives to No. 4 all the names I have for No. 2, which he calls *pokalá.*

* *A. paniculatus*, tall, thick-stemmed, leaves ovate lanceolate, spikes panicled, red, green, or yellow, sepals and stamens 5, bracts recurved, longer than the sepals. *Kahola-bháji.* Cultivated in India from time immemorial (*H.*). * *A. viridis*, erect, smooth, leaves ovate, the tip rounded or notched, spikes slender, panicled, flowers green, sepals and stamens 3, bracts and sepals membranous with green keel. A common weed in gardens and cultivated ground (*G.*). * *A. tenuifolius* (*Mengea t.* D.) smooth, branched, spreading from the root, leaves small oblong, very variable, clusters of flowers minute, axillary, sepals and stamens 2. *Ghol.*

A. caudatus is the old English garden flower "Love lies bleeding," a romantic name rather calculated to disappoint. *A. hypochondriacus* is Prince's feather. Dr. Gray mentions * *A. salicifolius*, with other species and vars., having brilliant crimson or deep-purple foliage, as common in Bombay gardens.

Deeringia, a shrub, stamens 4 or 5, stigmas 2 to 4, berry seated on the spreading perianth. * *D. celosioides* (*D. baccata*, D.) straggling, stem angled, leaves ovate or lanceolate acute, spikes long, slender, flowers greenish-white, bracts acute, berry round, scarlet. Konkan (*H.*).

4. Pupalia.

P. lappacea. A strong thick-stemmed plant tinged with red, more or less hairy all over, leaves ovate petioled, flowers in long terminal spikes, 2 together below, crowded above, sepals greenish-white, woolly, nerved, stamens pink, awns yellow, utricles large, roundish.

Nasik, common. Guzerat and Kattiawar (*D.*). It is very prickly and clinging in fruit.

* *P. atropurpurea*, described as common in Guzerat, has foliage dark-green, awns long, dark-purple, sepals and bracts broad, ovate, woolly. * *P. orbiculata*, spreading procumbent, leaves very broad, roundish, narrow at the base, spikes stout, clusters round, woolly, awns long and brown. Ghauts (*D.*).

5. Nothosærua.

N. brachiata (*Ærua b.* D.). Smooth, erect or procumbent, stems furrowed, leaves oval oblong entire, spikes short blunt, 3 or 4 often joined at the base, flowers white, bracts broad ovate, persistent.

Panch Mahals. Sind and the Konkan (*H.*). It is very like the next, but smooth.

6. Ærua.

Æ. lanata. Small whitish, branched, leaves oval or roundish, spikes short, solitary or 2 or 3 together, anthers yellow. *Kápur madhurá.*

Poona. A common weed (*G.*).

Æ. Javanica, two or three feet high, branched, leaves lanceolate, oblong, spikes long, flowers white, style and stigma long. Cambay (*D.*), Deccan (*H.*). * *Æ. scandens*, a climbing undershrub, leaves lanceolate, spikes round, ovate, or pyramidal, flowers whitish. Konkan, *Stocks* (*H.*). * *Æ. monsonia*, much-branched, prostrate or ascending, leaves linear, opposite or whorled, sessile, spikes solitary, ovate or cylindric, flowers pink, shining. Konkan and Deccan (*H.*).

7. Achyranthes.

A. aspera. Tall, erect, much-branched, ash-coloured and hairy, leaves obovate rounded, waved, soft above, spikes very long, twiggy, flowers shining, tinged red, pointing downwards, sepals and fruit rough and bristly. *Agára, Surúta, Kharmanjari.*

Poona and the Konkan. A common weed (*G.*). Mahableshwar (*Birdwood*), who calls it the burr plant. Throughout India and Ceylon (*H.*). He has 3 varieties and calls the leaves extremely variable.

* *A. bidentata*, "may prove a form of the last" (*H.*), but has bracteoles reduced to spines with scarcely a blade, or with a minute auricle on each side of the base, and staminodes not fringed. Not in *D.* or *G.* Konkan (*H.*).

8. ALTERNANTHERA.

A. sessilis. A common-looking creeping plant, nearly smooth, stems jointed, leaves ovate lanceolate or obovate, flowers in short conical or roundish spikes, white or pinkish. *Kánchari.*

Poona. A common weed (*D.*). Mahableshwar (*Dr. Cooke*). Throughout hotter India and Ceylon in damp places (*H.*).

The leaves are certainly not always sessile. *R.* called the plant *Achyranthes triandra.*

Cyathula, flowers in clusters much as in *Pupalia*, stamens 5, united below with the staminodes into a cup. * *C. prostrata*, stem creeping, leaves obovate rhomboid, flowers bluish, in small clusters on very slender spikes, the awns hooked, 10 to 20 together, yellowish. Deccan peninsula (*H.*).

Psilostachys, slender herbs with minute flowers all perfect, stamens 5, free. * *P. sericea* (*Psilotrichum s.*, D.). A very beautiful erect plant, leaves broad ovate, silky, flowers in spikes at the tips of the branches, outer sepals deeply ribbed, silky. Coast of Kattywar (*D.*).

Gomphrena globosa, globe amaranth, *jáfri gundi* is very common in native gardens, having large round heads of red flowers with two leafy bracts. "Cultivated in all countries, probably originating in America" (*H.*).

ORDER 95. CHENOPODIACEÆ. The Goosefoot Family.

Herbs or shrubs, mostly succulent, with small and inconspicuous flowers, generally green; leaves simple, alternate, without stipules, perianth of 3 to 5 sepals, united at the base, stamens usually 5, opposite the sepals, anthers 2-celled, ovary superior, stigmas 2 to 4, fruit a one-seeded achene, enclosed in the perianth, which is then often enlarged or fleshy.

This, like the last, is an unattractive order, but useful from many of its species being used as pot-herbs. Most of the order occur as weeds on the seashore or in saline desert regions, and very many species are tinged with red. The flowers are generally without the stiff dry bracts which distinguish the last order, and the leaves without the stipules which mark the next.

1. CHENOPODIUM. Stem angled, flowers minute, in axillary clusters.

2. ATRIPLEX. Flowers mostly unisexual, sepals of male flowers 5, of female none, but in their place 2 bracts, which unite and form a cover for the fruit, stigmas 2.

3. ARTHROCNEMUM. Fleshy and leafless, with jointed stems, flowers minute, 2 or 3 together in the joints of the short spikes perianth undivided, stamen one.

4. SUEDA. Leaves linear fleshy, flowers, minute axillary, sepals and stamens 5.

5. BASELLA. A much-branched fleshy twiner; flowers in spikes with 2 bracts united to the 5-lobed perianth; achene round included.

1. CHENOPODIUM. Goosefoot.

C. album. An erect plant, stems often striped with green, red or purple, leaves very variable, angled or egg-shaped, toothed or lobed, clusters of flowers in spikes, seed smooth, shining, and keeled. *Chákvit, ghánen.*

Not in *D.* Several varieties are cultivated as pot-herbs (*G.*). The cultivated forms vary from green to red (*H.*).

The leaves are often covered with meal, from which the plant gets in England the name of white goosefoot. It is there very common in waste places and cultivated fields, and was formerly used for food (as in India now), like many other wild plants. For in the seventeenth century Fuller wrote—"Weeds are counted herbs in the beginning of spring, nettles are put in pottage, and salads are made of elder buds."

C. ambrosoides, a tall, rank, aromatic, much-branched plant, Mr. Birdwood has in his Matheran list under the name of *Sherui*, and Dr. Dymock *Chandanbativá, vásuke.*

2. ATRIPLEX. Orache.

A. hortensis. Stout erect, leaves not mealy, triangular cordate, upper ovate lanceolate, flowers polygamous in axillary spikes and terminal panicles, bracts nearly free, roundish. *Juri.*

Cultivated as a spinach in several varieties, tinged with red or purple (*D.*). "Once very generally cultivated in England for the table, and called orach, orage, or mountain spinach, and still cultivated in Paris"—*Pratt.* Its cultivation in kitchen gardens in England has lately been revived.

* *A. Stocksii* (*Obione S.*, D.). Shrubby, leaves small, petioled, oblong or roundish, whitish or glaucous, male clusters axillary, or in short leafy spikes, fruiting bracts roundish from a narrow base. Guzerat, common near the sea (*D.*). Kurrachee (*H.*).

3. ARTHROCNEMUM.

* *A. Indicum.* Stem prostrate, spreading, half shrubby, branches alternate with short joints, spikes large cylindric. *Machur, ghuri.*

Common in salt ground (*D.* and *G.*). I have not seen this, but it appears to differ very little from the English jointed glass wort

(*Salicornia herbacea*), which looks as if made of green glass, and has spikes and branches very much alike.

4. Sueda. Sea blite.

1. *S. nudiflora.* A prostrate spreading heath-like plant, a good deal tinged with red, leaves narrow lanceolate or linear, becoming more fleshy and cylindrical as they get older, flowers in leafy spikes, 4 or 5 together, green or reddish, looking almost like a 5-lobed berry, styles 3. *Moras.*

The above is my description of *S. Indica*, D., which *H.* includes in this, though the two plants seem to me to be separate. Like others of the order this grows near the seashore in Salsette, Bassein, &c.; which might well be described by those who are not botanists as "wide flats where nothing but coarse grasses grow."

2. *S. maritima.* Erect plant, with woody stems, much branched from the root, glaucous tinged with red, leaves linear or cylindrical, flowers very numerous in slender spikes, the anthers alone conspicuous, styles 2.

Not in *D.* *G.* No. 1250: in similar situations as the last. *H.* makes it identical with the English annual sea blite, in which the leaves are generally half cylindrical, and the habit not shrubby.

5. Basella.

B. rubra (*B. alba*, D.). A pretty twiner, smooth, stems red or green, leaves broad ovate, heart-shaped or roundish, flowers in spikes, simple or branched, fruit size of a pea, red, white or black. *Miál ki bháji, yál chi bháji, velgond.*

Throughout India, wild or cultivated (*H.*).

There seem to be several varieties all cultivated and used as spinach.

To this order also belong *Beta vulgaris*, beetroot, wild on the English coast, *pálak, chukandar*, but generally known in W. India as *beet*: the mangel wurzel is a variety of the same; and *Spinacia oleracea*, spinach, *pálak*, but generally called, like other leaves used for the same purpose, *bháji*.

Order 96. POLYGONACEÆ. Buckwheats.

Herbs, rarely shrubs, leaves generally alternate, stipules conspicuous, chaffy or membranous, usually sheathing the stem, perianth inferior of 3 to 6 imbricated sepals, united at the base, nut hard, usually enclosed in the perianth, often triangular.

The remarkable stipules are generally enough to distinguish this order, which otherwise bears much resemblance to the last two. Many of the species are tinged with red. The flowers of some species are handsome, but most would ordinarily be called weeds. But then comes the question,—

> "Of all that deck the lanes, the fields, the bowers,
> What parts the kindred tribes of weeds and flowers?"—*Cowper.*

POLYGONUM. Flowers clustered or spiked with bracts, stems thickened at the nodes, and appearing to be jointed, stamens any number up to 8, styles 2 or 3.

H. calls this a very troublesome genus, and has 70 species, many of them with several varieties.

1. *P. plebeium* (*P. elegans*, D.). A small, prostrate plant, with numerous stems, leaves lanceolate, smooth, stipules large, white, ragged and hairy, flowers few in the axils, deep rose-coloured, stamens 3 to 8, very short.

In good specimens this is a very pretty heath-like little plant, sometimes red all over. I have had it at Mahableshwar, in Salsette, and the Panch Mahâls; but it is not plain whether *D.* thought it common or not. *H.* has 10 varieties, one or more found all over India.

2. *P. glabrum.* A tall, smooth, reddish plant, leaves long, lanceolate, oleander-like, flowers pink, in long-stalked spikes or racemes, stamens about 7, seeds ovate, compressed. *Raktrura, sheral.*

In river beds, in the Deccan, Konkan and Ghauts; and common in most parts of India (*H.*). He says it is difficult to separate this from smooth forms of *P. persicana*, which is so common in moist places in England; but this is much larger, and less branched. The English plant has generally a dark mark in the middle of the leaf, which, I believe, does not occur in Indian specimens.

3. *P. barbatum* (*P. rivulare*, D.). Smaller than the last, leaves slightly hairy, stems, stipules and bracts very much so, flowers pinkish, in long spikes, seeds triangular, stamens 5 to 8. *Dhâktâ sheral.*

In the same situations as the last. Throughout the hotter parts of India (*H.*).

4. *P. Chinense.* A climber, half shrubby, stems red, leaves oblong, subcordate, hairy, stipules long, lanceolate, entire, flowers in small, nearly round heads, white, with violet anthers, bracts auricled, stamens 8. *Paral, nárali.*

Mahableshwar, very common: confined to the Ghauts (*D.*). It seems from *H.* to be found everywhere in the hills in India. He calls it "a rambling, or erect shrub; a polymorphous plant."

* *P. alatum*, leaves ovate, narrowed into a broadly winged, often stem-clasping petiole, stipules tubular, obliquely truncate, flowers white, or pale purple, stamens 7 or 8 included, nut crowned by the sepals. Canara (*H.*) He has 7 vars. *P. pedunculare*, smooth stem, sometimes prickly, leaves elliptic, the base very variable, stamens 5 to 8, with alternating glands, nut roundish, included. Konkan (*H.*).

Rumex, stipules often disappearing with age, sepals 6, the inner 3 enlarging, and containing the fruit, stamens 6, styles 3, nuts triangular. * *R. dentatus*, leaves oblong, obtuse, often contracted above the rounded or cordate base, fruiting perianth with an oblong, smooth tubercle, and broad, irregularly-toothed wings. Konkan (*H.*). * *R. nepalensis*, tall and branched, radical leaves large, oblong, ovate, with broad, or cordate base, racemes long, tubercle as in the last, wings pectinated. Ghauts (*H.*). The last four are not in *D.*

To this genus belong the docks and sorrels. *R. vesicarius*, country sorrel, *chuka*, *chákvat*, is cultivated. "The numerous species of Polygonum and Rumex are scattered everywhere from the seashore to the snow line."—*Le Maout.*

Fagopyrum esculentum (*Polygonum fagopyrum*, D.) is the common buckwheat, supposed to belong originally to E. Asia, cultivated throughout N. Asia and Central Europe, growing in the poorest soil, and with little care. It is known to have been cultivated in England in the 16th century. It has the red stems and spikes or panicles of pinkish-white flowers characteristic of the *Polygonums*. *F. tataricum* (*Polygonum*, *t.* D.) is cultivated in the Deccan and Guzerat, the grain being eaten by Brahmins on fast days; leaves broad, spikes of flowers white, scarlet, or yellow, very handsome. *Rájagar.*

To this order also belongs *Rheum*, rhubarb, of which many species are found wild in the Himalayas. "The officinal rhubarb is the root of an undetermined species. The best is said to come from the very heart of Thibet, five or six hundred miles N. of Assam; but it is produced of one sort and another from many different species." —*Balfour.*

ORDER 97. PODOSTEMONACEÆ.

Aquatic plants growing on stones in streams, flowers usually enclosed in a spathe, inconspicuous, and generally very imperfect; filaments flat, anthers 2-lobed.

I know nothing of this order but from books, but in appearance the species seem to be more like lichens than flowering plants, and all known in India are of the smallest possible size.

1. TERNIOLA. Stems confluent into an expanded horizontal lobed frond, leaves minute, bristle-like, usually forming a sheath round the base of the pedicel, perianth transparent, 3-lobed, stamens and style 3, capsule ovoid.

2. Podostemon. Flowers sessile, in a little spathe, perianth of 2 or 3 scales, stamens 2, connate below, with 2 linear staminodes, capsule long-stalked, ovoid.

Of *Terniola* there are 5 species, attributed by *D.* to Konkan rivers on Mr. Law's authority, and for only one of these has *H.* any other habitat. The stems of all are frond-like and horizontal, and the size of the largest is put at ¼ of an inch in diameter.

Two *Podostemons* are given, one moss-like, from one to two inches broad; the other (not in *D.*) attributed by *H.* to streams of the W. Ghauts, but no size given.

Order 98. ARISTOLOCHIACEÆ. The Birthwort Family.

Herbs or shrubs, often climbing, leaves alternate, without stipules, perianth superior, generally large and tubular, anthers 6 or more, subsessile, inserted in a ring round the base of the style, which is short and columnar, stigma large and lobed, fruit a capsule or berry.

This is a small order, mainly of tropical America, with rather strong medicinal qualities. The perianth in Aristolochia is of an unusual shape, being rather like that of *Ceropegia*, and also resembling, to some extent, the pitchers of Nepenthes (pitcher plants) which belong to an allied order. In that case, however, the pitchers are appendages of the leaf. In this order the number and arrangement of the stamens are also distinctive. There is one of the genus in England, *A. clematitis*, generally considered to be wild.

Aristolochia. Petioles with dilated base, perianth with tube dilated at the base, then contracted and with a wide limb, obliquely one or two-lipped, anthers 6, style very short, 3 to 6-lobed, capsule 6-valved.

1. *A. bracteata.* A smooth glaucous plant, spreading nearly flat on the ground, leaves heart-shaped or kidney-shaped; flowers solitary axillary, green and claret-colour, hairy inside, lip strap-shaped, pedicel thick, with a heart-shaped or roundish bract attached, capsule oblong melon-shaped, seeds heart-shaped, thin. *Kiramár, gandáti.*

Guzerat and Deccan.

The thickened ribbed pedicel looks like an inferior ovary.

2. * *A. Indica.* Shrubby, smooth and twining leaves from linear to obovate, waved, flowers in racemes erect, dark green and brown, bract opposite the base of the penduncle, capsule oblong grooved, seeds flat, triangular, winged. *Sámpsan.*

Leaves exceedingly variable (*H.*).

Konkan hills, not very common (*D.* and *G.*). Throughout the low country of India (*H.*).

This is one of the plants said to be an antidote to the cobra's bite, sought out and used by the Mungoose.—*Tennent.* "In some American species, one or two of which are grown in Indian gardens, the perianth is almost large enough to form a bonnet for a child."—*Oliver.*

Bragantia, perianth shortly campanulate, equally 3-lobed, deciduous, stamens 6 to 12 in one series, connective thick, style short, stigmas 3 or more, capsule long, 4-cornered. * *B. Wallichii*, shrubby, diœcious, branches angled, leaves oblong lanceolate, large, flowers large in small irregular cymes, lobes of perianth broad ovate, stigmas 9, fruit like a silique, 4 inches long. Wári country and Canara (*D.*). * *B. Dalzelii* appears to depend on a single specimen found in Dalzell's herbarium, and to differ from the last in the leaves capsule and seeds being very much larger.

ORDER 99. PIPERACEÆ. Peppers.

Aromatic herbs or shrubs, leaves entire, flowers minute in catkin-like spikes, each supported by a peltate bract, perianth none, stamens 2 to 6 hypogynous.

Note.—In a true catkin the flowers are unisexual, here they are often hermaphrodite.

This order and the two next may be called the spice orders, containing between them—

> "Each spicy rind which sultry India boasts,
> Scenting the night air round her breezy coasts."
>
> *Dr. Darwin.*

1. PIPER. Shrubs with swollen nodes, leaves often unequal-sided, flowers generally diœcious, filaments short, stigmas 2 to 5, berry ovoid or roundish.

2. PEPEROMIA. Succulent herbs, flowers hermaphrodite, stamens 2, very short, stigma usually tufted, fruit minute.

1. PIPER.

H. has 45 species, but considers them very imperfectly identified.

P. nigrum (*P. trioicum*, D.). A large climber clinging very close to trees, leaves polished, ovate acute cordate, often unequal at the base, veined lighter, flowers in pendulous spikes, berries in racemes, rather fleshy, size of a pea, one-sided. *Kákar vel, rán miri.*

This, as *H.* has settled the species, produces, when cultivated, in the unripe dried berries, black peper, *kála miri*, and in the ripe fruit, with the outer covering removed, white pepper. Lanoli, Matheran, &c. *H.* seems doubtful as to it being often found wild.

* *P. Hookeri, D.* says, is easily distinguished by the rather long petioles being thickly clothed with whitish hairs. Common on the Mahableshwar hills (*D.*). *Dongri mirchi. D.* has also * *P. sylvestre*, which *H.* does not refer to, and I cannot make out the difference from *P. nigrum.* Mr. Birdwood has it at Matheran. * *P. tricho-stachyum*, smooth, stem stout and woody, leaves large, elliptic, spikes stout, 3 or 4 inches long, male flowers sunk in a fleshy sessile roundish receptacle, formed of the greatly enlarged bract. Not in *D.* or *G.* Konkan, Canara, and Khandalla (*H.*).

P. longum produces in the dried flower spikes, long pepper, *pipal, pipri, Bengáli-pipli;* the root *pipli mul* (*Dymock*). *P. betle, támbol,* supplies *pán* leaves for use with betel nut, and is extensively cultivated. "The Khásias, who are exceedingly addicted to *pán*, estimate distances by the number of mouthfuls they eat on the road."—*Hooker.*

2. Peperomia.

* *P. portulacoides.* Stem smooth, erect from a creeping base, leaves opposite, or upper ones whorled, obovate or oblong, spikes stout, longer than the leaves, axillary or terminal. *Mirwal.*

Common on the S. Ghauts on moist rocks and branches of trees (*D.*). *H.* does not refer to *D.*, and gives no habitat N. of Travancore.

* *P. Wightiana*, straggling, slender, smooth, leaves oblong or roundish, very variable, spikes very slender, one to three together. Not in *D.* or *G.* Konkan on trees (*H.*).

Order 100. MYRISTICEÆ. Nutmegs.

Evergreen, generally aromatic, trees, leaves alternate entire without stipules, flowers diœcious, small, regular, perianth 3-lobed, stamens several, monadelphous, or none; fruit fleshy, but opening like a capsule by 2 valves, seed one, nut-like, enclosed in a coloured aril.

"All parts of the Myristiceæ are aromatic."—*Le Maout.*

The fruit may be considered to characterize this small but important order, which is in many respects very like Anonaceæ. There are in W. India only two species, both more or less rare.

Myristica—as the order.

* *M. malabarica.* A tall tree, smooth with reddish bark, leaves large, narrow, oblong or lanceolate, more or less shining above, glaucous below, flowers in panicles, perianth round; male flowers with a persistent scale-like bract at the base, and

10 to 15 anthers united in a column, female flowers larger and fewer, fruit olong, pubescent, 2 or 3 inches long. *Ránjaiphal.*

Dense woods of the Ghauts (*D.*). Konkan, Canara, and Malabar only (*H.*). The aril of this is called *Máyapatri* or *Rámpatri.*

* *M. alternata*, apparently like the above, but young shoots and petioles covered with rusty meal, the male flowers fascicled on a short peduncle, perianth roundish, anthers 12 on the toothed edge of a stalked peltate disk, fruit ovate, beaked, rusty, 1½ inch long. Ghauts (*D.*). Deep ravines at Khandalla, but not common (*G.*). He calls it a very handsome tree, with something of the habit of Michelia champaca.

"The nutmeg tree (*M. fragrans, officinalis,* or *moschata*) has a one-seeded fruit like a peach, that splits open and exposes the nutmeg (*jaiphal*), surrounded by a brilliant scarlet aril; this aril, which is mace (*jayapatri*) no doubt attracts pigeons, which swallow the nutmegs, and transport them from island to island of the Moluccas" *Hooker*. Aromatic fruits, more or less resembling the nutmeg, are found in other species.

In the middle ages and later Arabia was looked on as the land of spices and perfumes, because these sweet-smelling products came to Europe through Arabia, or by the intervention of Arab merchants.

"All the perfumes of Arabia will not sweeten this little hand."
Macbeth.

But when the Portuguese in the sixteenth century had possession of the Moluccas, they got the name of the spice islands, and when the Dutch ousted the Portuguese, these islands were called the gold mines of the Dutch East India Company. To keep up the price the Dutch forced the native rulers to restrict the number of all spice-producing trees, and in many cases even to destroy great numbers of them. They thus managed to confine the production of each sort of spice to one or two islands.—*Raynal, Cook, &c.*

Order 101.—LAURINEÆ. Laurels.

Trees or shrubs (except *Cassytha*), leaves alternate, gland-dotted, without stipules, flowers regular, perianth tubular, usually 6-cleft, stamens on the tube in 2 or more rows, filaments flattened, some of them often with 2 glands at the base, anthers erect, ovary superior, at the base of the tube.

The trees and shrubs of this order are generally fragrant and valuable. They mostly possess in the bark and other parts an oil, which in different species has either stimulating or sedative qualities, represented in their maximum intensity by cinnamon and camphor respectively. From the beauty and celebrity of the true laurels, the name has been given to various trees of other orders, as the laurel and Portugal laurel of English gardens, which both belong to the genus Prunus. But the true laurel, in Greek Daphne, the tree of Apollo—

"the meed
Of mighty conquerors and poets sage" (*Spenser*),

is *Laurus nobilis*, called in England the bay-tree, and supposed to have been brought to Europe from Asia Minor in very early times; while the shrubs botanically termed Daphne (in English, Mezereon and Spurge laurel) belong not to this, but to the next order. See also under *Croton*.

1. CINNAMONUM. Flowers small in panicles, females usually the longest, often with fewer parts, perianth tube short, perfect stamens 9 or fewer in 3 rows, with a row of staminodes, anthers 4-celled, fruit seated on the enlarged perianth.

2. MACHILUS. Flowers in panicles, perianth tube short or none, perfect stamens 9 in 3 rows, with a row of staminodes, anthers 4-celled, berry seated on the perianth.

3. ALSEODAPHNE. Leaves more or less collected at the end of the branches, flowers in panicles, stamens, staminodes, and anthers as in the last, fruit seated on the thickened peduncle.

4. LITSÆA. Flowers diœcious, umbelled, with concave bracts, stamens 6 and upwards, anthers 4-celled, fruit seated on the often enlarged perianth tube.

5. CASSYTHA. Filiform twining leafless parasites, flowers minute with 3 bracts, perfect stamens 9, anthers 2-celled, fruit enclosed in the succulent perianth tube and crowned by its segments.

1. CINNAMONUM.

* *C. zeylanicum*, the cinnamon tree. A good-sized tree, leaves broad lanceolate or ovate, 3 to 5-nerved, panicle downy or silky, flowers small, greenish white, fruit oblong, dry. *Ohej, bojvár.*

"The cinnamon tree shoots forth its leaves in all shades from bright yellow to dark crimson."—*Tennent.*

The cultivated cinnamon tree is generally supposed to be found in India only in gardens; but *G.'s C. iners* (not in *D.*) is believed by Colonel Beddome, Dr. Dymock, and others, to be only a variety of the above, and *H.*, though giving *C. iners* as a separate species, seems to incline to the same opinion. *G.* makes it grow all along the range of Ghauts and in the hilly parts of the Konkans; it is not, however, in Mr. Birdwood's Matheran and Mahableshwar list, though he has a species, *C. tamala, Máhárukh,* which *H.* ascribes only to the Himalayas and N. India. Dr. Dymock thought that the further N. the cinnamon tree is found, the thicker and more mucilaginous is the bark.

C. cassia, or an allied species, produces the Cassia bark of China, which Sir J. Hooker believes to be the Cassia of Ex. xxx. 24 and Psl. xlv. 8. Camphor is produced from the wood of *C. camphora*, which *H.* says is commonly cultivated in India; but there are other native species, which produce inferior sorts. (For the drug Cassia, see p. 96.)

2. Machilus.

M. micrantha. A pretty tree, leaves oblong, lanceolate, smooth, glaucous beneath, flowers greenish, hairy, ovary round, fruit like a large black currant or small gooseberry. *Gulamb, Kurma, bobarsa.*

H. includes *D.'s M. glaucescens* in this. The panicles of flowers are much like those of the Mango. Lanoli, Matheran. The Ghauts (*D.*).

3. Alseodaphne.

* *A. semecarpifolia.* A small tree very variable in foliage, leaves obovate, smooth, glaucous beneath, often unequal-sided; panicles more or less umbellate, flower stalks rather long, fruit elliptical, as long as the swollen and warty peduncle. *Gulumbi, vivárana, ráni.*

Matheran (*Birdwood*). The Ghauts (*D.*). *H.* has four varieties; one of them, ascribed to the Konkan, has the young parts rufous and hoary.

4. Litsæa.

1. *L. Stocksii* (*Actinodaphne lanceolata*, D.). A pretty tree with bluish-grey leaves, lanceolate, drooping in tufts from the end of the branches, about 6 together, racemes of about 8 flowers, short, tawny and silky, bracts large obovate, deciduous, fruit oval like a small red acorn in a green cup. *Pesha, gulchai.*

The Ghauts; very common at Matheran and Mahableshwar. A remarkable tree from the colour and elegant shape and arrangement of the leaves. *H.* has 3 varieties.

Dr. Dymock agreed with me as to this identification of the *Pesha*, but Mr. Birdwood has it as *Actinodaphne Hookeri*, and Dr. King, of Calcutta, I am told, declared it to be *Litsæa fuscata*, with the description of which this appears to me not to agree at all, and which *H.* ascribes only to Ceylon, at an altitude of 6000 to 8000 feet! But as *H.* has 65 species of Litsæa there is evidently room for a good deal of difference of opinion.

* 2. *L. tomentosa* (*Tetranthera apetala*, D.). All downy except the upper side of the oblong petioled leaves, umbels large, solitary, many-flowered, involucre 4-leaved, flowers minute, perianth none or incomplete, stamens 18 to 20, fila-

ments long and slender, glands long-stalked, fruit round, smooth, black, size of a pea. *Chikná, wáras, miri.*

Matheran (*Birdwood*). Vingorla and Ghauts (*D.*). Of one variety of *L. sebifera*, which *H.* ascribes in one form or other to all the hotter parts of India, he says: "Except by the compound umbels, this is undistinguishable from *L. tomentosa*," and he favours the opinion of Dalzell and Gibson, that *tomentosa* and *sebifera* are forms of one species. "The bark is the *maida-lakri* of the shops" (*Dymock*).

* *L. Wightiana* (*Cylicodaphne W.*, D.), leaves broad-lanceolate, crowded about the ends of the branches, umbels racemed, covered with rusty hairs, bracts 4, stamens about 12, fruit like *L. Stocksii*, but the cup sometimes toothed. *Kengi.* Ghauts (*Lisboa*). Canara (*H.*). * *L. zeylanica*, a small tree, leaves variable, oblong, glaucous beneath, bracts and flowers yellowish, silky, fruit roundish on the disk-like perianth. Párwar Ghaut (*D.*).

5. Cassytha.

Nothing could be less like the family generally than this genus of leafless parasites, which, except for the species here given, is confined to Australia and S. Africa.

C. filiformis. All yellowish-green and downy, flowers very small in small spikes, the enlarged perianth white, fleshy, as large as a marble, containing the black pea-like fruit. *Akasvel.* (See *Cuscuta.*)

Common, especially in Guzerat. It runs over hedges in such a tangled mass as to be suggestive of seaweed left on the shore by the waves. It is larger in Guzerat than the Konkan. The fruit is like that of the garden nasturtium (*Tropæolum majus*). *G.* calls it the air plant.

Cryptocaria, flowers small in panicles, perianth ovoid or top-shaped, stamens as in Machilus, anthers 2-celled. * *C. Wightiana* (*C. floribunda*, D.), leaves oval oblong, glaucous beneath, flowers yellow, fruit black, glossy, round or oblong. Tullawárí, plentiful (*D.*). From Canara southwards (*H.*). * *C. Stocksii*, very similar, but the leaves much smaller and usually very obtuse, panicles short and dense, flowers larger, fruit smaller, ovoid. Not in *D.* or *G.* Canara (*H.*).

Beilschmiedia, flowers and stamens as in the last, perianth tube short, fruit quite free of the deciduous perianth. * *B. fagifolia* (*B. Roxburghiana*, D.), a large tree, leaves oblong or broad-lanceolate, shining, young flowers enclosed in broad, silky, deciduous scales, fruit one to two inches long, oblong or roundish. Common on the Ghauts (*D.*). *H.* doubts about the identification of this tree.

Actinodaphne, flowers diœcious, more or less umbelled, with densely-imbricated bracts, perfect stamens 6 to 9, in 3 series, anthers 4-celled, fruit seated on the enlarged perianth tube. * *A. Hookeri*, young leaves and branches almost woolly, leaves ovate lanceolate with long points, flowers silky, fruit very small. Not in *D.* or *G.* Konkan, Canara and Ghauts (*H.*).

Order 102. THYMELEACEÆ. The Daphne Family.

Shrubs or trees, with simple entire leaves without stipules, perianth regular, tubular, 4 or 5-lobed, ovary superior.

The Daphnes are known to many: "Small evergreens of great beauty and fragrance in the flower, and with a peculiar velvet texture in the leaf" (*Loudon*). They have also very tough barks. *H.* has three species as natives of the Himalayas, and one of Burmah, but I find no mention of any as introduced into gardens in W. India.

The single species of the order found here is easily recognizable.

Lasiosiphon. Silky shrubs, flowers in dense heads with broad bracts, perianth cylindric, lobes 5, small, spreading, with 5 to 10 scales above the 10 stamens, fruit small, dry, included in the base of the perianth.

L. eriocephalus (*L. speciosus*, D.). A large and pretty shrub with lanceolate rather acute leaves and dense heads of small yellow flowers surrounded by a large leafy involucre, perianth and bracts silky. *Rámetta.*

Very common and conspicuous on the Ghauts and Konkan hills. *H.* has it as a small tree or large bush, but it is only in the latter form, I believe, that it is known with us. *G.* calls it octandrous, and I believe that there may often be a confusion between the stamens and the scales. It seems in India to be confined to the Peninsula.

Order 103. ELÆAGNACEÆ. Oleasters.

Shrubs or trees, more or less covered with minute silvery or brown scurfy scales; flowers small, regular, perianth tubular, stamens adhering to the tube, ovary free, fruit enclosed in the perianth tube.

This is a small order, in characteristics much like the last. Only one species is known in W. India. The oleaster, or wild olive, *E. angustifolia,* was in ancient times nearly as famous as the olive itself. "The tree that grows carelessly, tufting the rocks with no vivid bloom, no verdure of branch; only with soft snow of blossom and scarcely full-filled fruit, mixed with grey leaf and thorn-set stem: . . . type of grey honour and sweet rest."—*Ruskin.*

Eleagnus. Stamens 4, style linear, stigma lateral.

E. latifolia. A large climber, all silvery with oval leaves, dotted above, white below, flowers several together, sessile, pale in colour, lobes 4, pistil within the tube, fruit oblong or oval, red, size of an olive. *Ámgul, nurgi.*

Matheran, Mahableshwar and Ghauts, common. *H.* has it as very variable in habit, bush, small tree, or climber, but it appears to be known in W. India only as the last. Mr. Birdwood says that the leaves are silvery-white or rusty-red beneath.

ORDER 104. LORANTHACEÆ. The Mistletoe Family.

It naturally puzzles students to find an order of plants, the flowers of which have a complete corolla as well as calyx, in the middle of the Monochlamydeous orders. Loranthaceæ, by Bentham and Oliver, as well as by other authorities less connected with Kew, was put among the calycifiorals near Araliaceæ and Rubiaceæ. *H.*, however, groups the order according to its less obvious affinities, and the reason is, I suppose, that which I find in another book—that the petals are looked on as being in reality sepals, and the calycine rim as being only an expansion of the pedicel. At the same time *H.*, in the description both of the order and of some of the species, writes of calyx and corolla in the ordinary way.

Parasitic shrubs, leaves usually opposite, often thick and fleshy, entire, without stipules; calyx adherent to the ovary, limb truncate, rarely toothed; petals 4 to 8 free or united, stamens as many as the petals and opposite to them, ovary inferior, fruit a one-seeded berry or drupe.

1. LORANTHUS. Flowers conspicuous, generally with bracts, corolla tube generally split on one side, lobes 4 or 5.

2. VISCUM. Flowers unisexual, very small and pale-coloured, calyx without any prominent border, petals 4, anthers broad, attached to the petals, stigma large, fruit fleshy and pulpy.

1. LORANTHUS.

Note.—H. has 58 species, of which 13 are found in W. India.

Brandis has *bánd* as a name for most of the plants of this order, which Dr. Dymock makes *wándá*, and calls a general name for all parasites. I noted *godmal* as a name generally given to the different species of Loranthus, amongst which there is a very strong similarity.

1. *L. obtusatus.* A large species, smooth, leaves oval obtuse, broad and thick, flowers in erect racemes at right angles to the stiff pedicels with a bract at the angle, corolla green with red lobes, flower bud 4-angled, fruit ovoid or roundish.

Mahableshwar. Ghauts (*H.*).

2. *L. longiflorus.* Large and handsome, all smooth, leaves oblong or ovate, flowers in racemes, tube long-curved, white or pink, lobes 5, curled back, green; stamens exserted, anthers red, fruit oval of a beautiful pink crowned by the calyx.

This is like honeysuckle. *H.* has 3 varieties, "leaves infinitely variable." Very common in the Konkan. Also in the Deccan and Guzerat. Nearly all over India (*H.*). Grows on most trees (*Brandis*)—but with us especially on the Mango, on which its roots make great unsightly knots.

3. *L. cuneatus.* A small species, smooth except the young parts ; leaves small obovate, narrowed at the base, flowers 3 or 4 together in short umbels, corolla tube green, lobes 5 red, throat streaked, bract small acute.

Common at Matheran, especially on *jámbul* trees; also at Mahableshwar. Ghauts (*D.*).

4. *L. elasticus.* A large woody smooth species, all olive-coloured and tinged with red, leaves broad and thick, flowers clustered on the branches, corolla long slender, white and green, the 5 lobes twisted, stigma and anthers bright red, fruit oval.

Dapoli and Kashedy (N.E. boundary of Rutnagherry Collectorate), where it is very common on *pipal* trees. Vingorla (*D.*). Mahableshwar (*Birdwood*).

5. *L. lageniferus.* Woody, leaves sessile or short-petioled, broad ovate or cordate at base, veined red ; a large bell-shaped reddish involucre with 5 shallow lobes is almost sessile on the branches, and contains 5 or 6 green flowers, long-tubed, erect, 5-lobed.

Matheran. Khandalla (*G.*). Pretty common on the higher hills (*D.*).

6. *L. loniceroides.* Smooth, leaves ovate lanceolate, flowers white, tinged with red, in short racemes, corolla tube long, curved, lobes 6 ; bracts 3, roundish, at the base of the ovary ; fruit smooth, oval, crowned by the calyx.

Common in the Konkan and Ghauts. This is much like No. 2 and also like honeysuckle.

* *L. capitellatus* is thought to be only a var. of this last, differing in the straight corolla and very long peduncle. Chorla Ghaut (*D.*). *L. Wallichianus*, smooth, leaves oval lanceolate, flowers in small short umbels, corolla green with 4 equal red lobes, much bulged at the base, fruit top-shaped: it comes nearest to No. 2. Mahableshwar. Rotanda Ghaut (*D.* and *G.*). * *L. scurrula* (*L. buddleioides*, D.). A large bush, very variable in pubescence, form and size of leaves, and inflorescence ; leaves elliptic to cordate ovate, peduncles very short, few-flowered, corolla buff or pink, tube split, lobes 4, fruit pear-shaped. On *ásana* and *karmal* trees at Khandalla (*D.* and *G.*). * *L. pulveruleutus*, stout, woody, young parts covered with dense white meal, leaves long petioled, ovate, flowers pale green in short racemes, corolla slender, curved, the tube split, 4-divided, fruit club-shaped. Not in *D.* or *G.* Konkan (*Stocks, Brandis*). * *L. involucratus*, woody with slender branches, leaves ovate or cordate, flowers in clusters, each in an involucre of 4 distinct leafy bracts, corolla tube split, lobes 5, style

and stigma large. Matheran (*Birdwood*). Bhimashankar (*D.* and *G.*).

The two following appear to be very slightly known; they are not in *D.* and *G.* *H.* ascribes the first to the Konkan, and the second to Canara. * *L. Stocksii*, leaves small opposite, covered with buff meal, flowers solitary, axillary, sessile, calyx limb truncate, fruit pear-shaped. * *L. trigonus*, smooth with very thick branches, branchlets 3-cornered, leaves very large, broad elliptic obtuse, flowers in short racemes, bracts forming a small cup, corolla 5-lobed.

2. Viscum. Mistletoe.

1. *V. angulatum.* Leafless with very numerous green jointed branches, lower ones round dichotomous, upper ones in verticils 3 or 4 angled, flowers sessile arranged round the joints.

S. Ghauts, not very common apparently. Mahableshwar, *Dr. Cooke*, who calls it Indian mistletoe. The peninsula (*H.*).

2. *V. articulatum.* Like the last, but the branches flat and flexible, broadening from each joint upwards, flowers several together at the joints, berry round tubercled when young, afterwards smooth and succulent.

Not in *D.* but in *G.* (No. 665), "common throughout the Konkans and in the Ghauts." I had it in S. Konkan, and in the Dhánu taluka, common. Deccan peninsula (*H.*).

G. has *V. Wightianum* with round stem and branches, and flat obtuse leaves, common on trees at Mahableshwar towards the Rotunda Ghaut; but this appears to be not otherwise known.

V. album is the European mistletoe, a plant much connected with ancient religious and superstitious rites.

> "Garlands of Spanish moss and of mystic mistletoe flaunted,
> Such as the Druids cut down with golden hatchets at Yule-tide."
> *Longfellow.*

The berries of the mistletoe, of *Loranthus albus*, and of other species of this order, produce the best and most tenacious bird-lime.

Order 105. SANTALACEÆ. Sandalwoods.

Leaves entire without stipules, flowers inconspicuous, regular, usually bracted, perianth more or less tubular of 3 to 8 divisions, stamens 3 to 6, ovary inferior, fruit a nut or drupe.

A small order, with much likeness to Thymeleaceæ and Eleagnaceæ.

1. SANTALUM. Smooth trees, perianth adherent to the base of the ovary with 4 or 5 lobes, stamens 5 or 4 with alternating scales, style long, stigma 2 or 3-lobed.

2. OSYRIS. Shrubs with angular branches, perianth with 3 or 4 triangular lobes, stamens 4 or 5, stigma 3 or 4-lobed.

1. SANTALUM.

S. album. Sandalwood tree. Leaves opposite, ovate elliptic acute at the base, petioles flat; flowers in panicles, small, brownish purple, drupe size of a large pea, dark purple or black, shining. *Chándan.*

H. makes the flowers first straw-coloured, then blood-red, and the drupe size of a cherry; habitat from Poona southwards, elsewhere planted. The Abbé Raynal describes it under the unromantic name of the Sanders tree. Some authorities consider that the algum or almug tree of Scripture (1 Kings x. 11; 2 Chron. ii. 8, &c.) was the Sandal (*Dictionary of the Bible*), but Hooker thinks it was probably either Pterocarpus santalinus, or Bombay blackwood (*Teachers' Bible*). The ancient Hindoos had no liking for the tree: Sir M. Williams quotes from the "Hitopadesa": "The root is infested by serpents, the blossoms by bees, the branches by monkeys, the summit by bears. In short, there is not a part of the sandal tree that is not occupied by the vilest impurities."

2. OSYRIS.

O. arborea (*O. Wightiana*, D.). Leaves alternate oval, fleshy, flowers minute green, the male and female on different racemes or heads, drupe long-stalked, round, orange or red, pretty. *Lotal, popli.*

Hills at Sattara. Mahableshwar and Khandalla (*Dr. Cooke*). Common on the Ghauts (*D.*).

I noted that the leaves are covered with white bloom, and was long before I could get this corroborated; but I believe that this bloom goes off as the leaves get older.

Note.—G.'s Osyris peltata is *Macaranga Roxburghii.*

ORDER 106. EUPHORBIACEÆ. The Spurge Family.

Herbs, shrubs or trees, generally with milky and acrid juice, leaves generally alternate, simple, and stipulate; flowers small, unisexual, unattractive, often surrounded by bracts or an involucre; perianth inferior with various glandular or scaly appendages, often wanting, sometimes double, the inner series being then often called petals; stamens very various, anthers 2-celled, often twin; ovary inferior, generally of 3 carpels more or less united, styles as many as the carpels; fruit of 3 cocci, separating from a persistent axis, or a drupe, generally 3-celled.

This is a very large and important order, chiefly tropical, though there are a good many herbaceous species of Euphorbia pretty well known in England. The order is, generally speaking, a very distinct one, but there is sometimes a difficulty in distinguishing the various parts of the flower, which some botanists describe as consisting of separate calyx and corolla. Hooker, however, calls the flower "a perianth, sometimes double," though he also occasionally lapses into calyx and corolla. "The family exhibits every gradation, from perfect corolliferous blossoms to the most degraded flowers in all nature."—*Grant Allen.*

The properties of the order are generally acrid, and often highly poisonous, but not unfrequently medicinal, as in the castor-oil plant and the crotons. The milky juice is the most offensive part, and there are many species (as there are of the English spurges) which, if handled at all, unpleasantly affect the lips and nostrils. The Manchineel tree of the W. Indies, *Hippomane manchinella*, bears the worst reputation. "The milky juice renders the cultivation of this tree, and even the coming near to it, very dangerous. One cannot sleep with impunity under the shade of it, and the water which drops from its leaves after a shower raises blisters upon the skin and excites a troublesome itching."—*Raynal.*

Note.—The species of Euphorbia and some other genera are easily identified by the remarkable ovary, which is round or nearly so, but deeply divided from top to bottom into 3 carpels topped by the styles. The fruit is then simply this ovary enlarged. This may be called the normal Euphorbiaceous ovary and fruit.

Note.—The leaves are alternate when not otherwise stated. They are lobed in *Bischofia*, *Jatropha*, *Givotia*, *Baliospermum*, and *Ricinus*; otherwise simple.

1. EUPHORBIA. Leaves often opposite; flowers monœcious a number of male flowers consisting only of a single-stalked stamen, and a single female, consisting of a stalked pistil of 3 carpels, are all enclosed in a cup-shaped involucre bordered with 4 or 5 glands sometimes resembling petals; capsule of 3 cocci, separating with elasticity.

Note.—This genus, by the involucre, differs very decidedly from all the rest, and is placed by *H.* in a tribe by itself. The above description requires explanation. The numerous male flowers and the single female being as above described, and the involucre being more or less like a perianth, the appearance of the whole is that of a single flower, with about 12 stamens and a single pistil; and, in fact, Linnæus thus described the flowers of a large section of Euphorbias.

2. BRIEDELIA. Flowers in clusters, bracted, sessile or nearly

so; calyx 5-cleft, petals much smaller, disk broad, stamens 5, united below, styles 2, forked, fruit a drupe, or of 2 cocci.

Nothing could be less like last genus than this, the flowers being of a very ordinary pentandrous type, much resembling some of the Rhamnaceæ.

3. PHYLLANTHUS. Leaves bifarious, flowers monœcious, sepals 4 to 6 in 2 series with a disk, stamens 3 to 5, fruit generally a capsule, sometimes a berry.

4. GLOCHIDION. Like the last, but flowers without disk, sepals generally 6 in 2 series, stamens 3 to 8 connate, styles connate in a more or less round column, lobed or toothed at the top, capsule often of 6 or more lobes.

5. FLUEGGIA. Shrubs, leaves small, flowers diœcious, sepals 5, stamens 3 to 5; the male flower has a large imperfect pistil, and in the female the long recurved styles are united below into an erect column.

6. BREYNIA. Shrubs or small trees, flowers minute, calyx of male flower truncate, of female 6-lobed, stamens 3 columnar, anthers adnate to the whole length of the column, styles 3.

7. PUTRANJIVA. Trees, male flowers clustered, females subsolitary, calyx unequally 3 to 6-lobed, stamens 2 to 4, styles short, dilated into broad fleshy arms, drupe 1-celled.

8. APOROSA. Trees, flowers minute, males in dense catkin-like spikes, females larger in short spikes, stamens 1 to 5, anthers twin.

Note.—This genus, differing from the rest of the order by the flowers being in catkins, was formerly in a separate order—Scepaceæ.

9. ANTIDESMA. Trees or shrubs, flowers diœcious in spikes or racemes, calyx 3 to 8-toothed, stamens 2 to 5 inserted on or round the disk, fruit a drupe crowned with stigmas.

Note.—This genus also belonged to a small separate order—Stilagineæ—connected by some authorities with Urticaceæ, and by others with Amentiferæ.

10. JATROPHA. Trees, shrubs or herbs, often glandular or prickly, leaves often lobed, flowers monœcious, sepals and petals 5, stamens many, anthers erect, fruit a capsule of 2 to 4 cocci.

11. CROTON. Trees or shrubs, leaves with 2 glands at the base, sepals, petals, and disk glands 4 to 6, stamens many on a

hairy receptacle, petals sometimes absent in female flowers, capsule of 3 cocci.

12. CHROZOPHORA. Herbs or undershrubs, rough or hairy; flowers in racemes with bracts, males crowded in the upper parts, females solitary stalked, male calyx round or ovoid, female of 5 narrow sepals; petals 5, in female flowers sometimes wanting, stamens 5 to 16, styles bifid, capsule of 3 cocci.

13. CLAOXYLON. Flowers in spikes or racemes, calyx roundish of 3 or 4 segments, stamens various, anthers erect, styles spreading, fringed, capsule various.

14. ACALYPHA. Flowers generally diœcious, male flowers very minute without bracts, females often at the base of large increasing bracts, stamens many or 8, styles long, fringed.

15. MALLOTUS. Trees or shrubs, leaves sometimes opposite, often with glands at the base, flowers racemed, males clustered, females solitary in the bracts, stamens 20 or more, capsule of 2 or 3 cocci.

16. MACARANGA. Trees or shrubs, flowers racemed, generally diœcious, males many clustered, females solitary or few under each bract, stamens 1 or more, styles entire.

17. HOMONOIA. Rigid shrubs, flowers usually diœcious, stamens numerous in a dense round head of branched filaments and anthers, styles spreading, capsule of 3 cocci.

18. BALIOSPERMUM. Erect shrubs, male flowers round, with 4 to 6 membranous sepals, females of 5 or 6 lanceolate sepals, stamens 10 to 30, anthers with a broad connective, styles stout bifid, capsules of 3 cocci.

19. TRAGIA. Twining herbs, flowers monœcious in racemes, male above, female few below; calyx of male flowers round or obovoid, 3 to 5 partite, sepals of female flowers 6; stamens 1 to 3, styles spreading above, capsule of 3 cocci.

20. SEBASTIANIA. Flowers monœcious, males minute, 1 to 3 in each bract, females solitary or at the base of the raceme, male calyx unequally 5-lobed, female 3-lobed; stamens 2 to 4, capsule round of 3 cocci separating from a central column.

1. EUPHORBIA.

Note.—I believe that the name *dudhi* is commonly applied to all small species of this genus. *H.* has 52 species, of which 15 are found in W. India.

I. Leaves opposite.

1. *E. elegans* (*E. strobilifera*, D.) Two or three feet high,

branched with smooth red stem; leaves none; bracts imbricated, leafy cordate, obliquely ovate, blunt, glands white, long-tubed, with 4 segments, 2 larger, capsule smooth or nearly so.

Hills above Lanoli. Rocks in Wári country (*D.*). The Konkan and Deccan peninsula (*H.*).

The above description is of my plant, which agrees with *D.'s*. *H.'s* description does not agree at all, the greatest, but not the only difference being that he describes both leaves and floral leaves; but as he makes the identification with *D.'s* plant without any mark of doubt, I have left it so.

To this section, in which the flowers are rather conspicuous, belong also * *E. pycnostegia*, a slender branched herb, smooth, leaves oblong, floral leaves ovate cordate or roundish, collected in an oblong head, limb of glands large obliquely obovate, cocci obtusely furrowed. W. Ghauts (*H.*). * *E. zornoides H.* calls probably a variety of this, with narrower cauline and smaller floral leaves. * *E. notoptera*, a foot high, smooth, leaves narrow linear oblong, distant, bracts with fringed lobes, cocci 2-winged. Konkan and Canara (*H.*). * *E. coccinea*, small, rigid, slender, with white hairs and purple stem, leaves obliquely elliptic or obovate, involucres in leafy roundish heads, two of the glands with conspicuous rosy or purple limbs, capsules woolly. Konkan (*H.*). None of these are in *D.* or *G.*

The next 3 species are small weeds, which may be found all together about Poona in the rains, and in other localities.

2. *E. hypericifolia* (*E. parviflora*, D.). Smooth, light green, leaves oval oblique blunt serrulate, involucres small in cymes, limb of the glands white tinged with pink. *Dudh mogra.*

Poona, Tanna, &c. Common throughout the hotter parts of India and the tropics of both hemispheres (*H.*).

3. *E. pilulifera* (*E. hirta*, D.). A coarse weed, hairy and of a dark hue, leaves oblong, very oblique acute serrulate, involucres in round sessile heads, limbs of glands not noticeable. *Náyati.*

Commonly distributed like the last.

4. *E. thymifolia.* A very small weed, all red and hairy, stems prostrate, leaves ovate oblique serrate, dark, involucres very small in close terminal cymes, white tinged with red. *Dhákti dudhi, hazárdáná.*

Throughout India and Ceylon and all hot countries (*H.*). To this section belongs * *E. microphylla* (*E. uniflora*, D.), slender, much-branched, smooth, leaves very short, obliquely oblong, involucres solitary all up the stem and branches. Konkan (*D.*). Rather rare.

II. Leaves alternate.

5. *E. Tirucalli.* Milk bush. An erect smooth shrub, consisting of much-branched smooth round stems without leaves, involucres clustered in the forks of the branches, inconspicuous, capsule velvety. *Nival, Sher, Kárá.*

A native of Africa, but quite naturalized.

A few small leaves may be found by close examination, but it is practically leafless. The milky juice is extraordinarily abundant and sticky, so that it can be used as gum when its great acridity is not an objection.

6. *E. neriifolia.* The common prickly pear (but see Opuntia). An erect fleshy shrub or small tree, branches jointed, cylindric or obscurely 5-angled, with short sharp thorns as stipules arising from thick tubercles, leaves obovate oblong, fleshy, involucres yellowish in short-stalked clusters, capsule smooth. *Thor, nival kánta, mingut.*

This is one of those shrubs which is too well known. A perfectly bare Deccan hill in the hot weather is scarcely less beautiful than one covered with this painfully hardy shrub. *H.* makes both this and the next natives of India. *E. canariensis,* described in Cook's voyages, seems to be very similar.

7. *E. nivulia.* Larger than the last, the leaves more fleshy, and the tubercles which bear the thorns set in spiral rows all up the stem.

This might easily be mistaken for the last, but neither could be mistaken for anything else. It is said to be more common than the other in Guzerat and Sind.

* *E. antiquorum,* of the same habit as the two last, but the branches 3 to 6-angled, with double rows of thorns along the angles; leaves none, or few and small, involucres about 3 to a peduncle. In the S. of the Presidency, rare. Through the hotter parts of India and Ceylon (*H.*).

8. *E. Rothiana.* A smooth glaucous, erect, slender plant, leaves oblong, lanceolate, involucres in terminal umbels with broad, cordate bracts at the forks, glands 2-horned, viscid.

Mahableshwar, Konkan, and Guzerat.

This, and also species Nos. 1 to 4, are quite of the character of the English spurges, the remarkable ovary (or capsule), often stalked, in the middle of the involucre, catching the eye at once.

* *E. fusiformis* (*E. acaulis,* D.). Stemless, leaves radical cuneiform with curled margins, often spotted with red, peduncles from the crown of the large spindle-shaped root, 5 to 7-flowered. Mahableshwar, Sawant Wári, &c. (*D.*). *E. splendens,* a small shrub, ex-

ceedingly thorny, with obovate leaves in whorls, and very pretty scarlet involucres in clusters, is very common in Indian gardens and English conservatories; a native of S. America.

2. Briedelia.

1. *B. retusa* (*B. montana*, D.). A handsome tree with spreading branches, leaves lanceolate ovate or obovate, pale beneath, flowers sessile axillary, fruit like a currant or larger, purple-black with persistent calyx. *Asanna, phatarphod, pále hasan.*

Common on the Ghauts: also in hilly parts of the Konkan. It is found with or without thorns, and *H.* has 4 varieties, in one of which the flowers are in spikes sometimes a foot long.

2. *B. stipularis* (*B. scandens*, D.). A scraggy diffuse shrub, leaves oblong or obovate, blunt, hard, downy with prominent nerves below, flowers greenish, axillary crowded, fruit oval seated in the calyx, turning from red to black. *Chikan.*

Konkan: common about Rajapore. Hotter parts of India (*H.*). *H.* has alternatively "flowers in long spikes often subtended by long stipular bracts."

* *B. Hamiltoniana*, straggling, nearly smooth, leaves small, oblong or obovate, flowers in minute axillary or spicate clusters, fruit roundish, seated on the calyx. Not in *D.* or *G.* Konkan and Ghauts, *Law*, *Stock*, &c. (*H.*).

3. Phyllanthus.

H. has 56 species, but only about 8 in W. India. All here given, except the first, have stamens 3, more or less columnar.

1. *P. reticulatus* (*Anisonema multiflora*, D.). A climbing shrub, with very small oval obtuse leaves, quite smooth, petioles red, flowers very small axillary reddish aggregated, stamens 5, berry when ripe like a small black currant. *Páwan.*

Sattara. Of great size in Sind, climbing to the tops of the highest trees (*D.*). Watercourses and other moist places in the Konkan (*G.*). Throughout tropical India (*H.*). He mentions a pubescent state of the plant.

2. *P. emblica* (*Emblica officinalis*, D.). A tree, leaves linear oblong obtuse, flowers small, yellowish, tinged with red in dense clusters on the branchlets, which look like spikes of flowers with leaves among them; perianth 6 or 7 divided, fruit waxy, roundish, only slightly lobed, size of a large gooseberry. *Awla, ámalak.*

Konkan and Deccan, often planted. Throughout tropical India (*H.*). The fruit is eatable, and is the Emblic Myrobolan of commerce.

3. *P. Lawii* (*P. polyphyllus*, D.). A rigid twiggy shrub, stems red, leaves oblong, very small, flowers subsessile, females above, fruit 3-lobed.

Banks of the Bhima, Gutpurba and Krishna (*G.*); and generally of rivers towards the Ghauts (*D.*).

I noted it as thorny, for which I find no confirmation.

* 4. *P. madraspatensis.* A herb or shrubby, leaves cuneate lanceolate or obovate, nearly sessile, flowers axillary, very small, females largest, sepals green with white margins, capsule dry, round. *Kánocha.*

Common in gardens and cultivated ground (*D.*). Drier parts of India, very variable in habit (*H.*).

5. *P. simplex.* Diffuse, smooth with red stems and flattened branches, leaves sessile lanceolate or oblong entire, flowers axillary sessile, capsule rough, seeds black muricated.

I had this as a small weed, and with branches rising from near the top of the short stem, which agrees with one of *H.'s* varieties, but he calls it a most variable plant, often shrubby, sometimes 3 feet high.

6. *P. niruri.* A much-branched smooth herb, leaves small, elliptic, narrow at the base, stipules 2, narrow, flowers very small, solitary in the axils, perianth persistent of 6 broad and blunt lobes, capsule nearly round of several shallow lobes. *Bhui áwali.*

A common weed. Throughout the hotter parts of India (*H.*).

The capsule is like a miniature edition of the fruit of Malva rotundifolia, and other mallows.

H. has another species, *P. scabrifolius*, known only in the Konkan on the authority of Stocks, which is near the last, but a leafy herb, roughish, with much larger flower and fruit. *G.* has also **P. urinaria*, which he calls much like *P. niruri*, but distinguishable by sessile flowers and rough capsules. *Lál bhui áwali.* *H.* calls it a low or tall diffusely branched erect or decumbent herb; throughout India. Common in Bombay (*G.*). * *P. Indicus* (*Prosorus I.* D.), a tree with oval or oblong leaves, male flowers very numerous, clustered, sepals generally 4, female flowers larger, capsules in 3's, bluish, roundish. S. Ghauts (*D.*).

P. distichus (*Cicca d.* D.), a tree, *harpharori, rayá wála,* is cultivated in gardens for the fruit, which is generally called "country gooseberry;" the flowers are minute red. It is a native of the Malay islands.

4. Glochidion.

1. *G. lanceolarium.* A small tree, leaves lanceolate acuminate, shining, flowers clustered, white, males on longish slender stalks with 4 to 6 anthers, females few and sessile, capsule small, 6-lobed, brown, splitting up like the capsule of a mallow. *Bhomá.*

Matheran, very abundant. Mahableshwar and the Ghauts generally.

2. *G. zeylanicum* (*G. nitidum*, D.). A small tree, leaves large sessile ovate oblong acute, shining, male and female mixed in short-stalked clusters, anthers 5 or 6, capsule nearly round, 6-lobed, larger than that of No. 1.

S. Konkan, near water. Very variable, there being a smooth and a hairy variety, pretty widely spread (*H.*).

The four following are small trees or shrubs, attributed to the Konkan or Canara by *H.*, but not in *D.* or *G.* * *G. tomentosum*, white with hairs, leaves ovate or oblong, flowers on short stout bent pedicels, anthers 5 to 7, capsule slightly 10 to 12-lobed. * *G. Hohlnackeri*, smooth, leaves ovate lanceolate, male flowers long-stalked, females sessile in clusters, capsule 6 to 8-lobed, the large round style in the sunk top. This and the next two have 3 anthers. * *G. Ralphii*, smooth, leaves lanceolate, male flowers on slender stalks, capsule 3 to 6-lobed with style as in the last. * *G. ellipticum*, smooth, branchlets angled, leaves elliptic, often unequal-sided, male flowers minute, short-stalked, females clustered, capsule obscurely 4 to 6-lobed.

5. Flueggia.

F. microcarpa (*F. leucopyrus*, D.). A pretty shrub, leaves small smooth obovate cuneate, stipules small pointed, flowers very small, crowded in the axils, berry pure white, round, size of a pea with calyx attached. *Pándharphali*, *Kánte puwan.*

Sattara. Konkan, common (*D.*). Matheran (*Birdwood*). Throughout India (*H.*).

H. has as another species, * *F. leucopyrus* (*F. virosa*, D.), a thorny shrub, differing more from the last in habit and foliage than in flowers and fruit, the leaves being smaller. But *D.*, who attributes the shrub to Malabar and Worlee hills only, says they are larger! Possibly the two plants are one, with trifling and casual differences.

6. Breynia.

B. patens (*Melanthesa turbinata*, D.). A smooth shrub with red stem and branches, leaves oval obtuse or oblong, sometimes unequal-sided, bifarious, female flowers greenish, calyx open flat, enlarging and growing red with the small melon-shaped fruit.

Bombay and the Konkan. The enlarged calyx looks like a miniature dish with the fruit in the middle.

7. Putranjiva.

P. Roxburghii. A very pretty tree, with drooping branches and bifarious leaves, lanceolate or ovate, rather blunt, smooth, sometimes unequal at the base; flowers in dense clusters, very small, stigmas 3, crescent-shaped, drupe from round to ovate, stalked, white, with persistent calyx. *Putrávanti, jivputrak.*

Nasik. Konkan, Khandalla, Belgaum (*D.*). Throughout tropical India (*H.*).

The generic name is from the Sanscrit, the drupes being used as charms to keep children in health.

8. Aporosa.

* *A. Lindleyana* (*Scepa L.*, D.). A much-branched tree, leaves oblong or lanceolate, smooth, with large hairy stipules; flowers yellowish, anthers 2, bracts broad ciliated, fruit round, smooth, tipped with the style, size of a pea. *Sálá.*

Very common in S. Konkan (*D.*). Deccan peninsula (*H.*).

9. Antidesma.

1. *A. Ghaesembilla* (*A. paniculatum* and *A. pubescens*, D.). A shrub or small tree, leaves oblong, broad, rounded at both ends, downy beneath, stipules small subulate; flowers sessile, greenish yellow in simple or compound spikes, the stamens (about 5) the most conspicuous part, berry small roundish, dark purple. *Jondri.*

Konkan, not common apparently, but widely spread through India (*H.*). The leaves in the specimens I had were of an uncommon shape, broad in comparison with the length, and equally broad throughout, but *H.* makes them vary from roundish to oblong.

2. *A. diandrum.* A laurel-like shrub or small tree, leaves oval entire smooth, stipules lanceolate, flowers greenish, very small, fruit minute succulent. *Amthi.*

Dapoli. Vingorla (*D.*). Khandalla (*G.*). Leafless in the hot weather (*Lisboa*). Leaves very variable (*H.*).

* *A. menasu* (*A. lanceolatum*, D.). Shrub or tree, leaves long lanceolate, smooth, flowers in spikes or racemes, stamens 3 or 4, fruit very small, ovoid. Tulkat Ghaut and Virdi (*D.*).

10. Jatropha. Physic Nut.

* *J. glandulifera.* A stout shrub or small tree, leaves simple ovate, or palmate, with 3 to 5 lanceolate lobes, the serratures bristle-tipped; flowers greenish yellow in glandular cymes, bracts bristly, stamens 8, capsule size of a cherry, slightly 6-lobed. *Tarkiyerand, andarbibi.*

Pundherpore, plentiful (*D.*). Deccan peninsula (*H.*). *D.* calls the capsule 3-lobed, and *G.* (if this is his No. 1325) calls it a strange-looking plant. "The flowers are not pale greenish yellow, as *D.* has it, but dull red, and the plant now grows everywhere on waste ground in Bombay island."—*Dr. Dymock.*

* *J. nana.* A small smooth shrub, leaves broad ovate, entire or 3-lobed, flowers with a subulate bract half-way up the pedicel, fruit obovate, slightly 6-furrowed. *Karkandi.* Stony places near Poona. —*Woodrow.* *J. Curcas, yerand, jepál,* is a large unbeautiful shrub, much used for hedges (but it makes very bad ones), in the Konkan. Throughout India and Ceylon, cultivated and naturalized, and throughout the tropics (*H.*). "The seeds taken inwardly act with great violence both upwards and downwards" (*R.*).

J. multifida is the coral plant of gardens, with much-divided leaves and red and yellow flowers, cultivated and naturalized in various parts of India. *Chini yerand.*

11. Croton.

* 1. *C. Gibsonianus.* A tree with smooth whitish bark, leaves oval pointed, often yellowish or reddish; flowers in long and slender racemes, distant, disk glands large, stamens 10, capsule greenish yellow, size of a cherry.

Canara and the Ghauts; common in moist forests of the S. Ghauts (*H.*).

* 2. *C. reticulatus* (*C. hypoleucos*, D.). A small tree, with much reddish down, leaves sometimes opposite, elliptic long-stalked, much covered with silvery scales, and with 2 or 3 stalked glands at the base; flowers in racemes, males above, females few below, stamens 15 to 18. *Pándhare.*

Shady jungles on the Konkan hills (*D.*). Matheran (*Birdwood*). Deccan peninsula (*H.*).

* *C. oblongifolius,* young parts scaly, leaves large oblong, serrate, flowers pale green in erect racemes, petals woolly, stamens 10 or 12, capsule round, fleshy, 6-furrowed. *Gansur.* * *C. Lawianus,* leaves oblong lanceolate or broad ovate, racemes short, few flowered, male flowers large, membranous, stamens about 20, capsule 3-lobed, sur-

rounded by the enlarged leafy sepals. Beemashankar, Mira hills and Canara (*D.*). * *C. tiglium*, leaves ovate serrate, flowers greenish-yellow in racemes, stamens 15 to 20, capsule large oblong or obovoid, 3-cornered, *jepál, jamalgota*, is the tree from which croton oil is produced; it is attributed by *G.* to the S. Konkan, but by *H.* only to the E. of India.

"The familiar 'laurel' of Bombay gardens, a shrub with green and yellow leaves, is *C. variegatum*, a native of the Indian archipelago" (*Dr. Gray*). Many species and varieties of croton are now cultivated both in India and England as foliage plants.

12. Chrozophora.

1. *C. plicata.* A tall handsome plant, all more or less rough and mealy, leaves long-petioled, broad cordate, waved; flowers in racemes, very small red, petals elliptic, scaly on the outside, hairy inside, ovary very large, capsule 3-sided. *Suryavarta.*

Konkan, Deccan, and Guzerat. Throughout India (*H.*). The leaves in shape and petiole are like those of scarlet geranium.

2. *C. prostrata.* Prostrate, rough and hairy all over, sometimes woolly, dark-coloured, with roundish leaves, much wrinkled and blistered; flowers as in the last, with bright yellow exserted stamens, capsule with styles and calyx persistent.

Poona. Found commonly in dried up water holes (*D.*). It is often pressed close to the ground, and is thus in habit, as well as in some details, as different as possible from the last, of which *H.* has put it as a variety. On sending a specimen to Kew the authority declared it to be *C. tinctoria*, though he confessed to not seeing how it differed from some large forms left by *H.* in *C. plicata*. *C. tinctoria*, which is attributed by *H.* to Sind and the Deccan as well as the Punjaub, he makes exceedingly like the larger states of *C. plicata*. The solution of the difficulty seems to be that they all three run into one another.

13. Claoxylon.

* *C. Mercurialis* (*Microstachys m.*, D.). Annual, nearly smooth, leaves ovate, sometimes cordate serrate or crenate; racemes axillary solitary, few-flowered, stamens 3 to 10, or very numerous in a round mass, capsule depressed, cocci round.

I do not know this, and *D.* gives no habitat. "Common in the rains, much like *Acalypha Indica*, and both of them bearing a strong resemblance to *Mercurialis perennis*, the English dog's mercury"—(a very common and unattractive plant of the early spring) (*G.*).

14. Acalypha.

1. *A. Indica.* Erect, smooth, leaves round ovate serrate, long petioled, flowers very small, whitish, in axillary spikes; involucre cup-shaped, toothed, concealing the capsule. *Kokati, Kupi.*

Poona. An annual common weed (*G.*). Hotter parts of India (*H.*).

2. *A. ciliata.* Differs from the last in being smaller, the ovate serrate leaves acuminate, the spikes more crowded, the involucre with narrow teeth; stem, petioles and involucre softly hairy.

Poona. Deccan peninsula (*H.*).

H. has named after Dalzell "a very remarkable shrubby species," smooth with 2 flowers in a very large round-reniform bract, but it is only known from female specimens and a drawing, and the locality is not given.

15. Mallotus.

1. *M. repandus* (*Rottlera dicocca*, D.). A large woody shrub, leaves large, round cordate pointed, waved or slightly-toothed, softly downy, racemes terminal and axillary; fruit almond-shaped, 2-lobed, about an inch long. *Petári.*

Konkan. Throughout India (*H.*). If this is *G.*'s No. 1333 the leaves fall in the cold weather. *H.* has it as sometimes a tree with trunk 60 to 80 feet. I noted the leaves as opposite, which *G.* has, but not *D.* or *H.*

2. *M. Philippensis* (*Rottlera tinctoria*, D.). Tree with oval oblong leaves, shining above, pale and covered with red glands below; flowers very inconspicuous in panicles, capsule 3-lobed, 3-seeded, covered with red meal, size of a pea. *Shendri, kamela, rohin, asli.*

Konkan, Ghauts and S. M. country (*D.*). Throughout tropical India (*H.*). I had what I thought to be this, a tree with smooth white bark, in the Panch Mahals. "Monkey-face tree, in allusion to their painting their faces red by rubbing them with the fruit."—*G.*, from Buchanan's "Mysore."

* *M. albus* (*Rottlera muppoides*, D.). Arboreous, leaves cordate peltate, long-petioled, white or reddish, hairy beneath, flowers clustered in panicles, capsule round, white, of 3 or 4 cocci, tubercled. Konkan, Canara and Ghauts. * *M. Lawii* (*Rottlera aureopunctata*, D.). A diœcious shrub, leaves opposite, oblong, with minute glands below, flowers in racemes, female calyx spathaceous, split on one side, capsule small, glandular. Konkan and Canara. * *M. stenanthus*, a small tree, leaves opposite, ovate lanceolate, racemes short and slender; anther tips with a broad connective, capsule 3-lobed, with yellow glands and tubercles.

16. Macaranga.

M. Roxburghii. A tree, leaves large peltate, round, pointed, long-petioled; flowers minute in panicles, stamens 2 to 5, capsules pea-like, sticky, in masses close to the trunk, seeds black. *Chánda, chandára.*

Matheran, Konkan, and the Ghauts. Deccan peninsula (*H.*). This is *G.*'s No. 1284.

17. Homonoia.

1. *H. riparia* (*Adelia neriifolia*, D.). A shrub, with linear lanceolate willow-like leaves; flowers red in slender axillary spikes, female flowers much smaller, with red 3-lobed stigma, capsule very small round, 3-lobed. *Sherni.*

In river beds, Deccan, Konkan and Mahableshwar, growing with tamarisk and *Polygonum glabrum*, and much resembling the latter.

* 2. *H. retusa* (*Adelia r.*, D.). A low shrub, leaves sessile obovate cuneate retuse, slightly crenate, spikes short and stout, flowers minute, capsules very small.

In river beds, Deccan (*D.*, *G.* and *H.*). Bears some resemblance to the sloe bush, and in foliage to *Sida retusa* (*G.*).

18. Baliospermum.

B. axillare (*B. polyandrum*, D.). A shrub, lower leaves ovate, sometimes lobed, upper oblong, small, all hairy and coarsely serrated; flowers in spikes yellowish, anthers broad, fruit green striped with white, 3-lobed, broader above, crowned with the 3-cleft style; seeds dark mottled and shining. *Jamálgota, dátarda, jáphalgota.*

S. Konkan. Ghauts.

The seeds are used in the same way as those of *Croton tiglium*: the root called *dántimul.*—*Dr. Dymock.*

19. Tragia.

T. involucrata. Leaves oblong cordate pointed, serrated, covered with stinging hairs, raceme long; male flowers each with a bract, white and green, female sepals pinnatifid, lobes of capsule round. *Kulti, thora ágiya, Kalávi.*

S. Konkan. Common on the Ghauts (*D.*). Throughout India, most variable (*H.*). The hairy 6-lobed calyx of the female flowers is the most prominent feature of the plant. It might easily be taken for one of the Menispermaceæ.

20. Sebastiania.

S. chamælea (*Microstachys c.*, D.). A small erect smooth plant, branched or with many stems from the root, leaves opposite linear sessile, capsule stalked.

Rutnagherry. Common about Vingorla (*D.*). Deccan peninsula (*H.*).

I noted this as very like a Euphorbia. Some specimens have grooved and ribbed stems (*H.*).

Actephila, like *Briedelia*, but flowers larger, petals sometimes wanting, filaments free, the male disks 5-lobed, the fruit or capsule of 3 cocci. * *A. excelsa* (*Anomospermum excelsum*, D.). An evergreen shrub or tree, leaves smooth and shining, elliptic, flowers axillary, long-pedicelled, sepals oblong, capsule smooth, broader than long. Fonda Ghaut (*D.*).

Sauropus, male calyx disciform, 6-lobed, female 6-cleft, persistent, increasing, stamens and styles 3, fruit with 6 indehiscent cocci. * *S. quadrangularis* (*Ceratogynum rhamnoides*, D.), a dwarf smooth shrub, leaves elliptic or broad ovate, male flowers very minute, racemed below, female solitary above, capsule size of a pea. *Chikli.* Vingorla, rare (*D.*) : Matheran (*Birdwood*).

Hemicyclia, stamens eight or more inserted round a disk, sepals 4 or 5, the inner usually larger, stigma large, otherwise as *Putranjiva.* * *H. sepiaria*, shrub or tree, leaves smooth, oblong, obovate, flowers minute, whitish, stigma concave, crenated, drupe nearly round, red. Konkan and Ghauts (*D.*). * *H. venusta*, tree with drooping branches, leaves oblong, smooth, male flowers clustered, females in pairs, stigma large disciform, fruit obovoid. Dharwar, Canara, &c. (*D.*).

Bischofia, a tree, leaves trifoliate, flowers diœcious, without petals, sepals and stamens 5, anthers large, fruit round, fleshy. * *B. Javanica* (*Stylodiscus trifoliatus*, D.), a large tree, leaflets oblong ovate, flowers in slender panicles, green, fruit size of a small cherry, blue-black, on long thickened stalk. *Boke.* Konkan and Ghauts.

Givotia, sepals 5, unequal, corolla 5-lobed, stamens 13 to 25 on a woolly receptacle. * *G. rottleriformis*, a small tree, leaves very large rounded and cordate, sometimes lobed, white and hairy beneath, very long-petioled, flowers in panicles, stamens about 15, fruit oblong hoary, size of a pigeon's egg. N. Deccan and S. M. Country (*D.*).

Blachia, smooth shrubs, sepals 4 or 5 enlarged and leafy in fruit, petals small in the male, absent in female, capsule of 3 cocci. * *B. denudata*, leaves ovate, oblong entire, flowers small, white, umbelled. Chorla Ghaut (*D.*). Konkan and Canara (*H.*). *Dimorphocalyx*, smooth trees, male calyx cup-shaped or 5-toothed, female of 5 distinct sepals enlarging greatly in fruit, petals 5, stamens 10 to 20; capsule of 3 cocci. * *D. Lawianus*, leaves ovate oblong, male flowers in cymes, female long pedicelled, stamens about 15, sepals in fruit very unequal. Not in *D.* or *G.* Konkan (*H.*).

Agrostistachys, smooth shrubs, male flowers several within each bract, female solitary, male calyx round, splitting into lobes, female 5 or 6 parted, petals 5 to 8, stamens 8 to 13. * *A. Indica*, leaves oblong, sharply serrated, very long, male flowers in grass-like spikelets, petals white, disk glands very large, capsule 3-celled. S. Ghauts (*D.*).

Trewia, trees, leaves opposite, flowers rather large, developing before the leaves, diœcious, males each with a bract, stamens numerous, styles very long. * *T. nudiflora*, more or less hairy or woolly, leaves heart-shaped, male flowers in drooping racemes, females generally solitary, long-stalked, fruit a berry, round, 3 or 4-celled. Konkan (*H.*). *Petári.* * *T. polycarpa*, female flowers in short racemes, the fruit smaller and ovoid. Konkan (*H.*).

Cleidion, male flowers in long racemes, females one or two on a long peduncle, stamens over 20, styles very long, bifid. * *C. javanicum* (*Rottlera uranda*, D.). Shrub or tree, leaves narrow, oblong, narrowed into the petiole, capsule of 3 round cocci. S. Ghauts (*D.*).

Sapium, flowers monœcious, males several in each bract, females solitary in the bracts, stamens 2 or 3. * *S. Indicum*, a small smooth tree, sometimes thorny, leaves elliptic, serrate, bract broad, obtuse, ciliated, female flowers larger, with long style and stigma, fruit round, hard, size of a nutmeg, 3-celled. S. Konkan, *Nimmo* (*H.*). * *S. sepiferum*, *vilayati pipal*, in Bombay gardens, &c., the China tallow tree; the fatty substance surrounding the seeds is used to make candles, but in India is produced in quantities too small to be of any practical use.

Excœcaria, smooth trees or shrubs, flowers diœcious or monœcious, males 1 to 3 in each bract, sepals 3, females at the base of the racemes, or in separate racemes, rachis with large glands near the bracts, stamens 3, capsule of 3 cocci. * *E. agallocha*, leaves about the end of the branchlets ovate or roundish, long-petioled, flowers fragrant, filaments lengthened after flowering. In salt marshes, with the mangroves, but not common apparently. The milky juice is said to be very dangerous. * *E. robusta*, leaves opposite, linear, oblong, spikes stout, sepals of the male flowers round, irregularly toothed, bracts broad, fleshy, bracteoles large. Konkan (*H.*), on Stock's authority, but apparently very imperfectly known.

The following are cultivated:

Ricinus communis, the castor oil plant, formerly called Palma Christi, *ránd*, *erandi*, probably indigenous in Africa (*H.*). Fields of it are very striking from the large, handsome leaves, and their peculiar bluish tint. The scarlet flowered species is a very ornamental shrub.

Pedilanthus tithymaloides, the slipper plant, with scarlet flowers (involucres) slipper-shaped, is commonly used as an edging in gardens. *Thor*, *vilayati thor*, *shend*.

Poinsettia pulcherrima, with scarlet or crimson bracts and yellow flowers, is known in every garden. It is a native of Mexico, and of comparatively recent introduction into India.

Aleurites molluccana, Belgaum walnut, *Jáphal ákhrot :* in the S. Sea Islands it is called the candlenut tree, the kernels themselves burning brilliantly, and lampblack being also obtained from the shell of the nut. In gardens, Bombay and Belgaum, and said, but apparently without reason, to grow wild in the latter neighbourhood (*D.*).

Manihot utilissima, a South American plant, produces (from the root) tapioca, and is grown in various places (e.g. Dapoli) with that object. From the same root, by another mode of preparation, is made the Cassava bread of Africa, and from another species Manioc.

* *Hura crepitans* is given both by *D.* and *G.* (though probably not common) as a garden tree. It is called the sand box tree; the capsules round, and consisting of many cocci, are in America boiled in oil to prevent dehiscence, and then being emptied used as sand boxes. The milky juice is said to be very dangerous, and to produce erysipelas (*Le Maout*). "The fruit is difficult to obtain even where the tree is plentiful, because, hanging at the end of long branches, it bursts when ripe with a crack like a pistol, scattering its seed far and wide."—*Kingsley.*

ORDER 107. **URTICACEÆ.**

Leaves generally alternate and stipulate, often oblique, generally rough with hairs, as the whole plant often is; flowers usually monœcious or diœcious, minute, often crowded on a fleshy involucre, perianth lobed; stamens generally as many as the perianth lobes, opposite to them, and inserted into the base, anthers 2-celled, ovary superior.

This, though not one of the largest, is a very important tropical order, and the number of species found in India is very large. Many of them are large and well-known trees, which makes the common English name of the order, "the nettle family," not appropriate here. The flowers in this order are absolutely and perhaps invariably without beauty. Its properties are very various, as will be seen from the names of trees and plants given below.

H. has the following tribes (here represented), all of which have by different botanists been considered as separate orders, but with distinctions so slight that except that tribes Nos. 4 and 5 have usually milky, and the others watery sap, I think it better not to attempt to describe them. Tribe 6 alone is obviously distinct from the rest.

Tribe 1. Ulmeæ—Elms—gen. Holoptelea.
Tribe 2. Celtideæ—gen. Celtis and Trema.

Tribe 3. Cannabineæ—gen. Cannabis, hemp.

Tribe 4. Moreæ—Mulberries—gen. Streblus.

Tribe 5. Artocarpeæ—gen. Ficus, Antiaris, Artocarpus.

All the above, except Cannabis and some species of Ficus, are trees.

Tribe 6. Urticeæ contains all the other genera here given, the species being mostly herbs and no trees. They have long coiled and elastic filaments, and round anthers, and leaves very frequently with stinging hairs.

1. HOLOPTELEA. Deciduous trees, leaves entire (except in young plants), with scarious stipules; flowers fascicled, perianth cleft to the base, stamens 4 to 8, fruit dry, flat, and winged.

2. CELTIS. Trees or shrubs, leaves bifarious, flowers polygamous, in cymes, females in the upper axils; sepals 4 or 5 imbricated, stamens short surrounding a woolly disk, drupe small ovoid or roundish.

3. TREMA. Trees or shrubs, sepals 4 or 5, drupe ovoid or roundish small, usually crowned with the style.

4. STREBLUS. Unarmed shrubs or trees, sepals 4, in the female flowers embracing the ovary, female flowers bracteate, fruit membranous roundish.

5. FICUS. Trees or shrubs, flowers minute, unisexual on the inner walls of a fleshy receptacle, the mouth of which is closed by imbricated bracts; flowers often mixed with bracteoles, stamens one or two, perianth of female flowers often imperfect.

6. ANTIARIS. Trees, leaves bifarious, male flowers crowded on the surface of an axillary fleshy receptacle, surrounded by imbricated bracts, female solitary, without perianth, in a many-leaved involucre; male sepals 4, stamens 3 to 8, ovary adherent to the involucre, fruit fleshy.

7. ARTOCARPUS. Trees, flowers densely crowded on receptacles, male perianth 2 to 4-lobed, stamen one erect; female perianth tubular, fruit large and fleshy, composed of a great number of enlarged perianths and carpels.

The remainder have sepals and stamens 4 or 5, but in Nos. 10 and 12 sometimes only three.

8. FLEURYA. Annual herbs with stinging hairs, flowers clustered and spiked.

9. ELATOSTEMMA. Herbs or undershrubs, leaves usually very

oblique, flowers very minute, crowded on fleshy involucrate receptacles, bracteoles densely crowded.

10. BOEHMERIA. Shrubs or small trees, leaves opposite or alternate, flowers in clusters, spiked racemed or panicled without involucres, male perianth 3 to 5-lobed, female tubular toothed.

11. POUZOLZIA. Like the last, but some are herbs, flowers in axillary clusters, never in naked spikes, the slender styles deciduous.

12. DEBREGEASIA. Shrubs or trees, flowers in clusters sessile or spiked, female perianth ovoid or obovoid, succulent in fruit.

1. HOLOPTELEA.

H. integrifolia. A large tree with ovate subcordate leaves, smooth and hard, bifarious, flowers very small, dark purple, in dense sessile clusters on the branches; sepals minute, ovary large and flat with two white stigmas, capsule nearly round, very thin, notched at the top, with one seed in the centre. *Waola, kewal, ainsádera.*

Konkan and Ghauts. Abundant at Ghorabunder.

G. calls it the Indian elm, and gives the stamens as 5; I noted 10, but they probably vary a good deal. *H.* has 3 varieties, in one of which the fruit is not notched. It is eatable and called *pápari.*

2. CELTIS.

* *C. tetrandra* (*C. Roxburghii*, D.). A small tree, leaves ovate oblique cordate, flowers in slender axillary softly hairy racemes, drupes solitary or twin.

On and below the Ghauts, common (*D.* and *G.*). The value of the specific name is reduced by *H.* saying flowers *usually* tetrandrous, and by his including in it a species which *R.* describes as pentandrous, as *D.* and *G.* call this.

H. has 4 species, one or other of which seems to be found in most parts of India, and he says "the species appear to me inextricable."

3. TREMA.

T. orientalis (*Sponia Wightii*, D.). A small twiggy tree with pretty, lanceolate leaves, heart-shaped and oblique at the base, finely serrated, rough above, white and prominently veined beneath, stigmas 2, large, covered with white hairs, capsule very small and black, top-shaped. *Gol, Kargol.*

Matheran and Mahableshwar. Common in the hilly parts of the Konkan (*D.*).

Called in Mysore the charcoal tree (*R. H. Elliot*). *R.* very tersely condemns it: "This tree is neither useful, nor ornamental, nor is it of long duration."

4. Streblus.

S. asper (*Epicarpus orientalis*, D.). A small scraggy tree, with ovate or obovate leaves very rough, serrated; flowers aggregated, nearly sessile, stamens long, folded up, opening elastically, anthers leafy, fruit yellow, compressed, size of a pea, succulent, with reflexed calyx attached. *Káru*, *Karoti*, *Sareru.*

Very common in Konkan hedges, also in Guzerat. Drier parts of India (*H.*). It has the general appearance of a thorn tree. The leaves vary much in shape; they are used to polish wood and ivory.

5. Ficus. Fig.

This is a very difficult genus to describe, for many of the species seem to run into one another. *H.* has 112 of them, divided into 7 sections, but I do not find much help from these divisions. *H.* lays great stress on the venation of the leaves, which I have accordingly given, mostly on his authority.

In all the species here given the flowers are monandrous, "and grow, closely packed, inside a pear-shaped receptacle, the mouth of which is closed by bracts. To see the flowers it is necessary to open the receptacle (commonly called the fruit) while still young and green. When it ripens, the true fruits (commonly called the seeds) are found shut up in it, mixed with a pulp formed of the remains of the flowers" (*Carnel*). Some writers give the name of syconus to this sort of aggregated fruit, of which the cultivated fig is the best example. *H.* always calls it the receptacle, but I think it better to retain the simple name of fruit.

* 1. *F. gibbosa* (*Urostigma ampelos* and *volubile*, D.). A tree or climbing shrub, trunk short, thick, often concealed by numerous small leafy branchlets, bark smooth, ash-coloured; leaves obliquely oval, rough, 3-nerved, the nerves prominent and pale, petioles channelled, male and female flowers in separate receptacles, fruit in pairs, size of a pea, yellow. *Dátir.*

Ghauts (*D.*). Throughout India (*H.*).
H. calls this a protean plant, and divides the forms into 4 groups. Mr. Birdwood calls *F. volubile* the climbing fig.

2. *F. Bengalensis* (*Urostigma*, *B.* D.). The banyan tree, called by some old writers "the Brahminee fig." Throwing out roots from the branches and thus making subsidiary stems, bark smooth, light ash-colour, leaves ovate, roundish, downy

beneath, smooth and shining when old, nerves about 5 pairs, fruit in pairs axillary sessile deep-red, size of a cherry, downy. *Wad.*

Planted in all the plains of India; wild only in the Sub-Himalayan forests and on the lower slopes of the Deccan hills (*H.*). There are various vast and famous banyan trees in this Presidency, the first of which is probably that at Kabirbhur in the Narbadda. Milton's description of this, "the fig-tree, not that sort for fruit renowned," is well known, with his mistake of giving it leaves "broad as Amazonian targe."

Southey's description is not so well known,—

"It was a goodly sight to see
That venerable tree,
For o'er the lawn, irregularly spread,
Fifty straight columns propt its lofty head:
And many a long depending shoot,
Seeking to strike a root,
Straight like a plummet grew towards the ground.

. . . .

Some to the passing wind at times, with sway
Of gentle motion swung,
Others of younger growth unmov'd were hung,
Like stone drops from the cavern's fretted height:

. . . .

So like a temple did it seem that there
A pious heart's first impulse would be prayer."

Sir E. Arnold speaks of

. . . "its ample shade
Cloistered with columned dropping stems, and roofed
With vaults of glistering green."

Roxburgh says that where a palmyra tree is seen, as it often is, apparently growing out of the trunk of a banyan, it is really the other way on, the palm being the older, and the seeds of the banyan being dropped in its fronds, and throwing its roots to the ground. "For such unions the Hindoos entertain a religious veneration, saying it is a holy marriage, instituted by Providence." (See as to this under the Vine).

3. *F. retusa* (*Urostigma retusum,* and *nitidum,* D.). A handsome compact tree, leaves broad ovate or obovate, shining, nerves 5 or 6 pairs; male flowers numerous, scattered, fruit axillary twin sessile, size of a pea. *Nándruk.*

Tolerably common, particularly about the Ghauts. Deccan peninsula (*H.*).

H. has a species very near this, but differing in the leaves being ovate, with narrow base and 3 to 5-nerved, found only in Canara. He has named it after Mr. Talbot, *F. Talboti.*

4. *F. religiosa* (*Urostigma r.*, D.). The Peepul tree. A large smooth handsome tree, leaves very long, petioled ovate cordate with long narrow points; nerves about 8 pairs with fine reticulations, fruit in pairs axillary sessile, like a black cherry. *Pipal, áshtá.* Sanscrit *Ashwat.*

Wild in the Sub-Himalayan forests, in Bengal and Central India. Universally planted (*H.*).

When in full growth and in good condition it is a noble tree, and is often seen to great advantage in front of temples, the base of the trunk surrounded by a stone platform. It is also in a very different form, the most destructive of those plants which flourish

"On gray but leafy walls, where ruin greenly dwells."—*Byron.*

"Where o'er some tower in ruin laid,
The peepul spreads its haunted shade."—*Heber.*

The sacred bo tree of Buddha was a peepul: "the age of the bo tree is matter of record, its conservancy has been the object of solicitude to successive dynasties, and the story of its vicissitudes has been preserved in a series of continuous chronicles among the most authentic that have been handed down by mankind" (*Tennent*). A famous pipal at Anarajpura was said to have attained in 1852 the age of 2147 years: (this is so stated on a label in the Museum at Kew).

The leaves in their perpetual motion and pleasing sound resemble those of the poplar and the aspen, celebrated by the poets of all ages:—

"Restless as the leaves of the tall poplar tree."—*Odyssey.*

"And in the meadows tremulous aspen trees
And poplars made a noise of falling showers."—*Tennyson.*

5. *F. Arnottiana* (*Urostigma cordifolium*, D.). A tree much like the last, leaves with very long petioles, broadly heart-shaped with long points, margin waved, 7-nerved, finely reticulated beneath, fruit like that of the last. *Pair.* This also is sometimes called *Ashta.*

On the Ghauts.

6. *F. tsiela* (*Urostigma pseudo-tsiela*, D.). A very large tree, all smooth, leaves long petioled ovate or oblong acute, shining, with numerous simple and parallel veins, fruit in pairs, axillary sessile, smooth, purple, size of a cherry. *Pipri.*

It is much like the pipal, but the leaves are narrower and without the long points.

The Ghauts (*D.* and *G.*). Deccan peninsula (*H.*). I noted it as common in Guzerat.

7. *F. infectoria* (*Urostigma i.* and *U. Lambertianum*, D.). A fine tree, all smooth, leaves rather long petioled oblong acute, nerves 5 to 7 pairs, anther broad ovate, fruit round, size of a marble, white. *Bassári, pákari lendva, kel, pipli.*

Salsette and the Konkans. Plains and lower hills of India; not common wild, frequently planted (*H.*).

8. *F. heterophylla.* A weak straggling shrub, mostly rough with short petioled leaves varying in shape, more or less oval, often 3-lobed, serrated or toothed, nerves 4 to 8 pairs, fruit sessile on the branches roundish or 2-lobed, yellowish, size of a cherry, rough.

Salsette. Common in moist places (*D.*). Throughout the hotter parts of India near water (*H.*).

9. *F. asperrima.* A shrub or small scrubby tree, leaves oblong lanceolate toothed or crenate, exceedingly rough, nerves 3 to 5 pairs, very prominent beneath, fruit round, hairy, rough, red, like a miniature fig. *Karoti, kál-umbar.*

Konkan and elsewhere. Central India and Deccan peninsula (*H.*). The leaves are used as sand-paper. (See Streblus asper.)

10. *F. hispida* (*Covellia oppositifolia* and *dæmonum*, D.). A shrub or small tree with opposite leaves, large, rough, oblong, cordate at the base, shining above, downy beneath, nerves 3 to 5 pairs; young shoots and branches hollow and jointed at the axils, fruit on the stem or branches round, hairy, size of a plum with several longitudinal ridges. *Kál-umbar, dhed-umbar, gándyá-umbar.*

The Konkan. Ghauts, pretty common (*G.*). Panch Mahâls common (*Lisboa*). Throughout India (*H.*). *D.* makes *C. dæmonum* common generally near the sea.

This is much like the last, but altogether larger, and the leaves not so very rough. The hollow branches are a peculiarity, and, in a lesser degree, the opposite leaves.

11. *F. glomerata* (*Covellia g.* D.). A large tree, leaves oblong or broad lanceolate, 3 to 6 nerved, opposite, fruit in clusters on the trunk or branches, like the cultivated fig, but small, red and downy, stamens 2. *Umbar, gular.*

Common in the Konkan and on the Ghauts. Widely spread through India (*H.*).

The fruit of this is eatable, and it is often called the wild fig-tree. The leaves are often covered with galls.

The only other species belonging to this side of India appear to be

F. mysorensis (*Urostigma dasyacarpum*, D.), a fine spreading tree, most parts densely downy, leaves broad ovate or elliptic, thick, veins very prominent beneath, fruit ellipsoid obtuse at both ends, generally twin. *Bhurwad.* Bhândup. Bombay (*D.*). Konkan (*Lisboa*). *F. Benjamina* (*Urostigma B.*, D.), a smooth tree with drooping branches, leaves broad ovate, leathery, male flowers very few, scattered; sepals 2, large, flat, females with shortly spathulate sepals, fruit like peas, smooth yellowish-green dashed with purple, sessile. S. M. country (*D.*). Dr. Cooke mentions *F. caricoides* as the only species besides *F. glomerata* growing at Mabableshwar. This is presumably *H.'s F. palmata*, ascribed to Abu by *H.*, a bush or small tree, leaves roundish-ovate, or obtusely 3—5 lobed, fruit roundish or pear-shaped, yellow.

F. carica, anjir, is the cultivated fig, which seems always to have been one of the most valued of fruits. It is mentioned in the "Odyssey." "There (in the garden of Alcinous) grow tall trees blossoming, pear trees, and pomegranates, and apple trees with bright fruit, and sweet figs, and olives in their bloom." (Bk. 8.) And in Judges ix. 8 it is mentioned with the olive and the vine, as if these three were the choicest of all trees.

The figs grown in India must be placed far below those of England, and these again are in flavour nowhere near the Italian figs; but the scientific cultivation of fruit in India must come in time.

F. elastica is the india-rubber tree, found in Bombay gardens, wild "in damp forests at the bâse of the Sikkim Himalayas," and further east (*H.*). "The close parallel straight nervation of the leaves and the enormous stipules" are its distinguishing marks. The true sycamore is *F. sycamorus.*

6. Antiaris.

* *A toxicaria* (*A. saccidora*, D.). A tree, leaves oblong elliptic acute toothed or serrated, flowers 4-androus on a convex fleshy receptacle, fruit like a small fig, purple or red, with one seed. *Jásund, chándul, chánd kuda.*

Konkan hills and Khandalla (*D.* and *G.*). Deccan peninsula, &c. (*H.*).

"A stately forest tree, truly majestic (*H.* says it attains 250 feet); the flowers are in very curious reflected aments something like a common mulberry" (*G.*). Its viscid juice, obtained by incisions in the bark, hardens into a gum resin, with which the Malays prepare the upas to poison their arrows. But a good many fables have grown up around the name upas, which is in fact only the Malay word for poison.

"The upas tree had reared its head,
And sent its baneful scions all around,
Blasting, where'er its effluent force was shed

In air and water and the infected ground,
All things wherein the breath and sap of life is found."
Southey.

In Coorg and Ceylon sacks are manufactured from its bark. —*Tennent.*

7. Artocarpus.

1. *A. hirsuta.* A handsome tree, leaves elliptic, obtuse or obovate, smooth above, hairy beneath, especially on the nerves; male flowers in pendulous heads 4 to 6 inches long, fruit round, size of a small melon, surface prickly. *Rán fanas, pát fanas, fansul.*

It seems doubtful from *D.* and *G.* whether this is wild in W. India, but it is often found planted. Deccan peninsula (*H.*). The foliage is very like that of the next.

2. *A. integrifolia.* The jack tree. Leaves oval oblong or obovate, rough below, male catkin size of a man's thumb; fruit growing on the trunk and main branches, very large and irregular in shape, rough, tubercled. *Fanas, kanthal.*

The immense fruit, the largest eatable fruit in the world (*Tennent*), sometimes attaining (it is said) the weight of 60 lbs. (*R.*) looks like a huge parasite on the trunk of the tree: the smell generally deters Europeans from tasting it, but having once ventured, I can state that the flavour is not disagreeable.

Colonel Beddome is said to have discovered it wild on the W. Ghauts: otherwise it is known in India only as a cultivated tree. The yellow wood is worthy of more attention for ornamental furniture than it has received.

It is said that the situation of the fruit varies with the age of the tree, being first borne on the branches, then on the trunk, and in very old trees on the roots. Its tenacious white juice makes the best bird-lime (*R.*).

* *A. lakucha* is a large tree, leaves oval entire, downy beneath, male aments about the size of a nutmeg; fruit nearly round smooth, yellow, size of an orange. *Lâni, áond, lákuch.* Caranja and Bassein (*D.*). Cultivated (*G.*).

* *A. incisa* is the bread-fruit tree of the South Seas. It has been grown in Bombay, and elsewhere in India. The fruit is not nearly so large as the jack.

"The bread-fruit, the jaca, and the mango vied with each other in the magnificence of their foliage. The landscape in the neighbourhood of Bahia almost takes its character from the two latter trees. Before seeing them I had no idea that any trees could cast so black a shade on the ground."—*Darwin's Naturalist's Voyage.*

8. Fleurya.

F. interrupta. A rough bristly plant, leaves long-petioled ovate cordate acute, coarsely serrated, flowers in interrupted sessile clusters on long spikes, stamens very elastic. *Khájoti, khájkul, vedekotti.*

S. Konkan; Matheran. A weed in waste places (*D.* and *G.*).

9. ELATOSTEMMA.

E. cuneatum. A very small plant, with leaves arranged in a rosette at the top of the stem, unequal-sided, narrow at the base, broad and toothed at the top, rough; flowers in sessile clusters.

Grows on walls: S. Konkan. Bombay and Belgaum (*D.*).

The description above is as I have seen it, but apparently under other conditions the stem lengthens and the leaves separate. "Base of leaf subauricled with sometimes a minute opposite leaflet" (*H.*).

10. BOEHMERIA.

B. platyphylla (*Splitgerbera scabrella*, D.). Shrubby, 3 or 4 feet high, all rough, leaves very large coarse, long-petioled ovate cordate serrated; spikes numerous, very long, fruit compressed or angled.

Dapoli. Matheran and Mahableshwar.—*Birdwood.* Common in hilly jungles of the Konkan (*D.*).

The above is my description, but *H.* calls it a most variable plant, and has nine varieties. The spike and flowers are suggestive of an amaranth.

B. nivea is the shrub from the bark of which "grass-cloth" is made: a native of the Eastern Islands, cultivated in Bengal.

11. POUZOLZIA.

P. Indica. A hairy plant tinged with red, with square stems and ovate pointed entire leaves, often long-petioled; flowers in sessile clusters within an involucre, hairy and reddish, stamens generally 4, very elastic, fruit winged or not.

The Konkans. Common in gardens as a weed (*D.*).

Throughout tropical and subtropical India (*H.*). It is very like the English pellitory of the wall, Parietaria, thought by many to be "the hyssop that springeth out of the wall" of 1 Kings iv. 33.

H. has 5 vars., some prostrate or creeping.

* *P. pentandra*, stem angled above, leaves entire narrow lanceolate, lower opposite; flowers in a terminal spike, stamens 5, fruit with 3 broad membranous wings. Caranja (*D.*). * *P. Bennettiana* (*P. Stocksii*, D.). Straggling, branched, 4-angled, stipules broad scarious,

leaves oval obtuse, flowers few axillary, stamens 5, fruit ovate ribbed or winged.

Belgaum and Deccan (*D.*). **P. integrifolia*, 3 or 4 feet high, stem slender, leaves opposite, sessile, lanceolate; stamens 3 or 4, fruit cordate or winged. Fonda Ghaut (*D.*), Canara and Deccan (*H.*).

12. Debregeasia.

* *D. velutina* (*Conocephalus niveus*, D.). A tall shrub, leaves ovate lanceolate acute serrated, rough or blistered above, prominently veined and white below, flowers clustered in cymes, drupes small round yellow, something like a mulberry. *Kápsi, kargul.*

Common in Konkan and Ghaut jungles (*D.*). Deccan peninsula (*H.*).

Conocephalus concolor, D., *H.* puts as a doubtful species.

Girardina, shrubs with stout stinging hairs, flowers clustered in spikes, achene broad compressed, seated on the perianth. * *G. heterophylla*, tall stout leaves large, long-petioled, broad cordate, 7-lobed, coarsely toothed, male spikes below panicled, female above and longer. *Moti kajoti, ágia, agarra.* Slopes of the Ghauts (*D.*). Matheran and Mahableshwar. S. Konkan (*G.*). "A formidable plant, the least touch of any part produces most acute pain" (*D.*).

Lecanthus, like Elatostemma, but leaves opposite. * *L. Wightii* (*Elatostemma oppositifolium*, D.). A succulent herb, leaves ovate or lanceolate, heads of flowers peduncled, receptacles flat, discoid, achene minute. Ghauts (*D.*).

The following are cultivated:—

Cannabis sativa, common hemp, *bháng*, producing also *gánja* and *charas*, cultivated throughout India, but wild in N. W. Himalayas (*H.*). The Egyptian haschish is a preparation from the husks of the seeds.

"Of all that Orient lands can vaunt
Of marvels with our own competing,
The strangest is the Haschish plant,
And what will follow on its eating."—*Whittier.*

Humulus lupulus, the hop, well-known in England, but a native of N. America, is cultivated in N. W. Himalayas. It belongs to the same tribe as the last.

The various mulberries, *Morus*, belong to the same tribe as *Streblus M. Indica, tut*, and *M. atropurpuræa, shaitut*, are found in gardens. The latter, a Chinese species, has a long cylindrical fruit, and *H.* considers that it may be only a form of *M. alba*, the sort most frequently cultivated for silkworms in China, and also in France and Italy.

Graham was very sanguine of the cultivation of mulberries and the production of silk in the Deccan, but the promising experiments of his time seem eventually to have come to nothing, like so many other attempts of the same sort.

The nettles, *Urtica*, as giving their name to this order, ought to be mentioned. Three are given by *H.* as occurring in the Himalayas and Thibet at high elevations, one of them in the Nilghiris, and he says, " *U. pilulifera*, the Roman nettle, a common European weed, occurs occasionally near Simla, and elsewhere near houses in the hills." We need not regret their absence from our territories, and in fact many of the species of tribe Urticeæ given above may reasonably be regarded in the same rather contemptuous way as that class of plants is in England.

> " We call a nettle but a nettle, and
> The faults of fools but folly."—*Coriolanus.*

The great order Amentaceæ formerly contained all plants having their flowers arranged in a catkin, a feature easily recognizable. The oaks, beeches, birches, willows, planes, chestnuts, hazels, and other trees were thus included in this order. It is, however, in *H.* split up into a number of orders, of which Casuarineæ and Salicineæ are alone represented here. To CASUARINEÆ belongs *Casuarina equisetifolia, suru, vilayati sáru*, a very well known tree, wild on the east side of the Bay of Bengal, and extending to Malaya and Australia. It is outwardly like a conifer, but is really leafless, the branchlets being green and cylindrical with sheaths of subulate scales at the nodes. It has, or had, a reputation for improving the climate of malarious places; and the branches when gently swayed by the wind give out a sound like that of the sea on a beach, very pleasing to the ears of exiled islanders. It is called in Australia the swamp oak, and in the Pacific Islands *Toa*. The genus is also known as Cassowary tree and Beefwood.

ORDER 108. **SALICINEÆ.** Willows.

Deciduous diœcious trees or shrubs, leaves alternate, with stipules, flowers in catkins, one under each bract, composed of a disk and two or more stamens; style short or none, stigma short, notched or lobed, capsule ovoid or lanceolate 2 to 4-valved, seeds with a pencil of long silky hairs.

This is a small order containing only two genera, but both well known, *Salix* (willow) and *Populus* (poplar). They are mostly trees of cold and temperate climates, found chiefly in damp situations. The greater part of the 26 species of willow given by *H.* belong to the Himalayas.

SALIX. Disk of one or two separate glands.

> "See the yellow catkins cover
> All the slender willows over."—*M. Howitt.*

S. tetrasperma, a small tree, leaves lanceolate, acute smooth, grey beneath, petioles red, male catkins lax and few-flowered, females dense and generally longer, stamens 5 to 10. *Wálunj, bucha, bitasa.*

This is the only wild species of W. India; it has all the appearance of the English willows, and, like many of them, is found on the banks of streams, but in this Presidency only, I believe, in or near the Ghauts, though *H.* gives it as throughout tropical and subtropical India. He calls it a polymorphous plant, and includes in it several different species of other authorities.

> "There is a willow grows aslant a brook,
> That shows his hoar leaves in the glassy stream."—*Hamlet.*

The willow is the tree of jilted lovers—

"I offered him my company to a willow tree, . . . to make him a garland, as being forsaken."—*Much Ado about Nothing.*

The weeping willow, *S. Babylonica* (so called apparently from Ps. cxxxvii. 1, 2) is said to be found in Bombay gardens, and this and other species are, it appears from *H.*, cultivated in N. India for the same purpose as willows at home.

Note.—The next order and Coniferæ belong to a separate class of Exogens, called Gymnospermæ, and differ from all the orders which have gone before in the seeds not being contained in an ovary. There is in fact no pistil, and the ovules, which are naked, are fertilized by the direct application of the pollen.

ORDER 109. GNETACEÆ.

Trees or shrubs with jointed branches, leaves opposite without stipules; filaments columnar, anthers roundish on the top of the column, seed dry or drupaceous.

A very small order: only one species known in W. India.

GNETUM. Flowers whorled in axillary spikes. The male flowers consist of a single stamen, the female of a naked ovule terminating above in a prolongation resembling a style, perianth scarcely distinguishable, seed drupaceous.

The above description is partly from Oliver.

G. scandens. A very large climber with a trunk like a tree, young shoots round and smooth, leaves oval, smooth, shining, entire; racemes containing 2 or 3 pairs of catkins, which are jointed, seed oblong, size of an acorn, orange-coloured with fibrous skin. *Kumbal, umbli.*

Ghauts and Konkan. "Very common in thick jungles" (*D.*).

Deocan and Ghauts (*H.*). The fallen catkins look exactly like green caterpillars with black rings, and legs all round.

Of the CONIFERÆ which come next the only species known in W. India is the Goa cypress, Cupressus glauca, or lusitanica, *sáru*, planted sometimes in gardens, and also in graveyards; the whole genus with the yews being always associated with death and mourning.

"Come away, come away, death,
And in sad cypress let me be laid."—*Twelfth Night.*

"Young flowers and an evergreen tree
May spring from the spot of thy rest,
But nor cypress nor yew let us see,
For why should we mourn for the blest?"—*Byron.*

VI. ENDOGENS.

With the conclusion of the Exogens the interest of our work may seem to decline: for the species of Endogens to be mentioned are not only few in comparison, but are in general, from their small size and the imperfection of their flowers, less attractive to the ordinary observer. "In northern regions everything included in this class of plants is herbaceous, and in hotter latitudes few deserve the name of bush or tree except the Palms, and a few Aroideæ and Asphodeleæ" (*Lindley*). But as Palms make a large exception when speaking of the absence of trees, so the Lilies, Irises, and Orchids (to mention no others), are certainly sufficient to glorify the whole class as regards beauty. And there are perhaps among Endogens, in proportion to the whole number of species, a larger number of flowers which may be called popular favourites, than in the much larger class of Exogens.

The parts of the flower in Endogens are generally in threes, or some multiple of three, which is rarely the case in Exogens.

CONSPECTUS OF ENDOGENOUS ORDERS.

I. Perianth 6-divided: stamens generally 6, but sometimes 3, either with or without staminodes.

ORDER 114. AMARYLLIDEÆ. Bulbous plants with radical leaves.

ORDER 115. TACCACEÆ. A herb with tuberous roots and large pinnatifid leaves.

ORDER 116. DIOSCORACEÆ. Twiners with unisexual flowers: leaves reticulated.

ORDER 117. LILIACEÆ. Herbs: fruit a 3-celled capsule or berry.

Tribe Smilaceæ has reticulated leaves.

Tribe Asparageæ has no real leaves, but much-divided green leaf-like branches.

ORDER 118. PONTEDERACEÆ. Herbs more or less aquatic, flowers from the sheaths of the leaves.

ORDER 119. XYRIDEÆ. A herb with radical leaves and scape of flowers from their sheaths.

ORDER 120. COMMELINACEÆ. Herbs with flat narrow leaves, and flowers from their sheaths or from aggregated bracts.

ORDER 121. FLAGELLARIEÆ. A large climber with small panicled flowers.

ORDER 122. PALMEÆ. Unbranched trees or shrubs with very large leaves collected at the top: flowers enclosed in spathes.

ORDER 126. ALISMACEÆ. Marsh or water plants with conspicuous flowers.

II. Perianth often but not always 6-divided, stamens not usually 6.

ORDER 110. HYDROCHARIDEÆ. Aquatic herbs, flowers unisexual in a spathe: stamens various.

ORDER 111. BURMANNIACEÆ. Herbs with bracted flowers: stamens 3.

ORDER 113. SCITAMINEÆ. Flowers irregular with petal-like bracts, stamen one with petaloid staminodes, leaves pinnately nerved from the midrib.

III. Perianth none, or sometimes (in Aroideæ) of scales, stamens various.

ORDER 123. PANDANACEÆ. Trees or shrubs, flowers on a spadix.

ORDER 124. AROIDEÆ. Herbs, flowers on a spadix, enclosed in a spathe.

ORDER 125. LEMNACEÆ. Very small floating plants, stamens 1 or 2.

IV. Not included in the above.

ORDER 112. ORCHIDEÆ. Herbs with very irregular conspicuous flowers, stamens and style united into a column.

ORDER 127. NAIADACEÆ. Aquatic plants with perianth and stamens various.

ORDER 110. HYDROCHARIDEÆ.

Aquatic herbs with undivided leaves, flowers unisexual, enclosed in a spathe, perianth 6-divided in two series, and therefore representing sepals and petals, stamens and styles 3 to 12, ovary inferior, fruit membranous or fleshy.

Many of the species of this order are so small that the parts of the flower are quite indistinguishable except when much magnified: in other species all the parts are of good size and well developed (*H.*).

1. HYDRILLA. A submerged diœcious herb, leaves whorled, sepals petals and stamens 3, styles 2 or 3, stigmas 3.

2. LAGEROSIPHON. Submerged diœcious herbs, leaves scattered, male flowers many together, female solitary; anthers 2 or 3 with often 3 staminodes, ovary oblong produced into a filiform beak, styles 3.

3. VALLISNERIA. A submerged tufted diœcious herb, leaves very long linear, male flowers very numerous, female solitary at the end of a very long thread-like spiral scape; sepals 3, petals none, stamens one to three, anthers twin, stigmas 3, fruit linear included in the spathe.

4. OTTELIA. Leaves crowded, the submerged narrow, the floating long-petioled broader, flowers solitary sessile on a tubular bifid spathe, stamens 6 to 15; ovary oblong, styles 6 bifid, fruit oblong 6-valved enclosed in the spathe.

1. Hydrilla.

* *H. verticillata.* Growing in large masses, leaves very small, sessile, oblong, serrulate, 4 to 8 in a whorl, with a short sheathing one at the base of each branch, and a short pair above this, linear or oblong; perianth segments very variable, fruit smooth or warty.

Common in tanks (*D.*). Still and slowly running waters throughout India and Ceylon (*H.*). *R.* has "male calyx 4-toothed, corolla 4-petalled, female calyx 4-parted."

2. Lagerosiphon.

* *L. Roxburghii* (*Nechmandra R.* D.). Stems filiform, leaves alternate, linear acute, grass-like, stem clasping, male spathe ovate enclosing many flowers, female tubular bifid at the apex, fruit many-seeded.

Common in tanks throughout India and Ceylon (*H.*). In both this and the last (as well as the next) the male flowers separate from the spadix and float away in search of the female flower.

3. Vallisneria.

V. spiralis. Leaves slightly spathaceous, flowers minute, males on short stalks, fruit long linear below the flower.

N. Konkan. In *G.* but not in *D.* Throughout India and Ceylon, and otherwise very widely distributed (*H.*). The remarkable arrangement by which the flowers of this plant are fertilized is described and figured in many botanical works. The best description that I have seen is Sir J. Lubbock's. "The female flower has a long spiral stalk, which by uncoiling enables the flower to reach the top of the water. The male flowers, which are small, numerous, and attached lower down, separate from the plant, rise to the surface and fertilize the female flower, around which they float. The spiral stalk of the female flower then contracts, and draws it down below the surface." "In the soft heaven of a translucent pool," the long spiral stalk is a beautiful object, and the minute male flowers floating on the surface of the water look more like pollen.

The plant is mentioned in 'Sákuntalá' under the name of *saivala.* "The lotus with the *saivala* entwined."—*Sir M. Williams*' translation.

4. Ottelia.

O. alismoides (*O. Indica*, D.). Leaves and peduncles all from the root, which is under water, floating leaves large oblong cordate, petioles 3-sided, flowers above the water white, rather large; the swelling ovary covered by the spathe is as much as 2½ inches long.

Deccan and Konkan. Tanks and ditches throughout India and Ceylon (*H.*). Leaves extremely variable; fruit 6-grooved, attaining 2 inches in diameter (*H.*).

Blyxa, stemless plants, bearing a spathe; leaves linear, male flowers several in a tubular 2-toothed spathe, sepals 3, petals 3, longer stamens 3 to 9, pistillodes 3, female flowers solitary sessile in the spathe, stigmas 3. * *B. Roxburghii*, a grasslike plant, leaves radical, sword-shaped, 8 to 24 inches long, flowers white, stamens 8, seeds tubercled, sometimes with short tails. **B. echinosperma*, leaves 6 inches to 4 feet long, like the last, stamens 3, capsule 2 or 3 inches long, seeds spiny, with a long thread-like tail at each end. **B. Talboti*, leaves 4 to 6 inches long, linear lanceolate, serrulate, narrowed from below the middle to the base, capsule an inch or two long, seeds with strong protuberances. These three are not in *D.* The first is attributed by *G.* (*Vallisneria octandra*, R.) to the margins of tanks throughout the Konkans; the two last have been found in Canara by Mr. Talbot.

ORDER 111. BURMANNIACEÆ.

Herbs with regular flowers, bracted, sepals and petals 3 each, or the latter wanting; stamens 3 on the tube, ovary inferior, capsule 3-valved, crowned by the perianth.

A very small order. "Natives of moist grassy places in the tropics."—*Balfour*.

BURMANNIA. Leaves radical sword-shaped or reduced to scales, calyx tube winged or angled, anthers sessile or nearly so, with a crested connective, style 3-lobed.

B. cœlestis (*B. triflora*, D.). About six inches high, scape square, leafless except for a few lanceolate scales, flowers terminal not more than 3, very pretty, the long 3-winged tube dark blue, the 3 lobes very small tipped with white.

Dapoli. Matheran and Mahableshwar (*Birdwood*). Mhar (*D.*). Widely distributed, and very variable in size, leafiness, and form of flowers (*H.*). **B. pusilla*, Konkan (*Law*), *H.* suspects to be a small state of the last, radical leaves very few, cauline none, or one or two. **B. disticha*, scape up to 20 inches, all the leaves radical, flowers crowded on a double spike, blue, sepals keeled at the back, capsule 3-winged. Neither of these are in *D.*, but the latter is in *G.*, S. Konkan.

Order 112. ORCHIDEÆ. Orchids.

Herbs, with simple quite entire leaves, either terrestrial with tuberous roots and annual simple stem, or epiphytes with perennial stems or branches thickened and shortened into a bulb-like mass (pseudo-bulbs). Flowers bisexual, perianth superior irregular with 6 segments arranged in two rows, the three outer (sepals) more or less alike; of the inner (petals) the two lateral are alike, the lower (lip) quite different, often large and lobed and provided with a spur at the base. The stamens and style are united in a column which is opposite the lip, and bears a single anther, free or adnate to it, with the pollen in two or more solid masses (pollinia); ovary inferior, usually linear and twisted, stigma a viscid surface on the top of the column, below the anther; fruit a capsule with 3 or 6 valves, containing many minute seeds.

"The orchis family (which consists of about 5000 species), is without question the most remarkable in the vegetable world. No plants unfold blossoms of more fantastic beauty, of odours more delicious, or of colours more vivid."—*Sowerby.*

To this it must be added that it is, at present, by far the most fashionable of floral families among English people.

The flowers of most, though not of all orchids, are so peculiar in shape, mainly in regard to the lip and staminal column, as to be at once recognizable. The twisted ovary might often be mistaken at first sight for the pedicel of the flower.

"In Mexico, where the language of flowers is understood by all, the Orchideæ seem to compose nearly the entire alphabet. Not an infant is baptized, not a marriage is celebrated, not a funeral obsequy performed, at which the aid of these flowers is not called in by the sentimental natives to assist the expression of their feelings. They are offered by the devotee at the shrine of his favourite saint, by the lover at the feet of his mistress, and by the sorrowing survivor at the grave of his friend; whether, in short, on fast days or feast days, on occasions of rejoicing or in moments of distress, these flowers are sought for with an avidity, which would seem to say that there was no sympathy like theirs."—*Bateman*—(quoted in *Contemporary Review*).

The most obvious distinction between the various orchids is into Epiphytes, or those which grow on trees, and terrestrial plants. Epiphytes differ from parasites in not deriving their sustenance from the tree or plant on which they grow, but mainly from the air. They are found almost exclusively in the moister parts of the tropics, while terrestrial orchids belong quite as much to the temperate regions of the world.

The genera of Orchideæ are divided by *H.* into 5 tribes, of which the first four, each divided into several subtribes, are here represented. I have thought it better to give the distinctions of these tribes, though confessing that I myself know little about the pollinia, which form so great a part of these descriptions.

TRIBE 1. EPIDENDREÆ. All here given are Epiphytes (except Microstylis, and perhaps Liparis). Anther cells distinct and parallel, pollinia waxy, one to nine in each cell, or those of each cell held together by a viscid appendage.

1. OBERONIA. Tufted: leaves distichous, sword-shaped, flowers very minute in dense spikes or racemes, sepals broad, ovate or oblong, petals smaller, lip sessile, concave, column very short.

Note.—"Tufted" is used of stems when very short, close, and many from the same root.

2. MICROSTYLIS. Terrestrial: flowers small in terminal racemes; sepals and petals about the same length; lip united to the base of the column, usually flat.

3. DENDROBIUM. Stems elongate or pseudo-bulbous; flowers racemose, often large and handsome, sepals about equal, the lateral obliquely united to the foot of the column, lip contracted at the base, similarly united, column short.

4. ERIA. Flowers not large or bright-coloured, sepals free, lip sessile on the foot of the column, spur various.

5. PHAJUS. Large stout herbs, leaves pleated, flowers large, handsome, racemed, sepals and petals about equal, lip embracing the column, erect, column long and stout.

TRIBE 2. VANDEÆ. Epiphytes (except Eulophia and Geodorum); anther cells generally confluent, pollinia waxy, usually 2 or 4 in superposed pairs, attached to a gland or process.

6. EULOPHIA. Terrestrial smooth herbs, leaves pleated, scape usually leafless, flowers racemose, sepals and petals free, spreading, lip erect from the base of the column, its disk crested or softly spinous, top of the column oblique, entire.

7. CYMBIDIUM. Generally epiphytes, scape loosely sheathed, flowers in racemes often large, sepals and petals about equal, free, lip embracing the column upwards, middle lobe recurved, column long.

8. RHYNCOSTYLIS. Stem stout, leafy, leaves very thick, linear, 2-lobed; flowers in long dense drooping racemes, sepals and petals spreading, lip produced into a broad dilated limb, without side lobes, column short and stout.

9. ÆRIDES. Stem leafy, leaves linear, flowers many in curved racemes, sepals and petals broad and spreading, column short.

10. SACCOLABIUM. Flowers usually small in simple or branched racemes, sepals and petals similar, free, united to the base of the column, spreading, lip with small lobes.

TRIBE 3. NEOTTIEÆ. Small terrestrial herbs. Anther cells distinct and parallel, pollen granular, powdery, or in small masses.

11. SPIRANTHES. Flowers small, often in twisted or spiral spikes, dorsal sepal and petals forming a hood, lip entire or 3-lobed, column short.

12. ZEUXINE. Flowers small spicate, hood as in the last, lip boat-shaped or saccate, the sac spurred within, column very short keeled or winged in front.

13. POGONIA. Herbs with one leaf, broad and pleated, appearing after the flowers; flowers racemed, sepals and petals about equal, narrow, lip with very short spur or sac, column rather long.

TRIBE 4. OPHRYDEÆ. Terrestrial; anther cells parallel or divergent below, often produced into a tube, pollinia one, rarely two, in each cell, granular, produced into short tails.

14. HABENARIA. Leafy herbs, flowers spicate or racemed, lip continuous with the base of the column, spurred, anther adnate to the very short column.

Note.—The very great majority of the species of W. India are found only in the Konkan and Ghauts. The proportion that I have seen is unusually small, and it will be noticed also that *H.* has a very large number of species which were not known to *D.*

1. OBERONIA.

O. recurva. A very small stemless plant, leaves fleshy oval, veinless, flowers minute, brick-red, dense, in a raceme 2 inches long, lip 3-lobed, the middle lobe 2 divided.

Tanna districts. Trees on the Ghauts (*D.*).

H. does not refer to *D.* either in this or *O. Lindleyana*, but there seems no reason for doubting the identity of the plants described.

* *O. Lindleyana* D. calls much larger than this, leaves short fleshy brown, somewhat falcate, spike very dense, flowers sessile, petals narrow linear, lip 2-lobed, flowers straw-coloured with orange lip. Trees on the Ghauts (*D.*).

* *O. Falconeri*, stem very short, leaves one or two inches long,

sword-shaped, bracts ovate, serrulate, flowers minute, greenish-yellow, lip with 2 small incurved lobes at the tip, lateral lobes small, capsule short-stalked. Konkan, Bombay, &c. (*H.*). * *O. platycaulon,* leaves narrow sword-shaped, 6 to 10 inches long, scape shorter, flowers densely imbricated, much larger than *O. recurva;* petals narrow, lip with broad rounded lateral lobes and a very short 2 or 3-divided terminal one. From the Konkan to the Nilghiris (*H.*). These two are not in *D.*

2. Microstylis.

* *M. Rheedii.* Stem 3 to 6 inches high, leafy, leaves broad ovate pleated, the base often unequal, flowers greenish-yellow or purple, fragrant, in a long slender raceme, bracts lanceolate, bent down, lip rounded, reniform or fan-shaped, finely toothed.

S. Konkan (*D.*). Common in the Ghauts (*H.*). Mahableshwar, "very like a Plantago.—*Birdwood.*

* *M. Stocksii.* Stem one or two inches high, leaves ovate lanceolate, bracts lanceolate bent down, flowers yellow, half an inch across, lip much broader than long, deeply lobed. Not in *D.* or *G.* Bababudin Hills, *Stocks* (*H.*).

3. Dendrobium.

H. has 158 species. "The name *bechu* is commonly given to all dendrobiums: *nángli* is another name," *Birdwood.*

1. *D. microbulbon.* Very small with one or two linear lanceolate or oblong leaves, or none, flowers few in racemes, the shape of a cornucopia, outer sepals and petals white, lip large 3-lobed, column green streaked with red.

On trees at Mahableshwar. Konkan (*D.*).

2. * *D. chlorops.* Stems 12 to 18 inches long, sometimes very stout, leaves oblong, lanceolate, soon falling; flowers white, greenish, or yellowish, middle lobe of lip round, fleshy, crenate, petals much broader than the lateral sepals.

Common in both Konkans (*D.*). Flowers very variable in size and colour (*H.*).

3. *D. barbatulum.* Six to fifteen inches high, very succulent, stems short and thick, leaves narrow lanceolate, but soon falling; flowers in racemes cream-coloured with some green, middle lobe of the lip flat, obtuse, bearded at the base with yellow hairs, spur short and thick.

S. Konkan and Mahableshwar. Common in the Konkans (*D.*).

* *D. Macraei*, much-branched, stems 2 or 3 feet long, leaf one terminal, oblong, flowers 2 or 3, small white, the middle lobe of the lip much dilated, and the disk crested. On *jámbul* trees at Rám Ghaut (*D.*). * *D. herbaceum* (*D. ramosissimum*, D.). Much-branched, branchlets leafy, leaves linear lanceolate, flowers few, small, yellow, lip narrow, middle lobe shorter than the side ones. Mahableshwar and Ghauts (*D.*). * *D. crepidatum* (*D. Lawianum*, D.). Stems stout, erect, leaves linear lanceolate, flowers in pairs, white or pink, lip yellow, roundish or broad ovate, concave. *Pátrika.* "The flowers are of a beautiful shining rose-colour" (*D.*). On trees on the Ghauts to the S. (*D.*). S. Konkan and Canara (*H.*).

All these six species are in Mr. Birdwood's Matheran list.

4. Eria.

E. Dalzellii (including *E. microchilos*, D.). One or two inches high, pseudo-bulbs lobed, reticulated with a white skin, spike many-flowered, one-sided; flowers minute, straw-colour with dull orange lip, bracts sepals and petals more or less lanceolate.

Sáwarda. Wári country and Ghauts (*D.*).

* *E. reticosa* (*E. braccata*, D.). Pseudo-bulbs round, enclosed in a net-like skin, stem none, leaves about 2, lanceolate, scape one-flowered with large boat-shaped bract; flowers rather large, white, lip yellowish, obscurely lobed and inconspicuous, spur broad incurved. S. Konkan and Ghauts (*D.*). Matheran (*Birdwood*). * *E. mysorensis*, leaves lanceolate, flowers from among them, curved, sepals petals and lip more or less lanceolate, the latter clawed. Not in *D.* Dharwar, &c. (*H.*).

5. Phajus.

* *P. albus.* Stems stout, pendulous, leaves in two rows, oblong, soft, glaucous beneath, sepals and petals oblong lanceolate, 2 or 3 inches long, white, lip shovel-shaped, middle lobe broad, toothed and crisped, white or yellow, veined darker, spur short.

Not in *D.* "Trees at Khandalla, rare; a very beautiful parasite" (*G.*). The Konkan. "Very variable in size of flower and colour of lip" (*H.*).

The following belong also to this tribe:—

Liparis. Lip united to the base of the column, usually broad, column long, bent in, margined or winged towards the top. * *L. paradoxa*, 6 to 18 inches high, leaves erect, sheathing, lanceolate, flowers racemed, yellow-brown, lip with the sides erect. * *L. Dalzellii*, stems 4 inches long, as thick as the thumb, leaves elliptic ovate, flowers half an inch across, lip fleshy, dark purple, broadly obcordate, tubercled at the base. Neither of these are in *D.*, and I have not been able to make out whether they are terrestrial or epiphytes. Konkan (*H.*).

Cirrhopetalum, scape arising from the pseudo-bulb, or distant from it, flowers in whorls, petals smaller than sepals, lip very small and stalked, column very short. * *C. fimbriatum*, leafless, umbels many-flowered, petals and dorsal sepal long-ciliated, lip tumid, fleshy: "lateral sepals cream-coloured with darker lines, the rest red" (*D.*); but 'flowers green with red cilia' (*H.*). "On trees on Parwar Ghaut—'the umbrella orchis' from the inflorescence: curious and beautiful" (*D.*). Konkan and Canara (*H.*). Matheran.—*Birdwood.*

Trias, small, scape lateral, one-flowered, petals and lip small, column short, broad, anther produced into a long horn. * *T. Stocksii*, leaves elliptic, an inch long, petals ovate lanceolate, erect, lip oblong, convex. Not in *D.* Canara and Konkan (*H.*).

Josephia, stemless, leaves radical, flowers very small in panicles, lip erect, fleshy, concave, 3-lobed, column erect, broad. * *J. lanceolata*, leaves linear lanceolate, narrowed into a petiole, bracts short, ovate, petals narrower than sepals, flowers white, tinged with purple. Not in *D.* W. Ghauts (*H.*). "Inflorescence like that of a Statice: Wight, on Jerdon's authority, mentions the curious fact of the persistent, continuously flowering spikes" (*H.*).

Pholidota, bracts in two rows, rigid, flowers small, round, sepals concave, petals flat, lip erect. * *P. imbricata*, leaf solitary, 6 to 12 inches long, oblong lanceolate, petioled, racemes long, drooping, slender, sepals united at the base, lip roundish hooded, the two terminal lobes smaller. Near Vingorla (*D.*).

Tribe 2. VANDEÆ. 6. EULOPHIA.

1. *E. pratensis.* One or two feet high, stem sheaths acute, flowers large, yellow and brown, petals and sepals much alike, lobes of the lip ovate rounded, the middle one with 3 crested veins.

Sholapore districts. Deccan pastures (*D.*). Mahableshwar.—*Cooke.*

D. has this as leafless, and I found it so—apparently—but *H.* says the leaves appear with the flowers.

2. * *E. nuda* (*E. bicolor*, D.). Tall and stout with lanceolate leaves coming after the flowers, which are large, green and purple, sepals and petals elliptic oblong, lip with obscure side lobes, the middle lobe crisped with many crested or tubercled veins. *Ambarkand.*

Ghauts (*D.*). Matheran (*Birdwood*). Many parts of India (*H.*). The root is like a potato.

* *E. herbacea D.* has something like the last, (but *H.* has it in a different group with "the column produced into a foot") the spike

shorter and thicker, spur shorter and flowers double the size. *H.* has petals very variable white with purple nerves, lip white with yellow nerves, bracts very long. The Konkan (*D.*). * *E. ochreata*, leaves elliptic with 3 broad loose sheaths, bracts lanceolate, petals broader than the sepals, acute, flat, lip oblong serrated, with all the veins fringed, spur small, hemispherical. "A small-flowered species with rather dense cylindrical raceme: all parts of the flower membranous" (*D.*). Konkan and Canara, and no other hab. (*H.*).

7. Cymbidium.

* *C. bicolor* (*C. aloifolium*, D.). Leaves long sword-shaped, the tip unequally lobed, racemes pendulous, many-flowered; petals and sepals lanceolate, yellowish-red, lip dark lilac or purple with saccate base and acute side lobes, disk with 2 curved thick side appendages.

Mahableshwar and Konkan (*D.* and *G.*). "One of our largest orchids, growing in great bunches on the branches of trees, and even on palms" (*D.*).

8. Rhyncostylis.

R. retusa (*Saccolabium guttatum*, D.). Stem stout, leaves thick linear channelled, ragged at the apex; flowers very many, in large and beautiful drooping racemes, pale with purple spots, sepals and petals closely joined and spreading, so as to make the flower as broad as long, lip long narrow, bending over to the column, spur short baggy.

Very frequent on mango trees in the Konkan, and spread more or less all over India. It is very conspicuous, and one of the most beautiful of the plants which "drink the bright shower, and feed upon the air" (*Dr. Darwin*).

9. Ærides.

Æ. maculosum. Leaves oblique at the point, obtuse, petals broader than sepals, lip ovate with a tubercle at the base of the middle lobe, and a short straight spur; flowers pale rose-colour, spotted with purple. *Ichwách.*

Rutnagherry and Mahableshwar. Pretty common in Konkan jungles (*D.*). Matheran (*Birdwood*). This also is a large and handsome species, and is no doubt *G.'s Æ. multiflorum*. *H.* seems to make the size much smaller, and does not refer to either *D.* or *G.*

* *Æ. crispum*, stem very stout, leaves strap-shaped, obliquely 2-lobed, panicle large, the terminal raceme long and drooping, sepals and petals very broad, mid-lobe of lip broad ovate crenate or toothed, spur short, obtuse, projecting forward, flowers rose-coloured, lip darker. *Rakhsing, pánsing.* S. Konkan and Wári (*D.*). W. Ghauts (*H.*).

Matheran (*Birdwood*). *H.* says he knows of no character whereby to separate *D.'s Æ. Lindleyana* from this. He also ascribes to the Konkan, but without any Bombay authority, *Æ. odoratum*, which has strap-shaped leaves, mid-lobe of lip incurved between the much larger side-lobes; flowers purple to nearly white, often purple-spotted or -tipped.

10. Saccolabium.

1. *S. Wightianum* (*S. papillosum,* D.). Stem 12 to 18 inches, leaves thick fleshy strap-shaped, unequal at the point; flowers fragrant, stiff and fleshy, nearly sessile on a short thick peduncle, sepals and petals nearly alike, greenish-yellow with horizontal purple bars, lip oval, pure white streaked with violet, saccate at base.

A very common species in the Konkan, but of little beauty. W. Ghauts (*H.*).

* *S. præmorsum,* "Near the last, but more slender, the leaves narrower, lip deeply lobed, very complicate, flowers small, papillose all over." Konkan, *Law* (*H.*) Not in *D.* or *G.*

2. *S. maculatum* (*Micropera m.* D.). Almost stemless, leaves flat linear, oblong, obliquely 2-lobed, spotted, racemes erect, many-flowered; flowers greenish-yellow, lip white spotted with purple, sepals erect, lateral petals turned down, side-lobes of lip erect horn-like, spur short and blunt.

S. Konkan. Talkat Ghaut (*D.*). Canara and W. Ghauts (*H.*).

The specimens that I had were very small, but *H.* gives the plant a larger size—leaves 4 to 6 inches long. "The whole flower like a side-saddle" (*D.*); a resemblance that may, perhaps, be discovered when pointed out.

* *S. viridiflorum.* Allied to the last (*H.*); very small, leaves 2 oblong, flat, flowers few fleshy, greenish-white, the lip variegated with rose-colour, sepals and petals clawed, obtuse, spur short conical, incurved.

Ghauts (*D.*). Also S. Konkan (*H.*).

To this tribe also belong :—

Geodorum, terrestrial, scape stout, erect, sheathed, racemes curved, lip boat-shaped erect, anther 2-celled with appendages after dehiscence. * *G. purpureum*, usually tall, leaves oval, flowers from white veined with red-purple to pale-purple with stronger veins, lip more or less fiddle-shaped, disk with a broad channelled ridge ending in a callosity. Wári country (*D.*). * *G. dilatatum* differs from the last in lower stature and broader petals and lip, the disk of which is smooth, granulate or sub-keeled. No hab. (*D.*).

Luisia, tufted epiphytes, stem sheathed, leaves more or less cylindric, flowers in short spikes drooping, bracts very short, thick, imbricated, petals narrower than sepals, column very short truncate. * *L. tenuifolia*, stem long and slender, flowers few and large, yellowish-green and purple, lip oblong auricled at the base, 2-lobed at the apex, with 3 callosities on the disk. S. Konkan (*D.*).

Cottonia, stem leafy, sepals and narrower petals widely spreading, lip much longer, more or less fiddle-shaped. * *C. macrostachya*, leaves strap-shaped, obliquely 2-lobed, scape 12 to 18 inches with branches, bearing a few short racemes on the apex, sepals broad ovate, lip purple with yellow border, velvety, furnished with bristly knobs and curious appendages (*D.*), like that of *Ophrys aranifera*, i.e. the English spider orchis (*H.*). Wári country and Chorla Ghaut (*D.*).

Vanda, stems leafy, sepals and petals about equal, spreading from a narrow base, lip large, mid-lobe short and stout. * *V. parviflora* (*Ærides Wightianum*, D.). Stem 4 to 6 inches, leaves strap-shaped, obliquely 2-lobed, racemes many-flowered, sepals and petals oval yellow and brown; lip with mid-lobe 2 or 3 divided at the tip, deep lilac, disk crested with fleshy blue lines, spur slender conical. S. Konkan (*D.*). * *V. Roxburghii*, leaves narrow, pleated, flowers large yellowish-green, or bluish, tesselated with brown and with white margins, disk of lip with fleshy ridges, spur conical. Not in *D.* Guzerat and Konkan (*H.*).

Sarcanthus, like Saccolabium, but petals and sepals fleshy, and spur with a callus or erect plate within. * *S. peninsularis*, stem leafy pendulous, leaves linear thick, racemes opposite the leaves, flowers bent down, green or yellow with pink margins and violet lip, side-lobes of lip erect, mid-lobe small acute, spur as long as the flower, obtuse. Wári country (*D.*). Ghauts (*H.*).

Tribe 3. Neottieæ. 11. Spiranthes.

* *S. australis.* Six to eighteen inches high, leaves very variable, linear lanceolate to sword-shaped, spikes twisted, slender, with very close-set white or reddish flowers, lip oblong crisp saccate, with 2 glands.

Chorla Ghaut (*D.*). Throughout India (*H.*), and widely spread over the world. *S. æstivalis*, ladies' tresses, is one of the common small English orchids, and the spirally twisted flowers mark the genus.

12. Zeuxine.

Z. sulcata. Stem leafy, leaves erect linear lanceolate, margins usually recurved, spike dense, flowers white, yellow, or pale rose, lip oblong tongue-shaped, dilated and 2-lobed at apex, or with a hammer-headed terminal lobe.

Sholapore. Throughout India in the plains and lower hills (*H.*). Not in *D.* or *G.* "The commonest Indian orchid: very variable in size" (*H.*). I had it about a foot high.

* *Z. longilabris* (*Monochilus l.*, D.). Very small, leaves ovate petioled, scape scaly, spike glandular pubescent, few-flowered, bracts roundish hooded as long as the ovary, lip much longer than the sepals, winged and toothed, flowers white with green sepals. Chorla Ghaut (*D.*). Ghauts and S. Konkan (*H.*).

13. Pogonia.

P. carinata. Erect, leaf cordate much pleated, quite separate from the stem, petals and sepals equal lanceolate, green, lip about the same length, white streaked with red or purple, mid-lobe broad, capsule oval, 6-winged.

Dapoli. Common in Konkan jungles (*D.*). Plains of India (*H.*).

* *P. flabelliformis* "differs from the last in the many-nerved leaf: the flowers are not readily distinguishable in dried specimens" (*H.*). *D.* also found no better distinctions—"Densest and shadiest thickets of the Konkan; also near Dharwar;" but he had never seen the flowers.

* *P. plicata*, leaf round cordate hairy, petiole often rusty purple, or brown; flowers one to three, yellowish-green with whitish or rose-coloured lip; sepals and petals spreading; lip embracing the column, the tip broad 2-lobed. Not in *D.* or *G.* Konkan (*H.*). "Growing under the thick shade of bamboos in the vicinity of Calcutta; immediately after the flowers decay the leaf from each bulb appears" (*R.*).

To this tribe also belongs *Cheirostylis*. Stem leafy, sepals combined in a tube, lip erect, base saccate, limb clawed and then dilated, column short with two appendages in front. * *C. flabellata*, scape glandular, pubescent, leaves ovate acute, flowers few white, limb of lip roundish, deeply 2-cleft, the divisions 4 or 5-lobed, the claw with two callosities at the base. Chorla Ghaut (*D.*). Konkan (*H.*). "The leaves are almost transparent and most beatifully veined" (*D.*).

Tribe 4. Ophrydeæ.

14. Habenaria.

To this tribe most of the well-known English orchids belong.

H. has no less than 106 species of *Habenaria* in his Flora, and divides them into two divisions and eight sections. Of the species given below all except the last four are in division A, which has "lateral sepals spreading, deflexed or reflexed." Division B has "lateral sepals erect or ascending, or forming a hood with the dorsal sepal and petals."

Note.—The flowers are nearly always white, though sometimes tinged with green or yellow.

Note.—Dr. Dymock gives *Mhenas* as the Marhatta name of the various species of this genus.

DIVISION A. *Section* 1. Petals truncate, bifid or bipartite, lip 3-lobed.

1. *H. digitata.* One or two feet high, leaves oblong ovate, waved, flowers greenish-white, the segments of the petals and of the lip linear and much alike, bract spur and ovary nearly the same length.

Dápoli. Caranjah (*D.*). W. Ghauts (*H.*).

Smell strong and sickly. *H.* makes *D.'s H. foliosa* a var. of this; it is smaller, and has the peculiarity of having the hinder divisions of the petals spirally twisted. I had it at Dápoli, *D.* in Salsette.

* *H. Gibsoni*, very stout and leafy, "much like a gigantic state of *H. digitata* with much longer leaves, and a few very large flowers" (*H.*). Not in *D.* or *G.* Near Kyreshwar, Konkan, and Khandalla, *Dr. Gibson* (*H.*).

2. *H. grandiflora* (*H. rotundifolia*, D.). All smooth, about six inches high, stem slender, arising from one round leaf pressed close on the ground; flowers few, divisions of the lip about equal, middle one broader.

Rutnagherry, on the rocks, and I believe very common at Dápoli, but I have made some mistake in my notes. Between Rám Ghaut and Belgaum, and Sivner Fort (*D.*). Konkan and Ghauts, and no other hab. (*H.*). The specific name is very misleading.

* 3. *H. rariflora.* Stem slender, leaves oblong lanceolate, radical, or on the lower part of the stem; flowers one or two with bracts shorter than the pedicels, lower segment of petals longer and narrower than the upper, lateral segments of lip long and very narrow, spur very long and stout.

S. Konkan (*D.*). Ghauts and Deccan peninsula; leaves and flowers very variable in size (*H.*).

* *H. stenopetala*, stem tall and stout, leaves oblong, raceme short dense, flowers very variable in size, greenish, segments of petals slender, sepals with filiform tips, segments of lip very variable, spur as long as the ovary. Not in *D.* or *G.* Konkan, *Stocks* (*H.*).

Section 2. Petals entire, lip 3-lobed, side-lobes broad, except *H. platyphylla*, mid-lobe narrow.

4. *H. Susannæ* (*Platanthera S.*, D.). The giant orchis. Two to four feet high, leaves ovate oblong acute, flowers very large, upper sepal very broad, 4-sided, petals linear acute, side-lobes of lip very broad, truncate, pectinated, mid-lobe linear, spur very long, bracts leafy.

Dápoli. Konkan and Ghauts in several places, but nowhere abundant (*D.*). "One plant has been found at Mahableshwar, and one at Matheran" (*Birdwood*).

There is no mistaking this grand plant, from its height and the size of the flowers, which *H.* puts at three or four inches in diameter. The deeply pectinated lobes of the lip are also very conspicuous.

"From the root
Springs lighter the green stalk, from thence the leaves
More aëry, last the bright consummate flower
Spirits odorous breathes."—*Milton.*

5. *H. longicalcarata.* Two feet high, leaves oblong, elliptic, stem clothed with sheaths of leaves, flowers white and green, with peduncles and bracts equal, mid-lobe of lip narrow lanceolate, side-lobes truncated, crenate, spur several times longer than ovary.

Dápoli. Grassy pastures near Belgaum, abundant (*D.*). Khandalla (*G.*). Ghauts (*H.*). This also is a large and handsome species.

* *H. platyphylla*, six to eighteen inches high, leaves three to six, sessile roundish or elliptic, pressed to the ground, flowers fragrant, sepals broader than petals, mid-lobe of lip lanceolate, spur slender, longer than ovary. Not in *D.* Mahableshwar (*Cooke*). Identified by *H.* with *G.'s* plant of the same name (Belgaum and Dharwar), which, however, he described as having a single round leaf pressed flat to the ground. * *H. suaveolens*, six inches high, leafy at base, leaves lanceolate acute folded, scape angled with one bract in the middle, flowers few, petals and sepals alike, mid-lobe of lip narrow, side-lobes obliquely truncated, slightly toothed, spur filiform as long as the ovary. This species depends on Dalzell alone, who had it between Vingorla and Malwan. * *H. crinifera*, very slender, leaves oblong lanceolate, sepals broader than petals, lip much longer, clawed and 4-partite, the side lobes tailed, spur much longer than the beaked ovary. Near Vingorla (*D.*). Ram Ghaut (*G.*). *D.* calls it three to five inches high.; *H.* up to eighteen inches.

Section 3. Petals entire, lip 3-partite, side-lobes very narrow, entire, filiform.

6. *H. commelinifolia.* Tall, robust, leaves oblong lanceolate, bracts longer than the beaked ovary, mid sepal roundish, lip with a linear blade, dividing into three very long filiform segments, spur incurved, green, very long.

Salsette. S. Konkan (*G.*). Canara also (*H.*). Not in *D.*

7. *H. Heyneana.* Stem short and stout, leaves narrow oval, bracts leafy, hooded, large, sepals broader than petals, lip thick, mid-lobe longer and broader than the side-lobes, spur about as long as ovary; flowers yellowish-green.

Lanoli. Wári country and Ghauts (*D.*).

* *H. subpubens* (*H. candida*, D.), perhaps only a form of this, but more slender, leaves linear, flowers white, lip spathulate, clawed, trifid (*H.*). S. Konkan (*D.* and *H.*). Mahableshwar (*Cooke*).

8. *H. marginata.* Eight inches to a foot high, leaves near the base, ovate with whitish margins, racemes dense, flowers yellow, sepals and petals about the same length, lip longer, mid-lobe obtuse, shorter than the linear side-lobes, spur short and stout.

Bandora and Dapoli. Caranjah and Ghauts about Junar (*D.*). S. Konkan (*G.*). The margins of the leaves in my specimens were very slight.

* *H. flavescens*, perhaps only a form of this, but a much more slender plant, turning yellow, with fewer and smaller flowers, and a distinctly beaked ovary (*H.*). Not in *D.* or *G.* The Konkan (*Law*), and known to no one else (*H.*).

9. * *H. crassifolia* (*Platanthera brachyphylla*, D.). Six inches to a foot high, leaves 2, radical, roundish, fleshy, scape with many sheaths, flowers many, small, white or greenish, sepals and petals short and broad, lobes of lip about equal, linear oblong obtuse, spur equal to the beaked ovary.

High hills about Junar (*D.*). From the Konkan to the Nilghiris, common (*H.*).

* *H. affinis*, one or two feet high, stem stout with many erect lanceolate sheaths, leaves large lanceolate, spikes long cylindric, flowers green, lip long, side-lobes longest, spur half as long as the ovary, slender incurved. Konkan and Canara (*H.*). Not in *D.* or *G.* * *H. viridifolia* (*Cæloglossum luteum*, D.), leaves radical, linear acuminate, spike very slender, many-flowered, flowers small greenish-yellow, lip longer than the sepals, lobes slender, variable in length, spur about as long as the beaked ovary. Near Malwan (*D.*). * *H. diphylla*, scape six inches high with many sheaths, leaves two, radical, round cordate margined, pressed flat on the ground, flowers greenish, sepals broader than petals, lobes of the lip filiform, lateral ones longest, spur about equal to the ovary. S. Konkan (*D.*).

Division B. *Section* 5. Petals entire, lip usually trifid; flowers usually very small, spur usually very short or saccate. The leaves in the species here given are collected about the middle of the stem.

10. * *H. Goodyeroides* (*Peristylus*, *G.*, D.). Stem stout, one or two feet high, leaves elliptic, lanceolate, spike long, dense, flowers yellowish-green or white, lateral sepals oblong obtuse, lip as long, recurved, spur minute.

S. Konkan (*D.*). Deccan peninsula (*H.*). The size of the flowers and the lobes of the lip are very variable (*H.*).

11. *H. Lawii* (*Peristylus, L.*, D.). Stem slender, with 3 or 4 leaves, elliptic or lanceolate, flowers very small, sepals narrower than petals, lip with 3 equal lobes, spur short and bladdery.

Lanoli. Belgaum (*D.*). Konkan and Mysore (*H.*). *H.* gives the flowers as yellow; I noted sepals brown, petals white.

* *H. Stocksii*, stem rather stout, 6 to 18 inches high, leaves obovate or elliptic, spike twisted, flowers on one side, yellowish, petals ovate obtuse, fleshy, lateral lobes of the lip incurved, claw broad, concave, spur as long as the sepals. Not in *D.* or *G.* Konkan and Mysore (*H.*), not elsewhere. **H. Wightii* (*Peristylus elatus*, D.). Stem one or two feet high, rather stout, leaves oblong, lanceolate, flowers greenish, crowded, dorsal sepal and petals broad, roundish, lip almost entire, shorter than the sepals, spur spheroidal. Málwan (*D.*).

D. had two species which *H.* cannot identify: * *H. Caranjensis*, flowers small, yellow, upper sepal rounded, petals half ovate, obtuse, mid-lobe of lip oblong, side-lobes shorter, truncate, spur club shaped, shorter than the ovary; Caranjah; and **H. modesta*, stem leafy at the base, flowers greenish-white, mid-lobe of the lip oval, shorter, cohering with the tip of the petals and upper sepals, and concealing the column, side-lobes linear lanceolate, spreading; spur filiform, a little longer than the ovary. Salsette.

I have no means of giving a list of orchids introduced into Bombay gardens and verandahs, of which there must be a great number.

Of useful products of plants of this order there seems to be only two: Vanilla, from the fleshy pod-like fruit of some species of the climbing genus *Vanilla*; one of these, *V. aromatica*, is said by *D.* to do well in Deccan gardens. *H.* has five species, mostly belonging to the south of India. The other product is Saloop, a nutritious starchy substance made from the roots of tubers of various species of *Orchis*, *Eulophia*, and probably other genera. It is known in England, and on this side of India is called *Sálap misri*. It is made from one species which grows commonly at Dápoli, but my note about it is not forthcoming.

ORDER 113. SCITAMINEÆ.

Herbs often large, rarely with woody stem; leaves simple, often radical, pinnately nerved from a midrib; flowers irregular, hermaphrodite (except *Musa*), arising generally from membranous spathaceous bracts, sepals free or tubular, sometimes spathaceous; corolla tubular with 3-partite limb; stamens (except in *Museæ*) one, with 5-petaloid staminodes; ovary inferior 3-celled, or imperfectly so, style slender, stigma entire, fruit usually a 3-celled capsule.

This order was formerly called the Ginger family; but is now made to include, as separate tribes, the arrowroots and plantains, formerly separate orders. It is a distinctly tropical order of large herbs, having in nearly all cases large handsome foliage, and very often showy flowers with many-coloured bracts. It might be thought from the mention in the above description of calyx and corolla, and leaves with nerves proceeding from the midrib, that the plants would have the appearance of belonging to the earlier orders; but this is not the case, the leaves being evidently endogenous, and not reticulated, and the peculiarity of flowers described below also making a distinction.

The roots of a large number of plants of this order are used for food, and some are medicinal.

"The peculiarity of the flowers is that most of the stamens are so developed as to look like petals, only one stamen generally retaining the normal appearance, and producing an anther. The perianth is usually of six lobes in two series (called calyx and corolla above), and within the perianth are the barren stamens (staminodes), which look like petals, are generally unequal in size and shape, and are variously combined. This arrangement makes the comprehension of the flowers difficult to beginners."—*Oliver.*

"In the Ginger order one outer whorl of stamens resembles the tubular corolla, so that the perianth seems to consist of nine lobes instead of six."—*Grant Allen.*

Note.—When there is a stem the leaves make a sheath to it, but in some cases there is no stem, the leaves being radical, and the scape of flowers then springs up, sometimes from the centre of the leaves, sometimes at a little distance from them, as if too proud to acknowledge the connection.

TRIBE 1. ZINGIBEREÆ. Gingers. Calyx tubular or spathaceous, staminodes various, style slender, embraced below the stigma by the anther.

1. GLOBBA. Stem erect, leafy, corolla tube long, filament slender, with two dorsal appendages, connective simple, winged or spurred, ovary one-celled.

(*a*) Lateral staminodes broad.

2. CURCUMA. Stem none, bracts hooded, enclosing several flowers, forming a cone-like spike, filament petaloid, anther cells spurred at the base.

Note.—Although having no stem, properly so called, many species have a spurious stem formed of the thick sheathing leaf-stalks, much as in the plantains; this is called by *H.* the "leafy stem," or the "leafy tuft."

3. KÆMPFERIA. Stem short or none, filament very short, connective crested.

4. HITCHENIA. Flowering stem leafy, filament long,

complicate, connective broad, not crested, inflorescence as in *Curcuma*.

(*b*) Lateral staminodes small or none.

5. ZINGIBER. Leafy stem elongated, spikes usually radical, bracts single-flowered, filament short, anther cells parallel, connective usually produced into a long appendage.

6. COSTUS. Stem and inflorescence as in the last, filament petaloid, anther adnate to its middle, cells parallel.

7. ALPINIA. Leafy stem long, with a terminal lax spike or panicle of flowers, filament long, connective various.

TRIBE 2. MARANTEÆ. Sepals free or loosely cohering, anther one-celled, staminodes connate into a 5 or 6-lobed inner perianth, of which one lobe is lip-shaped, two hooded, and one bears the anther.

8. PHRYNIUM. Stemless (in the species here given), spike compound from the side of the petiole, corolla tube cylindric, staminal tube longer, segments unequal, one bearing the one-celled anther on its margin.

TRIBE 3. MUSEÆ. Sepals free or connate in a split spathe, stamens 5, free, anthers linear, 2-celled, staminode one or none, style central, stigma 2 or 3-partite.

9. MUSA. Stem subarboreous, simple, leaves very large, flower spike erect, terminal, the flowers in clusters enclosed in a large spathaceous bract, calyx tube short.

Note.—Except in the last tribe, the following peculiarities are noticeable in this order, all of which tend to make the flowers of many species more conspicuous.

1. The calyx, petals, and petaloid staminodes are frequently all coloured.

2. The central staminode (lip) is frequently larger than the rest, often 3-lobed, and sometimes coloured differently.

3. The bracts are very conspicuous, often delicately coloured, particularly those which are without flowers, and which form the top of the raceme. This part is then called the coma.

1. GLOBBA.

* *G. bulbifera* (*G. marantina*, D.). 12 to 18 inches high, leaves bifarious, broad lanceolate with waved margins; spike terminal, bracts ovate cordate, with a small bulb in the axil; flowers yellow, fragrant, long-tubed, anthers with yellow bifid spreading wings.

Wári country (*D.*), *G.*, without hab.

2. Curcuma. Turmeric.

Note.—The species are very difficult of determination, and the characters are taken, almost without exception, from drawings (*H.*).

(*a*) Spike distinct from the leaves, usually appearing first.

1. *C. aromatica* (*C. zedoaria*, D.). Tubers yellowish inside, stem composed of leaf sheaths and bracts, corolla rosy or purple, the lip yellow, broad, 2-cleft. *Rán haldi, zadwár.*

The Konkans, springing up very commonly at the beginning of the rains, and known as wild arrowroot. Throughout India wild and frequently cultivated (*H.*). The produce of this, *C. Nilgherrensis*, and *Hitchenia*, is called East India arrowroot.

* *C. zedoaria* seems to be very like this, but larger, and the leaves have usually a dark mark down the middle; flowers shorter than the bracts. *Kachura, kápur*, said to produce the zedoaria of the *Materia Medica.* Cultivated throughout India (*H.*), but not given by *D.* or *G.*

* *C. Nilgherrensis* (*C. angustifolia*, D.). Root with small tubers, leaves petioled acute, narrowed to both ends; flowers large, bright yellow, longer than the bracts; coma pink or purple, flowering bracts pale yellowish-green. Rám Ghaut (*D.*). This yields Travancore arrowroot.—*Lisboa.*

(*b*) Spike in the centre of the tuft of leaves.

2. * *C. amada.* Leaves broad, lanceolate, long-petioled, spike about 6 inches high, flower-bracts pale green, coma pink, flowers about as long as the bracts, corolla whitish, lip pale yellow. *Amáda, kájura gauri.*

Konkans and Guzerat (*D.*). Widely cultivated (*H.*). "Mango ginger, so named from its fresh roots, something like green mangoes; the tube of corolla is slender, and the mouth shut by 3 yellow hairy glands" (*G.*).

3. * *C. longa.* *H.* says that herbarium specimens of this and the last are not distinguishable; but the leafy stem in this is given at 4 to 5 feet, and in the last at only 2 to 3 feet. "Conspicuous by its beautiful pink coma" (*D.*). *Haldi, alad.*

Cultivated in Guzerat and some parts of the Deccan for the root, which furnishes the turmeric of commerce. "Known in Bombay also by its Chaldaic or Hebrew name, *Karkam*" (*G.*).

"Curcuma, turmeric or Indian cane, brought to us from several parts of India by the company of merchants trading thither."—*Tournefort*, A.D. 1719.

4. * *C. montana* (*C. pseudomontana*, D.). Leafy, stem 2 to 3 feet, leaves with petiole as long, tapering to both ends, coma of a beautiful dark rose-colour, waved, flowers yellow, as long as the bracts, two or three to each. *Sindarbár, Sindarwáni, halaonda.*

Konkans (*D.*). "Grows in great abundance about Malhar in Salsette; tubers round, eaten by the natives when grain is dear" (*G.*).

* *C. decipiens*, tubers small almond-shaped, leaves broad, oval or cordate and cuspidate, spikes 6 to 8 inches, bracts and flowers purple; lip bifid, with curled margins. Malwan (*D.*), Konkan (*H.*); but the species is known only to Dalzell. He says that the earlier spikes are lateral, the later central.

H. identifies *G.'s* No. 1474, of which there is neither description nor hab., with * *C. strobilifera*, bracts all green, flowers pale yellow, about as long, corolla segments small, whitish, lip short, deflexed, roundish. Found otherwise only in lower Burmah.

Many species and vars. of *Curcuma* are grown in conservatories in England, and probably in gardens in India; the bracts, perianth and stamens are frequently all equally coloured.

3. Kæmpferia. Galangale.

K. scaposa (*Hedychium s.*, D.). Leaf-sheaths forming a stem, large, broad, lanceolate, scape 12 to 15 inches high, spike dense with pure white flowers, lip bifid, staminodes large and broad, anther very large, bracts green. *Jangli kácheru, kálla, sunka.* "The rice lily."

Rutnagherry, and (as *G.* says) very common in the plain between Kárli and Lanoli. S. Konkan (*D.*). *H.* has no other hab., and this differs from nearly all the other species of India proper, in having a leafy stem.

The other three species are stemless; the first two are not in *D.*

* *K. galanga*, leaves radical roundish, spread flat on the ground, spike central, flowers pure white, fragrant, lip with a lilac throat, deeply bifid, anther crest quadrate, lobes 2, rounded, bracts lanceolate green. S. Konkan (*G.*). Plains throughout India (*H.*). *Chanda mula.* This is the officinal Galanga. * *K. pandurata*, leaves large, oblong, erect, spike hidden in the dilated bases of the petiole. "A very beautiful plant, with pale pink-coloured flowers. Konkan and Guzerat" (*G.*). *H.* has no other Indian hab., but has "cultivated for its ginger-like rootstock." * *K. rotunda*, leaves oblong, erect, spikes appearing before the leaves, corolla segments long linear, lip with two deep roundish lobes, flowers of various shades of purple and white, fragrant. *Bhui champa.* Gardens (*D.* and *G.*). Throughout India, often cultivated (*H.*). Described and figured by Dr. Kirtikar in B.N.H.S. Journal, vii. 203.

4. Hitchenia.

H. caulina (*Curcuma caulina*, D.). Stem leafy, 3 feet high, radical leaves sheathing, oblong lanceolate, stem leaves much tinged with red, bracts large, green, coma white, flowers yellow, the tube slender. *Chawar, Nisham.*

Table land of Mahableshwar (*D.* and *G.*). The Konkan (*H.*); and no other hab. This is the plant from which arrowroot is made at Mahableshwar and Dapoli.—*Lisboa.*

5. Zingiber. Ginger.

1. **Z. nimmonii.* Stem 4 or 5 feet high, round, leaves lanceolate, acute, sheathing; spike just rising above the ground, at a little distance from the stem, bracts striped with red, corolla yellowish-red, lip yellow, 3-lobed, capsules size of a pigeon's egg.

The Konkans, common (*D.*). Abundant in Lanoli Grove (*G.*). No other hab. (*H.*).

2. *Z. officinale*, common ginger, *áleh, ádrakh*, the dried root *sunt*, cultivated in gardens in Guzerat and the Deccan, and generally throughout tropical Asia. Native locality unknown (*H.*).

3. **Z. zerumbet*, broad-leaved ginger; 3 to 4 feet high, leaves oblong, lanceolate, spike oval, oblong, very dense, bracts roundish, green, flowers large, sulphur-yellow; lobes of lip roundish, corolla tube as long as the bract. *Buteh, mahábán buteh.*

Common about old wells in the Konkan (*D.*). Throughout India: widely cultivated in the tropics of the Old World (*H.*).

4. *Z. macrostachyum.* Stem 2 or 3 feet high, it and the bracts red, leaves lanceolate, spikes long-peduncled, dense, flowers white, lip pale yellow, the middle lobe lined purple, corolla tube as long as the bracts, capsule red, size of a pigeon's egg. *Nisam.*

Rutnagherry. Konkan and Lanoli, growing near streams (*D.* and *G.*). No other hab. (*H.*). Has much the appearance of *Z. nimmonii*, but smaller (*G.*).

5. **Z. casumunar.* Stem 3 to 5 feet high, leaves bifarious, linear-lanceolate, spikes oblong, very dense, bracts reddish, flowers large, white, or pale yellow, corolla tube long. *Ban áda, rán ádu.*

In gardens Bombay, and wild in the Konkans (*D.* and *G.*). Throughout India, and widely cultivated in tropical Asia (*H.*).

Casumunar, the root of this plant, sometimes called yellow Zedoary, had a great reputation as a drug in Europe in the 17th century, which did not last. * *Z. cernuum*, leaves narrow, elliptic, spike as in *Z. nimmonii*, bracts yellowish-green, flowers a mixture of pink, white, and yellow. Ram Ghaut (*D.*). This is known to no one but Dalzell apparently.

6. Costus.

* *C. speciosus.* Stem 3 or 4 feet high, leafy, spike at the end of the stem, leaves spirally arranged, oblong, cuspidate, softly hairy beneath, bracts ovate, or obovate, bright red; flowers very large, pure white, the lip roundish, the margins incurved and meeting. *Kemuka, kut, wángchaora.*

One of the commonest as well as the handsomest of the order (*D.*). Throughout India (*H.*). *G.* also describes it as common in Salsette and the Konkans, so that I consider myself unfortunate never to have met with it.

7. Alpinia.

* *A. galanga.* Stems 6 or 7 feet high, leafy in the upper part, leaves lanceolate, smooth, flowers in a dense panicle, small, greenish white, the lip obovate, clawed, white veined with lilac, fruit size of a small cherry, orange-red. *Kulinjan.*

The margins of the leaves are white, and somewhat callous: the root is galanga major of the chemists (*D.*). Wild in the Wári country (*D.*). Throughout India, widely cultivated (*H.*).

The next two are ascribed to the Konkan, apparently on Nimmo's authority alone; but are widely cultivated (*H.*). The third is a native of the Eastern Islands, common in gardens.

* *A. allughas*, stem 3 to 6 feet high, covered with the smooth leaf-sheaths, panicle bending to one side, flowers large, of a beautiful rose-colour, capsule round, smooth, black when ripe. *Táraka.* This is *R.*, *D.* and *G.*'s description; but *H.* says, "flowers small, corolla segments linear, oblong, greenish-white, lip cuneate, pink." * *A. calcarata*, stem 2 to 4 feet high, leaves lanceolate, panicle dense, flowers middle size, corolla segments oblong, greenish-white, lip striped, and spotted with red and yellow, on a pale ground, base spurred; capsule round, red. *A. nutans*, very large, leaves oblong, lanceolate, flowers bell-shaped, red, yellow, and pink, very brilliant. *Puna champa, nág damani.*

Amomum, flowers in a dense spike, filament short, anther cells diverging above, connective crested or 2-lobed. The only species (out of 48) attributed to this Presidency, and that on Stocks' authority, as in the Konkan, is **A. microstephanum*, stem 4 feet high, leaves large, lanceolate, spike round, flowers white, corolla tube and lip each an inch long, lip obovate, anther crest small, round. Not in *D.* or *G.*

From various species of *Amomum*, and from *Elettaria cardomomum*, cultivated in the S., and sometimes found in gardens in W. India, the cardomums of commerce are produced, being the dry, membranous capsules, full of small black seeds. *Elchi.*

Hedychium, with long and slender filament, and broad lateral staminodes, is only known by *H. coronarium*, a garden plant, with pure white, fragrant flowers, which *R.* called the most charming plant of the order. *Sontukha, dulaba champa.* *H.* makes *D.'s H. flavum* with large yellow flowers, also called *Sontukha*, and *hema champa*, a var. of this.

Tribe MARANTEÆ.

8. PHRYNIUM.

P. capitatum. Leaves radical, large, long-petioled, oblong; flowers in short spikes, scarlet, capsule 3-lobed, seeds warted. *Kúdale.*

Common in shady jungles of the Konkan (*D.*). *H.* has omitted the reference to *D.*; but I think there is no doubt that his plant and *D.'s* are the same. It resembles *Canna Indica.* I have seen it only in gardens. **P. spicatum*, leaf oblong, petiole longer than the blade, spike oblong, one or two inches long; bracts green, flowers white.

Konkan, *Law* (*H.*). Otherwise only in Pegu. Not in *D.* or *G.*

Canna belongs to a separate tribe, Canneæ, in which the 1-celled anther is adnate to the single petaloid filament. *C. Indica*, Indian shot, one of the commonest of Indian garden plants, *deva keli, nána keli*; leaves large sheathing, flowers scarlet, seeds black, resembling, and said to be sometimes used as, shot.

"Tall Canna lifts his curled brow
Erect to heaven."—*Dr. Darwin.*

Throughout India (*H.*); but does not appear to be wild in W. India. There are various varieties, one of which has yellow flowers.

Tribe MUSEÆ.

9. MUSA. Plantain.

M. superba. Stem short, leaves petioled, lanceolate, bracts large, roundish, many-flowered, calyx 3-cleft, petals shorter, fruit oblong, dry when ripe, not eatable, full of large black seeds.

This is the wild plantain, *rán khela, kandera*, common on the Ghauts in the rains. The whole plant dies away to the ground each year. *H.* has no other hab. than W. Ghauts.

M. rosacea (*M. ornata*, D.). From 3 to 5 feet high, leaves petioled, linear oblong, bracts lilac, or pale red; calyx yellowish, white, 5-toothed, fruit oblong, pulpy, much as in *M. sapientium.* Konkan and Ghauts; also in the E. Himalayas (*H.*).

The cultivated plantain, *Khela*, is *M. sapientium*, said to be wild in Behar and the E. Himalayas. "The specific name conveys an allusion to a statement of Theophrastus concerning a fruit which served as food for the wise men of India, supposed to have been the plantain."

By far the best plantains in W. India are grown in the Bassein district; and at Agási, N. of Bassein, they have a way of drying them, which, if done scientifically, and for export, might probably make the fruit in that form as popular in England as dried figs. The banana of the W. Indies is not now considered a separate species; it has the honourable specific name of *Paradisiaca*, because of the tradition that Eve first saw Adam under one of these trees:—

> "Till I espied thee, fair indeed and tall,
> Under a platane."—*Paradise Lost.*

"Gerarde and other old authors name it Adam's apple, from a notion that it was the forbidden fruit of Eden; while others suppose the so-called grapes brought out of the Promised Land by the spies to have been bunches of plantains."—*Loudon.*

The poetical allusions to the tree are not always quite accurate, e.g.:—

> "Carved is her name in many a spicy grove,
> In many a plantain forest waving wide."—*Rogers.*

To its practical virtues H. M. Stanley bears witness in "Darkest Africa:"

"We had often wondered, during our life in the forest region, that natives did not appear to have discovered what valuable, nourishing, and easily digested food they possessed in the plantain and banana. All banana lands, Cuba, Brazil, the W. Indies, seem to me to have been specially remiss in this point. If only the virtues of the flour were known it is not to be doubted that it would be largely consumed in Europe. For infants, persons of delicate digestion, dyspeptics, and those suffering from temporary derangement of the stomach, the flour, properly prepared, would be in universal demand. During my two attacks of gastritis a light gruel of this, mixed with milk, was the only food that could be digested."

Ravenala Madagascarensis (*Urania speciosa*, D.), "the traveller's tree" of Madagascar, "the water tree" of the Dutch, is found in gardens in and about Bombay. It is a tree of remarkable appearance, having a woody stem, and very large, long-petioled plantain-like leaves, forming a semicircular head, like an open fan; flowers large, white, sessile.

"In Madagascar it forms a characteristic feature of the scenery in many parts. The lower leaves drop off as the stem grows, and in an old tree the lowest leaves are sometimes 30 feet from the ground. The fruit is filled with a fine silky fibre of the most brilliant blue or purple, among which are about 30 or 40 seeds. . . The leaf-stalks always contain water, even in the driest weather, more than a quart being readily obtained by piercing the thick part of the base of the leaf-stalk, and this water is pure and pleasant—hence the name."—*Chambers's Encyclopædia.*

"This tree, like the screw pine of the South Sea Islands, supplied most of the needs of the E. Coast natives: it provides roof, walls, floor, dishes, plates, spoons, drinking cups, covers for cooking pots, wrappings for parcels, and serves for various other purposes."—*Diary of a Missionary in Madagascar.*

Manilla hemp is made from a species very like the common plantain, but with an uneatable fruit.

Irideæ, the Iris family, have no representative in W. India, the very few species given in the Indian Flora belonging to the Himalayas. But one does not like to pass by quite without mention flowers with such associations as the fleur-de-lis and the crocus. The yellow flag, fleur-de-lis, or flower-de-luce, is the royal lily of France, borne for several centuries in the arms of England.

"Cropped are the flower-de-luces in your arms;
Of England's coat one half is cut away."—*King Henry VI.*

"O flower-de-luce, bloom on, and let the river
Linger to kiss thy feet;
O flower of song, bloom on, and make for ever
The world more fair and sweet."—*Longfellow.*

Order 114. AMARYLLIDEÆ. The Amaryllis Family.

Usually bulbous plants, leaves radical, more or less sword-shaped, scape naked, perianth petaloid, 6-divided, sometimes with a crown at the mouth; stamens 6 on the perianth, ovary inferior 3-celled, style one, stigma simple or cleft; fruit usually a 3-valved capsule.

This beautiful family is well known in Europe by the various species of Narcissus (including the daffodil), and by the snowdrop (Galanthus). The bulbs of many plants of the order are poisonous.

Tribe 1. Hypoxideæ. Rootstock tuberous.

1. Hypoxis. Perianth sessile on the top of the ovary, persistent, filaments short, anthers erect, style short, stigmas 3.

2. Curculigo. Flowers often unisexual, "perianth usually produced above the ovary as a solid stipes (stalk), bearing the rotate limb."

Tribe 2. Amaryllideæ. Rootstock bulbous, flowers from a spathe, umbelled.

3. Crinum. Flowers large, spathes 2, bracts linear, perianth

funnel or salver-shaped, stamens on the throat, filaments free, fruit large, rounded.

4. PANCRATIUM. Flowers large, spathes one or two, bracts few linear, perianth funnel-shaped, stamens on the throat, filaments united by a membrane forming a cup.

1. HYPOXIS.

* *H. aurea* (*Curculigo graminifolia*, D.). Small, diœcious, leaves narrow linear, keeled, scape slender with one or two long-peduncled yellow flowers.

Khandalla and the Ghauts (*D.* and *G.*). Subtropical Himalayas (*H.*).

2. CURCULIGO.

C. orchioides (*C. brevifolia*, D.). A pretty little plant with star-like yellow flowers on a short scape, among the lanceolate channelled leaves, which have a few long soft hairs; stigma 3-cleft, capsule with slender beak. *Musli Kand.*

Dapoli. S. Konkan (*G.*). Common at the beginning of the rains (*D.*).

In this *H.* includes *D.*'s *C. malabarica*, which *D.* distinguished chiefly by its greater size and hairiness, giving the leaves as 2 feet long and upwards; common on the Ghauts.

3. CRINUM.

1. * *C. asiaticum.* Leaves 3 to 4 feet by 5 to 7 inches, scape $1\frac{1}{2}$ to 2 feet compressed, flowers numerous white, perianth salver-shaped, tube 3 to 4 inches long, stamens often reddish, fruit usually one-seeded. *Nágdán.*

The Konkans (*D.* and *G.*). Throughout India (*H.*). The leaves are said to be equal as an emetic to the finest Ipecacuanha.

2. *C. ensifolium* (*C. Roxburghii*, D.). Leaves 12 to 18 inches by an inch broad, tapering to the tip, umbels with from 6 to 12 large, white, fragrant flowers with thread-like bracts among them, tube 4 to 6 inches long, stamens long, protruding.

S. Konkan and Ghauts. Common on banks of Deccan rivers (*D.*). *H.* attributes a very similar species, *C. defixum*, to swampy river banks throughout India.

Unscientific observers would call this a very beautiful lily,

"Stately, and lovely, and pure as truth."

* *C. brachynema*, bulb as large as the fist, leaves $1\frac{1}{2}$ to 2 feet long by 3 or 4 inches broad, strap-shaped, appearing long after the flowers, umbel of 15 to 20 white fragrant flowers, the tube $1\frac{1}{2}$ to 2 inches

long, anthers yellow. Found in the Konkan by Woodrow and Stocks (*H.*). No other authority. *D.* has what seems to be a very noble plant, * *C. augustum,* with lanceolate channelled leaves 3 to 5 feet long, scapes nearly as long, umbels of 30 to 40 pedicelled flowers, white or rosy, fragrant, corolla tube 2½ to 5 inches long. Banks of the Gatparba and Malparba rivers. I cannot find this in *H.* Another large species, * *C. latifolium,* is attributed by Nimmo in *G.* to both Konkans, rare. *H.* has it as throughout India wild or cultivated, but *D.* has not got it; the leaves and scape are 2 or 3 feet long, umbels of 10 to 20 white flowers, more or less streaked or tinged with red, corolla tube 3 to 6 inches long.

4. Pancratium.

P. parvum. A very pretty plant about 8 inches high, leaves blunt, flat, linear, scape compressed with 3 or 4 very long-tubed white flowers, staminal cup 12-toothed, anthers yellow, oblong linear.

Tungár and Bandora. Konkan and Ghaut Hills (*D.*). No other authority or hab. (*H.*)

G. has **P. parviflorum* without description. Common in both Konkans and on margins of Deccan rivers; not referred to by either *D.* or *H.*

Agave Americana, the American aloe, *pálkánde, jangli ánás,* is well known in gardens, "with leaves sharp-pointed like an Aztec knife," formerly believed to flower only once in a hundred years; also *A. vivipara,* and probably others.

Order Bromeliaceæ (not given in *H.*) must be mentioned for the sake of the pine-apple, *anánas, Bromelia ananas.* The fruit consists of numerous flowers and bracts grown together in a mass, and the crown of leaves, which looks so out of place, growing apparently out of the fruit, belongs really to the flowerless top of the spike.

The pine-apple was introduced into England about two centuries ago. The best pines from S. Konkan gardens (e.g. between Harni and Dapoli) are really good, though of course not equal to W. Indian or English hot-house fruit.

Order 115. TACCACEÆ.

Herbs, with tuberous roots, leaves radical, flowers umbelled, involucre of 2 to 6 spathes, bracts very long filiform; perianth superior, 6-lobed in 2 series, stamens 6 at the base of the lobes, anthers sessile within a hood, which forms the top of the filament, style short, stigmas 3 broad, or petaloid and reflexed like an umbrella over the style.

A very small order, containing only one genus.

Tacca, as the order.

T. pinnatifida. Leaves very large, smooth, pinnatifid, petioles erect 1 to 3 feet long, scape separate from the leaves, smooth, bearing at the top an umbel of insignificant greenish flowers, which only half open; capsule roundish with 6 prominent ridges, many-seeded. *Sardechámár devkandá.*

Common in the Konkans during the rains. It is a very noticeable plant. The tubers are eaten throughout Polynesia, after much washing, to get rid of the acridity. They yield what is called Tahiti arrowroot.

ORDER 116. **DIOSCORACEÆ.** The Yam Family.

Herbs, usually twining, with simple or digitate reticulated leaves; flowers small, rarely bisexual; perianth superior 6-lobed; male and female flowers alike, but the latter smaller; stamens 3 or 6, or 3 perfect and 3 staminodes; styles 3, very short; fruit a 3-valved capsule.

A small order, resembling in habit and the reticulated leaves tribe Smilaceæ of the Lily family. The tubers of some species are the yams of tropical countries. In England *Tamus communis*, black bryony, belonging to this order, is well known by its polished leaves and black berries.

DIOSCOREA. Flowers unisexual, fruit capsular, 3-winged.

1. *D. pentaphylla.* A large climber with digitate 3 or 5-lobed leaves, leaflets oblong or oval, pointed, smooth, male flowers very small and fragrant, white, in large panicles, with a cup-like bract below the flower, female spikes much smaller; stems and branches sometimes prickly. *Shendurvel.*

Common in the Konkans and Ghauts. Throughout tropical India (*H.*).

"The small flowers are sold in the bazaar and eaten as greens, and are said to be very wholesome and to resemble fish roes in flavour" (*G.*). The tubers are also eatable. *H.* includes in this *D.'s* (and apparently *G.'s*) *D. triphylla, Márchaina.* The root is intoxicating and intensely bitter, and is often used to render toddy more potent (*G.*).

* *D. Jacquemontii*, closely allied to the last, but the flowers much larger, and with the bracts streaked with brown. The Konkan, between Poona and Kárli (*Jacquemont.*) Belgaum, *Ritchie* (*H.*). Not in *D.* or *G.*

2. * *D. oppositifolia.* Leaves opposite, oval, waved; male flowers very numerous in panicles, female flowers few in spikes, both axillary.

The above is *D.'s* description. *H.* has male spikes short, leaves with a cartilaginous margin. *Mánda, páshpoli.* Common on the Ghauts (*D.* and *G.*). Tropical India (*H.*).

D. sativa is the yam most commonly cultivated (*D.*). *Konphal, Godri.* * *D. globosa,* "the white yam, nearly as common as the last" (*D.*). * *D. aculeata,* "Goa potato, common in Bombay, but imported from Goa; the smallest and most delicate of those cultivated" (*G.*). *Kángi, kánte kángi.* These two *H.* has not identified. * *D. alata,* stems short, variously angled or winged, leaves subhastate or deeply cordate, roundish, ovate, petiole stout, often winged. *H.* ascribes this to tropical India. * *D. dæmona* is apparently *D.'s Helmia d.*, stems twining, armed, leaves ternate, leaflets very large, obovate acute, petioles prickly, male spikes compound 6 to 18 inches long, female flowers on a different plant, solitary, pendulous. Vingorla and Konkan hills, rare (*D.*). Tropical forests throughout India (*H.*). *Helmia bulbifera,* D., is apparently *G.'s D. bulbifera,* put down by *H.* as undeterminable, *Káru karanda,* a smooth climber, leaves cordate, deeply nerved, flowers white, the male spikes panicled, bearing brown bulbs; fruit in racemes, oblong with 3 oval wings. Dapoli. Bombay and Konkans, common (*D.*). *H.* has not referred to these two. He says the species of this genus are "in a state of indescribable confusion."

Order 117. LILIACEÆ. The Lily Family.

Generally herbs with fibrous roots, or bulbs; leaves generally narrow with parallel veins; flowers generally bisexual; perianth coloured with 6 divisions in 2 series; stamens 6, rarely 3 or fewer; ovary 3-celled, fruit a 3-celled capsule or berry.

This great family contains such a number of plants quite unlike what are ordinarily known as lilies that it seems almost misleading to call it by that name. Among these are tulips, onions, squills, asparagus, aloes, Smilax, and Dracæna. *H.* has sixteen tribes, of which only seven are represented in W. India, and six of these by a single genus each.

Tribe 1. Smilaceæ. Climbing shrubs with reticulated and strongly-nerved leaves.

1. Smilax. Flowers diœcious, small, umbelled, anthers twin, or with cells separated by the forking of the filament: in the female flowers there are 3 or 6 staminodes; fruit a round berry.

Tribe 2. Asparageæ. No real leaves, but many much-divided, very slender branchlets, looking like feathery leaves, and so called by old botanists.

2. Asparagus. Flowers very small axillary, perianth bell-shaped, berry round.

The remaining tribes have parallel-veined leaves, and the distinctions would not be much help to my clients.

3. CHLOROPHYTUM. Flowers racemed; perianth segments distinct, capsule 3-winged.

4. ALLIUM. Strong-smelling bulbous herbs; scape bearing a head or umbel of flowers, at first enclosed in a spathaceous involucre.

5. DIPCADI. Root tuberous, flowers racemed, perianth cylindric, segments more or less recurved, stamens included.

6. URGINEA. Bulbous, flowers racemed, perianth bell-shaped of 6 unequal segments; stamens included, capsule 3-sided.

7. SCILLA. Bulbous, flowers racemed, perianth star-shaped or bell-shaped, segments recurved.

8. IPHIGENIA. Stem erect leafy, perianth segments equal, narrow, clawed, spreading; stamens hypogynous.

9. GLORIOSA. Climbing, leafy, leaves opposite or in threes, the tip elongated and tendril-like, flowers large axillary solitary, stamens hypogynous.

1. SMILAX.

Note.—The plants of this genus have no outward resemblance to Endogens.

S. macrophylla (*S. ovalifolia*, D.). A large smooth prickly climber, leaves large oval, strongly 5 to 7-nerved, entire, with a sudden acumination, petioles channelled and slightly winged, with tendrils in pairs; flowers small, greenish, in globular umbels, ovary and berries red. *Guti.*

Common in the Deccan and Konkan. Widely distributed in India (*H.*).

* *S. prolifera* (*S. macrophylla*, D.) is apparently very much like the last, and *H.* gives the identification with *D.'s* plant doubtfully; the sheathing part of the petiole usually forms 2 large auricles, and the umbels are much divided. S. Ghauts (*D.*). Widely distributed (*H.*).

Sarsaparilla is produced from the roots of *S. sarsaparilla* and other American species. (For Indian sarsaparilla, see *Hemidesmus.*)

2. ASPARAGUS.

A. racemosus (*A. sarmentosus*, D.). A very delicate smooth climber, with thorns turned downwards, branchlets divided into very fine segments, flowers small, white, in racemes, very fragrant, berries red, obscurely lobed. *Shatmuli, zatar, ásvel.*

Deccan, Konkan, and Guzerat. Throughout tropical India (*H.*).

H. makes the Bombay plant var. Javanica. Anyone would recognize this pretty climber as a near relation of the cultivated asparagus, *A. officinalis, haliyun.* That is a native of England, though not often found wild there. The young shoots, much enlarged by cultivation, are the edible part. "The asparagus, with its elegant stem and silky chevelure, all shining with the evening dew, seemed like a forest of Lilliputian fir-trees covered with silver gauze."—*G. Sand.*

* *A. Jacquemontii,* tall, much-branched, branches spreading, angled, ribbed and grooved, segments of the branchlets 2 to 5-divided, 3-sided, pointed; flowers solitary or in pairs on a short peduncle. Found by Jacquemont between Poona and Kárli. No other authority; not in *D.* or *G.*

3. Chlorophytum.

1. *C. breviscapum.* Tubers oblong from the fibrous roots, leaves flat sword-shaped, narrower at the base, margins wavy; flowers in a close raceme on a short round scape, white, petals much recurved, anthers long yellow, bracts long pointed, one to each pair of flowers.

D. had this at Málwan, I at Dapoli. Otherwise *H.* ascribes it only to the foot of the Sikkim Himalayas.

* *C. glaucum,* leaves glaucous, slightly folded, half the length of the scape, which is from one to two feet high, and scaly; flowers apparently much as the last. On the Ghauts (*D.*), rather rare. No other hab. or authority. * *C. tuberosum* (*C. anthericoideum,* D.), scape 2 feet high, longer than the sword-shaped slightly folded leaves, flowers large. District of Malwan (*D.*). Pretty common through Central and S. India (*H.*). *R.* says that the flowers are pure white, and like those of a snowdrop.

"Chaste snowdrop, venturous harbinger of spring,
And pensive monitor of fleeting years."—*Wordsworth.*

D.'s Phalangium tuberosum, which he calls very common in both Konkans and the Deccan, but which I have seen only at Rutnagherry, is apparently not mentioned by *H.* It may be included in the last, as *D.* says it is very like it. The leaves are waved on the margin, scape round, flowers small white in racemes or panicles. * *C. orchidastrum* (*C. Nimmonii,* D.), three feet high, leaves long, attenuated towards the base, scape round, branched, flowers twin, distant drooping white. Malwan, and Ghauts opposite Bombay (*D.*). * *C. laxum* (*C. parviflorum,* D.), 8 to 10 inches high, leaves erect grass-like, folded, longer than the scape; flowers minute solitary or twin, white, anthers green, bracts lanceolate. Rocky places near the sea in the Malwan district (*D.*).

To this tribe belong the Asphodels.

4. Allium. Onion.

There are a number of wild onions in the Himalayas, but

none of the tribe in W. or S. India. The cultivated species are the following:

A. ascalonium, the shallot.
A. ampeloperasum, the leek, *Korat.*
A. cepa, the onion, *piáz, kánda, kal.*
A. sativum, garlic, *lassan.*

The well-known superiority of the Bombay onions is due to their descent from Portuguese plants, though the size of the bulb has degenerated to that of the common English onion.

"In warmer climates the onion produces a larger bulb, and generally of a more delicate flavour than in England, and is more extensively used as an article of food. . . . In Spain and Portugal a raw onion is often eaten like an apple."—*Chambers.*

"There is an odour of sanctity about the onion and the garlic, turn up our noses as we may. The ancient Egyptians offered them as first-fruits upon the altars of their gods, and employed them also in the services for the dead; and such was their attachment to them that the followers of Moses hankered after them, despite the manna, and longed for 'the leeks, and the onions, and the garlic, which they did eat in Egypt freely.' Nay, even the fastidious Greeks not only used them as a charm against the evil eye, but ate them with delight."—*W. W. Story,* "Roba di Roma."

Some species of *Allium*, including *A. sativum* and a few other plants, have small bulbs (bulbils or bulblets) mixed up among the umbel of flowers. The flowers of several of the garlics are very pretty and pure-looking, and but for the strong smell in the roots and leaves would be very attractive as garden flowers. "Cloves of garlic" are the subordinate bulbs of which the bulbous root of the garlic plant is composed. Moly, the plant or root which Hermes gave to Ulysses to overcome the enchantments of Circe, is said to have been an Allium. Alphonse Karr says it was the yellow garlic, *A. aureum*, which has the reputation of being a preservative from enchantments, spells, and evil presages.

5. Dipcadi.

D. montanum (*Uropetalum m.*, D.). Scape about a foot high, leaves linear folded, about as long, flowers in a raceme, white, tubular or bell-shaped.

Ratnagherry. W. Deccan and Belgaum (*D.*).

* *D. minor*, a species found by Dalzell in rocky places at Malwan, and not otherwise known. *H.* says it is at once distinguished from the last by the small size of the flowers, the perianth of this being given at one-third to half an inch, and of the other three-quarters of an inch. * *D. Concanense* (*Uropetalum c.* D.). Scape six to twelve

inches, leaves fleshy, filiform half round, deeply grooved above; flowers an inch and a half in diameter, white, capsule 3-lobed. This also depends on Dalzell. The Konkan, and Hewra plains.

6. Urginea.

U. Indica. Bulb like an onion, white, leaves numerous, sword-shaped, smooth, a foot or more long, scape slender and delicate, sometimes two feet high; flowers remote, long-stalked, drooping, light-brown, petals lanceolate, stamens in pairs. *Jangli piáz.*

Common on the sandy shores of the Konkan, where "its early flowers anticipate the leaves." Also in the W. Himalayas and Behar (*H.*). He calls the flowers greenish-white with green nerves, but they are certainly as above in the Konkan. "Usually employed as a succedaneum for the true squill" (*G.*).

7. Scilla. Squills.

S. Indica (*Ledebouria hyacintha*, D.). Small smooth plant with oblong linear leaves, scape round, bearing a raceme of many small dull-pinkish flowers; ovary roundish, flat-topped, six-grooved. *Bhuikund.*

I had this at Mahableshwar, but *D.* thought it was confined to S. Konkan. *H.* includes in it *Ledebouria maculata*, which *D.* calls common in the Konkans and Deccan, and which springs up everywhere at Bandora as soon as the rain falls. The flowers are alike, but the leaves very different, ovate narrowing into a fleshy petiole, and with dark blotches. I noted as to this also that the pedicels and filaments were of a brighter colour than the perianth. *H.* calls the flowers (of the combined species) greenish purple with purple filaments, and adds that the leaves when the tips touch the ground produce bulbs; this, *D.* says, never occurs in *L. maculata.*

8. Iphigenia.

* *I. pallida.* This *H.* calls probably a variety of *I. Indica*, with white flowers and narrow linear leaves; bracts linear leafy. The Konkan, Mahableshwar, and Belgaum (*Ritchie*, &c.), and this is probably what Dr. Smith and Mr. Birdwood in their Matheran lists call *Anguillaria indica*. *H.'s* description of *I. Indica*, which he attributes to the whole of India, is very meagre, and he calls it "a sportive plant." *G.* had *A. Indica* under the name of *Márkallai* in the Konkans and at Khandalla. *D.* has not got it.

9. Gloriosa.

G. superba (*Methonia s.*, D.). A very handsome climber, leaves oblong to lanceolate with long curling tips; flowers axillary solitary long-stalked, petals about equal, long and narrow, spreading or reflexed, waved or crisped, a mixture of scarlet and bright yellow; stamens very long, yellow, standing out at right angles to the petals. *Bachnág, karianág, kalalávi.*

Common in the Konkans and Ghauts; also in Guzerat. Throughout tropical India (*H.*). This well-known plant is almost as remarkable as beautiful. The flowers go on changing in colour for several days before they finally die off. It is frequently seen in English conservatories, but in nothing like perfection. I always thought the name itself a work of genius; it is due apparently to Linnæus.

This plant, though a climber, is more like the typical lilies than any other of the order in W. India (but see *Crinum ensifolium*). The lilies which are so celebrated in poetry are generally white, *Lilium candidum* being the most typical. This, called in French fleur-de-Marie, is dedicated to the Virgin, as being the emblem of purity, and thus is constantly seen in religious pictures.

"Now by my maiden honour, yet as pure
As the unsullied lily."—*Love's Labour Lost.*

The lily of the valley, *Convallaria*, is similarly the emblem of modesty.

Travellers in Palestine are not agreed as to what flower our Lord alluded to when he said, according to our translation, "Consider the lilies of the field how they grow . . . even Solomon in all his glory was not arrayed like one of these," as there are several bulbous plants common there, which He might easily have pointed at. Sir E. Arnold calls it "the scarlet martagon," i.e. *L. Chalcedonicum.* But no doubt the translators, like many other unscientific writers, used the name lily as including many flowers, which do not belong to the botanical family. So Shakspeare:—

. . . "Lilies of all kinds,
The flower-de-luce being one."—*A Winter's Tale.*

Of cultivated plants of this order the commonest in India is probably *Polyanthes tuberosa, gulchhari, gulshábu.*

. . . "the sweet tuberose,
The sweetest flower for scent that blows."—*Shelley.*

Captain Cook, in describing the profusion of sweet-smelling flowers in Batavia, says, "The Malay name of the tuberose is 'Intriguer of the night,' and is not inelegantly conceived. The heat of this climate is so great that few flowers exhale their sweets in the day; and this in particular, from its total want of scent at that time, and its modesty of colour, seems negligent of attracting admirers; but as soon as night comes on it diffuses its fragrance, and at once compels the attention and excites the complacency of all who approach it."—*Voyages.* But it is now recognized that the particular office of white blossoms specially fragrant at night is to attract moths and other nocturnal insects for purposes of fertilization.

Yucca gloriosa, Adam's needle, is well known in gardens, with its erect panicle of white bells. It is sometimes found out of doors in favourable situations in England, as in Tennyson's garden in the Isle of Wight :—

"And marvel how in English air
My Yucca, which no winter quells,
Altho' the months have scarce begun,
Has pushed towards our faintest sun
A spike of half-accomplished bells."

Dracæna ferrea, a shrubby plant with copper-coloured leaves, crowded together at the top of the stem, and panicles of very small flowers, white or purplish : common in gardens. Tulips and hyacinths, of which the varieties may be counted by the hundred, belong also to this family; and the true Aloes, of which there are none given in the Indian Flora, nor in *D.*, either wild or introduced; but *G.* has *A. perfoliata* as common in gardens under the name of *kuar pur*, and there are probably others.

ORDER 118. PONTEDERACEÆ.

Herbs, more or less aquatic ; leaves erect or floating, flowers in spikes or racemes from the sheathing petioles, and with irregularly sheathing bracts ; perianth of six unequal divisions, stamens one to six inserted at the base of the lobes, capsule membranous, 3-valved.

A very small order, well marked (in the two Indian species) by the handsome flowers coming out of an opening in the petiole.

Monochoria. Leaves radical and solitary at the top of the branches, perianth bell-shaped ; one of the six stamens usually larger, with the filament toothed on one side, anthers at length elongating.

* 1. *M. hastæfolia* (*Pontederia hastata,* D.). Leaves triangular or arrow-shaped, very smooth and glossy, petioles of the radical leaves $1\frac{1}{2}$ to 2 feet long, swollen and splitting near the top to let the raceme come through : flowers numerous, bright blue or violet : the top flowers open first, and all wither on the stem ; the large anther is blue, the other yellow.

2. *M. vaginalis* (*Pontederia v.*, D.). A succulent plant with smooth glossy leaves, narrow cordate pointed, petioles long and hollow, flowers bright blue like hyacinths.

D. has for both of these, "margins of tanks and water holes, common." *H.* has "throughout India" for both. I have seen the last in dry rice-fields in the Konkan. *H.* calls it a very variable plant, the blue flowers sprinkled with red.

ORDER 119. XYRIDEÆ.

Herbs, with radical leaves sheathing at the base, and a spike of flowers on a naked scape ; sepals, clawed petals and stamens

3 each, and sometimes 3 staminodes; anthers sagittate, ovary free, style trifid.

Another very small order; in the only species occurring in W. India the scape of flowers bursts from the sheath of the leaves.

Xyris, characters of the order.

X. Indica. A small smooth rush-like plant, leaves linear, sword-shaped, all radical, the round scape bursting from the sheath of the leaf, and bearing an oval head of yellow flowers, each with a broad ovate convex brown bract, anthers twin. *Álu.*

Málwan. Salt marshes in S. Konkan, near Rairee fort (*D.*). Various parts of India (*H.*). I noted that the spathe and scape were light-yellow.

The natives of Bengal consider this plant a certain cure for ringworm (*R.*).

Order 120. COMMELINACEÆ. The Spiderwort Family.

Herbs, with flat narrow leaves sheathing at the base, perianth inferior 6-divided, the 3 outer segments herbaceous green, the three inner petaloid, coloured; stamens 6 on the base of the perianth, some of them sometimes reduced to staminodes; filaments often bearded, ovary free, capsule 2 or 3-valved.

Owing to the different colouring of the outer and inner sepals, the flowers of this order seem to have a more distinct calyx and corolla than most monochlamyds. This and the growth of the flowers (generally blue) from large bracts, or from the sheaths of the leaves, make the order tolerably easy of identification. Two or three spiderworts are well known in English gardens.

1. Commelina. Flowers in cymes included in a terminal spathe; petals larger than the sepals, one or more often clawed, stamens 3 perfect, with 2 or 3 staminodes.

2. Aneilema. Flowers in axillary and terminal panicles, with bracts but not spathes, stamens 2 or 3 with 3 or 4 staminodes.

3. Cyanotis. Usually prostrate or creeping; flowers in cymes, usually almost covered by large leafy imbricating bracts; limb of the petal roundish, stamens 6, all perfect, capsule 3-celled.

1. Commelina.

1. *C. nudiflora*? (*C. communis*, D.). Stem creeping, jointed, branchlets with a line of hairs, leaves sessile, sheathing, ovate

lanceolate, spathes opposite, the leaves rounded cordate, acute, folded; flowers handsome blue, one to three to each peduncle, two peduncles to each spathe.

2. *C. Bengalensis*? (So in D.). Like the last but much smaller, and most parts hairy, leaves petioled ovate elliptic, spathes short-peduncled, hooded, two peduncles in each, one longer than the other; flowers small, blue.

D. has these two as common everywhere, and they certainly are in the Konkan. My plants agreed with *D.'s* descriptions, and also with *R.'s C. cæspitosa* and *C. Bengalensis*, but *H.* has failed to recognize *D.'s* plants, and I cannot find that he has referred to *R.'s C. Bengalensis* at all. *H.* has his *C. nudiflora* as throughout the hotter parts of India, and *C. Bengalensis* throughout India.

* *C. hirsuta*, stem erect, 6 to 12 inches, branched, leaves linear lanceolate, spathes long-peduncled, hairy; flowers yellow, capsule one-seeded, the lateral cells being empty. Belgaum, Ritchie (*H.*). * *C. Forskalæi*, stem diffuse, rooting at the nodes, leaves sessile, narrow oblong obtuse, spathes short-peduncled, folded or hooded acute, broader than long, flowers blue. The Konkan, Jacquemont (*H.*). * *C. paleata*, stem stout branched, smooth, leaves elliptic or broad lanceolate, spathes short-peduncled, broad ovate, hooded, flowers blue. Konkan and Malabar, Law, Stocks, &c. (*H.*).

These last three are not in *D.*

2. Aneilema.

Note.—The flowers are blue except where otherwise stated.

1. *A. nudiflorum*. A grass-like plant with creeping stem and erect branches, leaves linear lanceolate acute, smooth, except the sheath, lower leaves very long, peduncles with several pale blue flowers collected at the end, anthers white.

S. Konkan. Common (*D.*). Throughout India (*H.*).

H. makes *D.'s A. compressum* a var. of this, and calls the petals rosy. *D.* makes the leaves shorter and darker in colour, and more seeds in the capsule. Málwan.

2. *A ochraceum*. Six inches high, leaves lanceolate, the upper broader and cordate, sheaths long and hairy, flowers several together with jointed pedicels, yellow; stamens 3, filaments much-bearded.

Dapoli. S. Konkan (*D.*): not much known otherwise apparently. *H.* describes the filaments as naked. * *A. versicolor* is the only other species of W. India with yellow flowers, leaves flat oblong lanceolate, stem-clasping: it would seem to be very like the last, and to be scarcely known except to Dalzell, who had it at Malwan. *H.*, however, puts this in the section with seeds in one row, the other with seeds in two rows.

3. *A. paniculatum.* (*A. semiteres*, D.). Two or three inches high, leaves radical, half-cylindric, fleshy, pointed; flowers in dichotomous panicles, calyx and pedicels red, anthers 3 white and 3 black.

Dapoli. At Bandora, on the rocks, it grows much larger, with round and jointed stems. *D.* has no hab., but identifies it with *G.*'s *Commelina nimmonia*, found in rocky parts of Malabar Hill, and about Rosa and Ellora. *H.* calls the leaves sometimes grass-like, and seems to have not much authority for it besides Dalzell.

* 4. *A. vaginatum.* (*A. pauciflorum*, D.). Two feet high, all smooth except the base of the long linear pointed leaves; sheaths of the upper leaves transformed into bracts, pedicels twice-jointed, one to three from the axils of the bracts; fertile stamens 2, anthers orange.

D. without hab. Throughout tropical India, in rice fields, and wet places (*H.*).

The remaining 3 species are attributed by *D.* to the S. Konkan. The last *H.* has throughout India, in pastures, &c.

* *A. lineolatum.* (*A. elatum*, D.). Three or four feet high, stem round, smooth, leafy, leaves large linear lanceolate or sword-shaped, with white margins; flowers three together in panicles, filaments bearded. * *A. dimorphum*, a foot high, nearly all smooth, leaves lanceolate to oblong, stem-clasping; flowers few, terminal, panicled, bracts small hooded, perfect stamens 3, their filaments bearded, anthers purple. * *A. spiratum* (*A. canaliculatum*, D.), small, branched, leaves lanceolate, oblong, stem-clasping, peduncle terminal, few-flowered; flowers long-pedicelled, bracts ovate, perfect stamens 3, filaments all bearded, anthers blue.

3. Cyanotis.

1. *C. papilionacea* (*C. hispida*, D.). A small plant with red stems, all covered with long hairs, leaves linear, sword-shaped, fleshy, bracts falcate semi-cordate; flowers violet in sessile heads, filaments bearded with blue hairs in the upper part.

Poona. On rocks, S. Konkan (*D.*). Deccan peninsula, in rocky places (*H.*).

D. gives the anthers as bright violet. I noted them as yellow.

2. *C. cristata.* Erect or procumbent, the stem with a line of hairs, which changes sides at each joint; leaves ovate lanceolate, smooth, except the margins and sheaths; flowers blue, bracts falcate, sepals narrow lanceolate, hairy, filaments bearded.

This is a larger and less hairy species than the last. S. Konkan. The commonest species in the rains (*D.*). Throughout tropical India in hilly districts (*H*).

3. *C. fasciculata.* Three to six inches high, all reddish and woolly, leaves fleshy, lanceolate, stem-clasping; flowers from the boat-shaped sheaths rose-coloured, filaments bearded with white and rose-coloured hairs.

Poona and Nasik. Common in rocky places in the Deccan (*D.*). It is a very pretty species, and *D.* says the only woolly one. *H.* has the flowers issuing from bracts, but *D.* has them, as I have found them, from sheaths.

* *C. tuberosa*, stems several creeping, radical leaves sword-shaped, large, stem leaves linear lanceolate, often purple beneath; flowers bluish-purple in peduncled heads, bracts falcate, ciliated. A large and coarse species compared with the others: W. Deccan, never seen in the Konkan (*D.*). *H.* includes in this as a var. *D.'s C. adscendens*, which is smaller and smoother.

* *C. vivipara*, a stemless epiphyte, radical leaves sword-shaped, fleshy, in a tuft, scapes numerous, very slender, with 2 or 3 white flowers, and small leaves and bracts. On trees at Parwar Ghaut (*D.*): not much known otherwise. *C. axillaris*, stem 6 to 18 inches, red, branched; leaves long linear, smooth, flowers blue, 2 or 3 together from the sheaths of the leaves, bracts small and hidden. Poona. W. Deccan (*D.*). Throughout India (*H.*). This *H.* makes the only species with flowers coming from the leaf-sheaths, but see No. 3.

Floscopa. Flowers in panicles with bracts, stamens 6 perfect, or one sometimes imperfect, filaments smooth, capsule 2-celled. * *F. scandens* (*Dithyrocarpus paniculatus*, D.). Stem creeping with erect branches, sheaths of the lanceolate leaves with woolly mouth, panicle roundish or pyramidal; flowers small, white lilac or rosy. On the Ghauts; might be easily mistaken for a grass at first sight (*D.*). Throughout tropical India in swamps (*H.*).

ORDER 121. FLAGELLARIEÆ.

Herbs, leaves with sheathing petioles, flowers small in terminal panicles, perianth segments 6 imbricated, stamens 6, ovary superior, styles 3, short, or one 3-cleft.

FLAGELLARIA. Stem climbing by the tendril-like tips of the leaves, flowers bisexual, sepals sub-petaloid, fruit a drupe.

F. Indica. A large climber with smooth jointed hollow stems; leaves alternate lanceolate, sub-cordate, flowers very fragrant, whitish, anthers and stigmas more conspicuous than the perianth, fruit roundish.

The stems are as thick as a walking cane, but quite green; the leaves like those of Gloriosa. It looks most like a rush, in which order some authors put it; others in Commelinaceæ.

Cliffs at Vingorla. Among rocks near the sea; S. Konkan (*D.*). Throughout India, chiefly near the coast (*H.*).

ORDER 122. PALMEÆ. Palms.

Trees or shrubs with unbranched trunks, marked with the scars of the leaves, which are collected at the top, pinnate or fan-shaped with sheathing petioles. Flowers small in panicles or spikes, enclosed in spathes, generally with3 bracts; perianth generally 6-divided in 2 series, stamens 3 or 6, ovary free, generally of 3 carpels. Fruit a drupe or hard berry, often with a fibrous covering.

The palms are a purely tropical order, and, being so different in appearance from all other trees, have a certain romantic celebrity of their own. They were called by Linnæus "the princes of the vegetable kingdom." Yet it is true that "masses of palms are far from having the grand and imposing look of our European forests. . . . The palm tree really displays all its splendours and its strength only when it shows itself in little groups in the midst of rocks."—*Pouchet.* On the other hand, to walk through a grove of fine palm trees, such as the cocoanut, must always be delightful. "The scene . . . is one of great interest: if, indeed, a person fresh from sea, and who has just walked for the first time in a grove of cocoanut trees, can be a judge of anything but his own happiness."—*Darwin.*

Old writers speak of "the palm tree" as if there were only one member of the family: "This tree is one of the most famous of all the forest, and is the usual emblem of constancy, fruitfulness, patience and victory; which the more it is oppressed, the more it flourisheth, the higher it grows, the stronger and broader it is in the top."—*Cruden.*

Palms in W. India are seen mostly about the coast, where we frequently find the combination mentioned by Tennyson,—

> " . . . Hills with peaky tops engrailed,
> And many a tract of palm and rice "—

but the islands and peninsulas nearer the line supply the great majority of the species found in the Indian Flora.

H. makes 6 tribes, which I name, though I think the descriptions are too technical for my purpose. In the generic descriptions he often speaks of the inflorescence as a spadix.

TRIBE 1. ARECEÆ.

1. ARECA. Leaves pinnate, spadices branched, male flowers many, minute, females much larger, few, at the base of the branches, stigmas 3, sessile, fruit oval or oblong.

2. PINANGA. Leaves pinnate, upper leaflets running together, flowers 3 together, a female between 2 males, the females much the smallest, stamens 6 or more, stigmas 3.

3. CARYOTA. Leaves few, very large, very deeply divided, leaflets very oblique, bases swollen at the insertion, spathes 3 to 5, spadices branched; flowers solitary, or in 3's, the middle one being female; stamens very numerous, filaments very short, anthers long, stigma 3-lobed, fruit round.

TRIBE 2. PHŒNICEÆ.

4. PHŒNIX. Flowers diœcious, leaves pinnate, leaflets sword-shaped; spadices several, calyx cup-shaped, stamens 6; female flowers with 6 staminodes or a 6-toothed cup, carpels 3.

TRIBE 3. LEPIDOCARPEÆ.

5. CALAMUS. Armed, erect or climbing, leaves pinnate, spadices long, much-branched, spathes many, tubular, persistent, calyx cup-shaped, 3-toothed, stamens 6, filaments short; in female flowers the staminodes form a cup, stigmas 3, fruit roundish.

TRIBE 4. BORASSEÆ.

6. BORASSUS. Leaves fan-shaped, spathes numerous, sheathing; flowers diœcious, males minute, sunk in the cavities of the catkin-like branches, stamens 6, females larger, sessile on the very short branches of a stout spadix; staminodes 6 to 9, stigmas 3, drupe large with 3 pyrenes.

TRIBE 5. COCCINEÆ.

7. COCOS. Leaves very deeply divided, leaflets narrow, spadix erect, panicled; flowers monœcious, spathes 2 or more, male flowers unsymmetric, stamens 6, females much larger, perianth increasing, fruit large ovoid one-seeded.

1. ARECA.

A. catechu. Betel nut tree. Leaves 4 to 6 feet long, spathe glabrous compressed, stamens 6; in the female the staminodes are united; fruit smooth, orange or scarlet. *Pophli;* the nut *supári.*

Grown in gardens about the coast; the most slender and elegant of Indian palms, "raising its graceful stem and feathery crown 'like an arrow shot down from heaven.'"—*Hooker.* The use of the nut with *pán* leaves is universal.

2. PINANGA.

P. Dicksonii. Leaves about 4 feet long, leaflets long, broadly linear, spadix with 4 to 8 branches, sepals subulate, nearly equalling the petals, stamens 20 to 30, fruit ovoid or oblong.

W. Ghauts (*H.*), but not in *D.* or *G.*

3. Caryota.

C. urens. Leaves bipinnate, leaflets triangular, spadices long, pendulous, berry size of a nutmeg. *Bhirli mhád ;* the fruit *ardhisupári.*

Jungles in the Konkans and Ghauts. Hotter parts of India (*H.*). This is a lofty and very noble palm, the great hanging clusters of flowers and fruit being very noticeable. It is one of the species called Sago palm.

4. Phœnix.

1. *P. sylvestris.* Wild date. Petiole spinous, leaflets one or two feet long, fruit yellow. *Sindi, Khájur.*

H. has "cultivated throughout India, wild in the Indus valley," but it certainly has all the appearance of being wild throughout N. Konkan and Guzerat. *G.* calls it the wild date.

"*P. dactylifera,* the true date, *Khurmá, Kárik,* has been introduced into Simla and N.W. India" (*H.*); but he makes it and *P. sylvestris* very close together.

"The date palms rustled not, the peepul laid
Its topmost boughs against the balustrade."—*Whittier.*

* 2. *P. acaulis.* Stem 6 to 10 inches in diameter, densely clothed with sheaths and bases of petioles; petiole a foot or more long, with many spines, fruit elliptic oblong, bright red to blue-black.

Common on the Ghauts (*D.*) ; not in *G.*

Notwithstanding the specific name, *D.* speaks of trees 6 or 8 feet high, and *H.* speaks of the stem.

5. Calamus.

Note.—This genus, which produces rattan canes, London calls the connecting link between palms and grasses, having the inflorescence of the former, and the habit of the latter.

*1. *C. pseudotenuis.* Stem slender, leaflets many, spathes flattened, spadix 2 or 3 feet long.

W. Ghauts (*H.*). Not in *D.* or *G.*

*2. *C. rotang.* The common rattan. Stem jointed, climbing to a great extent, enveloped in the thorny sheaths of the leaves, leaves 18 to 36 inches long, leaflets sessile, the margins with minute prickles ; fruit small, pale. *Bet.*

Pretty common in Southern jungles (*D.*). S. Konkan (*G.*). Deccan peninsula and Ceylon (*H.*).

6. Borassus.

B. flabellifer. The Palmyra or brab tree. Leaves very large, petioles serrated and spinous on the edges, fruit large, round. *Tád.*

Everywhere in N. Konkan; elsewhere sparingly. *H.* gives it only as cultivated. This is the largest and best known of the family in W. India. The fruit with its white pulp is eatable, and the sap is the commonest spirituous liquor of the Presidency.

G.'s B. dichotomus, Okemandal, which he says covers the whole island of Diu, and is found in various parts of Guzerat, is included by *H.* in this.

7. Cocos.

C. nucifera. The cocoanut tree. Unarmed, leaves pinnated, 10 to 15 feet long, leaflets sword-shaped. *Náral mhád.*

Cultivated, especially near the sea (*H.*). The cocoanut groves in the S. Konkan are planted by the Brahmins for the fruit, and by Bandháris for the liquor, but the other products of the tree are, as is well known, valuable.

> "And sweeter thy discourse is to my ear
> Than fruits of palm tree, pleasantest to thirst
> And hunger both."—*Paradise Lost.*

Captain Cook mentions that natives of the South Sea Islands peel off the outer rind of the cocoanut with their teeth.

Corypha, tall stout unarmed palms, dying after once flowering; leaves very large, roundish or fan-shaped, much-divided, calyx cup-shaped, 3-divided, stamens 6, ovary 3-lobed, fruit of 1 to 3 round fleshy drupes.

* *C. umbraculifera*, leaves palmately pinnatifid, 6 feet long, panicles pyramidal.

This is the talipot palm of Ceylon, found in gardens in India. The leaves are used for writing on with an iron style.

The allusions to palm trees generally in prose as well as poetry are numberless. Few similes are more striking, or more interesting from the circumstances under which the passage was composed,* than Heber's, with reference to the building of the Temple, in "Palestine:"

> "No hammer fell, no ponderous axes rung,
> Like some tall palm the mystic fabric sprung.
> Majestic silence!"

* See Lockhart's "Life of Scott," ii. 122, ed. 1839.

ORDER 123. **PANDANEÆ.**

Small diœcious trees or shrubs, spadices clothed with leafy spathes; flowers small, covering the whole spadix, perianth none, stamens numerous, ovary free or united with those of contiguous flowers; fruit a round mass of united woody or fleshy drupes.

PANDANUS, characters as abrove.

1. *P. fascicularis* (*P. odoratissimus*, D.). The screw pine. A large cactus-like shrub, with long sword-shaped sharply-toothed spinous leaves, growing round the stem in 3 spiral rows. The flowers, consisting apparently of innumerable threads, grow on a spadix 3 or 4 inches long, enclosed within large leaf-like bracts; fruit nearly round, something like a pineapple. *Kevri, khetki, bovdaga:* in Sanscrit poetry *Ketaka.*

Sandy places near the sea in the Konkan and elsewhere. "Throughout the hotter moister parts of India, and much planted for fences" (*H.*).

This is a well-known and widely-spread species, easily recognizable; many uses for various parts of it are found in the South Sea Islands. In Mauritius it grows 40 or 50 feet high, and is cultivated for the leaves, from which sugar bags are made.—*Kirby.* There is one in the palm house at Kew trying hard to get through the roof.

"The tender white leaves of the flowers (called spathes by *H.*), chiefly those of the male, yield the most delightful fragrance; of all perfumes it is by far the richest and most powerful" (*Loudon*). Roots are sent out from many parts of the stem, as in some of the mangroves, and look like artificial props.

* *P. furcatus.* "A large spreading bush, pretty much like the last, but with large compound fruit of an oblong shape, drupes cuneate, crowned with an incurved, polished, sharp-forked spine" (*D.*). "Spathes inodorous, golden-yellow" (*H.*).

Between Belgaum and Ram Ghaut (*D.*); but *H.* has no Western hab·

ORDER 124. **AROIDEÆ.** Arums.

Perennial herbs with radical leaves, or scandent shrubs. Flowers sessile on a spadix, which is enclosed in a spathe, perianth none, or of scales; male flowers with numerous anthers on the upper part of the spadix, females with sessile ovaries on the lower part, and often neuter flowers between.

A large order, easily known by the spadix, which conveys no particular idea of flowers, more or less enclosed in the spathe. The single English species, "Lords and ladies," is one of the commonest of wild flowers. The tubers of many of them produce nutritious starch or sago. I am not able to give *H.'s* tribal distinctions, but group such genera as I find possible.

Note.—When the upper part of the spadix is without flowers, it is called the appendage.

1. Cryptocorine. Aquatic or marsh herbs, spadix very slender, its top adhering to the spathe, anthers 2-celled, recurved; the female flowers form a single row of united ovaries; fruit of united 2-valved carpels.

2. Lagenandra. Like the last, but the female flowers form a spiral row of many free ovaries with peltate or discoid stigmas, and the fruit is a berry.

3. Pistia. A floating stemless herb, leaves sessile, forming an erect cup, spathe small, spadix united to its back; the male flowers consist of a few sessile connate stamens near the top of the spadix, the female of a solitary ovoid ovary.

4. Arisæma. Tuberous herbs, male flowers stalked, anthers 2 to 5, female densely crowded, the style short or none, the stigma disciform.

The two following genera are tuberous herbs, having pinnatifid leaves, which appear after the flowers.

5. Amorphophallus. Male and female flowers contiguous, without neuters, anthers 2 to 4 sessile, berries roundish.

6. Synantherias. Like the last, but male and female flowers distant with interposed neuters.

The next five genera belong to a tribe in which the leaves are undivided, often peltate, and the anthers sessile, densely crowded, with very thick connective.

7. Ariopsis. A small tuberous herb, male flowers cylindric, female adnate to the base of the spathes, berry 3 to 6-angled.

8. Remusatia. Leaf solitary entire peltate, spadix very short, male and female flowers separated by neuters, berry small.

9. Colocasia. Coarse herbs with stoutly peduncled spathe.

10. Rhaphidophora. Scandent shrubs rooting on trees, spadix sessile, perianth none, the berries many-seeded, confluent.

11. Pothos. Climbers, spathe small, sepals and stamens 6, berries 1 to 3-seeded.

12. Acorus. Aromatic marsh herbs, leaf sword-shaped, the spathe is the leaf-like continuation of the peduncle, sepals and stamens 6.

1. Cryptocorine.

* *C. Roxburghii.* Stemless, leaves linear lanceolate, spathe

about as long, erect, spirally twisted to a fine point, spotted with dark purple, capsule conical, 5-celled.

Banks of streams and other wet places, common (*D.*).

2. Lagenandra.

* *L. toxicaria.* A marsh plant 3 feet high, leaves long-petioled oblong, with long sheath, spathe slightly twisted, carpels free. *Vatsanáb.*

S. Konkan and Belgaum Collectorate, rare; it is a deadly poison (*D.*).

3. Pistia.

P. stratiotes. Leaves thick obovate, tapering to the base, the margins waved, the nerves spreading like a fan, but converging within the margin, spathe white, waved on the margin. *Gondali, prasni, shedvel.*

In tanks. Throughout India (*H.*).

"A good deal like the common Endive. It has a peculiar muriatic smell, and is said to be injurious to the water. Common throughout the Konkans" (*G.*).

4. Arisæma.

1. *A. tortuosum* (*A. curvatum*, D.). About 18 inches high, all smooth and greenish-yellow, leaves of 7 or more lanceolate leaflets joined at the base; flower stem arising from the leaf-sheath, spadix slender, curved outwards and then back over the spathe, which is much shorter.

Dapoli. No habitat in *D.*, and not given in *G.*

Appendage of the spadix long, like a rat's tail. Very common and varying in many points (*H.*).

2. *A. Murrayi.* Leaves peltate, palmate with lanceolate segments, spathe hooded, pointed, white tinged with purple, spadix scarcely longer than the tube of the spathe, nearly black. *Sarpá chá kándá.* The snake lily of Mahableshwar.

Konkans and Ghauts. Hills S.W. of Surat (*G.*).

* *A. Leschenaultii* (*A. erubescens*, D.), leaves peltate, with 10 to 12 linear lanceolate segments, spadix club-shaped, shorter than the pointed spathe. Between Rám Ghaut and Belgaum (*D.*).

The above is *D.*'s description, and as *H.* identifies *D.*'s plant doubtfully, it is better to give *H.*'s description separately. "Leaf solitary, petiole usually mottled and branded with red and brown, spathe green with broad dark-purple bands." W. Ghauts.

* *A. neglectum.* Monœcious, leaflets 4 to 7, elliptic, appendage twice as long as the spathe, remarkably like that of *A. tortuosum.* W. Ghauts (*H.*), but not in *D.* or *G.*

The following also belong to this group:—

Sauromatum. Tuberous herbs, leafing after flowering, leaf solitary, spadix sessile, very long; male and female flowers widely distant, with a few large neuters close above the females. * *S. guttatum,* leaves of 7 to 15 variable lobes, peduncle of spathe very stout, green or spotted, spathe one to two feet long, green or yellowish, with purple spots, spadix as long or nearly so, appendage 2 to 8 inches, green or dark purple. Attributed to the Konkan by *H.*, but doubtfully.

Typhonium. Spadix exserted, inflorescence as in the last, appendage long, smooth. * *T. trilobatum,* leaves 3-lobed, petiole up to a foot, spathe red-purple inside, appendage bright red. Not in *D.*, but in *G.* as *Arum trilobatum.* Widely spread (*H.*). * *T. bulbiferum,* leaves triangular, sagittate or cordate, spathe very slender, pale rose-colour, spadix as long, slender, yellow. The long petiole has usually a small bulb or tuber at the top. S. Konkan; *Stocks* (*H.*). Not in *D.* or *G.*

Theriophanum, like the last, but leaves undivided, cordate or arrow-shaped. * *T. crenatum,* spathe pale yellow-green, the margins waved and crenate, spadix half as long, appendage dark purple. Konkan (*G.* and *H.*).

5. Amorphophallus.

* 1. *A. campanulatus.* Tuber very large, leaves radical few thrice bifid, segments oblique oblong, spathe large, bell-shaped, spadix very stout, berries obovoid.

The cultivated *suran,* wild on the banks of streams in S. Konkan (*D.*). *H.* makes it wild throughout the plains of India. "The large dark-coloured flowers of this species have a very curious appearance" (*G.*). "The wild kind is *jangli suran,* and, when dried, *madanmast*" (*Dymock*).

* *A. commutatus,* spathe long-peduncled, spadix about as long, appendage very long, tuber and leaf unknown. The Konkan, *Stocks* (*H.*).

* *A. bulbifer,* spathe long-peduncled, spadix very stout and appendage not so long as in the last, leaves bearing bulbils at the base, forks and nerves above; leaflets obovate or lanceolate, petiole 3 or 4 feet long, peduncle 8 to 10 inches, green and pink, streaked with green or black. The Konkan (*G.*). Not in *D.*

Thomsonia has the characters of *Amorphophallus,* but the appendage is covered with tubercles at the top. * *T. nepalensis,* leaf once or twice ternate, leaflets oblong lanceolate, petiole long and stout, spathe boat-shaped, spadix very stout, greenish-brown or yellow. This is not in *D.* or *G.*, nor ascribed by *H.* to W. India, but it seems to be the poisonous plant described by Dr. Kirtikar in Journal B. N. H. S. vol. 7, under the name of *Pythonium Wallichii,* and said by him to be very common in Tanna jungles. Dr. Dymock gives it the name *Sherale,* which he says is applied to Arum flowers generally.

6. Synantherias.

S. sylvatica (*Amorphophallus s.*, D.). Scape two or three feet high, smooth, light with dark spots, petiole long, winged, with 3 or more leaflets radiating from the top, each of 2 or more lanceolate segments; spathe much shorter than the spadix, which is dark and tapering. *Luth, vajar muth, ujomuth.*

Dapoli. S. Konkan, common (*D.*). Indian peninsula (*H.*).

7. Ariopsis.

A. peltata. Small and pretty, all smooth, with one round peltate leaf, petiole 6 inches long, scape 2 inches high, hidden by the leaf, spathe hooded, pale buff, spadix shorter, club-shaped, capsules aggregated, pointed.

Dapoli. Common in the Konkan (*D.*). *H.* has spathe violet, with green dorsal ridge, paler within.

8. Remusatia.

R. vivipara. Growing in clefts of trees, sending up several stalks covered with minute scaly bulbs, leaves long-petioled, smooth, large, with prominent whitish veins, cordate, pointed; spathe with green tube and yellow limb; tubers pink. *Rukhálu.*

Sáwarda, Rutnagherry Collectorate. Ghaut jungles; it rarely flowers (*D.*). Both Konkans (*G.*).

9. Colocasia.

C. antiquorum, leaves large ovate sagittate, spathe pale yellow with green base, spadix shorter. *Alu.*

Everywhere in the S. Konkan at the beginning of the rains. Throughout the hotter parts of India, wild or cultivated (*H.*). Not in *D.* It is certainly, I think, *G.*'s No. 1622, and not, as *H.* makes it, his No. 1610.

Alocasia like the last in all outward respects. **A. macrorhiza,* leaves broad ovate sagittate, peduncles short, spathe hooded, spadix about the same length, with long appendage; berries size of a cherry. Not in *D.* or *G.* apparently. Tropical and subtropical India, wild or cultivated (*H.*): he has stem 6 to 16 feet, spathe 6 to 10 inches.

10. Rhaphidophora.

R. pertusa (*Scindapsus p.*, D.). A large climber, leaves very large, pinnatifid on one side and with large holes on the other, spathe shortly peduncled, yellow, spadix obtuse. *Ganesh-kand.*

Konkan jungles. Deccan peninsula (*H.*). It is easily known by the curious irregular holes in the leaves.

11. Pothos.

P. scandens. A smooth parasite with many thick stems; leaves lanceolate, jointed with the petiole, which is winged and the same shape as the leaf, with stem-clasping base; spadices axillary solitary, roundish, peduncle with a bract; berries red, nearly round.

Rajapore. Ghaut jungles, pretty common (*D.*). Konkan (*G.*). Throughout India on walls and tree trunks (*H.*).

12. Acorus. Sweet Sedge.

A. calamus. Sheath sword-shaped, several times longer than the spadix, which is thick and cylindrical; leaves three to six feet long, the margins waved. *Yekand.*

Cultivated in gardens (*D.*). Wild in S. Konkan (*G.*). Throughout India wild or cultivated (*H.*). It is an English aquatic plant, sometimes called the Sweet flag; it has been put in other orders, but the spadix is unmistakable. Linnæus called it the only aromatic plant of northern climates. The root is said to have been employed medicinally since the days of Hippocrates, and it is also said to be so offensive to the cobra as to act as a preservative.

Order 125. **LEMNACEÆ.**

Very small annual floating green scale-like plants, flowers naked or in a spathe, perianth none, stamens one or two.

These are what in England are called Duckweeds, and there being no distinction of stem and leaf, fronds are spoken of.

1. Lemna. Fronds with one or more roots, bearing the flowers in clefts on the margin.

2. Wolffia. Fronds like grains of sand, rootless, bearing the flowers on the upper surface.

1. Lemna.

* *L. trisulca.* Fronds joined crosswise, oblong lanceolate, toothed near the apex, roots solitary.

In standing water (*D.*). Konkan (*H.*).

This is the largest of the several Indian species, the fronds being as much as half an inch long. It is the ivy-leafed duckweed of English ponds, but does not seem so common in India as two or three other species, which however I do not find definitely ascribed to W. India. Balfour thus describes the genus: "The flowers are very simple, one male and the other female, without perianth, enclosed in a membranous bag; their roots are simple fibres covered with a sheath."

2. Wolffia.

D. arrhiza (*Lemna globosa*, D.). Fronds one or two together, roundish.

Common probably throughout India and Ceylon (*H.*). "Covering the surface of tanks like a green scum" (*G.*).

"The green mantle of the standing pool."—*King Lear.*

Order 126. ALISMACEÆ.

Marsh or water plants, leaves radical, entire; flowers regular, perianth segments 6, in 2 series, outer herbaceous, inner petaloid; stamens 6 or more; fruit of small achenes or follicles.

Having passed from plants with flowers barely recognizable as such to the scum that floats on ponds, we return in this order to tall herbs with handsome flowers, practically complete in all their parts, including the well-known English plants of brooks and ditches, Water plantain, Arrowhead, and Flowering rush.

1. Limnophyton. Flowers polygamous, stamens 6, fruit of 3 or more achenes, receptacle flat.

2. Wisneria. Flowers minute, monœcious in remote whorls, stamens 3; female flowers with staminodes, carpels 3 to 6, fruit as the last.

3. Butomopsis. Flowers in bracteate whorls, petals larger than sepals, deciduous, stamens 8 to 12, follicles 6 or 7, erect.

1. Limnophytum.

L. obtusifolium (*Sagittaria o.*, D.). All smooth, scape and petioles erect, thick, fleshy, obtusely angled, leaves broad, bluntly arrow-shaped, lower lobes long and tapering; flowers white in whorls on the scape, arising from 3 bracts, sepals and petals roundish ovate, drupes small, dry and wrinkled, collected in round heads. *Nalkut.*

Bassein. Guzerat (*D.*). Throughout the Konkans (*G.*). *H.* has stamens 6, and the same appears in other books; but *G.* calls the plant polyandrous, and I noted stamens numerous.

2. Wisneria.

* *W. triandra* (*Sagittaria t.*, D.). Leaves long-petioled

linear, spathulate obtuse, scape shorter than the petioles; flowers white in 3's, sepals linear oblong, petals much larger, achenes roundish.

Malwan taluka, *Stocks* and *Dalzell* (*D.* and *H.*).

To the same tribe as these two belongs *Sagittaria Sagittifolia*, "the common arrow-head" of English brooks and rivers, a handsome plant with white 3-petalled flowers. *H.* has it as growing in tanks throughout the plains of India, and it is otherwise a widely spread plant; but it is not in the Bombay books.

3. Butomopsis.

Note.—This genus has by other writers been put in a separate order, Butomaceæ, of which *Butomus umbellatus*, the flowering rush, is one of the handsomest of English aquatic plants. It is found also in the Punjaub and Cashmere.

* *B. lanceolata.* Leaves radical, long-petioled, lanceolate, scape as long as the leaves, 6 to 12-flowered; flowers in umbels erect, petals white.

Chickli in the Surat district (*D.* and *G.*), but *H.* has it as throughout the plains of India and the tropics of the Old World.

Order 127. NAIADACEÆ.

Aquatic or marsh herbs, with inconspicuous, usually green flowers, perianth various, stamens hypogynous, ovary of one to four carpels, fruit dry.

A small order of temperate and tropical lands, in no way remarkable. All here given are submerged plants.

1. Aponogeton. Scape long, bearing one or two spikes of bisexual flowers; perianth of one to three white segments, fruit of 3 or more follicles.

2. Potamogeton. Flowers in a spike, the scape rising from a membranous spathe, perianth of 4 green segments, anthers 4, essile on the sepals.

3. Naias. Flowers minute, male flowers with perianth of an outer and inner tube, stamen one adnate to the inner; female flowers without perianth.

1. Aponogeton.

* *A. monostachyon.* Leaves radical, long-petioled, linear

oblong cordate, 3 to 6 inches long, spikes densely flowered, sepals 2 concave, stamens 6, follicles smooth, pointed.

Tanks in S. M. country (*D.*). In Salsette and Konkans (*G.*). Throughout India (*H.*). The tubers are eatable.

2. Potamogeton. Pond weed.

1. *P. Indicus.* Stem branched, creeping, round, leaves lanceolate oval, shining, peduncles solitary, axillary or opposite the leaves; flowers on a crowded spike, styles 4.

Poona and N. Konkan. Pretty common in tanks (*D.*). Throughout the plains of India (*H.*).

2. * *P. crispus.* Stem branched, rather compressed, leaves smaller than the last, sessile, oblong linear, waved and finely toothed, spike very short, few-flowered, fruit oblique, broad ovate.

Tanks in the Konkans (*D.*). In tanks, common (*G.*). Plains of India (*H.*).

H. has two other species: * *P. perfoliatus,* leaves ovate, stem-clasping, peduncle short and stout, spike densely crowded. Streams around Dápori garden (*D.*). This is an English species, "remarkable for its brown, almost transparent leaves, which, when dry, have the appearance of gold-beaters' skin." * *P. pectinatus,* stem round, densely branched, the leaves extremely narrow, half round and channelled; flowers interruptedly whorled. *Phás.* Tank at Gogo, most plentiful (*D.*). Plains of India (*H.*).

There are many more species of Pond weed in England than in India; the flowers, I think, soon turn brown.

3. Naias.

* *N. minor* (*N. Indica,* D.). Stem round, much-branched, leaves narrow linear, remotely toothed, half an inch long or less, sheath dentate, ciliate, style bifid.

Common in tanks (*D.*). Throughout India in still sweet water, and distributed throughout the Old World generally (*H.*).

There are several other species of this order, all aquatic, which *H.* attributes to India generally, but as no references are given to Bombay books, and they are not in *D.*, I have not inserted them.

D. has **Zostera marina* (Zosteraceæ), the English grass-wrack, found in the salt-pans near Málwan, but I cannot find it in *H.* It is a submerged sea-water plant with slender stems and bright green grass-like leaves, the spadix coming out of a sheath in the leaves, the flowers consisting of one stamen and one pistil.

INDEX (LATIN AND ENGLISH).

Note.—*The names of orders are in capital letters.*

A.

D.

F.

G.

I.

J.

K.

L.

Q.

R.

INDEX (NATIVE NAMES).

A.

F.

G.

N.

O.

P.

R.

S.

T.

U.

V.